INTERNET PROGRAMMING

[A Complete Beginner's Guide]

Anuradha A. Puntambekar

M.E. (Computer)

Formerly Assistant Professor in

P.E.S. Modern College of Engineering,

Pune

INTERNET PROGRAMMING

First Edition : December 2020

Published by :

Amit Residency, Office No.1, 412, Shaniwar Peth, Pune - 411030, M.S. INDIA
Ph.: +91-020-24495496/97, Email : sales@technicalpublications.org
Website : www.technicalpublications.org

ISBN 978-93-332-2380-5

PREFACE

The importance of **Internet Programming** is well known in various engineering fields. Overwhelming response to our books on various subjects inspired me to write this book. The book is structured to cover the key aspects of the subject **Internet Programming**.

The book uses plain, lucid language to explain fundamentals of this subject. The book provides logical method of explaining various complicated concepts and stepwise methods to explain the important topics. Each chapter is well supported with necessary illustrations, practical examples and solved problems. All chapters in this book are arranged in a proper sequence that permits each topic to build upon earlier studies. All care has been taken to make students comfortable in understanding the basic concepts of this subject.

University questions have been added at the end of each section to help the students in picking important points from that section.

The book not only covers the entire scope of the subject but explains the philosophy of the subject. This makes the understanding of this subject more clear and makes it more interesting. The book will be very useful not only to the students but also to the subject teachers. The students have to omit nothing and possibly have to cover nothing more.

I wish to express our profound thanks to all those who helped in making this book a reality. Much needed moral support and encouragement is provided on numerous occasions by our whole family. I wish to thank the **Publisher** and the entire team of **Technical Publications** who have taken immense pain to get this book in time with quality printing.

Any suggestion for the improvement of the book will be acknowledged and well appreciated.

Author

A. A. Puntambekar

Dedicated to God

SYLLABUS

UNIT - I : Website Basics, HTML 5, CSS 3, WEB 2.0

Web Essentials : Clients, Servers and Communication - The Internet - Basic Internet protocols - World wide web - HTTP Request Message - HTTP Response Message - Web Clients - Web Servers. **(Chapter - 1)**

HTML5 - Tables - Lists - Image - HTML5 control elements - Semantic elements - Drag and Drop - Audio - Video controls. **(Chapter - 2)**

CSS3 - Inline, embedded and external style sheets - Rule cascading - Inheritance - Backgrounds - Border Images - Colors – Shadows - Text - Transformations - Transitions - Animations. **(Chapter - 3)**

UNIT - II : Client Side Programming

Java Script : An introduction to JavaScript-JavaScript DOM Model-Date and Objects,-Regular Expressions - Exception Handling-Validation-Built-in objects - Event Handling - DHTML with JavaScript - JSON introduction - Syntax - Function Files - Http Request - SQL. **(Chapter - 4)**

UNIT - III : Server Side Programming

Servlets : Java Servlet Architecture- Servlet Life Cycle - Form GET and POST actions- Session Handling - Understanding Cookies - Installing and Configuring Apache Tomcat Web Server - Database Connectivity : JDBC perspectives, JDBC program example.

JSP : Understanding Java Server Pages - JSP Standard Tag Library (JSTL)-Creating HTML forms by embedding JSP code. **(Chapters - 5, 6)**

UNIT - IV : PHP and XML

An introduction to PHP : PHP - Using PHP- Variables - Program control- Built-in functions - Form Validation - Regular Expressions - File handling - Cookies - Connecting to Database.

XML : Basic XML - Document Type Definition - XML Schema DOM and Presenting XML, XML Parsers and Validation, XSL and XSLT Transformation, News Feed (RSS and ATOM).

(Chapters - 7, 8)

UNIT - V : Introduction to AJAX and WEB Services

AJAX : Ajax Client Server Architecture-XML Http Request Object-Call Back Methods; Web Services : Introduction - Java web services Basics - Creating, Publishing, Testing and Describing a Web services (WSDL) - Consuming a web service, Database Driven web service from an application - SOAP. **(Chapters - 9, 10)**

TABLE OF CONTENTS

Unit - I : Website Basics, HTML 5, CSS 3, WEB 2.0

Unit - II : Client Side Programming

Unit - III : Server Side Programming

Unit - IV : PHP and XML

Unit - V : Introduction to AJAX and Web Services

Unit I

1 WebSite Basics

Syllabus

Web Essentials : Clients, Servers, and Communication. The Internet - Basic internet protocols, The World Wide Web, HTTP request message, HTTP response message, Web Clients, Web Servers.

Contents

1.1 Web Essentials

1.1.1 What is Web Technology?

- Web technology is a technology that acts as an interface between web client and web server. It includes markup languages, programming interfaces, online presentation tools, Java applets, video editing tools and so on.
- The commonly used client side scripting languages are HTML, JavaScript, CSS, XML and so on.
- The commonly used server side technologies are ASP, JSP, Java Servlets, PHP and so on.

1.1.2 Concept of Internet

Definition : Internet is global system in which millions of computers are connected together. It is basically a network of networks.

- Using internet many people can share resources and can communicate with each other. To have internet service one must go to the service providers. That means your computer must be connected to the Internet Service Providers (ISP) through phone-line modem or DSL.
- There are some privately owned internet service providers from which we can hire the internet services.

1.1.3 Concept of World Wide Web

Definition : World Wide Web (WWW) is collections of software and corresponding protocols used to access the resources over the network.

- The world wide web is a **information system** in which various documents containing information are interlinked together. User can access this information or write the information via computers. This information is typically stored on the web pages and through web browsers we can access these web pages.
- The web pages may contain the information in the form of text, audio, video, images and graphics. We can navigate between the web pages using hyperlinks.
- The concept of WWW was introduced by **Sir Tim Berners-Lee** the contractor at the **European Organization for Nuclear Research (CERN),** Switzerland in 1980. He built a personal database of people and software models and used hypertext so that each new page of information was linked to an existing page.

1.1.4 Internet or WWW?

- The term internet and WWW is often used interchangeably, but these are two different terms.
- The **internet** is collection of computers and other devices (such as printers, scanners etc.) connected together whereas World Wide Web (WWW) is collection of software and corresponding protocols used to access the resources over the network.
- The world wide web contains huge amount of documents, images and other resources which can be accessed using the hyperlinks.
- Thus people use internet through the Web.

1.2 Internet Protocol

Dec.-09, 11, May - 14

Various protocols used in internetworking are -

(1) File Transfer Protocol (FTP)

- The file transfer protocol sets the rules for transferring files between computers.
- When user wants to download a file from the server FTP is used.
- FTP uses **two connections** between client and server. One connection is used for actual **data transfer** and other is used for **control information** (used for commands). This separation of data and commands makes the FTP more efficient.

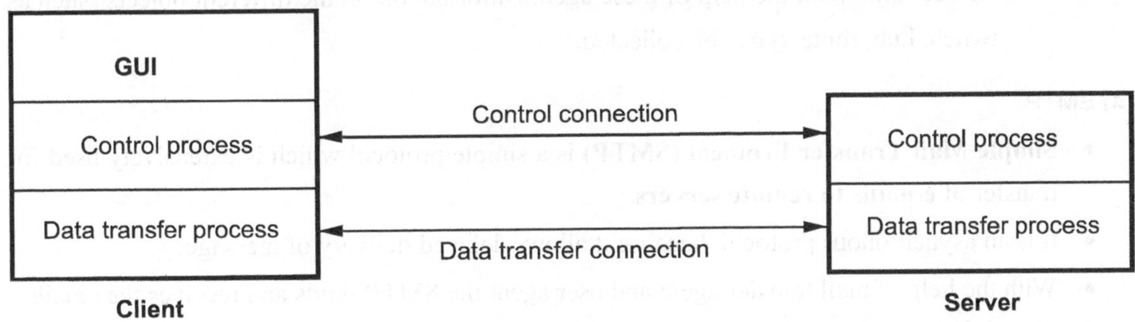

Fig. 1.2.1 Two connections used in FTP processing

- When client makes a request for particular file download then using the data transfer connection actual data gets transmitted from server to the client.
- At the same time server keeps track of how much data is sent so far and how much is remaining. This tracking can be done using the control transfer connection.
- Hence during the file downloading/uploading we can see a message about how many bytes are getting transferred and how much time is remaining.

(2) HTTP

- **The Hyper Text Transfer Protocol (HTTP)** is a **request/response** protocol.
- It is a **communication protocol** used to transfer the information on local area network and World Wide Web (WWW).
- It is the network protocol used to deliver virtually all files and other data (collectively called resources) on the World Wide Web, whether they're HTML files, image files, query results, or anything else. Usually, HTTP takes place through TCP/IP sockets.
- It is also called as a **stateless protocol** because this protocol is not able to maintain the previous conversation/information.

(3) SNMP

- **Simple Network Management Protocol (SNMP)** is a protocol which enables network administrators to manage network devices and to diagnose network problems.
- The network management system is based on two main elements : a **supervisor** and **agents**.
  - The supervisor is the terminal at which the network administrator requests for network management.
  - The agents are found at the level of each interface connecting the managed devices to the network. With the help of these agents information on the different objects (such as switch, hub, routers) can be collected.

(4) SMTP

- **Simple Mail Transfer Protocol (SMTP)** is a simple protocol which is extensively used for transfer of **e-mails to remote servers**.
- It is an asynchronous protocol, because it allows delayed delivery of message.
- With the help of mail transfer agent and user agent the SMTP sends and receives the emails.

(5) POP3

- **Post Office Protocol version 3 (POP3)** is used by local email clients (such as Microsoft Outlook Express).
- The POP3 protocol works only at the receivers end and has no work at the sender's end.
- The POP protocol has two parts, a client POP i.e. receiver's POP and a server POP i.e. reciever's email server. The client i.e. the receiver opens TCP connection with receiver's POP server. This client must be authenticated first by using the user name and password. Then the client can receive the emails from the mailbox.

(6) TCP

- The Transmission Control Protocol is used for,
  1. Safe delivery of data
  2. Error detection
  3. Assurance of the correct sequencing of data being received.
- This protocol is called **connection oriented protocol** because before sending the data this protocol requires that two computers have established connections.
- The TCP allows the transmission of arbitrary amount of data by breaking it into stream of separate **IP packets**.
- These IP packets are numbered so that it could be reassembled properly at arrivals. Along with the data an **acknowledgement** is also sent/received in order to know whether the **reliable connection** has occurred or not.

(7) UDP

- The user datagram protocol is a **connectionless** protocol without any error detection facility.
- This protocol is used for simply transmission of data.
- The UDP is known as an **unreliable protocol** however this is much faster than TCP.

(8) IP

- Internet Protocol (IP) is a network layer protocol which consists of addressing information.
- Using this information the communication between uniquely addressed computers is possible.

University Questions

1. *Explain the various Internet protocols used for client server communication.* **AU : Dec.-09, Marks 8,May-14, Marks 8**
2. *Explain TCP/IP in detail.* **AU : Dec.-11, Marks 8**

1.3 HTTP Request and Response Message

AU : June-09, May-12, 13,14, Dec.-12, 13, Marks 8

- The basic feature of HTTP protocol is that it follows the **request response** model.
- The client makes a request for desired web page by giving the URL in the address bar. This **request** is submitted to the web server and then web server gives the **response** to the web browser by returning the required web page.

1. HTTP Request Message Structure

The basic structure of request message is given by following general form -

```
<Start line>

<Header fields>

<Blank Line>

<Message Body>
```

<start Line>

The start line consists of three parts which are separated by a single space. These parts are -

i) **Request method** ii) **Request-URI** iii) **HTTP version**

(i) **Request Method :** Various methods used for making the request are enlisted in the following table

HTTP method	Description
GET	The GET method is used to retrieve information from a specified URI and is assumed to be a safe, repeatable operation by browsers.
POST	The POST method is used to request the server for desired web page and the request made is accepted as a new subordinate of the resource identified. The POST method is used for operations that have side effects and cannot be safely repeated. For example, transferring money from one bank account to another has side effects and should not be repeated without explicit approval by the user.
HEAD	The HEAD method is identical to GET. The only difference is that the server should not return a message-body in the response. The meta-information contained in the HTTP headers in response to a HEAD request should be similar to the information sent in response to a GET request.
OPTION	This method supports for the specified URL. It can be used to check the functionality of a web server by requesting '*' instead of a specific resource.
PUT	This method uploads a representation of the specified resource.
DELETE	This method is useful in deleting the specified resource.
TRACE	When request is made using TRACE method the server echoes back the received request so that a client can see what intermediate servers are adding or changing in the request.

(ii) Request-URI:

- The **U**niform **R**esource **I**dentifier (URI) is a string used to identify the names or resources on the Internet.
- The URI is a combination of URL and URN.
- The URL stands for **U**niform **R**esource **L**ocator and URN stands for **U**niform **R**esource **N**ame.
- The web address denotes the URL and specific name of the place or a person or item denotes the URN. For example

urn : ISBN 978-81-8431-123-2

specifies the address of some book.

- If the URI is written in the form of http: then it is both an URI and URL but there are some other URI which can also be used as URL. For example

URL	Intended server
ftp://ftp.mywebsite.com/index.txt	File can be located on FTP server
telnet://mywebsite.org	Telnet server
mailto:myself@mywebsite.org	Mail box
http://www.mywebsite.com	Web server

(iii) HTTP Version : The first HTTP version was HTTP/0.9 but the official version of HTTP was HTTP/1.1

<Header Field> and <Message Body>

- The host header filed is associated with the http request.
- The header fields are in the form of field name and field value.
- Thus typical structure of http request is given be following example -

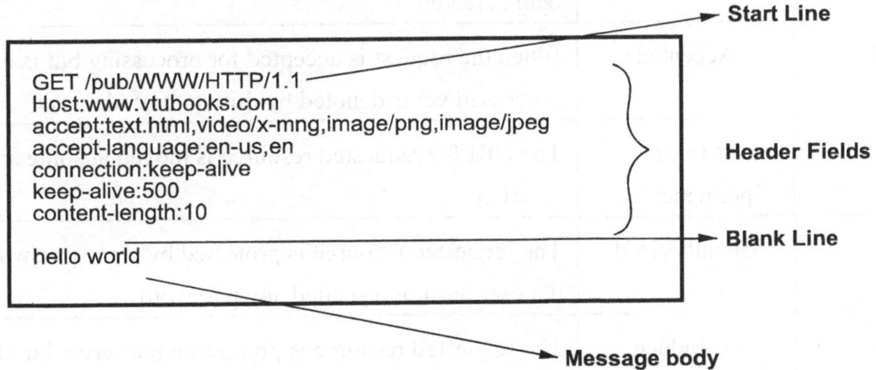

Fig. 1.3.1 HTTP request message structure

2. HTTP Response Message Structure

The basic structure of response message is given by following general form -

<Status line>
<Header fields>
<Blank Line>
<Message Body>

<Status Line>

Status line is similar to the start line in the request message. It consists of three fields.

HTTP version	Status code	reason phrase

The HTTP version denotes the HTTP version such as HTTP/1.1. The **status code** is a numeric code indicating the type of response. The **reason phrase** is in the text string form and presents the information about the status code.

For example -

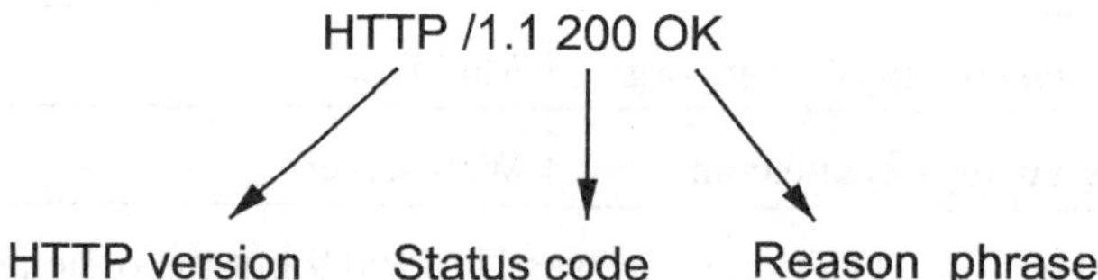

Following table explains some commonly used status codes.

Status code	Reason phrase	Description
200	OK	This is a standard response for successful request.
201	Created	It shows that the request is fulfilled and a new resource is being created.
202	Accepted	When the request is accepted for processing but is not processed yet is denoted by this status code.
301	Moved permanently	The URI for requested resource is moved at some another location.
401	Unauthorized	The requested resource is protected by some password and the user has not provided any password.
403	Forbidden	The requested resource is present on the server but the server is not able to respond it.

404	Not Found	The requested resource is not present currently but may be available in future.
500	Internal Server Error	It is a generic error message that appears due to software internal failure.

<Header Fields>

The **header field** in response message is similar to that of request message.

<Message Body>

The message body consists of response message.

For example

```
HTTP/1.1 200 OK
Date: Sat, 30 Mar 2019 07:59:01 GMT
Server: Apache/2.0.50 (Unix) mod_perl/1.99_10 Perl/v5.8.4
mod_ssl/2.0.50 OpenSSL/0.9.7d DAV/2 PHP/4.3.8
Last-Modified: Mon, 23 Feb 2009 08:32:41 GMT
Accept-Ranges: bytes
Content-Length: 2010
Content-Type: text/html
<!DOCTYPE HTML PUBLIC "-//W3C//DTD HTML 4.01 Transitional//EN">
<html>...</html>
```

The response header fields are enlisted in following table

Header field	Description
Date	It represents the date and time at which the response is generated.
Server	The name of the server which is responding
Last-Modified	The date and time at which the response is last modified.
Accept-ranges	It specifies the unit which is used by the client to accept the range request. For example if there is a large document and only a single web page is currently needed then this specifies the Accept-range.

University Questions

1. *Write short note on HTTP protocol* **AU : June-09, Marks 6**
2. *Explain the structure of HTTP request and response messages.* **AU : May-12, Dec.-12,Dec.- 13 Marks 8**
3. *Write and explain HTTP request message format.* **AU : May-13, Marks 4**
4. *Write the header format of Request and Response between Client/Server and explain it.* **AU : May-14, Marks 8**

1.4 Features of HTTP Protocol

1. It is a **communication** protocol used between web browser and web server.
2. This protocol is based on **request-response** messaging. That means client makes the request of desired web page and then the server responds it by sending the requested resource.
3. It is a **stateless protocol**. That means HTTP protocol can not remember the previous user's information nor it remembers the number of times the user has visited particular website.
4. The request-response message consists of plain text in fairly **readable form**.
5. The HTTP protocol has a **cache control**. This is an advanced feature of HTTP. Most of the web browsers automatically store(Cache) the recently visited web pages. This is very useful feature because if the user requests the same web page that has been visited already then it can be displayed from the cache memory instead of requesting the web server and bringing it from there.

1.5 Web Clients

AU : Dec.-11, Marks 8

- Web client is a kind of software that **runs on the clients machine**.
- This software sends the HTTP request to the server and then processes the HTTP response.
- Various forms of web client software are -
  (1) Web browsers
  (2) Browsers running on mobile phones
  (3) Software robots which crawl on the web for retrieving the information
  (4) User agents which assists the user in browsing the web.
- **Web browser** is a kind of software which is basically used to use resources on the web.
- Over the networks, two computers communicate with each other. In this communication, when request is made by one computer then that computer is called a **client** and when the request gets served by another computer then that computer is called **server**. Thus exchange of information takes place via Client-Server communication.
- When user wants some web document then he makes the request for it using the web browser.
- The browsers are the programs that are running on the clients' machines. The request then gets served by the server and the requested page is then returned to the client. It is getting displayed to the client on the web browser.
- The **commonly used web browsers** are (i) Internet explorer (ii) Mozilla Firefox (iii) Netscape Navigator (iv) Opera (v) Google Chrome (vi) Safari.
- Web browser supports variety of **protocols** but the most commonly used protocol on the web browser is Hyper Text Transfer Protocol(HTTP). This protocol is typically used when browser communicates with the server.

1.5.1 Functions Defined by Web Browser

Various functions of web browser are -

1. Reformats the URL and send a valid HTTP request.
2. When user gives the address of particular web site it is in the form of domain name. The web browser coverts the DNS to corresponding IP address.
3. The web browser establishes a TCP connection with the Web browser while processing the user's request.
4. The web browsers send the HTTP request to the web server.
5. The web server processes the HTTP request sent by the web browser and returns the desired web page to the client machine. The web browser on the client's machine displays this web page in appropriate format.

1.5.2 URL

- The **U**niform **R**esource **L**ocator (URL) is unique address for the file that has to be accessed over the internet.
- When we want to access some website we enter it's URL in the address bar of the web browser.
- For example if we want to access **www.google.com** then we must specify its URL in the address bar as shown

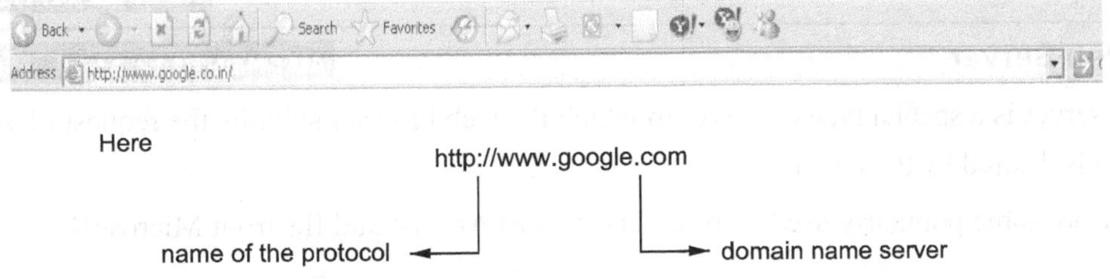

However any other file such as some text file or image file or some HTML file can also be specified. The URL contains name of the protocol such as **http://**

- The URL may contain the name of the protocol as such as ftp. For example
  ftp://ftp.funet.fi/pub/standards/RFC/rfc2166.txt
- The protocol identifier and the resource name are separated by a colon and two forward slashes. The syntax of writing URL is as given below,
  protocol://username@hostname/path/filename
- Sometimes instead of domain name servers IP addresses can also be use. For example,
  http://192.168.0.1

But use of IP address as URL is not preferred because human can not remember numbers very easily but they can remember names easily.

Absolute and Relative URL

- The absolute URL is a URL which directly point to a file. It exactly specifies exact location of a file or directory on the internet. Each absolute URL is unique. For example -
  http://www.vtubooks.com/home.aspx
- The relative URL points to the file or a directory in relation to the present directory. For example
- Consider the **absolute address** which refers an image mother.jpg
  http://www.mywebsite.com/myphotos/mother.jpg
- For the above given absolute address the **relative address** will be -
  ../myphotos/mother.jpg

That means from the current URL the directory **myphotos** will be searched for the image **mother.jpg**. The two peroids .. instruct the server to move up one directory which is the root directory, then enter myphotos directory **(/myphotos)** and finally point at **mother.jpg**. Thus using relative URL writing of long path name can be avoided.

University Question

1. *Explain the use of relative URL with example.* **AU : Dec.-11, Marks 8**

1.6 Web Server

AU : May-10,12,13,19 , Marks 12

- Web server is a special type of server to which the web browser submits the request of web page which is desired by the client.
- There are some popularly used web servers such as Apache and IIS from Microsoft.

Functions of web server

Various functions of web server are -

1. The web servers **accepts the requests** from the web browsers.
2. The user **request is processed** by the web server.
3. The web servers respond to the users by **providing the services** which they demand for over the web browsers.
4. The web servers **serve the web based applications.**
5. The DNS translate the **domain names into the IP addresses.**
6. The servers **verify** given address exists, **find necessary files** ,run appropriate scripts exchange cookies if necessary and returns back to the browser.
7. Some servers actively participate in **session handling techniques.**

Working Principle of Web Server

- When user submits a request for a web page, he/she is actually demanding for a page present on the web server.
- When web browser submits the request for a web page, the web server responds this request by sending back the requested page to the web browser of the client's machine.

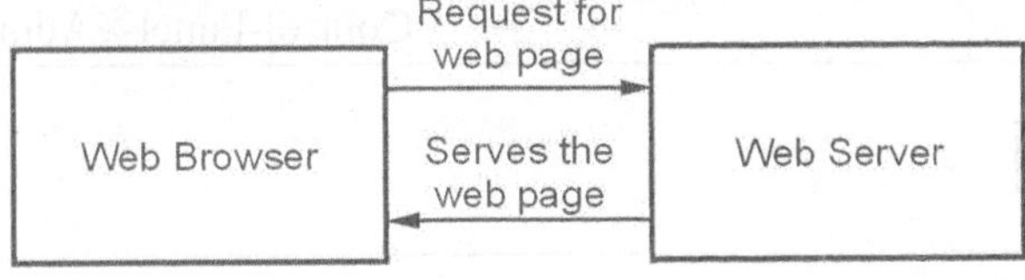

Fig. 1.6.1

Step 1 : Web client requests for the desired web page by providing the IP address of the website

Step 2 : The web server locates the desired web page on the website and responds by sending back the requested page. If the page doesn't exist, it will send back the appropriate error page.

Step 3 : The web browser receives the page and renders it as required.

1.6.1 Apache

- It is an excellent server because of its two important features : **Reliability** and **Efficiency**.
- Secondly it is more popular because it is an **open source software**. That means it is freely available to anybody. Apache web server is best suitable for UNIX systems but it can also be used on Windows box.

- The apache web server can be configured as per the requirements using the file **httpd.conf**. This file is present in the Apache software package.

1.6.2 IIS

- The **Internet Information Services** or Internet Information Server is a kind of web server provided by Microsoft.
- This server is most popular on Windows platform.

Following are some differences between Apache and IIS servers

Sr. No.	Apache web server	IIS web server
1.	Apache web server is useful on both Unix based systems and on Windows platform.	IIS web server is used on Windows platform.
2.	It is an open source product.	It is a vendor specific product and can be used on windows products only.
3.	The Apache web server can be controlled by editing the configuration file httpd.conf	For IIS server, the behaviour is controlled by modifying the window based management programs called **IIS snap in**. We can access IIS snap-in through the Control-Panel->Administrative Tools.

University Questions

1. *Explain briefly the IIS Web Server.* **AU : May-10, Marks 8**
2. *Explain in detail the functions of web server.* **May-12, Marks 8**
3. *Explain the capabilities of web client and web server.* **May-13, Marks 12**
4. *Explain the working principle of web server with neat sketch.* **May-19, Marks 8**

1.7 Client, Sever and Communication

- In this architecture, there are 3 components.
  1) Client PC or Web client
  2) An application server or web server
  3) A database server.

Working

Step 1 : The client PC or web client submits the request for desired web page to the web server.

Step 2 : The work of server is distributed among application server and database servers. Application server possesses the required communication functions.

Step 3 : The data required by this business logic is present on database server. The required data is returned to application servers

Step 4 : The web server or application server prepares the response page and sends it to the web client.

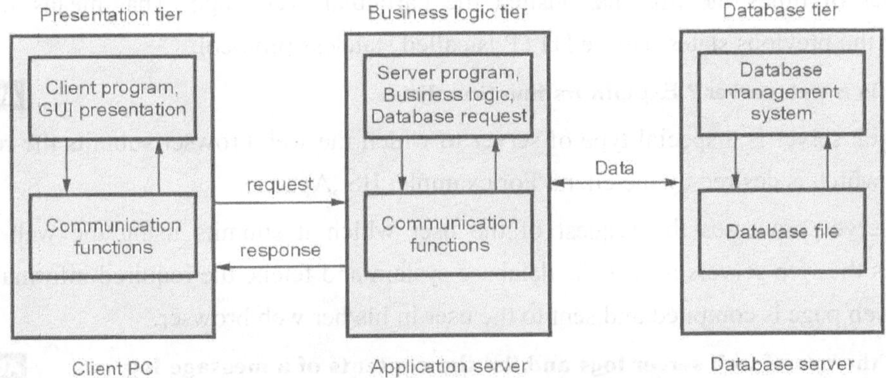

Fig. 1.7.1 Client Server Communication

Advantages :

1. High performance and persistent objects take part in communication.
2. This architecture is scalable. That means it can support increased number of users and resources.
3. High degree of flexibility in deployment platform and configurations.
4. Code/data reusability can be achieved.
5. Improved data integrity
6. Improved security as clients can not directly access the database.
7. The maintenance and modifications can be done effectively without disturbing other modules in the architecture.

Disadvantages :

1. The complexity gets increased.
2. Cost for network maintenance and deployment is increased.

Two Marks Questions with Answers

Q.1 List any two types of web servers with its application usage. **AU : May-09**

Ans. : There are two types of web servers one is vendor specific and another one is open source. The example of vendor specific web server is IIS and example of open source web server is Apache.

The IIS web server is used on Windows and Apache web server can be used on both Unix and Windows platform.

Q.2 Why is HTTP called as stateless protocol ? **AU : Dec.-09**

Ans. : The HTTP protocol can not remember the previous user's information nor it remembers the number of times the user has visited the particular web page. That means it can not remember the previous states. Hence HTTP is called stateless protocol.

Q.3 What is a web server ? Explain its functionalities. **AU : Dec.-09**

Ans. : Web server is a special type of server to which the web browser submits the request of web page which is desired by the client. For example: IIS ,Apache.

Web server processes the request of the user which it submits using the web browser. Sometimes the web servers access the database system and fetche the required information. The required web page is compiled and sent to the user in his/her web browser.

Q.4 State the use of web server logs and list the contents of a message log. **AU : May-11**

Ans. : Web server log records the information about the server activity. It stores the information about every http request processed by the server. A web server may produce more than one message logs.

Every message log contains variety of debugging information and other information generated by web application. Following information is present in the message log -

A. Host name or IP address of the client machine making the request.

B. Name of the user.

C. Date and time of response along with the time zone.

D. Start line of HTTP request.

E. HTTP status code of response.

F. Number of bytes sent in body of response.

Q.5 What is the use of cache control in HTTP response header ?

Ans. : Cache is used as a temporary repository. Use of cache improves the performance. Many web browsers store web pages viewed by the client in the cache memory. This brings efficiency in browsing the web page. The cache control help the user to display the web page quickly.

Q.6 List some basic internet protocols. **AU : May-13**

Ans. : Following are some basic Internet protocols.

i. http ii. ftp iii. smtp iv. pop3.

Q.7 For handling the mails which protocol is used ?

Ans. : There are two commonly used protocols for handling the emails. Simple Mail Transfer Protocol (SMTP) is a simple protocol which is used to transfer emails to remote servers. Another protocol is POP3 i.e. Post Office Protocol Version 3. This protocol works only at the receivers end and has no work at the sender's end.

Q.8 Give the functionalities of IP protocol.

Ans. : There are two functionalities provided by Internet Protocol -

Decomposition of the initial information flow into packets of standardized size and reassembling of data at the destination.

The Internet protocol **routes** the packet through successive networks, from the source machine to the destination which can be identified by its IP address.

Q.9 What is the difference between WWW and Internet ?

Ans. : The WWW and Internet are the two different terms. The Internet is a collection of computers and other devices such as printers, scanners etc. connected together whereas WWW is collection of software and corresponding protocol used to access the resources over the network. Thus World Wide Web (WWW) contains huge amount of documents, images and other resources which can be accessed using the hyperlinks. People use Internet through web.

Q.10 Explain any two functionalities of web browser.

Ans. : Various functions of web browser are -

1. Reformat the URL and send a valid HTTP request.
2. When user gives the address of particular website it is in the form of domain name. The web browser converts the DNS to corresponding IP address.
3. The web browser establishes a TCP connection with the web browser while processing the user's request.
4. The web browsers send the HTTP request to the web server.

Q.11 What is URL ? Write different parts of URL.

Ans. : The general format of URL is -

Scheme:Address

That is

protocol://username@hostname/path/filename

The scheme specifies the **communication protocol**. Different schemes have different forms of addresses.

Various schemes that are used are http, ftp, gopher, file, mailto, news and so on.

Example : http://www.vtubooks.com/index.aspx

Q.12 Define URI. AU : May-11

Ans. : The **U**niform **R**esource **I**dentifier (URI) is a string used to identify the names or resources on the Internet. The URI is a combination of URL and URN. The URL stands for **U**niform **R**esource **L**ocator and URN stands for **U**niform **R**esource **N**ame. The web address denotes the URL and specific name of the place or a person or item denotes the URN. For example

urn:ISBN 978-81-8431-123-2

specifies the address of some book.

Every URI consists of two parts, the part before the colon : denotes the **scheme** and the part after colon depends upon the scheme. The URIs are case insensitive but generally written in lower case. If the URI is written in the form of http: then it is both an URI and URL.

Q.13 What is GET and POST request ?

Ans. : The GET method is used to retrieve the information from a specified URI. The POST method is used to request the server for desired web page. This is supposed to be a safe method of retrieving the information.

Q.14 What is www ?

Ans. : The WWW is a World Wide Web which is a collection of software and corresponding protocols used to access the resources over the network. The WWW contains huge amount of documents, images, and other resources which can be accessed using hyperlinks. Thus Internet can be used through the web.

Q.15 What is TCP ?

Ans. : The TCP stands for Transmission Control Protocol. This is the connection oriented protocol which help in communicating two machines. Using TCP the message gets transferred in an orderly manner.

Q.16 List any four common browsers. AU : Dec.-11

Ans. : The common browsers are Internet Explorer, Mozilla Firefox, Google Chrome, Safari

Q.17 State the uses of Internet protocol. AU : May-12

Ans. : Following are the uses of Internet protocols -

i) The Internet protocol is used to decompose the initial information flow into packets of the standard size. At the destination these packets are reassembled back.

ii) The Internet protocol routes the data packets so that transmission of data is possible to the machine having desired IP address.

Q.18 State the functions of DNS and protocol used. **AU : Dec.-12**

Ans. : Following are the functions that are carried out by DNS –

1. Accepting and then requesting the programs to convert domain names to IP addresses.
2. Accepting and then requesting the other DNS servers to convert domain names to IP addresses.

Q.19 Explain the way in which a DNS server resolves the address ?

AU : Dec.-13, May-18, 19

Ans. : Using the domain name space the computer which is to be accessed is identified uniquely. The internet logically arranges the domain names in an hierarchical form. Secondly, the DNS server maintains the huge database of domain names. The desired address is searched in this database and if the IP address of corresponding name is found then IP address is returned to user computer.

Q.20 List the two forms of URL and its uses. **AU : May-14**

Ans. : The two forms of URL are Absolute URL and Relative URL. The absolute URL directly points to a file whereas the relative URL points to the file or directory in relation to the present directory. The URL is a unique address of the file which is accessed over the internet.

Q.21 Differentiate between internet and intranet. **AU : CSE : Dec.-15**

Ans. :

Sr. No.	Internet	Intranet
1.	Internet is a network of computers and it is open for all.	Intranet is a network of computers but it is designed for specific group of users.
2.	The number of users of internet are unlimited.	The number of users of intranet are limited.
3.	Internet contains different sources of information on variety of subjects.	The intranet contains limited information on limited subjects.
4.	Internet contains large number of intranets.	Internet can be accessed from the intranet but with restrictions.
5.	It is a collection of various LANs, WANs and MANs.	It is mostly any of LAN, WAN or MAN.

❑❑❑

Notes

Unit I

2 HTML5

Syllabus

HTML5 – Tables – Lists – Image – HTML5 control elements – Semantic elements – Drag and Drop – Audio – Video controls.

Contents

2.1 Introduction to HTML

- HTML stands for HyperText Markup Language. **Hypertext** is simply a piece of text that works as a link.
- **Markup Language** is language of writing layout information within documents.
- Basically an HTML document is a plain text file.
- It contains rich text. The rich text means text with tags.
- HTML is **not a case sensitive** language.
- Any HTML program can be written in simple Notepad or WordPad text editors. The extension to this program should be either **html** or **htm**.
- This program then can be opened in some web browser and the corresponding web page can be viewed. Let us create our first web page using HTML.

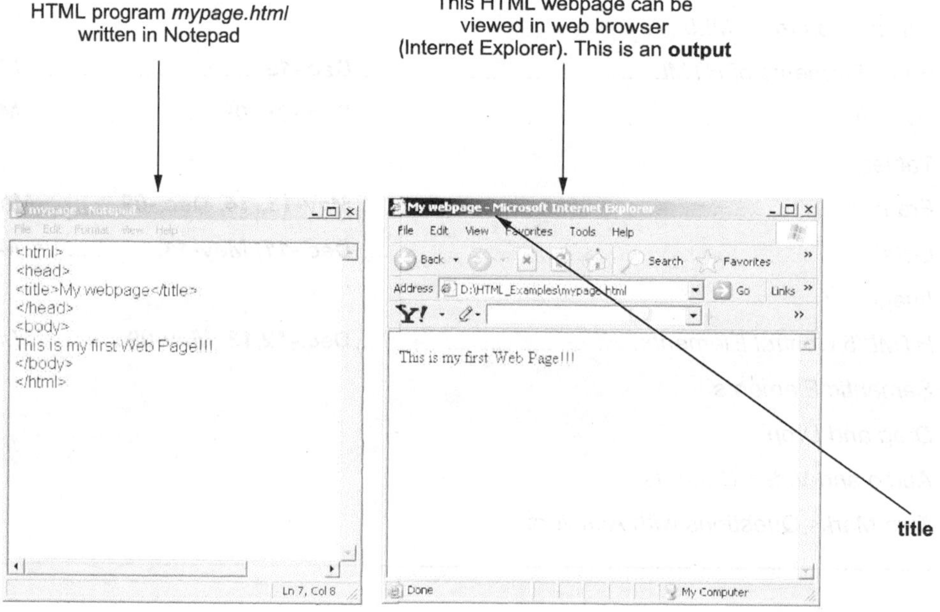

HTML Document

```
<html>
<head>
<title>My webpage</title>
</head>
<body>
This is my first Web Page!!!
</body>
</html>
```

Script Explanation

1) Note that the program consists of some strings enclosed within **angular brackets.** Such strings are called **tags.**

2) The HTML program should be written within **<html>** and **</html>.** The <html> indicates the start of html program and </html> denotes end of html program. Use of slash (/) in the angular bracket indicates end of that particular tag.

3) Any HTML program has two prominent parts : **head and body.** The head part acts as a header of a file and contains some information like setting the title of web page.

Comments in HTML

- The comment in HTML can be denoted as follows -

  <!--It is a comment statement -->

- There should **not be a space** between angular bracket and exclamation mark. This comment is beginning with <!-- and ending with -->. Also note one thing that there should not be any -- inside the comment.

2.2 Introduction to HTML5

- The HTML 5.0 is the fifth revision of HTML standard of World Wide Consortium(W3C) which is finalized in October 2014.
- The earlier version was HTML 4.0 which was released in 1997.
- The objective of this markup language version was - i) to provide support for latest multimedia and ii) to make the script readable and consistently understood by the developer.
- The HTML5 adds many new syntactic features. It includes the elements such as <video>, <audio> and <canvas> elements. It also has integration of Scalable Vector Graphics(SVG)contents and MathML for mathematical Formula.

2.2.1 Features of HTML 5.0

1. The XHTML doctype is just impossible to memorize (!DOCTYPE html PUBLIC "...). Hence a new HTML doctype is <!DOCTYPE html>
2. There are new graphic elements such as <canvas> and <svg> in HTML5.0
3. The support for multimedia elements such as <audio> and <video>
4. It has support for <header>, <footer>, <article>, and <section>
5. It has support for new form controls such as number, date, time, calendar, and range.
6. It has a rich set of Application Programming Interface(API) for geolocations, HTML Drag and Drop, Local Storage, Application cache and so on.

2.2.2 Difference between HTML and HTML5

Sr. No.	HTML	HTML5
1.	The DOCTYPE declaration is much longer such as <!DOCTYPE html PUBLIC "-//W3C//DTD XHTML 1.0 Transitional//EN" "http://www.w3.org/TR/xhtml1/DTD/xhtml11.dtd">	The DOCTYPE declaration is simple **<!DOCTYPE html>**
2.	<audio> and <video> tags are not supported.	<audio> and <video> tags are supported for playing audio and video files.
3.	Finding out geographic location is impossible using HTML	The HTML5 supports the API for identifying the **geographic location.**
4.	It supports the tag such as <applet>, <big>, <center>, <font>, <frame>, <strike>	The tags that are removed from HTML5 are <applet>, <big>, <center>, <font>, <frame>, <strike>
5.	Does not allow JavaScript to run in browser. JavaScript runs in same thread as browser interface.	It allows **JavaScript** to run in background.
6.	There is no support for <canvas>	The **<canvas>** tag is for 2D drawing.
7.	It needs external plugins such as flash.	The need for **external plugin is reduced.**

2.2.3 Structure of HTML

The structure of HTML document can be illustrated by following sample HTML document.

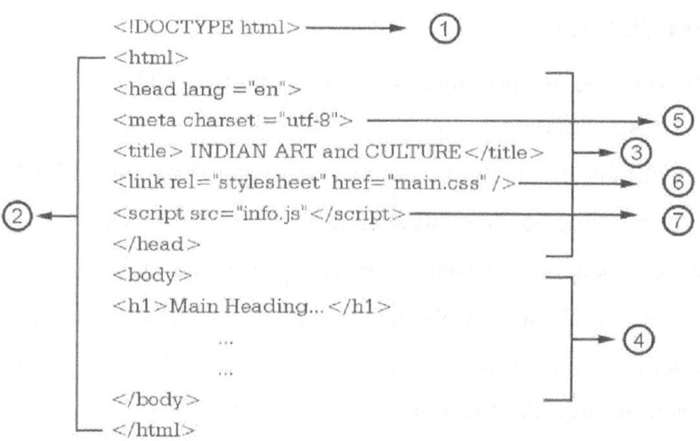

1. **Doctype :** The Doctype stands for Document type which tells the browser what type of document (HTML) it is about to process.
2. **HTML :** The <html> element is sometimes called the root element as it contains all the other HTML elements in the document.
3. **Head :** HTML pages are divided into two sections: the head and the body, which correspond to the <head> and <body> elements. The head contains descriptive elements about the document, such as its title, any style sheets or JavaScript files it uses.
4. **Body :** The body contains content (both HTML elements and regular text) that will be displayed by the browser.
5. **Character encoding :** The **<meta>** element specifies that the character encoding for the document is **UTF-8.** Character encoding refers to which character set standard is being used to encode the characters in the document. UTF-8 is a more complete variable-width encoding system that can encode all 110,000 characters in the Unicode character set.
6. **External style sheet :** The external stylesheet such as css can be used with HTML document. We can specify the name of the CSS stylesheet.
7. **External scripts :** Sometimes external JavaScript files can be associated with HTML document.

2.3 Basic Elements of HTML

AU : Dec.-13, Marks 8

- In all HTML/XHTML documents the root element is **<html>** which has two children : head and body.
- Any text contained within the head element does not appear directly in the **client area** of web browser. The head element is used for providing certain information to web browser. The **<title>** element is used to give title to the web page. Note that this **title** does not appear in client area. Rather it appears at the top of web browser.
- The **<body>** element contains the information which is to be displayed in the client area of web browser.
- The body element can contain several fundamental elements such as <p>, <h1>, <div>, <a>, <hr>, <br> and so on. The elements within the body part is for deciding the layout of your web page.

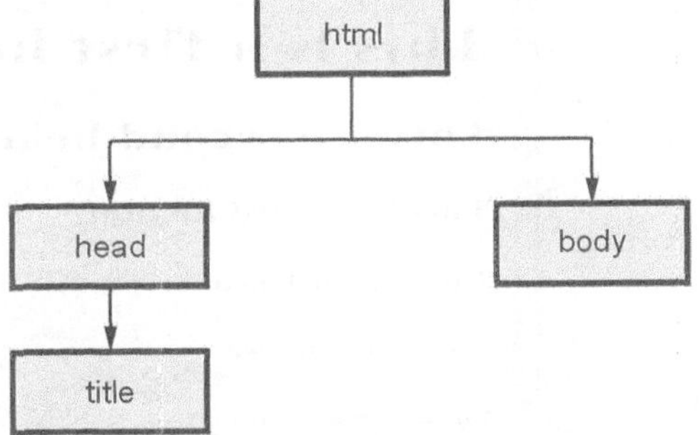

Fig. 2.3.1 Element tree

2.3.1 Heading

- There are header tags which help to display the text as some header.
- The header tag is denoted by h1, h2 and so on upto h6.
- Following HTML document along with its output is itself self explanatory.

HTML Document [headerDemo.html]

```
<!DOCTYPE html>
<html>
    <head>
    </head>
    <body>
        <h1>  This is a first header </h1>
        <h2>  This is a second header </h2>
        <h3>  This is a third header </h3>
        <h4>  This is a forth header </h4>
        <h5>  This is a fifth header </h5>
        <h6>  This is a sixth header </h6>
    </body>
</html>
```

Output

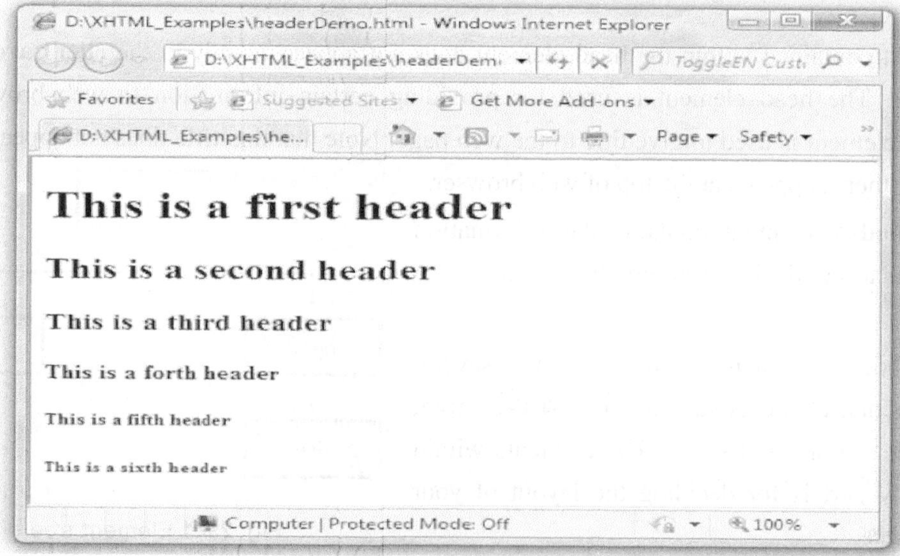

2.3.2 Paragraphs

Following are the tags that are used for creating paragraphs

Tag	Meaning
<p>	This tag should be put at the end of every paragraph.
<pre>	This tag is used to preserve the white spaces and lines in the text.
<div>	This tag is used to make division of sections in the XHTML document.

For example

HTML Document[TextFormat.html]

```
<!DOCTYPE html>
<html >
        <head>
        </head>
        <body>
                <p>
                Once upon a time, there was a king who kept a monkey as a pet.
                The monkey served the king by all the possible ways.
                </p>
                <div>
                It was very hot in those days. So one day, when the king was sleeping, monkey was
                fanning the king. Suddenly monkey noticed a fly on the chest of the king. The monkey
                tried to swish it away. But fly would go away for one moment and come back again.
                </div>
                <div> So monkey decided to teach a lesson to the fly.</div>
<pre>
The monkey then looked for something to hit a fly.
It then found a stick.
It picked up the stick and tried to beat the fly using stick.
Hmmm     at last it found a fly and
with all the force it hit the fly as a result of which the king died.

Lesson from the story:Never keep a fool servant !!!
</pre>
        </body>
</html>
```

Output

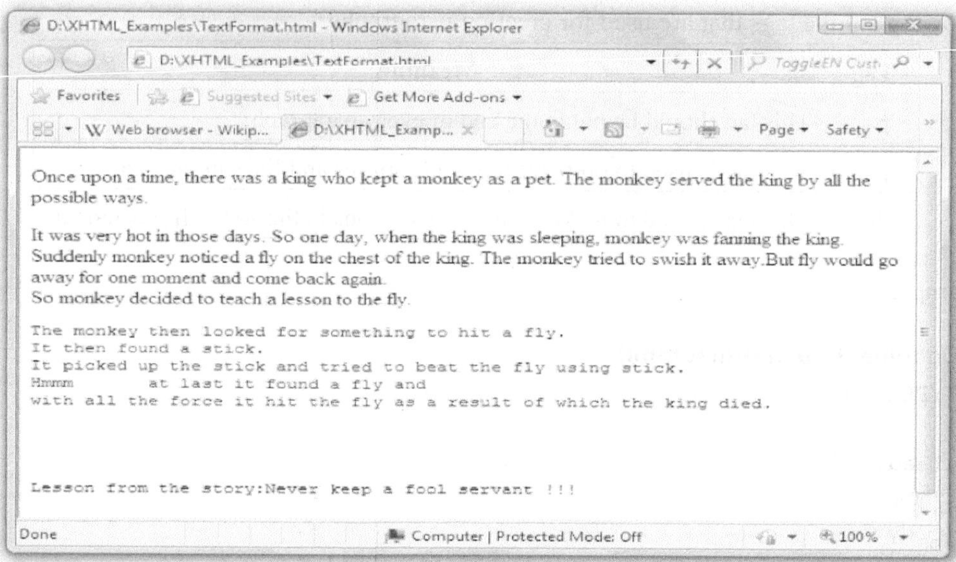

2.3.3 Line Break

For the line break the **
 tag** is used. This is a single line break tag. Generally this tag is kept at the end of every line.

For example

```
<!DOCTYPE html>
<html>
    <head>
      <title>Line Break Demo</title>
    </head>
    <body>
        <p>
            Here the line breaks <br/> and new line starts.
            Again line breaks<br/> Bye.
        </p>
    </body>
</html>
```

Output

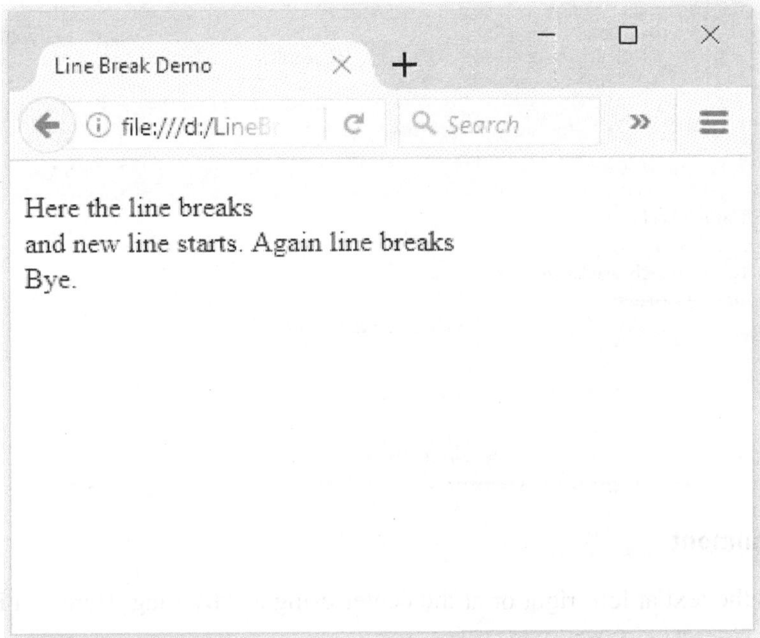

2.3.4 Setting Font Style

The font style can be of various types such as boldface, italics, and strikethrough.

Tag	Purpose
<b> </b>	Displays the text in bold
<i> </i>	Displays the text in italics
<strong </strong>	Displays the text in bold
<strike> </strike>	Displays the text with strike

Following HTML document illustrates this –

HTML Document [FontStyle.html]

```
<!DOCTYPE html>
<html>
        <head>
          <title>Font Style Demo</title>
        </head>
        <body>
                <b> This is a bold text </b> <br/>
                <i> This is in italics</i> <br/>
                <strong> This is strongly emphasized text</strong> <br/>
                <strike> This is striked text </strike>
                <center> This will appear at the center</center> <br/>
        </body>
</html>
```

Output

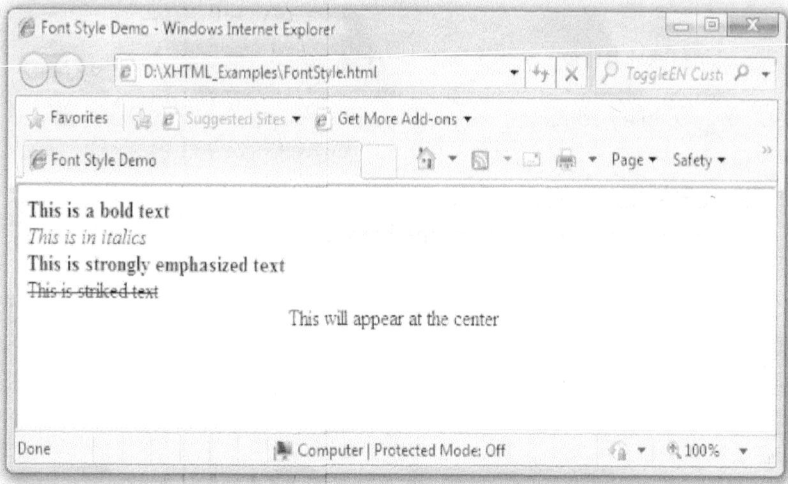

2.3.5 Text Alignment

We can align the text at left, right or at the center using a **<div>** tag. Here is a HTML program which shows the text aligned left, right and centre.

HTML Document[TextAlign.html]

```
<!DOCTYPE html >
<html>
    <head>
      <title>Font Style Demo</title>
    </head>
    <body>
            <div align="center">This line is aligned at center</div>
            <div align="left">This line is aligned at left</div>
            <div align="right">This line is aligned at right</div>
    </body>
</html>
```

Output

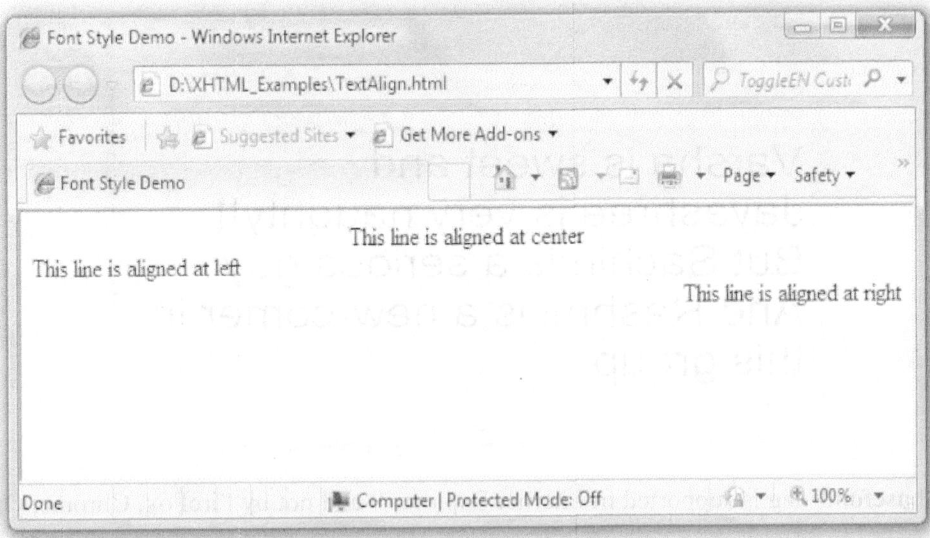

2.3.6 Setting the Font and Color

We can set the font, size and color of the text in the web page. The tag **<basefont>** is used for this purpose. The optional attributes used with <basefont> tag are as given below :

Attribute	Value	Purpose
color	Color value such as "red", "yellow" and so on.	It displays the text with specified color.
face	Font-family such as "arial", "verdana","sans-serif" and so on.	It displays the text with specific font family.
size	Number	The text of specified size will be displayed using this attribute value.

For example –

HTML Document[SetFont.html]

```
<!DOCTYPE html>
<html >
        <head>
                <title>Setting the Text </title>
        </head>
        <body>
                        <basefont face="arial" size="10">
                        Varsha is sweet  and <br/>
                        Jayashree is very naughty!!<br/>
                        But Sachin is a serious guy<br/>
                        And Rashmi is a new-comer in this group
</body>
</html>
```

Output

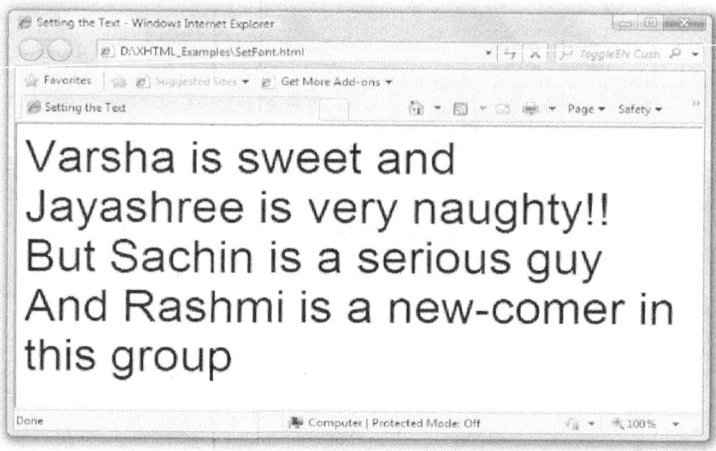

The **<basefont>** tag is supported in Internet Explorer 9 and not by FireFox, Chrome, Opera and so on.

Most of the web designers prefer to have their web pages white in color. HTML allows the web developer to use **color** attribute for coloring the text or for setting the background color.

First of all we will learn how to display a text colourful on the webpage.

HTML Document[ColorFont.html]

```
<!DOCTYPE html>
<html>
    <head>
        <title>coloring the text</title>
    </head>
    <body>
            <basefont face="arial" size="5" color="blue">
        Great people are simple and <br>
        <font face="Times new roman" color="red" size="8">
        Simple people are great!!!<br>
        <font face="GoudyHandtooled BT" color="green" size="14">
        Great people rule the world.
    </body>
</html>
```

Output

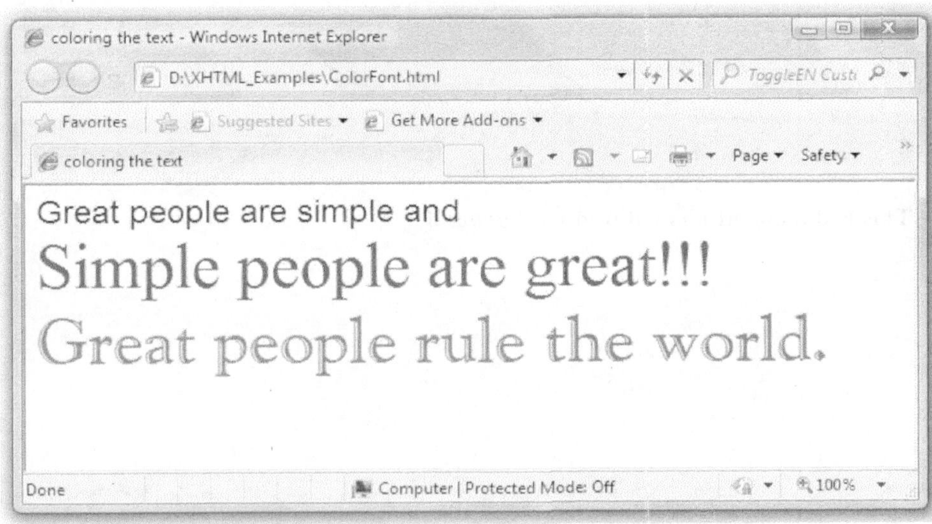

Script Explanation :

1) In the above HTML document, we have used **font face** tag to set the font.
2) Using the attributes **color** and **size** we can specify values color and size in double quotes.

We can set the **background color** of the web page using the attribute **bgcolor.** Following program sets the background color of the web page to red.

HTML Document[BgColor.html]

```
<!DOCTYPE html>
<html>
    <head>
        <title>Coloring the background</title>
    </head>
    <body bgcolor="#FFFF00">
    <h3>This is document has colored background</h3>
    </body>
</html>
```

Script Explanation :

1) In above document we have specified background color using the **bgcolor** attribute.
2) The color can be specified by either using the color name in double quotes or using the hex.code as given in above document.
3) The first two digits of Hex code represents the Red value, then next two digits specify the green value and final two digits specify the blue value. Hence the corresponding output will be as follows -

Output

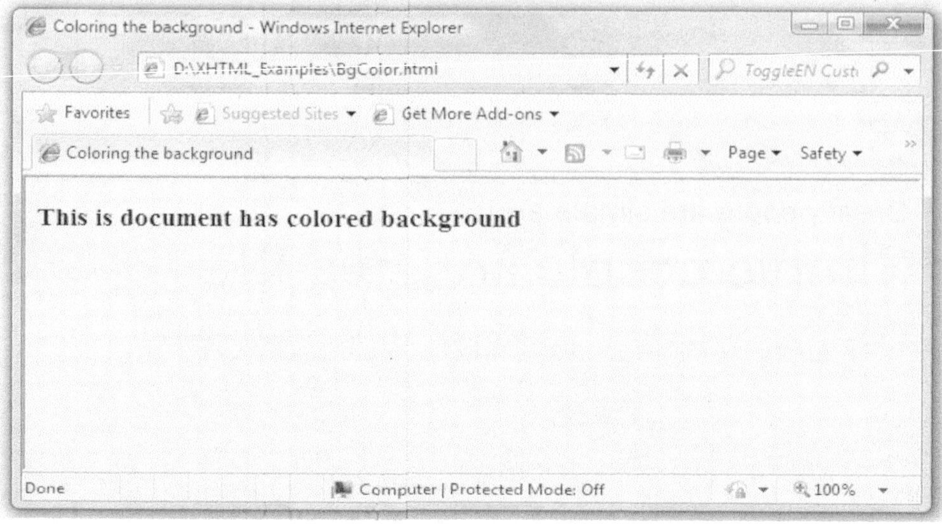

Note that the background color is specified by the hexadecimal value. Following table shows the hex. and corresponding decimal values -

Decimal value	Hexadecimal value
1	1
2	2
3	3
4	4
5	5
6	6
7	7
8	8
9	9
10	A
11	B
12	C
13	D
14	E
15	F

In HTML, the colors are specified by beginning with # and the FF denotes 255. In this color code first two digits specify the amount of red color then next two digits specify the green color and the last two digits specify blue color.

FF 00 00

red colour

Hence is used to set the background color red. Each pair of digits specifies 0 to 255 color values. Thus hexadecimal color coding helps us to specify.

$$256 * 256 * 256 = 16777216 \text{ colors.}$$

The color can also be specified by its name as follows -

```
<html>
<body bgcolor=yellow>
</html>
```

Following is a list of colors that can be specified for setting the background colors

Aqua	Navy
Black	Olive
Blue	Purple
Fuchsia	Red
Gray	Silver
Green	Teal
Lime	White
Maroon	Yellow

2.3.7 Special Character

- In HTML certain symbols are treated as special. For example - < i.e. less than symbol is considered as special symbol because it is used as the beginning of the tag.
- Hence we cannot directly use certain symbols such as <, >, “,© and so on.
- To print these symbols we use the units which are called as **reference.** This reference always begins with ampersand (&) sign. Such reference is called as **entity reference.**
- Following table enlists some characters and entity references –

Character	Meaning	Entity Reference
<	less than	<
>	greater than	>
&	ampersand	&
“	double quote	"
’	apostrophes	'
©	copyright	©

- Another type of entity reference that is used frequently is ** ** that is **non breaking space character.**
- This entity reference is useful for defining the space between two string and informing browser for not performing the word wrapper between the strings.
- Following is a sample script that makes use of ** .**

HTML Document[SpaceDemo.html]

```
<!DOCTYPE html>
<html>
	<head>
	<title>Space Demo</title>
	</head>
	<body>
	<h3>
	Method 1:
	</h3>
	<p>
	Jony Jony Yes Papa     Eating
	 sugar no  Papa   Open Your 
	mouth       Ha!Ha!Ha
	</p>
	<h3>
	Method 2:
	</h3>
	<p>
	Jony Jony Yes Papa      Eating sugar no Papa   Open Your mouth        Ha!Ha!Ha
	</p>
	</body>
</html>
```

Output

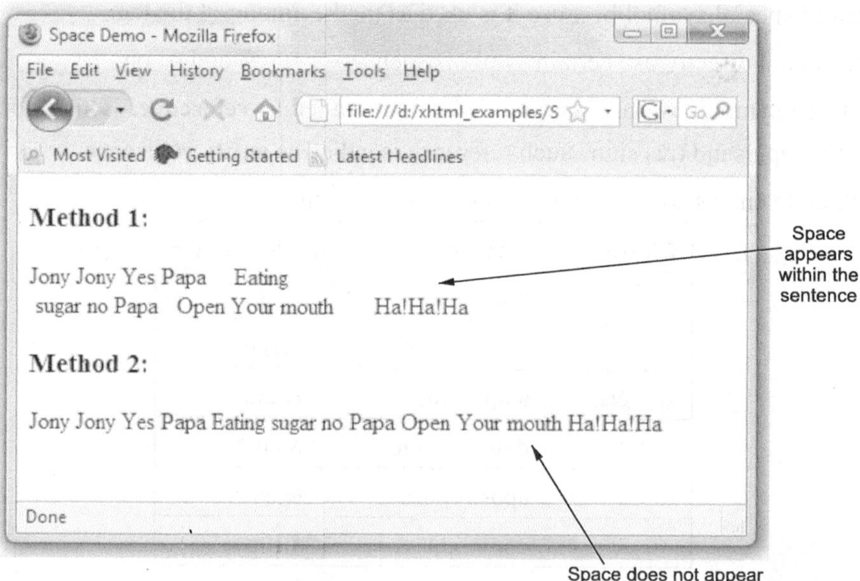

Ex. 2.3.1 : How Divide and Pound symbol can be put on HTML document ?

Sol. : With the help of entity references denoted using & these two symbols can be put in HTML document. The code can be

```
<html>
<head>
</head>
<body>
<p>This &divide symbol</p>
<p>This &pound symbol</p>
</body>
</html>
```

Output

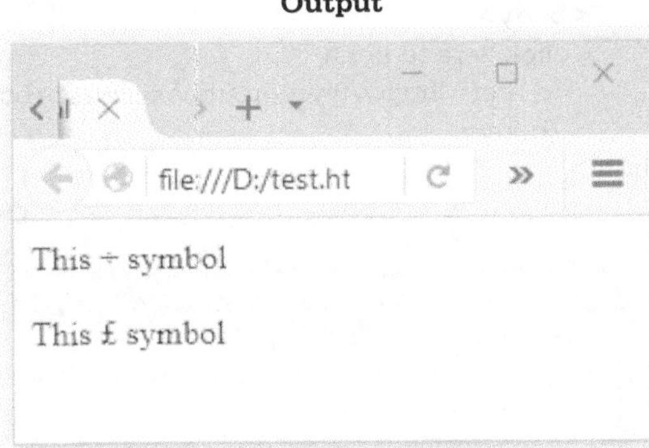

University Question

1. *State and explain any four HTML elements in detail.* **AU : Dec.-13, Marks 8**

2.4 Hyperlink

AU : Dec.-08, 09, Marks 2

- There is a common practice to specify the web link in the web page. The link acts as a pointer to some web page or some resource.
- Use of hyperlink in the web page allows that page to link logically with other page.
- We can use hyperlinks by using a tag **<a>** and by specifying the URL for **href.**
- The value assigned to **href** specifies the target of the link.
- The <a> means beginning of the web link and **</a>** means end of the web link.
- The most important attribute of the <a> element is the **href** attribute, which indicates the link's destination.
- By default, links will appear as follows in all browsers :
  1) An unvisited link is underlined and blue.
  2) A visited link is underlined and purple
  3) An active link is underlined and red
- Following are the steps to be followed to specify web link in the web page.

Step 1 : The beginning of web link can be specified by the tag <a href = " ". Inside the double quotes mention the URL of desired link.

Step 2 : Write some text that should act as a hyperlink.

Step 3 : End the web link </a>

Here is a sample program which implements the above given idea -

HTML Document [HyperlnkDemo.html]

```
<!DOCTYPE html>
<html>
        <head>
                <title> Use of Hyperlink on the web Page </title>
        </head>
        <body>
          click here to get a
         <a href="http://www.vtubooks.com">book</a> on engineering
        </body>
</html>
```

Output

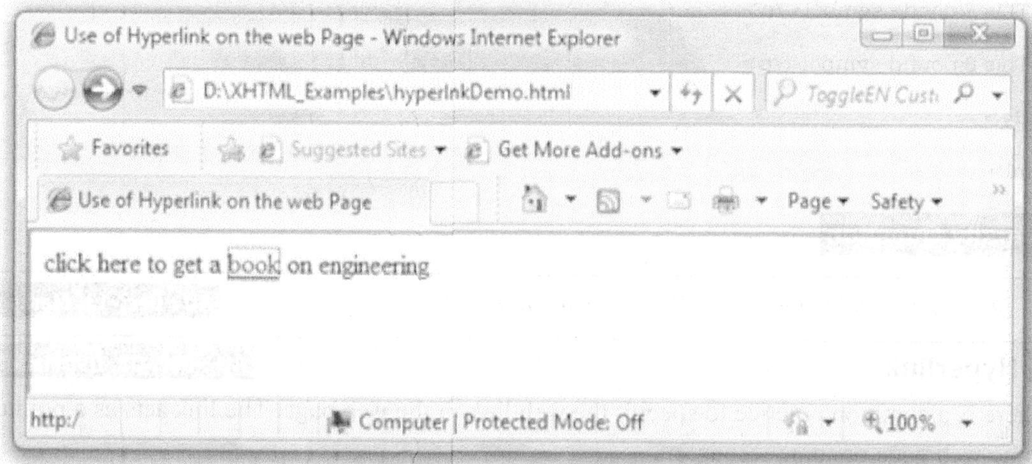

If you click on the hyperlink book then you will get the following output.

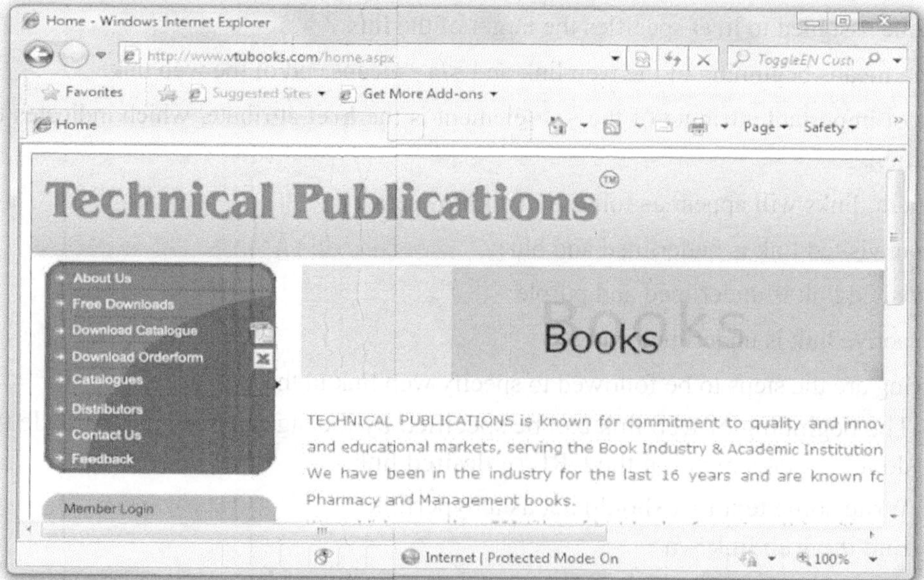

The target attribute

- If we want to get that link opened in another window we can mention _**target** property. Various targets can be -
- _**self** loads the page into the current window.
- _**blank** loads the page into a new separate browser window.

Ex. 2.4.1 : Develop a HTML page to use image as a link to another page. **AU : Dec.-08, Marks 2**

Sol. :

Step 1 : Write the HTML document containing an hyperlink to an image. When we click on the image the html page referred by the **<a href>** tag must get opened.

XHTML Document[ImgLink.html]

```
<!DOCTYPE html>
<html>
    <head>
     <title> Image Demo </title>
    </head>
    <body>
     <h1> Indian Heritage </h1>
     </p>
     <a href="TajMahal.html" target ="_blank">
     <img src= "TajMahal.jpg" alt= "Taj Mahal!!" />
     </a>
     <br/>History of Taj Mahal
     <br/>
    </body>
</html>
```

Step 2 : Write the HTML document(TajMahal.html) mentioned by the <a href> tag in Step 1 as follows.

HTML Document[TajMahal.html]

```
<!DOCTYPE html>
<html>
    <head>
     <title> Information on TajMahal </title>
    </head>
    <body>
     <h1> Indian Heritage </h1>
     <p>
     Taj Mahal is one of the wonders of the World. It is located in Agra,India.
     <br/>
```

```
        Taj Mahal is built by <strong>Shah Jahan</strong> in memory of his wife <strong>Mumtaz
Mahal</strong>
        <br/>
        It is considered to be the excellent example of Mughal Architecture
        </p>
        <br/>
      </body>
</html>
```

Step 3 : Open some web browser and specify the file name **ImgLink.html** in the address bar and you will get following output.

Output

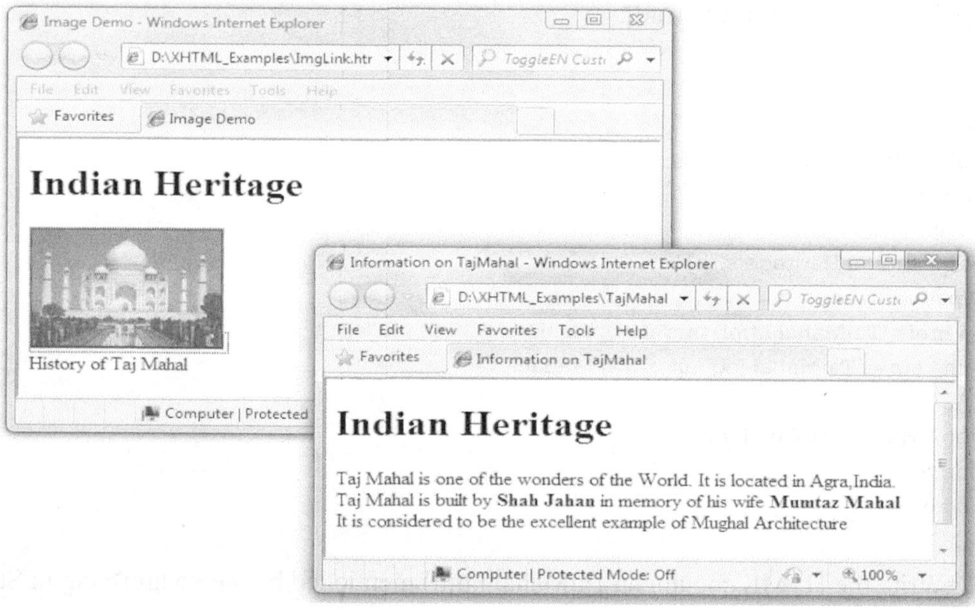

2.4.1 Playing an Audio File

Using HTML script we can play the audio files. The simplest way to play audio file is the use of hyperlinks. Following script shows how simple it is to a play a sound file using HTML

```
<html>
 <body>
  <h2>Playing The Audio</h2>
  <form>
    <a href="chimes.wav">Click here to Play the sound</a>
  </form>
 </body>
</html>
```

The above script executes in almost all the web browsers such as Internet explorer, Mozilla Firefox, Opera and so on. But the above HTML document launches the Media player software and then the audio file is played within it. For playing the audio files using hyperlinks it is necessary to get the audio file downloaded first.

2.4.2 Uses of Links

Following are the uses of the hyperlinks for a web document -

1. One can link logically related documents together using the links in the web page.
2. Use of link enhances the readability of the web document.
3. User can click on the link and can learn more about a subtopic and then can return to the main topic. This navigation within the web pages is possible due to the links.

University Question

1. *How are audio files played through HTML? Explain with an example.* **AU : Dec.-09, Marks 2**

2.5 Tables

- For systematic arrangement of information we often require tabular structure. HTML allows us to create tables on the web pages.
- Many web designers are using invisible tables on the web pages.
- The **biggest advantage of using tables** on the web pages is that the information gets arranged systematically.
- The table is a matrix of rows and columns and the area formed due to intersection of a row and a column is called cell.

2.5.1 Basic Table Structure

- To create a table on the web page the table beginning tag is <table> and </table> tag is used for ending the table.
- Within <table> … </table> tag we can create rows and columns.
- The rows are created using <tr> </tr> and columns are created using <td> </td>
- For example –

<table>

<tr>	One **<td>**	Two **<td>**	Three **<td>**
<tr>	Four **<td>**	Five **<td>**	Six **<td>**
<tr>	Seven **<td>**	Eight **<td>**	Nine **<td>**

HTML Document[TabDemo.html]

```
<!DOCTYPE html>
<html>
    <head>
        <title> Table Demo </title>
    </head>
    <body>
    <br/><br/>
    <center>
    <table border="5">
    <caption align="bottom">
        <b> Table Demo </b>
```

```
    </caption>
    <tr>
        <td>This is Left cell-row 1</td>
        <td>This is Right cell -row 1</td>
    </tr>
    <tr>
        <td>This is Left cell-row 2</td>
        <td>This is Right cell-row 2</td>
    </tr>
    </table>
    </center>
    </body>
</html>
```

Output

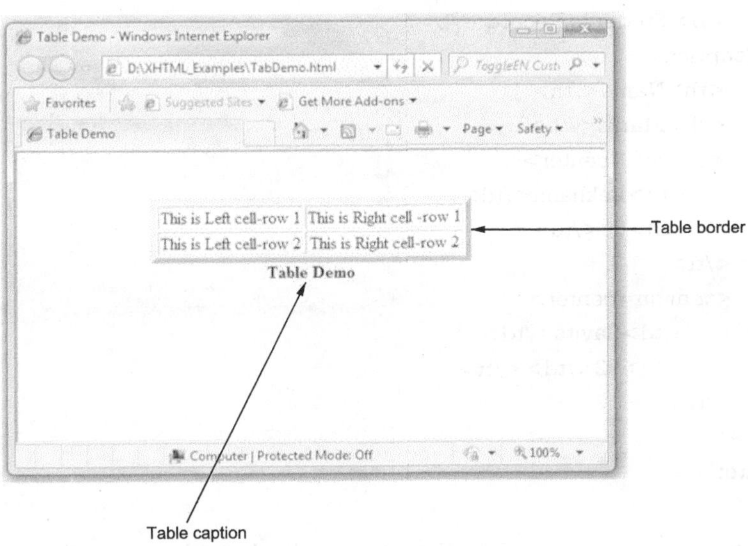

Script Explanation

1) In above program, the parameter border = "5" is set in order to set the table border. You can give any value to set the desired border.
2) The caption to the table is given by the parameter caption, we can set this caption either at the top or at the bottom by using the parameter align.
3) Then using the tag <tr> the table row can be set. The <td> tag is used to create columns from left to right.
4) Thus in the above program we are filling up the table values from top to bottom and from left to right. Just refer the output provided along with the program for clear understanding of look and feel of the table.

Ex. 2.5.1 : Write HTML document to create a table with header to each column.

Sol. : We can set the **header** to each column of the table by **<th>** tag. Here is a simple HTML program that simply adds the header to each column.

HTML Document [TabDemo1.html]

```
<!DOCTYPE html >
<html >
        <head>
                <title> Table Demo </title>
        </head>
        <body>
        <br/><br/>
        <center>
        <table border="3">
        <caption align="bottom">
            <b> Students Record </b>
        </caption>
            <th>Name</th>
            <th>Marks</th>
            <tr align=center>
                <td>Lekhana</td>
                <td>89</td>
            </tr>
            <tr align=center>
                <td>Savita</td>
                <td>92</td></tr>
            </tr>
    </table>
    </center>
</html>
```

Output

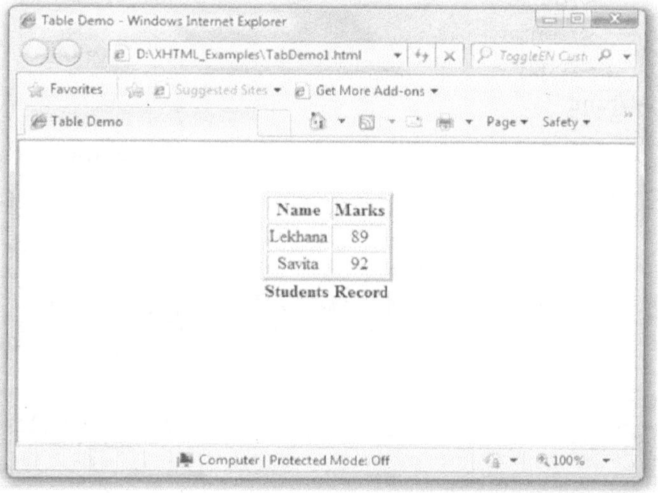

Name	Marks
Lekhana	89
Savita	92

Students Record

The data in each row can be aligned centrally by using **<tr align=center>** Other types of alignment can be left or right by **<tr align=left>** or **<tr align=right>** respectively.

Ex. 2.5.2 : Discuss the process of dividing the table into columns with an example. How would you give headers to the table columns ?

Sol. : The process of dividing the table into column is as follows :

1. Create a table using the tag <table>
2. Set the border to the table using attribute border="some value"
3. Create rows using the tag <tr> and for each row create the columns using <td> </td> tags.
4. The header for the table column can be given using the tag <th> </th>

Ex. 2.5.3 : Following HTML document divides the table in columns and gives the header to the column.

```
<!DOCTYPE html>
<html>
<head>
<title>Table Demo</title>
</head>
<body>
    <table border ="1">
    <th>Name</th>
    <th>Marks</th>
            <tr>
            <td>AAA</td>
            <td>50</td>
        </tr>
        <tr>
            <td>BBB</td>
            <td>90</td>
        </tr>
   </table>
 </body>
 </html>
```

Output

Name	Marks
AAA	50
BBB	90

2.5.2 RowSpan and ColSpan

- Sometimes we may require adding sub-columns or sub-rows to categorize the information properly. In such a situation colspan and rowspan can be used.
- The **rowspan** is used to extend the **row vertically** and **colspan** is used to extend the **column horizontally**.

For example –

When **rowspan**=2 then the **row can be extended vertically by two cells.**

rowspan	First	Second	<td rowspan=2>First
		Third	<td>Second</td><td>Third</td>

When **colspan**=2 then the **column can be extended** horizontally by two cells.

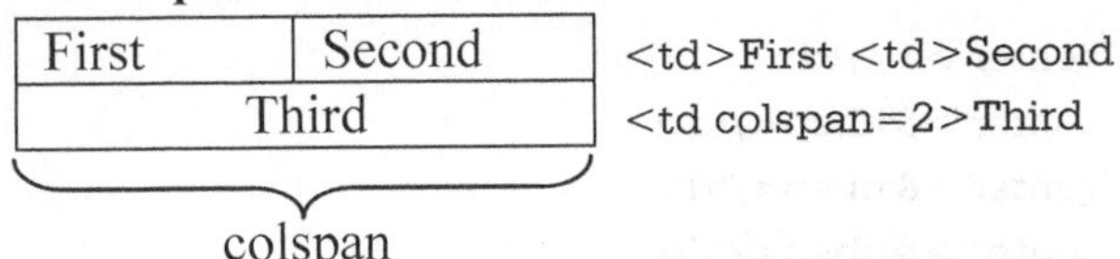

Ex. 2.5.4 : Explain the structure of HTML documents, write code to display following table :

<table border="1">
<tr><td rowspan="3">Sr. No.</td><td colspan="4">College Name</td></tr>
<tr><td colspan="2">Section A</td><td colspan="2">Section B</td></tr>
<tr><td>X</td><td>Y</td><td>X</td><td>Y</td></tr>
<tr><td>1</td><td></td><td></td><td></td><td></td></tr>
<tr><td>2</td><td></td><td></td><td></td><td></td></tr>
<tr><td>3</td><td></td><td></td><td></td><td></td></tr>
</table>

Sol. :

```
<html>
     <head>
          <title>My Table</title>


     </head>
     <body>
          <table border=1>
               <tr>
                    <td rowspan="3">
                    <p align=center>Sr.No.</p>
                    <p> </td>
                    </td>

                    <td colspan="4">
                         <p align="center">College Name</p>
               </td>
               </tr>
               <tr>
               <td width="40%" colspan="2" align="center">Section A</td>
               <td width="40%" colspan="2" align="center">Section B</td>
               </tr>
               <tr>
                   <td align="center">X</td>
                   <td align="center">Y</td>
                   <td align="center">X</td>
                   <td align="center">Y</td>
               </tr>
               <tr>
                   <td align="center">1</td>
                   <td align="center"> </td>
                   <td align="center"> </td>
                   <td align="center"> </td>
```

```
                <td align="center"> </td>
            </tr>
            <tr>
                <td align="center">2</td>
                <td align="center"> </td>
                <td align="center"> </td>
                <td align="center"> </td>
                <td align="center"> </td>
            </tr>
            <tr>
                <td align="center">3</td>
                <td align="center"> </td>
                <td align="center"> </td>
                <td align="center"> </td>
                <td align="center"> </td>
            </tr>
        </table>
    </body>
</html>
```

Output

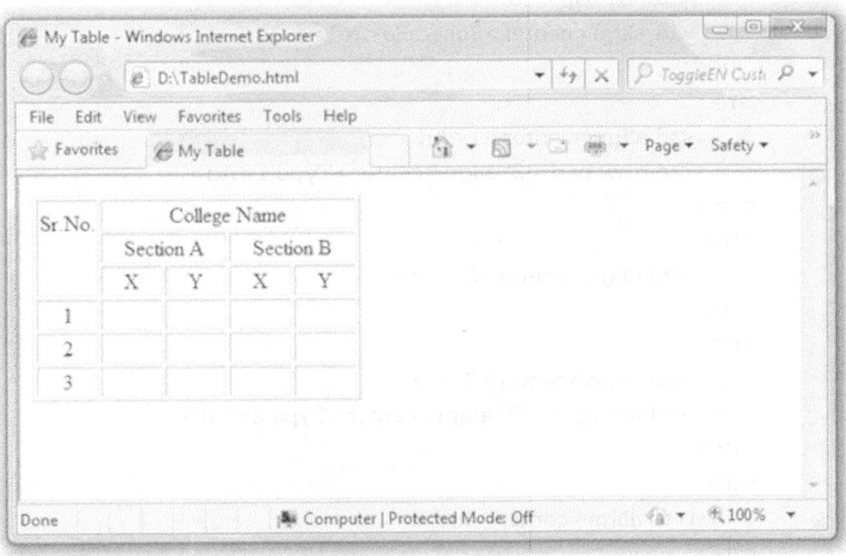

Ex. 2.5.5 : Write HTML code to draw table given below :

Image (20%)	Company Name (80%)
	Schedule
1	Type 1
2	
3	Type 2
4	

Sol. :

ImageDemo.html

```
<html>
      <head>
            <title>My Table</title>
      </head>
      <body>
            <table border=1>
                  <tr>
                        <td width="20%" align=center><img src="logo.jpg"/></td>
                        <th width="80%" align=center>TopTech Solutions</th>
                  </tr>
                  <tr>
                        <td> </td>
                        <td align=center>Schedule</td>
                  </tr>
                  <tr>
                        <td align=center>1</td>
                        <td rowspan="2" align=center>Type 1</td>
                  </tr>
                  <tr>
                        <td align=center>2</td>
                  </tr>
                  <tr>
                        <td align=center>3</td>
                        <td rowspan="2" align=center>Type 2</td>
                  </tr>
                  <tr>
                        <td align=center>4</td>
                  </tr>
            </table>
      </body>
</html>
```

Output

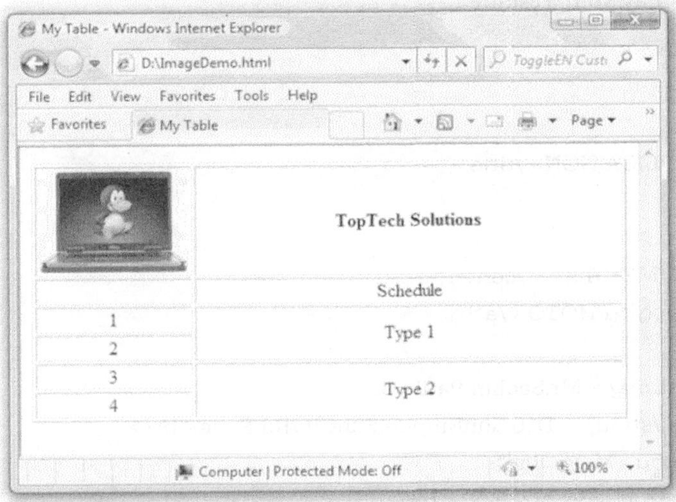

Ex. 2.5.6 : Write HTML code to draw table given below.

<table>
<tr><th colspan="2">Items</th><th>Price</th></tr>
<tr><th>Shirt</th><th>Trouser</th><td rowspan="2">₹. 1000/-</td></tr>
<tr><td>₹. 400/-</td><td>₹. 600/-</td></tr>
</table>

Sol. :

```
<html>
<head>
<title>Item-Price List</title>
</head>
<body>
<table border=1>
<tr>
<th colspan="2"><center>Items</center></th>
<th>Price</th>
</tr>
<tr>
<th><center>Shirt</center></th>
<th><center>Trouser</center></th>
<td rowspan="2"><center>Rs.<br/>1000/-</center></td>
<tr>
<td><center>Rs.400/-</td>
<td><center>Rs.600/-</td>
</tr>
</table>
</body>
</html>
```

Output

Ex. 2.5.7 : Write HTML code which includes table, Hyperlink, character formatting ordered and unordered list to display your resume.

Sol. : resume.html

```
<html>
<head>
<title>RESUME APPLICATION</title>
</head>
<body>
<center><h2>RESUME</h2></center>
<a href="my_photo.jpg">PHOTO</a>
<br/><br/>
<strong>Name: </strong> Mr.Sachin Patil<br/>
<strong>Address: </strong> D10,SunEmpire,SunCityRd,Pune<br/>
<strong>Sex: </strong>Male<br/>
<strong>Phone: </strong>9229229221<br/>
<strong>Email: </strong>puntambekar_a@rediffmail.com
<br/><br/>
<strong>Educational Qualification:</strong>
<table border=2>
<tr>
<th>Examination</th>
<th>Year Of Passing</th>
<th>Board/University</th>
<th>Marks obtained</th>
</tr>
<tr>
<td>S.S.C</td><td>1991</td><td>Pune</td><td>93%</td>
</tr>
<tr>
<td>H.S.C</td><td>1993</td><td>Pune</td><td>90%</td>
</tr>
<tr>
<td>B.E.(Computer)</td><td>1997</td><td>Pune</td><td>72%</td>
</tr>
<tr>
<td>M.Tech(Computer)</td><td>2001</td><td>IIT(Kanpur)</td><td>A grade</td>
</tr>
</table>
<strong>
<br/><br/>
```

```
Programming Languages known :
</strong>
<ul>
<li>Cobol
<li>C
<li>C++
<li>Visual C++

<li>Visual Basic
<li>Java
</ul>
<br/><br/>
<div align=left>Date:</div>
<div align=right>Place:</div>
<br/>
<div align=left>Signature</div>
</body>
</html>
```

Output

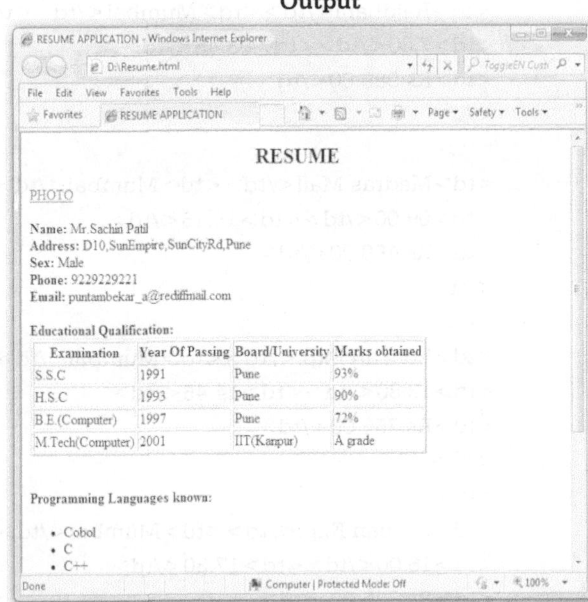

Ex. 2.5.8 : Create the following table using HTML tags

Name of Train	Place	Destination	Time Arrival Departure		Fare
Rajdhani	Mumbai	Delhi	07.30	08.45	Rs. 989.00
Madras Mail	Mumbai	Madras	09.00	10.15	Rs. 450.00
Konkan Exp.	Mumbai	Manglore	13.30	14.45	Rs. 756.00
Deccan Exp.	Mumbai	Pune	16.00	17.30	Rs. 345.00

Sol. :

```
<html>
<head>
        <title> Train Time Table </title>
</head>
<body>
        <table border="1">
        <tr>
        <th rowspan=2>Name of Train</th>
        <th rowspan=2>Place</th>
        <th rowspan=2>Destination</th>
        <th colspan=2>Time</th>
        <th rowspan=2>Fare</th>
        </tr>
        <tr><th>Arrival</th><th>Departure</th></tr>
        <tr>
```

```
        <td>Rajdhani</td><td>Mumbai</td><td>Delhi</td>
        <td>7.30</td><td>08.45</td>
        <td>Rs.989.00</td>
        </tr>
        <tr>
        <td>Madras Mail</td><td>Mumbai</td><td>Madras</td>
        <td>09.00</td><td>10.15</td>
        <td>Rs.450.00</td>
        </tr>
        <tr>
        <td>Konkan Exp.</td><td>Mumbai</td><td>Manglore</td>
        <td>13.30</td><td>14.45</td>
        <td>Rs.756.00</td>
        </tr>
        <tr>
        <td>Deccan Exp.</td><td>Mumbai</td><td>Pune</td>
        <td>16.00</td><td>17.30</td>
        <td>Rs.345.00</td>
        </tr>

        </table>
</body>
</html>
```

Output

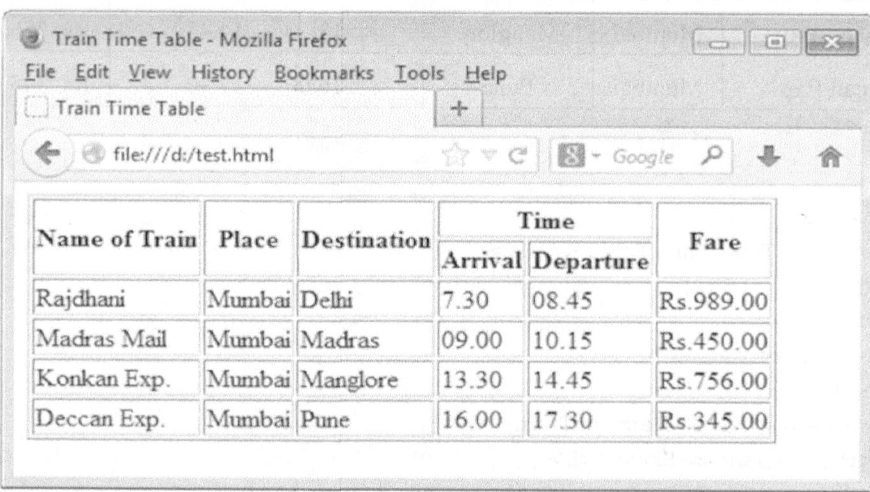

Name of Train	Place	Destination	Time		Fare
			Arrival	Departure	
Rajdhani	Mumbai	Delhi	7.30	08.45	Rs.989.00
Madras Mail	Mumbai	Madras	09.00	10.15	Rs.450.00
Konkan Exp.	Mumbai	Manglore	13.30	14.45	Rs.756.00
Deccan Exp.	Mumbai	Pune	16.00	17.30	Rs.345.00

Ex. 2.5.9 : Differentiate between <table width="400" height="200"> and <table width="100%" and height="50%">

Sol. : (i) <table width="400" height="200"> denotes that the table width is 400 pixels and height is 200 pixels. It denotes the **absolute value.**

For example

```
<html>
<head>
</head>
<body>
        <table border="1" width="100" height="50">
        <tr>
        <th>Name</th>
        <th>City</th>
        <th>Age</th>
        </tr>
        <tr>
        <td>AAA</td><td>Mumbai</td><td>10 yrs.</td>
        </tr>
        <tr>
        <td>BBB</td><td>Pune</td><td>20 yrs.</td>
        </tr>
        <tr>
        <td>CCC</td><td>Chennai</td><td>50 yrs.</td>
        </tr>
        </table>
</body>
</html>
```

Output

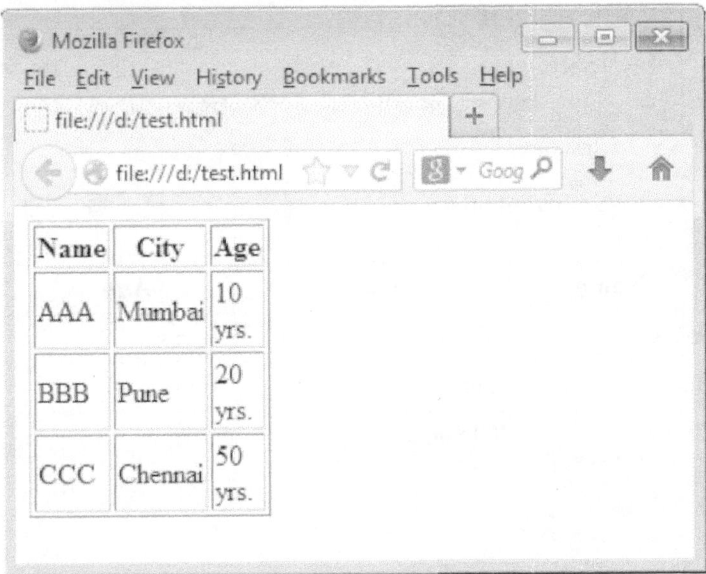

ii) On the other hand **<table width="100%" and height="50%">** denotes the width of the table is 100% of the screen and height is 50% of the browser screen. It denotes the **relative value**

For example

```
<html>
<head>
</head>
<body>
        <table border="1" width="100%" height="50%">
        <tr>
        <th>Name</th>
        <th>City</th>
        <th>Age</th>
        </tr>
        <tr>
        <td>AAA</td><td>Mumbai</td><td>10 yrs.</td>
        </tr>
                <tr>
        <td>BBB</td><td>Pune</td><td>20 yrs.</td>
        </tr>
        <tr>
        <td>CCC</td><td>Chennai</td><td>50 yrs.</td>
        </tr>
        </table>
</body>
</html>
```

Output

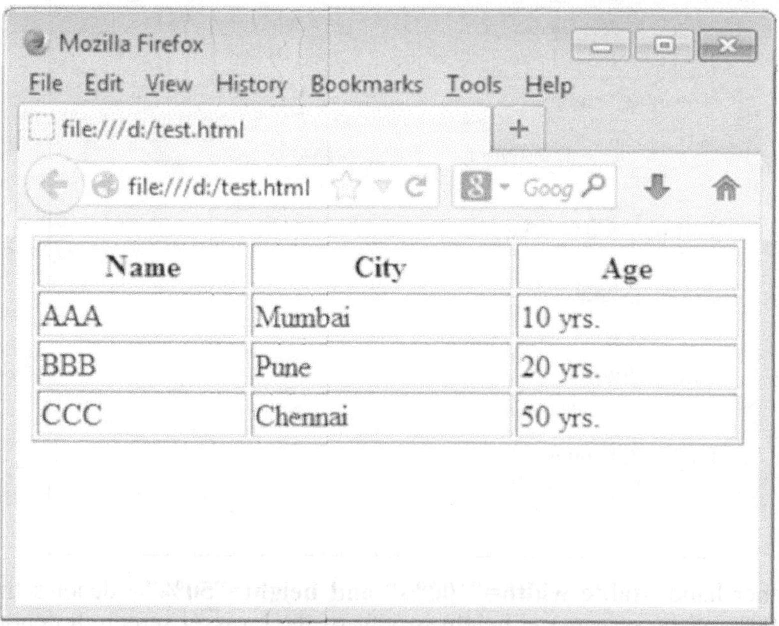

2.5.3 Additional Table Elements

There are some additional tables that can add additional meaning and accessibility to the table. For example –

1. The <caption> element :

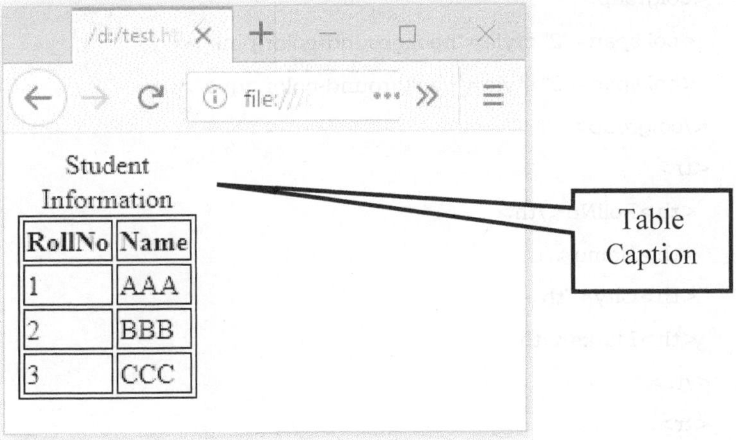

- The <caption> tag defines a table caption.
- The <caption> tag must be inserted immediately after the <table> tag.
- For example –

```
<!DOCTYPE html>
<html>
<head>
<style>
table,th,td{
   border:1px solid black;
}
</style>
</head>
<body>
<table>
  <caption>Student Information</caption>
  <tr>
    <th>RollNo</th>
    <th>Name</th>
  </tr>
  <tr>
    <td>1</td>
    <td>AAA</td>
  </tr>
  <tr>
    <td>2</td>
    <td>BBB</td>
  </tr>
  <tr>
    <td>3</td>
    <td>CCC</td>
  </tr>
</table>
</body>
</html>
```

Output

Student Information

RollNo	Name
1	AAA
2	BBB
3	CCC

Table Caption

2. The <col>and <colgroup> element :

- The <col> tag specifies column properties for each column within a <colgroup> element.
- The **<col> tag** is useful for **applying styles to entire columns**, instead of repeating the styles for each cell, for each row.
- For example –

```
<!DOCTYPE html>
<html>
<head>
<style>
table, th, td {
  border: 1px solid black;
}
</style>
</head>
<body>

<table>
 <colgroup>
  <col span="2" style="background-color:pink">
  <col span="2" style="background-color:aqua">
 </colgroup>
 <tr>
  <th>RollNo</th>
  <th>Name</th>
  <th>City</th>
  <th>Marks</th>
 </tr>
 <tr>
  <td>1</td>
  <td>AAA</td>
  <td>Pune</td>
  <td>78</td>
 </tr>
 <tr>
  <td>2</td>
```

```
    <td>BBB</td>
    <td>Mumbai</td>
    <td>88</td>
  </tr>
  <tr>
    <td>3</td>
    <td>CCC</td>
<td>Bangalore</td>
    <td>97</td>
  </tr>
  <tr>
    <td>4</td>
    <td>DDD</td>
    <td>Hyderabad</td>
    <td>84</td>
  </tr>
</table>
</body>
</html>
```

Output

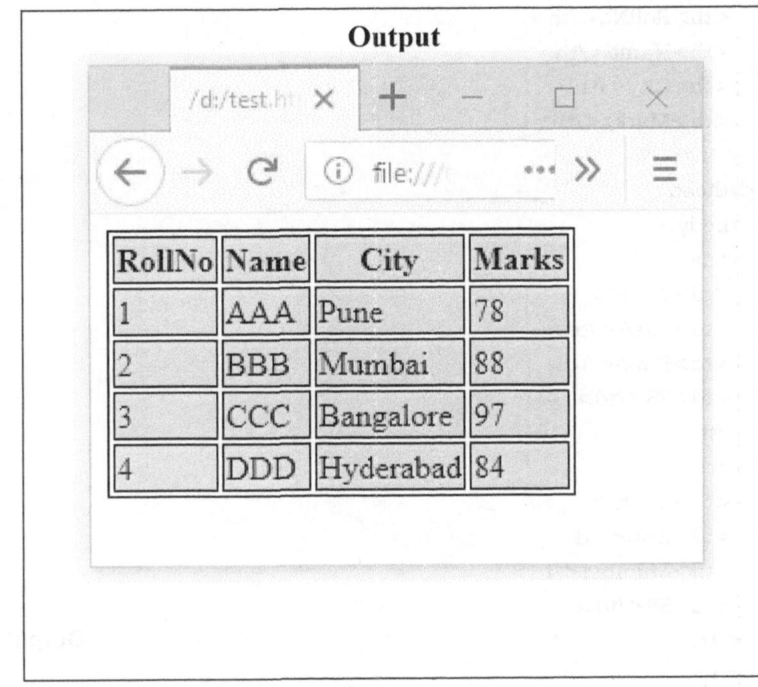

RollNo	Name	City	Marks
1	AAA	Pune	78
2	BBB	Mumbai	88
3	CCC	Bangalore	97
4	DDD	Hyderabad	84

3. The <tbody>,<thead> and <tfoot>elements

- The <tbody> tag is used to group the body content in an HTML table.
- The <tbody> element is used in conjunction with the <thead> and <tfoot> elements to specify each part of a table such as body, header, and footer.
- For example –

```
<!DOCTYPE html>
<html>
<head>
<style>
table, th, td {
  border: 1px solid black;
}
thead {color:red;}
tbody {color:green;}
tfoot {color:blue;}
</style>
</head>
<body>

<table>
<thead>
  <tr>
```

```
    <th>RollNo</th>
    <th>Name</th>
    <th>City</th>
    <th>Marks</th>
  </tr>
</thead>
<tbody>
  <tr>
    <td>1</td>
    <td>AAA</td>
    <td>Pune</td>
    <td>78</td>
  </tr>
  <tr>
    <td>2</td>
    <td>BBB</td>
    <td>Mumbai</td>
    <td>88</td>
  </tr>
  <tr>
    <td>3</td>
    <td>CCC</td>
    <td>Bangalore</td>
    <td>97</td>
  </tr>
  <tr>
</tbody>
<tfoot>
    <td>4</td>
    <td>DDD</td>
    <td>Hyderabad</td>
    <td>84</td>
  </tr>
</tfoot>
</table>
</body>
</html>
```

Output

RollNo	Name	City	Marks
1	AAA	Pune	78
2	BBB	Mumbai	88
3	CCC	Bangalore	97
4	DDD	Hyderabad	84

2.6 Frames

AU : May-13, 14, Dec.-09, Marks 16

- HTML frames allow us to present documents in **multiple views.**
- Using multiple views we can keep certain information visible and at the same time other views are scrolled or replaced.

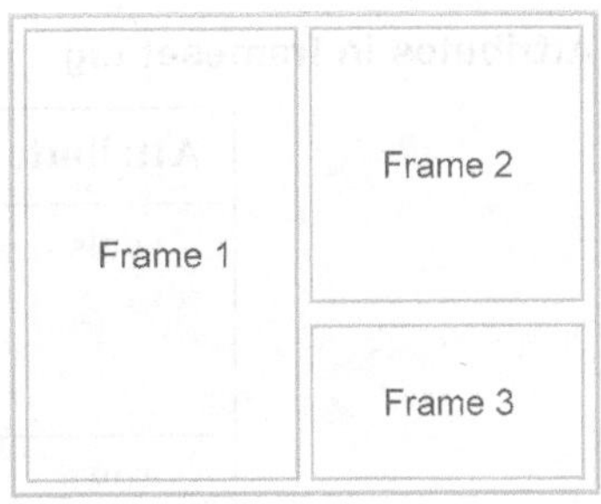

Fig. 2.6.1 Frames

- For example, within the same window, one frame can display a company information, a second frame can be a navigation menu and a third frame may display selected document that can be scrolled through or replaced by navigating in the second frame.
- Various frames can be set in one browser window.
- To set the frames in the browser window we use **frame set.**
- **For example -**

```
<frameset cols="150,*">
```

will allow us to divide the window into two columns (i.e. in two vertical frames). One frame occupying the size of 150 pixels and the other occupies the remaining portion of the window. Here * means any number of pixels.

- Similarly

```
<frameset rows="*,120">
```

will divide the window into two rows (i.e. in two horizontal frames). The second part of horizontal frame will be of 120 pixels and upper horizontal frame will occupy remaining portion of the window.

- Similarly we can also specify the frameset in percentage form. For example

```
<frameset rows="30%,70%">
```

Using frameset we can divide the rows and columns in any number of frames. For example

```
<frameset rows = “20%,30%,50%” cols = “30%,*”>
```

This will create a frames in the browser's window as follows -

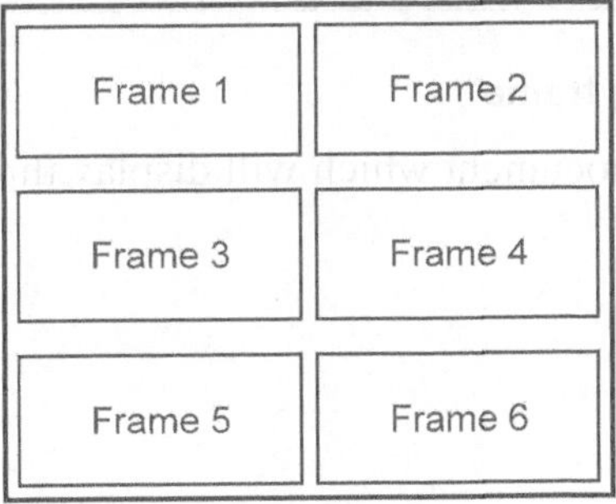

Fig. 2.6.2 Frames

- In every layout frame we can load the desired html page by using **frame src.** For example

```
<frame src="D:\\html_examples\\bulleted1.html" name="Left_Vertical">
```

By this statement we are loading the web page **bulleted1.html** in the specific frame and the frame is named as **Left_Vertical.**

Attributes in frameset tag

Attribute	Value	Purpose
cols	pixels % *	It specifies the number and size of columns in a frameset
rows	pixels % *	It specifies the number and size of rows in a frameset.

Attributes of frame tag

The <frame> tag has no end tag. The <frame> tag defines one frame within a <frameset> tag. Various attributes of frame tag are

Attribute	Value	Purpose
frameborder	0 or 1	Value 1 specifies that the frame is displayed with border and 0 indicates that there is no border.
name	Some name	It specifies name of the frame
Nosize		Due to this attribute we cannot resize the particular frame.
scolling	yes, no or auto	It specifies whether or not to display the scrollbar along with the frame.
src	URL	It specifies the name of the Document to be displayed within the frame.

Example of Browser containing frame

Step 1 : Create a main HTML document which will display three HTML documents in three vertical frames

FrameSet.html

```
<!DOCTYPE html>
<html>
<frameset cols="25%,*,50%">
  <frame src="frame1.html">
  <frame src="frame2.html">
  <frame src="frame3.html">
</frameset>
</html>
```

Step 2 : Create frame1.html, frame2.html and frame3.html files as follows –

Frame1.html

```
<!DOCTYPE html>
<html>
<body>
        <h1> Frame 1 </h1>
</body>
</html>
```

Frame2.html

```
<!DOCTYPE html>
<html>
<body>
        <h1> Frame 2 </h1>
</body>
</html>
```

Frame3.html

```
<!DOCTYPE html>
<html>
<body>
        <h1> Frame 3 </h1>
</body>
</html>
```

Output

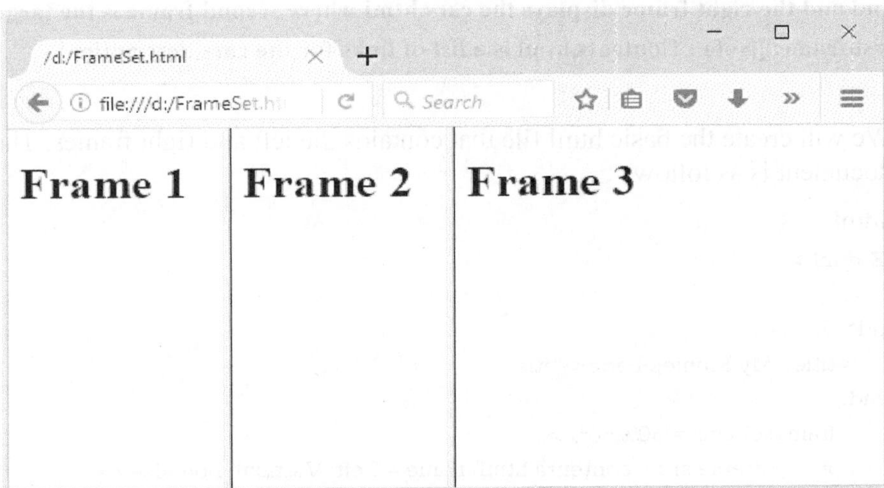

Script Explanation : The above HTML document, the <frameset> tag is used to define frameset. The **col** attribute is used to create the three column frames.

2.6.1 Frames with Scrollbars

```
<!DOCTYPE html>
<html>
<frameset cols="25%,*,50%">
 <frame src="frame1.html" scrolling=no>
 <frame src="frame2.html" scrolling=auto>
 <frame src="frame3.html">
</frameset>
</html>
```

Output

To set the scroll bar we should assign the value **auto** to the **scrolling** parameter and if we do not want the scroll bar accompanying the frame then we must assign the value **no** to the scrolling parameter.

Ex. 2.6.1 : Create XHTML document that has two frames. The left frame displays the contents.html and the right frame displays the cars.html where second frame is the target of link from the first frame. [Note : Contents.html is a list of links for the cars description]

Sol. :

Step 1 : We will create the basic html file that contains the left and right frames. The HTML document is as follows :

CarDemo.html

```
<!DOCTYPE html >
<html>
        <head>
                <title>My Frames Page</title>
        </head>
                <frameset cols="50%,50%">
                        <frame src="contents.html" name="Left_Vertical" noresize />
                        <frame src="Description.html" name="Right_Vertical" scrolling=no/>
                </frameset>
</html>
```

Step 2 : Following is a HTML document that displays the contents that are loaded at first. The left frame HTML document is as follows –

contents.html

```
<!DOCTYPE html >
<html >
        <head>
                <title>My Frames Page</title>
        </head>
        <body>
        <h3>
        <a href="Innova.html" target="Right_Vertical">Toyota Innova</a>
        <h3/>
        <h3>
        <a href="Scorpio.html" target="Right_Vertical">Mahindra Scorpio</a>
        <h3/>
        <h3>
        <a href="Etios.html" target="Right_Vertical">Toyota Etios Liva</a>
        <h3/>
        </body>
</html>
```

The right frame HTML document is as follows-

Description.html

```
<!DOCTYPE html >
<html >
        <head>
                <title>My Frames Page</title>
        </head>
        <body>
        <center>
        <h3> WELCOME <h3/>
        This page displays the details of a car you have chosen.
        </center>
        </body>
</html>
```

Step 3 : Following are the three html documents each containing the description of each car.

Innova.html

```
<!DOCTYPE html >
<html>
        <head>
                <title>My Frames Page</title>
```

```
        </head>
        <body>
        <h2> TOYOTA INNOVA</h2>
        <ul type="disc">
        <li>Price: Rs.9,35,731-Rs.14,82,852</li>
        <li><td>Mileage: </td><td>10Kmpl(City) and 13 Kmpl(hwy)</li>
        </ul>
        </body>
</html>
```

Scorpio.html

```
<!DOCTYPE html>
<html >
        <head>
                <title>My Frames Page</title>
        </head>
        <body>
        <h2> MAHINDRA SCORPIO</h2>
        <ul type="disc">
        <li>Price: </td><td>Rs.7,49,583-Rs.12,85,479</li>
        <li>Mileage: </td><td>12Kmpl(City) and 16 Kmpl(hwy)</li>
        </ul>
        </body>
</html>
```

Etios.html

```
<!DOCTYPE html>
<html >
        <head>
                <title>My Frames Page</title>
        </head>
        <body>
        <h2> TOYOTA ETIOS LIVA</h2>
        <ul type="disc">
        <li> Price: </td><td>Rs.4,46,276-Rs.6,86,426</li>
        <li> Mileage: </td><td>17Kmpl(City) and 19 Kmpl(hwy)</li>
        </ul>
        </body>
</html>
```

Step 4 : Open the suitable web browser and invoke the CarDemo.html(created in Step 1), the output will be as follows -

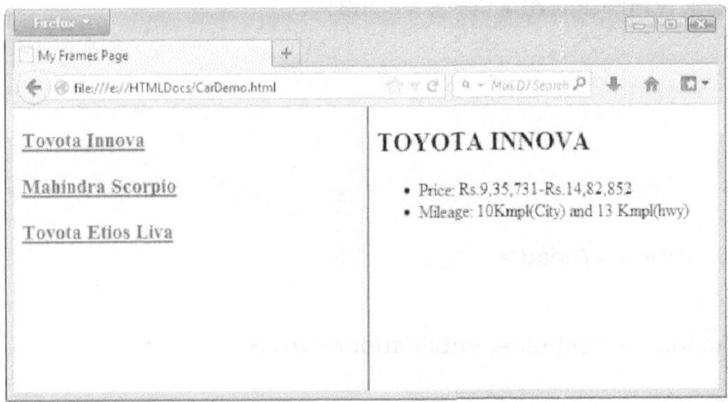

Ex. 2.6.2 : Create a HTML document for a company home page and explain.

AU : May-13, Marks 16

Sol. : For creation of this web page the frames are used.

Step 1 : The main page is created as follows -

Main.html

```
<?xml version = "1.0" encoding ="utf-8"?>
<!DOCTYPE html PUBLIC "-//W3C//DTD XHTML 1.0 Frameset//EN"
    "http://www.w3.org/TR/xhtml1/DTD/xhtml1-frameset.dtd">
<html xmlns="http://www.w3.org/1999/xhtml">
  <frameset rows="20%,80%">
    <frame src="logo.html">
     <frameset cols="30%,70%">
       <frame src="menu.html">
       <frame src="contents.html">
    </frameset>
  </frameset>
</html>
```

Step 2 : In the main page a layout of the company home page is created. Various html files that are called in this HTML document are as given below -

Menu.html

```
<html>
<head><title>LOGO</title></head>
<body bgcolor="aqua">
<h3><a href="about.html"> About us<a/></h3>
<h3><a href="download1.html"> Free Downloads<a/></h3>
<h3><a href="download2.html"> Download Catalogue<a/></h3>
<h3><a href="download3.html">Download Orderform<a/></h3>
<h3><a href="catalogues.html">Catalogues<a/></h3>
<h3><a href="distributors.html">Distributors<a/></h3>
<h3><a href="Contacts.html">Contact Us<a/></h3>
```

```
<h3><a href="feedback.html">Feedback<a/></h3>
</body>
</html>
```

Logo.html

```
<html>
<head><title>LOGO</title></head>
<body bgcolor="magenta">
<h1><img src="books.jpg"/> Technical Publications</h1>
</body>
</html>
```

Contents.html

```
<html>
<head><title>LOGO</title></head>
<body bgcolor="khaki">
<center>
  <h2>BOOKS</h2>
</center>
  <p>TECHNICAL PUBLICATIONS is known for commitment to quality and innovation. We are Leaders in our chosen scholarly and educational markets, serving the book Industry & Academic Institutions.
  </p>
  <p>We have been in the industry for the last 18 years and are known for the quality and scholarly publications in Engineering books. We publish more than 1000 titles of text books, for various Universities across the India.
  </p>
  <p>We are specialized in Engineering text books and have been publishing titles for various Engineering branches such as Electrical, Electronics, Computer Science, Information Technology,Mechanical etc. and other management
    books.
  </p>
</body>
</html>
```

Step 3 : Open the suitable web browser and type the address for **main.html.** The output will be as follows -

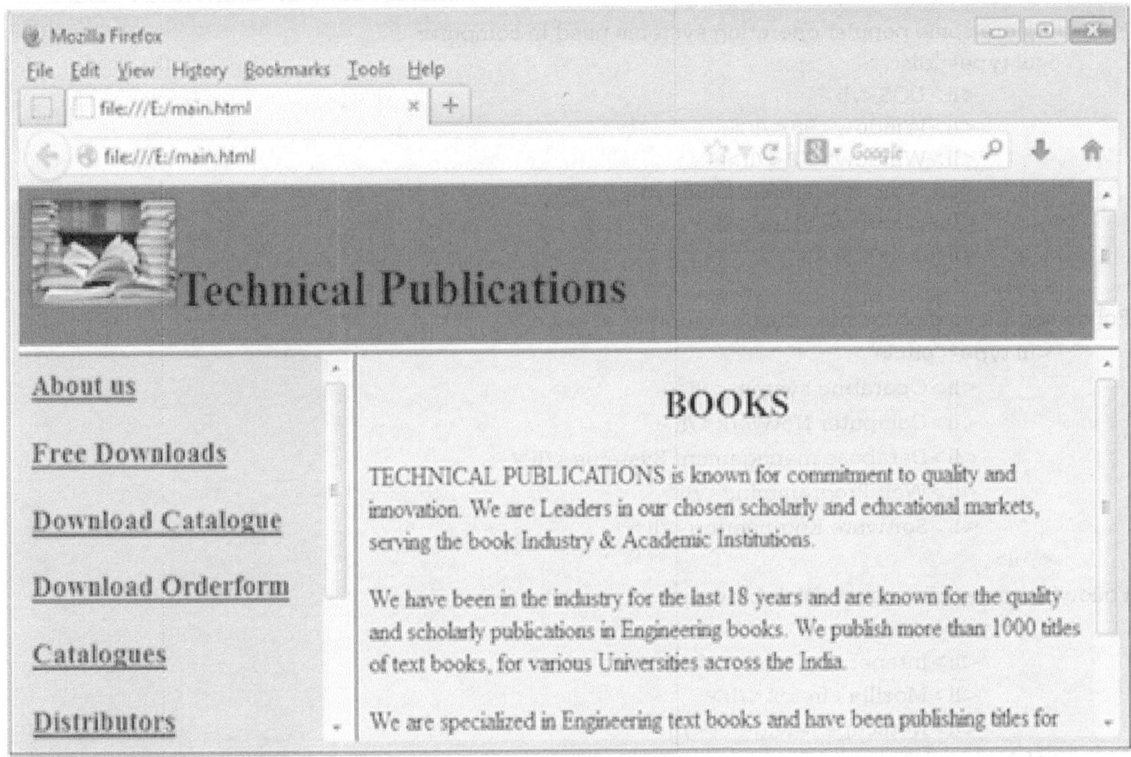

University Questions

1. *Explain FRAME and IFRAME tags and attributes.* **AU : May-14, Marks 8**
2. *Write down HTML tags to explain frame within a frame.* **AU : Dec.-09, Marks 2**

2.7 Lists

AU : Dec.-11, May-11, Marks 8

- List is nothing but the collections of items or elements. There are two types of lists - **unordered lists** and **ordered lists.**
  - The unordered list is useful for simply listing the items but if we want the items in some specific sequence then the ordered lists are used. Let us discuss how to use these types lists in the HTML document.

2.7.1 Unordered List

Following HTML document makes use of unordered list.

HTML Document [UnordLstDemo.html]

```
<!DOCTYPE html>
<html>
        <head>
                <title> Use of Unordered List </title>
        </head>
        <body>
        <h2>All About Computer ...</h2>
```

```
Following are some popular operating systems used in computer
        <ul type="disc">
                <li>DOS</li>
                <li>Windows 98</li>
                <li>Windows XP</li>
                <li>Windows Professional</li>
                <li>Windows Vista</li>
                <li>Unix</li>
        </ul>
Following are some core subjects on computer science
        <ul type="circle">
                <li>Operating system</li>
                <li>Computer Network</li>
                <li>Database management Systems</li>
                <li>Web Programming</li>
                <li>Software Engineering</li>
        </ul>
Following are some popular Web browsers
        <ul type="square">
                <li>Intenet Explorer</li>
                <li>Mozilla Firefox</li>
                <li>Netscape Navigator</li>
        </ul>
        </body>
</html>
```

Output

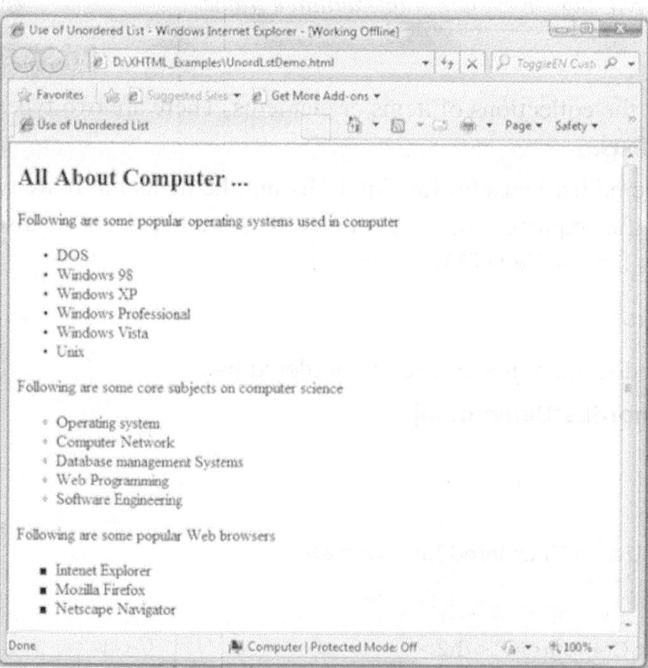

Script Explanation :

In above script we have used the tag <ul> for specifying the unordered list. The list items can be mentioned using the tag <li> Due to which the list items can appear in bulleted form. The style of the bullet can be as given below -

tags	meaning
<ul> and </ul>	Beginning and end of the bulleted list
<li> and </li>	Displays the bulleted text on separate line.
<ul type="circle">	Displays the circular bullets.
<ul type="disc">	Displays the solid round bullets.
<ul type="square">	Displays the squared bullets.

2.7.2 Ordered List

The ordered list is a list of items which must follows some specific sequence. We can number the text using **<ol>** tag. Following table shows various styles by which the list can be numbered.

tags	meaning
<ol> and </ol>	Beginning and end of the numbered list
<li> and </li>	Displays the numbered text on separate line.
<ol type="A">	Displays the list in following manner
	A.
	B.
	C.
	...
<ol type="i">	Displays the list in following manner
	i.
	ii.
	iii.
	...
<ol type="I">	Displays the list in following manner

	I.
	II.
	III.
	…
<ol type=“1”>	Displays the list in following manner
	1.
	2.
	3.
	…

Here is one illustrative program -

HTML Document [OrdLstDemo.html]

```
<!DOCTYPE html>
<html>
        <head>
                <title> Ordered List Demo </title>
        </head>
        <body>
                <h4>This is a typical List</h4>
                <ol type="A">
                <li>First</li>
                <li>Second</li>
                <li>Third</li>
                <li>Forth</li>
                <li> and so on</li>
                </ol>
                <h4>The list is starting from 5</h4>
                <ol start="5">
                <li>Ice cream</li>
                <li>Mango</li>
                <li>Juice</li>
                <li>Pop Corn</li>
                <li> and so on</li>
                </ol>
        </body>
</html>
```

We can have the nested ordered list. Here is an example of it

Output

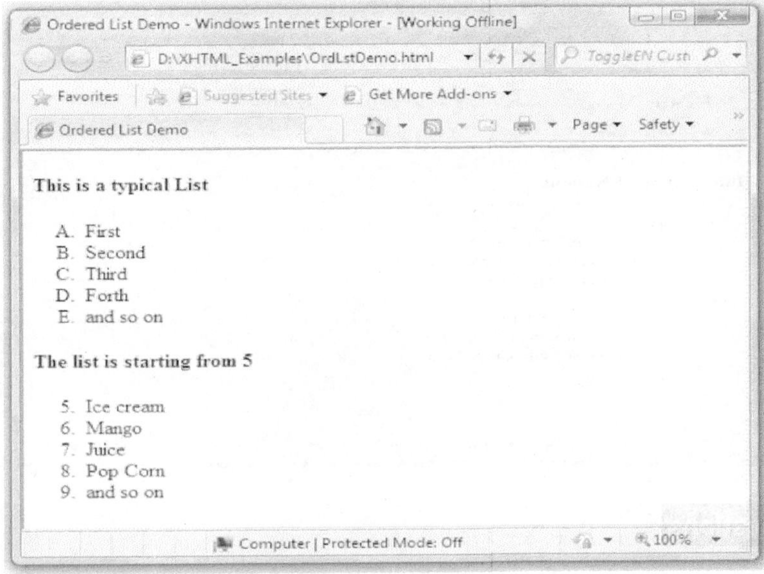

HTML Document [OrdLstDemo1.html]

```
<!DOCTYPE html>
<html>
        <head>
                <title> Ordered List Demo </title>
        </head>
        <body>
                <h4>Information of Nations</h4>
                <ol type="1">
                <li>India
                        <ol type="i">
                                <li>National Bird: Peacock</li>
                                <li>National animal:Tiger</li>
                                <li>National game:Hockey</li>
                        </ol>
                </li>
                <li>Australia
                        <ol type="i">
                                <li>National Bird: Emu</li>
                                <li>National animal:Kangaroo</li>
                                <li>National game:Cricket</li>
                        </ol>
                </li>
                </ol>
        </body>
</html>
```

Output

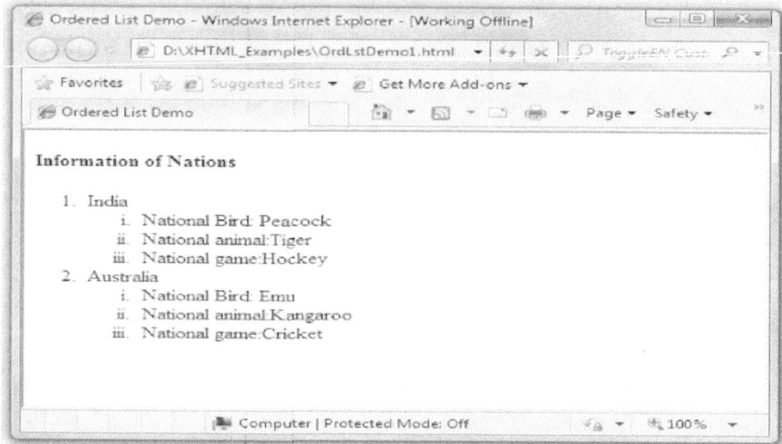

University Questions

1. *Explain the purpose and way of creating lists in HTML documents.* **AU :Dec.-11, Marks 8**
2. *State the types of lists supported by HTML and explain them in detail.* **AU : May-11, Marks 8**

2.8 Image

- We can display images as a link. We have to use the **<img src =" ">** tag for this purpose.
- Within the double quotes image file should be mentioned. Normally .gif or .jpg files are used to display the images on the web browser.
- **Example**
- Following HTML Script shows how to insert an image in the web page.

HTML Document [imagedemo.html]

```
<!DOCTYPE html>
<html>
<head>
    <title> Image Demo </title>
</head>
<body>
    <h1> Indian Heritage </h1>
    <p>
    In India, People celebrate the festival of light <br/>
    Which is called as <strong>Diwali</strong>
    </p>
    <img src= "lamp1.jpg" alt= "Light!!" />
```

```
    <br/>
    Diwali suggests us to enlighten our life with hope,health and wealth
    <br/>
  </body>
</html>
```

Output

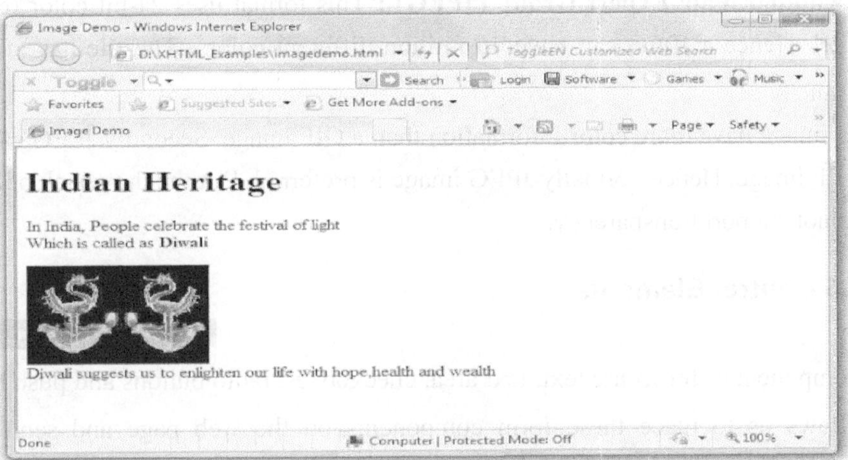

Script Explanation : In above script we have used **<img />** tag in order to display an image. The image tag has two attributes -

- The **src** suggests us to give the **image file name**. If the desired image is not present in the current directory of web page then the complete path where the image is located must be given.
- The **alt** attribute displays the text when it is not possible to display the image. For instance - in above given **imagedemo.html** script if, the **lamp1.jpg** is not present then we will get following output.

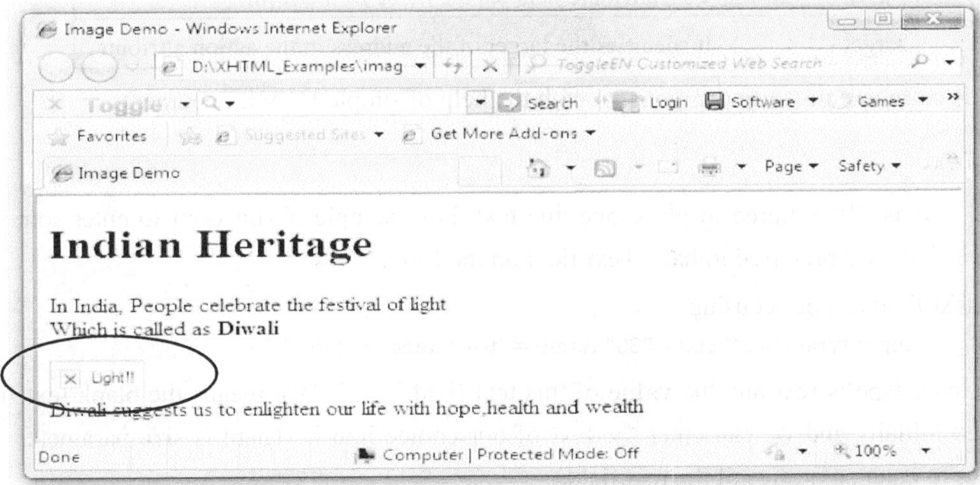

Types of Images

- There are two types of images that are more commonly used -

1. **Graphic Interchange Format (GIF) :** It uses 8-bit color representation for pixels. Hence a single pixel can have 256 different colors. This file have the extension **.gif.**
2. **Joint Photographic Expert Group (JPEG) :** This format uses 24-bit color representation for pixel. Hence a JPEG can have 16 million different colors. The file have the extension .jpg or .jpeg.

The JPEG image have more color information than a GIF image. Secondly JPEG can be smaller than GIF image. Hence normally JPEG image is preferred. But the drawback of JPEG is that it does not support transparency.

2.9 HTML5 Control Elements

AU : May – 09, Dec.-12, Marks 6

- Typical component of forms are text, text area, checkboxes, radio buttons and push buttons.
- HTML allows us to place these form components on the web page and send the desired information to the destination server.
- All these form contents appear in the <form> tag.
- The form has an attribute action which gets executed when user clicks a button on the form.
- Various attributes of form are –

Attribute	Description
action	It specifies the url where the form should be submitted.
method	It specifies the HTTP methods such as GET, POST
name	This attribute denotes the name of the form.
target	It specifies the target of the address in the action attribute.

Let us learn various form components with the help of simple HTML documents.

2.9.1 Text

- **Text** is typically required to place one line text. For example if you want to enter some name then it is always preferred to have Text field on the form.
- The text field can be set using

```
<input type="text" size="30" name ="username" value=" ">
```

The input type is **text** and the **value** of this text field is " " That means the blank text field is displayed initially and we can enter the text of our choice into it. There is **size** parameter which allows us to enter some size of the text field.

- Some other parameters or attributes can be
    - o **maxlength** that allows us to enter the text of some maximum length.
    - o **name** indicates name of the text field.
    - o **align** denotes the alignment of the text in the text field. The alignment can be left, right, bottom and top.

Example Code

HTML Document [TextDemo.html]

```
<!DOCTYPE html>
<html>
 <head>
     <title>My Page</title>
 </head>
 <body>
 <form>
      <b>Input String:</b><br/><input type="text" size="25" value="">
 </form>
 </body>
</html>
```

Output

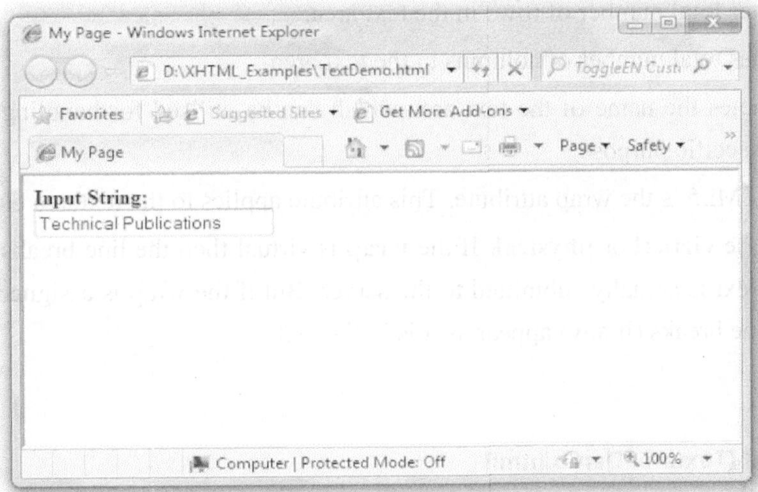

Script Explanation :

In above document

1) we have the label "Input String" just before the **<input>** tag. We can also specify the label by using the **<label>** tag as follows -

```
<label>Input String: <br/><input type="text" size="25" value=""></label>
```

2) Thus the label gets bound to the text box. This aspect is always beneficial for a web

programmer because using label control we can focus on the corresponding text box contents.

3) Initially the text box field is blank. We can type some text inside this text box.

Ex. 2.9.1 : How will you create password field in a HTML form ?

Sol. : The password field is typically created on the form. Hence following code can be written to create it -

```
<form name="form1">
 Password:<input type="password"/>
</form>
```

2.9.2 Textarea

- Text field is a form component which allows us to enter single line text, what if we want to have multiple line text? Then you must use textarea component.
- In HTML 4, we were required to specify a textarea element's size by specifying values for the rows and cols attributes. In HTML5, these attributes are no longer required; you should use CSS to define a textarea's width and height.
- Various parameters that can be set for the text area can be
  - **row** denotes total number of rows in the text area.
  - **col** specifies total number of columns in the text area.
  - **name** denotes the name of the text area which can be utilised for handling that component for some specific purpose.
  - New in HTML5 is the wrap attribute. This attribute applies to the textarea element
  - **wrap** can be **virtual** or **physical.** If the **wrap** is virtual then the line breaks get disappeared when the text is actually submitted to the server. But if the wrap is assigned to the **physical** then the line breaks (if any) appear as it is in the text.

Example code

HTML Document [TextareaDemo.html]

```
<!DOCTYPE html>
<html>
<head>
 <title>My Page</title>
</head>
<body>
 <form>
   Enter the Desired text here
```

```
    <textarea cols="40" rows="5" name="myname">
    </textarea>
    </form>
  </body>
  </html>
```

Output

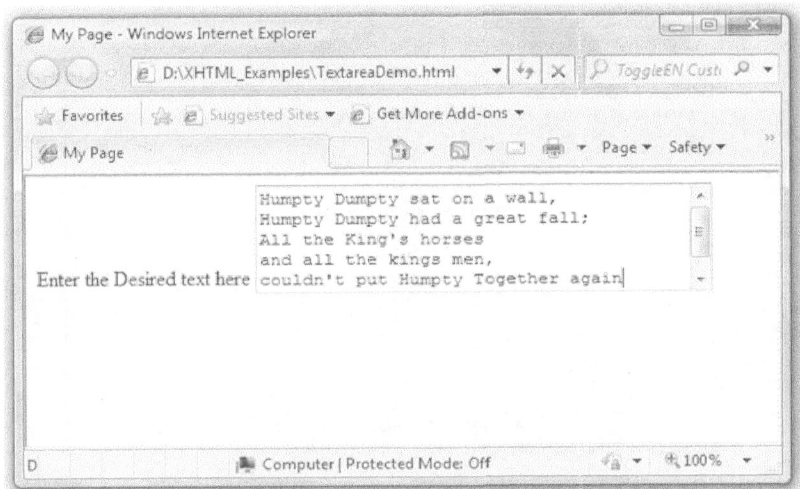

2.9.3 Checkbox

- It is the simplest component which is used particularly when we want to make some selection from several options.
- For having the checkbox we have to specify the input type as **checkbox**. For example

```
<input type="checkbox" name="option1" value="mango" checked="checked">Mango<br/>
```

- If we want to get the checkbox displayed as checked then set **checked="checked"**

Example Code

HTML Document[ChkBoxDemo.html]

```
<!DOCTYPE html>
<html>
 <head>
    <title>My Form with Check box</title>
 </head>
 <body>
    <form name ="checkboxForm">
    <div align="center"><br>
    Select the fruit(s) of your choice<br/>
    <input type="checkbox" name="option1" value="mango" checked="checked">Mango<br/>
```

```
        <input type="checkbox" name="option2" value="apple">Apple<br/>
        <input type="checkbox" name="option3" value="guava">Guava<br/>
        </div>
        </form>
    </body>
</html>
```

Output

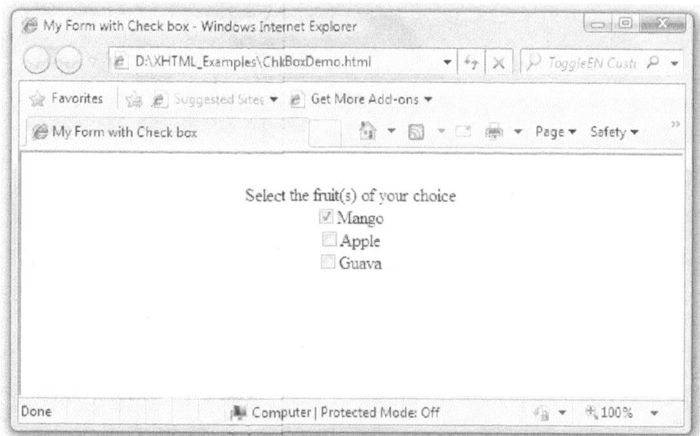

Script Explanation

1) In the above program to set some checkbox in checked state we can mention the attribute **checked** as **checked.**
2) We can set the **value** attribute as " " but this then the checkbox will not get associated with any value. The **Mango, Apple** and **Guava** are the labels of the checkboxes.

2.9.4 Radio Button

- This form component is also use to indicate the selection from several choices.
- Using **input type="radio"** we can place radio button on the web page.
- This component allows us to make only one selection at a time.
- We can create a group of some radio button component.
- Following HTML document displays the radio buttons for two different groups.

HTML Document[RadioButDemo.html]

```
<!DOCTYPE html>
<html >
<head>
      <title>My Form with radio buttons Page</title>
</head>
<body>
```

```
<form name="myform">
      <div align="left"><br>
      <b>Select Fruit which you like the most</b><br/>
      <input type="radio" name="group1" value="Mango">Mango<br/>
      <input type="radio" name="group1" value="Apple" checked> Apple<br/>
      <input type="radio" name="group1" value="Grapes"> Grapes
      <br/><br/><br/>
      <b>Select Flower which you like the most</b><br/>
      <input type="radio" name="group2" value="Rose"> Rose<br/>
         <input type="radio" name="group2" value="Lotus">Lotus<br/>
         <input type="radio" name="group2" value="Jasmine" checked>Jasmine<br/>
 </div>
</form>
</body>
</html>
```

Output

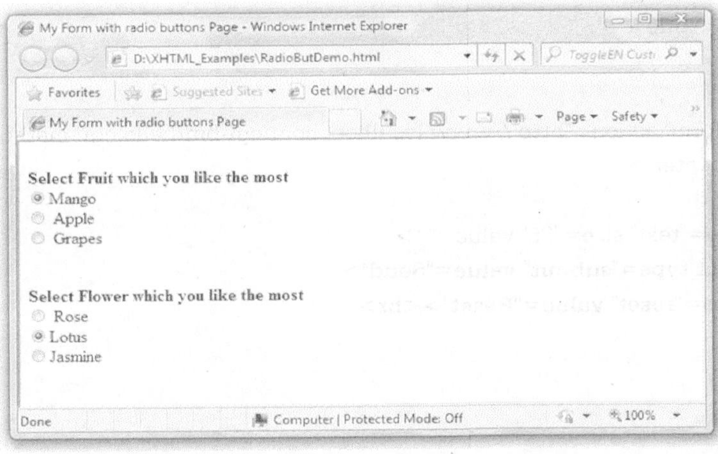

Ex. 2.9.2 : What is the difference between group of checkbox buttons and group of radio buttons ?

Sol. :

- The checkbox and radio buttons are used for making the selection from a group of choices.
- When a user selects (checks) a checkbox, its value gets assigned as the current value of the checkbox group's control name.
- A checkbox group's control name may get paired with several current values if the user selects more than one checkbox.
- Radio buttons work just like checkboxes except they are typically set up to be mutually exclusive of one another, i.e. when one is selected, all the others are automatically deselected.

2.9.5 Button

- We can create the button using **<input type ="button">** tag.
- There are two types of buttons that can be created in HTML. One is called **submit** button and the another one is **reset** button.
- Various parameters of submit button are

1) **name** denotes the name of the submit button.
2) **value** is for writing some text on the text on the button.
3) **align** specifies alignment of the button.

Example Code

HTML Document[Button.html]

```
<!DOCTYPE html>
<html >
 <head>
 <title> My Page </title>
 </head>
 <body>
<form name="myform" action="http://www.localhost.com/cgi-bin/hello.cgi" method="POST">
      <div align="center">
      <br/><br/>
         <input type="text" size="35" value=" ">
         <br><input type="submit" value="Send">
         <input type="reset" value="Reset"><br>
      </div>
      </form>
  </body>
  </html>
```

Output

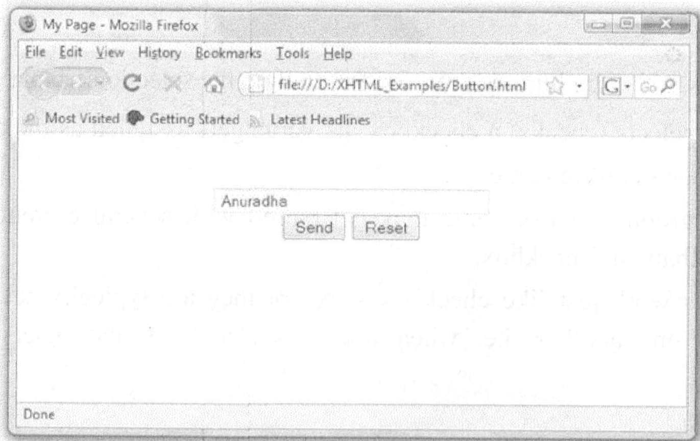

Script Explanation

1) In above HTML document, we have used the form whose name is **"myform".**

2) There are two attributes associated with the **form** tag and those are **action** and **method.** The **action** parameter indicates the address and the cgi script where the contents should go and **method** parameter is for the methods for submitting the data. The **method** can be **get** or **post.** Thus by specifying the action and method for a form we can send the desired data at desired location.

2.9.6 Menu

- HTML allows us to have pop down menu on the web page so that the desired selection can be made.
- The parameter **select** is for the menu component and **option** parameter is for setting the values to the options of drop down menu.
- We can make some specific option selected by **selected value =** .
- In the following HTML document we have created one drop down menu in which various fruits are enlisted. By default "Banana" is set as selected.

Example code

HTML Document [Menu.html]

```
<!DOCTYPE html>
<html >
 <head>
   <title> My Page </title>
 </head>
 <body>
 <form name="myform">
 <div align="center">
   <select name="My_Menu">
     <option value="Mango">Mango</option>
     <option value="Strawberry">Strawberry</option>
     <option selected value="Banana">Banana </option>
     <option value="Apple">Apple</option>
   </select>
 </div>
 </form>
 </body>
</html>
```

Output

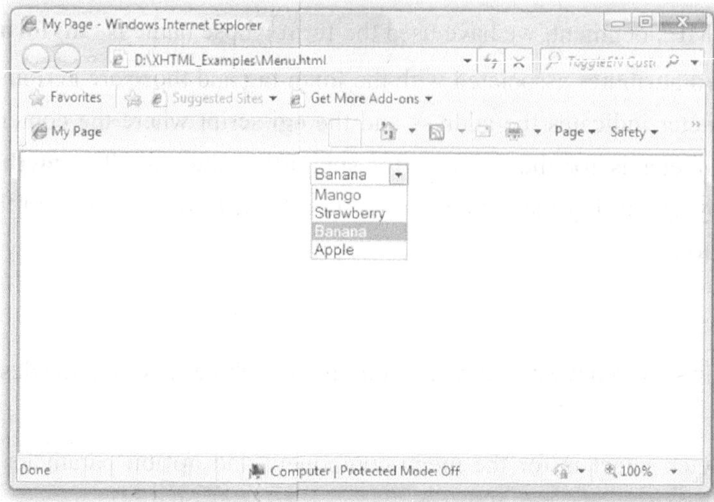

Ex. 2.9.3 : Create a HTML document that has the form with the following controls

a) A text box to collect the customer name.

b) Four checkboxes, one for the following items :

i. Four HTML textbooks for ₹ 1000 ii. Eight XML textbooks for ₹ 2000

iii. Four Javabeans books for ₹ 2500 iv. Eight UML textbooks for ₹ 1500

c) A collection of radio buttons that are labelled as follows –

i. Cash ii.Cheque/DD iii Creadit card.

Sol. :

```
<!DOCTYPE html>
<html >
 <body>
<center><h2>REGISTRATION FORM</h2></center>
<hr/>
<form>
<table>
<tr>
<td>Name:</td>
<td><input type="text" size="25"value=""></td>
</tr>
<tr>
<td>Select the desired Items:</td>
<td>
<select name="f">
<option value="4 HTML Books(Rs. 1000)">4 HTML Books(Rs. 1000)</option>
<option value="8 XML Books(Rs. 2000)">8 XML Books(Rs. 2000)</option>
```

```
<option value="4 JavaBeans Books(Rs.2500)">4 JavaBeans Books(Rs.2500)</option>
<option value="8 UML Books(Rs.1500)">8 UML Books(Rs.1500)</option>
</select>
</td>
</tr>
<tr>
<td>
Mode of Payment:
</td>
</tr>
<tr>
<td><input type="radio" name="group1" value="Cash">Cash</td>
</tr>
<tr>
<td><input type="radio" name="group1" value="Cheque/DD">Cheque/DD</td>
</tr>
<tr>
<td><input type="radio" name="group1" value="Credit Card">Credit Card</td>
</tr>
<tr></tr><tr></tr><tr></tr>
<td><input type="submit" value="Submit"></td>
<td><input type="reset" value="Reset"></td>
</tr>
</table>
</form>
</body>
```

Ex. 2.9.4 : Write a form to collect details of a user such as name, address, radio button to choose subject of book he wants to buy, dropdown to choose favorite author, comments for the last book he read.

Sol. :

```
<!DOCTYPE html >
<html >
 <head>
  <title>My Page</title>
</head>
  <body>
    <form>
<b>Name:</b><input type="text" size="20" value=""><br/>
        <b>Address:</b><input type="text" size="35" value=""><br/>
        <b>Subjects:</b><br/>
        <input type="radio" name="authors" value="Web Programming">Web Programming<br/>
        <input type="radio" name="authors" value="Computer Network">Computer Network<br/>
        <input type="radio" name="authors" value="Software Engineering">
         Software Engineering<br/>
```

```
        <input type="radio" name="authors" value="Data Structures">Data Structures<br/>
        <b>Select favorite Author:</b>
        <select name="MyMenu">
         <option value="AAA">AAA</option>
         <option value="BBB">BBB</option>
         <option value="CCC">CCC</option>
         <option value="DDD">DDD</option>
        </select>
        </br>
        <b>Comments:</b></br>
        <textarea cols="30" rows="10" name="comments">
        </textarea>
        <br/><br/>
        <input type="submit" value="Submit"/>
        <input type="reset" value="Clear"/>
        </form>
        </body>
</html>
```

Output

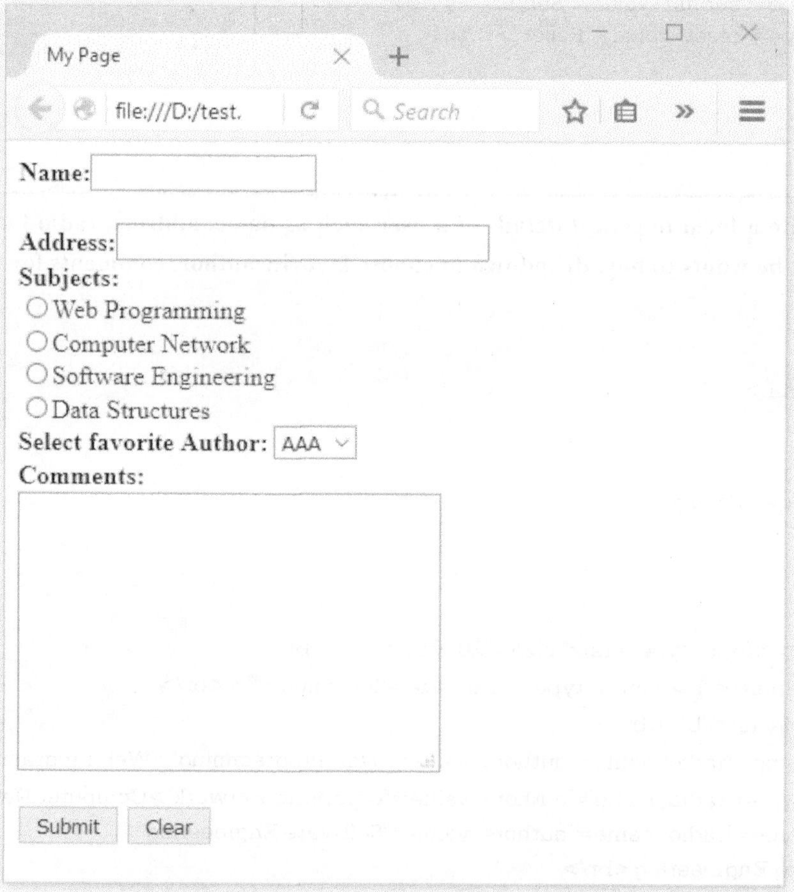

My Page

file:///D:/test.

Search

Name:

Address:

Subjects:

○ Web Programming

○ Computer Network

○ Software Engineering

○ Data Structures

Select favorite Author: AAA

Comments:

Submit Clear

Ex. 2.9.5 : Design a simple HTML form for registration of a student.

Sol. : HTML Form for Student Registration

```
<!DOCTYPE html>
<html >
 <head>
  <title>My Page</title>
</head>
  <body>
    <form>
      <b>Student Name:</b><input type="text" size="20" value=""><br/><br/>
      <b>Address:</b><input type="text" size="35" value=""><br/><br/>
      <b>Email:</b><input type="text" size="20" value=""><br/><br/>
      <b>Password:</b><input type="password" size="10" value=""><br/><br/>
      <b>Select Course:</b><br/><br/>
      <input type="radio" name="courses" value="Computer Engineering">
      Computer Engineering<br/><br/>
      <input type="radio" name="courses" value="E&TC Engineering">
      E&TC Engineering<br/><br/>
      <input type="radio" name="courses" value="Mechanical Engineering">
      Mechanical Engineering<br/><br/>
      <input type="radio" name="courses" value="Civil Engineering">
      Civil Engineering<br/><br/>
      <b>Select Payment Mode:</b>
      <select name="MyMenu">
       <option value="Cheque">Cheque</option>
       <option value="Cash">Cash</option>
       <option value="Card">Card</option>
      </select>
      <br/><br/><br/>
      <input type="submit" value="Submit"/>
      <input type="reset" value="Clear"/>
      </form>
      </body>
</html>
```

Output

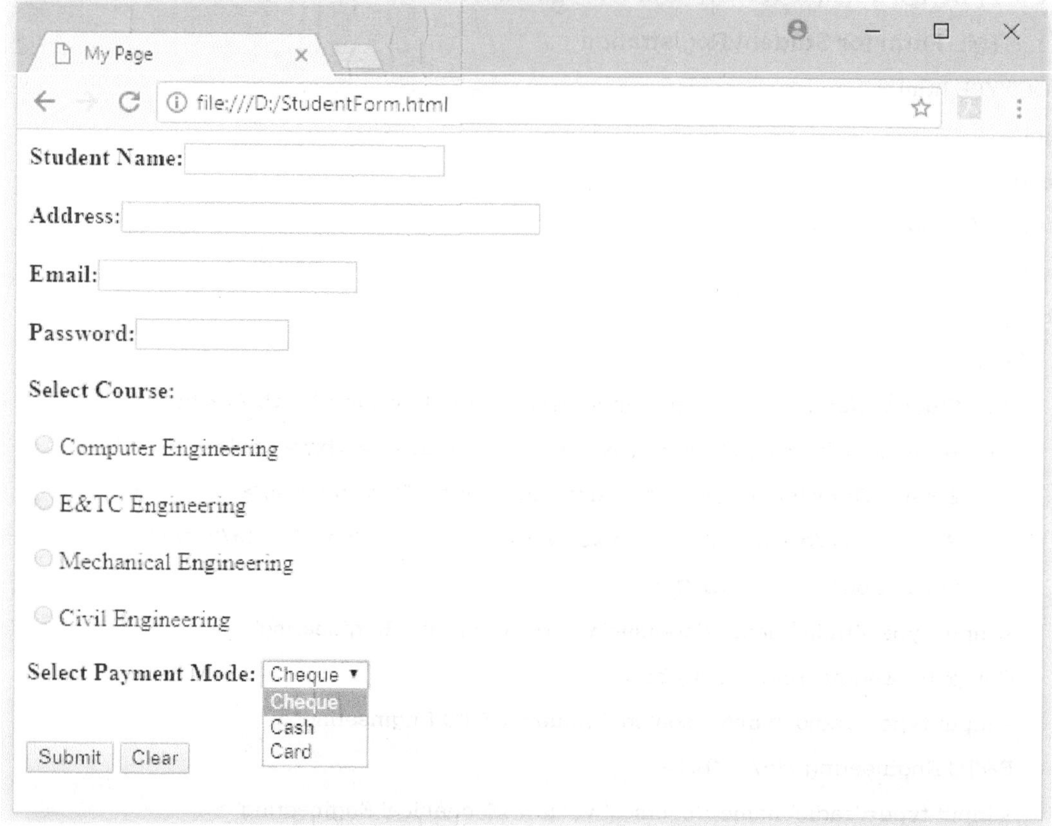

My Page
file:///D:/StudentForm.html

Student Name:

Address:

Email:

Password:

Select Course:

Computer Engineering

E&TC Engineering

Mechanical Engineering

Civil Engineering

Select Payment Mode: Cheque

Cheque
Cash
Card

Submit Clear

Ex. 2.9.6 : Write and explain any five HTML form objects for a typical online user registration process.

AU : May-09, Marks 8

Sol. : The five objects that can be used in the registration form are -

1. Text Field
2. Radio Button
3. Check Box
4. Submit Button
5. Reset Button

A sample application using all these form objects is as given below -

Registration.html

```
<html>
<head>
<title>Online Baking System</title>
</head>
<body bgcolor="khaki">
<center>
<h2>On-line Registration Form</h2>
</center>
```

```
<form name="form1">
<table>
<tr><td><b>Name:</b></td><td><input type="text" name="userName"></tr>
<tr><td><b>Password:</b></td><td><input type="password"name="pwd"></tr>
<tr>
<td><b>Sex:</b></td>
<td><input type="radio" name="group1" value="Male">Male</td>
<td><input type="radio" name="group1" value="Female">FeMale</td>
</tr>
<tr><td><b>Account Type:</b></td>
<td><select name="MyMenu">
   <option value="Savings Account">Savings Account</option>
   <option value="Current Account">Current Account</option>
   </select>
</td>
</tr>
<tr><td><b>Account Number:</b></td><td><input type="text" name="AccNo"></tr>
<tr><td><b>Facilities:</b></td>
<td><input type="checkbox" name="option1" value="ATM card">ATM Card</td></tr>
<tr><td></td><td><input type="checkbox" name="option2" value="Cheque book">
Cheque book</td></tr>
</table>
<br/><br/>
<center>
<input type="submit" value="Submit">
<input type="reset" value="Clear">
</center>
</form>
</body>
</html>
```

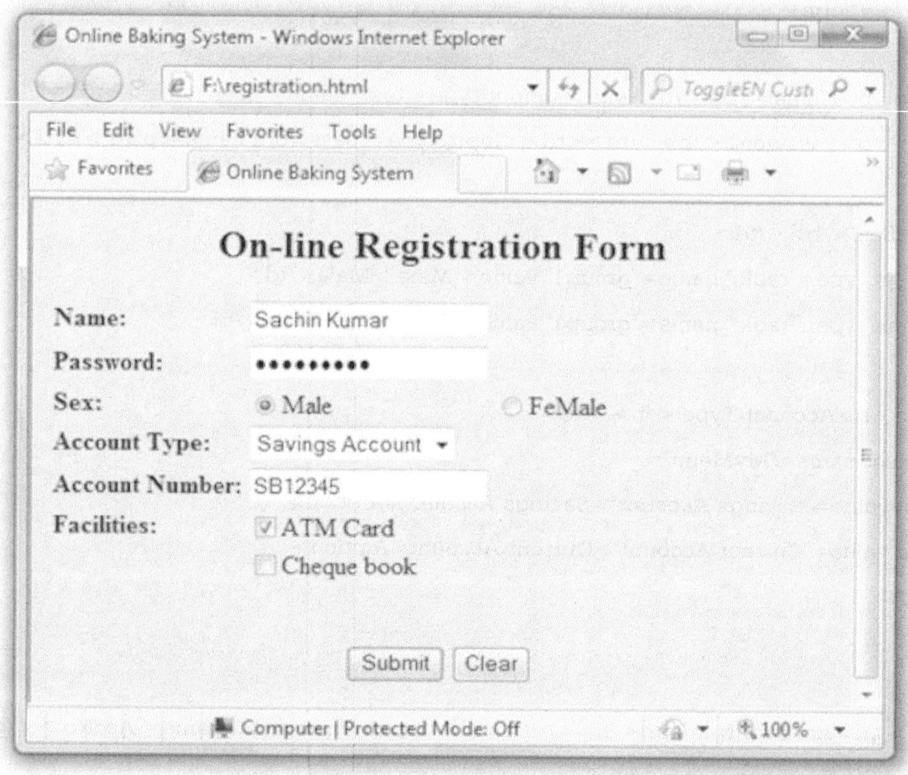

Ex. 2.9.7 : Create a registration form for an educational web site with E-learning resources. All form controls should have appropriate name attributes. Use the GET method for form submission and specify an empty string for the action attribute. **AU : Dec.-12, Marks 16**

Sol. :

```
<!DOCTYPE html>
<html>
  <head><title>My Form </title></head>
  <body>
    <h3> E-learning Resource Registration Form</h3>
    <form name="myform" action ="" method="get" >
        <div align="left"><br>
        Name:<input type="text" name="name" value="">
        <br/><br/>
        Address:<input type="text" name="add" value="">
        <br/><br/>
        Phone:<input type="text" name="ph" value="">
        <br/><br/>
```

```
        Sex:
        <input type="radio" name="group1" value="Male">Male
        <input type="radio" name="group1" value="Female">Female<br/>
        <br/><br/>
        Select the Course of your choice:
        <select name="My_Menu">
          <option value="Computer">Computer</option>
          <option value="Information Technology">Information Technology</option>
          <option selected value="Mechanical">Mechanical </option>
          <option value="Electronics and Telecommunication">
             Electronics and Telecommunication</option>
          <option value="Electrical">Electrical</option>
        </select>
        <br/><br/><br/>
        <input type="button" value="Submit">
        </div>
    </form>
  </body>
</html>
```

2.9.7 Specialized Controls

There are two special purpose form controls that are available in all browsers.

(i) <input type="hidden"> element

This control is used to define the hidden element. As the name suggests, this field and the data value assigned to this field is not visible to the user. Following is an HTML document that makes use of hidden element –

HTML Document

```
<!DOCTYPE html>
<html>
<body>
<p>The name and hidden marks will be submitted</p>
<form action="ProcessPg.php">
 Name : <input type="text" name="fname"><br>
 <input type="hidden" id="marks" name="Smarks" value="98">
 <input type="submit" value="Submit">
</form>
</body>
</html>
```

Output

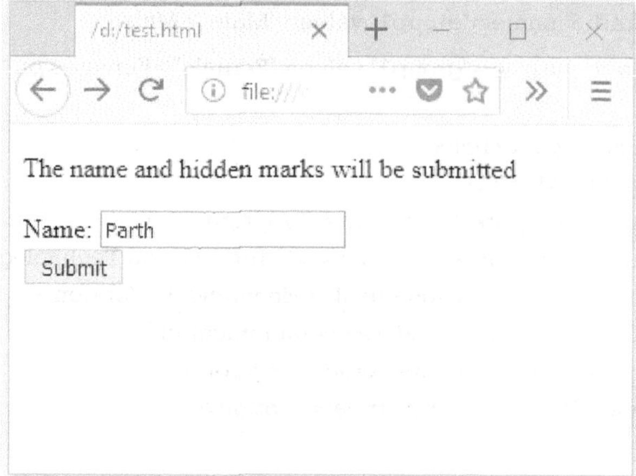

The address bar contains

file:///d:/ProcessPg.php?fname=Parth&Smarks=98

A hidden field often stores what database record that needs to be updated when the form is submitted.

(ii) <input type="file"> element

This element defines a file select field and **Browse** button to upload a file.

For selecting multiple files we need to add the attribute **multiple** in the <input> element.

Here is the illustrative HTML document which allows to select single and multiple files both.

HTML Document

```
<!DOCTYPE html>
<html>
<body>
<h4>Selection of Single file:</h4>
<form>
    Select a file: <input type="file" name="myFile"><br><br>
</form>
<h4>Selection of multiple files:</h4>
<form>
    Select files: <input type="file" name="myFile" multiple><br><br>
</form>
</body>
</html>
```

Output

/d:/test.html

file:///

Selection of Single file:

Select a file: Browse... No file selected.

Selection of multiple files:

Select files: Browse... No files selected.

/d:/test.html

file:///

Selection of Single file:

Select a file: Browse... DailyLog.xlsx

Selection of multiple files:

Select files: Browse... 2 files selected.

2.9.8 Number and Range

- HTML5 introduced two new controls for the input of numeric values.
- When input via a standard text control, numbers typically require validation to ensure that the user has entered an actual number and, because the range of numbers is infinite, the entered number has to be checked to ensure it is not too small or too large.
- The number and range controls provide a way to input numeric values that eliminate the need for client-side numeric validation.

HTML Document

```
<!DOCTYPE html>
<html>
<body>
<form action="ProcessPg.php">
 Scale your Performance from Poor to Excellent :(1 to 5)
 <input type="number" min="1" max="5"><br>
 <input type="submit">
</form>
</body>
</html>
```

/d:/test.html

Scale your Performance from Poor to Excellent:(1 to 5)

3

Submit Query

Range Selector

- To provide option to select a value between range, we can set type attribute to "range".
- Slider control is a very intuitive user interface to set a number within a range.
- In order to specify the minimum and maximum value, we can set min and max attribute.
- For example -

HTML Document

```
<!DOCTYPE html>
<html>
 <body>
 <p>Range slider</p>
 <form>
 Select value:
      <input type="range" id="myRange" name="myRange"
     min="0" max="50" value="24"/>
 </form>
</body>
</html>
```

Output

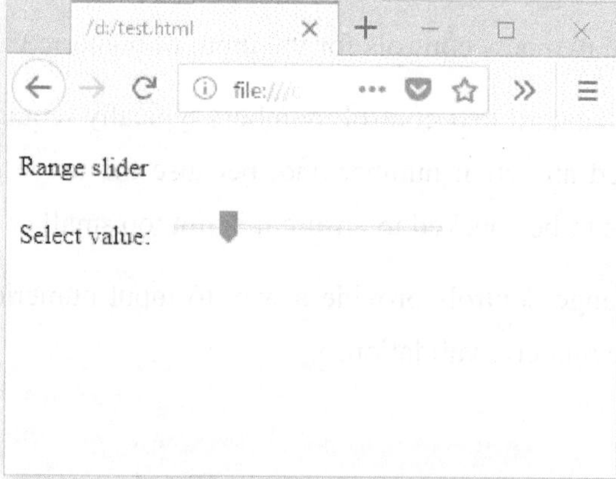

2. Color

- The HTML5 allows input> elements of type "color" provide a user interface element that lets a user specify a color, either by using a visual color picker interface or by entering the color into a text field in "#rrggbb" hexadecimal format.
- For example –

```
<!DOCTYPE html>
<html>
 <body>
 <p>Color Element</p>
 <form>
 Select color: <input type="color" value="#ff0000"/>
 </form>
</body>
</html>
```

Output

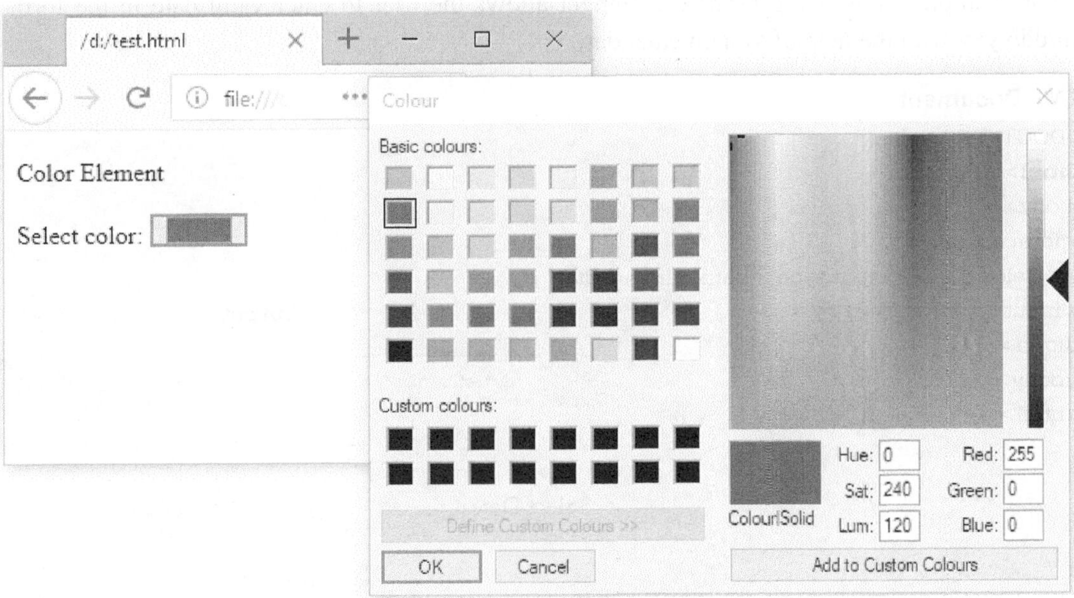

The **value** of an <input> element of type "color" is always a string specifying an RGB color in hexadecimal format.

2.9.9 Date and Time Controls

- Asking user to enter date is a common web activity. The date and time input often need validation while gathering the input from the user.

- There are different input types to handle date and time requirement in the User Interface provided by HTML5. All these types run on only those browsers which support HTML5.

Type	Description
date	Creates a general date input control. The format for the date is "yyyy-mm-dd."
time	Creates a time input control. The format for the time is "HH:MM:SS," for Hours : minutes : seconds.
datetime	Creates a control in which the user can enter a date and time.
datetime-local	Creates a control in which the user can enter a date and time without specifying a time zone.
month	Creates a control in which the user can enter a month in a year. The format is "yyyy-mm."
week	Creates a control in which the user can specify a week in a year. The format is "yyyy-W##."

For example – Following HTML document allows the user to enter valid date in the form of mm/dd/yyyy with the help of system calendar.

HTML Document

```
<!DOCTYPE html>
<html>
<body>
 <form action="">
   Select Date <input type="date" name="dt">
 <input type="submit">
</form>
</body>
</html>
```

Output

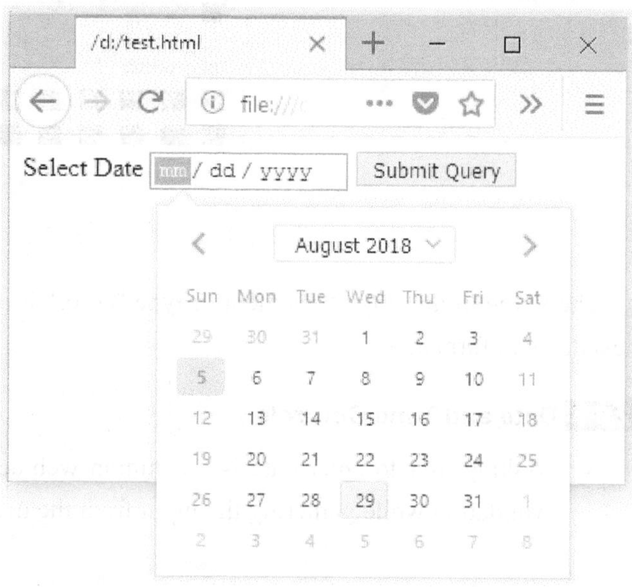

Similarly using **time** control, the user can enter the time in HH:MM:SS form. Here is the illustration.

HTML Document

```
<!DOCTYPE html>
<html>
<body>
<form action="">
 Select time <input type="time" name="tm">
  <input type="submit">
</form>
</body>
</html>
```

Output

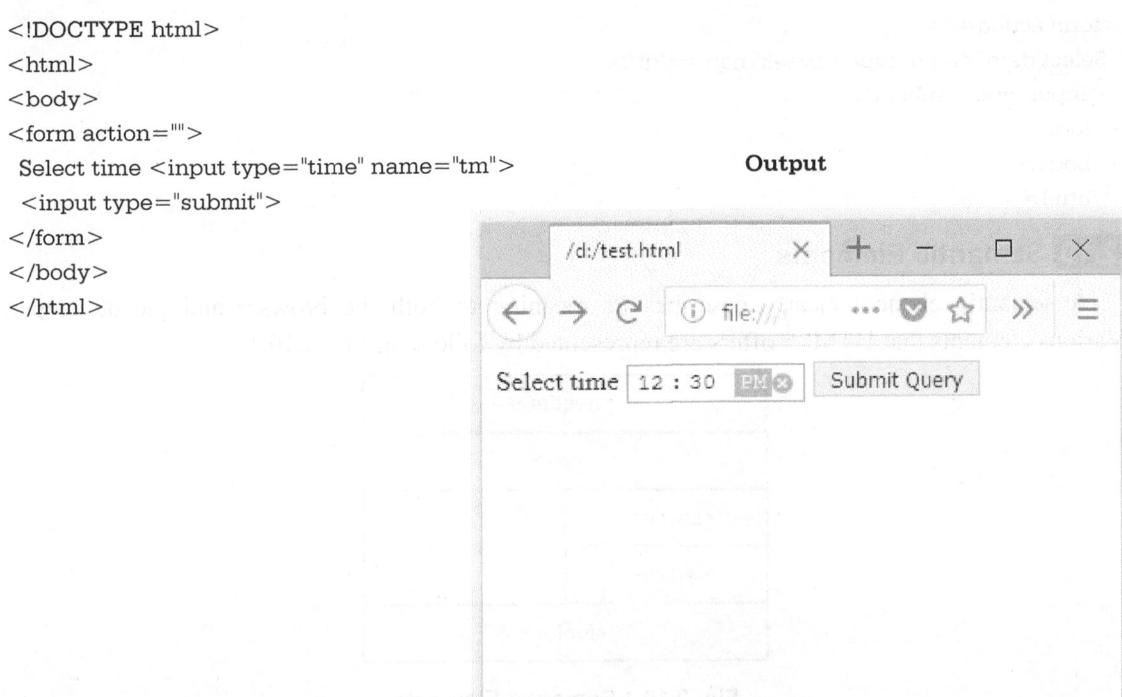

The input type datetime provides the time zone and with that we can select date globally. It provides date and time both values. For instance -

HTML Document

```
<!DOCTYPE html>
<html>
<body>
<h3>datetime Demo in HTML5</h3>
<form action="">
 Select Date <input type="datetime" name="dt">
  <input type="submit">
</form>
</body>
</html>
```

The **Week** is also an interesting input type. While selecting date, it provides a specific column for week. User easily can identify that which date is week days.

HTML Document

```
<!DOCTYPE html>
<html>
<body>
<form action="">
 Select date <input type="week" name="dt">
  <input type="submit">
</form>
</body>
</html>
```

2.10 Semantic Elements

A semantic element clearly describes its meaning to both the browser and the developer. Various elements that HTML5 offers are represented by following Fig. 2.10.1.

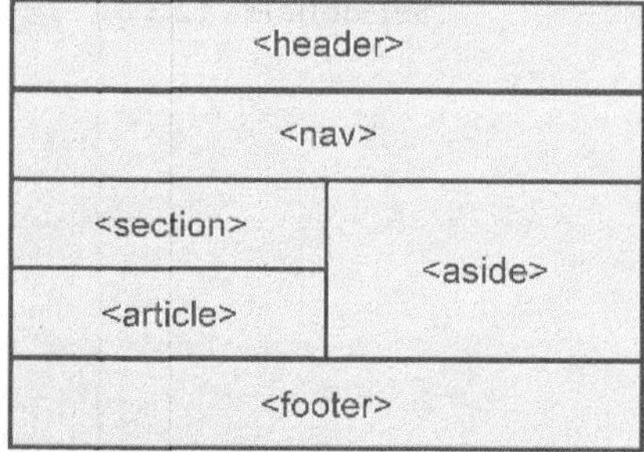

Fig. 2.10.1 Semantic Elements

2.10.1 Header and Footer

- The <header> element specifies the header for the document or section.
- There can be several header elements present on a page.

HTML Document

```
<!DOCTYPE html>
<html>
<body>
<article>
  <header>
    <h1>Art and Culture </h1>
    <h3>Introduction:</h3>
  </header>
  <p> India has one of the world's largest collections of songs, music, dance, folk traditions, performing arts,paintings and writings that are known, as the 'Intangible Cultural Heritage' (ICH) of humanity.  </p>
</article>
</body>
</html>
```

Output

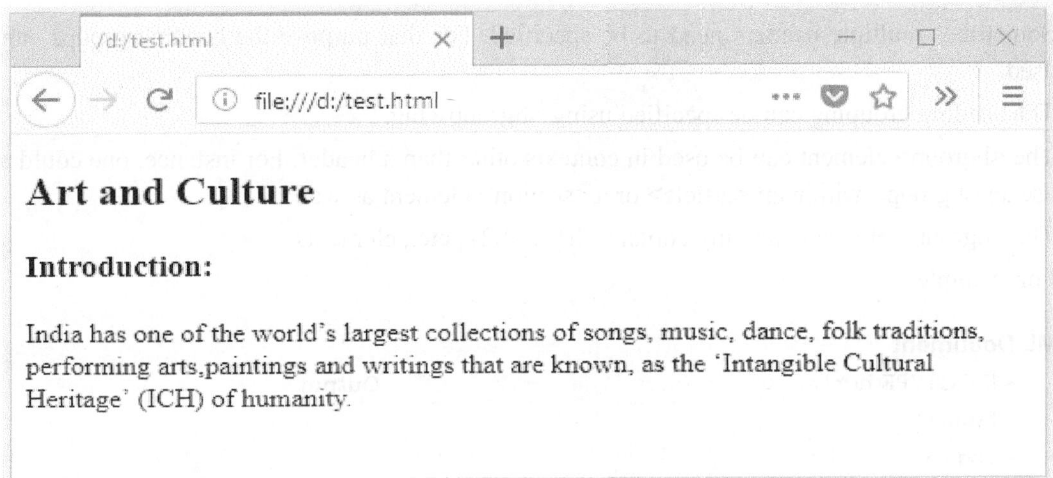

- The <footer> element specifies a footer for a document or section.
- A <footer> element should contain information about its containing element.
- A footer typically contains the author of the document, copyright information, links to terms of use, contact information, etc.
- You may have several <**footer**> elements in one document.

HTML Document

```
<!DOCTYPE html>
<html>
<body>
<footer>
<p>All Rights Reserverd.2018</p>
<p>Reproduction of materials found on this site, in any form, without explicit permission is prohibited.</p>
</footer>
</body>
</html>
```

Output

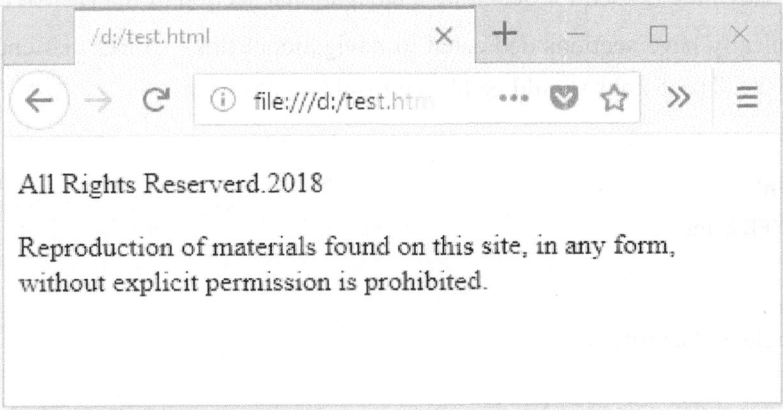

2.10.2 Heading Groups

- Sometimes multiple headers need to be specified. For that purpose the heading groups can be used.
- The heading grouping can be specified using <hgroup> tag.
- The <hgroup> element can be used in contexts other than a header. For instance, one could also use an <hgroup> within an <article> or a <section> element as well.
- The <hgroup> element can only contain <h1>, <h2>, etc., elements.
- For example –

HTML Document

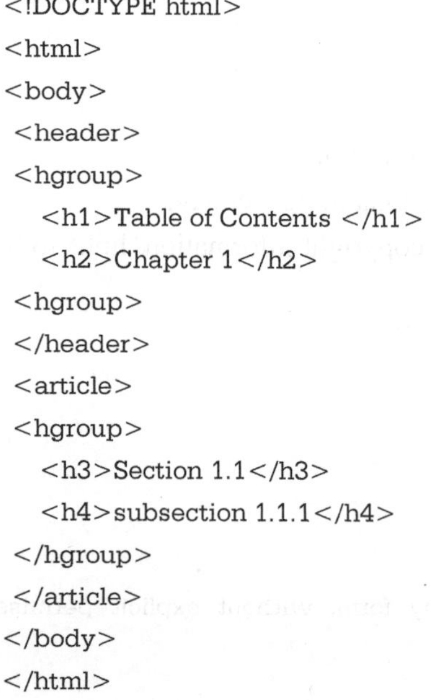

```
<!DOCTYPE html>
<html>
<body>
 <header>
 <hgroup>
   <h1>Table of Contents </h1>
   <h2>Chapter 1</h2>
 <hgroup>
 </header>
 <article>
 <hgroup>
   <h3>Section 1.1</h3>
   <h4>subsection 1.1.1</h4>
 </hgroup>
 </article>
</body>
</html>
```

Output

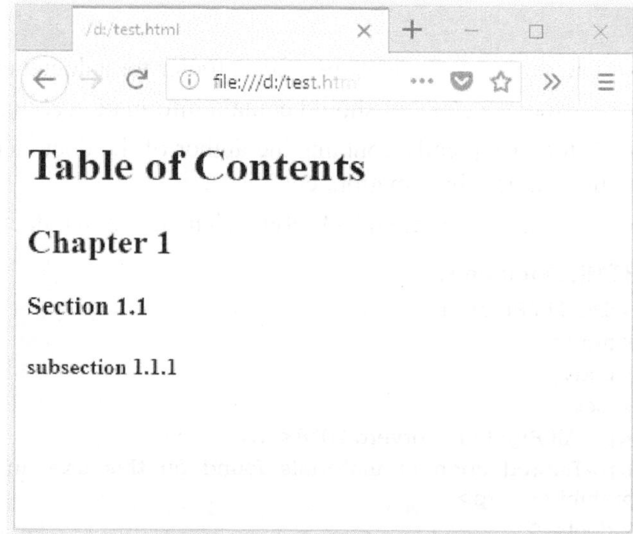

2.10.3 Navigation

- The HTML <nav> tag is used for declaring a navigational section of the HTML document.
- Websites typically have sections dedicated to navigational links - links that enable the user to navigate the site. These links should be placed inside a <nav> tag.
- For example :

HTML Document

```
<!DOCTYPE html>
<html>
<body>
 <h1>Table of Contents </h1>
 <nav>
```

```
    <a href="/ch1/">Chapter 1</a> |
    <a href="/ch2/">Chapter 2</a> |
    <a href="/ch3/">Chapter 3</a> |
    <a href="/ch4/">Chapter 4</a>
   </nav>
  </body>
  </html>
```

Output

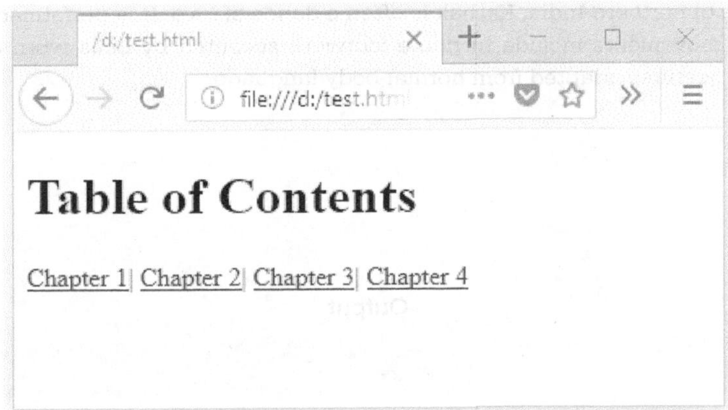

2.10.4 Articles and Sections

- The **<article>** element specifies independent, self-contained content.
- The **<section>** element defines section in a document.
- There can be HTML documents with <section> elements containing <article> elements, and <article> elements containing <section> elements.
- **Example of article -** Forum Post, Newspaper article, Blog Post
- **Example of section -** A home page could normally be split into sections for introduction, content, and contact information.

HTML Document

```
<!DOCTYPE html>
<html>
<body>
 <article>
 <h1>Classical Dances In India </h1>
 <section>
       <h2>Bharatanatyam</h2>
         <p>Bharatanatyam is a dance of Tamil Nadu in southern India. It traces its origins back to
         the Natyashastra, an ancient treatise on theatre written by the mythic priest Bharata.</p>
 </section>
```

```
<section>
    <h2>Kathakali</h2>
    <p>Kathakali comes from southwestern India, around the state of Kerala. Like
     bharatanatyam, kathakali is a religious dance. It draws inspiration from the Ramayana and
     stories from Shaiva traditions.
  </p>
</section>
<section>
  <h2>Kathak</h2>
   <p>A dance of northern India, Kathak is often a dance of love. It is performed by both men and
   women. The movements include intricate footwork accented by bells worn around the ankles
   and stylized gestures adapted from normal body language.
  </p>
  </section>
  </article>
 </body>
</html>
```

Output

Classical Dances In India

Bharatanatyam

Bharatanatyam is a dance of Tamil Nadu in southern India. It traces its origins back to the Natyashastra, an ancient treatise on theatre written by the mythic priest Bharata.

Kathakali

Kathakali comes from southwestern India, around the state of Kerala. Like bharatanatyam, kathakali is a religious dance. It draws inspiration from the Ramayana and stories from Shaiva traditions.

Kathak

A dance of northern India, Kathak is often a dance of love. It is performed by both men and women. The movements include intricate footwork accented by bells worn around the ankles and stylized gestures adapted from normal body language.

2.10.5 Figures and Figures Captions

The <figure> element can be used to group the image and figure caption. The figure caption gives the information about the image. For example –

HTML Document

```
<!DOCTYPE html>
<html>
<body>
<h2>Proud of India</h2>
<p>Konark Sun Temple is a 13th-century CE sun temple at Konark.The name Konark derives from the combination of the Sanskrit words Kona (corner or angle) and Arka (the sun).</p>
<figure>
  <img src="Konark.jpg" alt="KonarkTemple" style="width:50%">
  <figcaption>Fig.1 - Konark Temple, India</figcaption>
</figure>
</body>
</html>
```

Output

Proud of India

Konark Sun Temple is a 13th-century CE sun temple at Konark.The name Konark derives from the combination of the Sanskrit words Kona (corner or angle) and Arka (the sun).

Fig.1 - Konark Temple, India

2.10.6 Aside

- The <aside> element is used to identify **content that is related to the primary content** of the webpage, but does not constitute the primary content of the page.
- For example – Author information, related links, related contents, and advertisement, are the examples of the contents that may be found in an aside element.
- Asides are frequently presented as sidebars or call-out boxes.

HTML Document

```
<!DOCTYPE html>
<html>
<body>
<p>Android is a mobile operating system developed by Google, based on a modified version of the Linux kernel and other open source software and designed primarily for touchscreen mobile devices such as smartphones and tablets.</p>
<aside>
  <h4>Note:</h4>
  <p>Android Inc. was founded in Palo Alto, California, in October 2003.</p>
</aside>
</body>
</html>
```

2.11 Drag and Drop

- The HTML5 drag and drop feature allows the user to drag and drop an element to another location.
- While dragging an element a translucent representation of the element is follow the mouse pointer.
- A number of events are fired during the various stages of the drag and drop operation. But mouse events such as **mousemove** are not fired during a drag operation.
- The HTML5's drag and drop feature is supported in all major modern browsers like Firefox, Chrome, Opera, Safari and Internet Explorer 9 and above.
- The following table provides you a brief overview of all the drag and drop events.

Event	Description
ondragstart	This event gets fired when the user starts dragging an element.

ondragenter	This event gets fired when draggable element is moved into the target element.
ondragover	This event gets fired when user drags an element over the drop listener or target element.
ondragleave	This event gets fired when the user drags an element out of drop listener.
ondrag	When user drags an element this event gets fired.
ondrop	When user drops an element over the target element, this event is fired.
ondragend	This event gets fired when the drag action is complete.

Following is an HTML script that illustrates the drag and drop action of an image.

HTML Script

```
<!DOCTYPE html>
<html>
<head>
<script>
function during_dragdrop(e) {
    e.preventDefault();
}
function begin_drag(e) {
    e.dataTransfer.setData("text/html", e.target.id);
}
function end_drop(e) {
    e.preventDefault();
    var code = e.dataTransfer.getData("text/html");
    e.target.appendChild(document.getElementById(code));
}
</script>
</head>
<body>
<p>Drag the image into the rectangle:</p>
```

```
<div id="div1" style="float:left;width:300px;height:300px;padding:10px;border:1px solid red;"
ondrop="end_drop(event)" ondragover="during_dragdrop(event)"></div>
<br>
<img id="drag1" src="mickey.jpg" alt="Cartoon image"
style="float:left;width:300px;height:300px;padding:10px;border:1px solid blue;"
draggable="true" ondragstart="begin_drag(event)"/>
</body>
</html>
```

Output

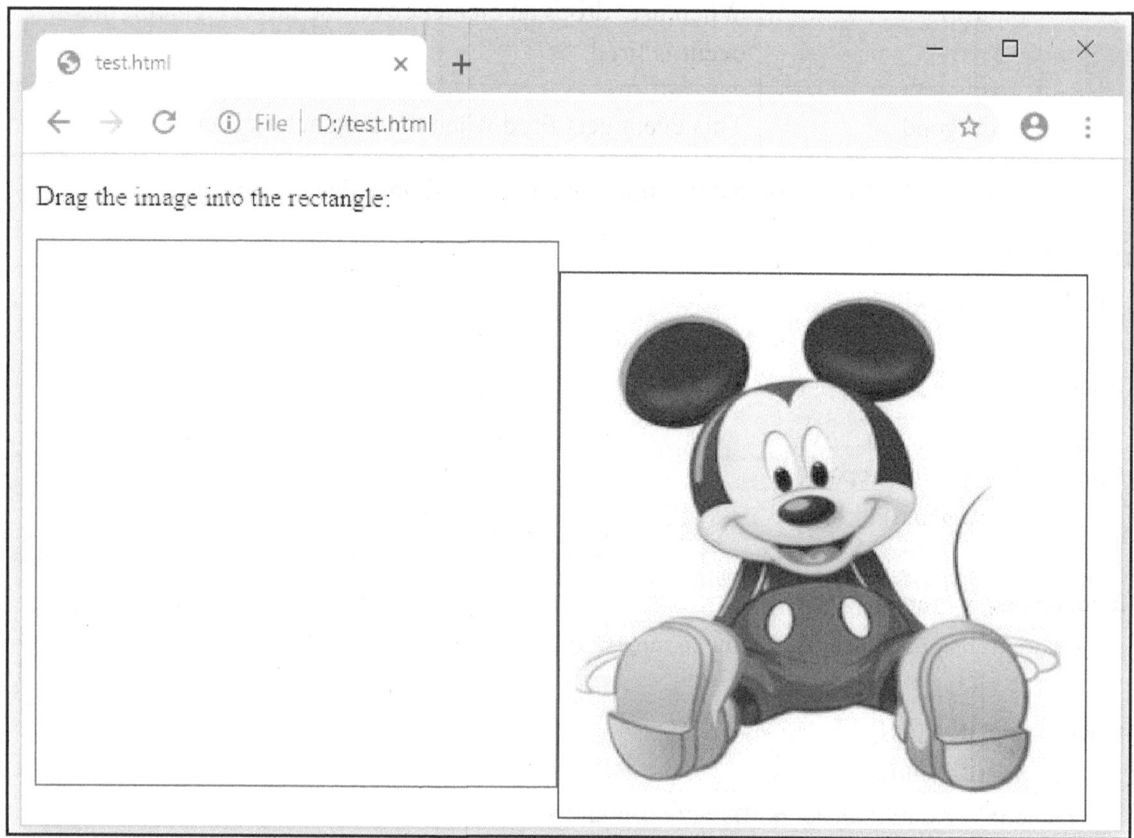

On dragging and dropping the image into the rectangle we get

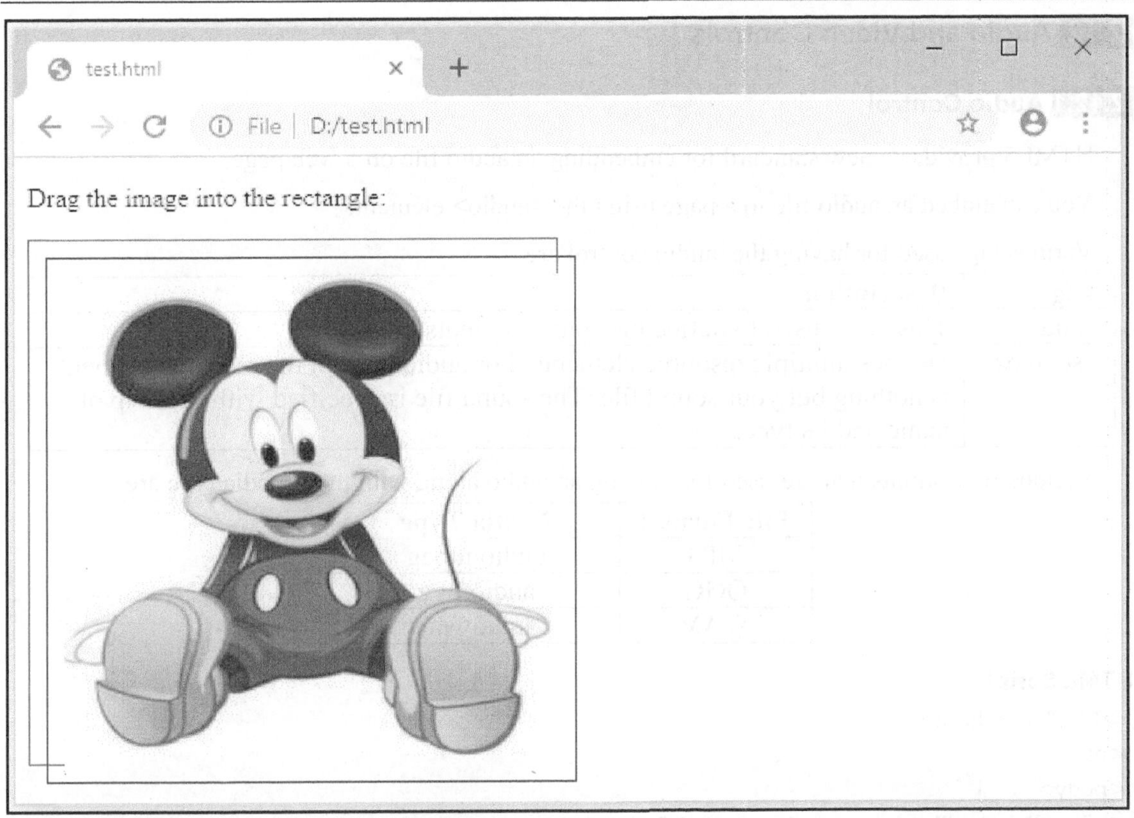

Script Explanation : In above HTML,

(1) There are two rectangles created – one rectangle is with red border and other rectangle is with blue rectangle in which image is placed.

(2) You can make an element draggable by setting the draggable attribute to true, like **draggable="true"**.

(3) When we want to drag an image into the red rectangle we fire an even ondragstart. This event is handled by a user defined function **begin_drag.**

(4) Inside the **begin_drag** function we invoke a method named **dataTransfer.setData**. The **DataTransfer** object holds data about the drag and drop operation. Using **setData** method, the specified data is added.

(5) For a red rectangle, the ondrop event is triggerd. This event is handled using the function **end_drop.** Inside this method, the data hold during drag operation is acquired using **getData** method of **dataTransfer** object.

(6) During the drag operation and before drop, the event **ondragover** is raised. This event is simply handled by using **e.preventDefault()** method. This method prevents the browser default handling of the data.

2.12 Audio and Video Controls

2.12.1 Audio Control

HTML5 provides a new standard for embedding an audio file on a web page.

You can embed an audio file to a page using the <audio> element.

Various tags used for having the audio control are

Tag	Description
<audio>	This tag is used to define the sound contents
<source>	Defines multiple resource elements. For audio control the resource element is nothing but your sound file. The sound file is specified with the help of name and its type.

Various file formats that are used for playing an audio along with their media type are –

File Format	Media Type
MP3	audio/mpeg
OGG	audio/ogg
WAV	audio/wav

HTML Script

```
<!DOCTYPE html>
<html>
<body>
<h2> Click the Play button to listen...</h2>
<audio controls>
 <source src="bell_ringing.mp3" type="audio/mpeg">
Your browser does not support the audio element.
</audio>
</body>
</html>
```

Output

2.12.2 Video Control

The <video> control allows us to add a video in an HTML page. The controls attribute adds video controls, like play, pause, and volume.

The height and width attributes are specified for this control.

The <source> element allows you to specify alternative video files which the browser may choose from. The browser will use the first recognized format.

HTML Video File format with media type are –

File Format	Media Type
MP4	video/mp4
WebM	video/webm
Ogg	video/ogg

HTML Script

```
<!DOCTYPE html>
<html>
<body>
<video width="320" height="240" autoplay>
 <source src="SampleVideo.mp4" type="video/mp4">
Your browser does not support the video tag
</video>
</body>
</html>
```

Output

Two Marks Questions with Answers

Q.1 How to write comment statements in HTML ?

Ans. : The comments in HTML can be denoted as follows -

<!- -It is a comment statement -->

There should not be a space between angular bracket and exclamation mark. This comment is beginning with <!-- and ending with -->. There should not be any character such as -- inside the comment.

Q.2 What is the use of <pre> tag in HTML ?

Ans. : The pre tag can be used to preserve the white spaces and lines in the text.

Q.3 What is non breaking space character in HTML ?

Ans. : The &nbps is a non breaking space character. This entity is useful for defining the space between two strings and informing browser for not performing the word wrapper between the strings.

Q.4 What is cellpadding and cell spacing attributes ?

Ans. : The cellpadding allows to have some space between the contents of each cell and its borders. The distance between each cell is called cell spacing.

Q.5 What is the need of using form in HTML ?

Ans. : Form is a typical layout on the web page by which user can interact with the web page. The components that can be placed on the form are text box, check box, radio buttons, push buttons and so on. Thus form is typically used to create an interactive Graphical User Interface.

Q.6 What is the purpose of using frames in HTML?

Ans. : The XHTML frames allows the web designer to present the web document in multiple views. Using multiple views one can keep the information visible and at the same time other views can be scrolled or replaced. For example, within the same window, one frame can display a company information, the second frame can be a navigation menu and third frame may display selected document that can be scrolled through or replaced by navigating in the second frame.

Q.7 What is the use of markup language in Web technology ? Give examples of some markup languages.

Ans. : The markup language is used to layout the information on the web page. Various markup languages are HTML, XHTML, DHTML, JavaScript.

Q.8 How will you create password field in a HTML form ? **AU : Dec.-11**

Ans. : The password field is typically created on the form. Hence following code can be written to create it -

```
<form name="form1">
 Password:<input type="password"/>
</form>
```

Q.9 List and explain any two HTML elements. AU : May -12

Ans. :

Element	Meaning
<title>	This element is used to specify the title of the web page. This element is defined within the <head> part.
<p>	This element is generally defined in the <body> part. It is used to create a paragraph.

Q.10 List and explain any two special characters in HTML

Ans. :

Special Character	Entity Reference	Meaning
<	<	To display the less than character.
&	&	To display the ampersand.

Q.11 How would you insert an image file named elephant.jpg at the very top of a web page ?

Ans. :

```
<!DOCTYPE html PUBLIC "-//W3C//DTD XHTML 1.0 Transitional//EN"
"http://www.w3.org/TR/xhtml1/DTD/xhtml11.dtd">
<html xmlns="http://www.w3.org/1999/xhtml">
<body>
<p>
<img src= "elephant.jpg" alt= "Light!!" />
</p>
</body>
</html>
```

Q.12 Is it possible to insert white space in the web page while writing some paragraph ?

Ans. : Yes. We can insert the white space in the paragraph by using the entity reference &nbps i.e. non breaking character space.

Q.13 What are the uses of hyperlinks in HTML ?

Ans. : Following are the uses of hyperlinks for the web document -

i) To logically link one page with another

ii) Use of link to enhance readability of the web document.

iii) The navigation from one page to another is possible.

Q.14 What is the advantage of using tables on the web document ?

Ans. : Using tables the information can be arranged systematically in row-wise and column-wise manner.

Q.15 Write HTML code to display an image. AU : Dec.-12

Ans. :

```
<html>
    <head>
     <title> Image Demo </title>
    </head>
    <body>
     <img src= "lamp1.jpg" alt= "Light!!" />

    </body>
</html>
```

Q.16 List and explain the three flavors of HTML AU : May -13

Ans. : The three flavors of HTML are as follows -

1. **XHTML 1.0 Strict :** When we want a clean markup code or markup then this type is used. To get the font, color, layout effects this flavor can be used along with the CSS.
2. **XHTML 1.0 Transitional :** By this type we can use the deprecated or presentational elements but frames are not allowed.
3. **XHTML 1.0 Frameset :** We can use this type when we want to use Frames to partition the browser window into two or more frames.

Q.17 How XHTML is more advantageous than HTML ? Specify. AU : May-14

Ans. : The XHTML is convenient to use if some one needs to reprocess the document using XML. This reprocessing is always needed when we want to send the XHTML document on some other devices say PDA. XML's stricter syntax rules make automatic processing of XHTML much easier and cheaper than ordinary HTML.

Q.18 Enlist any five features of HTML5.0.

Ans. :

1. It has a rich set of Application Programming Interface(API) for geolocations, HTML Drag and Drop, Local Storage, Application cache and so on.
2. There are new graphic elements such as <canvas> and <svg> in HTML5.0
3. The support for multimedia elements such as <audio> and <video>
4. It has support for <header>, <footer>, <article>, and <section>

5. The XHTML doctype is just impossible to memorize(!DOCTYPE html PUBLIC "...). Hence a new HTML doctype is <!DOCTYPE html>

Q.19 How do the hyperlinks appear by default ?

Ans. : By default the hyperlinks are unvisited, underlined and blue.

Q.20 Mention the HTML tag that can be used to make a picture a link.

Ans. : The href tag around **img** can be used to make a picture a link. For example -

```
<a href = "http://www.myhome.com"> <img src =
http://myhome.com/gallery/sampleflat.jpg></a>
```

Q.21 What are HTML forms ?

Ans. : HTML form is an element used to allow a user to input data on the web page. The element used in <form>. The main attributes are **action** and **method.** For example

```
<form action =http://www.mywebpage.com/ method=get></form>
```

Q.22 What do you mean by row spanning and column spanning ?

Ans. : The row spanning is used to combine two or more rows and columns spanning is used to combine two or more columns.

Q.23 Explain the format of HTML document.

Ans. : The format of HTML document is as follows -

```
<html>
  <head>
    <title>
    </title>
  </head>
  <body>
    ... HTML statements
  </body>
</html>
```

Q.24 What are the uses of HTML form ?

Ans. : The HTML forms can be used in variety of applications such as

1. For creating registration forms
2. For creating the login forms
3. For gathering user information
4. For conducting surveys.

Q.25 How you use Form's Action Attribute and Submit Button in HTML ?

Ans. : The action attribute specifies where to send the form-data when a form is submitted.

For example - On clicking the submit button, the **mypage.php** page will be invoked for further processing.

```
<form action="mypage.php" method="get">
First name: <input type="text" name="name"><br>
<input type="submit" value="Submit">
</form>
```

Q.26 How to use Line Break and Horizontal Line tags in HTML ?

Ans. : • The line break tag is denoted by

- The horizontal line can be inserted in the HTML document by <hr> tag.

Q.27 How you define href, target and name Attributes ?

Ans. : The href tag is used to have hyperlink in the HTML document. The **target** attribute specifies where to open the linked document. For example - Following created hyperlink helps the user to open the web document in another page.

```
<a href="/" target="_blank">The home page will open in another tab.</a>
```

Q.28 Why we use XHTML ? **AU : Dec.-17**

Ans. : The XHTML is used for following reasons -

i) It creates strict standard for making web pages.

ii) It reduces the incompatibility between various web browsers, and hence is compatible for almost all the web browsers.

iii) It creates a standard that can be used on variety of different devices without change.

Q.29 What is HTML canvas and what are the uses of it ? **AU :Dec.-18**

Ans. :

- The < canvas > is an element in HTML 5.0 which creates rectangular area on HTML page on which we can draw graphs.
- The uses of it are

i) For drawing graphics such as boxes, circles, text, adding images.

ii) Online, offline games.

iii) Animations

iv) Interactive video and audio.

Q.30 When user enters a Uniform resource Locator (URL) address into a web browser ? How is the specific document retrieved from a web server ? **AU :May-18**

Ans. : Refer section 1.6

❑❑❑

Unit I

3 CSS3 and Web 2.0

Syllabus

CSS3 – Inline, embedded and external style sheets – Rule cascading – Inheritance – Backgrounds – Border Images – Colors – Shadows – Text – Transformations – Transitions – Animations

Contents

3.1 Introduction to CSS

AU : May-11, 14

- The CSS stands for Cascading Style Sheet.
- The Cascading Style Sheet is a markup language used in the web document for presentation purpose.
- The **primary intension of CSS** was to separate out the web content from the web presentation.
- Various elements such as text, font and color are used in CSS for presentation purpose. Thus CSS specification can be applied to bring the styles in the web document.

3.1.1 Features of CSS

- By combining CSS with the html document, considerable amount of **flexibility** into the content submission can be achieved.
- Similarly, separating out the style from actual contents help in **managing** large-scale complex sites. Thus CSS facilitates publication of content in multiple presentation formats.
- If CSS is used, effectively then **global style sheet** can be applied to a web document. This helps in maintaining the **consistency in the web document**.
- If a **small change** needs to be done in the style of web content, then CSS makes it more convenient.
- All above mentioned advantages of CSS show the need for it in web development.

3.1.2 Features of CSS3

CSS3 is the latest version of CSS and contains a number of exciting, new features that make it easier for web developers to create great styling for websites.

Features

1. The CSS3 is a latest version of CSS.
2. It is completely backward compatible with older version of CSS.
3. It support for selectors, box model, Background and borders, Text effects, animations, multiple column layout, 3D transformations and so on.

University Question

1. *Explain the features of cascading style sheets.* **AU : May-11,14, Marks 8**

3.2 Core Syntax

- The style specification is specified differently for each different level. For instance :
- For inline cascading style sheets the **style** appears in side the tag for defining the value.

  <p style="font-size: 30pt ;font-family:Script">

- For the document cascading style sheet the **style** specification appear as the content of a style element within the header of a document.

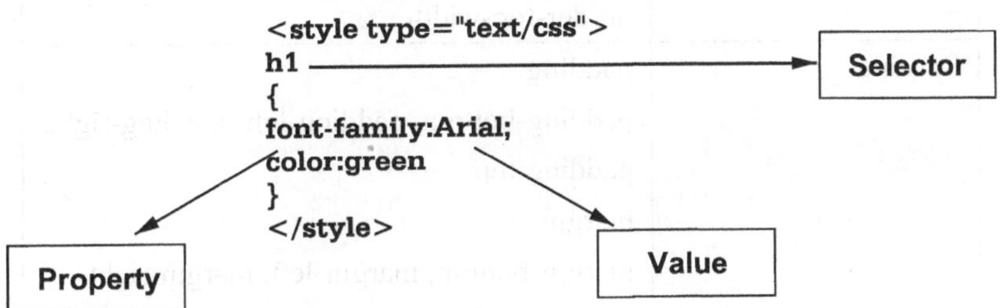

The **type** attribute tells the browser that what it is reading is text which is affected by the Cascading Style Sheet. The type specification is necessary because there is one more specification used in JavaScript.

- The External style sheet makes use of **style** specification in the same manner as in document cascading style sheet.

The most commonly used CSS properties are enlisted in the following table -

Property Type	Property
Fonts	font font-family font-size font-style font-weight @font-face
Text	letter-spacing line-height text-align text-decoration text-indent
Color and background	background background-color background-image background-position background-repeat color

Borders	border border-color border-width border-style border-top border-top-color border-top-width
Spacing	padding padding-bottom, padding-left, padding-right, padding-top margin margin-bottom, margin-left, margin-right, margin-top
Sizing	height max-height max-width min-height min-width width
Layout	bottom, left, right, top clear display float overflow position visibility z-index
Lists	list-style list-style-image list-style-type

3.3 Selector

3.3.1 Simple Selector Form

- The simple selector form is a single element to which the property and value is applied.
- We can also apply property and value to group of elements.
- Following is an illustration for simple selector form.

HTML Document[SimpleSel.html]

```
<!DOCTYPE html>
<html >
<head>
     <title>Simple Selector Form</title>
     <style type="text/css">
     h1
     {
      font-family:Arial;
color:green;
     }
     h2,h3
     {
      font-family:Monotype Corsiva;
      color:red;
      font-size: 28pt;
     }
     </style>
     </head>
     <body>
      <h1>India is My Country</h1>
      <h2>All the Indians are my brothers and sisters</h3>
      <h3>I love my country</h3>
     </body>
</html>
```

We can apply style to more than one selector

output

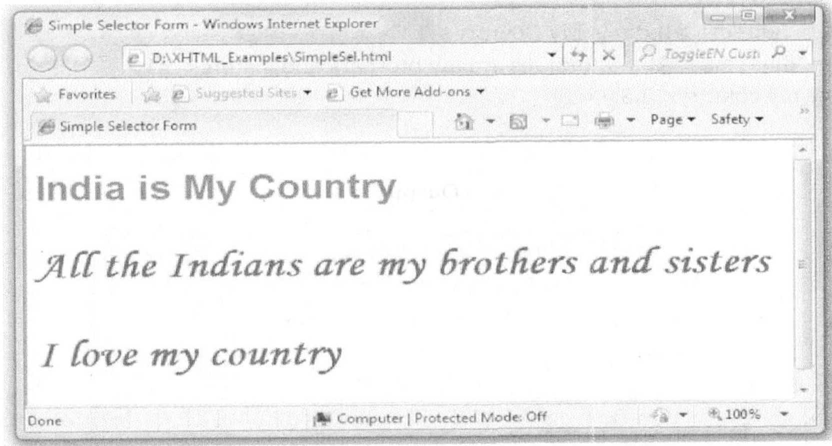

Similarly the style can also be applied to the elements at specific positions.

For example :

```
body b p {font-size:18pt;}
```

Note that there are more than one element to which the style is applied and these elements are separated by the white spaces.

3.3.2 Class Selectors

- Using class selector we can assign different styles to the same element.
- These different styles appear on different occurrences of that element.

For example

HTML Document[ClassSel.html]

```
<!DOCTYPE html>
<html>
<head>
<title>Class Selector Form</title>
<style type="text/css">
    h1.RedText
    {
     font-family:Monotype Corsiva;
     color:red;
     font-size: 14pt;
    }
h1.BlueText
    {
     font-family:Arial;
     color:blue;
     font-size: 10pt;
    }
</style>
</head>
<body>
    <h1 class ="RedText">India is My Country</h1>
    <h1 class="BlueText">All the Indians are my brothers and sisters</h1>
    <h3>I love my country</h3>
</body>
</html>
```

Output

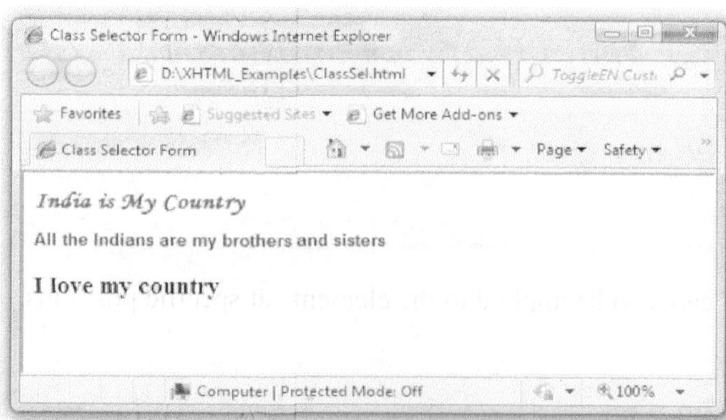

Script Explanation :

Note that in above given script we have used two different classes for the element h1. One class selector is for displaying the string in red color and another is for displaying the string in blue color. This definition is given in the head section. In the body section these class names appear in double quotes inside the h1 tag.

Ex. 3.3.1 : Create a HTML document that displays a table of basketball scores at national games in which the team names have their respective team colors. The score of the leading/wining team should appear larger and in different font than the losing team. Use CSS.

Sol. : Football.html

```
<!DOCTYPE html>
<html >
<head>
<style type="text/css">
tr.one
{
 background-color:pink;
 color:blue;
}
tr.two
{
 font-family:cursive;
 background-color:black;
 color:yellow;
 font-size:50px;

}
tr.three
{
background-color:green;
color:white;
}
</style>
</head>
<body>
<table border="3">
<th>Team</th>
<th>Score</th>
<tr class="one"><td>ABC</td><td>7</td>
</tr>
<tr class="two"><td>XYZ</td><td>10</td>
</tr>
<tr class="three"><td>PQR</td><td>5</td>
```

Output

```
</tr>

</body>
</html>
```

3.3.3 Generic Selectors

- We define the class in generalised form.
- In the sense, that particular class can be applied to any tag.
- Here is the HTML document which makes use of such generic selector.

HTML Document [ClassSel1.html]

```
<!DOCTYPE html>
<html>
    <head>
    <title>Generic Class Selector Form</title>
    <style type="text/css">
     .RedText
     {
      font-family:Monotype Corsiva;
      color:red;
     }
     </style>

</head>
    <body>
    <center>
    <h1> Tongue Twister</h1>
    </center>
     <h2 class="RedText">
     She sells sea shells on the sea shore.
    </h2>
    <h3 class="RedText">
     The shells she sells are sea shells, I'm sure.
    </h3>
    <h4 class="RedText">
     And if she sells sea shells on the sea shore,
     </h4>
    <p class="RedText">
    Then I'm sure she sells seashore shells.
    </p>
    </body>
</html>
```

Output

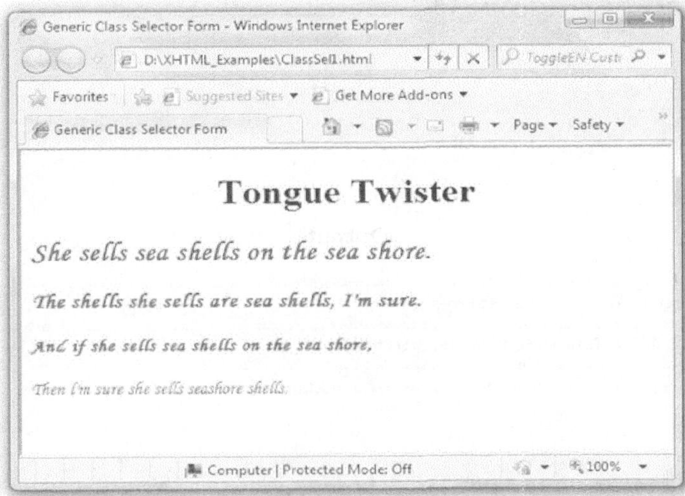

Note that the class selector must be preceded by a dot operator.

3.3.4 Id Selectors

- The id selector is similar to the class selector but the only difference between the two is that class selector can be applied to more than one elements where as using the id selector the style can be applied to the one specific element.
- The syntax of using id selector is as follows -

```
#name_of_id {property:value list;}
```

- Following HTML document makes use of id selector

HTML Document[IdSel.html]

```
<!DOCTYPE html>
<html>
    <head>
    <title>id Selector</title>
    <style type="text/css">
     #top
     {
      font-family:Monotype Corsiva;
      color:blue;
      font-size:16pt;
     }
     </style>
    </head>
    <body>
    <div id="top">
```

```
    It is the mark of an educated mind to be able to
    entertain a thought without accepting it.
    </div>
    <p>
     -Aristotle
    </p>
    </body>
</html>
```

Output

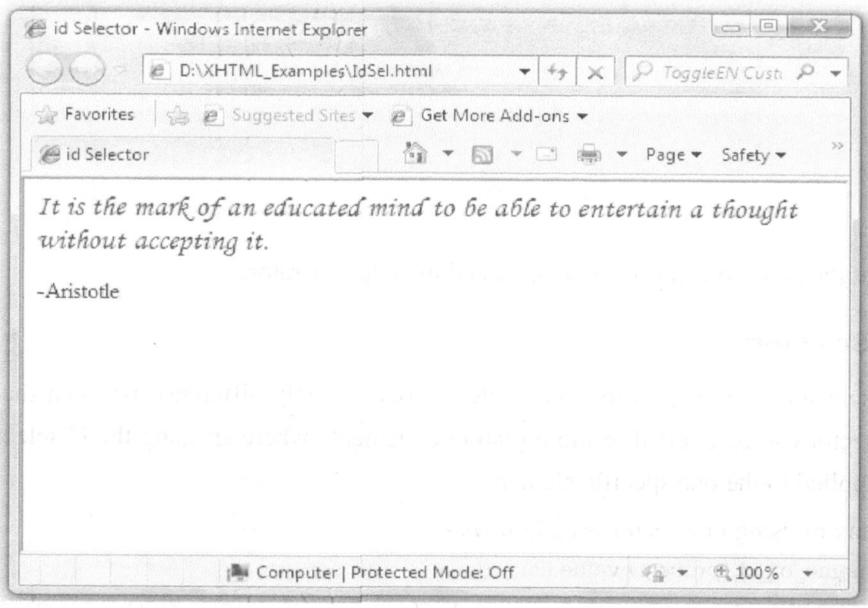

3.3.5 Universal Selectors

This selector is denoted by * (asterisk). This selector can be applied to all the elements in the document.

HTML Document[UniverSel.html]

```
<!DOCTYPE html>
<html >
    <head>
    <title>Universal Selector</title>
    <style type="text/css">
     * {
     color:green;
      }
     </style>
    </head>
<body>
```

```
<h2> Famous Proverbs</h2>
    <hr/>
    <ul type="disc">
    <li>A friend in need is a friend indeed</li>
    <li>Cleanliness is next to Godliness</li>
    <li>All is fair in love and war</li>
    <li>An apple a day keeps the doctor away</li>
    <li>God helps them who help themselves</li>
    <br/><br/>
    <em>
     -From My Collection.
    </em>
    </body>
</html>
```

Output

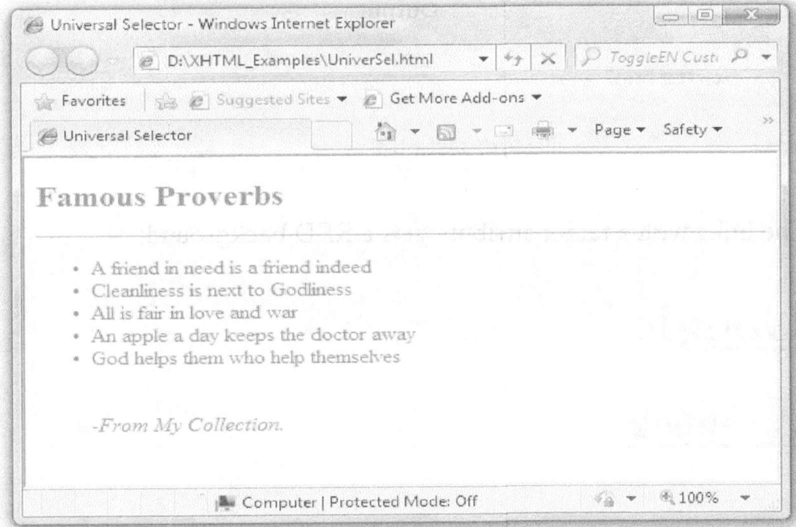

As we have defined the universal selector that sets the green color. Hence the text that is appearing on the above web page is in green color.

3.3.6 Attribute Selector

- CSS allows authors to specify rules that match elements which have certain attributes defined in the source document.
- The syntax is

  [att] - Match when the element sets the "att" attribute, whatever the value of the attribute.

  [att=val] - Match when the element's "att" attribute value is exactly "val".

- Example : In the following example all the <a> elements get selected with a target attribute.

```
<!DOCTYPE html>
```

```
<html>
<head>
<style>
   a[target] {
   background-color: red;
 }
</style>
</head>
<body>
<p>The links with a target attribute gets a RED background:</p>
<h1><a href="https://www.google.com">Google</a> </h1>
<h2><a href="http://www.facebook.com" target="_blank">Facebook</a></h2>
</body>
</html>
```

Output

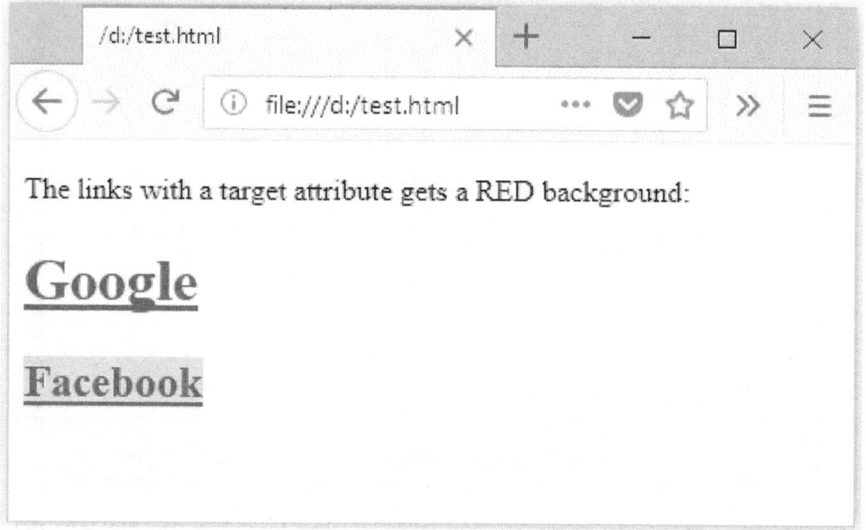

3.3.7 Pseudo Classes

Using pseudo classes we can give special effects on the selectors. There some pseudo classes which are more commonly used and those are -

- Focus
- Hover
- Hyperlink

In the following XHTML documents we have used these pseudo classes.

HTML Document[PsedoCls.htmll]

```
<!DOCTYPE html>
<html>
    <head>
    <title>Pseudo classes</title>
    <style type="text/css">
     input:focus

     {
     background-color:skyblue;
     color:white;
     }
    </style>
    </head>

    <body>
     <form>
     Enter some string:<input type="text" name="my_txt"/>
     <br/>
     <input type="submit" value="Enter"/>
     </form>
    </body>
</html>
```

Output

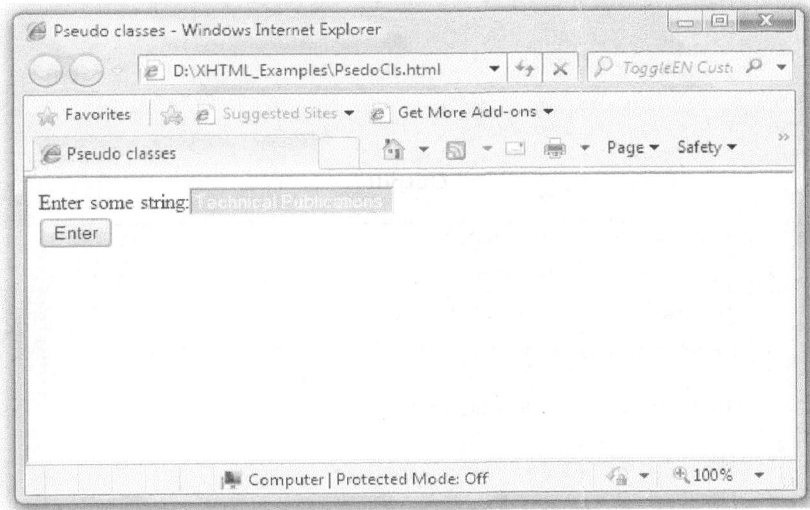

Let us now see one more illustration in which the pseudo class is used.

HTML Document[PsedoCls1.html]

```
<!DOCTYPE html>
<html>
```

```
<head>
      <title>Pseudo classes for hyperlinks</title>
      <style type="text/css">
      a.ColoredTxt:link {color: red}
      a.ColoredTxt:visited {color: blue}
      a.ColoredTxt:hover {color: green}

      a.BigTxt:link {color: red}
      a.BigTxt:visited {color: blue}

      a.BigTxt:hover {font-size: 200%}

</style>
      </head>
      <body>
       <h3>Move Mouse over following text</h3>
       <p>
       <em>
          <a class="ColoredTxt" href="mypage.html" target="_blank">The text
          changes color
          </a>
       </em>
       </p>
       <p>
       <em>
<a class="BigTxt" href="mypage.html" target="_blank">The text is getting
          Big in size
          </a>
       </em>
       </p>
</body>
```

We have defined two pseudo classes named ColoredTxt and BigTxt

Output

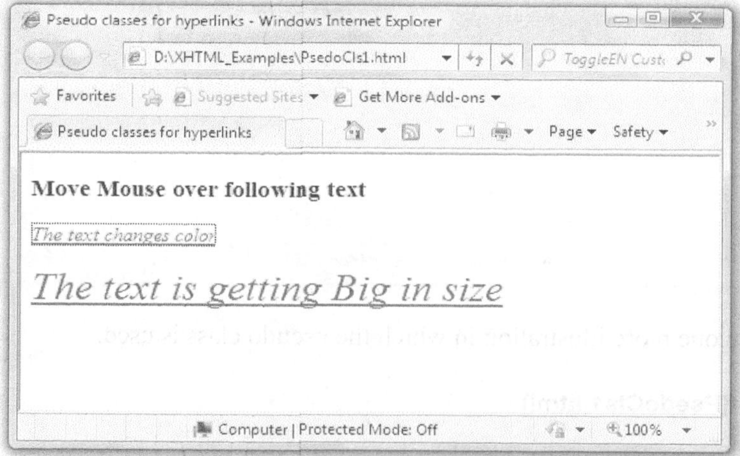

3.3.8 Contextual Selector

- "Contextual selectors" in CSS allow you to specify different styles for different parts of your document.
- You can assign styles directly to specific HTML tags, or you can create independent classes and assign them to tags in the HTML.

For example –

```
<!DOCTYPE html>
<html>
<head>
<style>
    p b {
     font-family: Times, serif; /* Font family */
     font-weight: bold; /* heavy faced type*/
     color: blue; /* blue colour of the text */
    }
</style>
 </head>
  <body>
  <div><b>This line is in bold face font</b></div>
  <p><b>This line is in bold face with the color of the text - blue </b></p>
   <p> Good Bye</p>
 </body>
</html>
```

Output

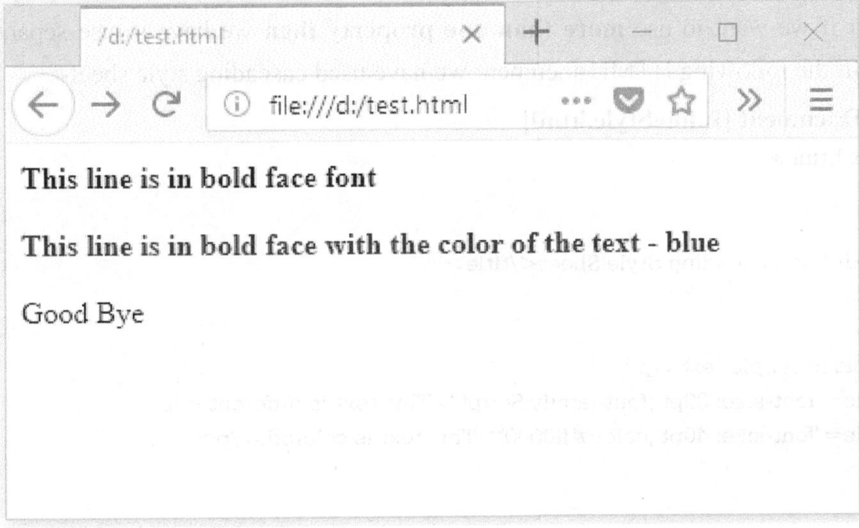

3.3.9 At Rules

The @import rule is used to import one style sheet into another. The syntax for using @import is

```
@import url("mystyles.css")
```

3.4 Inline Embedded and External Style Sheet

There are three levels of cascading style sheets -

- Inline style sheet
- Document level style sheet
- External level style sheet

3.4.1 Inline Style Sheet

The inline cascading style sheet is a kind of style sheet in which the styles can be applied to HTML tags. This tag can be applied using following rule -

```
Tag
{
property: value
}
```

For example :

```
<p style="font-family: Arial;color:red" >
```

Here for the tag **p** two properties are used such as **font-family** and **color** and those are associated with the values such as Arial and red respectively.

Note that if we want to use **more than one property then** we have to use separator such as **semicolon**. In the following HTML document we have used cascading style sheet-

HTML Document [InlineStyle.html]

```
<!DOCTYPE html >
<html>
    <head>
     <title>Inline Cascading Style Sheet</title>
    </head>
    <body>
     <p>This is simple text</p>
     <p style="font-size: 30pt ;font-family:Script">This text is different </p>
     <p style="font-size: 40pt ;color:#ff0000">This text is colored.</p>
    </body>
</html>
```

Script Explanation

1) In this document, in the body section the style sheets are created.
2) In this section first of all we have displayed a simple sentence This is simple text. There is no style for this sentence.
3) In the next line, we have applied style in which **font-size** is set to the size of 30 point and **font-family** is set by the font name "Script".
4) Then colored text will be displayed by **color:#ff0000"**. The first two digits ff denote the red color, there is no green and blue color as the values next to ff are 00. Hence the text will be displayed in red.

This can be very well illustrated in output.

Output

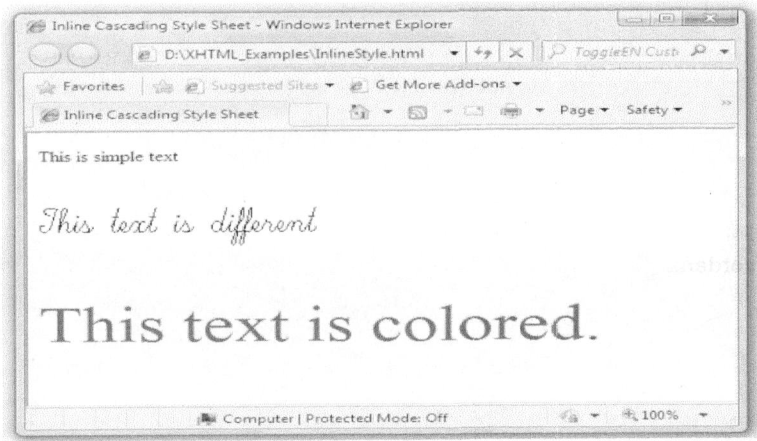

3.4.2 Document Level Style Sheet

- This type style sheet appears only in the head section and in the body section newly defined Selector tags are used with the actual contents.
- For example : In the following HTML script we have defined **h1, h2, h3** and **p** selectors. For each of these **selectors** different property and values are set. Such setting will help us to represent our web page in some decorative form.
- The most important thing while writing document level style sheet is that we should mention the **style type="text/css"** in the head section. By this the browser will come to know that the program is making use of cascading style sheet.

HTML Document [DocLevelCSS.html]

```
<!DOCTYPE html>
<html >
```

```
<head>
    <title>Document Level style sheet</title>
    <style type="text/css">
     h1
     {
      font-family:Arial;
      color:green
     }
     h2
     {
      font-family:Arial;
      color:red;
      left:20px
     }
     h3
    {
      font-family:arial;
      color:blue;
     }
     p
     {
      font-size:14pt;
      font-family:verdana
     }
    </style>
    </head>
    <body>
     <h1>
<center>
      This page is created using Document Level Style Sheet
      </center>
        </h1>
     <h2>
      This line is aligned left and red colored.
     </h2>
     <p>
      The embedded style sheet is the most commonly used style sheet.
      This paragraph is written in Verdana font with font size of 14.
     </p>
     <h3>
    This is a blue <a href="colorname.html">colored</a> line.
     </h3>
</body>
</html>
```

Output

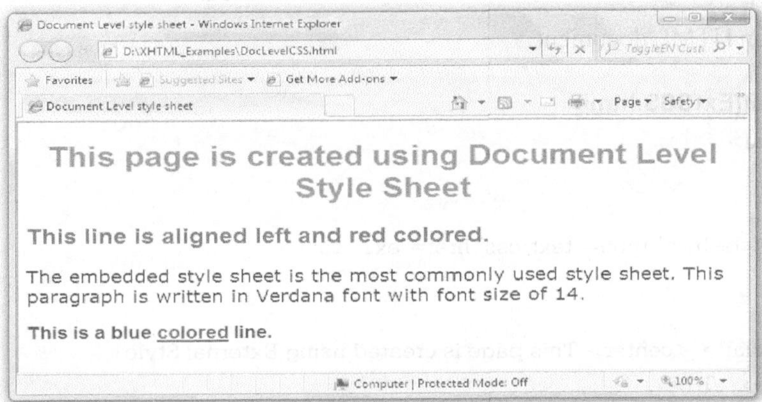

Script Explanation

1) In above program, we have defined all the selectors in the head sections only. And these HTML elements are then used along with the web page contents.

2) The setting defined in the selectors will affect the web page contents. For example we have defined the selector h2 as

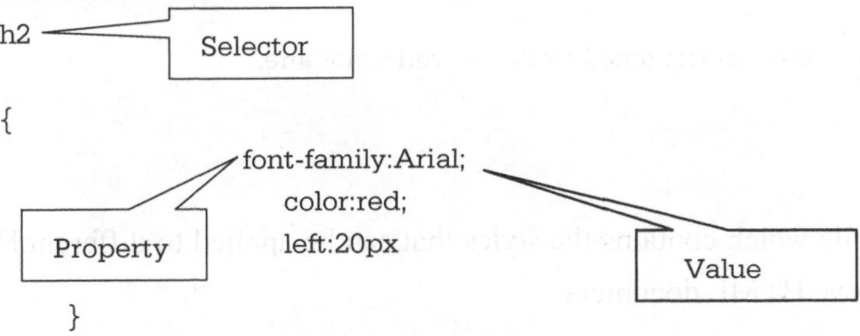

and then in the body section we have written -

<h2> This line is aligned left and red colored.</h2>

3) Now as h2 defines font to be "Arial" with color as "red" having left alignment of 20 pixels, the sentence "This line is aligned left and red colored." will be displayed in Arial font, which is red colored and aligned from left by 20 pixels. Surely we can see this effect on our web browser.

3.4.3 External Stylesheet

- Sometimes we need to apply particular style to more than one web documents in such cases external style sheets can be used.
- The central idea in this type of style sheet is that the desired style is stored in one .css file. And the name of that file has to be mentioned in our web pages.
- Then the styles defined in .css file will be applied to all these web pages.

- Here is a sample program in which external style sheet is used.

Step 1 : Create an HTML document

HTML Document[ExtCSS.html]

```
<!DOCTYPE html>
<html >
     <head>
     <link rel="stylesheet" type="text/css" href="ex1.css" />
     </head>
     <body>
<h1 class="special"> <center> This page is created using External Style
Sheet</center> </h1>
     <h2>
        This line is aligned left and red colored.
     </h2>
     <p>
     The External style sheet is the compact representation of Cascading Style Sheets.
     This paragraph is written in Monotype Corsiva font with font size of 14.
     </p>
     <h3>
        This is a blue <a href="colorname.html">colored</a> line.
     </h3>
     </body>
</html>
```

Step 2 : Create a css file which contains the styles that can be applied to different HTML elements present in the above HTML document.

The cascading style sheet ex1.css can be

```
<!- - The file name ex1.css and can be opened in notepad.-->
h1
{
 font-family:Arial
}
h2
{
 font-family:times new roman;
 color:red;
left:20px
}
h3
{
font-family:arial;
color:blue;
}
```

```
p
{
 font-size:14pt;
 font-family:Monotype Corsiva
}
```

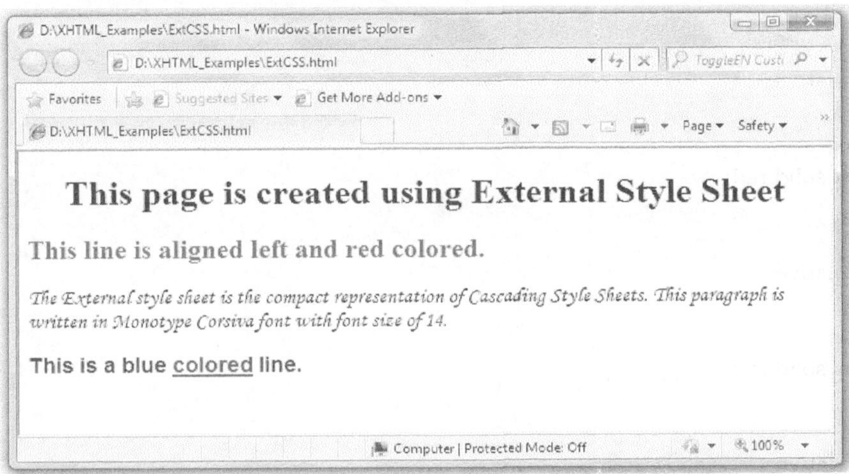

Script Explanation

When we want to link the external style sheet then we have to use **<link>** tag which is to be written in the head section.

- **link** tells the browser some file must be linked to the page.
- **rel=stylesheet** tells the browser that this hyperlink is a style sheet.
- **href="   "** denotes the path name of style sheet file.
- **type="text/css"** tells the browser that what it is reading is text which is affected by the cascading style sheet.

3.5 Positioning Elements

- It is possible to move an item from its regular position in the normal flow.
- The position property specifies the type of positioning method used for an element.
- The left, right, top, and bottom properties are used to indicate the distance the element will move; the effect of these properties varies depending upon the **position** property.

3.5.1 Relative Positioning

- An element with position: relative; is positioned relative to its normal position.
- Setting the top, right, bottom, and left properties of a relatively-positioned element will cause it to be moved away from its normal position.

- For example -

HTML Document

```
<!DOCTYPE html>
<html>
<head>
<style>
div.box1 {
   position: relative;
   top: 20px;
   width:80px;
   border: 3px solid red;
}
div.box2 {
   position: relative;
   left: 60px;
   width:80px;
   border: 3px solid red;
}
div.box3 {
   position: relative;
   bottom: -10px;
   right: 20px;
   width:80px;
   border: 3px solid red;
}
</style>
</head>
<body>
<h2>position: relative;</h2>
<p>An element with position: relative;
is positioned relative to its normal position:</p>
<div class="box1">
Box1
</div>
<div class="box2">
Box2
</div>
</div>
<div class="box3">
Box3
</div>
</body>
</html>
```

Output

/d:/test.html

file:///d:/test.html

position: relative;

An element with position: relative; is positioned relative to its normal position:

Box1 Box2

ox3

3.5.2 Absolute Positioning

- The absolute is the trickiest position value.
- The absolute behaves like fixed except relative to the nearest positioned ancestor instead of relative to the viewport.
- If an absolutely-positioned element has no positioned ancestors, it uses the document body, and still moves along with page scrolling.
- For example

HTML Document

```
<!DOCTYPE html>
<html>
<head>
<style>
div.box1 {
   position: relative;
   width: 400px;
   height: 200px;
   border: 3px solid red;
}
div.box2 {
   position: absolute;
   top: 80px;
   right: 0;
   width: 200px;
   height: 100px;
   border: 3px solid green;
}
</style>
</head>
<body>
<div class="box1">Box1
  <div class="box2">Box2</div>
</div>
</body>
</html>
```

Output

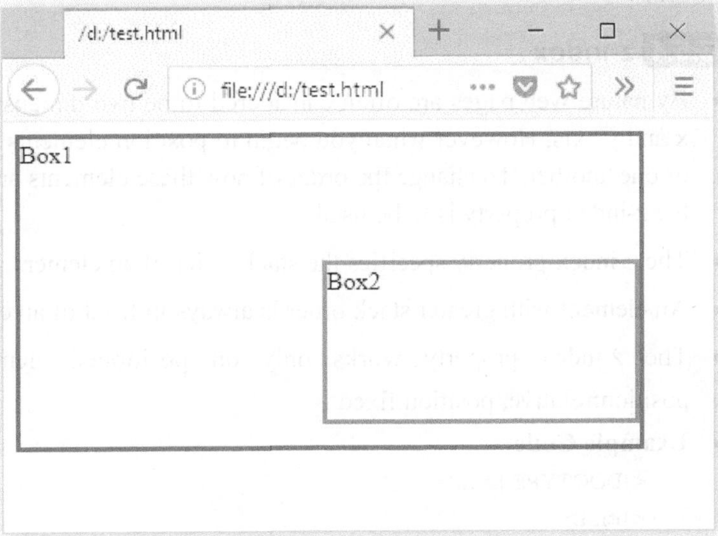

/d:/test.html
file:///d:/test.html
Box1
Box2

3.5.3 Fixed Position

- A fixed element is positioned relative to the viewport, which means it always stays in the same place even if the page is scrolled

- For example :

HTML Document

```
<!DOCTYPE html>
<html>
<head>
<style>
div.box1 {
    position: fixed;
    bottom: 10;
    right: 10;
    width: 50px;
    border: 3px solid red;
}
</style>
</head>
<body>
<div class="box1">
Box1
</div>
</body>
</html>
```

Output

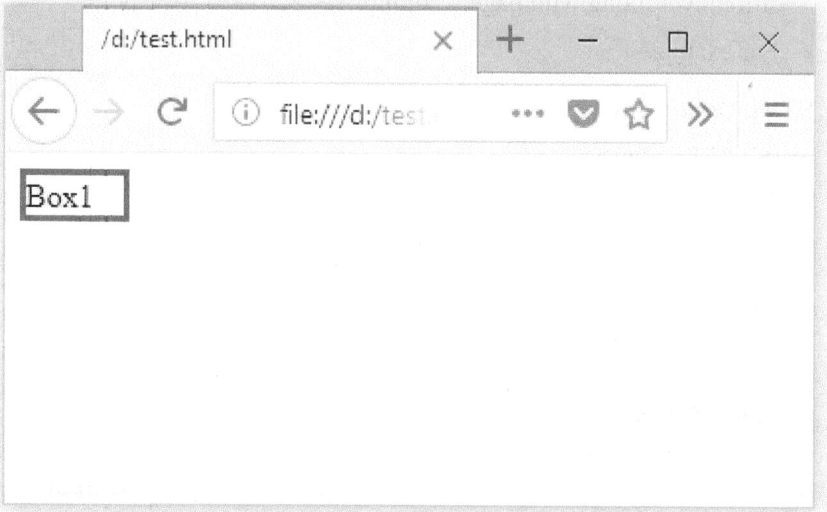

3.5.4 z-index

- By nature web pages are often considered to be two dimensional, displaying elements upon the x and y axis. However when you begin to position elements they are occasionally placed on top of one another. To change the order of how these elements are stacked, also known as the z-axis, the z-index property is to be used.
- The z-index property specifies the stack order of an element.
- An element with greater stack order is always in front of an element with a lower stack order.
- The z-index property works only on positioned elements i.e. with position:absolute, position:relative, position:fixed.
- **Example Code**

```
<!DOCTYPE html>
<html>
<head>
<style>
img {
  position: absolute;
  left: 0px;
  top: 0px;
```

```
    z-index: -1;
  }
  </style>
  </head>
  <body>
  <img src="img1.jpg" width="100" height="140">
  <p> This line will appear behind image as z-index of image is -1</p>
  </body>
  </html>
```

Output

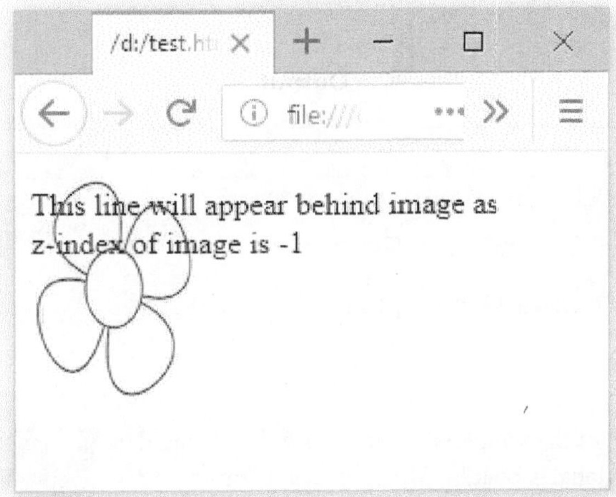

3.5.5 Float Position

The float position is used to shift an image to one side and wrap the text around it.

In the following example, the image is shifted to the right and the text is wrap around it. We have used **float:right** for this pupose. If one wants to shift the image to the left he can simply declare the style as **float:left.**

XHTML Document[FloatPosDemo.html]

```
<!DOCTYPE html >
<html >
<head>
 <title>Float Positioning</title>
  <style type="text/css">
   img.Rightfloat
   {
    float:right;
     margin: 4px;
   }
  </style>
```

```
</head>
<body>
  <img src="TajMahal.jpg" class=" Rightfloat"/>
  <p>Taj Mahal is one of the wonders of the World. It is located in
Agra,India.Taj Mahal is built by Shah Jahan in memory of his wife
Mumtaz Mahal.
</p>
<p>It is considered to be the excellent example of Mughal
Architecture.</p>
</body>
</html>
```

Output

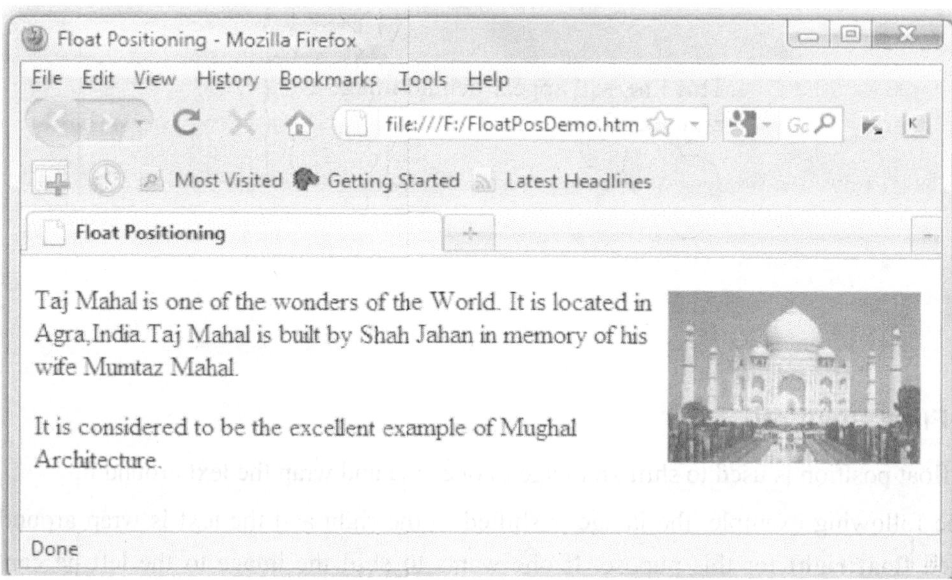

3.6 Rule Cascading and Inheritance

3.6.1 Style Rule Cascading

- When there are two or more values for the same property then conflict occurs. There are various levels of style sheets such as embedded CSS and external CSS. Out of which **embedded CSS** have **more precedence over the external CSS**.
- There are some sorting order rules that are used to decide the precedence. These are based on two things, importance (important or normal) of the property and origin (author origin, user origin and user agent origin). Let us first understand the terms important and origins.

- The keyword **!important** can be applied to specify that particular property is important. For example :

```
p.myclass {font-family:Arial !important ;font-style:bold;}
```

specifies that the font being Arial is one property but font-style being bold is a important property.

- When the specification is marked by !important then it actually specifies the weight. The weight can be either important or normal.
- The origin can be author origin, user origin and user agent origin. These terms can be defined as follows -
  - o **Author** is a person who writes the XHTML document and associated style sheets.
  - o **User** is a person who interacts with user agent and use the web document along with the associated style sheets.
  - o **User agent** is a program that interprets the web document written in scripting language and applies the style sheet according to the specification. For example, HTML is an user agent.
- The sorting order can be determined by applying following rules with highest precedence to lowest -
  1. Important declaration having user origin.
  2. Important declaration having author origin.
  3. Normal declaration having author origin.
  4. Normal declaration having user origin.
  5. Any declaration (either important or normal) with user agent (i.e. browser) origin.
- Following rules are also be used to decide the sorting order of the elements from highest precedence to lowest -
  1. **id** selectors have the highest precedence.
  2. **class** and **pseudo class** selectors
  3. Contextual selectors
  4. Universal selectors
- If the conflict still occurs then it can be resolved writing the properties in the specification. The rules that are defined later in the document tree have the highest precedence than those defined earlier.
- **Style rule cascading** can be defined as the process which is used to resolve the conflicts in the style specification. Fig. 3.6.1 shows the steps in CSS cascade.

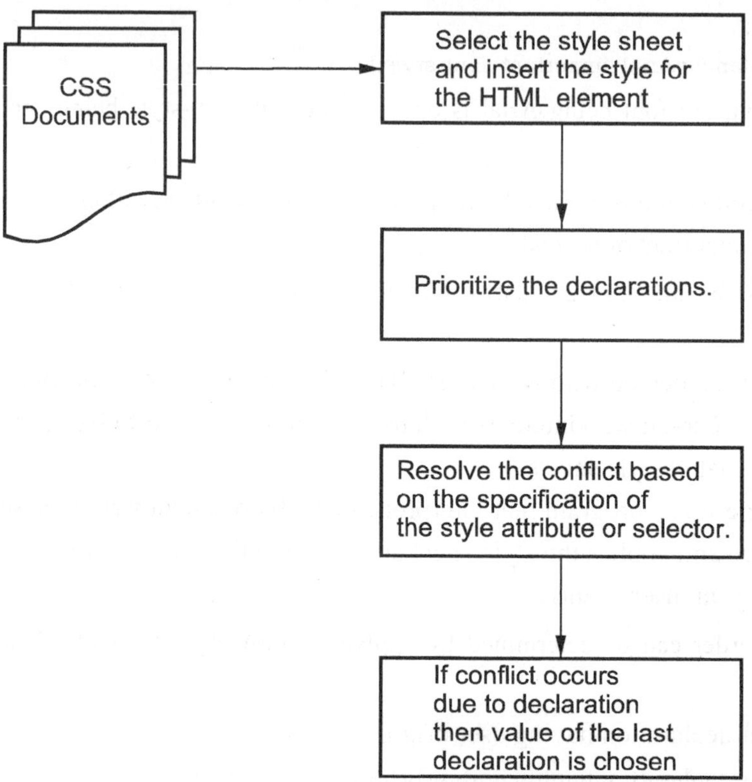

Fig. 3.6.1 Steps in CSS cascade

3.6.2 Inheritance

- In CSS, if a property of an element has no associated declarations then using inheritance technique the value for this property can be obtained.
- In an HTML document, the tags have parent-child relationships. For example, <title> tag is always inside the <head> tag, so the <head> tag is the parent of the <title> tag. Similarly <p> tag is defined inside the <body> tag. Then <body> becomes parent of <p> tag.
- In cascading style sheets, inheritance is based on **tree structure** of the document itself.
- An element inherits the value for its properties by checking the parent element. If the parent has the value for the property demanded by the child then this property value can be inherited. If the parent down not have this value, then its parent (i.e. grandparent) is checked. If this parent has no such property value then its parent is checked. This process is continued until a root element is obtained.
- Thus the search will be made in upward direction from the parent of the element to the root of the tree or to the <html> tag of the document.

Inheritance can be defined as a concept in which child always inherits the properties of parent tag along with its own properties.

Following is an HML document in which inheritance is demonstrated.

HTML Document

```
<!DOCTYPE html>
<html>
<head>
    <title>Inheritance Demo</title>
     <style type="text/css">
        p
        {
         font-family:Arial;
         color:blue;
         background-color:yellow;
        }
        strong
        {
        font-size:24px;
        }
     </style>
</head>
<body>
    <center>
     <p>This is a blue text <strong>with</strong> yellow background</p>
    </center>
</body>
</html>
```

Output

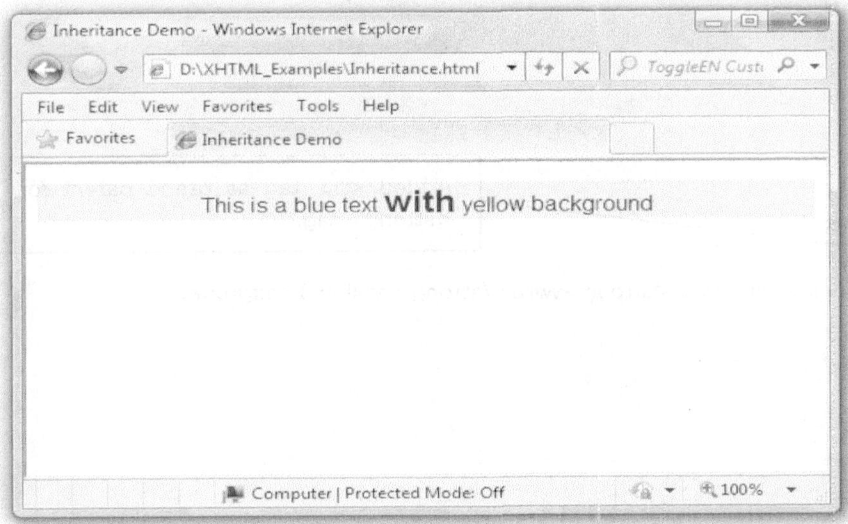

Script Explanation :

In above, script <p> tag has some properties as **Arial** font, blue font color and **yellow** background. The <strong> tag has only one property can that is font-size which is assigned by the value **24px**. But in the body section, <strong> tag is the child of <p> tag. And note that <strong> inherits the properties of <p> tag. Hence the text defined under<strong> tag is also blue colored with yellow background.

Now just modify by the above script as follows and observe the sample output.

HTML Document [inheritance1.html]

```
<!DOCTYPE html>
<html>
<head>
    <title>Inheritance Demo</title>
     <style type="text/css">
       li
       {
       font-style:italic
       }
       p
       {
        font-family:Arial;
        color:blue;
        background-color:yellow
       }
       strong
       {
       font-size:24px
       }
     </style>
</head>

<body>
    <center>
    <li>
     <p>This is a blue text <strong>with</strong> yellow background</p>
    </li>
    </center>
</body>
</html>
```

Added <li> tag as grand parent for <strong> tag.

Output

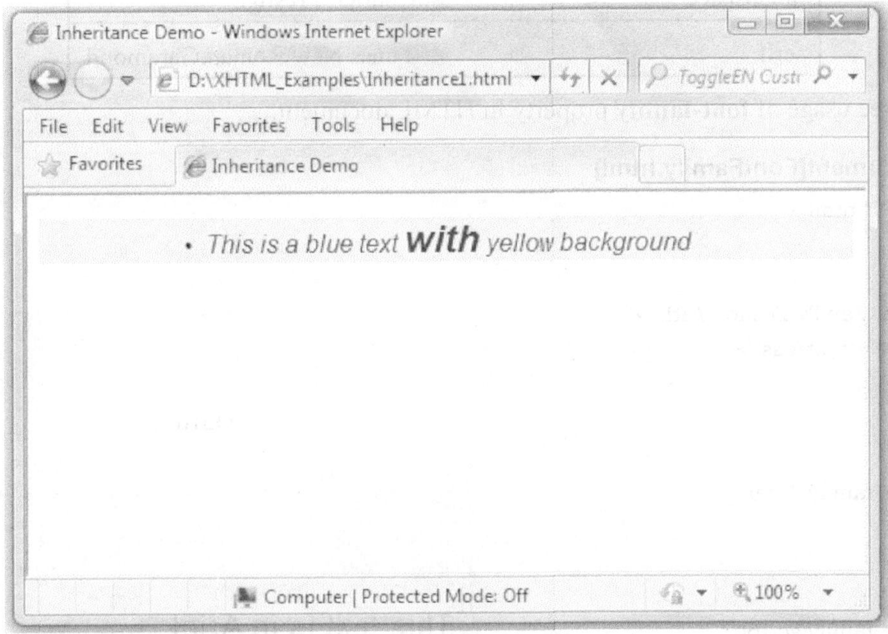

Note that the above style sheet contains the nested tags -

```
<li>
.....<p>
............<strong>
............</strong>
.....</p>
</li>
```

The <li> tag contains the italic property. Hence the text inside the <strong> tag becomes italic. That means <strong> tag has inherited the italic property from its grandchild.

3.7 Text Properties

AU : Dec.-11, Marks 8

The font properties can be setting different types of fonts, styles and sizes.

3.7.1 Font Families

The **font-family** denotes different types of fonts such as Arial, Times New Roman, Script, monospace and so on. Following are some examples of generic fonts

Generic Font Name	Example
sans-serif	Arial, Helvetica, Futura
cursive	Zapf-chancery
fantasy	Critter, Cottonwood

monospace	Courier, Prestige
serif	Times New Roman,Garamond

Let us see usage of **font-family** property in HTML document.

HTML Document[FontFamily.html]

```
<!DOCTYPE html>
<html>
<head>
<title>Font Family Demo</title>
<style type="text/css">
   h1
    {
      font-family:Arial;
    }
   h2
    {
      font-family:script;
    }
   h3
    {
      font-family:'Times New Roman';
    }
   h4
    {
     font-family:fantasy;
    }
   h5
    {
      font-family:Garamond;
    }
</style>
</head>
<body>
<h1>This text is in Arial </h1>
<h2>This text is in script </h2>
<h3>This text is in Times New Roman</h3>
<h4> This text is in fantasy</h4>
<h5> This text is in Garamond</h5>

</body>
</html>
```

Output

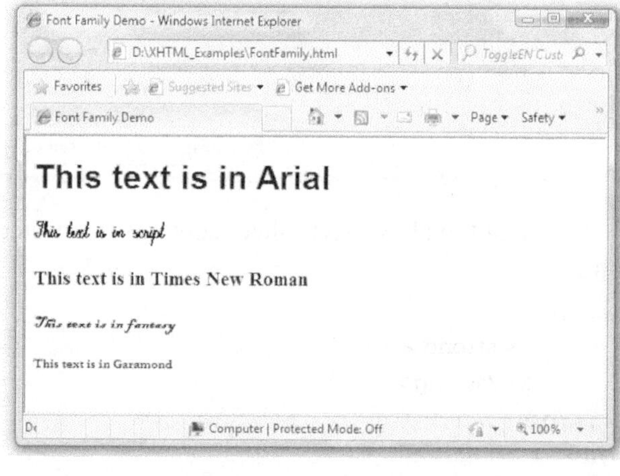

If the font name has more than one word then the name should be enclosed by the single quotes. Although quotes are not mandatory, it is a good practice to use quotes for specifying the font name.

3.7.2 Font Sizes

This property is used to specify the size of the font. One can specify the font size in points (pts), pixels (px) or in percentage (%). We can also specify the font size using the relative values such as **small**, **medium**, **large**. Use of font size in such a way is relative. And the disadvantage of using such relative sizes is that one cannot have the strict control over the font-size. Different browsers may have different font size values.

In the following HTML document we will use the font-size property.

HTML Document[FontSize.html]

```
<!DOCTYPE html>
<html>
   <head>

<title>Font-Size Demo</title>
   <style type="text/css">
    h1
    {
     font-size:10pt;
    }
    h2
    {
     font-size:20px;
    }
    h3
    {
     font-size:xx-large;
    }
    h4
    {
     font-size:250%;
    }

   </style>
   </head>
   <body>
   <h1>Programming the Web</h1>
    <h2>Programming the Web</h2>
    <h3>Programming the Web</h3>
    <h4>Programming the Web</h4>
```

Output

```
   </body>
</html>
```

3.7.3 Font Variants

The font variation can be achieved by making setting the font in upper case or in lower case. We use **font-variant** property for this purpose.

Value	Meaning
normal	The font can be displayed in normal form.
small-caps	The font can be displayed in small capital letters.

HTML Document[FontVariant.html]

```
<!DOCTYPE html>
<html>
   <head>
   <title>Font-Variant Demo</title>
   <style type="text/css">
    h1

{
     font-variant:small-caps;
    }

   </style>
   </head>
   <body>
    <h1>Programming the Web</h1>
   </body>
</html>
```

Output

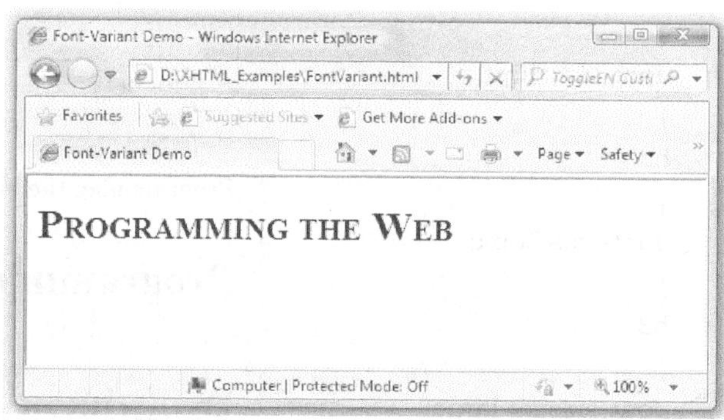

3.7.4 Font Styles

Various font styles are -

- normal
- italic
- oblique

The illustration is as given below -

HTML Document[FontSt.html]

```
<!DOCTYPE html>
<html
```

```
    <head>
    <title>Font-Style Demo</title>
    <style type="text/css">
     h3.normal { font-style:normal;}
     h3.italic { font-style:italic;}
     h3.oblique { font-style:oblique;}
    </style>
    </head>
    <body>
     <h3 class="normal">Programming the Web</h3>
     <h3 class="italic">Programming the Web</h3>
     <h3 class="oblique">Programming the Web</h3>
    </body>
</html>
```

Output

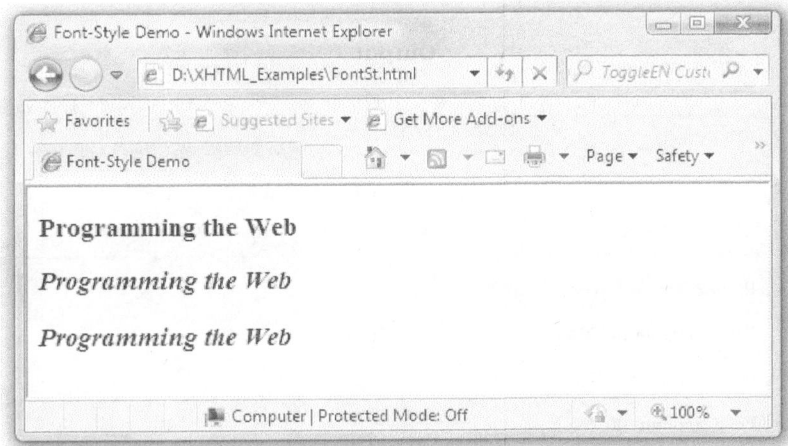

3.7.5 Font Weights

Various font styles are -

- Normal (by default)
- Bold
- Bolder
- Lighter

The illustration is as given below –

HTML Document[FontWt.html]

```
<!DOCTYPE html>
<html>
    <head>
```

```
    <title>Font-Weight Demo</title>
    <style type="text/css">
     p.normal { font-weight:normal;}
     p.bold { font-weight:bold;}
     p.bolder { font-weight:bolder;}
     p.lighter { font-weight:lighter;}
    </style>
    </head>
    <body>
     <p class="normal">Programming the Web</p>
     <p class="bold">Programming the Web</p>
     <p class="lighter">Programming the Web</p>
     <p class="bolder">Programming the Web</p>
    </body>
</html>
```

Output

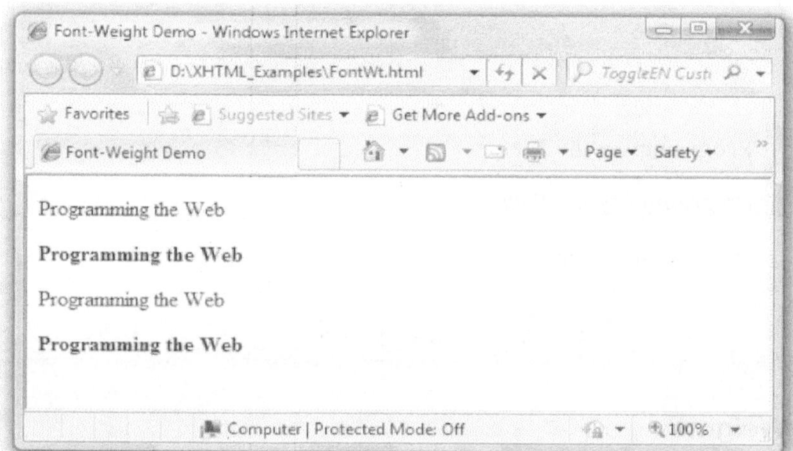

3.7.6 Font Shorthands

We can specify more than one font properties in a list

For example

HTML Document[Fontshrthnd.html]

```
<!DOCTYPE html>
<html>
    <head>
    <title>Font Properties</title>
    <style type="text/css">
     p.myfont {font-family:Courier New;
```

```
font-style:italic;
font-weight:bold;
font-size:28pt;
}
</style>
</head>
<body>
<p class="myfont">I Love my Country!!!</p>
</body>
</html>
```

Output

3.7.7 Text Decoration

Using text decoration property we can include special features in the text. Various properties of text decoration are

- underline
- overline
- line-through

HTML Document[TxtDecor.html]

```
<!DOCTYPE html>
<html>
<head>
<title>Text Decoration</title>
<style type="text/css">
p.linethrough {text-decoration:line-through;}
```

```
        p.underline {text-decoration:underline;}
        p.overline {text-decoration:overline;}
        p.normal {text-decoration:normal;}

</style>
    </head>
    <body>
     <p class="linethrough"> This text is having linethrough </p>
     <p class="overline"> This text is having overline </p>
     <p class="underline"> This text is having underline </p>
     <p class="normal"> This text is a normal text </p>

    </body>
</html>
```

Output

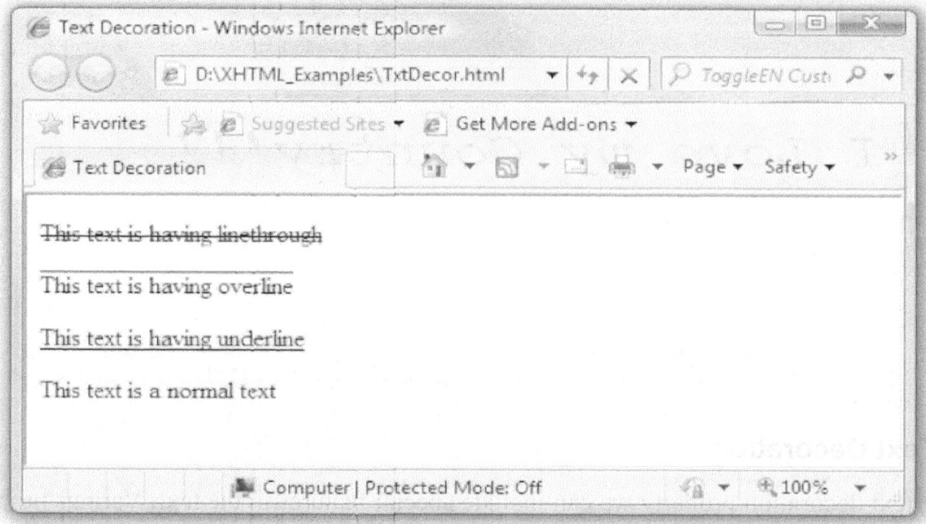

3.7.8 Alignment of Text

Using cascading style sheets we can align the text. This alignment can be done using following properties such as -

Property	Value	Meaning
text-align	left	Aligning the text to the left.
text-align	right	Aligning the text to the right
text-align	center	Alignment of text at the centre.
text-indent	value in inches	Desired indentation of the text can be applied.

Following is script which uses various text alignment properties.

HTML Document[TextAlignCSS.html]

```
<!DOCTYPE html>
<html>
    <head>
     <title>Text Alignment Demo</title>
     <style type="text/css">
    h1
    {
     font-family:Arial;
     font-size:15px;
     text-align:left;
    }
    h2
    {
     font-family:Arial;
     font-size:15px;
     text-align:right;
    }
   h3
    {
     font-family:Arial;
     font-size:15px;
     text-align:center;
    }
    </style>
    </head>

    <body>
     <h1>This line is aligned at left</h1>
     <h2>This line is aligned at right</h2>
     <h3>This line is aligned at center</h3>
    </body>
</html>
```

Output

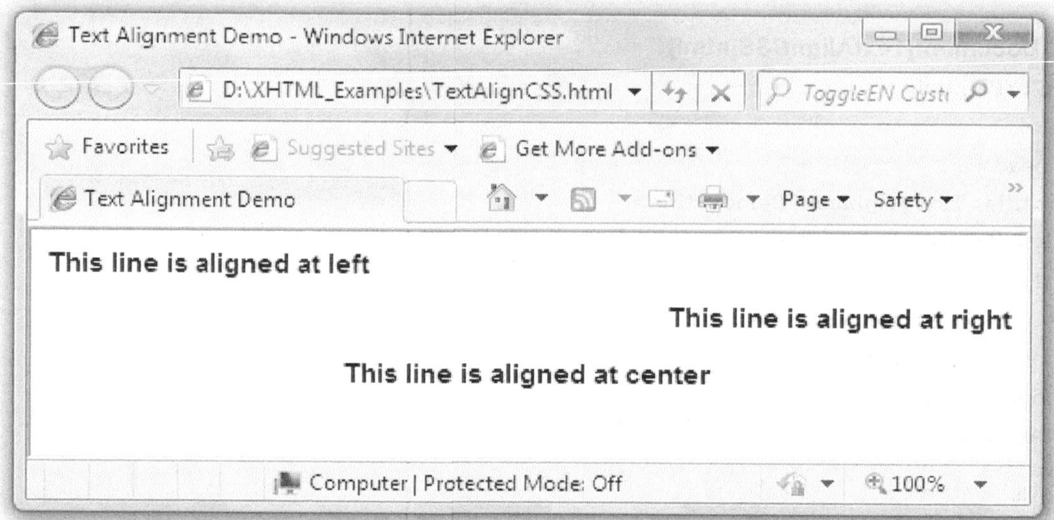

University Question

1. *Explain any eight CSS text properties.* **AU : Dec.11, Marks 8**

3.8 Box Model

The box comes in picture when we put the contents within some rectangle. The box model represents the contents, inner edge, outer edge, margins and padding. It is as shown in Fig. 3.8.1.

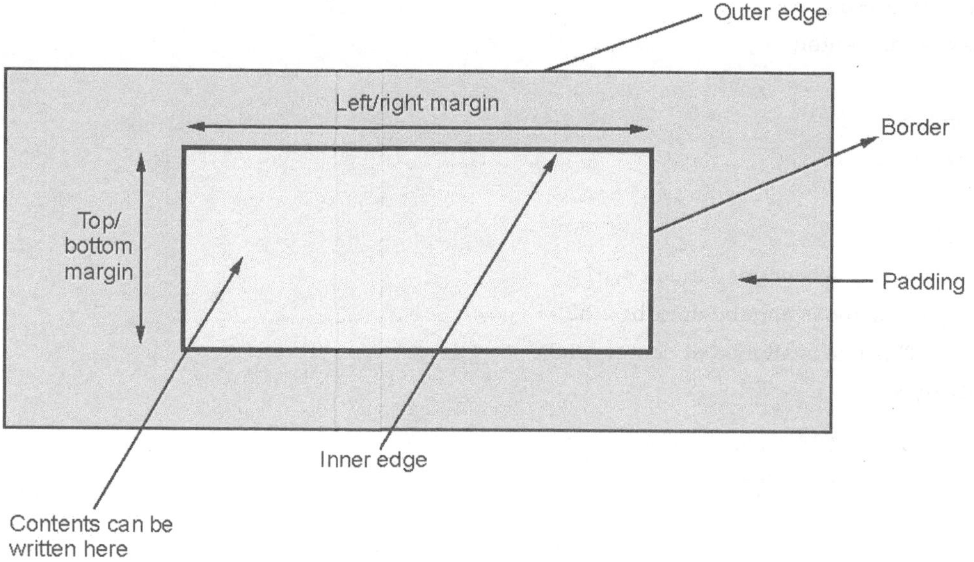

Fig. 3.8.1 The box model

Let us understand each of these terms along with suitable illustrations

3.8.1 Borders

There is a property called border-style which controls the element's content border.

HTML Document[BorderStyle.html]

```
<!DOCTYPE html >
<html >
 <head>
  <title>A Border Style Demo</title>
  <style type="text/css">
   h4.none {border-style:none}
   h4.dotted {border-style:dotted}
   h4.dashed {border-style:dashed}
   h4.solid {border-style:solid}
   h4.double {border-style:double}
   h4.groove {border-style:groove}
   h4.ridge {border-style:ridge}
   h4.inset {border-style:inset}
   h4.outset {border-style:outset}
   h4.hidden {border-style:hidden}
  </style>
 </head>
 <body>
  <h4 class="none">This text has no border</h4>
  <h4 class="dotted">This text has a dotted border.</h4>
  <h4 class="dashed">This text has dashed border.</h4>
  <h4 class="hidden">This text has hidden border.</h4>
  <h4 class="double">This text has double border.</h4>
  <h4 class="solid">This text has solid border.</h4>
  <h4 class="groove">This text has groove border.</h4>
  <h4 class="ridge">This text has ridge border.</h4>
  <h4 class="inset">This text has inset border.</h4>
 </body>
</html>
```

Output

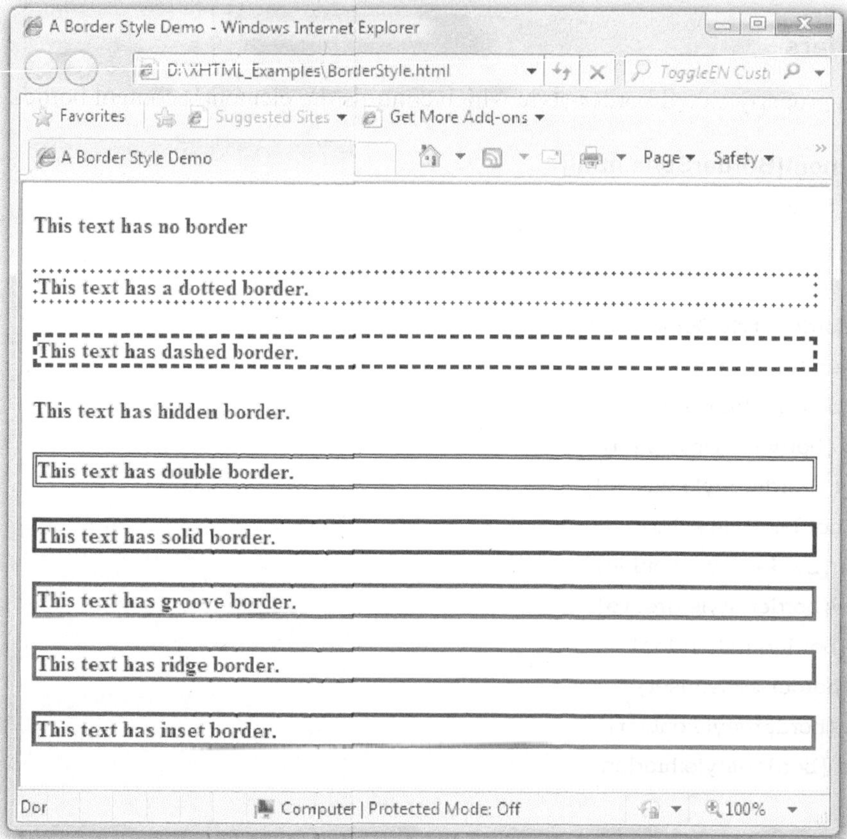

There is another property and that is **border-width** which defined the width of the border. The width can be specified in terms of pixels. The border-width property is illustrated in the following example.

HTML Document[BorderWidth.html]

```
<!DOCTYPE html >
<html >
  <head>
   <title>A Border Width Demo</title>
   <style type="text/css">
    h4.thick
    {
     border-style:solid;
     border-width:3px;
    }
```

```
    h4.thicker
    {
     border-style:solid;
     border-width:5px;
    }
    h4.thickest
    {
     border-style:solid;
     border-width:7px;
    }
   </style>
  </head>
  <body>
   <h4 class="thick">Thick.</h4>
   <h4 class="thicker">Thicker.</h4>
   <h4 class="thickest">Thickest.</h4>
  </body>
</html>
```

Output

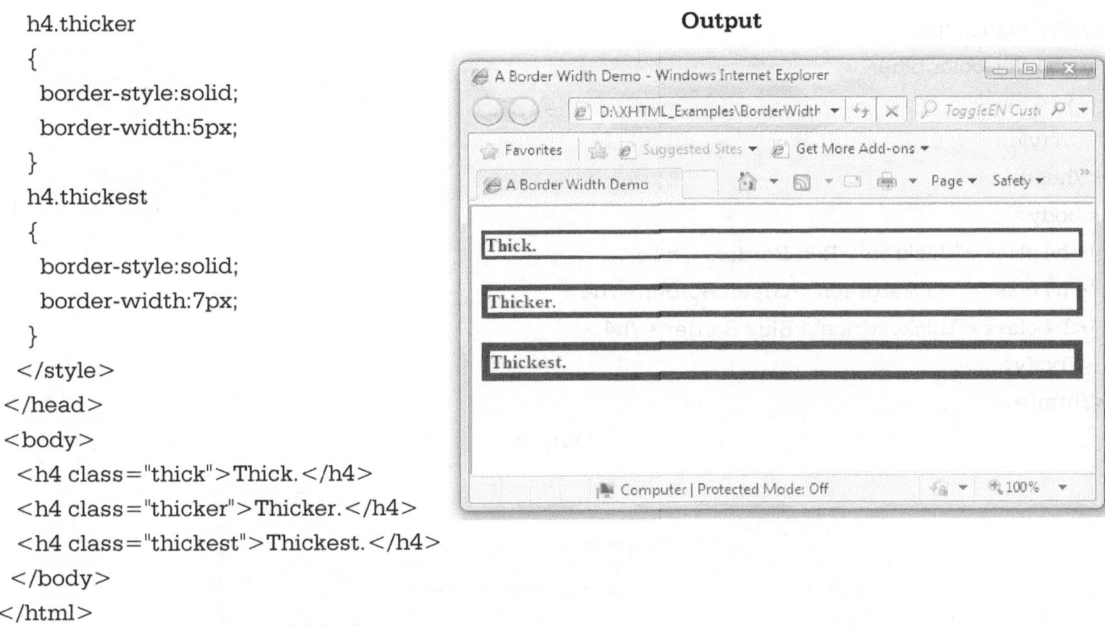

We can make the borders colourful using **border-color** property. Following script displays the colored borders.

HTML Document[BorderColor.html]

```
<!DOCTYPE html>
<html>
  <head>
   <title>Colored Border Demo</title>
   <style type="text/css">
    h4.thickred
    {
     border-style:solid;
     border-width:3px;
     border-color:red;
    }
    h4.thickergreen
    {
     border-style:solid;
     border-width:5px;
     border-color:green;
    }
    h4.thickestblue
    {
     border-style:solid;
```

```
border-width:7px;
      border-color:blue;
    }
  </style>
 </head>
 <body>
  <h4 class="thickred">Red Border.</h4>
  <h4 class="thickergreen">Green Border.</h4>
  <h4 class="thickestblue">Blue Border.</h4>
 </body>
</html>
```

Output

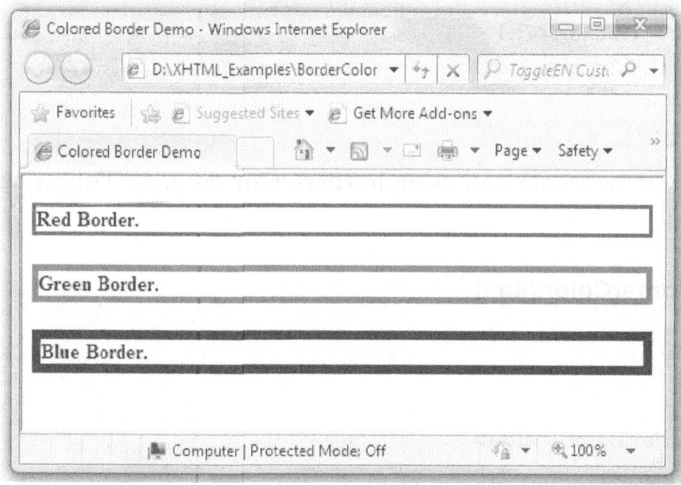

We can also specify the individual side of the box by some particular style. For example we can display a box with the solid border on the top and right, dashed border on the bottom and dotted border on the left. Thus any possible combinations with all four sides can be made using the individual border style property.

Hence we can use -

- border-top-style:solid;
- border-right-style:solid;
- border-bottom-style:dashed;
- border-left-style:dotted;

OR

- border-style:solid solid dashed dotted

HTML Document[EachBorder.html]

```
<!DOCTYPE html>
<html>
 <head>
  <title>Setting Indivudual borderBorder Demo</title>
  <style type="text/css">
   h4.method1
   {
    border-top-style:solid;
    border-right-style:solid;
    border-bottom-style:dashed;
    border-left-style:dotted;
   }
   h4.method2
   {
    border-style:solid solid dashed dotted;
    border-color:green;
   }
  </style>
 </head>
 <body>
  <h4 class="method1">Box by One Method</h4>
  <br/><br/>
  <h4 class="method2">Box by another Method</h4>
 </body>
</html>
```

Output

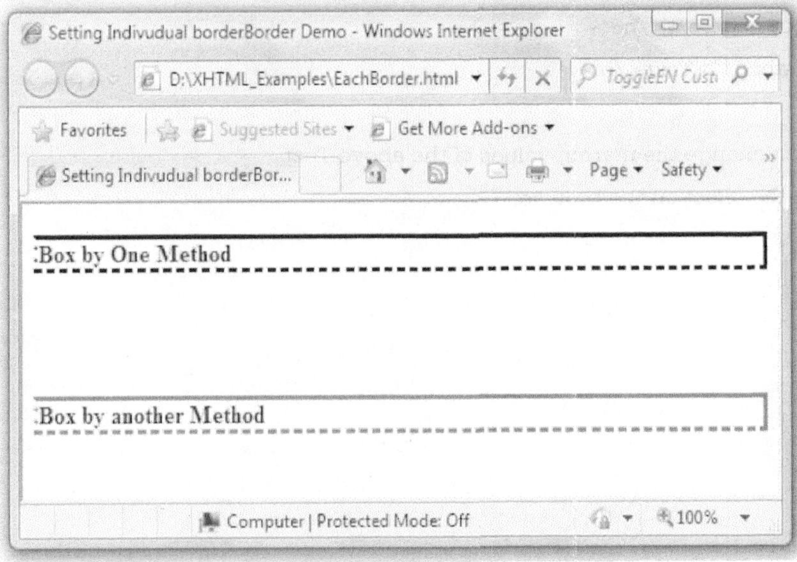

3.8.2 Margins and Padding

Margin means the space between the content and its neighbouring content. There can be top margin, bottom margin, left margin and right margin. Hence various properties of margins are margin-top, margin-bottom, margin-left and margin-right. The values of these properties can be given in **px** and **in**.

HTML Document[MarginDemo.html]

```
<!DOCTYPE html>
<html>
 <head>
  <title>Margin Demo</title>
  <style type="text/css">
   p.method1
   {
    border-style:solid;
    margin-top:80px;
    margin-bottom:60px;
    margin-left:30px;
    margin-right:70px;
   }
   </style>
 </head>
 <body>
  <h3>Neighbouring Text</h3>
  <p class="method1">Text</p>
<em>
 <pre>Note:Just change the margin values of the above Text
       and notice the effect on the browser
 </pre>
</em>
 </body>
</html>
```

Output

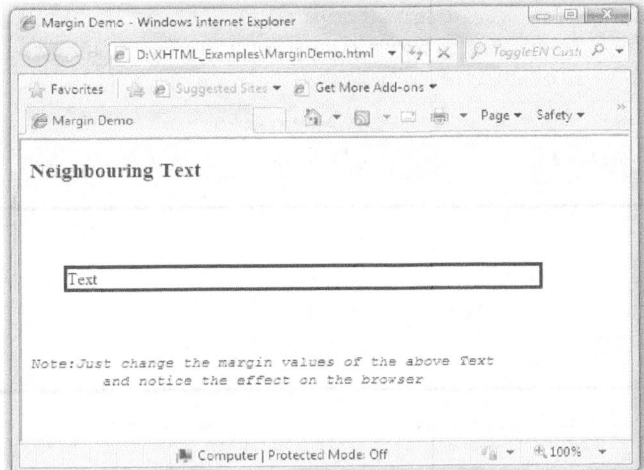

Just change the values of the properties such as margin-top, margin-bottom, margin-left and margin-right of the above given XHTML document and observe the change in the web browser. Thus by experimenting the above script in this way, you can understand the actual meaning of the margin.

Padding means the space between the contents and its border. Various properties of padding are padding-left, padding-right, padding-top and padding bottom. These values can also be given in **px** or in **in**.

HTML Document[PaddingDemo.html]

```
<!DOCTYPE html>
<html>
 <head>
  <title>Padding Demo</title>
  <style type="text/css">
  p.method1
  {
   border-style:solid;
   padding-top:70px;
   padding-bottom:50px;
   padding-left:120px;
   padding-right:60px;
  }
  </style>
 </head>
 <body>
    <p class="method1">My Text</p>
<em>
 <pre>Note:Just change the padding values of the above Text
       and notice the effect on the browser
 </pre>
</em>
  </body>
</html>
```

Output

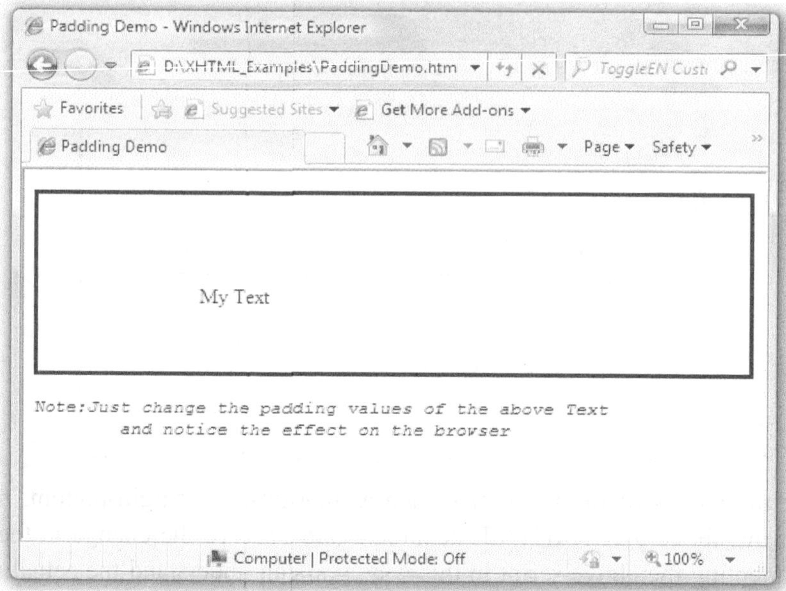

Just change the values of the properties such as padding-top, padding-bottom, padding-left and padding-right of the above given XHTML document and observe the change in the web browser. Thus by experimenting the above script in this way, you can understand the actual meaning of the padding.

University Question

1. *Explain the box modeling of CSS.*

3.9 Colors

3.9.1 Color Groups

There are three groups of colors. Those are as given below -

1. This is the **smallest group** of colors. In this group there are **16 colors.** These are named colors. The colors in this group are enlisted as follows.

Sr. No.	Color Name	Hexadecimal Value
1	black	000000
2	red	FF0000
3	lime	00FF00
4	blue	0000FF
5	yellow	FFFF00

6	fuchsia	FF00FF
7	aqua	00FFFF
8	white	FFFFFF
9	silver	C0C0C0
10	gray	808080
11	maroon	800000
12	purple	800080
13	green	008000
14	olive	808000
15	navy	000080
16	teal	008080

These colors get displayed as it is on the web browsers. And all the web browsers support these colors.

2. There is a set of **216** colors which is called **web palette**. The elements of such colors are red, green and blue. The values of these elements can be 00, 33, 66, 99, CC and FF.
3. These are **16 millions colors.** These are **24-bit** colors.

3.9.2 Color Properties

Using **color** property we can set the foreground color and using **background-color** the background color can be set. The use of these properties is shown in XHTML document.

HTML Document [colorProperties.html]

```
<!DOCTYPE html>
<html>
    <head>
    <title>Color Properties</title>
    <style type="text/css">
     h1
     {
      font-family:Arial;
      color:green;
      background-color:yellow;
     }
    </style>
    </head>
    <body>
     <center>
     <h1>This is a green text with yellow background</h1>
```

```
    </center>
   </body>
</html>
```

Output

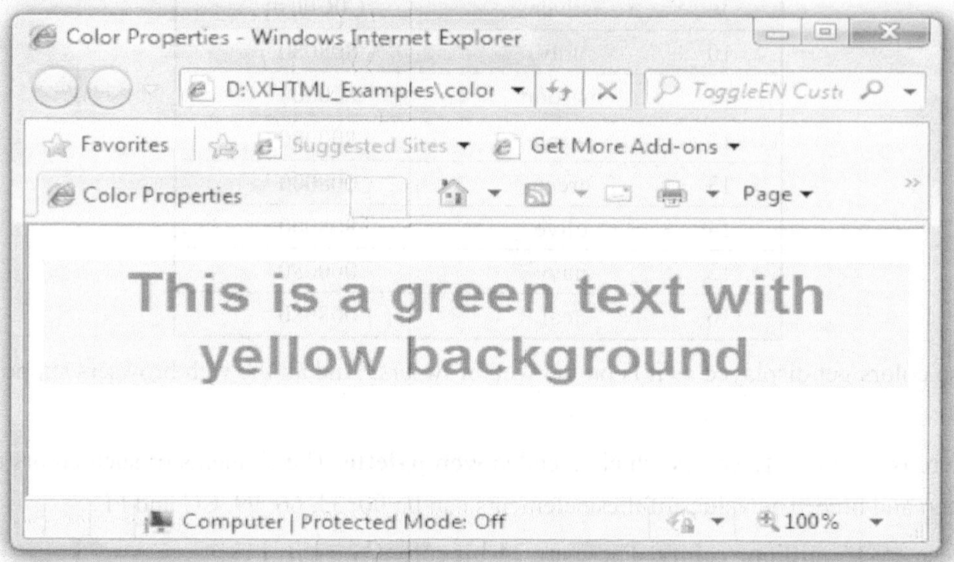

3.10 Backgrounds

AU : May-09, 13, Marks 8

Using **background-image** property an image can be set as background.

HTML Document[BackImg.html]

```
<!DOCTYPE html>
<html>
   <head>
   <title>Background Image</title>
   <style type="text/css">
    body {background-image:url(victoriafalls.jpg);
        background-repeat:no-repeat; }
    p
    {
     font-family:Arial;
     font-size:20px;
    }
   </style>
   </head>
   <body>
   <center>
   <h2>Wonder of the World</h2>
   </center>
   <p>
```

```
    The Vicorial waterfall is one of the greatest waterfalls in the world.
    It lies on the Zimbezi river which is between the border of Zambia and Zimbabwe.
    The Victoria fall can be seen from 25 to 40 miles away.
    The roaring of the water can be heard from a long distance.
    The native people call it as "mosi-oa-tunya", that means "smoke that thunders".
    Victoria falls was discovered by David Livingstone in 1855.
    The falls were named in honor of Queen Victoria.
    </p>
    </body>
</html>
```

Output

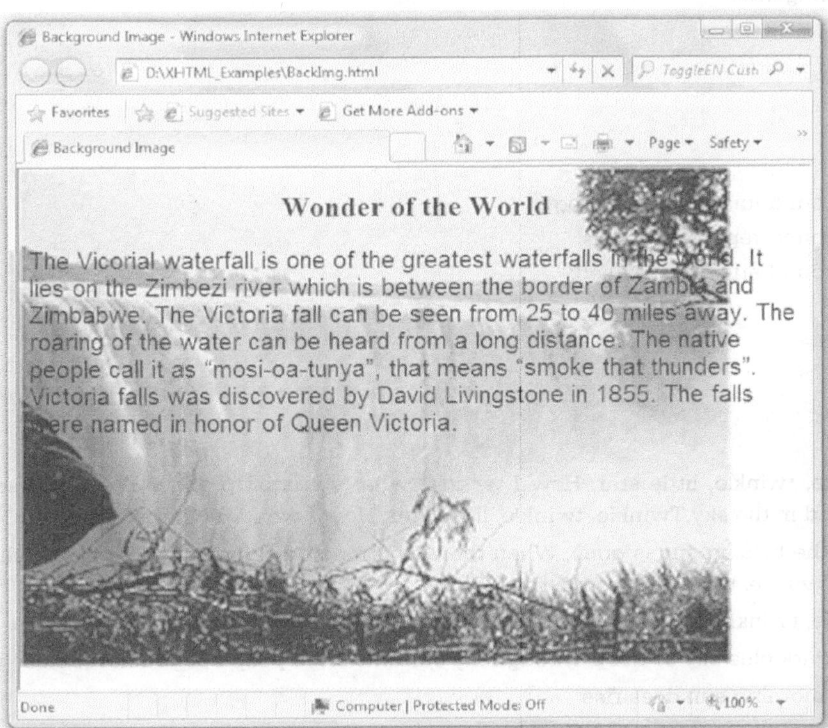

It is expected that the foreground text over the image should be visible. That means the color of the background image must not be the same as the color of the text written over it.

- **Background-repeat property**

  The **background-image** property sets the background image with repetition. If we want to control the repetition of the image then we must set the **background-repeat** property. The values of this property could be no-repeat, repeat-x, repeat-y or repeat(default). The repeat-x means the background image gets repeated over the x-axis(horizontally) and repeat-y means the background image gets repeated over the y-axis(vertically).

- **Background-position property**

  Various values for back-ground position property could be **top**, **bottom**, **left** and **right.**

Ex. 3.10.1 : Write a CSS rule that places a background image halfway down the page, tilting it horizontally. The image should remain in place when the use scrolls up or down.

Sol. :

```
<!DOCTYPE html>
<html>
<head>
<style type="text/css">
p
{
 font-size:40px;
 color:magenta;

}
body
{

background-image:url(baby.jpg);
background-repeat:repeat-x;
background-attachment:fixed;
}
</style>
</head>
<body>
<p>
Twinkle, twinkle, little star, How I wonder what you are.Up above the world so high, Like a diamond in the sky.Twinkle, twinkle, little star, How I wonder what you are!
When the blazing sun is gone, When there's nothing he shines upon,Then you show your little light, Twinkle, twinkle, through the night.
Twinkle, twinkle, little star, How I wonder what you are!
In the dark blue sky so deep Through my curtains often peep For you never close your eyes
Til the morning sun does rise
Twinkle, twinkle, little star How I wonder what you are Twinkle, twinkle, little star How I wonder what you are
</p>
</body>
</html>
```

Ex. 3.10.2 : Create a web page to create a fixed background image.

AU : May-09, Marks 2

Sol. :

```
<html>
    <head>
     <style type="text/css">
```

```
body
{
background-image:url("Myimg.jpg");
background-repeat:no-repeat
}
</style>
</head>
<body>
<center>
<h1>Life is beautiful!!!</h1>
</center>
</body>
</html>
```

No repeat creates fixed background image

Output

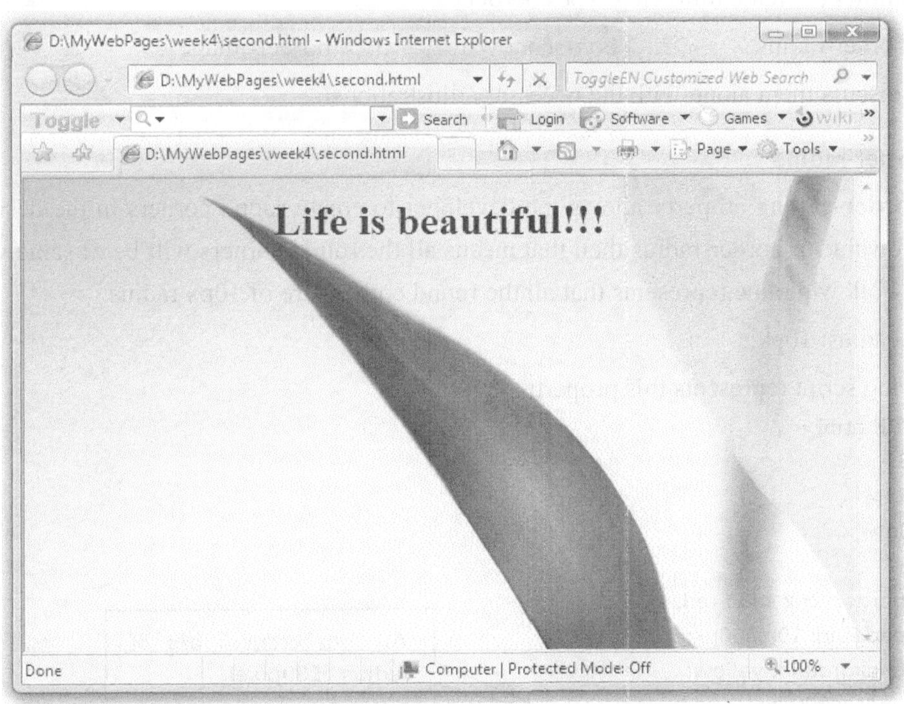

Ex. 3.10.3 : Write a CSS which adds background images and indentation.

AU : May-13, Marks 8

Sol. :

```
<html>
  <head>
   <style type="text/css">
  body
  {
```

```
background-image:url("Rose.jpg");
background-repeat:no-repeat
}
p {text-indent:50px;}
</style>
</head>
<body>
<center>
<p>Roses are beautiful.</p>
</center>
</body>
</html>
```

3.11 Border

CSS3 allows to create following types border

1. border-radius 2. box-shadow 3. border-image

Let us discuss them along with the necessary illustrations.

1. The border-radius

The **border-radius** property allows the developer to create round corners in the design. If we set a single value to border-radius then that means all the round corners will be of same value. For example - Following line represents that all the round corners are of 10px radius.

border-radius: 10px;

Following script represents this property

```
<!DOCTYPE html>
<html>
<head>
<style>
div {
    border: 3px solid red;
    padding: 10px 60px;
    background: yellow;
    width: 300px;
    border-radius: 30px;
}
</style>
</head>
<body>
  <div>This design has round corner</div>
</body>
</html>
```

All four corners are of radius of 30pixel.

Output

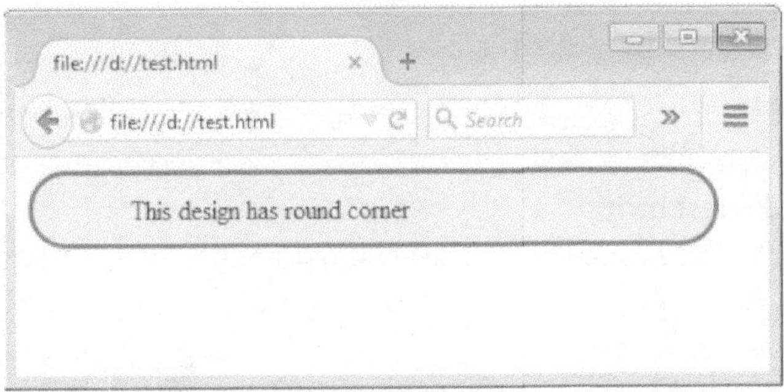

2. The border shadow

The **border-shadow** property represents the shadows around the border. For example-

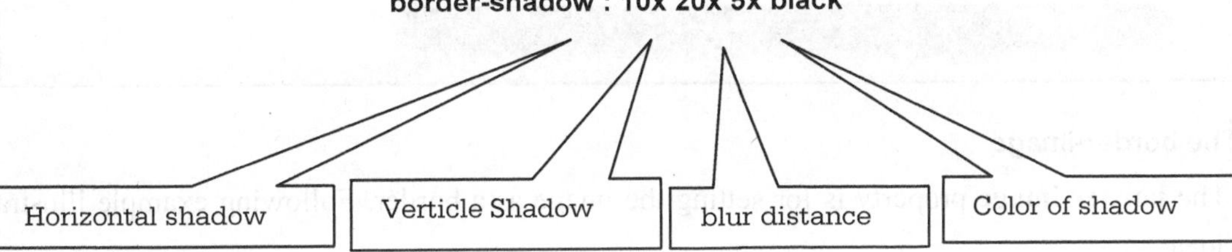

Following script represents this property

```
<!DOCTYPE html>
  <html>
   <head>
   <style>
   div {
      width: 300px;
      height: 100px;
      background-color: yellow;
      box-shadow: 10px 20px 5px blue;
    }
   </style>
   </head>
   <body>
      <div> </div>
   </body>
  </html>
```

Output

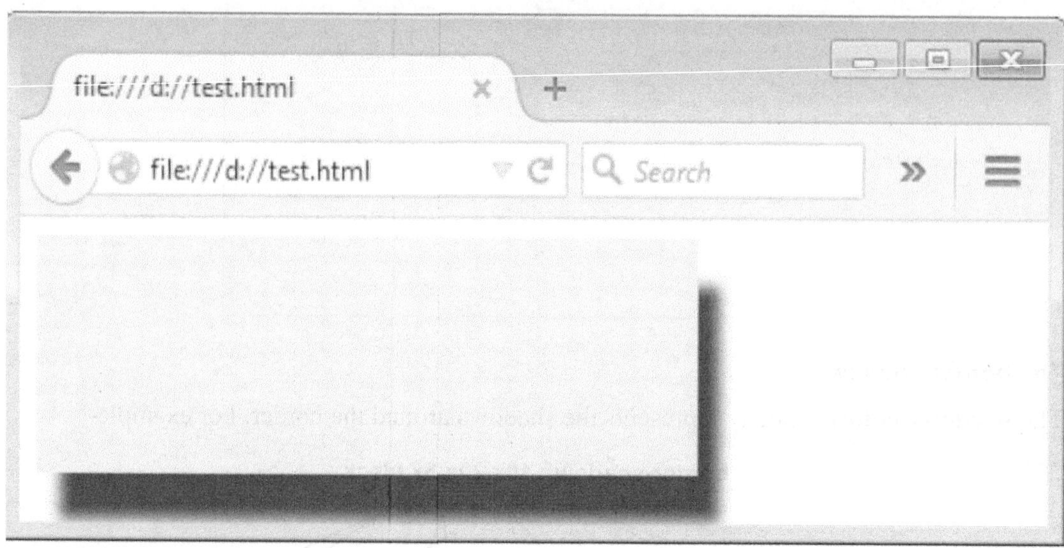

3. The border-image

The **border-image** property is for setting the image as a border. Following example illustrates the idea

```
<!DOCTYPE html>
   <html>
    <head>
    <style>
      div {
         background-color: pink;
         border: 20px solid transparent;
         border-image-source: url('flower.png');  //image as a border
   // The inward offsets of each side of image-border is specified by image-slice
               border-image-slice: 20;
         border-image-repeat: repeat;  //repeat the image border
      }
    </style>
    </head>
    <body>
      <div>
         This design has a image border
      </div>
    </body>
</html>
```

Output

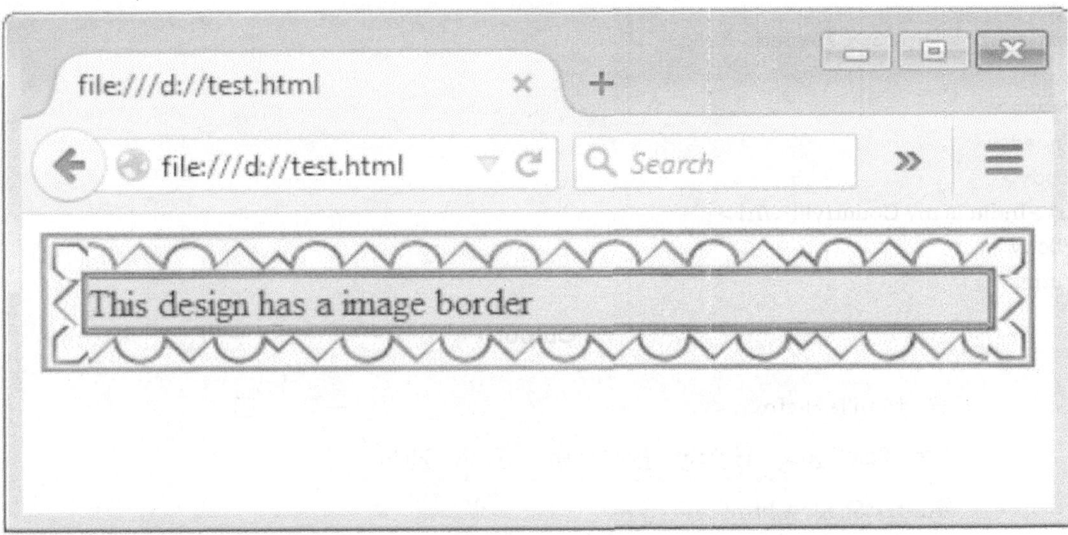

Explanation

The image file can be provided to the **border-image-source** style using the **url**. The **border-image-slice** specifies the inward offset of each side of the border image. It can be denoted by a value or percentage. The syntax for border-image-slice is given by following example.

```
border-image-slice: 20% 30% 30% 20%; /* top right bottom left*/
```

If a single value is provided then that means all the four corners are sliced using the same number.

By the **border-image-repeat** property the slice gets repeated from the center of the side to fill the space.

3.12 Shadows

The shadow effect in CSS3 can be created for two categories -

(1) Text Shadow and (2) Box Shadow

Let us discuss them

(1) Text Shadow: The text shadow property applies shadow to the text.

Syntax :

```
text-shadow: [x-coordinate] [y-coordinate] [blur radius] [color of shadow];
```

For example

```
<!DOCTYPE html>
<html>
<head>
```

```
<style>
h1 {
  text-shadow: 5px 5px 7px red;
}
</style>
</head>
<body>
<h1>India is my Country!!!</h1>
</body>
</html>
```

Output

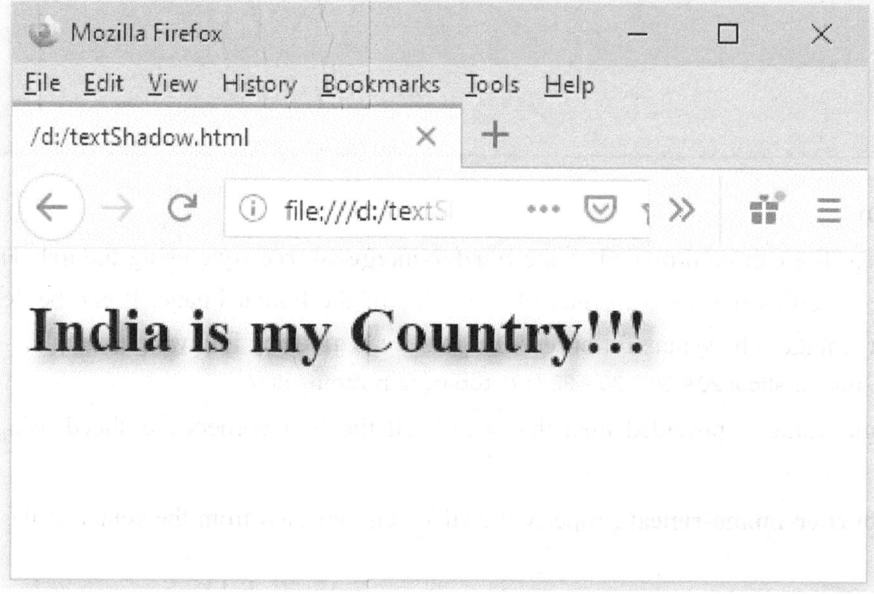

If we simply apply the style as

```
<style>
h1 {
text-shadow: 3px 3px;
}
</style>
```

Then output will be -

India is my Country!!!

(2) Box Shadow: The CSS box-shadow property applies shadow to elements.

Syntax :

box-shadow: [horizontal offset] [vertical offset] [blur radius] [optional spread radius] [color];

1. The **horizontal offset** (required) of the shadow, positive means the shadow will be on the right of the box, a negative offset will put the shadow on the left of the box.
2. The **vertical offset** (required) of the shadow, a negative one means the box-shadow will be above the box, a positive one means the shadow will be below the box.
3. The **blur radius** (required), if set to 0 the shadow will be sharp, the higher the number, the more blurred it will be, and the further out the shadow will extend. For instance a shadow with 5px of horizontal offset that also has a 5px blur radius will be 10px of total shadow.
4. The **spread radius** (optional), positive values increase the size of the shadow, negative values decrease the size. Default is 0 (the shadow is same size as blur).
5. Color (required) - takes any color value, like hex, named, rgba or hsla. If the color value is omitted, box shadows are drawn in the foreground color (text color).

For example

```
<!DOCTYPE html>
<html>
<head>
<style>
 div {
  width: 200px;
  height: 50px;
padding: 15px;
  background-color: khaki;
  box-shadow: 20px 20px;
}
</style>
</head>
<body>
<div>Box-shadow</div>
</body>
</html>
```

Output

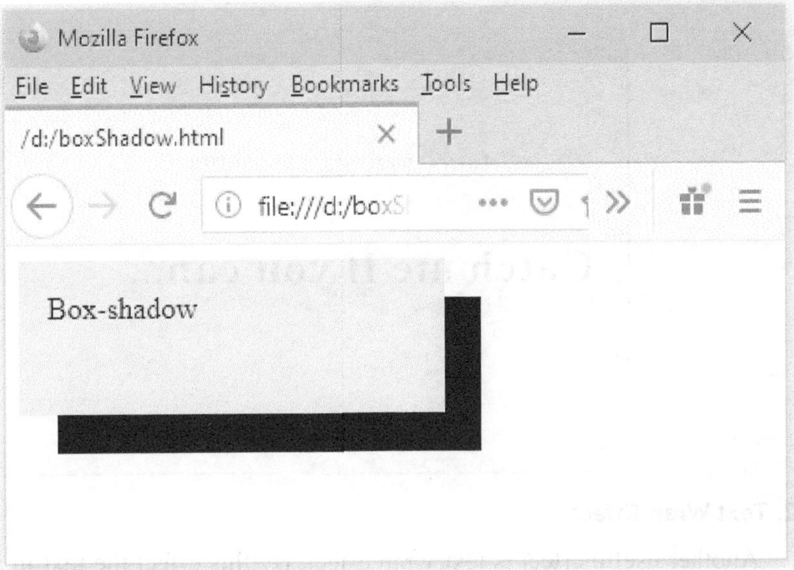

Mozilla Firefox

File Edit View History Bookmarks Tools Help

/d:/boxShadow.html

file:///d:/boxS

Box-shadow

3.13 Text Effects

In this section we will discuss various text effects mainly used in CSS3.

1. Text Shadow Effect

The CSS3 allows to incorporate many advanced text effects in the web design. Out of which the text shadow effect is very commonly used.

The text-shadow property can be as given below -

text-shadow: horizontal_shadow vertical_shadow blur_distance color_of_shadow

Let us now understand how to apply and experience this text style.

```
<!DOCTYPE html>
<html>
<head>
  <style>
    h2 {
    text-shadow: -5px 15px 3px gray;
    }
  </style>
</head>
<body>

<h2>Catch me If you can...</h2>
</body>
</html>
```

Output

2. Text Wrap Effect

Another useful effect is text wrap effect. By this effect the text in a paragraph gets wrapped on the next line. This effect can be achieved by breaking the word -

word-wrap: break-word

Following is a simple CSS script in which the text wrap effect is used.

```
<!DOCTYPE html>
<html>
<head>
  <style>
    div.wrapdemo
    {
    width: 130px;
    border: 1px solid red;
    word-wrap: break-word;
    }
  </style>
</head>
<body>

<div class="wrapdemo"> There was once a Merchant who had three daughters, the youngest of whom was so beautiful that everybody called her Beauty. This made the two eldest very jealous; and, as they were spiteful and bad-tempered by
nature, instead of loving their younger sister they felt nothing but envyandhatredtowardsher.</div>
</body>
</html>
```

Output

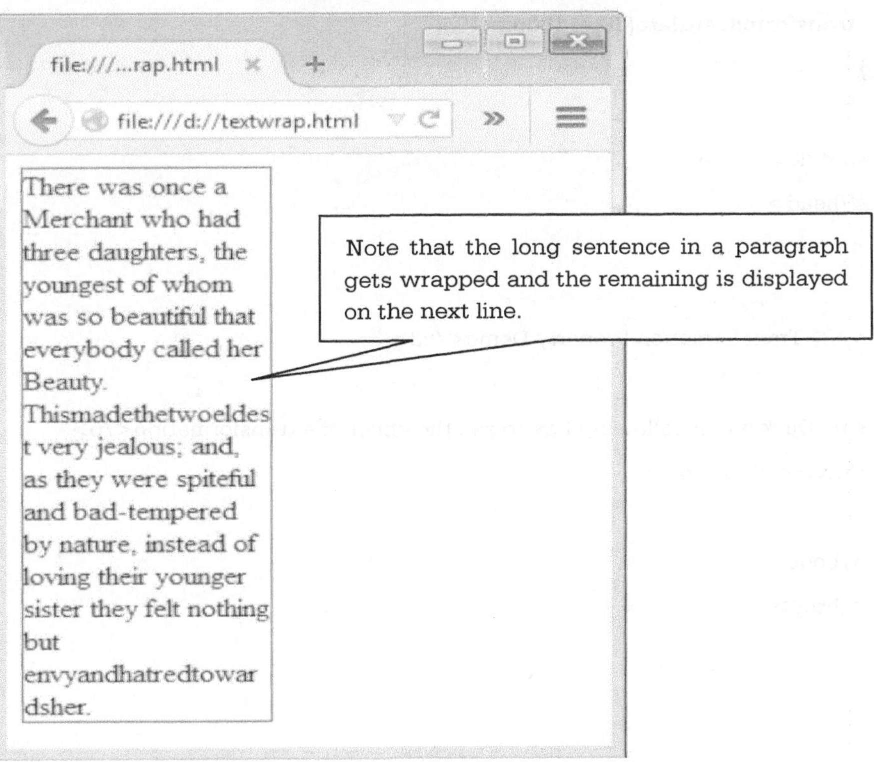

3.14 Transformation

Transformation is a property by which the object can be rotated, scaled, or skewed. The transformation can be of two types – 2D transformation and 3D transformation.

(1) The 2D transformation

- **Translate Property :** The translate() method moves an element from its current position

For example : Following example shows that the **div** block can be moved for 30PX along the X-axis and 100px along the Y-axis.

```
<!DOCTYPE html>
<html>
<head>
<style>
div {
 width: 70px;
 height: 30px;
 background: blue;
}
div:active {
 transform:translate(30px,100px);
}

</style>
</head>
<body>

<h3>Transformation Property Demo</h3>

<p>Click on the following box to see the effect of a transformation</p>
<div></div><br/>

</body>
</html>
```

Output

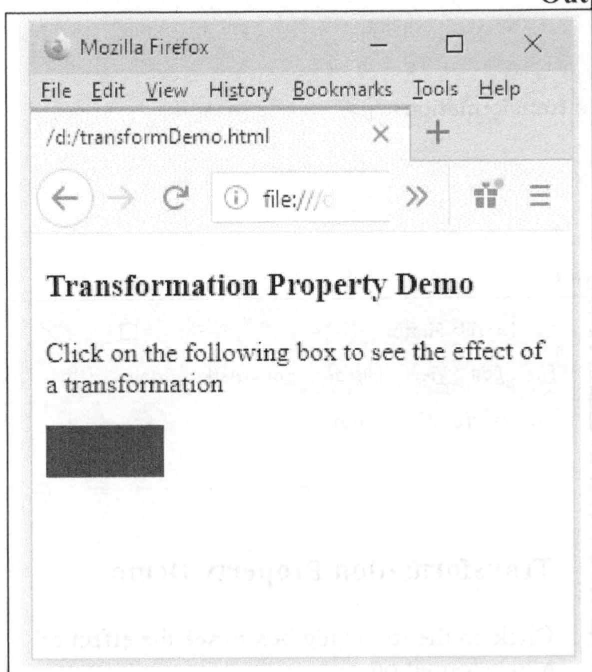

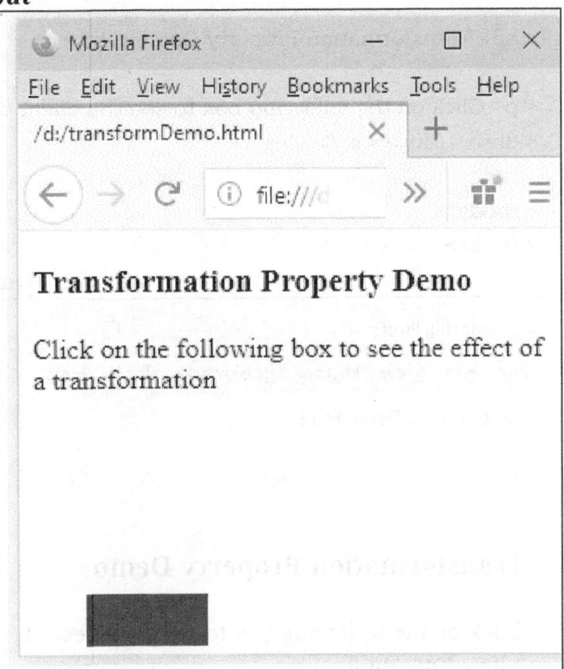

- **rotate()** method is used to rotate the element in clockwise or anti-clockwise manner to given degree. The positive value of degree indicates rotation in clockwise manner and negative value of degree indicates rotation in anti-clockwise manner.

For example

```
<!DOCTYPE html>
<html>
<head>
<style>
div {
 width: 70px;
 height: 30px;
 background: blue;

}
div:active {
 transform:rotate(45deg);
}

</style>
</head>
<body>
```

```
<h3>Transformation Property Demo</h3>

<p>Click on the following box to see the effect of a transformation</p>
<div></div><br/>

</body>
</html>
```

Output

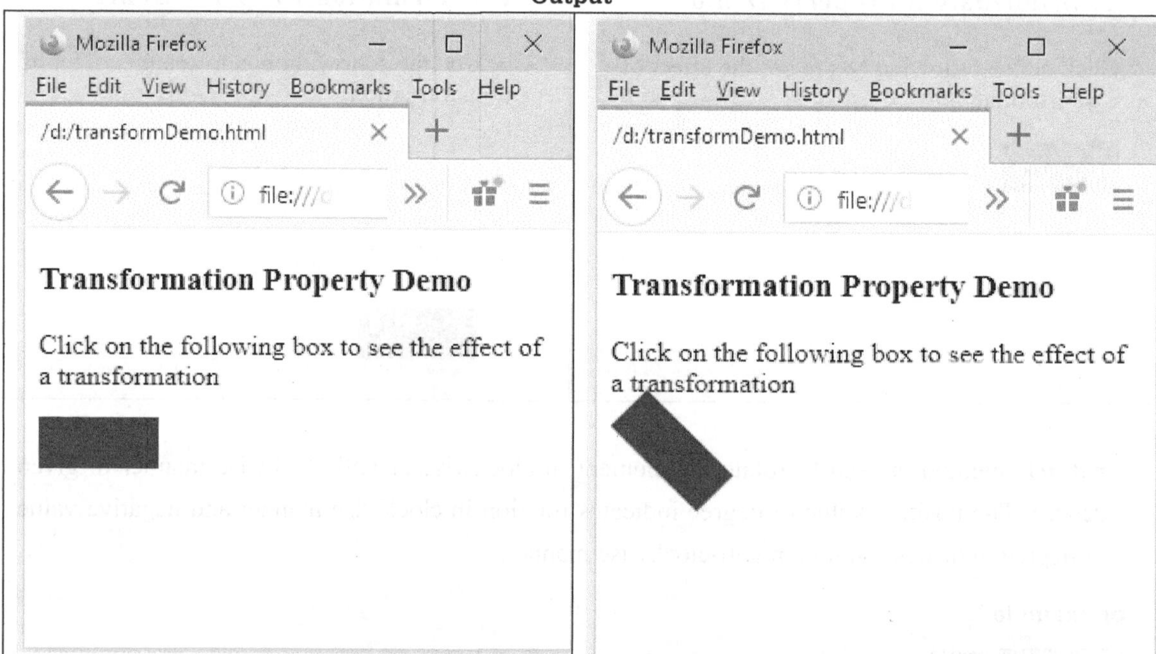

- **Scale () :** The scale method is used to increment or decrement the size of the element. The scaleX() method increases or decreases the width of element. The scaleY() method increases or decreases the height of the element.

For example

```
<!DOCTYPE html>
<html>
<head>
<style>
div {
 width: 70px;
 height: 50px;
 background: blue;

}
#div1:active {
 transform:scaleX(3);
```

```
}
#div2:active {
 transform:scaleY(3);
}

</style>
</head>
<body>

<h3>Transformation Property Demo</h3>

<p>Click on the following box to see the effect of a transformation</p>
<div id="div1">Increase the width</div><br/><br/><br/>
<div id="div2">Increase the height</div><br/>
</body>
</html>
```

Output

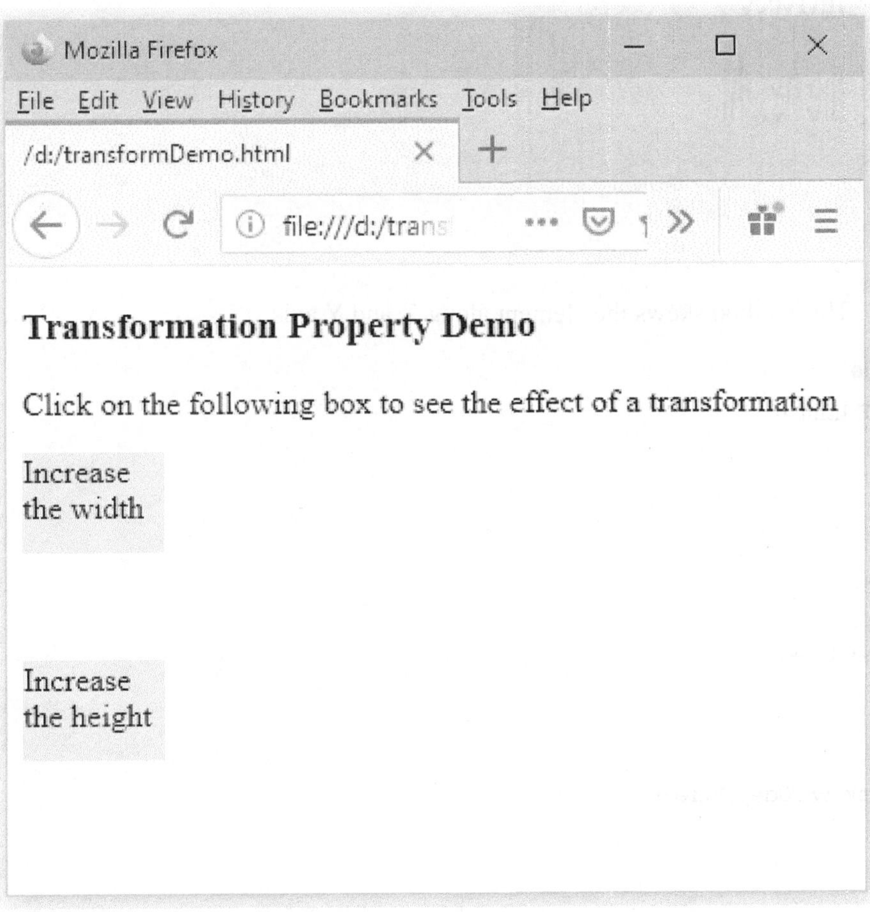

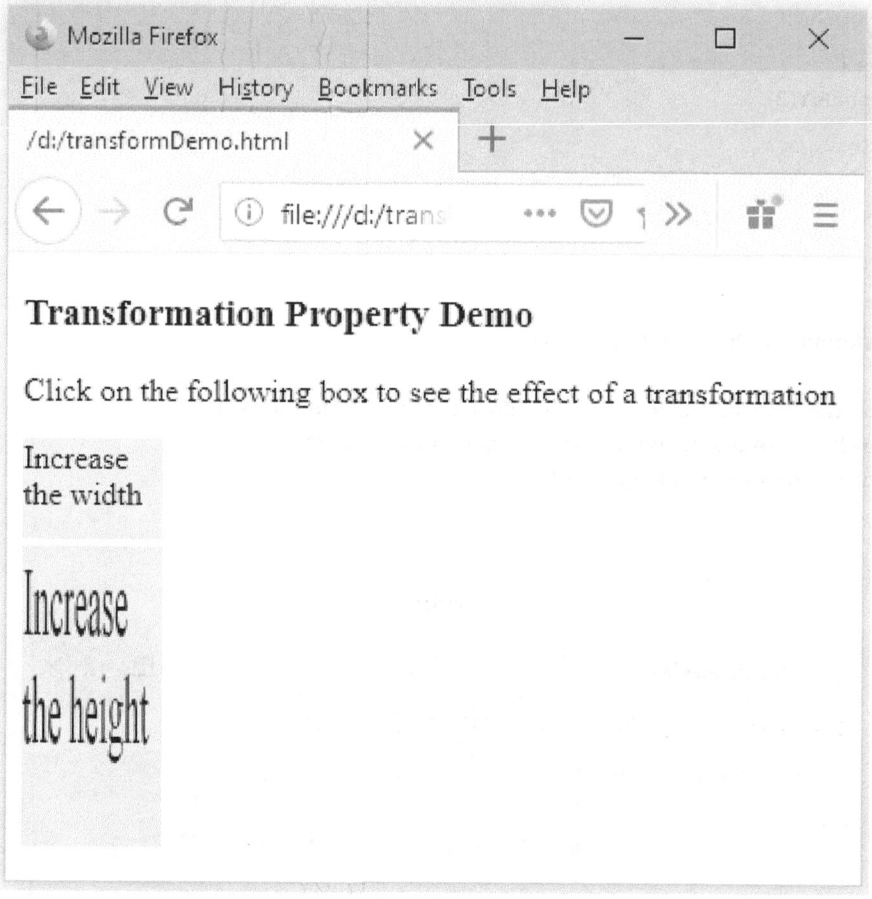

- **Skew ()** : This method skews the element along X and Y axis.

For example

```
<!DOCTYPE html>
<html>
<head>
<style>
div {
 width: 70px;
 height: 50px;
 background: khaki;

}
div:active {
 transform:skew(30deg,45deg);
}

</style>
```

```
</head>
<body>

<h3>Transformation Property Demo</h3>

<p>Click on the following box to see the effect of a transformation</p>
<div>Skew</div>

</body>
</html>
```

(2) The 3D transformation

- The 3D transformation can be applied by rotating the element along x, y or a axis.
- The rotateX() method rotates an element around its X-axis at a given degree: For example

  transform:rotateX(45deg);
- The rotateX() method rotates an element around its Y-axis at a given degree: For example

  transform:rotateY(45deg);
- The rotateZ() method rotates an element around its Z-axis at a given degree: For example

  transform:rotateZ(45deg);
- The rotate3d() function rotates the element in 3D space by the specified angle around the [x,y,z] direction vector. This can be written as rotate(x, y, z, angle).
- For example

```
<!DOCTYPE html>
<html>
<head>
<style>
div {
 width: 100px;
 height: 50px;
 background: khaki;

}
div:active {
 transform:rotate3d(0,1,0,100deg);
}

</style>
</head>
<body>
<h3>Transformation Property Demo</h3>
```

```
<p>Click on the following box to see the effect of a transformation</p>
<div>Rotate 3D</div>
</body>
</html>
```

Output

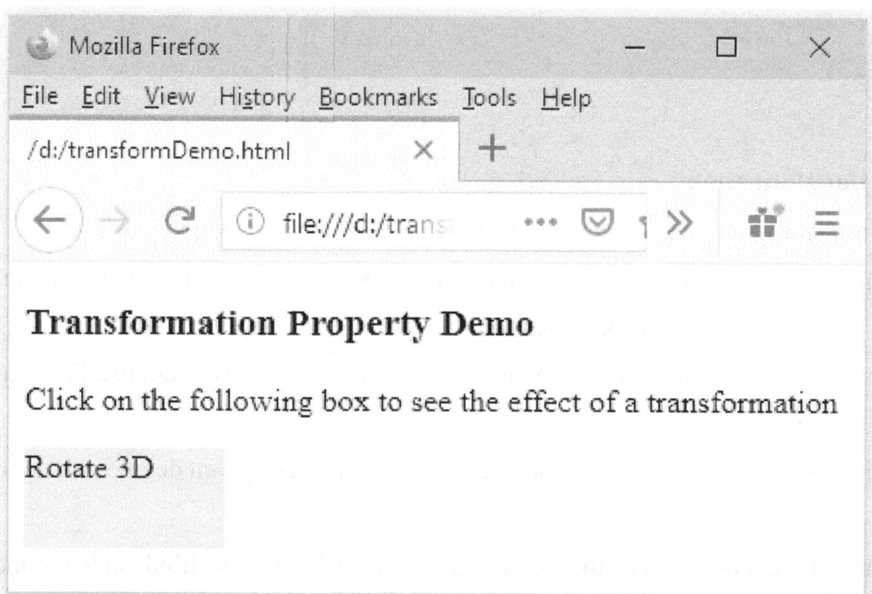

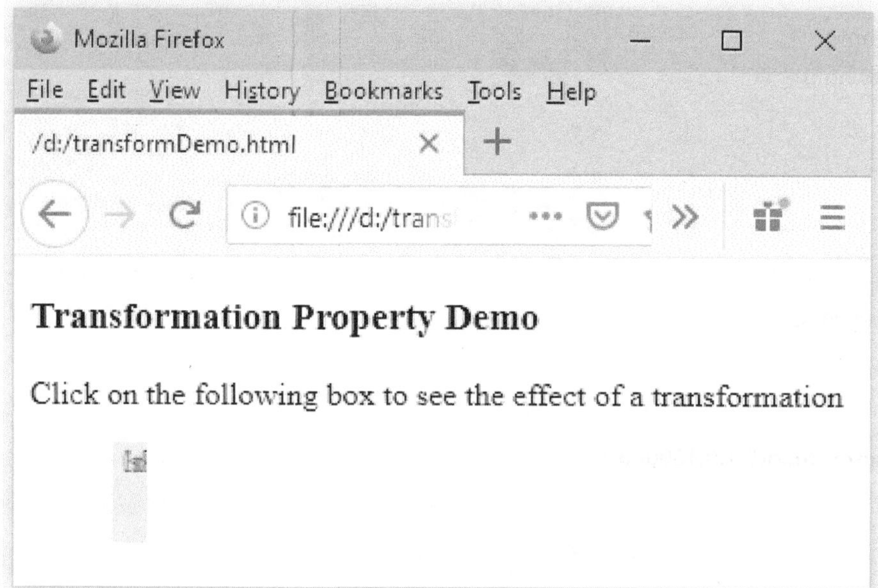

3.15 Transitions

- The CSS3 transition allows the user to alter the appearance and behavior of an element whenever a state change occurs. This state change can be focus on, active, targeted or hovered on.
- During the transition, an element must have a change in state, and different styles must be identified for each state.
- The styles can be applied at different states such as :hover, :focus, :active and :target pseudo classes.
- There are five transition related properties :
  - o Transition
  - o Transition-property
  - o Transition-duration
  - o Transition-timing-function
  - o transition-delay

  Not all of these are required to build a transition; with the first three are the most popular.

  For example

```
<!DOCTYPE html>
<html>
<head>
<style>
.box {
  width: 50px;
  height: 50px;
  background: blue;
  transition: width 2s;
}

.box:hover {
  width: 200px;
 background: green;
}
</style>
</head>
<body>
<h3>Transition Property Demo</h3>
<p>Hover over the following box to see the effect of a transition</p>
<div class ="box"></div>
</body>
</html>
```

Output

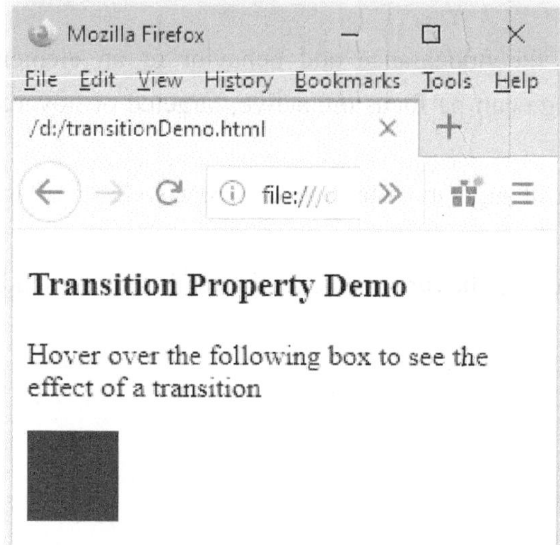

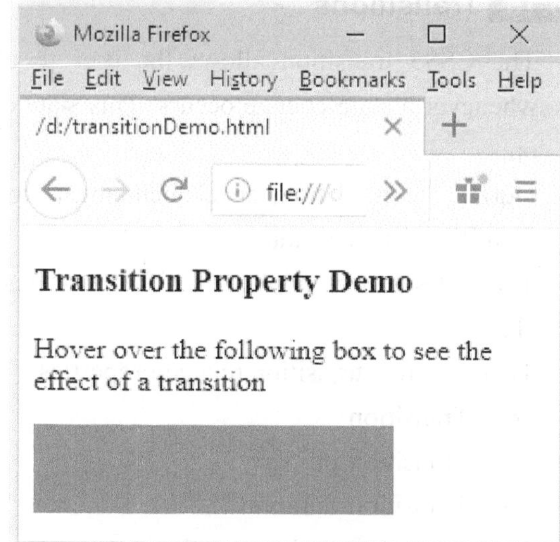

1. The **transition-delay** property specifies the delay in seconds for transition effect. This delay is introduced before the transition effect takes place.

For example

```
<!DOCTYPE html>
<html>
<head>
<style>
.box {
 width: 50px;
 height: 50px;
 background: blue;
 transition: width 2s;
 transition-delay:2s;
}
.box:hover {
 width: 200px;
 background: green;
}
</style>
</head>
<body>
<h3>Transition Property Demo</h3>
<p>Hover over the following box to see the effect of a transition</p>
<div class ="box"></div>
</body>
</html>
```

2. The **transition-timing-function** is a property that specifies the speed curve of the transition effect. The transition-timing-function property can have following values -

Values	Description
ease	It specifies a transition effect. This effect can be slow start, then fast and then end slowly.
linear	It specifies a transition effect. This effect is with same speed from start to end.
ease-in	It specifies a transition effect. This effect is with slow start.
ease-out	It specifies a transition effect. This effect is with slow end.
ease-in-out	It specifies a transition effect. This effect is with slow start and slow end.

For example

```
<!DOCTYPE html>
<html>
<head>
<style>
div {
 width: 70px;
 height: 30px;
 background: blue;
 transition: width 2s;
}
div:hover {
 width: 200px;
}
#box1{
 transition-timing-function:linear;
}
#box2:hover {
 transition-timing-function:ease;
}
#box3:hover {
 transition-timing-function:ease-in;
}
#box3:hover {
 transition-timing-function:ease-out;
}
```

```
</style>
</head>
<body>

<h3>Transition Property Demo</h3>
<p>Hover over the following boxes to see the effect of a transition</p>
<div id ="box1">Linear</div><br/>
<div id ="box2">ease</div><br/>
<div id ="box3">ease-in</div><br/>
<div id ="box4">ease-out</div><br/>
</body>
</html>
```

Output

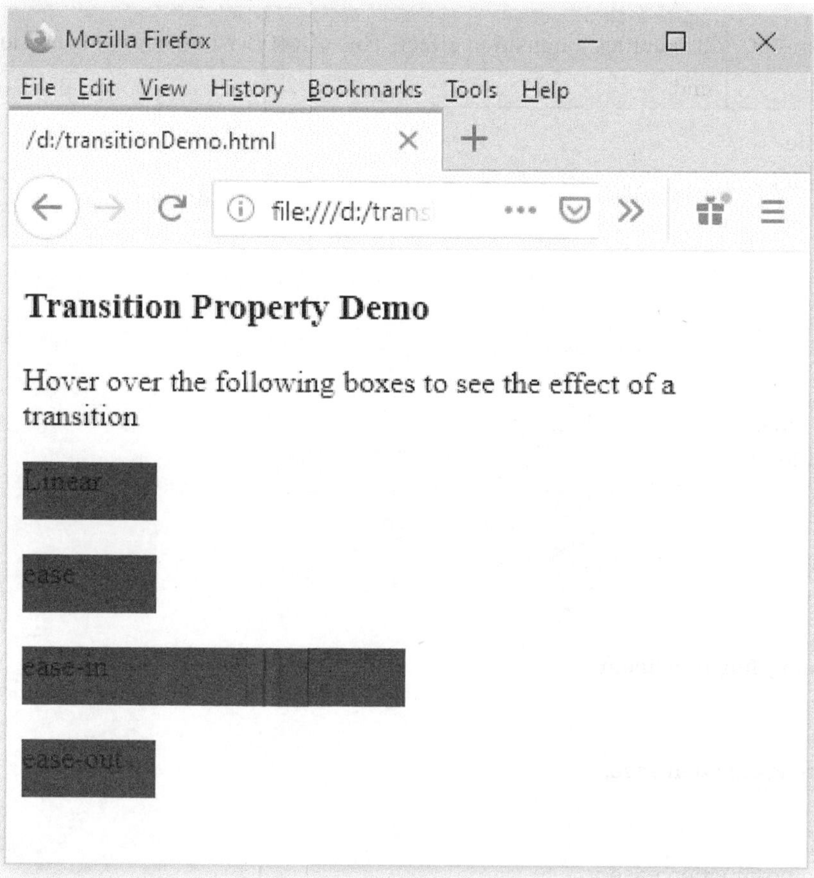

3.16 Animations

- Animation is a technique of changing the element from one style to another. This change can be in position, or in appearance of the element.

- Creating CSS animations is a two step process, as shown in the example below:

1. The first step of building a CSS animation is to defining individual **keyframes** and naming an animation with a keyframes declaration. Using @keyframe rule the animation from one style to another will occur.
2. The second step is referencing the keyframes by name using the **animation-name property** as well as adding **animation-duration** and other **optional animation properties** to control the animation's behavior.

For example

```
<!DOCTYPE html>
<html>
<head>
<style>
div {
  width: 70px;
  height: 30px;
  background-color: khaki;
  animation-name: myanimation;
  animation-duration: 4s;
}

@keyframes myanimation {
  from {top:0;}
  to {top: 50%;}
}
</style>
</head>
<body>

<div></div>

</body>
</html>
```

Defining Keyframes

The keyframe selector for a keyframe style rule starts with a percentage (%) or the keywords from (same as 0 %) or to (same as 100 %). The selector is used to specify where a keyframe is constructed along the duration of the animation.

Percentages represent a percentage of the animation duration, 0 % represents the starting point of the animation, 100 % represents the end point, and 50 % represents the midpoint and so on.

For example

```
<!DOCTYPE html>
<html>
<head>
<style>
div {
 width: 70px;
 height: 30px;
 background: green;
 position: relative;
 animation: myanimation 5s infinite;
}

@keyframes myanimation {
 0%   {left: 0px;}
 25%  {left: 50px;}
 75%  {left: 100px}
 100% {left: 200px;}
}
</style>
</head>
<body>
<div></div>
</body>
</html>
```

Output

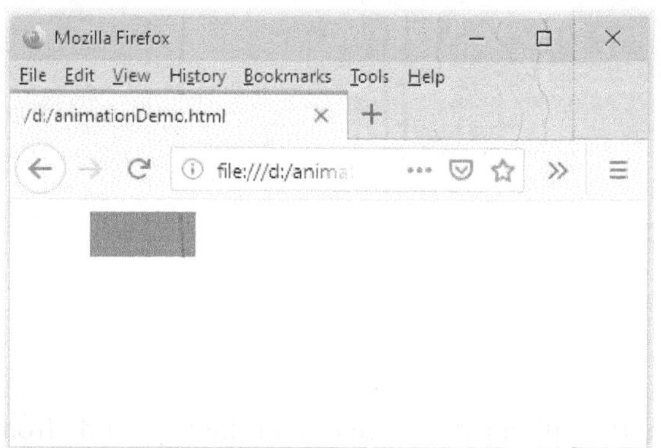

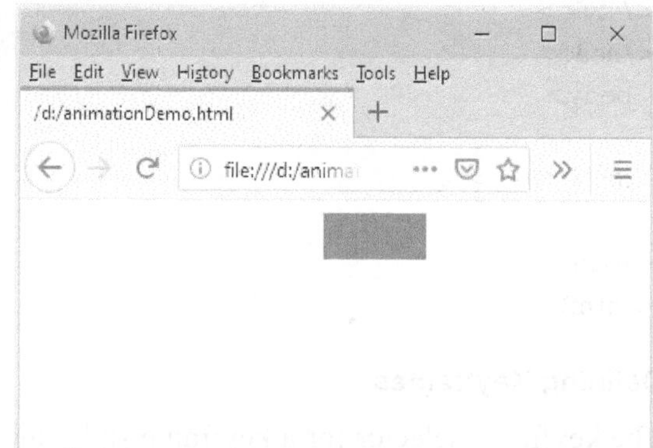

3.17 Web 2.0

- Web 2.0 allows the user to do more than simply retrieving the information. Instead of merely reading user can write their own contents to the web pages by means of Web 2.0.

- Web 2.0 is the term given to describe the web technology that is used to focus on the ability for people to collaborate and share information online.
- Web 2.0 basically refers to the transition from static HTML Web pages to a more dynamic Web that is more organized and is based on serving Web applications to users.
- The most popular functionality of Web 2.0 is that it includes open communication with an emphasis on Web-based communities of users and more open sharing of information. Web 2.0 offers all users the same freedom to contribute.
- It also increases the incidence of **spamming** and **trolling** by destructive users.
- **Blogs, wikis** and **Web services** are all seen as components of Web 2.0.

Features

1. Users can collectively classify and find the desired information using Web 2.0
2. User can obtain the dynamic contents. They can also get the appropriate responses based on their input.
3. The information entered by one user can be shared by multiple users. Contributions are available for the world to use, reuse, or re-purpose.
4. Web 2.0 allows mass participation in particular discussion.

Technologies used

At the client side AJAX and JavaScripts are used.

At the server side various technologies such as PHP, Ruby, Python, Microsoft .NET framework is used.

Web 2.0 can be described in three parts -

1. **Rich internet applications :** It is a web application that has many of the characteristics of desktop application software, typically delivered by way of a site-specific browser, a browser plug-in, or a virtual machine.
2. **Web oriented architecture :** It defines how Web 2.0 applications expose their functionality so that other applications can integrate their functionality providing a set of much richer applications. Examples are feeds, RSS, Web services.
3. **Social web :** It tends to interact much more with the end user and make the end-user an integral part of the application.

3.17.1 Rich Internet Application (RIA)

Users are dissatisfied with the capabilities and performance of simple HTML based web applications. They need desktop type interactions from the web applications.

Rich internet applications are intended to bring the interactivity and intuitiveness in web applications.

Features of RIA

1. RIA can work on web.
2. Information in RIA always appears to users eliminating distractive page refreshes.
3. RIA retains the ability of web to present complex information to users but adds to this capability by incorporating richness and user interactivity. RIA applications support a rich set of visual elements like images, graphics, and video.
4. RIA works in real time enabling business services as well as on-demand services.
5. RIA helps users to understand and use complex business applications by reducing unnecessary navigations from one page to another.

Examples of rich application framework

1. Apache Flex
2. Quick PHP
3. .Net Framework

Benefits of RIA

1. RIA allows users to perform multiple tasks in a simple and intuitive way from a single integrated interface. As a result more transactions can be carried out.
2. RIA development is based on a traditional development model that is easy to learn, follow and deliver. This makes RIA development highly productive.
3. Since RIA framework enables client-end processing, it improves overall performance of the application and reduces the burden on server.
4. It adds value to existing customers by presenting information in new and improved format.

Two Marks Questions with Answers

Q.1 What is CSS file ?

Ans. : The cascading style is many times defined in a separate file. This file is called CSS file. In CSS file one or more style rules are given.

Q.2 Give the syntax of CSS rule. AU : Dec.-11, May-12

Ans. :

```
<style type="text/css">
    h1
```

```
{
    font-family:Arial;
     color:green
}
</style>
```

Q.3 What are style sheets ?

Ans. : The style sheets are the collection of styles that can be either embedded within the HTML documents or can be externally applied. The Cascading style sheet is a markup language used to apply the styles to HTML elements.

Q.4 What is selector string ? Specify any three forms of selectors.

Ans. : The ruleset in CSS consists of selector string which is basically an HTML element. These selectors can be defined with the help of properties and values.

Q.5 How do you provide uniform access to structured documents in diverse applications ?

AU : Dec.-08

Ans. : Style sheets allow the user to decide the style of presentation. This presentation can be defined in a separate file. And simply by including this file in various web documents the designated style can be applied to the corresponding tag. For example - If we define

```
h1
{
 font_size : 20 pt
 color : red
}
```

Then every line defined by h1 tag will be of size 20 pt and red in color.

Q.6 Mention the need for cascading style sheet. **AU : May-11**

Ans. : The cascading style sheet allows separation between the information contained in a document and its presentation. Hence any change in presentation can be made without disturbing the information of the document. The cascading style sheet allows the developer to give the consistent appearance to all elements of the web page.

Q.7 What do you mean by the term ruleset ?

Ans. : The styles are defined in separate file. This file is called CSS file. The collection of rules in a CSS file is called **ruleset**.

Q.8 Enlist various categories of properties used in CSS

Ans. : The various categories of properties in CSS are -

1) Fonts 2) List 3) Alignment of Text 4) Color

5) Margins 6) Background 7) Borders.

Q.9 What is the use of universal selector ?

Ans. : Using the universal selector the values can be defined for all the elements in the document. It is denoted by *.

Q.10 What is generic class selector ?

Ans. : The generic class applied to any tag in the HTML document. And thus the values defined within that generic selector can be applied to the corresponding tag. The class selector must be preceded by the dot operator.

Q.11 Enlist the three commonly used pseudo classes.

Ans. : The three commonly used pseudo classes are -

1. focus 2. hover 3. hyperlink

Q.12 Define the hover element.

Ans. : The hover is associated with anchor element and the selector for this element is specified by a:hover. When the mouse is moved over the element then the pseudo class get activated.

Q.13 What are the advantages of external style sheet ?

Ans. : When we use external style sheet then the style is defined in one file and actual contents of the web page are defined in another file. Hence if we want to change the style of presentation of web page then we can simply modify the file in which the style is defined.

Q.14 What is the difference between the external style sheet and embedded style sheet ?

Ans. : The external style sheet is a kind of style sheet in which the styles are defined in a separate .css file and this file is mentioned at the beginning of the HTML document. When we need to apply the a method in which the style is specified (or embedded) within the HTML document itself. It is not defined in separate file. Due to embedded style sheet unique style can be applied to all the elements.

Q.15 What is the significance of Box Model in CSS ?

Ans. : The box model in CSS represents the contents, inner edge, outer edge, margins and padding.

Q.16 What do you mean by margin and padding ?

Ans. : Margin means the space between the content and its neighbouring contents. Padding means the space between the contents and its border.

Q.17 What is the use of float position ?

Ans. : The float position is used to shift an image to one side and wrap the text around it.

Q.18 What is CSS padding ? **AU : Dec.-09**

Ans. : CSS padding is a property that allows to have space between the border and actual content. This space can be at the top, bottom, left and right. For example - Following is a CSS script that creates padding around the sentence.

```
<html>
<head>
<style type="text/css">
h3
{
 background-color:green;
}
h3.padding
{
padding-top:50px;
padding-bottom:50px;
padding-right:50px;
padding-left:50px;
}
</style>
</head>
<body>
<h3>This is a simple text without padding</h3>
<h3 class="padding">This text have padding around it</h3>
</body>
</html>
```

This text coil have padding at top bottom left and right

Q.19 If you do not want repeated background images then how will you apply the style ?

Ans. : For not repeated background images the following style can be set :

```
body
{
  background-image:url("Myimg.jpg");
  background-repeat:no-repeat
}
```

Q.20 What do you mean by the term inline element ?

Ans. : The inline elements are those elements that do not form new blocks of content. The content is distributed in lines.

Q.21 List two forms of style rules with an example. **AU : Dec.-12**

Ans. : 1. Universal Selector

This selector is denoted by * (asterisk). This selector can be applied to all the elements in the document.

For example -

```
<style type="text/css">
 * {
 color:green;
 }
 </style>
```

2. Class Selector

Using class selector we can assign different styles to the same element. These different styles appear on different occurrences of that element.

For example :

```
<style type="text/css">
 h1.RedText
 {
  font-family:Monotype Corsiva;
  color:red;
  font-size: 14pt;
 }
 h1.BlueText
 {
  font-family:Arial;
  color:blue;
  font-size: 10pt;
 }
</style>
```

Using the **dot Operator** particular class is defined

Q.22 List the ways of positioning an element within a browser window. **AU : Dec.-12**

Ans. : There are three ways of positioning the element within the browser window. These are -

1. Absolute positioning 2. Relative positioning 3. Float positioning

Q.23 Give example for inline style sheet. **AU : May-13**

Ans. : Using the style tag we can embed the css style within the web document. Such type of style sheet is called inline style sheet. For example -

```
<html>
<head>
 <style type="text/css">
  h1
   {
    color:green
   }
 </style>
</head>
<body>
 <h1> This page contains an inline style sheet</h1>
</body>
</html>
```

Q.24 Define cascading.

Ans. : Cascading is the collection of rules that the browsers use to determine how to use the style information.

Q.25 What are different variations of CSS ?

Ans. : 1) CSS 1 2) CSS 2 3) CSS 2.1 4) CSS 3 5) CSS 4

Q.26 What are the features of CSS3 ?

Ans. : Various features of CSS3 are -

1. It allows simple arithmetic calculations using calc() function.
2. There are many powerful selectors available using which the style sheet can be fancy.
3. There is introduction of new pseudo classes such as only-child, empty, root, first-child, after, before.
4. It supports 2D/3D transformations.
5. It has a support for multiple backgrounds. The background-size property is also introduced in CSS3. That means designer can specify the size of background image using either length or percentage.

Q.27 Write appropriate inline CSS to show a section of the HTML document with a font size 20. **AU : May-16**

Ans. : The inline CSS can be written with the tag **style**.

```
<!DOCTYPE html>
<html>
<head>
    <title>Display Section with Specific Font Size</title>
</head>
<body>
    <div style="font-size:20px;">
  India is my country.All Indians are my brothers and sisters.I love my country, and I am proud of its rich and varied heritage.I shall always strive to be worthy of it.I shall respect my parents, teachers and all elders and treat everyone with courtesy.To my country and my people, I pledge my devotion.In their well being and prosperity alone lies my happiness.
</div>
</body>
```

Q.28 List out the limitations of CSS **AU : May-18**

Ans. : 1) CSS work differently on different browser.

2) One can not read files using CSS.

3) It is unable to interact with CSS.

4) The CSS can not invoke a web page.

❑❑❑

Notes

Unit II

4 Client Side Programming

Syllabus

Java Script : An introduction to JavaScript – JavaScript DOM Model–Date and Objects, –Regular Expressions – Exception Handling – Validation – Built-in objects – Event Handling – DHTML with JavaScript – JSON introduction – Syntax – Function Files – Http Request – SQL.

Contents

Part I : Introduction to JavaScript

4.1 Features of JavaScript

Following are some features of JavaScript

1. **Browser Support :** For running the JavaScript in the browser there is no need to use some plug-in. Almost all the popular browsers support JavaScripting.
2. **Structure Programming Syntax:** The Javascript supports much commonly the structured language type syntax. Similar to C-style the programming blocks can be written.
3. It automatically inserts the semicolon at the end of the statement, hence there is no need to write semicolon at the end of the statement in JavaScript.
4. **Dynamic Typing :** It supports dynamic typing, that means the data type is bound to the value and not to the variable. For example one can assign integer value to a variable say 'a' and later on can assign some strg the ing value to the same variable in JavaScript.
5. **Run Time Evaluation :** Using the **eval** function the expression can be evaluated at run time.
6. **Support for Object :** JavaScript is object oriented scripting language. However handling of objects in JavaScript is somewhat different that the conventional object oriented programming languages. JavaScript has a small number of in-built objects.
7. **Regular Expression :** JavaScript supports use of regular expressions using which the text-pattern matching can be done. This feature can be used to validate the data on the web page before submitting it to the server.
8. **Function Programming :** In JavaScript functions are used. One function can accept another function as a parameter. Even, one function can be assigned to a variable just like some data type. The function can be run without giving the name.

4.2 Writing First JavaScript

The JavaScript can be directly embedded within the HTML document or it can be stored as external file.

Directly embedded JavaScript

The syntax of directly embedding the JavaScript in the HTML is

```
<script type="text/javascript">
        ...
        ...
        ...
</script>
```

Ex. 4.2.1 : Write a JavaScript to display Welcome message in JavaScript

Sol. :

```
<!DOCTYPE html >
<html >
```

```
    <head>
        <title> My First Javascript </title>
    </head>
    <body>
        <center>
        <script type="text/javascript">
        /*This is the First JavaScript*/
        document.write(" Welcome to First Page of Javascript");
        </script>
        </center>
    </body>
</html>
```

Output

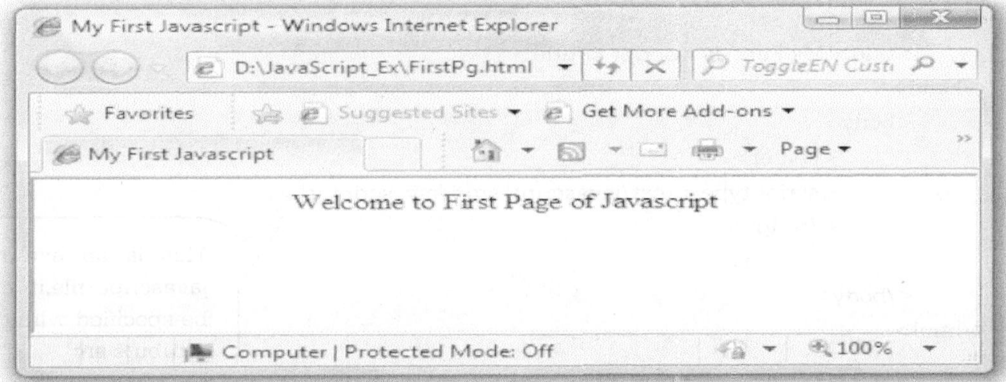

Script Explanation :

In above script

(1) we have embedded the javaScript within

```
<script type="text/javascript">
...
</script>
```

(2) a comment statement using /* and */. Note that this type of comment will be recognized only within the <script> tag. Because, JavaScript supports this kind of comment statement and not the XHTML document.

(3) Then we have written document.write statement, using which we can display the desired message on the web browser.

Indirectly Embedding JavaScript

If we want to embed the JavaScript indirectly, that means if the script is written in some another file and we want to embed that script in the HTML document then we must write the script tag as follows -

```
<script type="text/javascript" src="MyPage.js">
    ...


    ...
    ...
</script>
```

Javascript is which is to be embedded is in the file **MyPage.js**

We will follow the following steps to use the external JavaScript file.

Step 1 : Create an XHTML document as follows -

XHTML Document[FirstPg.html]

```
<!DOCTYPE html >
<html>
    <head>
        <title> My First Javascript </title>
    </head>
        <body>
            <center>
            <script type="text/javascript" src="my_script.js">
            </script>
            </center>
        </body>
    </html>
```

This is an external javascript file,it can be specified with the attribute **src**

Step 2 :

JavaScript[my_script.js]

```
/*This is the First JavaScript*/
        document.write(" Welcome to First Page of Javascript");
```

Step 3 : Open the HTML document in Internet Explorer and same above mentioned output can be obtained.

Advantages of indirectly embedding of JavaScript

1. Script can be hidden from the browser user.
2. The layout and presentation of web document can be separated out from the user interaction through the JavaScript.

Disadvantages of indirectly embedding of JavaScript

1. If small amount of JavaScript code has to be embedded in XHTML document then making a separate JavaScript file is meaningless.
2. If the JavaScript code has to be embedded at several places in XHTML document then it is

complicated to make separate JavaScript file and each time invoking the code for it from the XHTML document.

4.3 Identifier, Keywords and Comments

1. Identifiers

Identifiers are the names given to the variables. These variables hold the data value. Following are some conventions used in JavaScript for handling the identifiers -

1. Identifiers must begin with either letter or underscore or dollar sign. It is then followed by any number of letters, underscores, dollars or digits.
2. There is no limit on the length of identifiers.
3. The letters in the identifiers are case-sensitive. That means the identifier INDEX, Index, index, inDex are considered to be distinct.
4. Programmer defined variable names must not have upper case letters.

2. Reserved words

Reserved words are the special words associated with some meaning. Various reserve words that are used in JavaScript are enlisted as below –

break	Continue	delete	for	in	return	throw	var	with
case	default	else	function	instanceof	switch	try	void	
catch	do	finally	if	new	this	typeof	while	

3. Comments

JavaScript supports following comments

1. The // i.e a single line comment can be used in JavaScript.
2. The /* and */ can be used as a multi-line comment.
3. The XHTML <!--> and <--> is also allowed in JavaScript

4. Semicolon

While writing the JavaScript the web programmer must give semicolon at the end of the statements.

4.4 Data Types

JavaScript defines two entities primitives and objects. The primitives are for storing the values whereas the object is for storing the reference to the actual value.

There are following primitive types used in JavaScript

1. Number 2. String 3. Boolean
4. Undefined 5. Null

There are three type of predefined objects in JavaScript

1. Number 2. String 3. Boolean

These objects are called **wrapper objects**. These wrapper objects provide properties and methods which can be used by primitive types.

Fig. 4.4.1 (a) Representation of primitive type

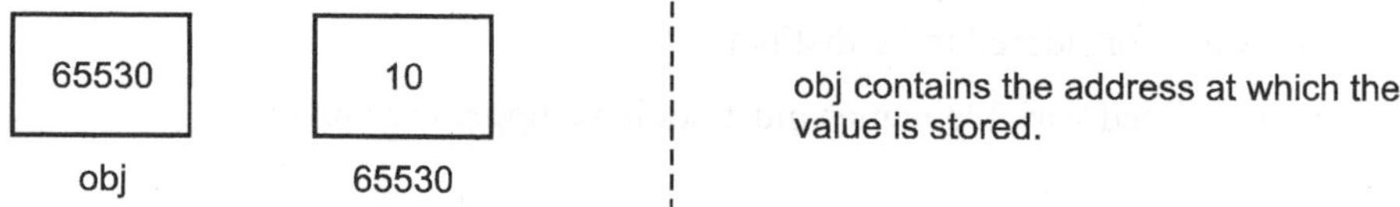

Fig. 4.4.1 (b) Representation of object

4.5 Variable

In JavaScript we can declare the variable using the reserved word var. The value of this variable can be any thing; it can be numeric or it can be string or it can be a Boolean value.

JavaScript[VarDemo.html]

```
<!DOCTYPE html >
<html >
 <head>
 <title> Variables in Javascript </title>
</head>
 <body>
  <script type="text/javascript">
   var a,b,c;
   var string;
   a=2;
   b=3;
   c=a+b;
   string ="The result = ";
   document.write("Performing addition of 2 and 3.  "+"<br/>");
   document.write(string);
   document.write(c);
  </script>
</body>
</html>
```

Variable declaration is done using **var**. Note that there is no data type required for handling variables.

Output

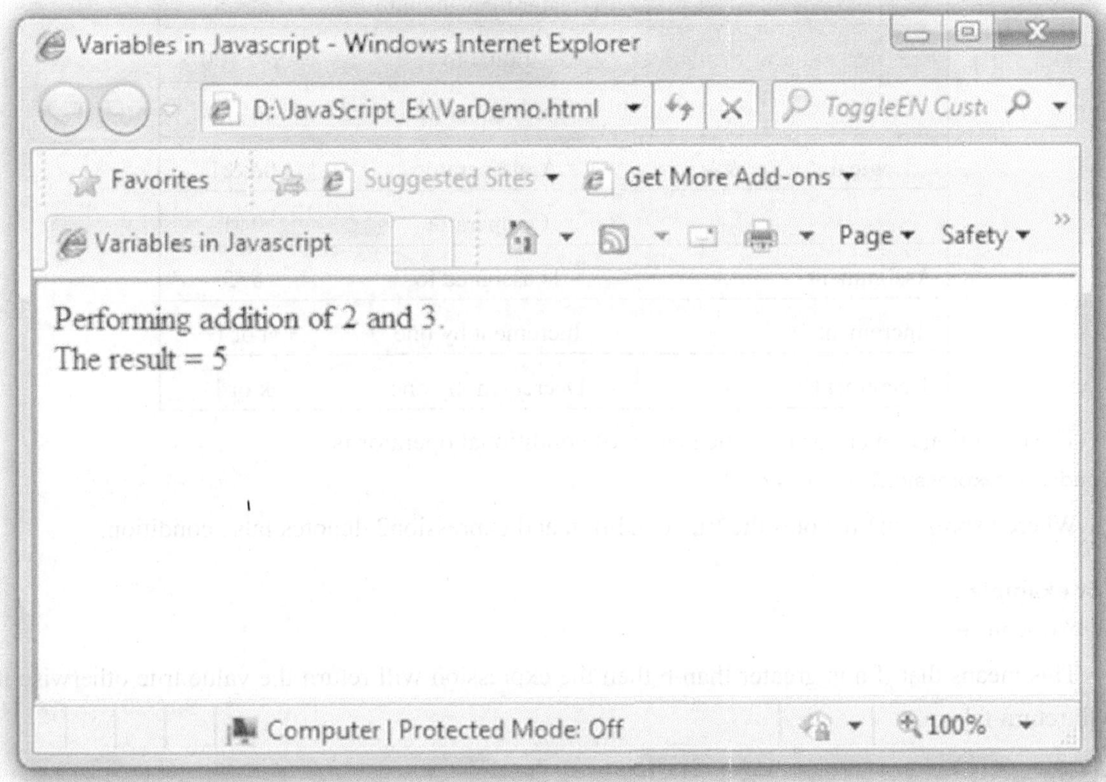

Note that using **var** we can define the variable which is of type numbers(2 , 3 or 5) as well as the string "The result".

4.6 Operators

Various operators used by JavaScript are as shown in following table -

Type	Operator	Meaning	Example
Arithmetic	+	Addition or unary plus	c = a+b
	–	Subtraction or unary minus	d = –a
	*	Multiplication	c=a*b
	/	Division	c=a/b
	%	Mod	c=a%b
Relational	<	Less than	a<4
	>	Greater than	b>10

	<=	Less than equal to	b<=10
	>=	Greater than equal to	a>=5
	==	Equal to	x==100
	!=	Not equal to	m!=8
Logical	&&	And operator	0&&1
	||	Or operator	0 ||1
Assignment	=	Is assigned to	a=5
Increment	++	Increment by one	++i or i++
Decrement	--	Decrement by one	– – k or k– –

The conditional operator is ? The syntax of conditional operator is

```
Condition?expression1:expression 2
```

Where expression1 denotes the true condition and expression2 denotes false condition.

For example :

```
a>b?true:false
```

This means that if a is greater than b then the expression will return the value true otherwise it will return false.

4.6.1 String Concatenation Operator

Two string can be concatenated using the + operator. A variable can be concatenated with the string using + operator also.

JavaScript[StrOper.html]

```
<!DOCTYPE html >
<html >
 <head>
  <title>String Concatenation Demo</title>
</head>
<body>
 <center>
  <script type="text/javascript">
   var first_string;
   first_string="Programming";
   document.write("<h3>"+first_string+" the web"+"</h3>");
  </script>
 </center>
</body>
</html>
```

Output

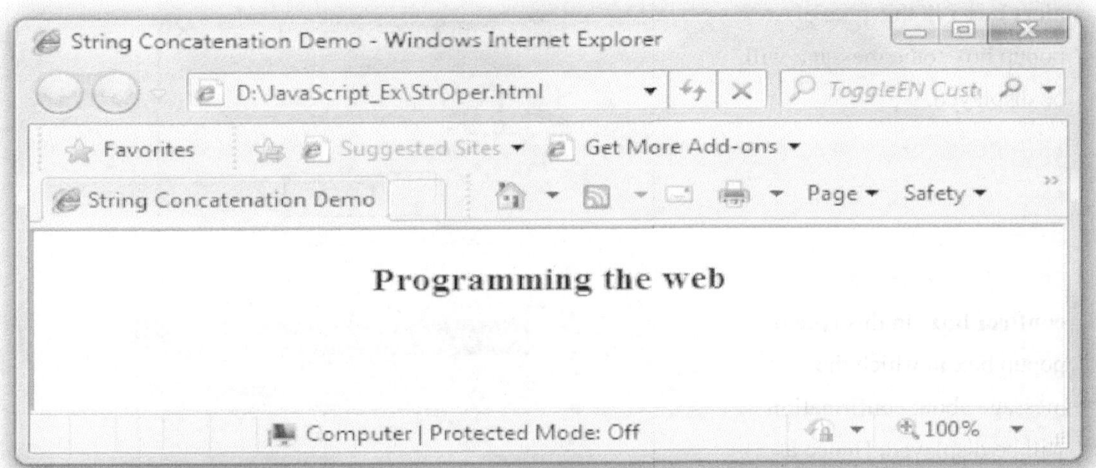

4.7 Input and Output

4.7.1 The document.write

- For displaying the message on the web browser the basic method being used is **document.write**. To print the desired message on the web browser we write the message in double quotes inside the document.write method.
- **For example**

```
document.write("Great India");
```

- We can pass the variable instead of a string as a parameter to the document.write.

For example

```
var my_msg="Great India";
document.write(my_msg);
```

Note that the variable my_msg should not be passed in double quotes to document.write otherwise the result the string "my_msg" will be printed on the browser instead of the string "Great India" .

- We can combine some HTML tags with the variable names in document.write so that the formatted display can be possible on the web browser.

For example – if we want to print the message "Great India" on the web browser in bold font then we can write following statements-

```
var my_msg="Great_India";
document.write("<strong>"+my_msg+"</strong>");
```

4.7.2 Popup Box

- One of the important features of JavaScript is its **interactivity** with the user.
- There are **three types of popup boxes** used in JavaScript by which user can interact with the browser.

alert box : In this type of popup box some message will be displayed.	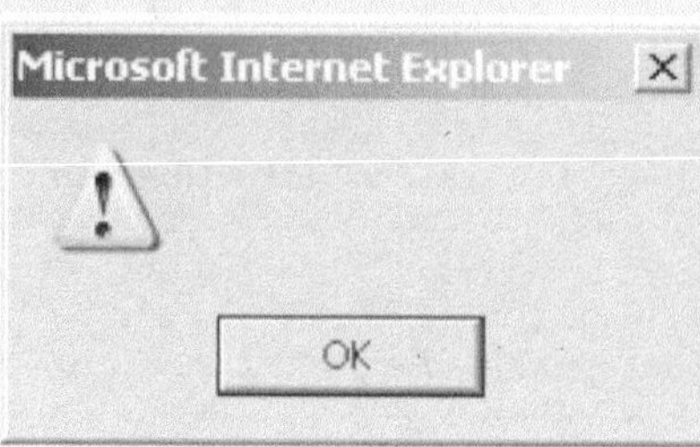
confirm box: In this type of popup box in which the message about confirmation will be displayed. Hence it should have two buttons **Ok** and **Cancel.**	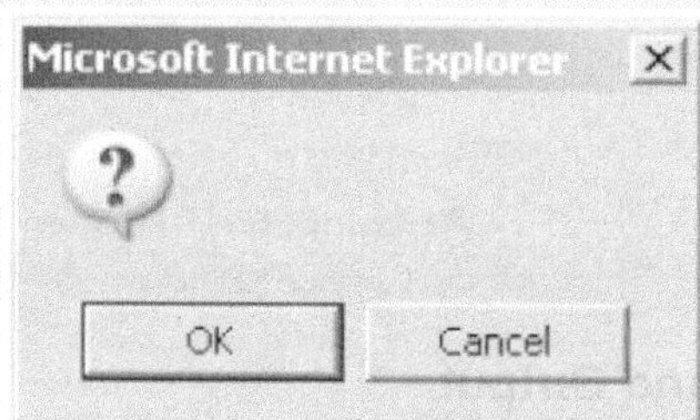
Prompt box is a type of popup box which displays a text window in which the user can enter something. Hence it has two buttons **Ok** and **Cancel**.	

JavaScript[PopupBox.html]

```
<!DOCTYPE html>
<html >
 <head>
   <title>Introduction to pop up box</title>
</head>
<body>
<p>Experiment with the popup boxes by clicking the buttons(OK and Cancel) on them</p>

   <script type="text/javascript">
    if(confirm("do you agree?"))
       alert("You have agreed");
    else
       input_text=prompt("Enter some string here..."," ");
    /*the value entered in prompt box is returned
    and stored in the variable text */
       alert("Hi "+input_text);
```

```
    </script>
</body>
</html>
```

Output

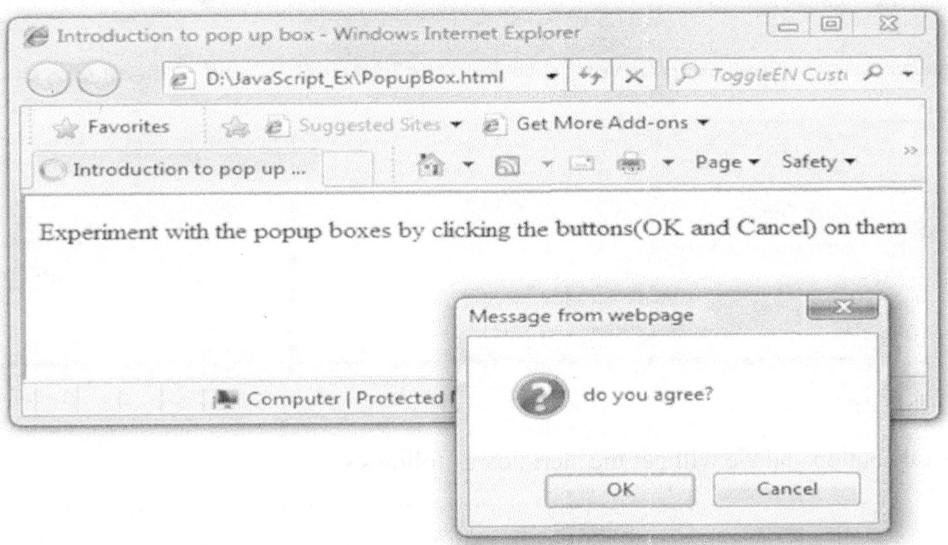

If we click on OK button then an alert box will appear.

On load, the confirm box appears and if we click on Cancel button then the prompt box will appear. We can type some string within it.

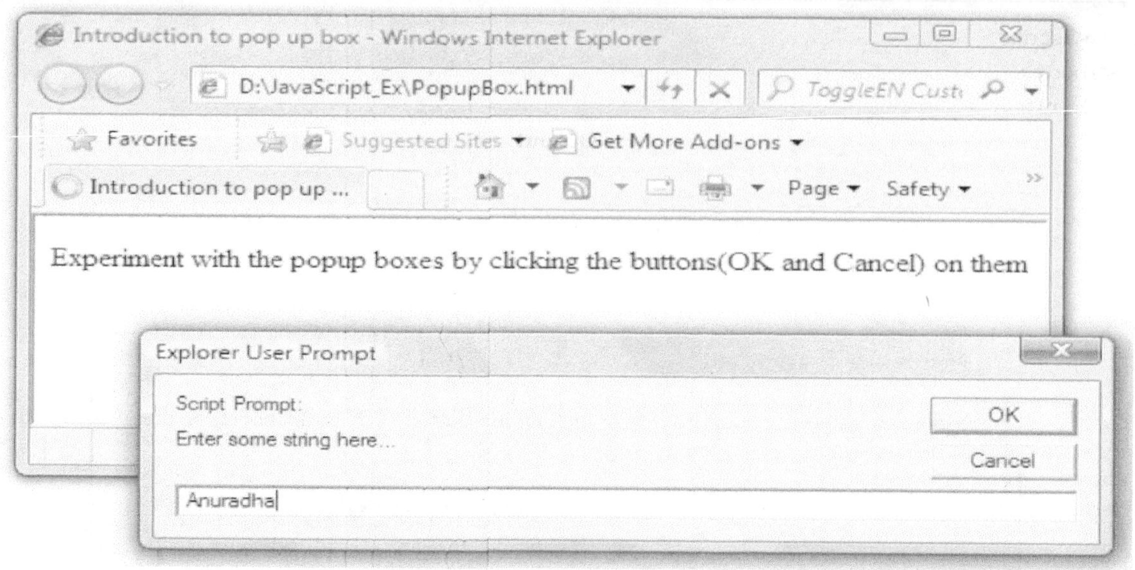

Click OK button and we will get the alert box as follows -

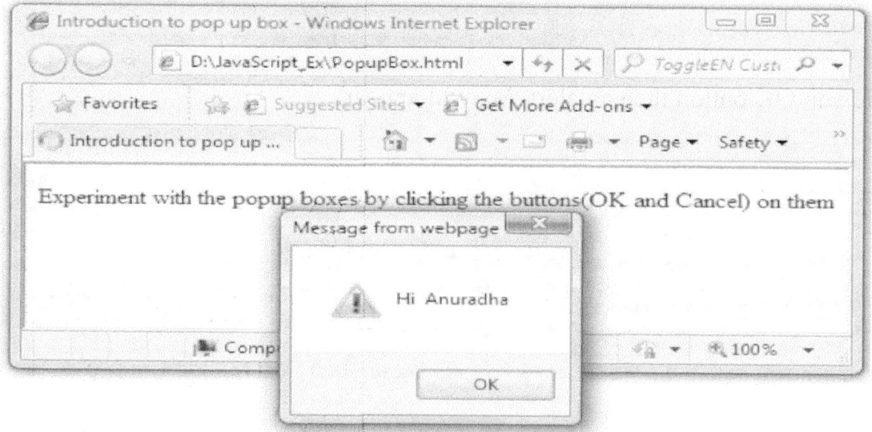

Thus alert, confirm and prompt boxes cause the browser to wait for user response. The user responds by clicking the button on these popup boxes.

Script Explanation

On loading this script using web browser first of all a confirm box will be displayed. If we click on OK button an alert box will appear. Otherwise a prompt box will be displayed. Again if we click on the OK button of prompt box again an alert box will appear which will display the string which you have entered on prompt box. If you run the above script you will get all these effects.

4.8 Control Structures

AU : Dec.-08,18, May- 10, 11, Marks 9

Various control structures used in JavaScript are

Statement	syntax	Example

if-else	if(condition)
	statement
	else
	statement
		if(a>b)
		document.write(" a is greater than b");
		else
		document.write("b is greater than a");

while	while(condition)
	{
	statements
	}
		while(i<5)
		{
		i=i+1;
		document.write("value of i"+i)
		}

do..while	do
	{
	}while(condition);
		do
		{
		i=i+1;
		document.write("value of i"+i)
		}while(i<5);

for	for(initialization;test condition;stepcount)
	{
	statements
	}
		for(i=0;i<5;i++)
		{
		document.write(i);
		}

switch...case	switch(expression)
	{
	case 1: statements
	break;
	case 2: statements
	break;
	...
	default:
	statements
	}
		switch(choice)
		{
		case 1: c=a+b;
		break;
		case 2:c=a-b;
		break;
		}

break :
Similar to C or C++, the break statement is used to break the loop.
	break;	for(i=10;i>=0;i--)
		{
		if(i==5)
		break;
		}

continue:
The continue statement is used in a loop in order to continue(skip). The keyword **continue** is used to make use of continue statement in a loop.
	continue;	for(i=10;i>=0;i--)
		{
		if(i==5)
		{
		x=i;
		continue;
		}

Control structure is essential part of JavaScript. The Control Structures in JavaScript are just similar to that of C or C++. Various control structures are -

1. if statement 2. While 3. Do-while 4. for
5. switch case 6. break 7. Continue

Let us discuss various examples that make use of control structures.

Ex. 4.8.1 : Develop a javascript to generate 'ARMSTRONG NUMBERS' between the range 1 to 100. [Eg : 153 is an Armstrong number, since sum of the cube of the digits is equal to the number i.e. [13+53+33=153]

Sol. :

```
<html>
<body>
<table border="1" allign="center">
<th>Armstrong Numbers</th>
<script type="text/javascript">
var num,i,temp,sum;
var n=0;
i=1;
do
{
 num=i;
 sum=0;
 while(num>0)
 {
  n=num%10;
  n=parseInt(n);
  num=num/10;
  num=parseInt(num);
  sum=sum+(n*n*n);
 }
 if(sum==i)
 {
  document.write("<tr><td>"+i+"</td></tr>");
 }
 i++;
}while(i<=1000);
</script>
</table>
</body>
</html>
```

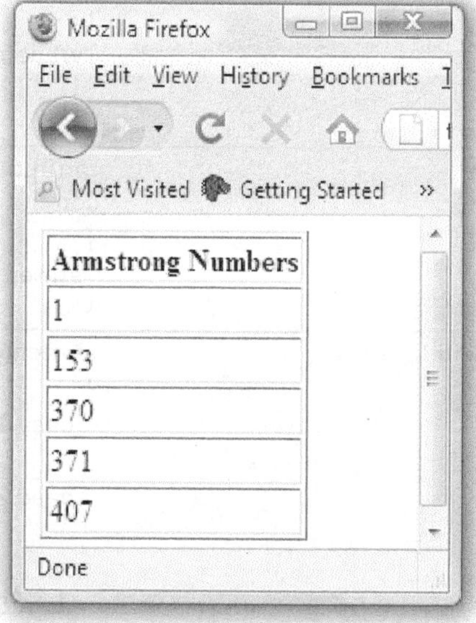

Ex. 4.8.2 : Write a javascript that displays the as per following :

(Calculate the squares and cubes of the numbers from 0 to 10)

Number	Square	Cube
1	1	1
2	4	8
3	9	27
4	16	64
5	25	125
6	36	216
7	49	343
8	64	512
9	81	729
10	100	1000

Sol. :

```
<html>
<head>
<title>Sqaure and Cube value table</title>
</head>
<body>
<table border=1 align="center">
<th>Number</th><th>Square</th><th>Cube</th>
<script type="text/javascript">
for (i=1; i<=10; i++)
{
document.write("<tr><td>"+i+"</td><td>"+(i*i)+"</td><td>"+(i*i*i)+"</td></tr>");
}
</script>
</table>
</body>
</html>
```

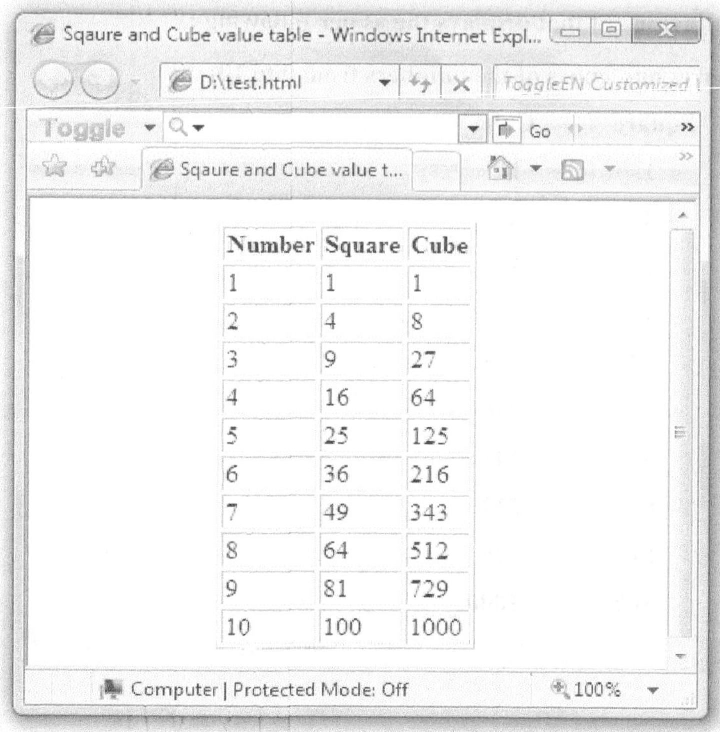

Number	Square	Cube
1	1	1
2	4	8
3	9	27
4	16	64
5	25	125
6	36	216
7	49	343
8	64	512
9	81	729
10	100	1000

Ex. 4.8.3 : Write a script that reads an integer and displays whether it is a prime number or not.

Sol. :

```
<html>
  <head>
   <title>PRIME NUMBER DEMO</title>
  </head>
 <body>
   <script type="text/javascript">
   var num=prompt("Type number here.","");
   var b;
   var flag=1;
   for(i=2;i<num;i++)
   {
     b=num%i;
     if(b==0)
     {
      flag=0;

     break;
     }
   }
```

```
    if(flag==0)
      alert(num+" is not a prime number");
    else
      alert(num+" is a prime number");
</script>
</body>
</html>
```

Output

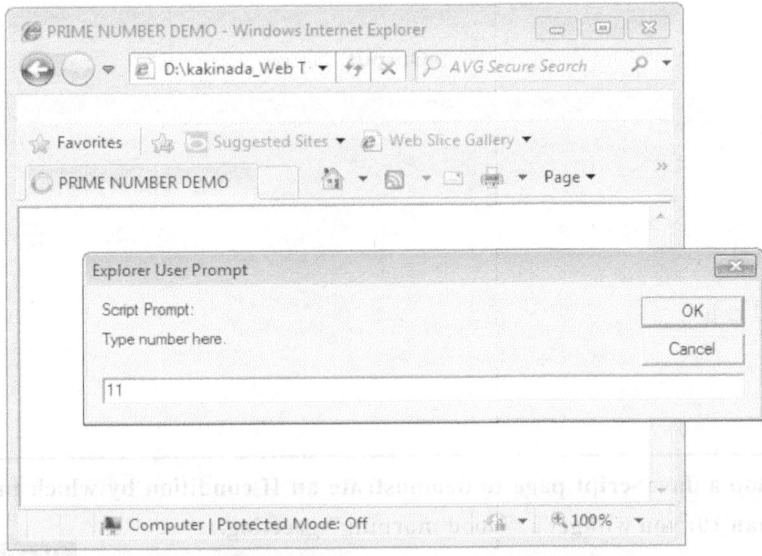

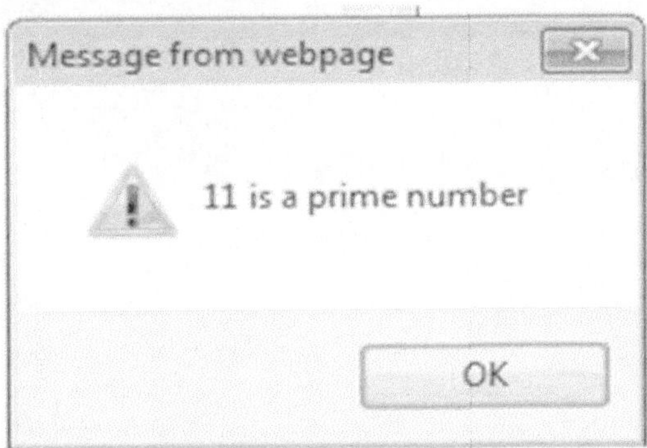

Ex. 4.8.4 : Write a JAVAScript to print characters of a string at odd positions. (for example for the string India, I, d and a should get printed).

Sol. :

```
<html>
<body>
<script>
var str="India";
var k=str.length;
```

```
for(i=0;i<=k;i=i+2)
{
 n=str.charAt(i);
 document.write(n);
 document.write(" ");
}
</script>
</body>
</html>
```

Output

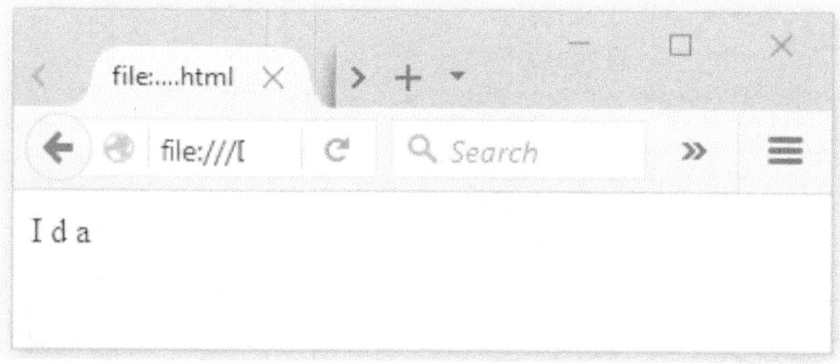

Ex. 4.8.5 : Develop a JavaScript page to demonstrate an If condition by which the time on your browser is less than 10; you will get a "Good morning" greeting.

AU : Dec.-08, Marks 2

Sol. : Goodmorning.html

```
<html>
<head>
<script type="text/javascript">
function GreetMsg()
{
 var today=new Date();
 var h=today.getHours();
 var m=today.getMinutes();
 var s=today.getSeconds();
 if(h<10)
  alert("Good Morning!!!(Time "+h+":"+m+":"+s+")");
 else
  alert("Have a Good Day!!!(Time "+h+":"+m+":"+s+")");
}
</script>
</head>
<body onload="GreetMsg()">
</body>
</html>
```

Output

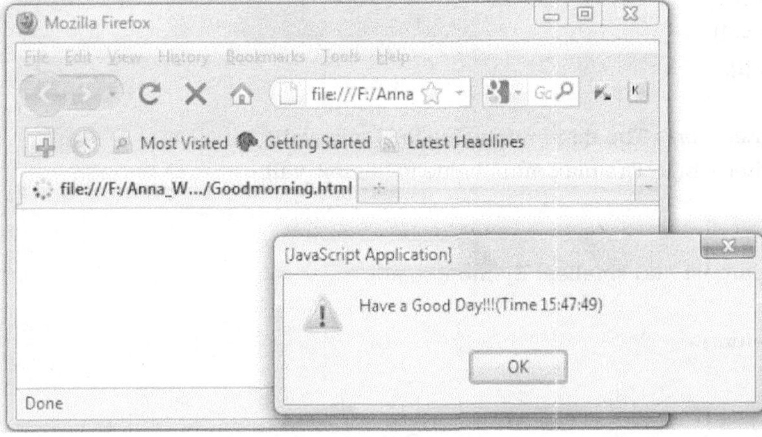

Ex. 4.8.6 : Write a JavaScript to find and print the largest and smallest values among 10 elements of an array.

AU : May-10, Marks 8

Sol. : largestsmallest.html

```
<html>
 <head>
 <script type="text/javascript">
  function fun()
  {
   a=new Array(10);
   a[0]=20;
   a[1]=10;
   a[2]=-1;
   a[3]=50;
   a[4]=70;
   a[5]=120;
   a[6]=40;
   a[7]=60;
   a[8]=90;
   a[9]=100;
   document.write("<br/>The elements of array are...<br/>");
   max_val=a[0];
   for(i=0;i<10;i++)
    document.write(" "+a[i]);
   min_val=a[0];
   max_val=a[0];
   for(i=0;i<10;i++)

   {
```

```
      if(a[i]<min_val)
        min_val=a[i];
      if(a[i]>max_val)
        max_val=a[i];
    }
    document.write("<br/>The minimum value is "+min_val);
    document.write("<br/>The maximum value is "+max_val);
  }
  </script>
 <title>Finding largest and smallest Element</title>
 </head>
 <body onload=fun()>
 </body>
</html>
```

Output

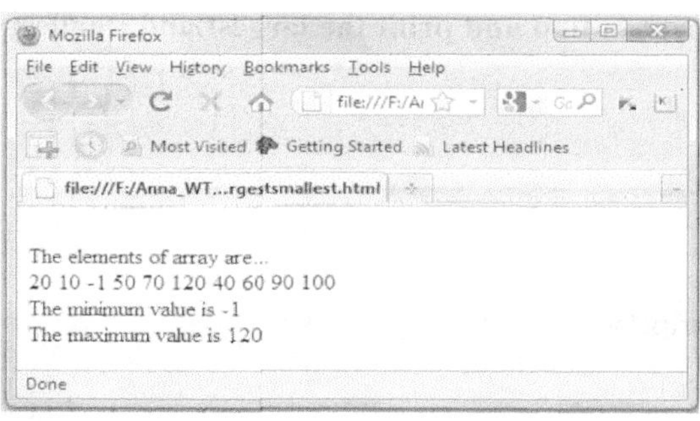

Ex. 4.8.7 : Write a JavaScript to find the product of first 15 even numbers.

Sol. :

```
<html>
<body>
<script type="text/javascript">
prod=1;
for(i=1;i<15;i++)
{
    if(i%2)
    {
     prod=prod*i;
    }
}
document.write("Product of odd numbers between 1 to 15 is "+prod);
</script>
</body>
</html>
```

Ex. 4.8.8 : Write a JavaScript program to print Prime Numbers from 1 to 100.

AU : Dec.-18, Marks 9

Sol. :

```
<!DOCTYPE html>
<html>
<head>
<script type="text/javascript">

function primeNumber(from, to){
          var flag=false;
          for(i = from; i <= to; i++)
        {
          for( j = 2; j < i; j++)
          {
            if(i % j == 0)
            {
                flag = false;
                break;
            }
            else
            {
                flag = true;
            }
          }
          if(flag)
          {
            document.write(" "+i);
          }
        }
  }
</script>
</head>
<body>
<h4> Prime Numbers from 1 to 100 are...</h4>
<script type="text/javascript">
primeNumber(1, 100)
</script>
</body>
</html>
```

Output

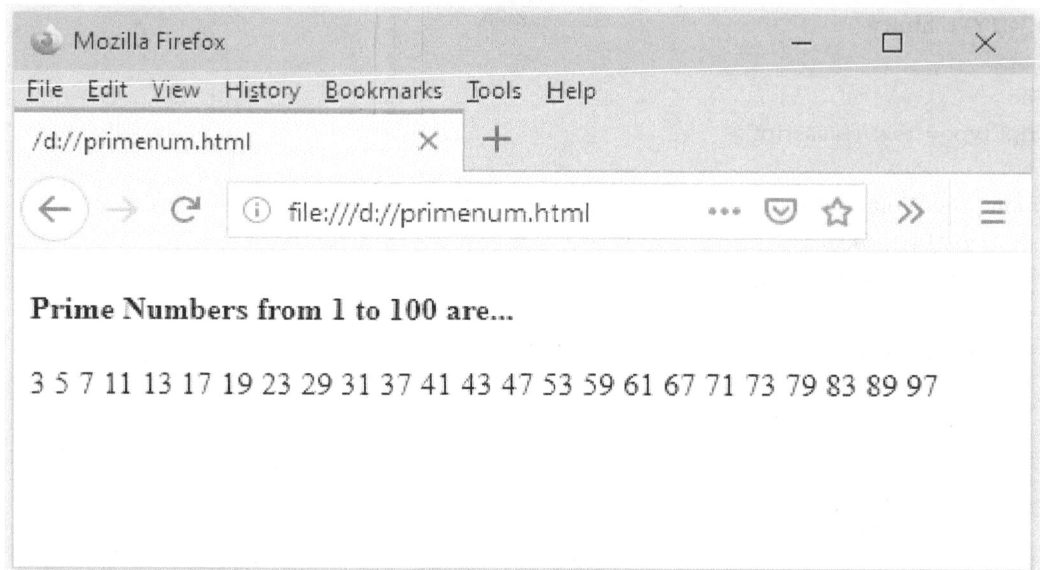

University Question

1. *State and explain the types of statements in JavaScript.* **AU : May-11, Marks 8**

4.9 Functions

AU : Dec.-07, 08, May-11,12,13, Marks 16

- We can write the functions in the JavaScript for bringing the modularity in the script.
- Separate functions can be created for each separate task. This ultimately helps in finding the bug from the program efficiently.
- We can define the function anywhere in the script either in head or body section or in both. But it is a standard practice to define the function in the head section and call that function from the body section.
- The keyword **function** is used while defining the function.
- The syntax for defining the function is

```
function name_of _function (arg1,arg2,...argn)
{
 ...
 Statements
}
```

Here is a simple illustration in which we have written a function **my_fun()**

JavaScript[FunDemo.html]

```
<!DOCTYPE html>
<html>
```

```
<head>
 <title>Function Demo</title>
 <script type="text/javascript">
  function my_fun()
  {
    document.write("This statement is within the function");    } Definition of function
  }
</script>
</head>
<body>
<center>
  <script type="text/javascript">
    document.write("This statement is before a function call");
    document.write("<br>");
    my_fun();
  call to the function
  </script>
</center>
</body>
</html>
```

Output

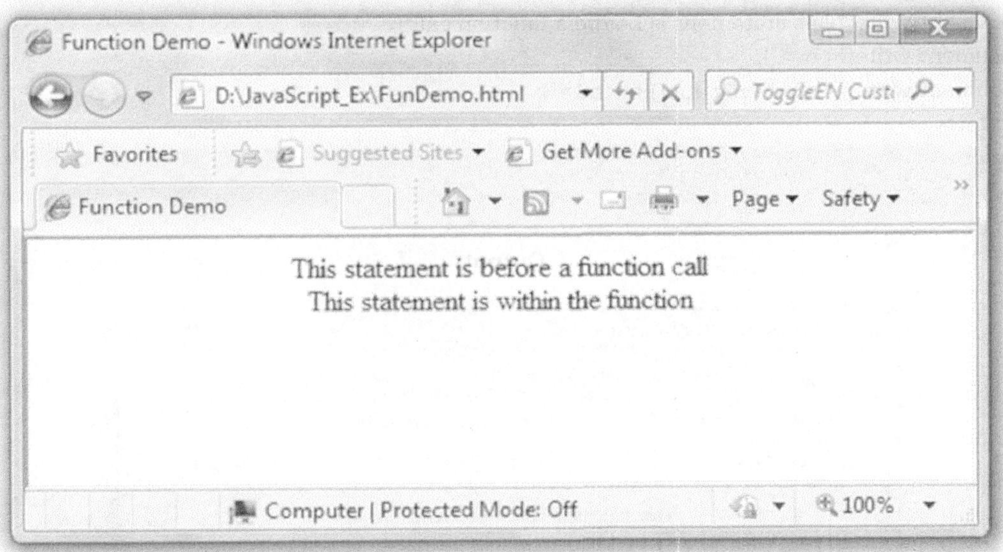

Script Explanation

The above code is pretty simple. We have defined one function named **my_fun** in the **head** section of the HTML document and called it from the **body** section. The corresponding **write** statements are used to display the messages on the browser window.

4.9.1 Returning Value from the Function

- We can return some value from the function using a keyword **return**.
- This return value is either stored in variable or directly displayed on the browser window.
- Following is a simple illustration in which the value is returned from the function and is directly displayed on the browser window using **document.write.**

JavaScript[FunRetDemo.html]

```
<!DOCTYPE html>
<html>
<head>
 <title>Function Demo</title>
 <script type="text/javascript">
  function my_fun()
  {
    str="I am function returned value";
    return str;
  }
</script>
</head>
<body>
<center>
 <script type="text/javascript">
   document.write("This statement is before a function call");
   document.write("<br>");
   document.write("<h3>"+my_fun()+"<h3>");
 </script>
</center>
</body>
</html>
```

Output

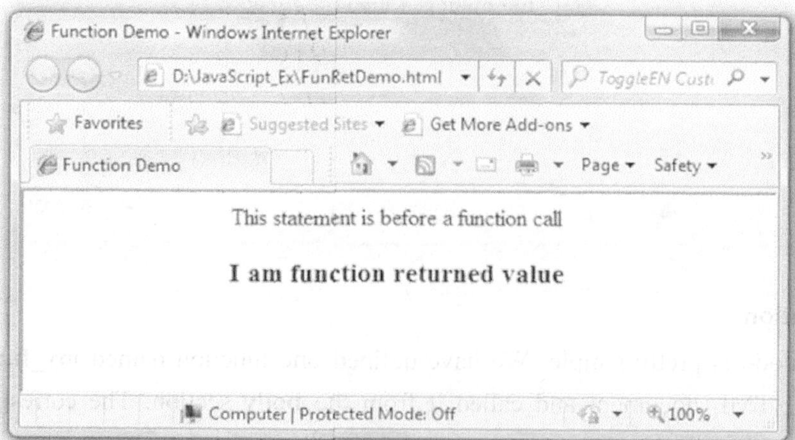

4.9.2 Passing the Parameters to the Function

- Similarly we can pass some arguments to the function.
- The syntax is

```
function function_name(aregument1, argument2...,argumentn)
{
//body of function
}
```

- In the following program, we have passed two arguments to the function and returning some value from the function.

JavaScript[FunPassRet.html]

```
<!DOCTYPE html >
<html>
 <head>
 <title>Function Demo</title>
 <script type="text/javascript">
  function my_fun(str1,str2)//two atrguments str1 and str2 are passed
  {
    str="I am function returned value."+" "+str1+" "+str2 ;
    return str; //returning one string value from function
  }
</script>
</head>
<body>
<center>
 <script type="text/javascript">
   document.write("This statement is before a function call");
   document.write("<br>");
   document.write("<h3>"+my_fun("Hello!!","How are to you?")+"<h3>");
 </script>
</center>
</body>
</html>
```

Output

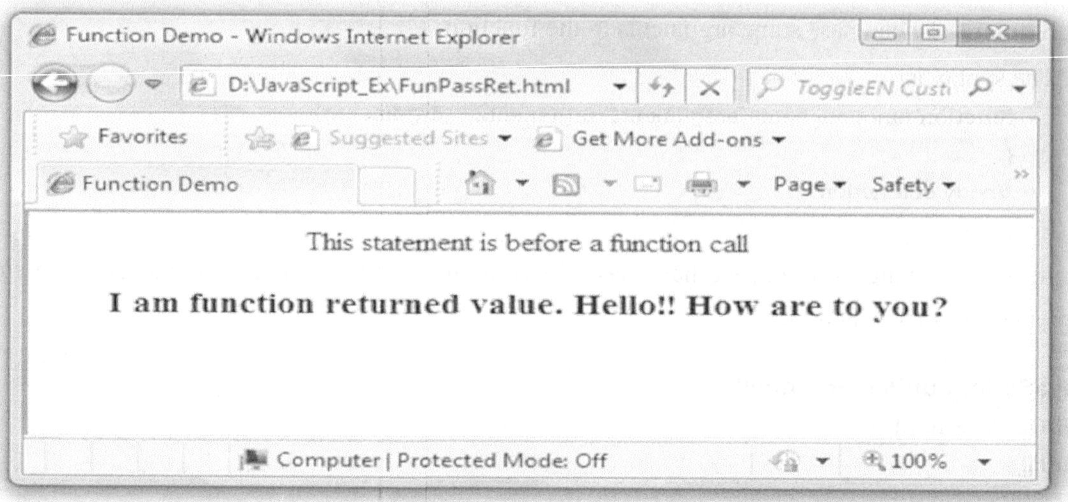

4.9.3 Passing an Array to the Function

- Similar to C or C++ we can pass an entire array as a parameter to the function.
- This method of array passing is called as **call by reference.**
- When an array is passed to the function the array name is simply passed.
- In the following JavaScript we have initialized an array in the body part and to display those contents of an array we have called a **display()** function. And to this function an array is passed as an argument. Let see the JavaScript.

JavaScript[FunPassArr.html]

```
<!DOCTYPE html>
<html>
<head>
 <title>Passing an Array to the function</title>
 <script type="text/javascript">
  function display(a)
  {
   document.write("The contents of the array are..."+"<br>");
   i=0;
   for(i in a)
   {
    document.write(a[i]+"<br>");
    i++;
   }
  }
</script>
</head>
<body>
```

Function definition with array as an argument

```
<center>
 <script type="text/javascript">
  var ar=new Array(10);
  for(i=0;i<=9;i++)
  {
    ar[i]=i;
  }
  display(ar);         Function call
 </script>
</center>
</body>
</html>
```

In above given script we have called a **display** function by passing an array as a parameter to it. Hence we will get following output.

Output

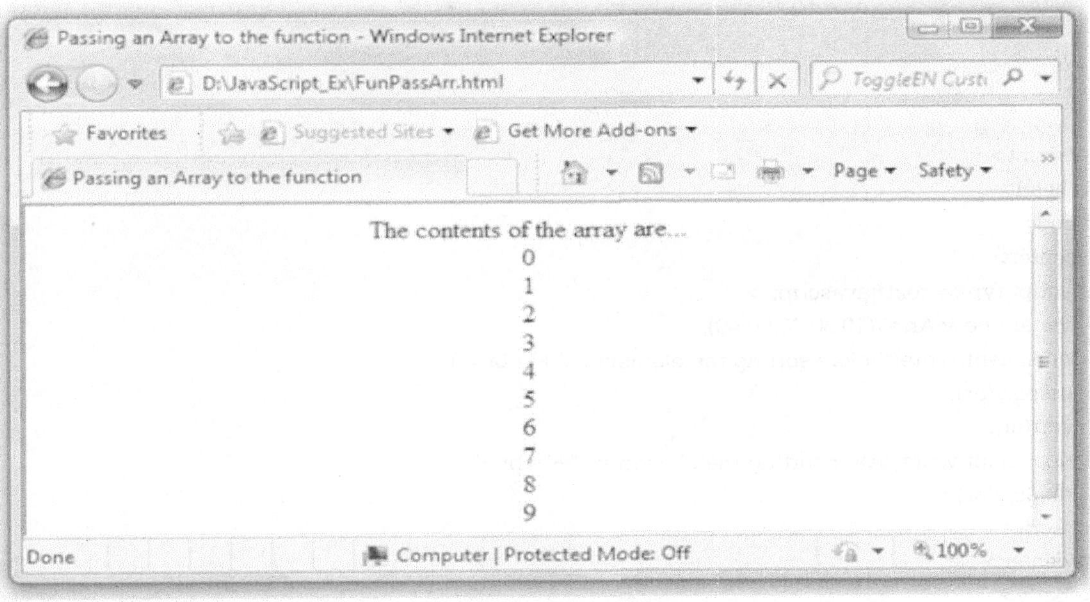

Ex. 4.9.1 : Write a JavaScript to sort the elements of an array in ascending order

Sol. :

```
<!DOCTYPE html>
<html>
<head>
 <title>Sorting the Numbers</title>
 <script type="text/javascript">
 function display(a)
 {
  i=0;
  for(i in a)
```

```
  {
  document.write(a[i]+"<br>");
  i++;
  }
 }
 function sort(a)
 {
  for(i=0;i<a.length-1;i++)
  {
  for(j=i+1;j<a.length;j++)
  {
   if(a[i]>a[j])
   {
    temp=a[i];
    a[i]=a[j];
    a[j]=temp;
   }
  }
 }
 }
</script>
</head>
<body>
<center>
 <script type="text/javascript">
  var ar=new Array(10,30,20,50,40);
  document.write("Before sorting the elements..."+"<br>");
  display(ar);
  sort(ar);
  document.write("After sorting the elements..."+"<br>");
  display(ar);
 </script>
</center>
</body>
</html>
```

Script Explanation

1. In the above program we have stored some values in the array in the body part.
2. Then in order to display the contents of an array we have called **display** function.
3. Then we have called one more function called **sort** in which the elements of an array are sorted.
4. Note that in the sort function we have used *length* property which returns total number of elements in an array.
5. The simple bubble sort method is used to sort the array in an ascending order.

6. Again the display function is called in order to display the sorted array.

Output

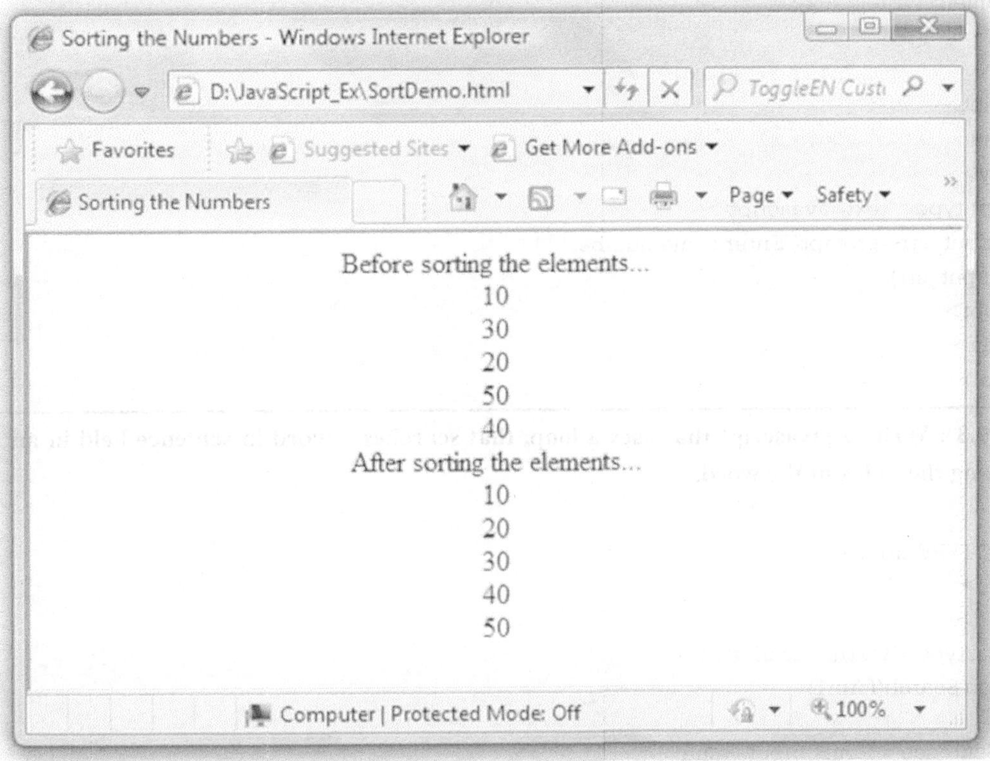

Ex. 4.9.2 : Write an HTML and JavaScript program which accepts N as input and displays first N Fibonacci numbers as list.

Sol. :

```
<!DOCTYPE html>
<html>
<head>
<script type="text/javascript">
function fun(str)
{
 var num=Number(str);
 var i,j,k,count;
 document.write("<h3>"+" The Fibonacci series is as follows..."+"</h3>");
 i=0;
 j=1;
 document.write(j);
 for(count=0;count<=num;count++)
 {
  k=i+j;
```

```
 i=j;
 j=k;
 document.write(","+k);
 }
}
</script>
</head>
<body>
<script type="text/javascript">
 var input_str=prompt("Enter some number","");
 fun(input_str);
</script>
</body>
</html>
```

Ex. 4.9.3 : Write a javascript that uses a loop, that searches a word in sentence held in an array, returning the index of the word.

Sol. :

```
<!DOCTYPE html>
<html >
 <head>
<script type="text/javascript">
function Search(form1)
{
 var Sentence= form1.input.value;
 var pattern=prompt("Enter the word to be searched for: ","");
 alert(pattern);
 temp=Sentence.split(" ");
 for(i=0;i<temp.length;i++)
 {
  if(temp[i]==pattern)
  {
   alert("The word is at position: "+(i+1));
  }
 }
}
</script>
</head>
<body>
<form name="form1">
 <b> Enter the sentence </b>
 <input type="text" name="input"><br/>
 <input type="button" value="Click Me" onclick="Search(form1)">
</form>
</body>
</html>
```

Output

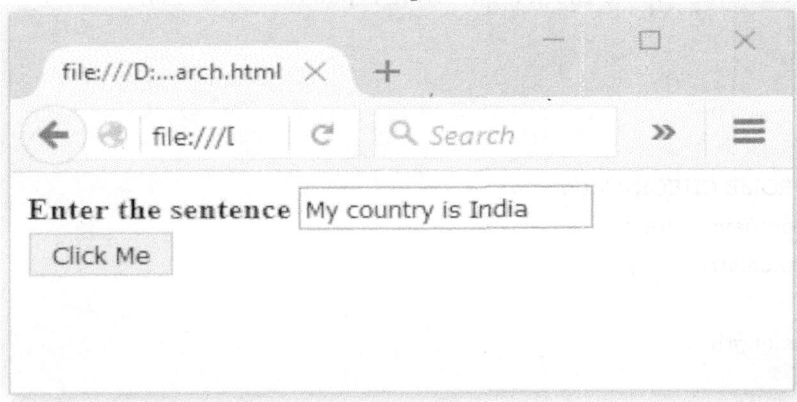
file:///D:...arch.html
file:///I
Search
Enter the sentence
My country is India
Click Me

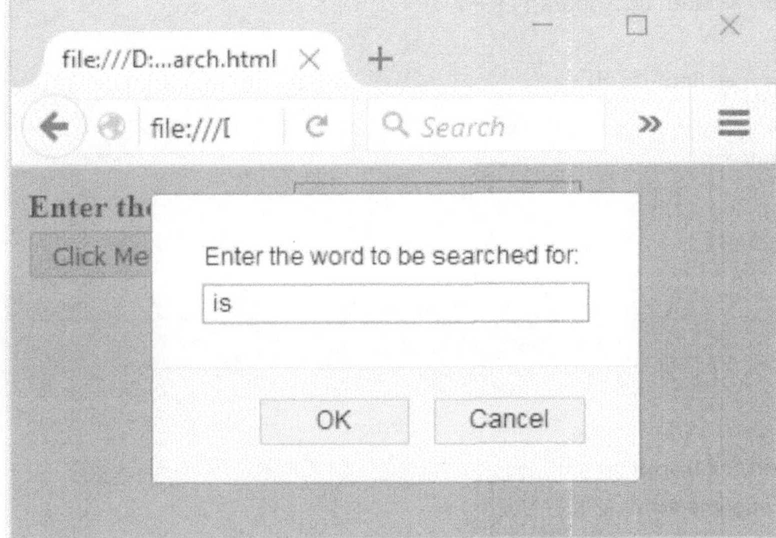
file:///D:...arch.html
file:///I
Search
Enter the word to be searched for:
is
OK
Cancel

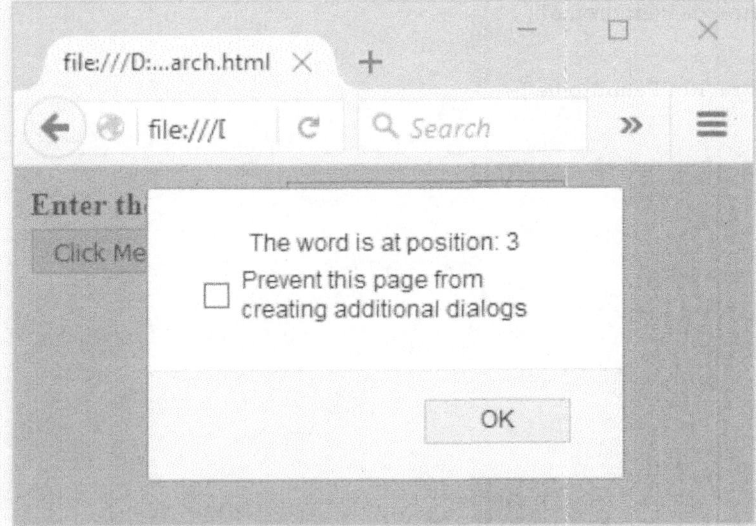
file:///D:...arch.html
file:///I
Search
The word is at position: 3
Prevent this page from creating additional dialogs
OK

Ex. 4.9.4 : Write a JavaScript to check input string is palindrome or not.

Sol. :

```
<html>
<head>
<title>PALINDROME CHECK</title>
<script type="text/javascript">
function palindrome(str)
{
    var len = str.length;

    for ( var i = 0; i < Math.floor(len/2); i++ )
    {
        if (str[i] !== str[len - 1 - i])
        {
            return false;
    }
        }
    return true;
}
</script>
</head>
<body>
<script type="text/javascript">
str=prompt("Enter some string","");
if(palindrome(str))
 document.write(str+" is Palindrome");
else
 document.write(str+"Not Palindrome");
</script>
</body>
</html>
```

Output

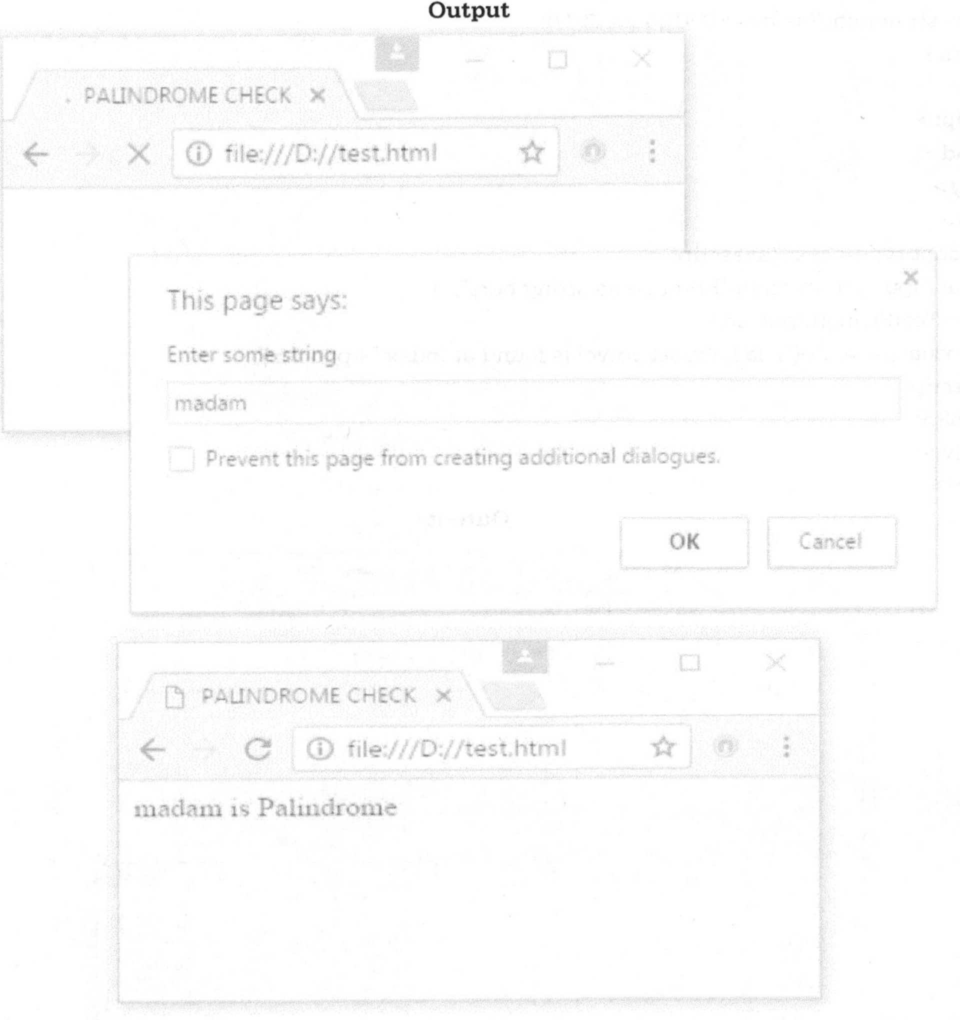

Ex. 4.9.5 : Develop and demonstrate a HTML file that includes JavaScript that uses a function for the following problems :

(a) Parameter : A string Output : The position of the string of the left-most vowel

(b) Parameter : A number Output : The number with digits in the reverse order.

Sol. : (a) [RegExpDemo4.html]

```
<!DOCTYPE html>
<html >
 <head>
<title>Pattern Matching using Regular Expression </title>
<script type="text/javascript">
function TestString(str)
{
  document.write("The given string is ");
  document.write("<em>"+str+"</em>"+"<br/>");
```

```
    var i=str.match(/[aeiouAEIOU][a-zA-Z]*/);
    return i;
}
</script>
</head>
<body>
  <h3>
    <script type="text/javascript">
      var input_str=prompt("Enter some string here","");
      p=TestString(input_str);
      document.write("The leftmost vowel is found at index "+p.index);
    </script>
    </h3>
</body>
</html>
```

Output

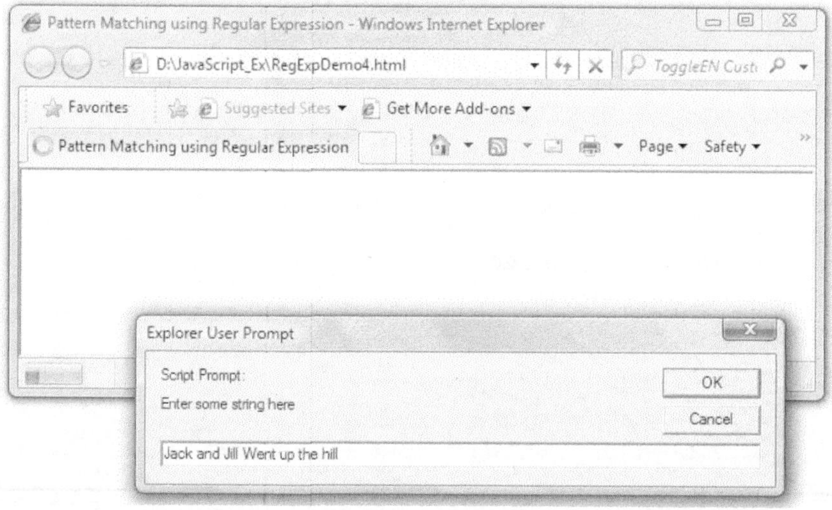

b) [RevNum.html]

```
<!DOCTYPE html>
<html >
 <head>
<script type="text/javascript">
function fun(str)
{
 var num=Number(str);
 var n=0;
 document.write("<b>"+"The reversed number is "+"</b>");
 while(num>0)
 {
  n=num%10;
  n=parseInt(n);
  num=num/10;
  num=parseInt(num);
  document.write(n);
 }
}
</script>
</head>
<body>
<script type="text/javascript">
 var input_str=prompt("Enter some number","");
 fun(input_str);
</script>
</body>
</html>
```

Output

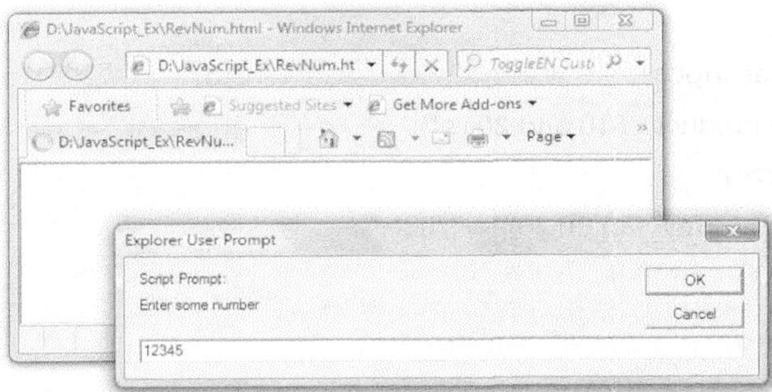

Click OK button and you will get the reversed number as follows -

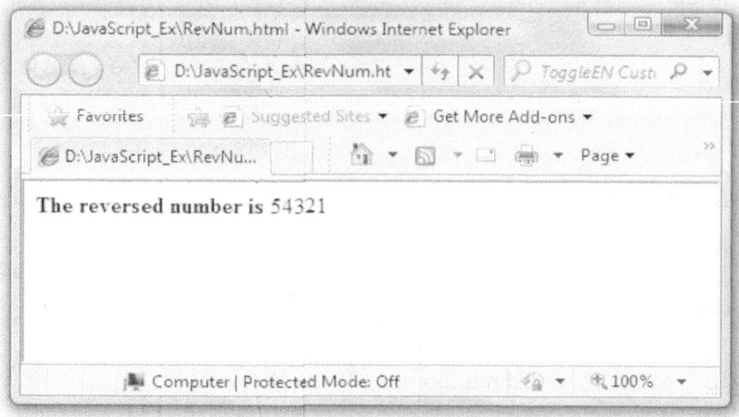

Ex. 4.9.6 : Write a JavaScript function to find the product of two arguments and return the result.

AU : Dec.-08, Marks 5

Sol. :

```
<!DOCTYPE html>
<html>
 <head>
 <title>Function Demo</title>
 <script type="text/javascript">
  function my_fun(num1,num2)
  {
   return num1*num2;
  }
</script>
</head>
<body>
<center>
 <script type="text/javascript">
   document.write("The product of 10 and 20 is ");
   document.write("<br>");
   document.write("<h3>"+my_fun(10,20)+"</h3>");
 </script>
</center>
</body>
</html>
```

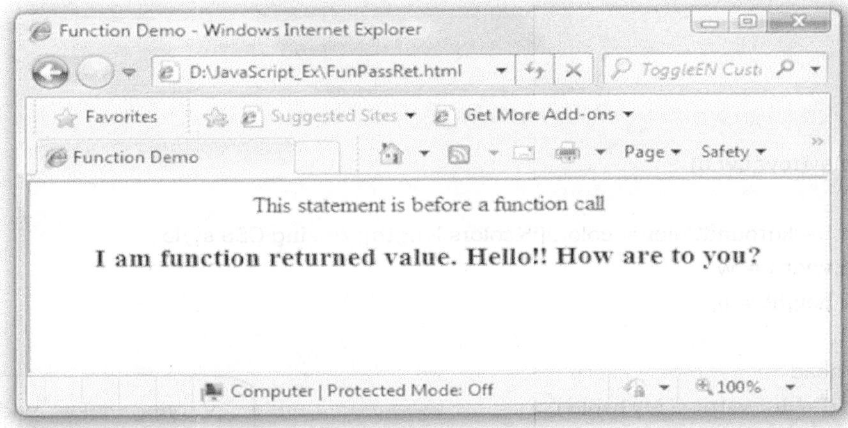

Ex. 4.9.7 : Write a JavaScript function named drawstripes that will draw a number of colored strips by generating an HTML table in which each row has (possibly) different color. Your function must have 3 parameters :

- **Width, the width of each strip**
- **Height, the height of each strip**
- **Colors an array in which each element is the name of color. Each color name is a valid HTML color (can be used as the value of BGCOLOR attribute or CSS color property)**

AU : Dec.-07, CSE, Marks 16

Sol. : **[stripeDemo.html]**

```
<html>
<head>
<title></title>
<script>
var colors = new Array('#ff0000','#00ff00','#0000ff','#ff00ff');
function drawstrips(id)
{
   if(document.getElementById)
   {
    var table = document.getElementById(id);//get the table
    var rows = table.getElementsByTagName("tr");      //get the row of table
    var wd,ht;
    for(i = 0; i < rows.length; i++)
    {
      wd=prompt("Enter the width of the strip"+i,"");
      ht=prompt("Enter the height of the strip"+i,"");
        w=Number(wd);
        h=Number(ht);
      display(rows[i],i,w,h);
```

```
        }
      }
}
function display(row,i,w,h)
{
      row.style.backgroundColor = colors[i%colors.length]; //using CSS style
      row.style.width = w;
      row.style.height = h;
}
</script></head>
<body onLoad="drawstrips('MyTable')">
<table id="MyTable" cellspacing="10" cellpadding="10">
        <tr><td>Strip 1</td></tr>
        <tr><td>Strip 2</td></tr>
        <tr><td>Strip 3</td></tr>
      </table>
</body>
```

Varying color, width and height of each

Note : For the sake of understanding following output is given for the above application]

Ex. 4.9.8 : Write a JavaScript to find the sum of first n even numbers and display the result. Get the value of n from the user.

AU : May-13, Marks 8

Sol. :

```
<html>
<head>
<script type="text/javascript">
function EvenNumSum(str)
{
```

```
        var n=Number(str);
        sum=0;
        for(i=1;i<n;i++)
        {
        if(i%2==0)
         sum=sum+i;
        }
        document.write("<br>"+" Sum of first "+n+" even numbers is "+sum+"<br>");
}
</script>
</head>
<body>
<script type="text/javascript">
        var n=prompt("Enter the value of n","");
        EvenNumSum(n);
</script>
</body>
</html>
```

4.9.4 Global Functions of JavaScript

Global functions are the top-level functions in JavaScript that are independent of any specific object. These functions use the built in objects of the JavaScript. Following are some global functions -

1. encodeURI(URI)

This function is used to encode the URI.This function encodes special characters, except: , / ? : @ & = + $ #.

For example

globalfun1.html

```
<html>
  <body>
    <script type="text/javascript">
     var uri="my example.jsp?name=< >ggg"
     document.write(encodeURI(uri)+ "<br />");
    </script>
  </body>
</html>
```

Output

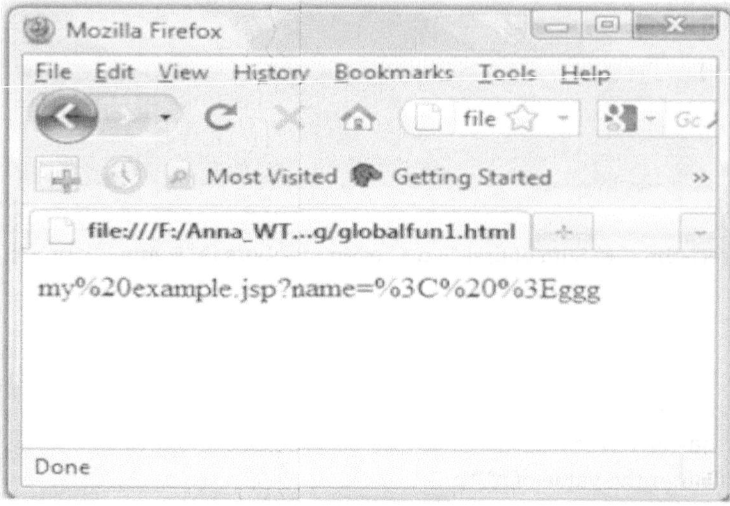

2. decodeURI

This function decodes the encoded URI.

For example

globalfun2.html

```
<html>
  <body>
    <script type="text/javascript">
      var uri="my example.jsp?name=< >ggg"
      document.write(encodeURI(uri)+ "<br />");
      document.write(decodeURI(uri)+ "<br />");
    </script>
  </body>
</html>
```

Output

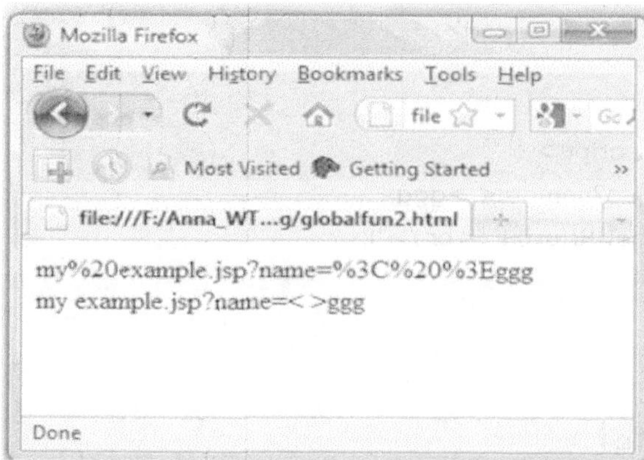

3. parseInt

This function parses a string and returns the integer value.

The syntax is -

parseInt(string,radix)

String is parsed to obtain integer value	It represents the numerical system such as octal, decimal or hexadecimal. It is optional parameter.

Example

globalfun3.html

```
<html>
 <body>
  <script type="text/javascript">
   document.write(parseInt("100"));
  </script>
 </body>
</html>
```

The output of above code will be 100.

Similar to the **parseInt** function the **parseFloat** function is used to obtain the real value from the string.

4. eval

The eval function is used to evaluate the expression.

The syntax is

eval(string);

Example

globlafun4.html

```
<html>
 <body>
  <script type="text/javascript">
   document.write(eval("2+3*5"));
  </script>
 </body>
</html>
```

The output of above code will be **17.**

University Questions

1. *Explain how functions can be written in JavaScript with an example.* **AU : May-11, Marks 8**
2. *Explain how local and global functions can be written using JavaScript.* **AU : May-12, Marks 8**

4.10 Arrays

AU : May- 08,12, Dec.-13, Marks 8

- Arrays is a collection of similar type of elements which can be referred by a common name.
- Any element in an array is referred by an array name followed by "[" followed by position of the element followed by].
- The particular position of element in an array is called array index or subscript.

For example –

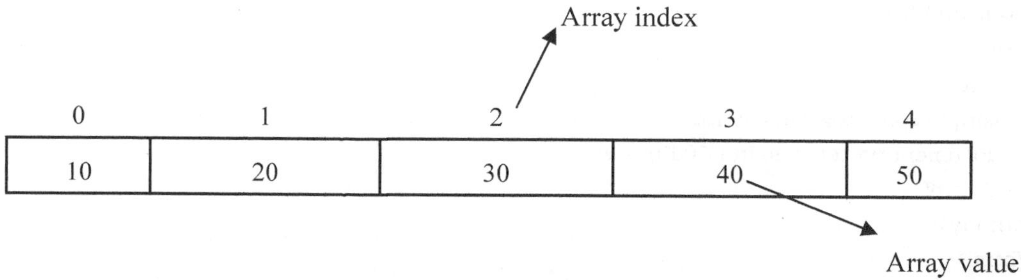

Fig. 4.10.1 Arrays

- Normally the first element in an array is stored at 0th location, however we can start storing the element from any position.

4.10.1 Array Declaration

- In JavaScript the array can be created using **Array** object.
- Suppose, we want to create an array of 10 elements then we can write,

```
var ar = new Array(10);
```

- Using new operator we can allocate the memory dynamically for the arrays.
- In the brackets the size of an array is mentioned and the var ar denotes the name of the array. Thus by the above sentence an array ar will be created in which we can store 10 elements at the most. Sometimes the above statement can be written like this

```
var ar;
 ar=new Array(10);
```

4.10.2 Array Initialization

Let us see how to store some elements in an array.

- **JavaScript Program [ArrayDemo.html]**

```
<!DOCTYPE html>
<html>
<head>
  <title>Array Demo</title>
</head>
<body>
<strong>
  <script type="text/javascript">
    a=new Array(5);//creation of array
    for(i=0;i<5;i++)
    {
     a[i]=i;
     document.write(a[i]+"<br>");//displaying array
    }
    document.write("Another way of initialization"+"<br>");
    b=new Array(11,22,33,44,55);//creation of array
    for(i=0;i<5;i++)
    {
     document.write(b[i]+"<br>");//displaying array
    }
    document.write("Yet another way of initialization"+"<br>");
    var c=[100,200,300,400,500];//creation of array
    for(i=0;i<5;i++)
    {
     document.write(c[i]+"<br>");//displaying array
    }
  </script>
 </strong>
</body>
</html>
```

As you can notice that, in above JavaScript an array can be initialized in three different ways which is shown by boldface. Hence an output of above script will be

Output

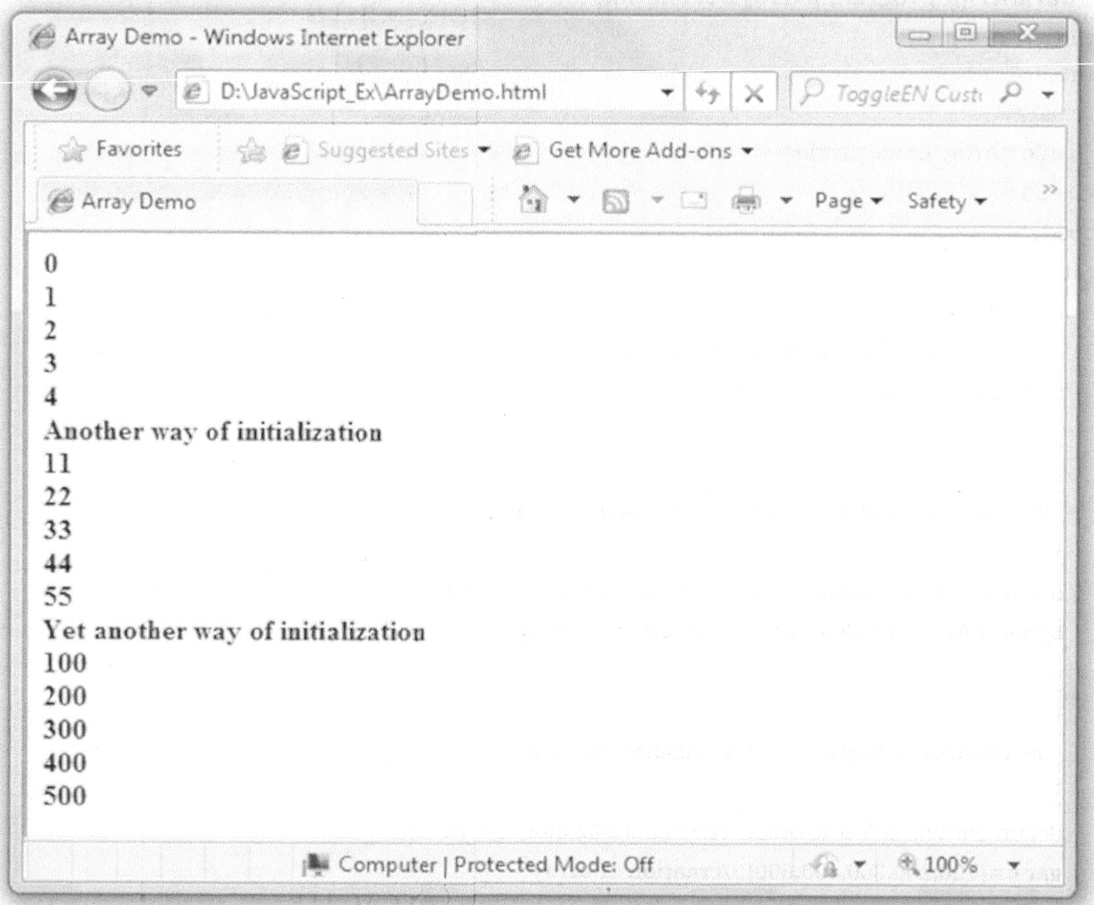

There is one control structure in JavaScript which is closely associated with array elements and such a control structure is **for...in**. Let us see a simple JavaScript which makes use of **for-in** control structure to display elements of an array.

JavaScript [for_inDemo.html]

```
<!DOCTYPE>
<html>
<head>
  <title>for-in Demo</title>
</head>
<body>
<strong>
  <script type="text/javascript">
   Days=new Array();
   Days[0]="Sunday";
   Days[1]="Monday";
   Days[2]="Tuesday";
```

```
    Days[3]="Wednesday";
    Days[4]="Thursday";
    Days[5]="Friday";
    Days[6]="Saturday";
    for(i in Days)
    {
     document.write(Days[i]+"<br>");
    }
  </script>
 </strong>
</body>
</html>
```

Output

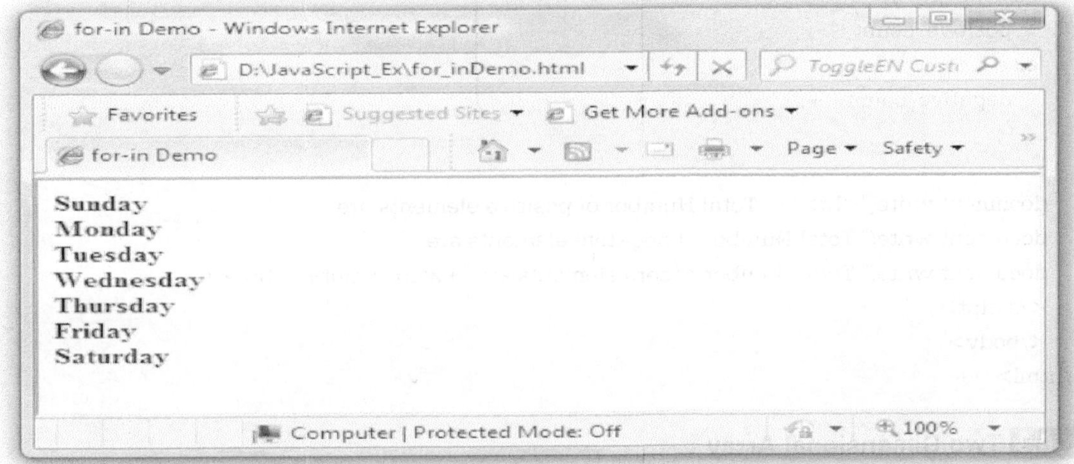

Ex. 4.10.1 : Write a javascript that reads ten numbers and displays the count of negative numbers, the count of positive numbers and the count of zero from the list.

Sol. :

```
<html>
    <body>
    <script type="text/javascript">
    ar=new Array();
    ar[0]=10;
    ar[1]=0;
    ar[2]=-9;
    ar[3]=0;
    ar[4]=20;          Reading ten numbers
    ar[5]=30;
    ar[6]=3;
    ar[7]=88;
    i=0;
    for(i in ar)
```

```
{
 document.write(ar[i]+"<br/>");
 i++;
}
```

Displaying the ten numbers

```
positive_count=0;
negative_count=0;
zero_count=0;
i=0;
for(i in ar)
{
 if(ar[i]==0)
    zero_count++;
 else if(ar[i]>0)
    positive_count++;
 else
    negative_count++;
i++;
}
```

Computing the count for zero, positive and negative numbers

```
document.write("<br>"+" Total Number of positive elements are
document.write(" Total Number of negative elements are
document.write(" Total Number of zero elements are "+zero_count+"<br/>");
</script>
</body>
</html>
```

4.10.3 Two Dimensional Array

Actually JavaScript does not support the multidimensional arrays. Hence for defining the 2D array we make use of single dimensional array, how? Here it is -

JavaScript[TwoDArray.html]

```
<!DOCTYPE html>
<html>
<head>
  <title>Two Dimensional Array</title>
</head>
<body>
 <center>
 <h3> Demonstration of 2D array</h3>
 <script type="text/javascript">
   a=new Array();//creation of rows of array
   for(i=0;i<5;i++)
   a[i]=new Array();//creating columns of array
   for(i=0;i<5;i++)
   {
```

```
    for(j=0;j<5;j++)
    {
     a[i][j]=i+j;
     document.write(a[i][j] +"  ");
    }
    document.write("<br>");
   }
  </script>
</center>
</body>
</html>
```

Output

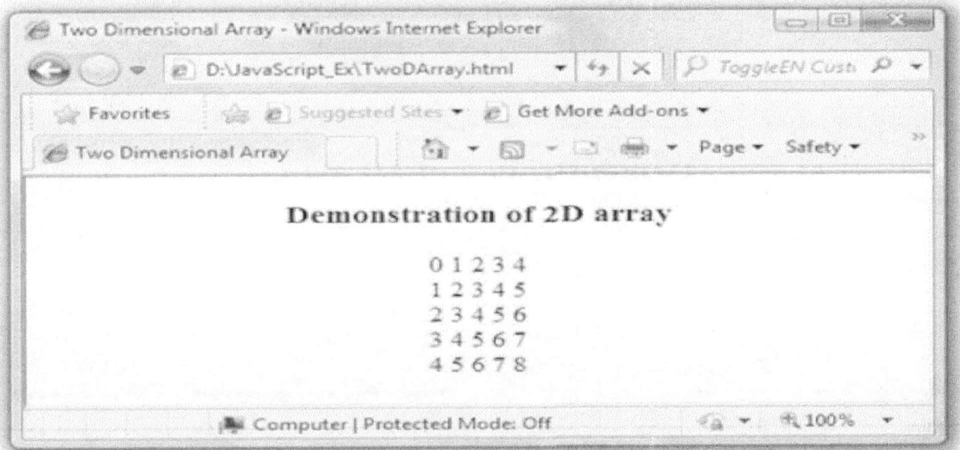

There is another way by which the two dimensional array can be initialized. This method is represented in the following Script

JavaScript[TwoDArray1.html]

```
<!DOCTYPE html>
<html>
<head>
  <title>Two Dimensional Array</title>
</head>
<body>
 <center>
 <h3> Demonstration of 2D array</h3>
 <script type="text/javascript">
  var a=[ [1,2,3],
          [4,5,6],
          [7,8,9]
      ]; //creation of array
  for(i=0;i<3;i++)
```

```
  {
  for(j=0;j<3;j++)
  {
   document.write(a[i][j] +"  ");
  }
   document.write("<br>");
  }
 </script>
</center>
</body>
</html>
```

Output

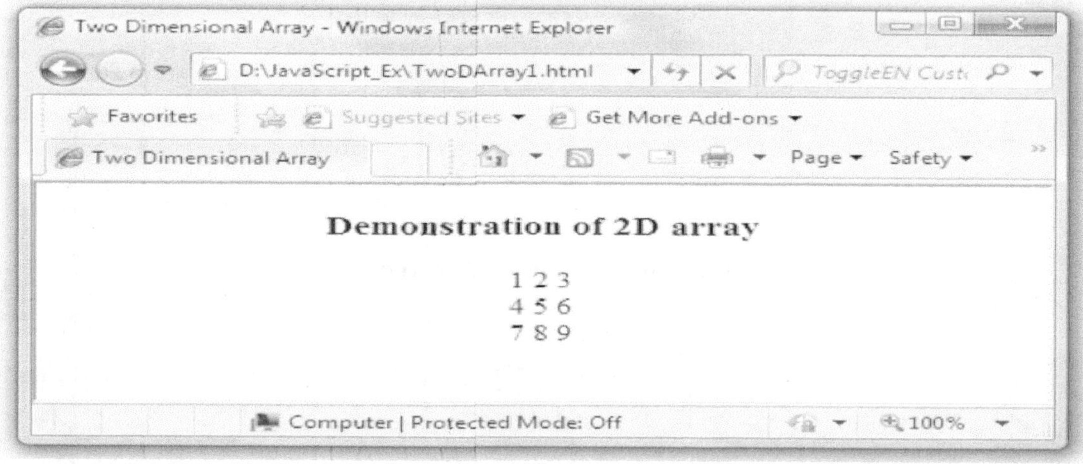

Ex. 4.10.2 : Use a one-dimensional array and write a script to solve following problem . Read in 20 numbers, each of which is between 1 and 100. As each number is read, print it only if it is not a duplicate of a number that has already been read.

AU : May-08, Marks 8

Sol. : duplicate.html

```
<html>
 <head>
 <script type="text/javascript">
  function change()
  {
   a=new Array(20);
   for(i=0;i<=19;i++)
   {
    var input_str=prompt("Enter the any number between 1 to 100","");
    var val=Number(input_str);
    a[i]=val;
   }
   for(i=0;i<=18;i++)
   {
```

```
    for(j=i+1;j<=19;j++)
    {
     if(a[i]>a[j])//before checking duplicate elements
     {
      temp=a[i]; //arrange them in sorted order
      a[i]=a[j];
      a[j]=temp;
     }
    }
   }
   document.write("The elements (without considering duplicate elements)are...");
   for(i=0;i<=18;i++)
   {
    flag=0;
    for(j=i+1;j<=19;j++)
    {
     if(a[i]==a[j])//checking if two adjacent elements are duplicate
     {
      a[j]=-1;//-1 is assigned to duplicate elements
      flag=1;//flag indicates a[i] and a[j] are duplicate
     }
    }
    if(flag==1)//flag=1 represents that a[i] element
    a[i]=-1;//needs to be marked as duplicate
   }
   for(i=0;i<=19;i++)
   {
    if(a[i]>0) //-1 means duplicate elements
    document.write(a[i]+",");//elements that are not -1 are unique elements
   }
  }
 </script>
<title>Eliminating Duplicate Elements</title>
</head>
 <body onload=change()>
 </body>
</html>
```

University Questions

1. *Explain the way in which javaScript handles arrays with example.* **AU : May-12, Marks 8**
2. *Explain the JavaScript array handling and array methods.* **AU : Dec.-13, Marks 8**

Part II : Introduction to DOM Model

4.11 Definition of DOM

- The **D**ocument **O**bject **M**odeling (DOM) is for defining the standard for accessing and manipulating HTML,XML and other scripting languages.
- It is the **W3C recommendation** for handling the structured documents.
- Normally the structured information is provided in XML, HTML and many other documents.
- Hence DOM provides the standard set of programming interfaces for working with XML and XHTML and JavaScript.

What is DOM?

Document Object Model (DOM) is a set of platform independent and language neutral Application Programming Interface (API) which describes how to access and manipulate the information stored in XML,HTML and JavaScript documents.

4.12 The Document Tree

AU : May-11,12, Dec.-13, Marks 8

- Basically DOM is an **Application Programming Interface (API)** that defines the interface between HTML document and application program. That means, suppose application program is written in Java and this Java program wants to access the elements of HTML web document then it is possible by using a set of Application Programming Interfaces (API) which belongs to the DOM.
- The DOM contains the **set of interfaces** for the document tree node type. These interfaces are similar to the Java or C++ interfaces. They have **objects, properties and methods** which are useful for respected node type of the web document.
- The documents in DOM are represented using a tree like structure in which every element is represented as a node. Hence the tree structure is also referred as DOM tree.
- **For example :** Consider following XHTML document.

```
<html>
    <head>
       <title>This is My Web Page </title>
    </head>
    <body>
       <h1>Hello Friends </h1>
       <h2>How are you?</h2>
       </h3>See you</h3>
    </body>
    </html>
```

- The DOM tree will be

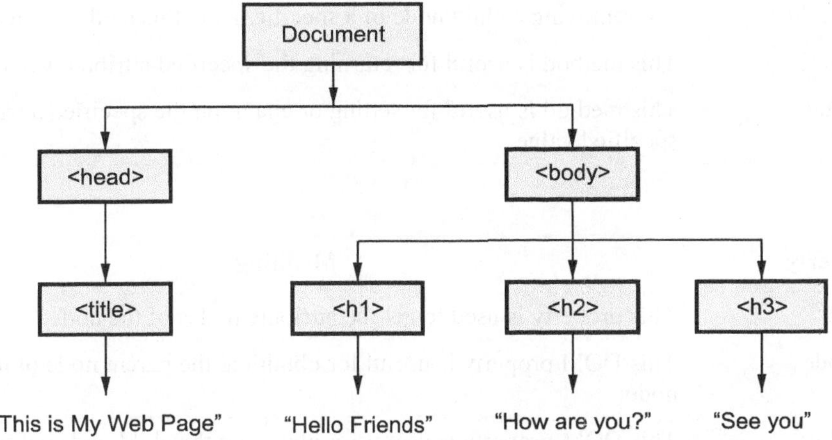

Fig. 4.12.1 DOM structure for simple web document

- We can describe some basic terminologies used in DOM tree as follows -
  1. Every element in the DOM tree is called **node**.
  2. The topmost single node in the DOM tree is called the **root**.
  3. Every child node must have a parent **node**.
  4. The bottommost nodes that have no children are called **leaf nodes**.
  5. The nodes that have the common parent are called **siblings**.

University Questions

1. *Explain about document tree in detail.* **AU : May-11,12**
2. *List and explain the various types of document nodes* **AU : Dec.-13, Marks 8**

4.13 Modifying Element Style

AU : Dec.-12, 15, Marks 16

We can access or change the contents of document by using various methods. Some commonly used properties and methods of DOM are as follows :

Methods

Method	Meaning
getElementById	This method is used to obtain the specific element which is specified by some id within the script.
createElement	This method is used to create an element node.
createTextNode	Useful for creating a text node.
createAttribute	Useful for creating attribute.
appendChild	For adding a new child to specified node, this method is used.

removeChild	For removing a child node of a specific node, this method is used.
getAttribute	This method is useful for returning the specified attribute value.
setAttribute	This method is useful for setting or changing the specified attribute to the specified value.

Properties

Property	Meaning
attributes	This property is used to get the attribute nodes of the node.
parentNode	This DOM property is useful for obtaining the parent node of the specific node.
childNodes	This DOM property is useful for obtaining the child nodes of the specific node.
innerHTML	It is useful for getting the text value of a node.

4.13.1 Accessing Elements using DOM

- There are several ways by which we can access the elements of the web document.
- To understand these methods of accessing we will consider one simple web document as follows.

```
<html >
<head>
    <title>This is My Web Page </title>
</head>
<body>
<form name="form1">
    <input type="text" name="myinput"/>
</form>
</body>
</html>
```

Method 1

- Every XHTML document element is associated with some address. This address is called **DOM address.**
- The document has the collection of **forms** and **elements**. Hence we can refer the text box element as

```
var Dom_Obj=document.forms[0].elements[0];
```

- But this is not the suitable method of addressing the elements. Because if we change the above script as

...

```
<form name="form1">
     <input type="button" name= "mybutton"/>
     <input type="text" name="myinput"/>
</form>
...
```

then index reference gets changed. Hence another approach of accessing the elements is developed.

Method 2

- We can access the desired element from the web document using JavaScript method **getElementById**. The element access can be made as follows -

```
var Dom_Obj=document.getElementById("myinput");
```

- But if the element is in particular group, that means if there are certain elements on the form such as radio buttons or check boxes then they normally appear in the groups. Hence to access these elements we make use of its index. Consider the following code sample

```
<form id="Food">
   <input type="checkbox" name="vegetables" value="Spinach" />Spinach
   <input type="checkbox" name="vegetables" value="FenuGreek" />FenuGreek
   <input type="checkbox" name="vegetables" value="Cabbage" />Cabbage
</form>
```

- For getting the values of these checkboxes we can write following code.

```
var Dom_obj=document.getElementById("Food");
for(i = 0 ; i < Dom_Obj.vegetables.length ; i++)
     document.write(Dom_Obj.vegetables[i]+"<br/>");
```

4.13.2 Modifying Elements using DOM

Appending an element Using DOM

We can add new node in the HTML document using the DOM method **appendChild** method

Following example illustrates the idea

```
<!DOCTYPE html>
<html>
<body>

<div id="div1">
<p id="p1">The first sentence in HTML document.</p>
<p id="p2">The second sentence in HTML document.</p>
</div>
```

```
<script>
var pnode = document.createElement("p");
var node = document.createTextNode("This is newly added sentence in HTML document.");
pnode.appendChild(node);
var element = document.getElementById("div1");
element.appendChild(pnode);
</script>
</body>
</html>
```

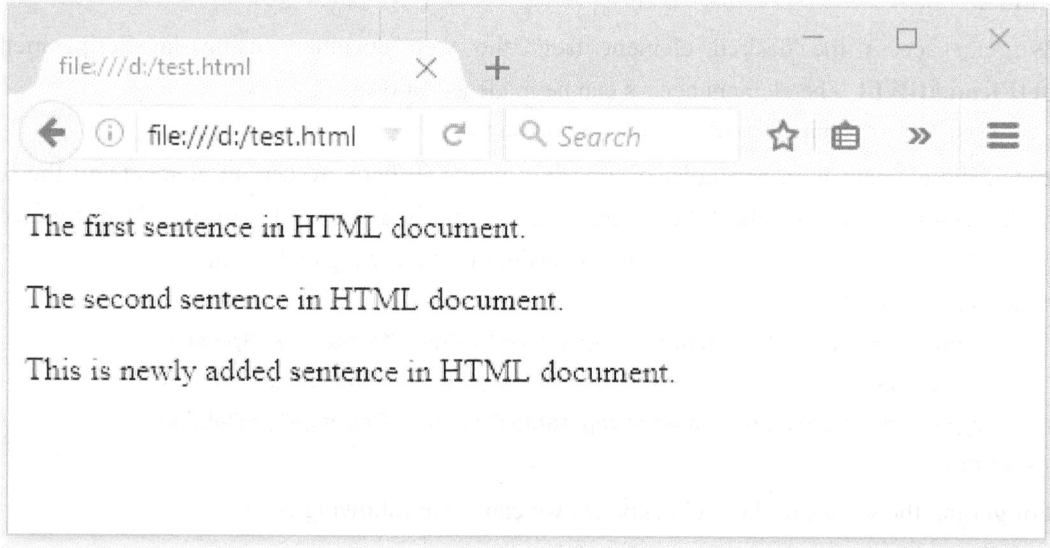

Inserting an element Using DOM

We can insert a node in between the nodes by using appendChild and insertBefore method. For example

```
<!DOCTYPE html>
<html>
<body>

<div id="div1">
<p id="p1">First Sentence</p>
<p id="p2">Second Sentence</p>
</div>

<script>
var pnode = document.createElement("p");
var node = document.createTextNode("Newly Added Sentence!!!");
pnode.appendChild(node);
var element = document.getElementById("div1");
```

```
var nextnode = document.getElementById("p2");
element.insertBefore(pnode,nextnode);
</script>

</body>
</html>
```

Output

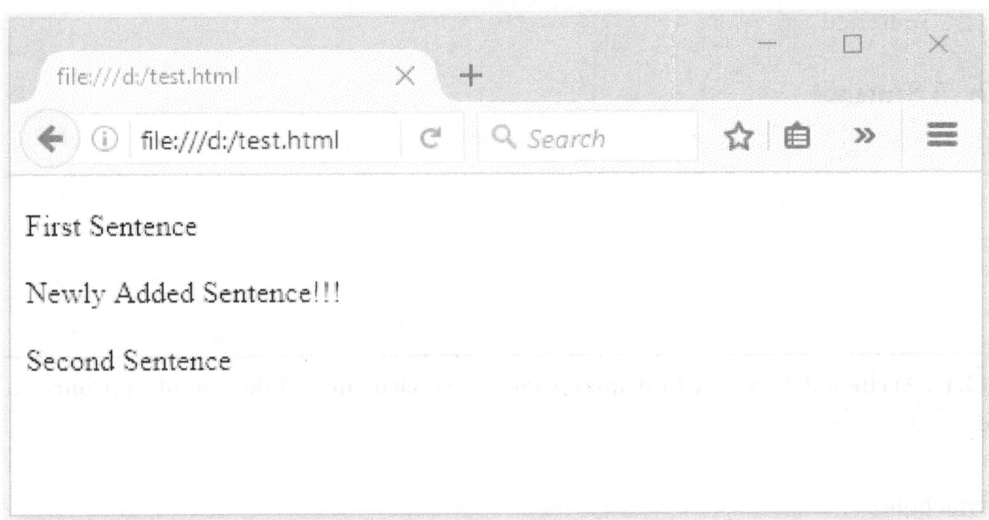

Removing an element Using DOM

We can remove or delete particular from HTML document using DOM's **removeChild** method.

Here is the illustration

```
<!DOCTYPE html>
<html>
<body>

<div id="div1">
<p id="p1">First Sentence</p>
<p id="p2">Second Sentence</p>
<p id="p3">Third Sentence</p>
</div>

<script>
var parentnode = document.getElementById("div1");
var node = document.getElementById("p2");
parentnode.removeChild(node);
</script>
</body>
</html>
```

Output

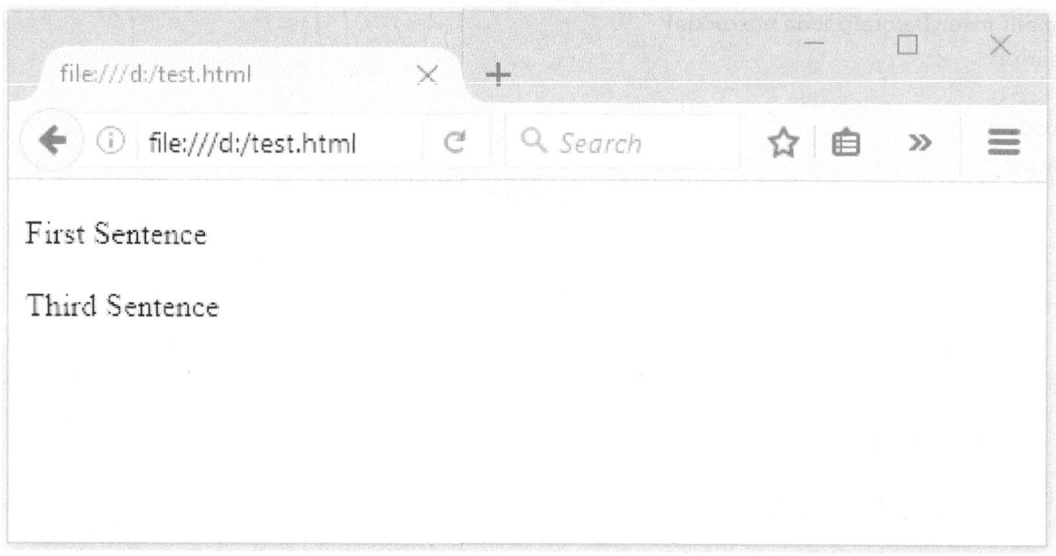

Ex. 4.13.1 : Write a JavaScript to display sum of two elements. Make use of appropriate DOM method.

Sol. :

```
<!Doctype html>
<html>
<head>
<script type="text/javascript">
function getSum()
{
    var number1=document.getElementById("number1").value;
    var number2=document.getElementById("number2").value;
    var num1=Number(number1);
var num2=Number(number2);
    alert(num1+num2);
}
</script>
</head>
<body>
<form>
Enter Num1:<input type="text" id="number1" /><br/> <br/>
Enter Num2:<input type="text" id="number2" /><br/>
<input type="button" value="SUM" onclick="getSum()"/>
</form>
</body>
</html>
```

Output

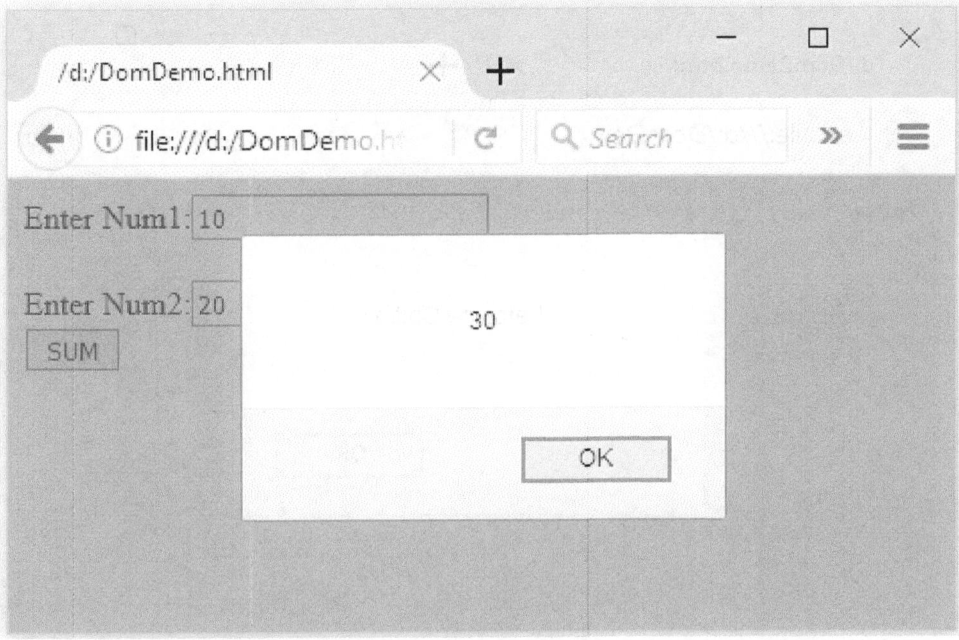

Ex. 4.13.2 : Write a JavaScript to welcome the user by his/her name when he enters his/her name in textbox. Make use of appropriate DOM method.

Sol. :

```
<!Doctype html>
<html>
<head>
<script type="text/javascript">
function display()
{
    var name=document.getElementsByName("user");
alert("Welcome "+name[0].value);
}
</script>
</head>
<body>
<form>
Enter Name:<input type="text" name="user" /><br/> <br/>
<input type="button" value="Greet" onclick="display()"/>
</form>
</body>
</html>
```

Output

University Questions

1. *With a simple example illustrate how the elements of the HTML document tree structure can be accessed using Javascript.* **AU : Dec.-12, Marks 16**
2. *Explain DOM model.* **AU : Dec.-15, Marks 8**

4.14 Objects in JavaScript **AU : Dec.-09, 11, 13, Marks 16**

In JavaScript object is a collection of properties. These properties are nothing but the members of the classes from Java or C++. For instance - in JavaScript the object Date() is used which happens to the member of the class in Java.

4.14.1 Math Objects

- For performing the mathematical computations there are some useful methods available from **math** object.
- For example if we want to find out minimum of two numbers then we can write -

```
document.write(math.min(4.5,7.8));
```

The above statement will result in 4.5. Thus using various useful methods we can perform many mathematical computations.

- Here are some commonly used methods from **math** object.

Method	Meaning
sqrt(num)	This method finds the square root of num.
abs(num)	This method returns absolute value of num.
ceil(num)	This method returns the ceil value of num. For example ceil(10.3) will return 11.
floor(num)	This method returns the floor value of num. For example floor(10.3) will return 10.
log(num)	This method returns the natural logarithmic value of num. For example log(7.9) will return 2.
pow(a,b)	This method will compute the ab. For example pow(2,5) will return 32.
min(a,b)	Returns the minimum value of a and b.
max(a,b)	Returns the maximum value of a and b.
sin(num)	Returns the sine of num.
cos(num)	Returns the cosine of num.
tan(num)	Returns the tangent of num.
exp(num)	Returns the exponential value i.e. enum .

JavaScript Program[MathDemo.html]

```
<!DOCTYPE html>
<html >
 <head>
  <title>Math Demo</title>
</head>
<body>
 <center>
  <h3>Square root of 100 is </h3>
  <script type="text/javascript">
   var num=100;
   document.write("<h3>"+Math.sqrt(num)+"</h3>");
  </script>
 </center>
</body>
</html>
```

Output

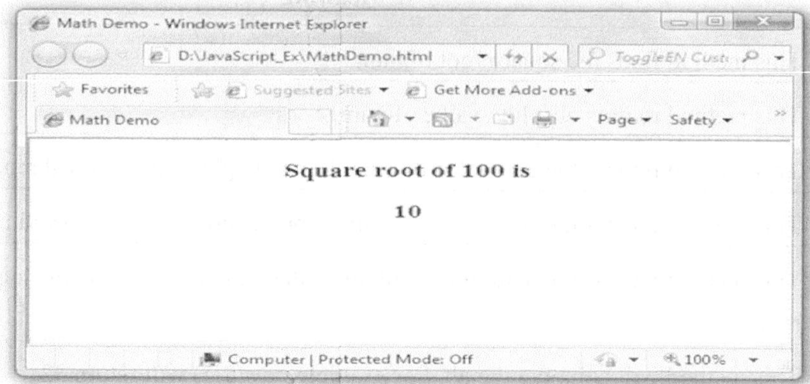

4.14.2 Number Objects

Various properties of number object are -

Property	Meaning
MAX_VALUE	Largest possible number gets displayed.
MIN_VALUE	Smallest possible number gets displayed.
NaN	When not a number then NaN is displayed.
PI	The value of PI gets displayed.
POSITIVE_INFINITY	The positive infinity gets displayed.
NEGATIVE_INFINITY	The negative infinity gets displayed.

Using **Number**.*property_name* we can display the property value. Following JavaScript uses the property of negative infinity.

JavaScript[NumberDemo.html]

```
<!DOCTYPE html>
<html>
<head>
  <title>Number Object Demo</title>
</head>
<body>
 <center>
  <script type="text/javascript">
  document.write(Number.NEGATIVE_INFINITY);
  </script>
 </center>
</body>
</html>
```

Output

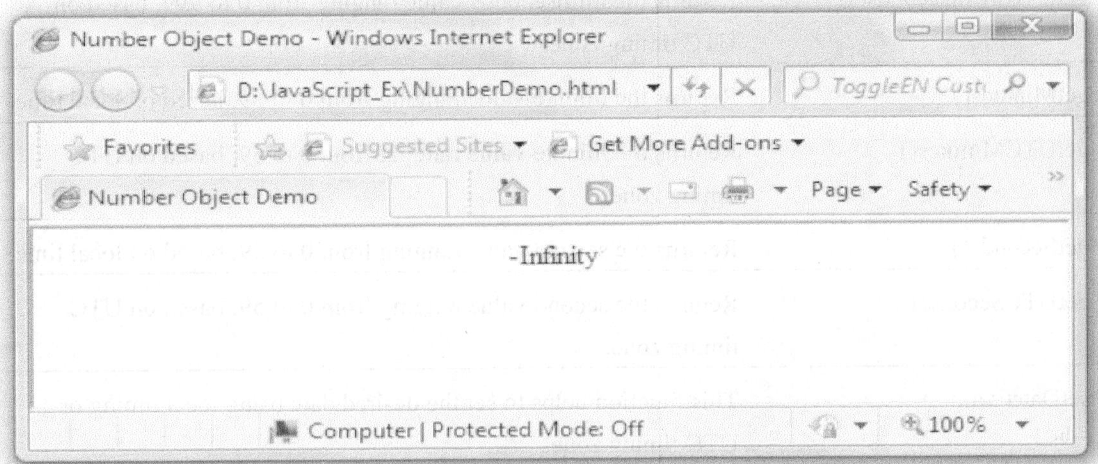

4.14.3 Date Objects

- This object is used for obtaining the date and time.
- This date and time value is based on computer's local time (system's time) or it can be based on GMT(**G**reenwich **M**ean **T**ime).
- Nowadays this GMT is also known as UTC i.e. **U**niversal **C**o-ordinated **T**ime. This is basically a world time standard.
- Following are the commonly used methods of Date object.

Method	Meaning
getTime()	It returns the number of milliseconds. This value is the difference between the current time and the time value from 1st January 1970.
getDate()	Returns the current date based on computers local time.
getUTCDate()	Returns the current date obtained from UTC.
getDay()	Returns the current day. The day number is from 0 to 6 i.e. from Sunday to Saturday.
getUTCDay()	Returns the current day based on UTC. The day number is from 0 to 6 i.e. from Sunday to Saturday.
getHours()	Returns the hour value ranging from 0 to 23, based on local time.
getUTCHours()	Returns the hour value ranging from 0 to 23, based on UTC timing zone.
getMilliseconds()	Returns the milliseconds value ranging from 0 to 999, based on local time.

getUTCMilliseconds()	Returns the milliseconds value ranging from 0 to 999, based on UTC timing zone.
getMinutes()	Returns the minute value ranging from 0 to 59, based on local time.
getUTCMinutes()	Returns the minute value ranging from 0 to 59, based on UTC timing zone.
getSeconds()	Returns the second value ranging from 0 to 59, based on local time.
getUTCSeconds()	Returns the second value ranging from 0 to 59, based on UTC timing zone.
setDate(value)	This function helps to set the desired date using local timing or UTC timing zone.
setHour(hr,minute,second,ms)	This function helps to set the desired time using local or UTC timing zone. The parameters that can be passed to this function are hour,minute,seconds and milliseconds. Only hour parameter is compulsory and rest all are the optional parameters.

In the following web document we are making use of **Date()** object and some useful methods of it.

JavaScript[DateDemo.html]

```
<!DOCTYPE html>
<html>
<head>
  <title>Date Demo</title>
</head>
<body>
  <script type="text/javascript">
  var my_date=new Date();
  document.write("The date is: "+my_date.toString()+"<br>");
  document.write("Today's date is "+my_date.getDate()+"<br>");
  document.write("This is the month of  "+my_date.getMonth()+"<br>");
  document.write("The current year is "+my_date.getFullYear()+"<br>");
  document.write("Now, Hour = "+my_date.getHours()+"<br>");
  document.write("Minutes = "+my_date.getMinutes()+"<br>");
  document.write("Seconds = "+my_date.getSeconds()+"<br>");
  </script>
</body>
</html>
```

Output

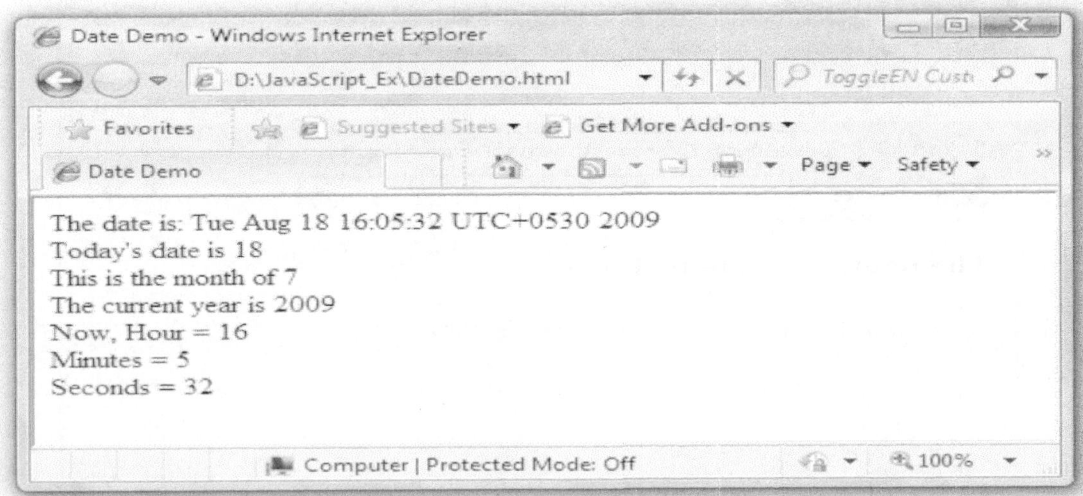

Script Explanation :

1. In the above script we have created an instance *my_date* of the object **Date().**
2. Then using **my_date.toString()** method we can display the current date along with the time.
3. Then using the functions like getDate(), getMonth(), getFullYear() we are displaying the date, month and year separately.
4. Similarly using the functions getHours(), getMinutes() and getSeconds() we can display the current hour, minute and seconds separately.

4.14.4 Boolean Objects

- This object is the simplest kind of object which is used especially when we want to represent **true** and **false** values.
- Here is a simple javascript in which the Boolean type variable is used -

Javascript Program

```
<html>
<body>
<script type="text/javascript">
var temp=new Boolean(false);
document.write("<b>"+"The boolean value is:  ");
document.write(temp.toString());
</script>
</body>
</html>
```

Output

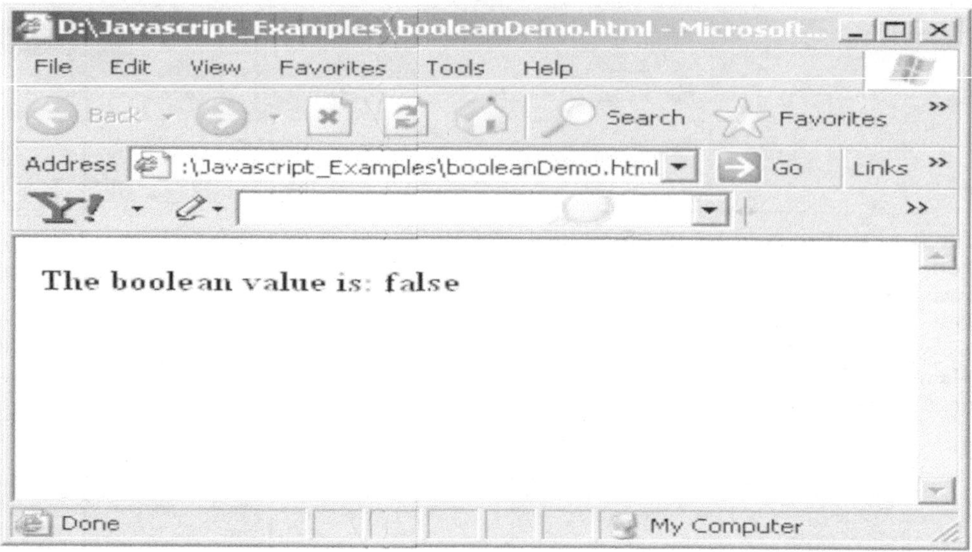

4.14.5 String Objects

- String is a collection of characters.
- In JavaScript using **string** object many useful string related functionalities can be exposed off.
- Some commonly used methods of string object are concatenating two strings, converting the string to upper case or lower case, finding the substring of a given string and so on.
- Here is a listing of some methods of string.

Method	Meaning
concat(str)	This method concatenates the two strings. For example s1.concat(s2) will result in concatenation of string s1 with s2.
charAt(index_val)	This method will return the character specified by value index_val.
substring(begin,end)	This method returns the substring specified by begin and end character.
toLowerCase()	This function is used to convert all the uppercase letters to lower case.
toUpperCase()	This function is used to convert all the lowercase letters to upper case.
valueOf()	This method returns the value of the string.

There is one important property of string object and that is **length**. For example

```
var my_str="Hello";
 var len;
 len=my_str.length;
```

Length of the string "Hello" will be stored in the variable len

Here is sample program in which some methods of string object are used.

JavaScript[StringDemo.html]

```
<!DOCTYPE html>
<html>
<head>
  <title>String Properties and Methods Demo</title>
</head>
<body>
<strong>
   <script type="text/javascript">
    var s1="Hello ";
    var s2="Parth!";
    document.write("First string is: "+s1+"<br>");
    document.write("Second string is: "+s2+"<br>");
    document.write("Concatenating two strings: "+s1.concat(s2)+"<br>");
    document.write("Finding length of Second string : "+s2.length+"<br>");
    document.write("The character at 0th position of First string is : "+s1.charAt(0)+"<br>");
    document.write("The First string can be converted to upper case as : "+s1.toUpperCase());
   </script>
  </strong>
</body>
</html>
```

Output

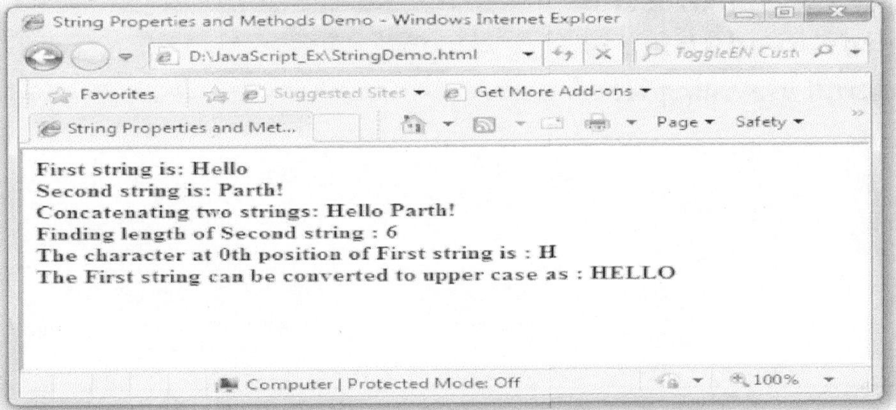

Ex. 4.14.1 : Write a script that inputs a line of text, tokenizes it with String method split and displays the tokens in reverse order.

Sol. :

```
<html>
<body>
<script type="text/javascript">
```

```
var str=new String("I like writing in javascript");
var a=new Array();
a=str.split(' ');
document.write("<strong>The original string is</strong>"+"<br/>");
for(i=0;i<a.length;i++)
document.write(a[i]+" ");
document.write("<br/>");
document.write("<strong>The reversed string is</strong>"+"<br/>");
for(i=a.length-1;i>=0;i--)
document.write(a[i]+" ");
</script>
</body>
</html>
```

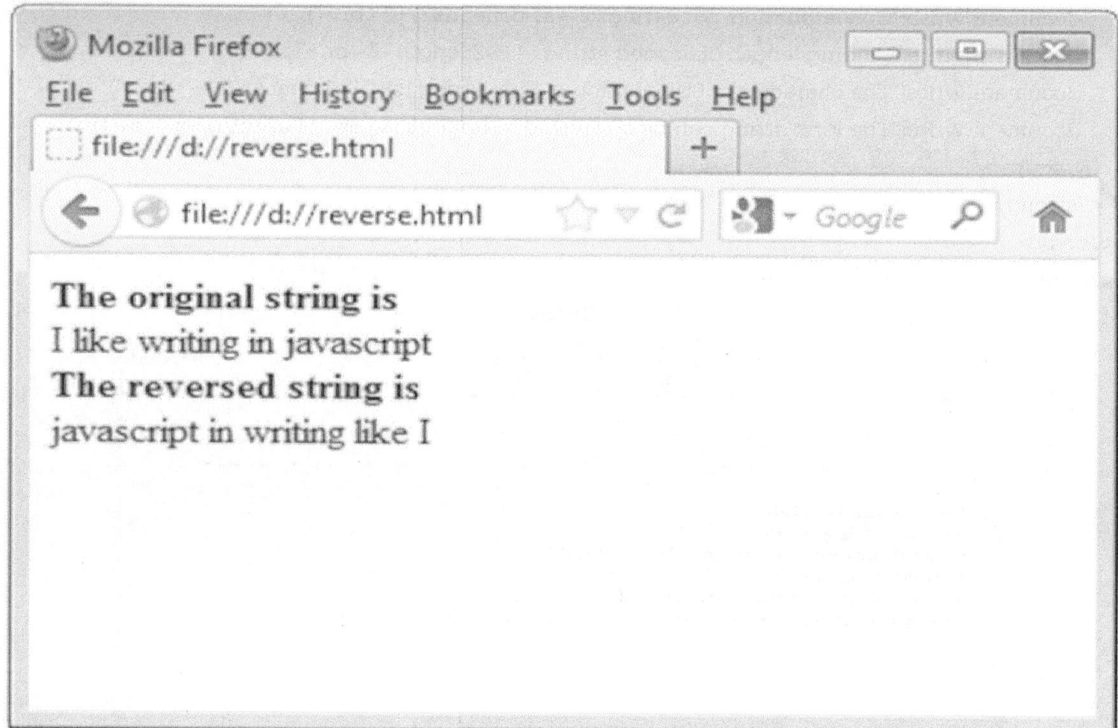

4.14.6 Object Creation and Modification

- The web designer can create an object and can set its properties as per his requirements.
- The object can be created using new expression.
- Initially the object with no properties can be set using following statements

```
Myobj=new Object();
```

- Then using dot operator we can set the properties for that object.

- The object can then be modified by assigning the values to this object.

JavaScript[ObjectDemo.html]

```
<!DOCTYPE html>
<html>
<head>
  <title>Object Creation Demo</title>
</head>
<body>
<strong>
  <script type="text/javascript">
    var Myobj;
    var n,i;
    //creating an object
    Myobj=new Object();
    //setting the propertis for newly created object
    Myobj.id=10;
    Myobj.name="Anuradha";
    document.write("The ID is "+Myobj.id+"<br/>");
    document.write("The Name is "+Myobj.name);
  </script>
 </strong>
</body>
</html>
```

Output

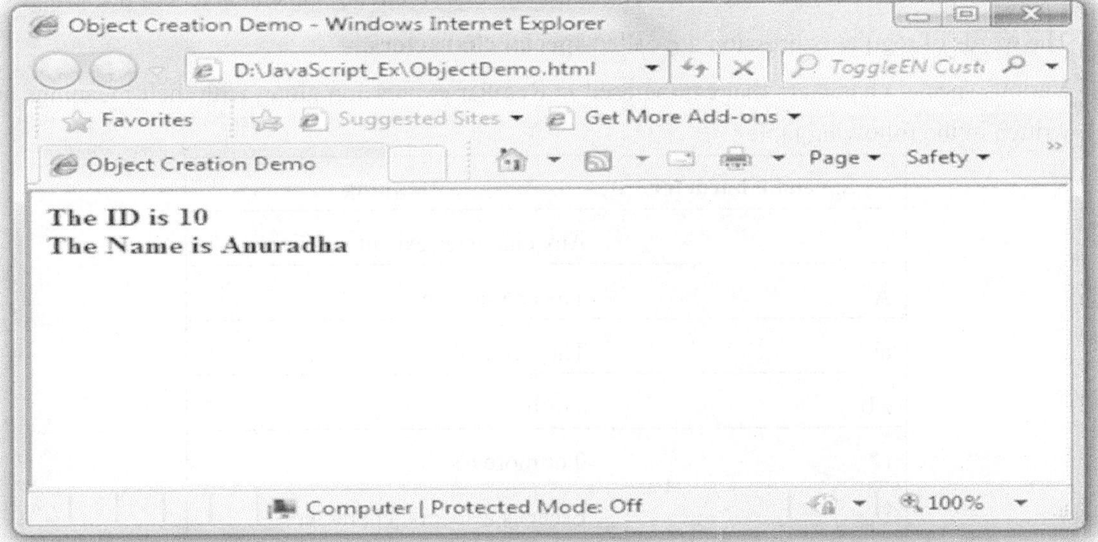

Alternative method of creating an object and modifying the properties is as given below -

```
var Myobj={name:"Anuradha",id:10};
```

Then using **document.write** statement we can display the property values as follows -

```
document.write("The ID is "+Myobj.id+"<br/>");
document.write("The Name is "+Myobj.name);
```

The property of created object can be deleted using an expression **delete**. Normally the property of an object is deleted in order to free the allocated memory so that this memory can be reused by other process.

University Questions

1. *Discuss javascript array object in detail.* **AU : Dec.-11, Marks 8**
2. *Explain the javascript object Math.* **AU : Dec.-13, Marks 8**
3. *What are the methods associated with array object in JavaScript ? Explain each one with example.* **AU : Dec.-09, Marks 16**

4.15 Regular Expressions

AU : May-08, Marks 8

- **Definition :** Regular Expression is a special text string that defines the search pattern. It is a logical expression.
- **For example** – For counting specific characters in a string or to replace some substring by another substring we need to create a regular expression.
- We can create a regular expression pattern using forward slash /. For instance -

  re = /abc/
- Regular expression is a powerful way for searching and replacing the characters in the string.
- The words of regular expression are called **special characters**.
- Various special characters that can be used in Regular expression along with their meanings are written in the following table :

Special Character	Meaning
.	Any character except newline
A	The character a
ab	The string ab
a|b	a or b
a*	0 or more a's
\	Escapes a special character
[ab-d]	One character of: a, b, c, d
[^ab-d]	One character except: a, b, c, d

[\b]	Backspace character
\d	One digit
\D	One non-digit
\s	One whitespace
\S	One non-whitespace
\w	One word character
\W	One non-word character
*	0 or more
+	1 or more
?	0 or 1
{2}	Exactly 2
{2, 5}	Between 2 and 5
{2,}	2 or more
(...)	Group of pattern
^	Start of string
$	End of string
\b	Word boundary
\n	Newline
\r	Carriage return
\t	Tab
\0	Null character

Methods that use regular expressions

Method	Description
exec	A RegExp method that executes a search for a match in a string. It returns an array of information or null on a mismatch.
test	A RegExp method that tests for a match in a string. It returns true or false.

match	A String method that executes a search for a match in a string. It returns an array of information or null on a mismatch.
matchAll	A String method that returns an iterator containing all of the matches, including capturing groups.
search	A String method that tests for a match in a string. It returns the index of the match, or −1 if the search fails.
replace	A String method that executes a search for a match in a string, and replaces the matched substring with a replacement substring.
split	A String method that uses a regular expression or a fixed string to break a string into an array of substrings.

4.15.1 Finding Non Matching Characters

We can find the non matching characters from the given text by placing ^ as the first character within a square [ ].

Ex. 4.15.1 : Write a Java program that checks whether the string entered by the user contains digit or not.

Sol. :

```
<!DOCTYPE html>
<html>
<head>
    <script type="text/javascript">
        function TestString(str)
        {
          re=/[^[0-9]]/; // [0-9] indicates any digit
          if(re.test(str))
           {
            alert("The string does not contain
           any digit");
          }
             else
          {
            alert("String contains some digit(s)");
```

```
        }
    }
  </script>
</head>
<body>
<h2>Example of Regular Expression</h2>
<script type="text/javascript">
    var input_str=prompt("Enter some input","");
    TestString(input_str);
</script>
</body>
</html>
```

Output

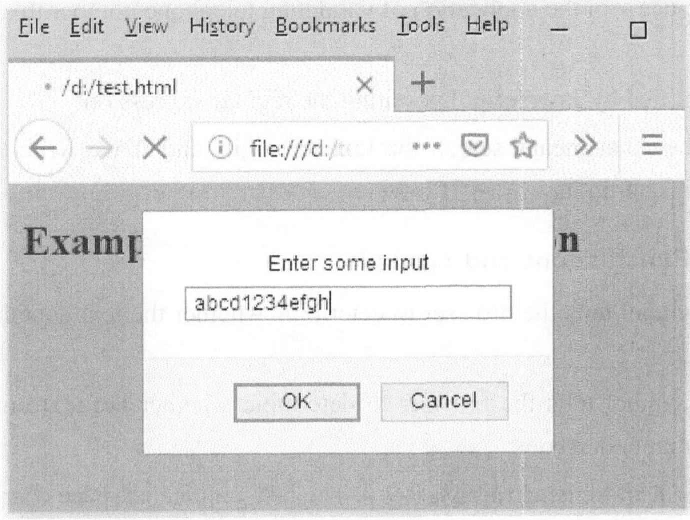

Click OK button and you will get

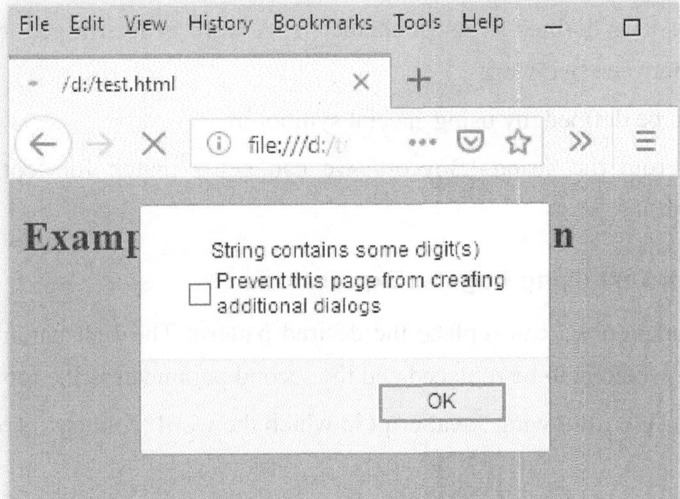

4.15.2 Entering the Range of Characters

- For matching any digit we need not have to enter every digit right from 0 to 9. Similarly for matching letters we need not have to test with every single alphabet. We can achieve this by entering range of characters.
- For example – To match a digit we must have a regular expression as [0-9]. Thus placing the range within a square bracket helps us to evaluate a complete range of set of characters.
- Suppose we enter [j-s] then that means match the characters j, k, l, m, n, o, p, q, r and s.

4.15.3 Matching Digits and Non Digits

- Determining whether the string contains digits or non digits is a common task in any search pattern. For instance – in the application of validating telephone number this is the most wanted task.
- This can be simplified by JavaScript by writing the regular expression.
- If we write \d then that means search the text for digits and if we write \D then that means search the text for non-digits.

4.15.4 Matching Punctuations and Symbols

- The \w special symbol tells the browser to determine whether the text contains a letter, number, or an underscore.
- The \W special symbol tells the browser to determine whether the text contains other than a letter, number, or an underscore.
- Using \W is equivalent to using [a-zA-Z0-9_]. The last _ indicates space character.

4.15.5 Matching Words

- Any word in the text is defined as set of characters. A word is determined by a word boundary that is the space between two words.
- The boundary can be defined by using special symbol \b
- For example – From the string 'Boycott' we can get a match for 'cot' by using regular expression /\bcot\b/

4.15.6 Replacing a Text using Regular Expressions

Using **replace** function we can replace the desired pattern. The first parameter in the replace function is the string which is to be replaced and the second parameter is the replacing string.

For example- Consider following JavaScript in which the word 'country' is replaced by 'India'

```
<!DOCTYPE html>
<html>
<head>
    <script type="text/javascript">
      function TestString(str)
      {
         new_str=str.replace("country","India");
         document.write(new_str);
      }
    </script>
</head>
<body>
    <script type="text/javascript">
    str="I love my country";
    document.write(str);
    </script>
    <form name="form1">
       <input type="button" value="Replace"
       onclick="TestString(str)">
    </form>
</body>
</html>
```

Output

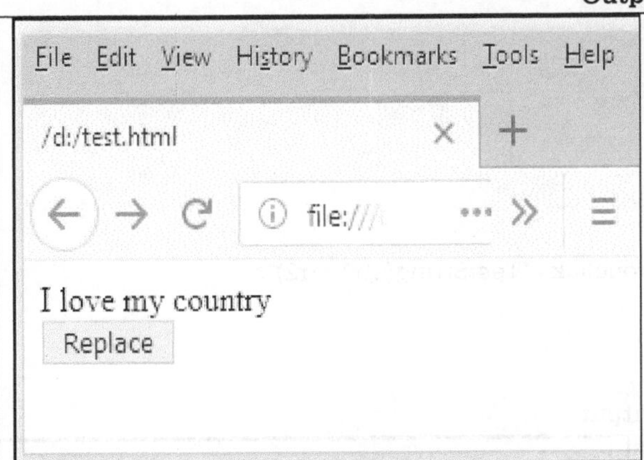

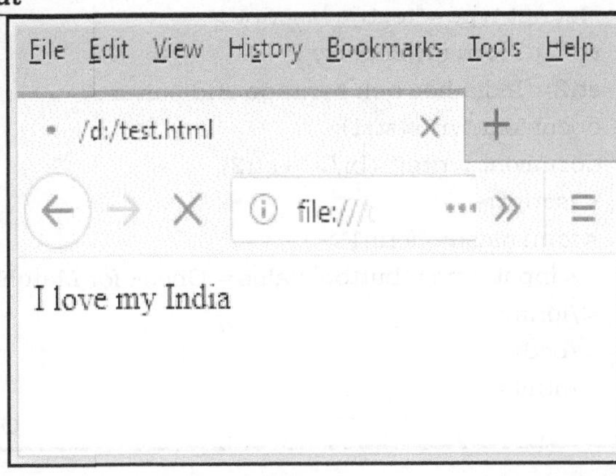

4.15.7 Returning a Matched Character

The **exec()** method searches string for text that matches with the regular expression. If it finds a match , it returns an array of results, otherwise it returns null.

If we want to search for particular pattern from a text then exec() method can be used as follows -

```
pattern.exec(text)
```

This function returns an array of matched result.

Example Program

```
<!DOCTYPE html>
<html>
<head>
    <script type="text/javascript">
      function TestString(str1,str2)
      {
        re=/India/g;
        result1=re.exec(str1);
        result2=re.exec(str2);
        if(result1)
        document.write("<br/>The First text contains the word "+result1);
        else
        document.write("<br/>The First text does not contain the word 'India' ");

        if(result2)
        document.write("<br/>The Second text contains the word "+result2);
        else
        document.write("<br/>The Second text does not contain the word 'India' ");
      }
</script>
</head>
<body>
<script type="text/javascript">
str1="I love my country";
str2="India has rich heritage and culture";
document.write(str1);
document.write("<br/>"+str2);
</script>
<form name="form1">
  <input type="button" value="Check for Match" onclick="TestString(str1,str2)">
</form>
</body>
</html>
```

Output

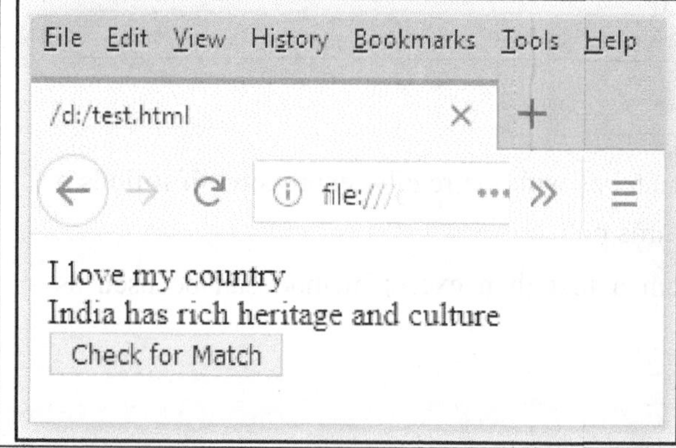

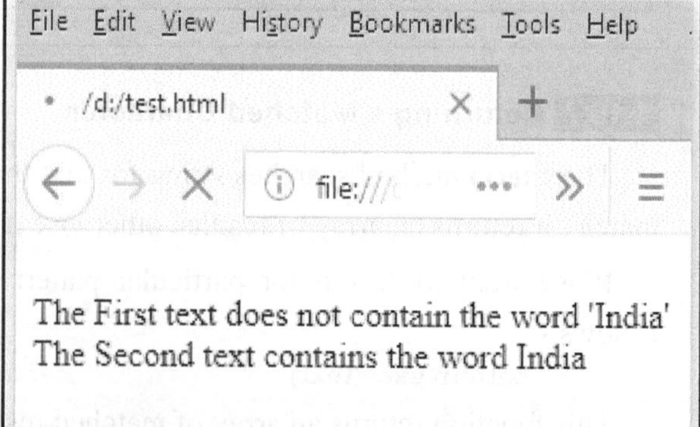

4.15.8 Regular Expression Object Properties

There are various regular expression object properties that help in matching particular word, character, last character, index at which to start the next match and so on. These properties are enlisted in the following table -

Regular Expression Object	Properties
$1 (through $9)	Parenthesized substring matches
$_	Same an input
$*	Same as multiline
$&	Same as lastMatch
$+	Same as lastParen
$`	Same as leftContent
$'	Same as rightContext
global	Search globally (g modifier in use)
ignoreCase	Search case-insensitive (i modifier in use)
input	The string to search if no string is passed
lastIndex	The index at which to start the next match
lastMatch	The last match characters
lastParen	The last parenthesized substring match
leftContext	The substring to the left of the most recent match
multiline	Whether strings are searched across multiple lines
prototype	Allows the addition of properties to all objects
rightContext	The substring to the right of the most recent match
source	The regular expression pattern itself

Example Program

```
<!DOCTYPE html>
<html>
<head>
    <title>Pattern Matching using Regular Expression </title>
    <script type="text/javascript">
      function TestString(str)
      {
      // for each Sunil - replace it with Mr. and then Sunil
      alert(str.replace(/Sunil/g, 'Mr.$&'));
      }
    </script>
</head>
<body>
```

```
    <script type="text/javascript">
      str= "Sunil kumar, Sunil Shetty,Sunil Kale";
      document.write(str);
    </script>
    <button onclick="TestString(str)">Change</button>
</body>
</html>
```

Output

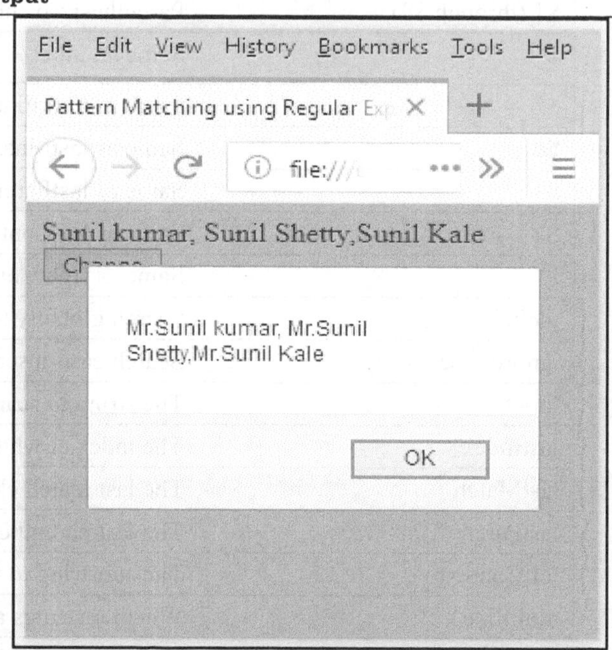

Ex. 4.15.2 : Develop and demonstrate, using Javascript document that collects USN(the valid format is : A digit from 1 to 4 followed by two upper-case characters followed by two digits followed by two upper case characters followed by three digits:no embedded spaces allowed) of the user. Event handler must be included for the form element that collects this information to validate the input. Message in the alert windows must be produced when errors are detected.

Sol. :

```
<!DOCTYPE html>
<html>
<head>
<title>Pattern Matching using Regular Expression </title>
<script type="text/javascript">
function TestString(str)
{
  document.write("The given string is: ");
  document.write("<em>"+str+"</em>"+"<br/>");
  var i=str.match(/[1234][A-Z]{2}\d{2}[A-Z]{2}\d{3}/);
```

```
if(i==null)
 return false;
else
return true;
}
</script>
</head>
<body>
 <h3>
  <script type="text/javascript">
   var input_str=prompt("Enter Your University Seat number here","");
   if(TestString(input_str))
    document.write("valid Seat Number");
   else
    document.write("Invalid Seat Number");
  </script>
  </h3>
</body>
</html>
```

Output

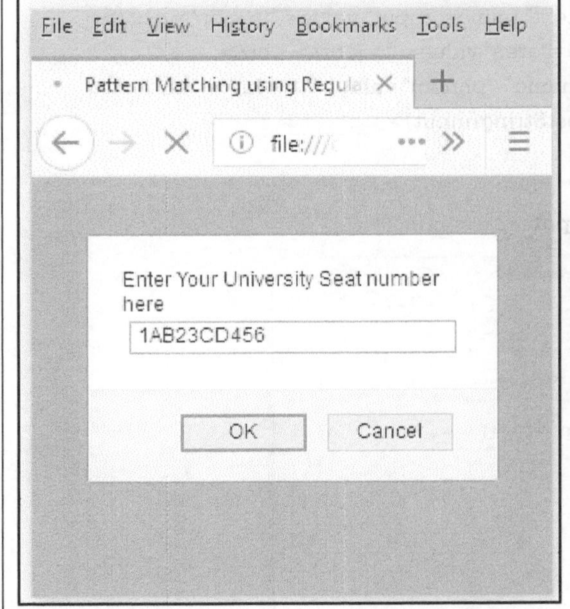

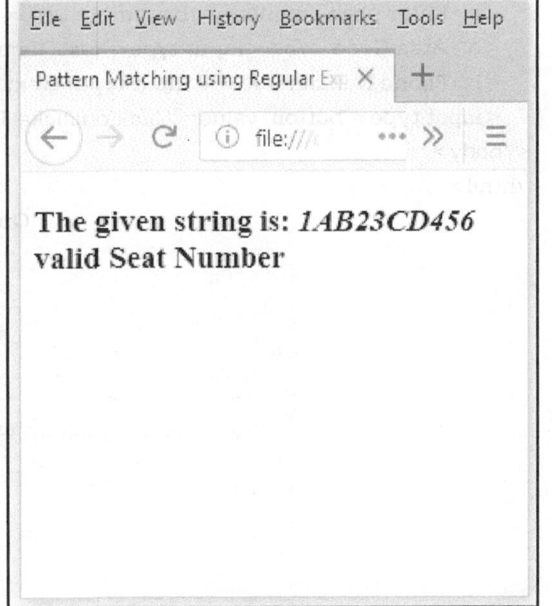

Ex. 4.15.3 : Write a Javascript that inputs a telephone number as a string in the form of (555) 5555555. The script should use string method split to extract the area code as a token, the first 3 digits of the phone number as a token, the last 4 digits of the phone number as a token. Display the area code in one text field and seven digit phone number in another text field.

AU : May-08, CSE, Marks 8

Sol. : HTML Document[phNo.html]

```
<html>
<head>
   <title>Phone Number Demo</title>
   <script type="text/javascript">
   function TestString()
    {
    var str=document.form1.input.value;
    var i=str.match(/"("\d{3}")"\" "\d{3}"-"\d{4}/);
    var temp1=str.split("(");
    var temp2=temp1[1].split(")")
    document.form1.area.value=temp2[0];
    var temp3=temp2[1].split(" ");
        var temp4=temp3[1].split("-")
    document.form1.phnum.value=temp4[0]+temp4[1];
    }
   </script>
</head>
 <body>
    <form name="form1">
    <b>Enter phone number:</b><input type="text" name="input" value=""><br/><br/>
    <b>Area Code:</b><input type="text" name="area" value=""><br/><br/>
    <b>Phone Number:</b> <input type="text" name="phnum" value=""><br/><br/>
    <input type="button" value="Click"onclick=TestString(input)>
 </body>
</html>
```

Output

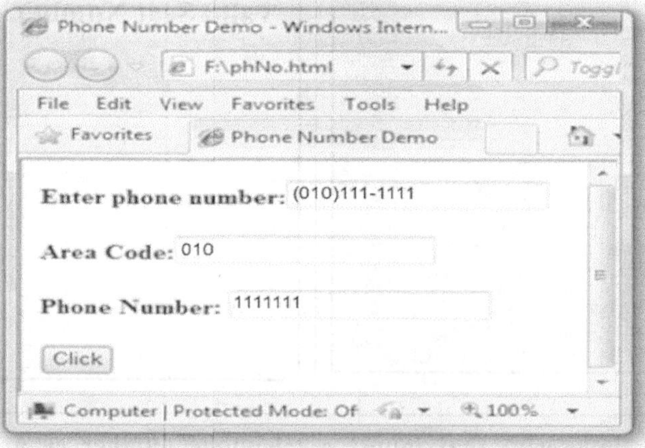

4.16 Exception Handling

- **Definition:** Exception handling is a mechanism that handles the runtime errors so that the normal flow of the application can be maintained.

- Basically an exception is an event that disrupts the normal flow of the program. It is an object which is thrown at runtime.
- The exception handling in JavaScript can be performed with the help of following types of statements –
  1. The try statement lets you test a block of code for errors.
  2. The catch statement lets you handle the error.
  3. The throw statement lets you create custom errors.
  4. The finally statement lets you execute code, after try and catch, regardless of the result.
- Basic syntax of try-catch block is

```
try {
 Block of code to try
}
catch(err) {
Block of code to handle errors
}
```

- When error occurs, JavaScript will normally throw an exception so that appropriate error message can be displayed and it will avoid a crash of a program.
- Following example illustrates the exception handling mechanism in JavaScript

```
<!DOCTYPE html>
<html>
<body>

<p>Enter Some Number:</p>

<input id="demo" type="text">
<button type="button" onclick="GetPositiveNumber()">Click</button>
<p id="myID"></p>

<script>
    function GetPositiveNumber() {
    var message, num;
    message = document.getElementById("myID");
    message.innerHTML = "";
    num = document.getElementById("demo").value;
    try {
          if(num == "")
             throw "empty";
          if(isNaN(num))
            throw "not a number";
          num = Number(num);
          if(num < 0)
            throw "Negative";
```

```
            if(num == 0)
                throw "Zero";
        }
        catch(err) {
            message.innerHTML = "Input is " + err;
        }
}
</script>
</body>
</html>
```

Output

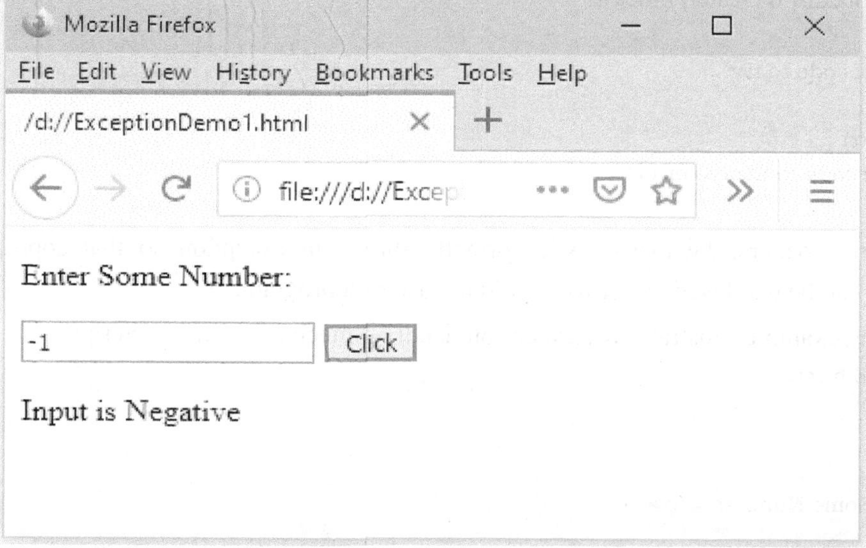

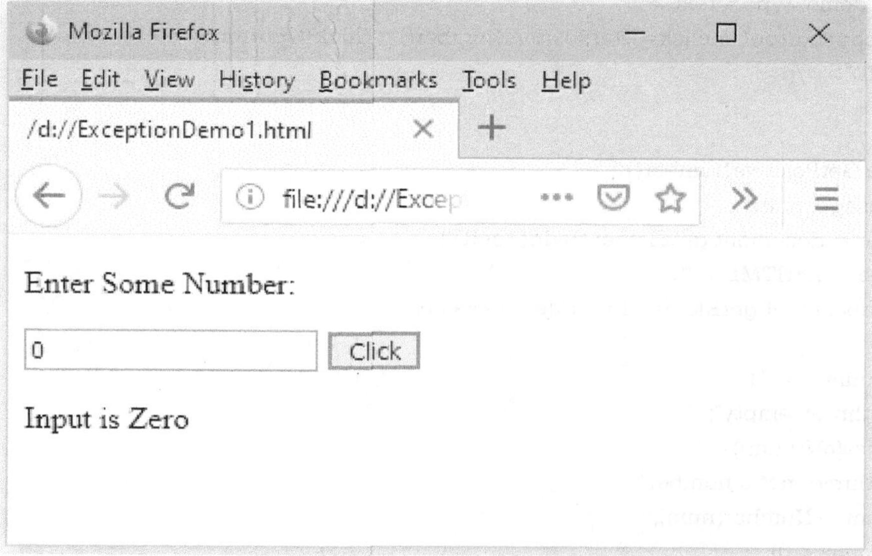

Ex. 4.16.1 : Write a JavaScript to handle divide by zero error using exception handling mechanism.

Sol. :

```
<!DOCTYPE html>
<html>
<body>

<p>Enter Some Number:</p>
<input id="numerator" type="text">
<input id="denominator" type="text">
<button type="button" onclick="divide()">Click</button>
<p id="myID"></p>

<script>
    function divide() {
    var n,result, message, num;
    message = document.getElementById("myID");
    message.innerHTML = "";
    d = document.getElementById("denominator").value;
    try {
        if(d == "")
            throw "empty";
        if(isNaN(d))
            throw "not a number";
        num = Number(d);
        if(num == 0)
            throw "Divide By Zero!!!";
        else
        {
            n = document.getElementById("numerator").value;//obtaining numerator
            n=Number(n);//converting text string to number
            ans=n/num;//performing division
            message.innerHTML = ""+ans;
        }

      }
      catch(err) {
        message.innerHTML = "Error: " + err;
    }
}
</script>
</body>
</html>
```

Output

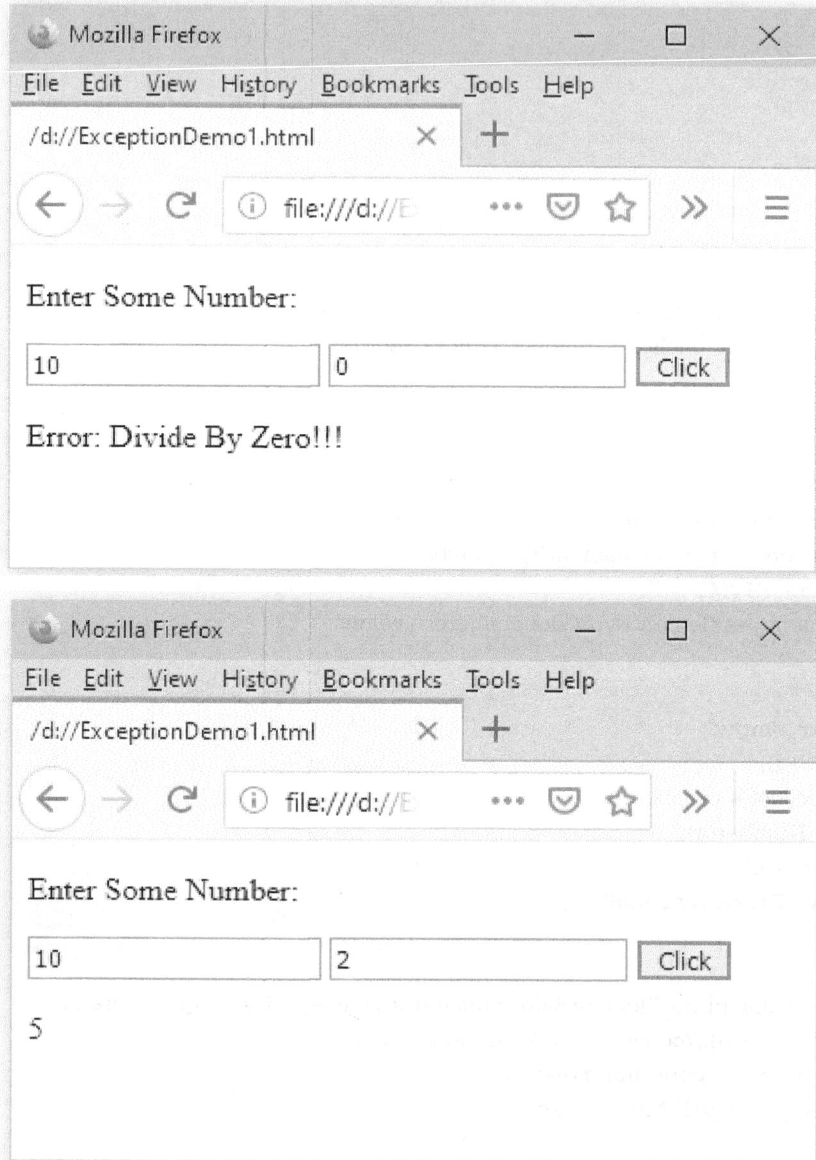

4.17 Validation

AU : May-14, Marks 8

- Various control objects are placed on the form. These control objects are called **widgets.**
- These widgets used in JavaScript are – Textbox, Push button, Radio button, Checkbox and so on.
- In JavaScript the **validation of these widgets** is an important task.

  Let us understand the validation of form elements with the help of examples –

Ex. 4.17.1 : Write a JavaScript for password verification.

Sol. :

```
<!DOCTYPE html>
<html>
<head>
 <title>Demo of onlclick Tag Attibute</title>
<script type="text/javascript">
 function my_fun()
 {
  var mypwd=document.getElementById("pwd");
  var my_re_pwd=document.getElementById("re_pwd");
  if(mypwd.value=="")
  {
    alert("You have not entered the password");
    mypwd.focus();
    return false;
  }
  if(mypwd.value!=my_re_pwd.value)
  {
    alert("Password is not verified, Re-enter both the passwords");
    mypwd.focus();
    mypwd.select();
    return false;
  }
  else
  {
    alert("Congratulations!!!");
    return true;
  }
 }
</script>
</head>
<body>
 <center>
 <form id="form1">
  <label> Enter your password
  <input type="password" value="" id="pwd" />
  </label>
  <br/><br/>
  <label> Re-Enter the password
  <input type="password" value="" id="re_pwd" onblur="my_fun();"/>
  </label><br/>
  <input type="submit" value="Submit" name="submit" onsubmit="my_fun();"/>
   <input type="reset" value="Reset" name="reset"/><br/>
```

```
  </form>
 </center>
</body>
</html>
```

Output(Run1)

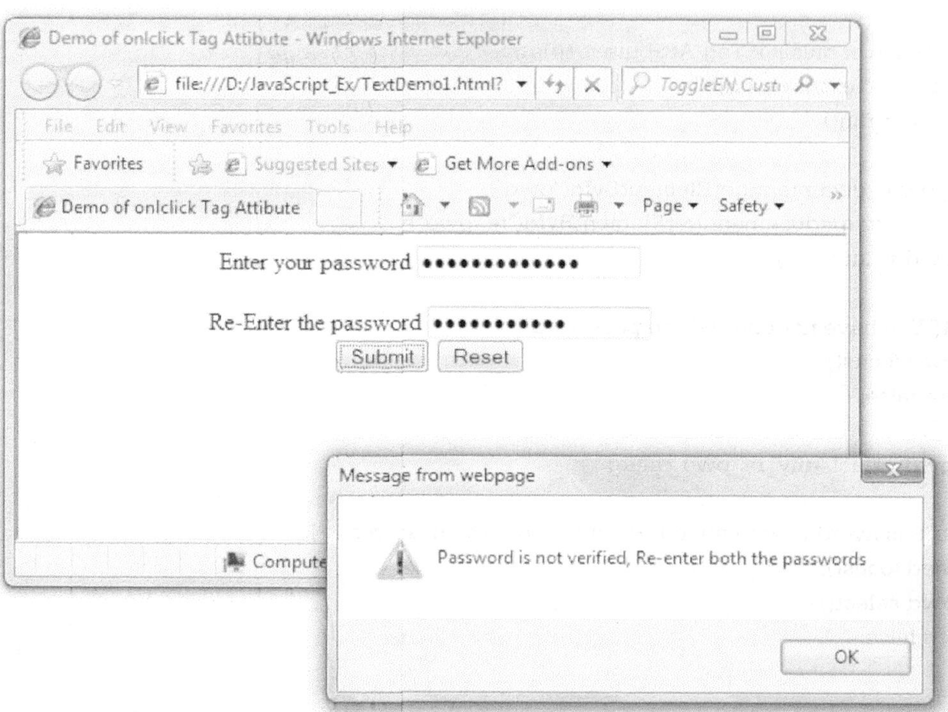

Output(Run2)

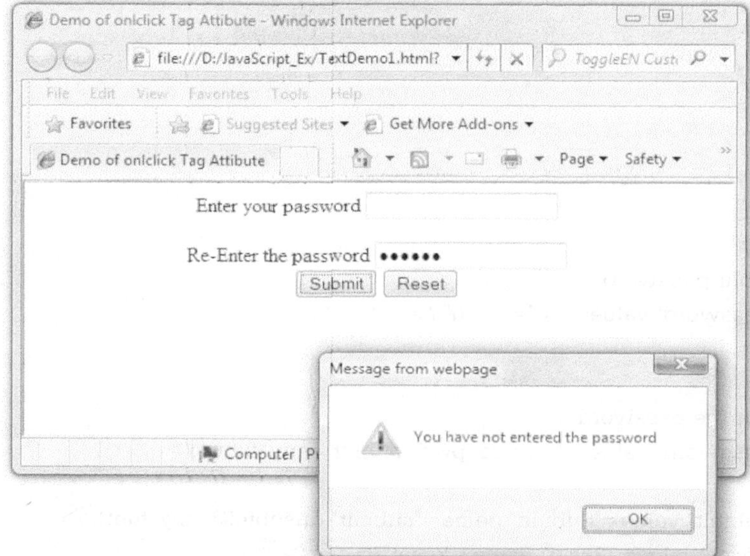

Output(Run3)

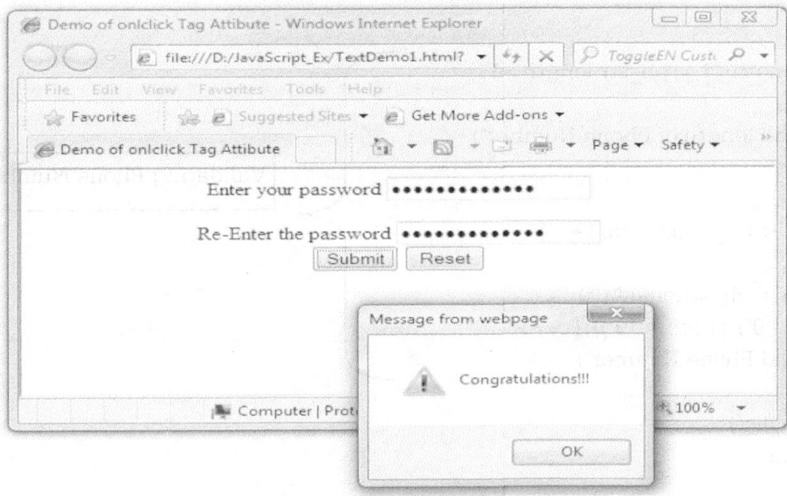

Ex. 4.17.2 : Write JavaScript to validate a for consisting of Name, Age, Address, EmailID, hobby (check box), Gender(radio box), country(Drop down menu).

Sol. : ApplicationForm.html

```
<html>
<head>
<title>The Student Registration Form</title>
<script type=text/javascript>
function validate()
{
    var i;
    var name_str=document.my_form.name;
    var phoneID=document.my_form.ph_txt;
    var ph_str=document.my_form.ph_txt.value;
    var str=document.my_form.Email_txt.value;
    if((name_str.value==null)||(name_str.value==""))
    {
    alert("Enter some name")                          Validating Name
    return false
}
     if(document.my_form.Age_txt.value=="")// validating age
    {
    alert("Enter Some Age")
    return false
    }
         if((document.my_form.Age_txt.value<"5")&&(document.my_form.Age_txt.value>"21"))
    {
    alert("Invalid Age")
```

```
return false
}

if(ph_str.length<1 ||ph_str.length>11)
{
alert("Invalid length of Phone Number")
return false
}
for (i = 0; i < ph_str.length; i++)
{
      var ch = ph_str.charAt(i);
   if (((ch < "0") || (ch > "9"))){
alert("Invalid Phone Number")

phoneID.focus()
 return false
}
}

var index_at=str.indexOf("@")
var len=str.length
var index_dot=str.indexOf(".")
var emailID=document.my_form.Email_txt
if ((emailID.value==null)||(emailID.value==""))
{
alert("Please Enter your Email ID")
emailID.focus()
return false
}
if (str.indexOf("@")==-1)
{
  alert("Invalid E-mail ID")
  return false
}
  if (str.indexOf(".")==-1 || str.indexOf(".")==0
          || str.indexOf(".")==index_at)
{
  alert("Invalid E-mail ID")
  return false
}

 if (str.indexOf("@",(index_at+1))!=-1)
 {
  alert("Invalid E-mail ID")
  return false
 }
 if (str.indexOf(" ")!=-1)
```

Validating Phone Number

Validating Email ID

Validating Email ID

```
    {
        alert("Invalid E-mail ID")
        return false
     }
    if (!document.my_form.group1[0].checked && !document.my_form.group1[0].checked)
     {
        alert("Please Select Sex");
        return false;
     }
    if (!document.my_form.group1[0].checked && !document.my_form.group1[0].checked)
     {
        alert("Please Select Sex");
        return false;
     }
      return true

}
</script>
</head>
<body bgcolor=aqua>
<center><h3>Application Form</h3></center>
<form name=my_form onsubmit=validate()>
<strong>Name: </strong>
<input type=text name=name><br/>

<strong>Age: </strong>
<input type=text name=Age_txt><br/>

<strong>Phone No:</strong>
<input type=text name=ph_txt><br/>
<strong>Email: </strong>
<input type=text name=Email_txt><br/><br/>
<strong>Sex:  </strong>
<input type="radio" name="group1" value="Male">Male
<input type="radio" name="group1" value="Female">Female<br/><br/><br/>
<strong>Hoby: </strong>
<input type="checkbox" name ="option1" value="Singing">Singing<br/>
<input type="checkbox" name ="option1" value="Reading">Reading<br/>
<input type="checkbox" name ="option1" value="T.V.">Watching T.V<br/>
<br/><br/>
<strong>Country:</strong>
<select name="My_Menu">
<option value="India">India</option>
<option value="China">China</option>
```

```
<option value="Shrilanka">Shrilanka</option>
</select>
<center>
<input type=submit value=Submit></br>
</center>

</body>
</html>
```

Output

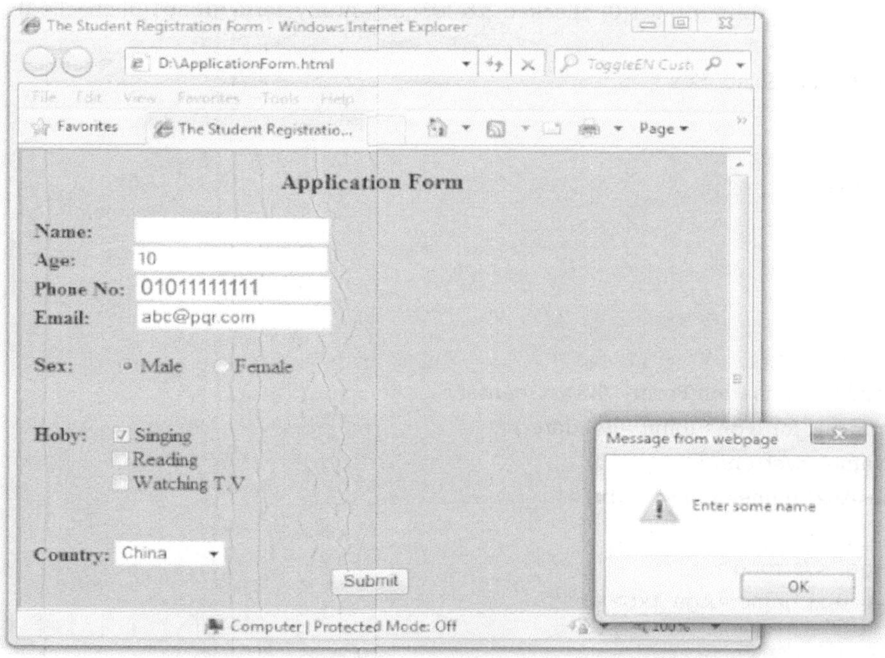

Ex. 4.17.3 : Design a HTML form for validation the users with fields user name and password and ok button which should receive the input from the user and responses as authorized or invalid user name or invalid password. **AU : May-14, Marks 8**

Sol. :

```
<head>
  <title>HTML FORM</title>
  <script type=text/javascript>
   function validate()
    {
     var user=document.form1.username;
     var pass=document.form1.password;
    if((user.value==null)||(user.value==""))
    {
     alert("Enter some user name");
```

```
      }
    if((pass.value==null)||(pass.value==""))
     {
      alert("Enter some password");

      }
      if(user.value=="admin")
      {
      alert("Valid user name");

      }
      if(pass.value=="password")
      {
      alert("Valid password");
      }
      else
      alert("Invalid username/password");
     }
  </script>
 </head>
 <body>
  <form id="form1" name="form1" onsubmit=validate()>
  <table width="510" border="0" align="center">
  <tr>   <td>Username:</td>
  <td><input type="text" name="username"/></td>
  </tr>
  <tr>    <td>Password</td>
  <td><input type="password" name="password"/></td>
  </tr>
  <tr>
  <td> </td>
  <td><input type="submit" name="button" value="OK"  /></td>
  </tr>
  </table>
  </form>
 </body>
</html>
```

Ex. 4.17.4 : Write a Javascript to validate radio button, operator field and check box.

Sol. :

JavaScript Program

```
<html>
<head>
<script LANGUAGE="JavaScript">

function ValidateForm(form)
{

if ((form.gender[0].checked == false ) && ( form.gender[1].checked == false ))
 { alert ( "Please choose your Gender: Male or Female" );
  return false;
 }
 if ((form.status[0].checked == false ) && ( form.status[1].checked == false ))
 { alert ( "Please choose your choice: AC or non AC" );
  return false;
 }
 if ( form.course.selectedIndex == 0 )
 { alert ( "Please select Some Course." );
  return false;
 }
 return true;
}
</script>
</head>
<body>
<br>
<form>
 Your Gender: <input type="radio" name="gender" value="Male"> Male
 <input type="radio" name="gender" value="Female"> Female
 <br/>
 Choice: <input type="checkbox" name="status">AC
 <input type="checkbox" name="status"> Non AC
 <br/>
 Course:
 <select name="course">
  <option value="">Select an Option:</option>
  <option value="Computer">Computer</option>
  <option value="Mechanical">Mechanical</option>
  <option value="E&Tc">E&Tc</option>
 </select>
 <br/><br/>
<input type="button" name="SubmitButton" value="Submit"
 onClick="ValidateForm(this.form)">
 <input type="reset" value="Reset">
</form>
</body>
</html>
```

Validating Radio Button

Validating Checkbox

Validating Option

4.18 Event Handling

AU : Dec-09,12, May-10,11, Marks 8

- **Definition of Event :** Event is an activity that represents a change in the environment. For example mouse clicks, pressing a particular key of keyboard represent the events. Such events are called intrinsic events.
- **Definition of Event Handler :** Event handler is a script that gets executed in response to these events. Thus event handler enables the web document to respond the user activities through the browser window.
- JavaScript support this special type of programming in which events may occur and these events get responded by executing the event handlers. This type of programming is called event-driven programming.
- Events are specified in lowercase letters and these are case-sensitive.
- **Event Registration :** The process of connecting event handler to an event is called event registration. The event handler registration can be done using two methods -
  - o Assigning the tag attributes
  - o Assigning the handler address to object properties.

Internet Programming

On occurrence of events the tag attribute must be assigned with some user defined functionalities. This will help to execute certain action on occurrence of particular event.

Commonly used events and tag attributes are enlisted in the following table -

Events	Intrinsic event attribute	Meaning	Associated tags
blur	onblur	Losing the focus.	<button> <input> <a> <textarea> <select>
change	onchange	On occurrence of some change.	<input> <textarea> <select>
click	onclick	When user clicks the mouse button.	<a> <input>
dblclick	ondblclick	When user double clicks the mouse button.	<a> <input> <button>

focus	onfocus	When user acquires the input focus.	<a> <input> <select> <textarea>
keyup	onkeyup	When user releases the key from the keyboard.	Form elements such as input,button,text,textarea and so on.
keydown	onkeydown	When user presses the key down	Form elements such as input,button,text,textarea and so on.
keypress	onkeypress	When user presses the key.	Form elements such as input,button,text,textarea and so on.
mousedown	onmousedown	When user clicks the left mouse button.	Form elements such as input,button,text,textarea and so on.
mouseup	onmouseup	When user releases the left mouse button.	Form elements such as input,button,text,textarea and so on.
mousemove	onmousemove	When user moves the mouse.	Form elements such as input,button,text,textarea and so on.
mouseout	onmouseout	When the user moves the mouse away from some element.	form elements such as input,button,text,textarea and so on.
mouseover	onmouseover	When the user moves the mouse away over some element.	Form elements such as input,button,text,textarea and so on.
load	onload	After getting the document loaded.	<body>
reset	onreset	When the reset button is clicked.	<form>
submit	onsubmit	When the submit button is clicked.	<form>
select	onselect	On selection.	<input> <textarea>
unload	onunload	When user exits the document.	<body>

The use of these tag attributes for handling the events is illustrated by following code sample

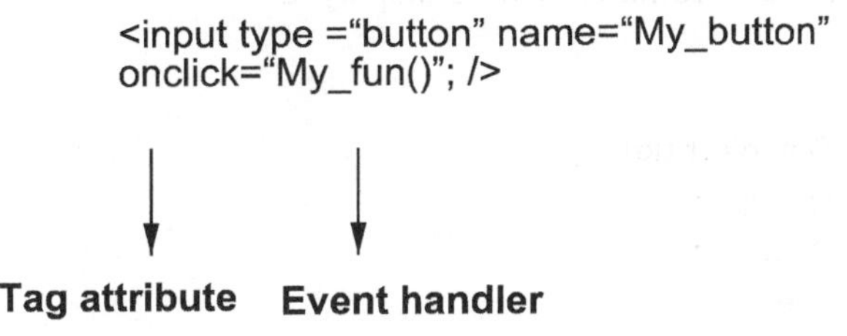

That means when the user clicks the **button** then as an event handler a user defined function **My_fun()** gets called. Basically in this function user writes the instructions that need to be executed on the button click event.

Ex. 4.18.1 : Discuss the properties of mouse events associated with DOM2 with an example.
AU : Dec-12, Marks 8

Sol. : Various types of mouse events associated with DOM2 are click, mousedown, mouseup, mouseout and mouseover.

Events	Intrinsic event attribute	Meaning	Associated tags
mousedown	onmousedown	When user clicks the left mouse button.	Form elements such as input,button,text,textarea and so on.
mouseup	onmouseup	When user releases the left mouse button.	Form elements such as input,button,text,textarea and so on.
mousemove	onmousemove	When user moves the mouse.	Form elements such as input,button,text,textarea and so on.
mouseout	onmouseout	When the user moves the mouse away from some element	form elements such as input,button,text,textarea and so on.
mouseover	onmouseover	When the user moves the mouse away over some element	Form elements such as input,button,text,textarea and so on.
click	onclick	When user clicks the mouse button.	<a> <input>
dblclick	ondblclick	When user double clicks the mouse button.	<a> <input> <button>

Following is an example in which image can be dragged and dropped anywhere in the HTML document. Accordingly the co-ordinates will be displayed.

```
<html>
<head>
 <title> Drag and Drop Demo</title>
 <script type = "text/javascript">
  var X_offset, Y_offset, Item;
  function Catch_function(e)
  {
    Item = e.currentTarget;
    var posX = parseInt(Item.style.left);
    var posY = parseInt(Item.style.top);
    X_offset = e.clientX - posX;
    Y_offset = e.clientY - posY;
    document.addEventListener("mousemove", Move_function, true);
    document.addEventListener("mouseup", Drop_function, true);
    e.stopPropagation();
    e.preventDefault();
  }
  function Move_function(e)
  {
    Item.style.left = (e.clientX - X_offset) + "px";
    Item.style.top = (e.clientY - Y_offset) + "px";
    e.stopPropagation();
  }
  function Drop_function(e)
  {
    document.removeEventListener("mouseup", Drop_function, true);
    document.removeEventListener("mousemove", Move_function, true);
    e.stopPropagation();
  }
 </script>
</head>
<body>
 <h3>
  Click on image below-drag it, move it and then drop anywhere!!!
  <br /><br />
  <img src="lamp1.jpg"
   style = "position: absolute;
```

Registering the mouse event with the help of **addEventListener** function.

```
    top: 100px;
    left: 100px;
    border:2px solid;"
    onmousedown = "Catch_function(event);" />
  </h3>
</body>
</html>
```

Output

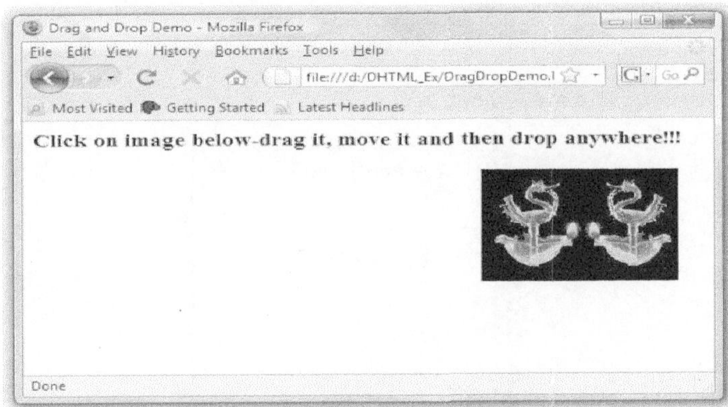

4.18.1 Handling Events from the Body Elements

To understand how events works in JavaScript let us put some Form components on the JavaScript. The **onload** event gets activated as soon as the web page gets loaded in the browser's window. Following script along with its output illustrate the **onload** tag attribute.

JavaScript[OnloadDemo.html]

```
<!DOCTYPE html PUBLIC "-//W3C//DTD XHTML 1.0 Transitional//EN"
"http://www.w3.org/TR/xhtml1/DTD/xhtml11.dtd">
<html xmlns="http://www.w3.org/1999/xhtml">
<head>
  <title>Demo of onload Tag Attibute</title>
  <script type="text/javascript">
   function my_fun()
   {
   //This message will be displayed on page loading
  alert("Welcome");
   }
  </script>
</head>
<body onload="my_fun()">
```

When web document gets loaded on the browser window then **my_fun()** will be called

```
</body>
</html>
```

Output

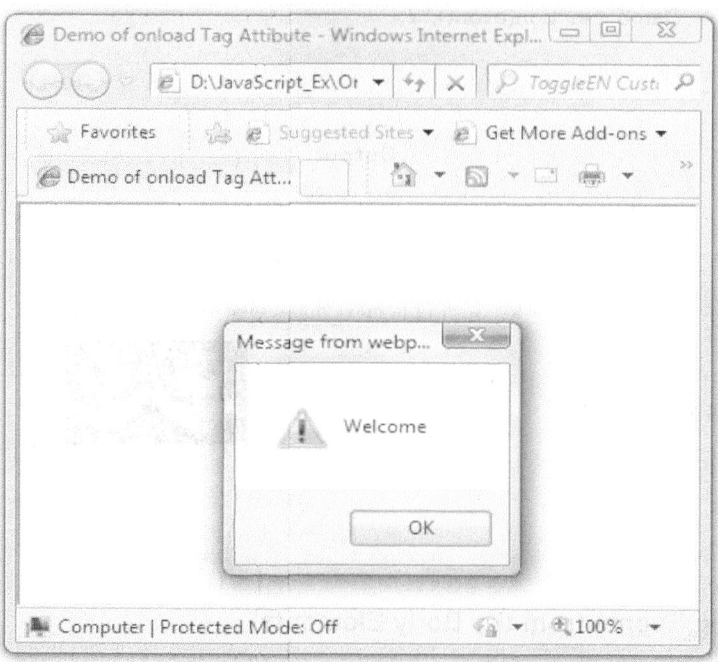

University Questions

1. *Explain the process of event registration.*
2. *Explain DOM event handling in detail.* **AU : May-11, Marks 8**
3. *Describe the event object properties.* **AU : May-10, Marks 8**
4. *Explain any four intrinsic event attributes.*
5. *Write a javascript to demonstrate the onload event.* **AU : Dec.-09, Marks 6**

Part III : DHTML

4.19 DHTML with JavaScript

AU : Dec.-16, Marks 8

- The DHTML stands for **D**ynamic **H**ypertext **M**arkup **L**anguage.
- Basically with DHTML a web developer can control how to display and position HTML elements in a browser window.
- The first important difference between HTML and DHTML is that HTML is used to create **static web pages** and DHTML is used to create **dynamic web pages.**

- The HTML consists of simple HTML tags, on the other hand DHTML is made up of **HTML tags + Cascading Style Sheets(CSS) + JavaScripts.**
- The HTML does not allow to alter the text and graphics on the web page unless web page gets changed. But in DHTML you can alter the text and graphics of the web page and for that matter you need not have to change the entire web page.
- Creation of HTML web pages is **simplest** but less interactive. Creation of DHTML is **complex but more interactive.**

Difference between HTML and DHTML

Sr. No.	HTML	DHTML
1.	HTML stands for Hypertext Markup Language. HTML is used to create **static web pages.**	DHTML stands for Dynamic Hypertext Markup Language. DHTML is used to create **dynamic web pages.**
2.	HTML sites work slowly upon the client server technology.	DHTML sites work fast upon the client server technology.
3.	HTML does not make use of the technology for making the pages dynamic.	DHTML makes use of CSS, events, methods and so on to make the page dynamic.
4.	HTML does not require any processing from the browser.	DHTML requires processing from the browser.

4.19.1 Moving Elements

- The position attribute decide the position of an element on the web browser , we can change this position by simply changing its **left** and **top** values.
- Note that only **absolute** or **relative** elements can be moved because static elements just neglect the top and left values.
- In the following example, we have placed two input boxes and one button element on the form. With the help of these elements we want to move the image **"fruit.jpg"** which is placed on the web document.
- For moving this image we have invoked one function "my_fun()". This function takes the values of X and Y co-ordinates through two text boxes that are supplied with and accordingly change the left and top values of the positioned element.
- The output shown along with this script itself is illustrative.

DHTML Document[MovingDemo.html]

```
<!DOCTYPE html>
<html>
<head>
<title>Moving the element</title>
<script type="text/javascript">
 function my_fun(x_pos,y_pos)
 {
  var Dom_obj=document.getElementById("my_img").style;
  Dom_obj.top=y_pos+"px";;
  Dom_obj.left=x_pos+"px";
 }
</script>
</head>
<body>
 <form>
  <label>X Co-ordinate:
  <input type="text" value="10" id="x"/>
  </label>
  <label>Y Co-ordinate:
  <input type="text" value="50" id="y"/>
  </label>
  <input type="button" value="Move" onclick="my_fun(x.value,y.value);"/>
 </form>
 <div id="my_img" style="position:absolute;top:50px;left:10px;">
  <img src="fruit.jpg" />
 </div>
</body>
</html>
```

Output

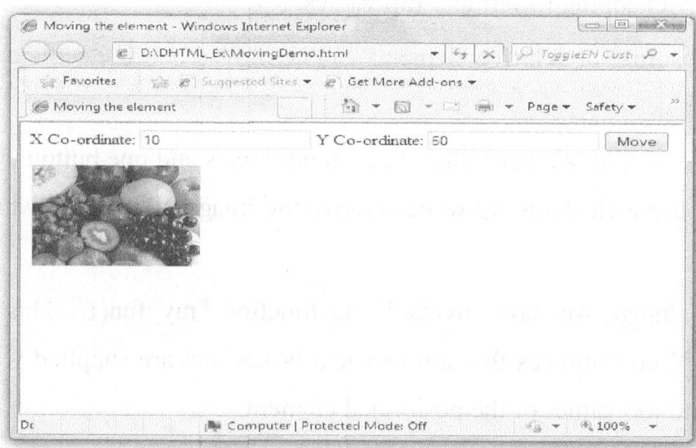

Just change the values in two text boxes meant for X and Y co-ordinates, then click the Move button and you can see following sort of output.

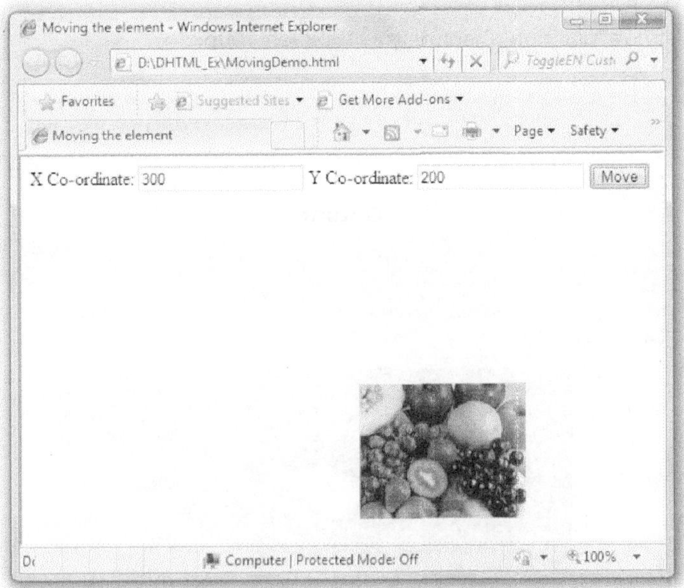

4.19.2 Elements Visibility

We can have control over the visibility of particular element on the web document. This can be done using the property **visibility.** There are two values that can be set to the "visibility" and those are **visible** for getting the element displayed and **hidden** for hiding the element. Following is a simple DHTML document which makes use of this property.

DHTML Document[VisibilityDemo.html]

```
<!DOCTYPE html>
<html>
<head>
<title>Visibility Of Element</title>
<script type="text/javascript">
 function my_fun()
 {
  var Dom_obj=document.getElementById("my_img").style;
  if(Dom_obj.visibility=="visible")
   Dom_obj.visibility="hidden";//Image will be as hidden
  else
   Dom_obj.visibility="visible";//image will be displayed
 }
</script>
</head>
```

```
<body>
 <form>
  <input type="button" value="Show/Hide" onclick="my_fun();"/>
 </form>
 <div id="my_img" style="position:absolute;top:10px;left:100px;">
  <img src="bird.jpg" />
 </div>
</body>
</html>
```

Output

Just click Show/Hide button repeatedly and get the effect of visibility demo.

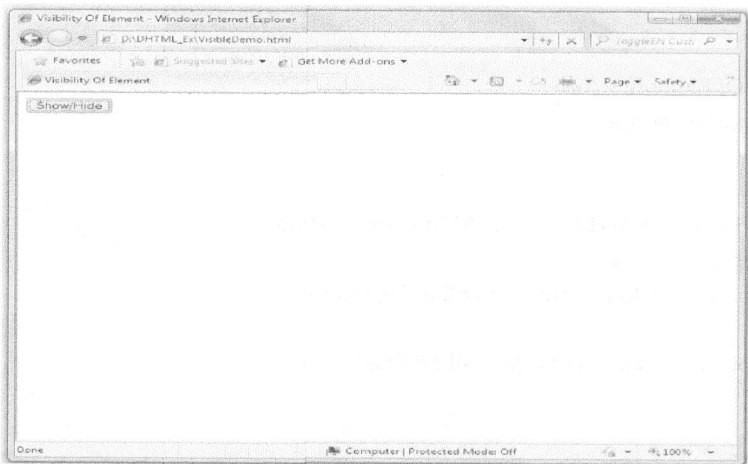

4.19.3 Changing Colors

There are two important properties – **backgroundColor** and **color** using which the background and foreground color can be changed.

In the following script we have put two text boxes in which the name of desired color can be written *(note that this name should be strictly in lower case letters)* and then user must click the button in order to get the effect. Illustrative output is given along with this script.

DHTML Document[ChangeColor.html]

```
<!DOCTYPE html>
<html>
<head>
<title>Change Color Demo</title>
<script type="text/javascript">
 function my_fun()
 {
  var F_color=document.getElementById("fore_color").value;
  var B_color=document.getElementById("back_color").value;
  document.body.style.backgroundColor=B_color;
  document.body.style.color=F_color;
 }
</script>
</head>
<body>
 <h2>Change Color!!!</h2>
  <form>
   <label>Enter foreground color
   <input type="text" value="" id="fore_color"/>
  </label>
  <br/><br/>
  <label>Enter Background color
   <input type="text" value="" id="back_color"/>
  </label>
  <br/><br/>
   <input type="button" value="click to change the color"  onclick="my_fun();"/>
  </form>
</body>
</html>
```

Output

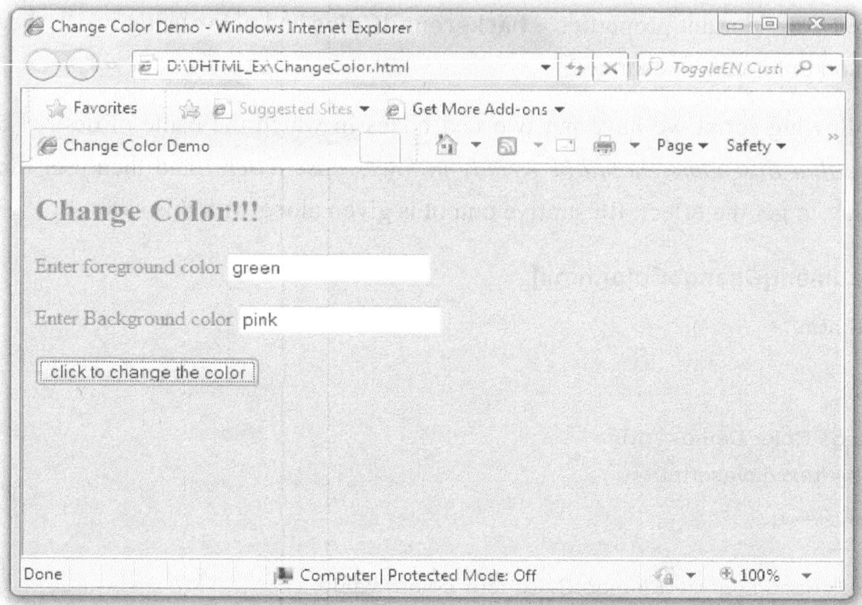

4.19.4 Locating the Mouse Cursor

We can locate the position of the mouse with the help some mouse event. The mouse click event is implemented by **MouseEvent** interface. The mouse position can be denoted by two co-ordinates i.e. x and y co-ordinates.

There are two ways of specifying the position of the mouse.

- **Co-ordinates with respect to browser window**

  Using the clientX and clientY the x and y positions of mouse event can be obtained. These positions are calculated from the upper left corner of browser window.

- **Co-ordinates with respect to computer screen**

  Using the screenX and screenY the x and y positions of mouse event can be obtained. These positions are calculated related to clients computer screen.

  But normally used of clientX and clientY is preferred for obtaining the x and y positions when some mouse event occurs on the browser window.

In the following document we are displaying both the types of co-ordinates.

DHTML Document[MouseCursorPos.html]

```
<!DOCTYPE html>
<html>
<head>
 <title>Mouse Cursor Demo</title>
```

```
<script type="text/javascript">
function my_fun(e)
{
 points1.innerText="With in client area"+"\n"+"X-Position:"+e.clientX+"\n"+
 "Y-Position:"+e.clientY;
 points2.innerText="\n"+"Relative to origin of screen"+"\n"+"X-Position:"
 +e.screenX+"\n"+"Y-Position:"+e.screenY;
}
</script>
</head>
<body onclick="my_fun(event);">
 <span id="points1">(0,0)</span>
 <br/>
 <span id="points2">(0,0)</span>
 <div align="center">
  <img src="lamp1.jpg"/>
 </div>
</body>
</html>
```

Output

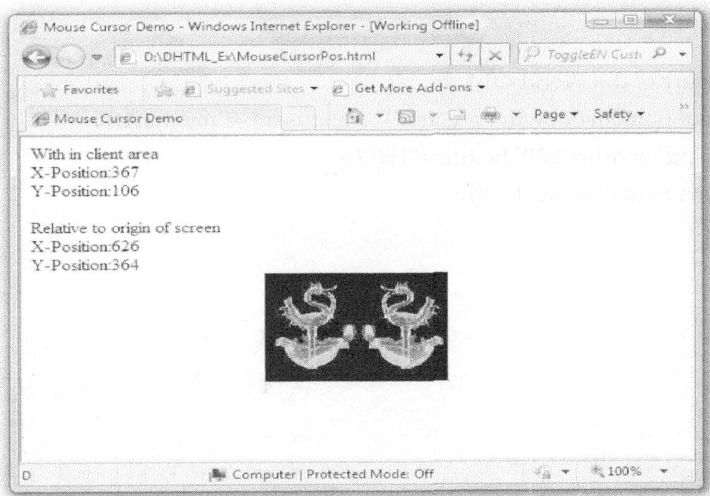

In above script we have used **innerText** attribute. If certain block of text gets displayed and may get changed repeatedly then the innerText property is used. Onclick event we are passing the object **event** to the event handler function. Hence we can obtain the current positions.

4.19.5 Reacting to a Mouse Click

AU : Dec.-16, Marks 8

When we click the mouse button it goes down and then comes back. These activities can be caught using the **onmousedown** and **onmouseup** events respectively.

Following is an example in which we will display one image when user presses mouse button and another image gets displayed when user releases the mouse button.

DHTML Document[MouseClick.html]

```
<!DOCTYPE html>
<html>
<head>
  <title>Response to mouse click</title>
<script type="text/javascript">
function my_fun()
{
 my_img.src="waterfall.jpg";
}
function my_fun1()
{
 my_img.src="TajMahal.jpg";
}
</script>
</head>
<body>
 <center>
  <h1> Two Wonders of the World</h1>
  <img id="my_img" onmousedown="my_fun()" onmouseup="my_fun1()"
   src="TajMahal.jpg" width="200" height="150"/>
  <p> Click this image to change it</p>
 </center>
</body>
</html>
```

Output

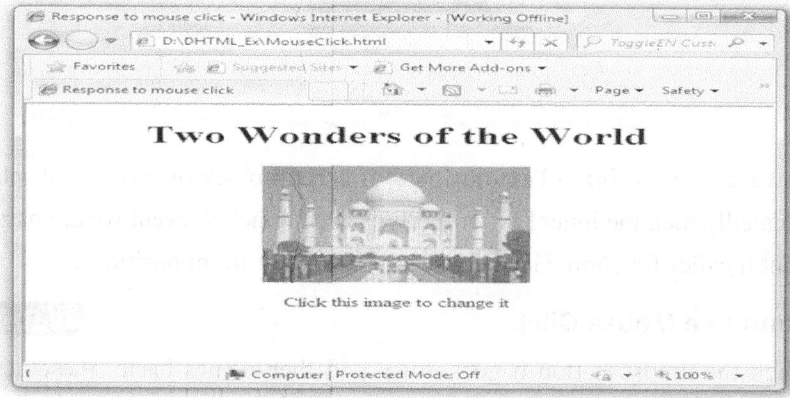

If click on the image we will get another image being displayed.

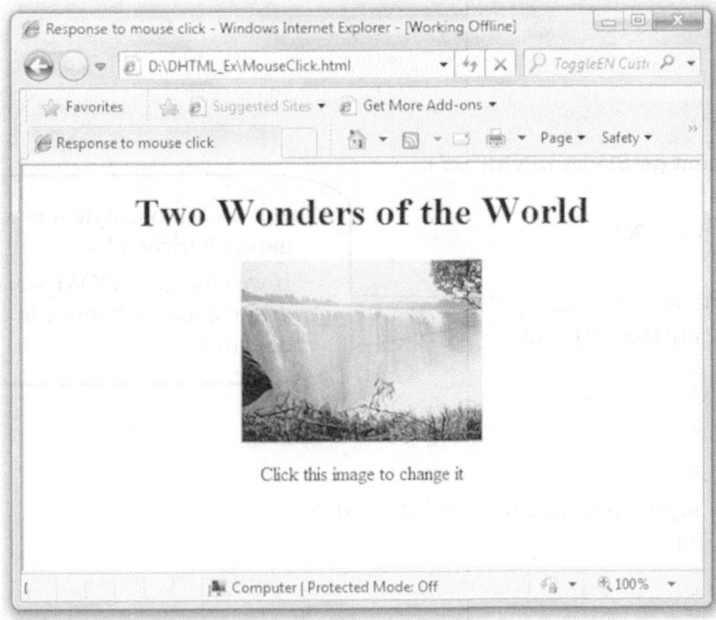

4.19.6 Slow Movements of Elements

- The element can be moved by changing the left and top properties.
- For moving an element slowly we have to move it by small amount repetitively.
- Each move must be separated by some amount of time.
- There are two methods defined by an object window which are responsible for moving an element. These methods are setTimeout and setInterval.
- The setTimeout function takes two parameters. The first one is the function which is responsible for moving an element. And the second parameter is the delay time given in milliseconds. The function which is responsible for moving an element can be called with the specified amount of delay. For example

  ```
  setTimeout("Move1();",10)
  ```

  means the function **Move1()** can be called after 10 milliseconds repeatedly.
- Following is a simple DHTML document in which the text is moved in forward and backward direction using setTimeout function.

DHTML Document[TxtMove.html]

```
<!DOCTYPE html>
<html>
<head>
<title>Moving Text Example</title>
<script language="javascript">
```

```
var x=0;
var direction=1;
function Move1()
{
  Dom_obj=document.getElementById("txt");
  x += dir;
  if (x >= 300 || x <= - 300)
     dir = 0 - dir;
  Dom_obj.style.left=x;
  window.setTimeout("Move1();",10);
 }
</script>
</head>
<body onload="Move1();">
<h3 align="center" style="position: relative;" ID="txt">
 King is on the move!!!
</h3>
</body>
</html>
```

Due DOM_obj.style.top=x the element moves horizontally.
If we change to DOM_obj.style.top=x then the text will move in vertical direction.

Output

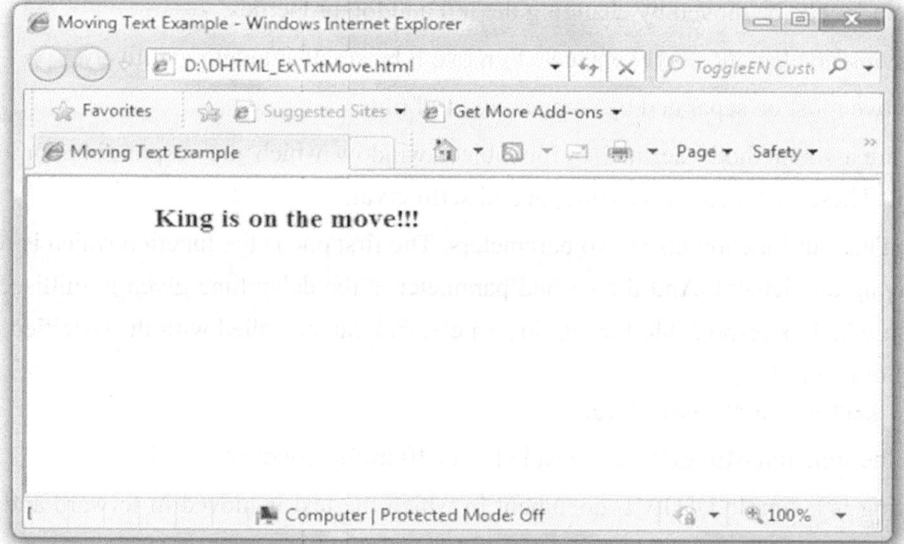

- In above script, we have called a **Move1()** function in which we are accessing the <h3> elements whose id is "txt".
- Then an object **Dom_obj** is created. The value of x will be incremented by one each time and is assigned to the left property of the object **Dom_obj.**
- Then **setTimeout** function will be called. This method calls the function **Move1()** again with the time delay of 10 milliseconds.

- Thus on each call of **Move1()** function the value of x will be incremented and is assigned to the **left** property of **Dom_obj.** This continues until the value being reached is 300.
- On reaching the value to 300, the value of x gets decremented. This causes this to move the element in backward direction.
- Hence as an output we get the text is moving forward and backward.

Review Question

1. *Write a DHTML program to handle the user click event.* **AU : Dec.-16, Marks 8**

4.20 Programming Examples

AU : May-08,16, June-09, Dec.-08,09, Marks 16

Ex. 4.20.1 : Design web page to create a clock with a timing event. **AU : June- 09, Marks 4**

Sol. : clock.html

```
<html>
<head>
<script type="text/javascript">
function Display()
{
 var today=new Date();
 var h=today.getHours();
 var m=today.getMinutes();
 var s=today.getSeconds();
 h=ConvertTwelve(h);
 m=SingleDigit(m);
 s=SingleDigit(s);
 document.getElementById("mytext").value=h+":"+m+":"+s;
 t=setTimeout('Display()',500);
}
 function ConvertTwelve(h)
 {
  if(h>=12)
  h=h-12;
  return h;
 }
 function SingleDigit(i)
 {
  if (i<10)
  {
  i="0" + i;//writing 0 before single digit number
  }
  return i;
```

```
}
</script>
</head>
<body onload="Display">
  <input type="text" value="" size="5" id="mytext"/>
</body>
</html>
```

Output

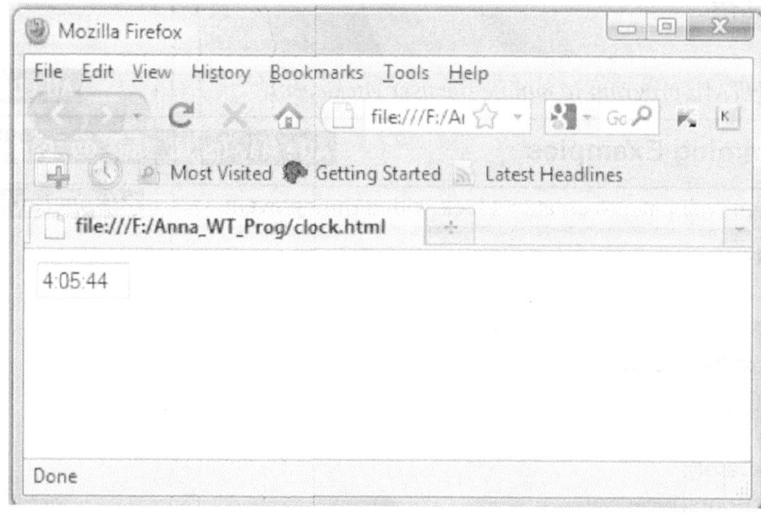

Ex. 4.20.2 : Write HTML program for the registration of new customer to the online banking system (Customer Data collected using a form, after submitting account number and type of account and username, password is displayed as output) **AU : May-08, CSE, Marks 8**

Sol. : HTML Document[bank.html]

```
<html>
<head>
  <title>Online Banking System</title>
  <script type="text/javascript">
  function fun()
  {
   alert("Name: "+form1.userName.value);
   alert("Password: "+form1.pwd.value);
   alert("Account Type: "+form1.MyMenu.value);
   alert("Account Number: "+form1.AccNo.value);
  }
  </script>
</head>
<body bgcolor="khaki">
  <form name="form1" onsubmit="fun()">
   <table>
```

```
    <tr><td><b>Name:</b></td><td><input type="text" name="userName"></tr>
    <tr><td><b>Password:</b></td><td><input type="password" name="pwd"></tr>
    <tr><td><b>Account Type:</b></td>
    <td><select name="MyMenu">
        <option value="Savings Account">Savings Account</option>
        <option value="Current Account">Current Account</option>
    </select>
    </td>
    </tr>
    <tr><td><b>Account Number:</b></td><td><input type="text" name="AccNo"></tr>
  </table>
  <br/><br/>
  <center>
    <input type="submit" value="Submit">
    <input type="reset" value="Clear">
  </center>
 </form>
</body>
</html>
```

Output

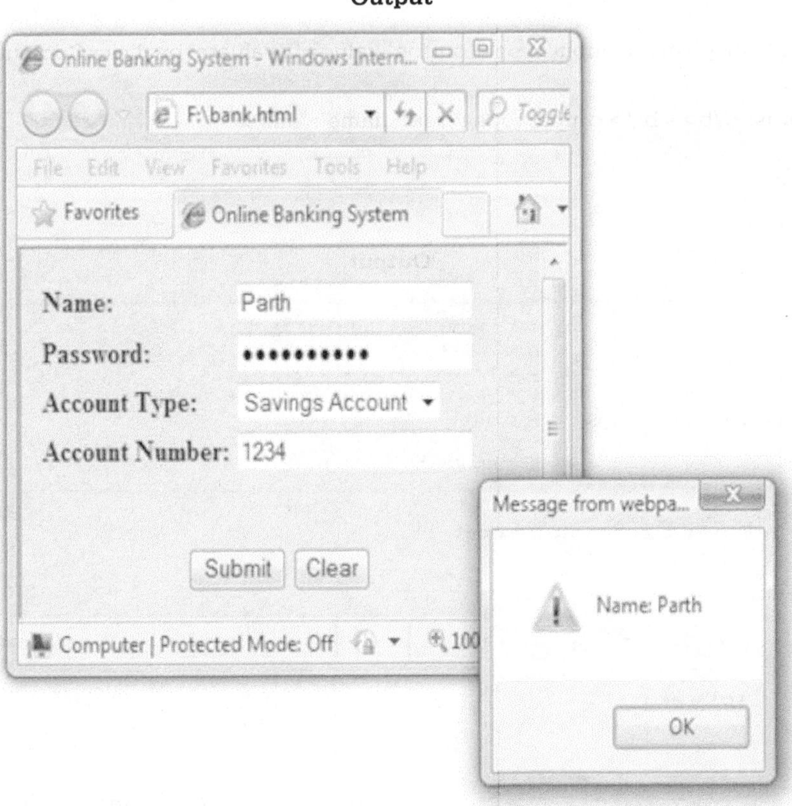

Ex. 4.20.3 : Develop a HTML page which accepts

- Any mathematical expression
- Evaluate the expression
- Displays the result of the evaluation.

AU : Dec.-08, CSE, Marks 16

Sol. : HTML Document[eval.html]

```
<html>
<head>
 <title>Expression Evaluation</title>
 <script type="text/javascript">
  function Compute()
  {
   document.form1.ans.value=eval(document.form1.my_exp.value);
  }
  </script>
</head>
<body>
 <form name="form1">
 <b>Enter Expression here:</b><br/><input type="text" name="my_exp">
  <br/><br/>
      <input type="button" value="Evaluate" onclick=Compute()>
  <br/><br/>
  <b>Answer is: </b><br/><input type="text" name="ans">
 </form>
</body>
</html>
```

Output

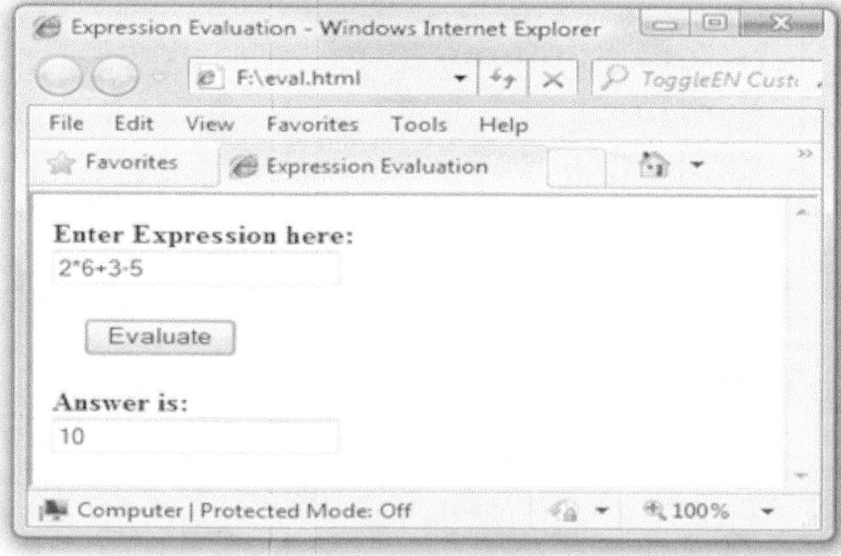

Ex. 4.20.4 : Develop a simple online shopping application using JavaScript.
(Assume your own data) **AU : Dec.-09, CSE, Marks 16**

Sol. :

Step 1 : We will first write a simple JavaScript which will allow user to enter the personal details and items to be purchased.

HTML Document[shopping.html]

```
<!DOCTYPE html PUBLIC "-//W#C//DTD XHTML 1.0 Transitional//EN"
"http://www.w3.org/TR/xhtml1/DTD/xhtml11.dtd">
<html xmlns="http://www.w3.org/1999/xhtml">
<head>
<script language="JavaScript">
var cost;
function fun()
{
 cost=0;
 if(document.myform.Item1.checked){cost=cost+20.15;}
 if(document.myform.Item2.checked){cost=cost+10.10;}
 if(document.myform.Item3.checked){cost=cost+26;}
 if(document.myform.Item4.checked){cost=cost+29;}
 document.myform.total.value="$"+cost;
}
</script>
</head>
<body bgcolor="pink">
<form name="myform" action="http://localhost/cgi-bin/purchaseInfo.cgi" enctype="text/plain"
method="post">
<center><h2>Online shopping Application</h2></center>
<strong>Personal Details:</strong>
<table>
<tr><td>name:</td><td> <input type="text" name="customer"/></td></tr>
<tr><td>City:</td><td> <input type="text" name="city"/></td></tr>
<tr><td>Phone:</td><td> <input type="text" name="phone"/></td></tr>
<tr><td>Email_Id:</td><td> <input type="text" name="email"/></td></tr>
</table>
<hr/>
<strong>Description:</strong>
<p>Following are some items with their prices.</p>
<p>Choose the required items by checking the chekboxes.</p>
</div>
```

```
<hr/>
<strong>Items to be chosen:</strong>
<br/>
<input type="checkbox" name="Item1" value="Item1_chosen" onclick="fun()"> Item One($20.15)
<p><input type="checkbox" name="Item2" value="Item2_chosen" onclick="fun()"> Item Two($10.10)
<p><input type="checkbox" name="Item3" value="Item3_chosen" onclick="fun()"> Item Three($26)
<p><input type="checkbox" name="Item4" value="Item4_chosen" onclick="fun()"> Item Four($29)
<input type="text" name="total" value="0"/>
<br/><br/>
<center>
<input type="submit" value="Place the Order" />
<input type="reset" value="Clear" />
</center>
</form>
</body>
</html>
```

Step 2 : When user click the Place the order button the submitted input can be collected in a cgi file. The sample cgi file can be written as follows -

CGI Document[purchaseInfo.cgi]

```
#!/program files/perl/bin/perl
use CGI qw(:standard);
print header;
print start_html(-BGCOLOR =>"Khaki");
print h2("Thank you for spending your valuable time with us!!!<br/>");
my($name)=param("customer");
print"<b>Order submitted is...</b>$name";
print end_html;
```

Step 3 : The output can be viewed as follows -

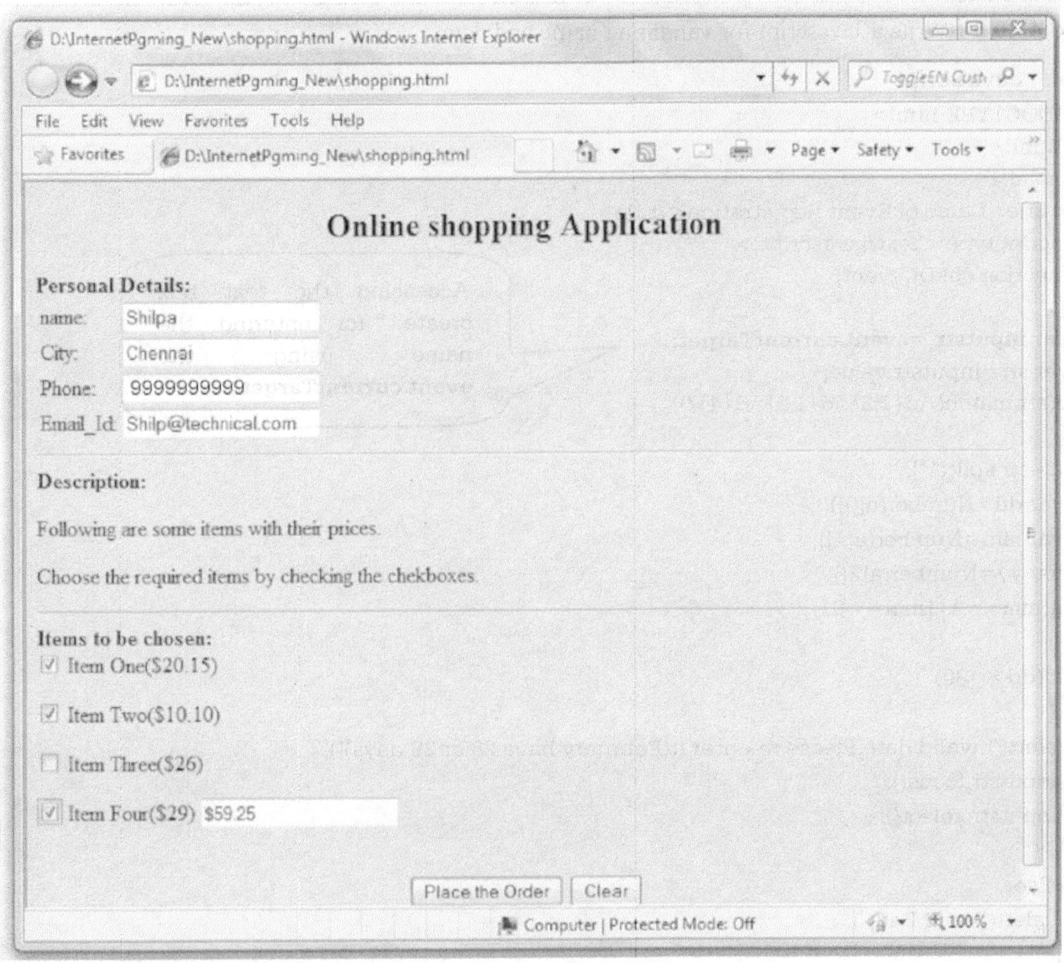

D:\InternetPgming_New\shopping.html - Windows Internet Explorer

D:\InternetPgming_New\shopping.html

File Edit View Favorites Tools Help

Favorites D:\InternetPgming_New\shopping.html Page Safety Tools

Online shopping Application

Personal Details:

name: Shilpa

City: Chennai

Phone: 9999999999

Email_Id Shilp@technical.com

Description:

Following are some items with their prices.

Choose the required items by checking the chekboxes.

Items to be chosen:

☑ Item One($20.15)

☑ Item Two($10.10)

☐ Item Three($26)

☑ Item Four($29) $59.25

Place the Order Clear

Computer | Protected Mode: Off 100%

Click the 'Place the order' button and following output can be seen

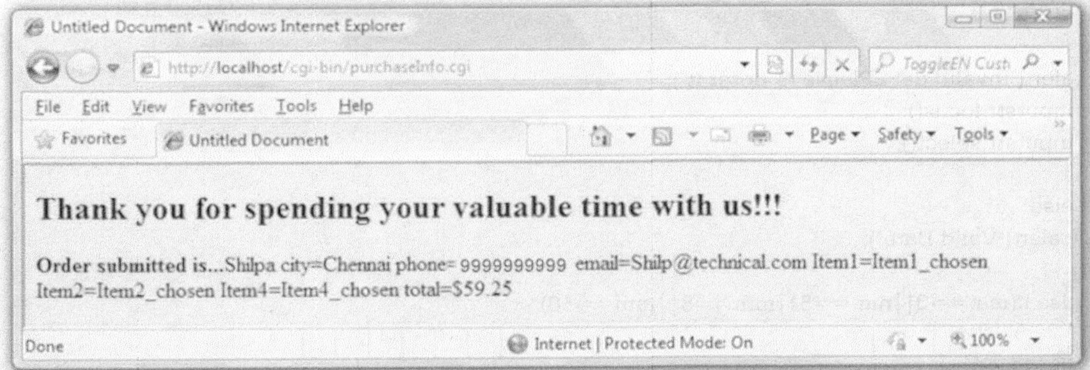

Ex. 4.20.5 : Write a Javascript for validating name and date.

Sol. : JavaScript

```
<!DOCTYPE html>
<html>
<head>
 <title>Demo of Event Registration</title>
<script type="text/javascript">
 function chkDt(event)
 {
 var inputstr =event.currentTarget;
 var str=inputstr.value;
 if(str.match(/\d{1,2}:\d{1,2}:\d{4}/))
 {
  a=str.split(":");
  var dd=Number(a[0]);
  var mm=Number(a[1]);
  var yy=Number(a[2]);
  if(mm==1||mm==01)
  {
   if(dd>=30)
   {
   alert("Invalid date,Please re-enter it(February have 28 or 29 days)");
   inputstr.focus();
   inputstr.select();
   }
   else
    alert("Valid Date");
  }
  else if(mm==0||mm==2||mm==4||mm==6||mm==7||mm==9||mm==11)
  {
   if(dd>31)
   {
   alert("Invalid date,Please re-enter it");
   inputstr.focus();
   inputstr.select();
   }
   else
    alert("Valid Date");
  }
  else if(mm==3||mm==5||mm==8||mm==10)
  {
   if(dd>30)
   {
   alert("Invalid date,Please re-enter it");
   inputstr.focus();
```

Accessing the text box created for entering the name using the **event.currentTarget**

```
   inputstr.select();
   }
   else
    alert("Valid Date");
  }
 }
 else
  {
   alert("invalid Input format!!,Please try again");
   inputstr.focus();
   inputstr.select();
  }

}
function chkName(event)
{
 var inputstr =event.currentTarget;
 var str=inputstr.value;
 if(str.match(/[a-zA-Z]+\s[a-zA-Z]\s[a-zA-Z]+/))
 {
  a=str.split(" ");
  var First_name=a[0];
  var Mid_initial=a[1];
  var Last_name=a[2];
  if(First_name.match(/^[a-zA-Z]{1,15}$/))
  {
   if(Mid_initial.match(/[a-zA-Z]$/))
   {
    if(Last_name.match(/^[a-zA-Z]{1,15}$/))
     alert("Valid name, now enter date");
    else
     alert("InValid Last Name");
   }
   else
     alert("InValid Middle name initial");
  }
  else
    alert("InValid First name");
 }
 else
   alert("You have entered wrong input");
 }
 </script>
</head>
```

Accessing the text box created for entering the name using the **event.currentTarget**

```
<body>
  <form id="form1">
   <label>Enter Name:
     <input type="text" value="" id="Name_chk" />(firstname mid_initial lastname)
   </label>
   <br/><br/>
   <label>Enter date:
   <input type="text" value="" id="Dt_chk" />(dd-dd-dddd)
   </label>
   <br/>
  </form>
<script type="text/javascript">
  var name_node=document.getElementById("Name_chk");
  var dt_node=document.getElementById("Dt_chk");
 dt_node.addEventListener("change",chkDt,false);
  name_node.addEventListener("change",chkName,false);
</script>
 </body>
</html>
```

Getting the object for each element and then registering the event handlers

Output

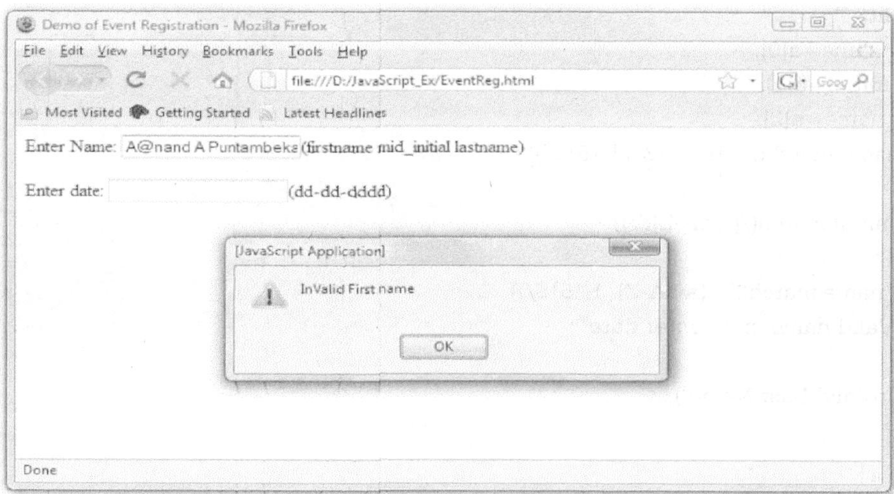

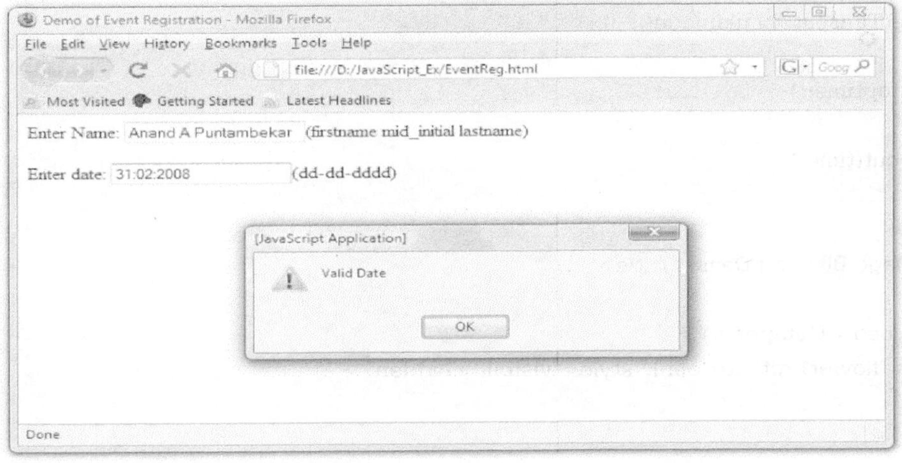

Thus document object model is useful in handling objects and events.

Ex. 4.20.6 : Create a script that repeatedly flashes an image on the screen. Do this by changing the visibility of the image. Allow users to control the "blink speed". **AU : May-08, Marks 8**

Sol. : Blinking.html

```
<html>
<head>
<script type="text/javascript">
function GetSpeed()
{
var input_str=prompt("Enter the speed value here:","");
var i=Number(input_str);
blinkImage(i);
}
function blinkImage(i)
{

 if(!document.getElementById('blink').style.visibility)
  {
    document.getElementById('blink').style.visibility="visible"
  }
  if(document.getElementById('blink').style.visibility=="visible")
  {
    document.getElementById('blink').style.visibility="hidden";
  }
  else
  {
    document.getElementById('blink').style.visibility="visible";
  }
  j=i;
```

```
timer=setTimeout("blinkImage(j)",i);
}
function stoptimer()
{
clearTimeout(timer);
}
</script>
<title>Image Blinking Demo</title>
</head>
<body onload="GetSpeed()">
<img src="flower1.gif" id="blink" style="visibility:hidden" >
</body>
</html>
```

Ex. 4.20.7 : Develop a DHTML page to change the background color using mouse over event on three squares containing different colors. **AU : Dec.-08, Marks 2**

Sol. : backgroundcolor.html

```
<html>
<head>
<script type="text/javascript">
function changeColor(color)
{
 document.getElementById('B').style.background=color;
}
</script>
</head>
<body id="B">
 <p>Move mouse over the color strips</p>
 <p> </p>
 <table width="50%">
  <tr>
   <td bgcolor="red" onmouseover="changeColor('red')"
              onmouseout="changeColor('transparent')">RED</td>
   <td bgcolor="yellow" onmouseover="changeColor('yellow')"
               onmouseout="changeColor('transparent')">YELLOW</td>
   <td bgcolor="aqua" onmouseover="changeColor('aqua')"
               onmouseout="changeColor('transparent')">AQUA</td>
  </tr>
 </table>
</body>
</html>
```

Output

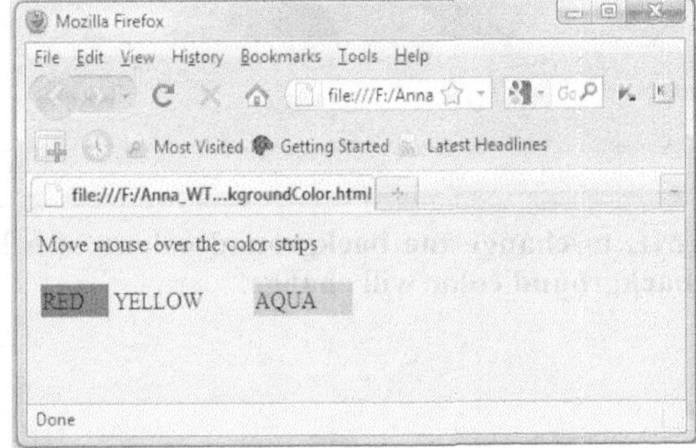

Ex. 4.20.8 : Write a DHTML to shake the window of a button click. Make use of two buttons one button used to start the shaking and another button used to stop the shaking of window.

AU : Dec.-08, Marks 10

Sol. : shake button.html

```
<head>
<script language="JavaScript1.2">
function shake(n)
{
 if(parent.moveBy)
 {
  for (i = 100; i > 0; i--)
  {
   for (j = n; j > 0; j--)
   {
    parent.moveBy(0,i);
    parent.moveBy(i,0);
    parent.moveBy(0,-i);
    parent.moveBy(-i,0);
   }
  }
 }
}
function Stop_Shake(obj)
{
 parent.moveBy=0;
 obj.style.left=0;
 obj.style.top=0;
}
</script>
</head>
<body>
<center>
<form>
<input type="button" onClick="Stop_Shake(this)" value="Stop">
```

```
<input type="button" onClick="shake(100)" value="Shake">
</form>
</center>
</ form>

</body>
```

Ex. 4.20.9 : Write a DHTML to change the background colour of a button, Mouse over three colored table cells and the background color will change. **AU : Dec.-08, Marks 10**

Sol. : buttoncolor.html

```
<html>
<head>
<script type="text/javascript">
function changeColor(color)
{
 document.getElementById('MyButton').style.background=color;
}
</script>
</head>
<body>
 <p>Move mouse over the color strips</p>
 <p> </p>
 <table width="50%">
  <tr>
   <td bgcolor="red" onmouseover="changeColor('red')">RED</td>
   <td bgcolor="yellow" onmouseover="changeColor('yellow')">YELLOW</td>
   <td bgcolor="aqua" onmouseover="changeColor('aqua')">AQUA</td>
  </tr>
 </table>
<form>
<input id="MyButton" type="button" value="Changing Color of Button">
</form>
</body>
</html>
```

Output

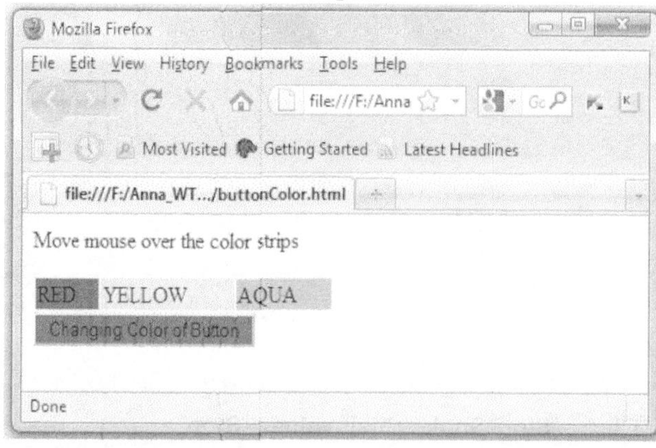

Ex. 4.20.10 : Write a JavaScript for displaying the context menu. The context menu is one that is shown when user right clicks anywhere in the document.

Sol. :

test1.html

```
<div id="ContxtMenu"
style="width:150px;border:1px solid black;background
color:yellow;visibility:hidden;position:absolute;line-height:30px; padding-left: 10px">
  <a href="http://www.google.com">Search Engine</a><br />
  <a href="http://www.facebook.com">Social Networking</a><br />
  <a href="http://www.gmail.com">Email Service</a><br / >
</div>

<script type="text/javascript">
var browserObj=document.getElementById && !document.all
var visibility=0

function Display(e)
{
 el=document.getElementById("ContxtMenu")
 visibility=1
 if (browserObj)
 {
  el.style.left=pageXOffset+e.clientX+"px"
  el.style.top=pageYOffset+e.clientY+"px"
  el.style.visibility="visible"
  e.preventDefault()
  return false
 }

}

function Hide()
{
 if (typeof el!="undefined" && visibility)
 {
  el.style.visibility="hidden"
  visibility=0
 }
}
if (browserObj)
{
 document.addEventListener("contextmenu", Display, true)
 document.addEventListener("click", Hide, true)
}
</script>
```

Output

[Note that the Mozilla FireFox browser is used to get the following output]

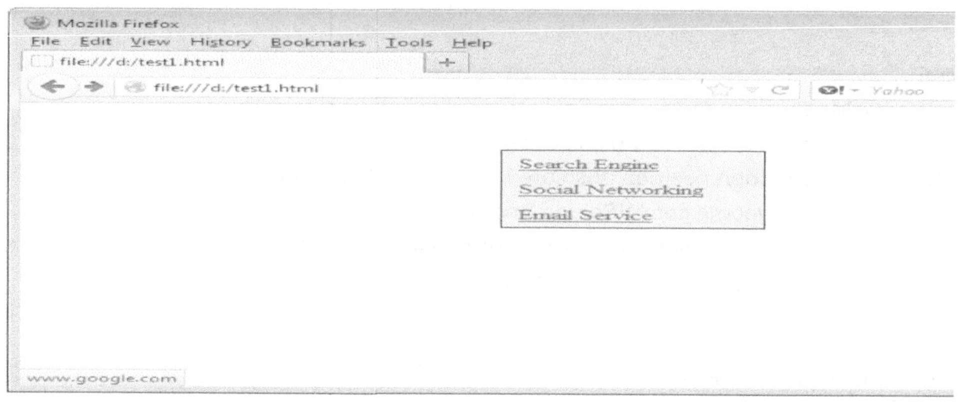

Ex. 4.20.11 : Use Javascript and HTML to create a page with two panes. The first pane (on the left) should have a text area where HTML code can be typed by the user. The pane on the right side should display the preview of the HTML code typed by the user, as it would be seen on the browser. **AU : May-16, Marks 16**

Sol. :

Step 1 : Create the Main Window containing two frames. The code for this document is as follows -

```
MainWindow.html
<!DOCTYPE html>
<html>
<head>
   <title>Frameset Example</title>
</head>
   <frameset cols="50%,50%">
      <frame src="Left.html" name="left"/>
      <frame src="Right.html" name="right"/>
   </frameset>
<body>
</body>
</html>
```

Step 2 : Create the left frame containing the textarea in which we can write any HTML code. This document is named as Left.html. It is as follows -

```
Left.html
<!DOCTYPE html>
<html>
<head>
</head>
<body>
```

```
<form>
<textarea name="data" cols=45 rows=6></textarea>
     <br>
     <input type="button" value=" view "
onclick="javascript:parent.right.displayHTML(this.form)">
</form>
</body>
</html>
```

Step 3 :

```
<!DOCTYPE html>
<html>
<head>
<script type="text/javascript">
function displayHTML(form)
{
     var inf = form.data.value;
win = window.open('', '', 'right', 'toolbar = no, status = no');
      win.document.write("" + inf + "");
}
</script>
</head>
<body>
</body>
</html>
```

Step 4 : Open Web browser and open the MainWindow.html document(created in step1). The sample output will be as follows -

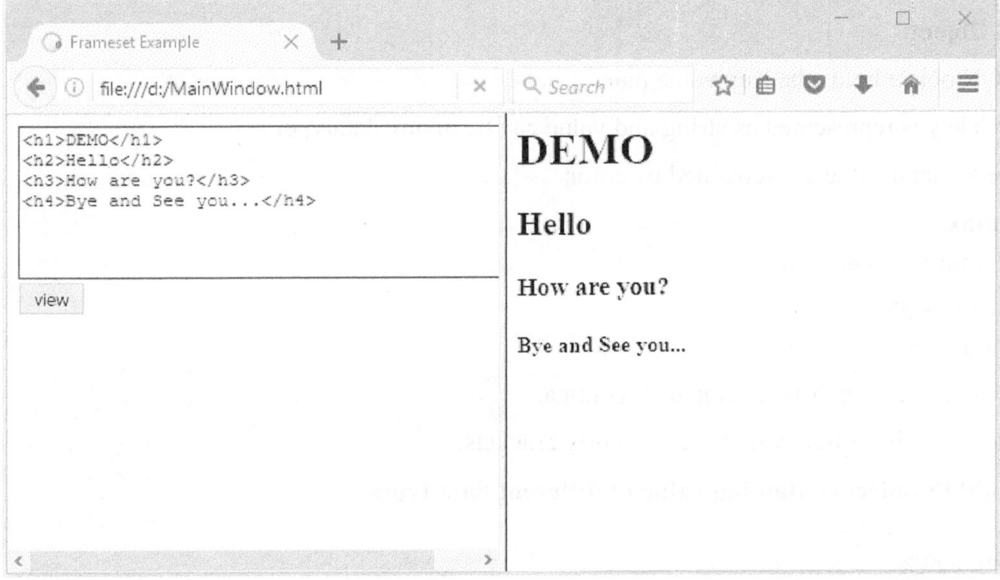

Part IV: Introduction to JSON

4.21 What is JSON ?

- JSON stands for JavaScript Object Notation.
- Using JSON we can store and retrieve data. This text based open standard format.
- It is extended from JavaScript language.

Features of JSON

1. It is **text based, lightweight data interchange format.**
2. It is **language independent.**
3. It is **easy to read and write.**
4. It is **easy** for machines **to parse and generate.**
5. It uses the conventions that are **familiar** to the languages like C, C++, Java, JavaScript, Perl, Python and so on.

4.21.1 Syntax

JSON is built on **two structures :**

1. A collection of name/value pairs. In various languages, this is realized as an object, record, struct, dictionary, hash table, keyed list, or associative array.
2. An ordered list of values. In most languages, this is realized as an array, vector, list, or sequence.

JSON Object

- JSON object holds the Key value pair.
- Each key is represented as string and value can be of any datatype.
- The key and value are separated by colon.
- **Syntax**

```
{ string : value, .......}
```

- **For example**

```
"Age":38
```

- Each key value pair is separated by comma.
- The object is written within the { } curly brackets.

1) JSON object containing value of different data types

```
{
    "student":
```

```
    {
     "name":        AAA",       ←— String value
     "roll_no": 10,             ←— Numeric value
     "Indian": true        ←— Boolean value
    }
}
```

2) JSON Nested Object

```
{
    "student":
    {
     "name":  "AAA",
     "roll_no": 10,
     "address":
        {
        "Street": "Shivaji Nagar",
        "City": "Pune",
        "Pincode": 411005
        }
    }
}
```

3) Creation of JSON object with JavaScript

In JavaScript we can write the JSON object and store it in some variable. For example

```
var stud = { "name":"AAA", "roll_no":10, "city":"Pune" };
```

Here the object named stud is created.

Example

Let us understand how to create an JSON object and obtain its value, and get it displayed on the web browser using JavaScript. The code is as follows -

Test.html

```
<html>
  <head>
    <title>JSON DEMO</title>
    <script language = "javascript" >
      var stud1 = { "name":"AAA", "roll_no":10, "city":"Pune"};
      document.write("<h3>Data of Student1</h3>");
      document.write("<h4>Name : " + stud1.name+"</h4>");
      document.write("<h4>roll_no : " + stud1.roll_no+"</h4>");
      document.write("<h4>city : " + stud1.city+"</h4>");

      var stud2 = { "name":"BBB", "roll_no":20, "city":"Mumbai"}
      document.write("<h3>Data of Student2</h3>");
```

```
        document.write("<h4>Name : " + stud2.name+"</h4>");
        document.write("<h4>roll_no : " + stud2.roll_no+"</h4>");
        document.write("<h4>city : " + stud2.city+"</h4>");
      </script>
   </head>
   <body>
   </body>
</html>
```

Output

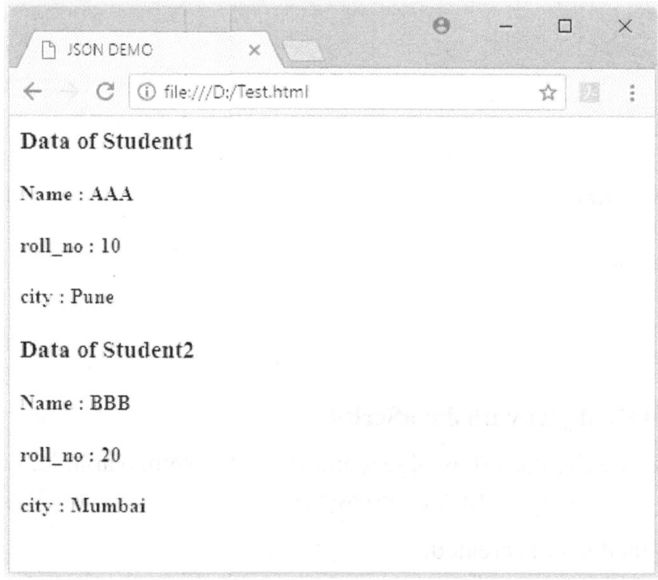

JSON with Arrays

JSON array represents the collection of values. It is denoted within [ ]. The elements of array are separated by comma.

Syntax

[value, ...]

Example

```
<html>
   <head>
      <title>JSON DEMO</title>
      <script language = "javascript" >
        var obj = {"Student":[
          { "name":"AAA", "roll_no":10, "city":"Pune"},
          { "name":"BBB", "roll_no":20, "city":"Mumbai"},
          { "name":"CCC", "roll_no":30, "city":"Chennai"},
          { "name":"DDD", "roll_no":40, "city":"Kolkatta"}
```

```
        ]};
var i = 0
        document.writeln("<table border = '2'><tr>");
    for(i = 0;i<obj.Student.length;i++)
    {
        document.writeln("<td>");
        document.writeln("<table border = '1' width = 100 >");
        document.writeln("<tr><td><b>Name</b></td><td width = 50>"+
        obj.Student[i].name+"</td></tr>");
        document.writeln("<tr><td><b>Roll</b></td><td width = 50>" + obj.Student[i].roll_no
        +"</td></tr>");
        document.writeln("<tr><td><b>City</b></td><td width = 50>" + obj.Student[i].city
        +"</td></tr>");
        document.writeln("</table>");
        document.writeln("</td>");
    }
    </script>
  </head>
  <body>
  </body>
</html>
```

Output

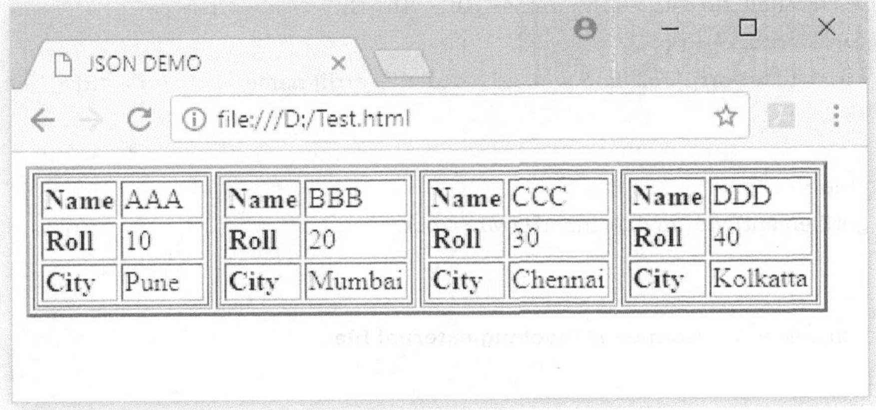

4.21.2 Function Files

Using JSON, it is possible to define a function in a separate external JS file and we can access this functionality from HTML document.

Following example illustrates this idea

Example Code

Step 1 : We can write a JavaScript file containing an array of Student's information. This file is saved with .js extension. The code for it is as follows -

myFile.js

```
Student([
    { "name":"AAA", "roll_no":10, "city":"Pune"},
    { "name":"BBB", "roll_no":20, "city":"Mumbai"},
    { "name":"CCC", "roll_no":30, "city":"Chennai"},
    { "name":"DDD", "roll_no":40, "city":"Kolkatta"}
])
```

Step 2 : Now we will invoke this file in our JSON script to access the elements of an array. The code is as follows -

JSON_File_Demo.html

```
<!DOCTYPE html>
<html>
<body>

<div id="myID"></div>
<script>
function Student(arr) {
 var out = "";
 var i;
 out+='<table border=1>'
 out+='<tr><th>Roll_No</th><th>Name</th><th>City</th></tr>'
 for(i = 0; i<arr.length; i++) {
 out += '<tr><td>'+arr[i].roll_no + '</td><td>' +arr[i].name + '</td><td>' +arr[i].city +
'</td></tr>';
 }
 out+='</table>'
 document.getElementById("myID").innerHTML = out;
}
</script>
<script src="myFile.js"></script> // Invoking external file

</body>
</html>
```

Output

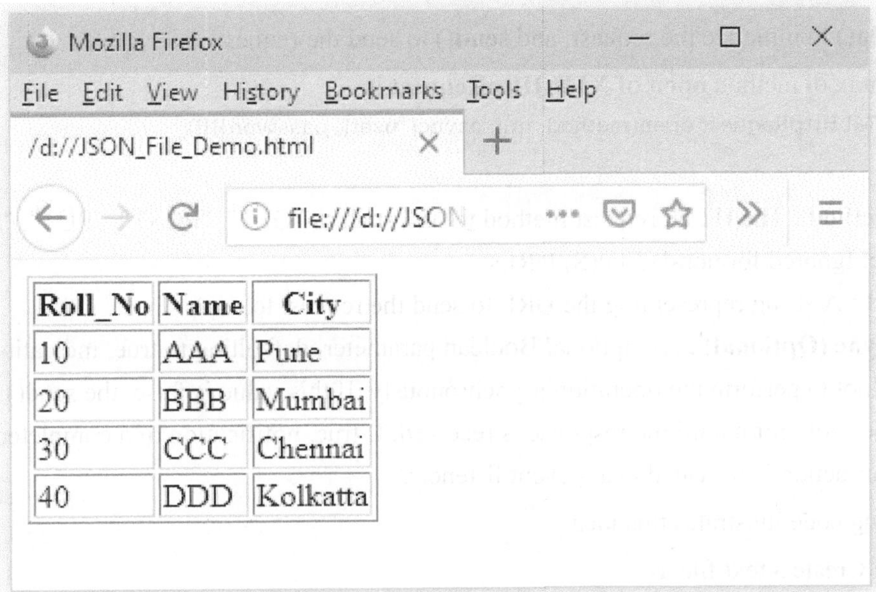

Script Explanation :

In above script,

1. We have written the Student function in a file named **MyFile.js**
2. This function defines an array of three fields Roll_No, Name and City. There are four elements in that array
3. In our HTML file, the JSON code refers to the external JS file as shown below

```
<script src="myFile.js"></script>
```

4. Then the elements of array are accessed and displayed on the browser as follows

```
for(i = 0; i<arr.length; i++) {
    out += '<tr><td>'+arr[i].roll_no +
  '</td><td>' +arr[i].name +
  '</td><td>' +arr[i].city + '</td></tr>';
}
```

4.21.3 HTTP Request

- JSON is most commonly used in asynchronous HTTP requests. This is where an application pulls data from another application via an HTTP request on the web.
- **XMLHttpRequest** is an API that provides scripted client functionality for transferring data between a client and a server.
- It allows you to get data from an external URL without having to refresh the page

XMLHttpRequest includes a number of methods and attributes.

- We use two functions of XMLHttpRequest - **Open()** and **send().**
- The **open()** to initialize the request, and **send()** to send the request.
- The Syntax of method **open of XMLHttpRequest** is

  ```
  XMLHttpRequest.open(method, url[, async[, user[, password]]])
  ```

  where

  - **Method :** The HTTP request method to use, such as "GET", "POST", "PUT", "DELETE", etc. Ignored for non-HTTP(S) URLs.
  - **url :** A string representing the URL to send the request to.
  - **async (Optional) :** An optional Boolean parameter, defaulting to true, indicating whether or not to perform the operation asynchronously. If this value is false, the send() method does not return until the response is received. If true, notification of a completed transaction is provided using event listeners.
- Following code illustrates this idea

  Step 1 : Create a text file as

  myfile.txt

```
[
    { "name":"AAA", "roll_no":10, "city":"Pune"},
    { "name":"BBB", "roll_no":20, "city":"Mumbai"},
    { "name":"CCC", "roll_no":30, "city":"Chennai"},
    { "name":"DDD", "roll_no":40, "city":"Kolkatta"}
]
```

Step 2 : The JSON code to invoke above text file using Http Request is as follows -

JSON_HttpReq_Demo.html

```
<!DOCTYPE html>
<html>
<head>
  <meta charset="UTF-8">
</head>
<body>

<div id="myID"></div>
<script>

var xmlhttp = new XMLHttpRequest();
var url = "file:myfile.txt";

xmlhttp.onreadystatechange = function() {
    if (this.readyState == 4 && this.status == 200) {
     var stud_arr = JSON.parse(this.responseText);
```

```
    Student(stud_arr);
   }
};

xmlhttp.open("GET", url, true);
xmlhttp.send();

function Student(arr) {
 var out = "";
 var i;
 out+='<table border=1>'
 out+='<tr><th>Roll_No</th><th>Name</th><th>City</th></tr>'
 for(i = 0; i<arr.length; i++) {
out += '<tr><td>'+arr[i].roll_no + '</td><td>' +arr[i].name + '</td><td>' +arr[i].city +
   '</td></tr>';
 }
 out+='</table>'
 document.getElementById("myID").innerHTML = out;
}
</script>
</body>
</html>
```

The output as obtained in previous section is displayed on the browser.

4.21.4 SQL

It is possible to retrieve data from database table. For that purpose we can use following steps -

(i) PHP script to read the contents of database table.

(ii) This PHP file can be invoked and accessed using **XMLHttpRequest** API.

Let us understand this concept with following example

Step 1 : Create a Database table named Student_table in MySQL as follows

Roll_No	Name	City
10	AAA	Pune
20	BBB	Mumbai
30	CCC	Chennai
40	DDD	Kolkatta

Step 2 : Now write a PHP script as follows

DBSelect.php

```
<html>
<head>
<title>PHP-Database Connectivity</title>
</head>
<body>
<?php
    $servername = "localhost";
    $username = "root";
    $password = "";
    $dbname="Student_DB";

    // Create connection
    $conn = new mysqli($servername, $username, $password,$dbname);

    // Check connection
    if ($conn->connect_error) {
     die("Connection failed: " . $conn->connect_error);
    }
    echo "Connected successfully";
    $sql = "SELECT * FROM Student_table";
    $result = $conn->query($sql);
    if ($result->num_rows > 0)
    {
        $outp = "[";
     while($rs = $result->fetch_assoc())
     {
            if ($outp != "[") {$outp .= ",";}
            $outp .= '{"Roll_No":"' . $rs["Roll_No"] . '",';
            $outp .= '"Name":"'  . $rs["Name"]       . '",';
            $outp .= '"City":"'. $rs["City"]    . '"}';
     }
    }
    else
    {
     echo "0 results";
    }
    $conn->close();
?>
```

Step 3 : Now write JSON code in the following file

JSON_SQL_Demo.html

```
<!DOCTYPE html>
<html>
```

```
<head>
  <meta charset="UTF-8">
</head>
<body>

<div id="myID"></div>
<script>

var xmlhttp = new XMLHttpRequest();
var url = "localhost:8089/php-examples/DBSelect.php";

xmlhttp.onreadystatechange = function() {
    if (this.readyState == 4 && this.status == 200) {
     var stud_arr = JSON.parse(this.responseText);
     Student(stud_arr);
    }
};

xmlhttp.open("POST", url, true);
xmlhttp.send();

function Student(arr) {
  var out = "";
  var i;
  out+='<table border=1>'
  out+='<tr><th>Roll_No</th><th>Name</th><th>City</th></tr>'
  for(i = 0; i<arr.length; i++) {
    out += '<tr><td>'+arr[i].Roll_No + '</td><td>' +arr[i].Name + '</td><td>' +arr[i].City +
'</td></tr>';
  }
  out+='</table>'
  document.getElementById("myID").innerHTML = out;
}
</script>
</body>
</html>
```

The output as obtained in previous section is displayed on the browser.

Two Marks Questions with Answers

Q.1 What is the benefit of using JavaScript code in an HTML document ? AU : Dec.-07, CSE

Ans. : Following are some significant benefits of using JavaScript code in an HTML document

1. The client side data validation can be possible using JavaScript.
2. We can access the HTML elements. That means we can have control over HTML, BODY, TITLE tags.
3. Since JavaScript is based on the programming constructs we can control the logic of a simple scripting language. For example if a mouse pointer is moving over a text then change its colour.
4. JavaScript can determine the visitor's browser and can load the page accordingly.

Q.2 What is the need for client side scripting ? AU : May-09, CSE

Ans. : Following are the issues that get handled using client side scripting -

1. Simple scripting language like HTML or XML represents the data on the web page in simplest manner.
2. The scripting languages like JavaScript and DHTML are useful for enhancing the interactivity of the user with the web browser.
3. Mathematical evaluation is also possible using the client side scripting.
4. Using client side scripting languages the web page which gets designed for the user provides a graphical user interface using which the user can input his data in an elegant manner. This data can then be submitted to database or any server side scripting language in order to process it further.
5. The input validation can also be possible using client side scripting language like JavaScript.
6. Using cascading stylesheets with the client scripts the look and feel of the web page can be enhanced.

Q.3 List out the objects used in JavaScript with its purpose. AU : May-09, CSE, May-12

Ans. : Various objects that can be used in JavaScript are -

1. **Math Object** - This object provides useful methods that are required for mathematical computations.

   For example : For computing square root of some number sqrt(num) method is used.

   For finding out minimum value of a and b min(a,b) method is used.

2. **Number Object** - This object is used has various numeric properties.

   For example : Largest possible number gets displayed using MAX_VALUE, for displaying the pi value PI property is used.

3. **Date Object** - This object is used for obtaining date and time. For example using getTime() function the number of milliseconds can be obtained.
4. **Boolean Object** - This is the simplest object used to obtain true or false values.
5. **String Object** - This object provides many useful string related functionalities.

   For example : For finding out the substring of a given string substring(begin,end) method can be used.

Q.4 Comment on the statement. "Each object of a class has its own instance of static member variable." **AU : Dec.-08**

Ans. : When we create an object for a class then each object has its own distinct copies of variables. Such variables are called instance variables. For example if declare a class MyCar as follows

```
class MyCar
 {
private String color;
private String model;
private double price;
 }
```

This class has instance variables color, model and price. Now, each object of class MyCar will have its own values for these variables. These values will be static in nature. These objects can be stored at different memory locations. Thus every instance of the class(object) shares a class variables. Hence it is said that every object of a class has its own instance of static member variable.

Q.5 What is JavaScript statement ? Give an example. **AU : Dec.-11**

Ans. : The assignment statement in JavaScript is very much similar to C. For example

```
Sum+=10
Sum=sum+10
```

Can be written in JavaScript.

Q.6 Give any three uses of JavaScript.

Ans. :

1) The JavaScript can be used to create some web applications such as Calculator, Calender, Paint like applications.
2) JavaScript can be used to detect the visitor's browser.
3) JavaScript can be used to validate the data.

Q.7 What kind of comments are supported by the JavaScript ?

Ans. : JavaScript supports following comments -

The // is used to specify the single line comment.

The /* and */ can be used to specify the multi-line comments.

The XHTML <!- -> and <- -> is used in JavaScript.

Q.8 Explain how the string literals are used in JavaScript ?

Ans. : The string is a collection of characters. The string literal is used within the single quote or double quotes.

Q.9 What is the use of the word 'var' in the JavaScript ?

Ans. The word var is used to define the variables of numeric or string type.

Q.10 What do you mean by Coercion ?

Ans. : JavaScript supports the automatic type conversion. The coercion is a type conversion method. This is implicit type of conversion.

Q.11 What is the use of parseInt() and parseFloat() methods ?

Ans. :

The parseInt() and parseFloat() methods are used to separate out the integer and float values respectively from the string. For example parseInt("12abc") will return 12 from the string.

Q.12 What is the use of pop up boxes in JavaScript ?

Ans. : There are three types of popup boxes used in JavaScript. Using these popup boxes the user can interact with the web application.

Q.13 What is the use of toString method with respect to arrays ?

Ans. : The toString method converts the array to string.

Q.14 What are the advantages of indirectly embedding the JavaScript in the Web document ?

Ans. : Following are the advantages of indirectly embedding the JavaScript in the web document -

1. Script can be hidden from the browser.
2. The layout and presentation of web document can be separated out from the user interaction through the JavaScript.

Q.15 What are the properties and methods object window for screen output ?

Ans. : Following are some properties and methods of object window -

1. The property **write** of object window is used to display something on the screen.
2. The methods **alert, prompt** and **confirm** are useful for handling screen output and keyboard input.

Q.16 Explain array creation in JavaScript with example. **AU : May-11**

Ans. : In JavaScript the array can be created using Array object. Suppose, we want to create an array of 10 elements then we can write,

```
var ar = new Array(10);
```

Using new operator we can allocate the memory dynamically for the arrays. In the brackets the size of an array is mentioned and the var ar denotes the name of the array. Thus by the above sentence an array ar will be created in which we can store 10 elements at the most. Sometimes the above statement can be written like this

```
var ar;
ar=new Array(10);
```

Q.17 What are global functions in JavaScript ?

Ans. : The global functions are the top level functions in JavaScript that are independent of any specific object. These functions are built in objects of JavaScript. Examples of global functions are –

Name of the Function	Purpose
encodeURI	This function is used to encode URI
decodeURI	This function is used to decode the encoded URI
parseInt	This function parses the string and returns the integer value.
eval	The eval function is used to evaluate the expression.

Q.18 What is the meaning of widgets ?

Ans. : Various graphical controls such as text box, check box,radio buttons, push buttons and so on can be placed on the form for user interactivity. These control objects are called the widgets.

Q.19 State the types of java script statements with examples. **AU : Dec.-13**

Ans. : Various types of javascript statements are -

1. Simple assignment statements
2. Conditional statements
3. Object manipulation statements
4. Comment statements
5. Exception handling statements

Q.20 Write a Java Script to print "Good Day" using IF-ELSE condition. **AU : May-14**

Ans. :

```
<html>
<head>
```

```
<script>
function MyMessage()
{
   var today=new Date();
   var h=today.getHours();
   if(h<12)//After 12 O'clock Say Good Bye
       //Before 12 O'clock say Good Day
    document.write("Good Day");
   else
       document.write("Good Bye");
}
</script>
</head>
<body onload="MyMessage()">
</body>
</html>
```

Q.21 List any four methods of date object. AU : Dec.-16

Ans.

Method	Meaning
getTime()	It returns the number of milliseconds. This value is the difference between the current time and the time value from 1st January 1970.
getDate()	Returns the current date based on computers local time.
getDay()	Returns the current day. The day number is from 0 to 6 i.e. from sunday to saturday.
getHours()	Returns the hour value ranging from 0 to 23, based on local time.
getSeconds()	Returns the second value ranging from 0 to 59, based on local time.

Q.22 How exceptions are handled in JavaScript ? AU : May 17

Ans. : The exceptions are handled in Javascript using try… catch block.s

For example –

```
<html>
  <head>
    <script type="text/javascript">
      <!--
        function myFunc()
        {
```

```
        var a = 100;
        var b = 0;
        try{
          if ( b == 0 ){
            throw( "Divide by zero error." );
          }
          else
          {
            var c = a / b;
          }
        }
        catch ( e ) {
          alert("Error: " + e );
        }
      }
    //-->
  </script>
</head>
```

Q.23 What are object literal in JavaScript. **AU : Dec.-18**

Ans. : The object literal in javascript is a name-value pair wrapped in curly braces.

For example -

```
Var myobj = {
              name : "AAA",
              rollno : 2,
              marks : 82
            };
```

Q.24 What is DOM ?

Ans. : Document Object Model (DOM) is a set of platform independent and language neutral application programming interface (API) which describes how to access and manipulate the information stored in XML,XHTML and JavaScript documents.

Q.25 Define DOM Tree.

Ans. : The documents in DOM are represented using tree like structure in which every element is represented as a node. Such a tree like structure is called DOM Tree.

For example -

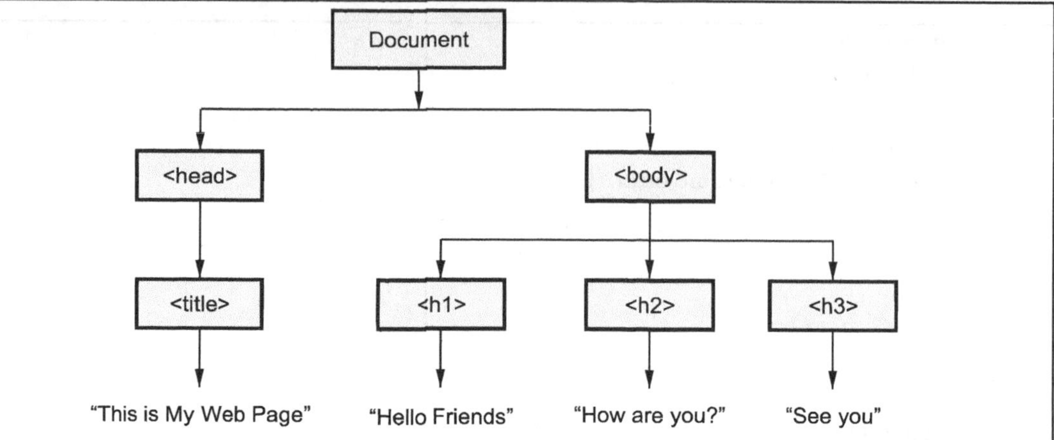

Q.26 List the different methods defined in document and window object of JavaScript.

AU : May-11, 13

Ans. : Methods in document object

Methods	Description
document.createAttribute()	Creates an attribute node.
document.createElement()	Creates an element node .
document.createTextNode()	Creates a text node.
document.getElementById()	Returns the element that has ID attribute with the specified value.
document.getElementByName()	Returns the element specified by its name.
document.write()	Writes HTML expression to a document.

Methods in window object

Methods	Description
alert()	Displays the alert box containing some message and OK button.
confirm()	Displays a dialog box with a message and OK and Cancel button.
createPopup()	Creates a pop up window.
moveTo()	Moves a window to some specific position.
open()	Opens a new window.
print()	Prints the contents in the window.

Q.27 What is the use of 'all' in DOM tree traversal ?

Ans. : The all is a object model collection which is used to refer all the HTML elements. For representing all the elements present on the HTML document the 'all' is used.

Q.28 List out various level of Document Object Modelling.

Ans. : Various levels of DOM are -

DOM0 DOM1 DOM2 DOM3

Q.29 What is getElementById method ?

Ans. : The getElementById is a method which is defined in DOM1. The element access can be made by using this method. For example -

```
var Dom_Obj=document.getElementById("myinput");
```

Q.30 What is the drawback of the DOM0 event Model ?

Ans. : The main drawback of DOM0 event model is that two different event handlers can not be assigned to the same event. This drawback is overcome in DOM2 event model.

Q.31 What do you mean by the term event registration ?

Ans. : The process of connecting event handler to an event is called event registration. The event handler registration can be done using two methods -

- Assigning the tag attributes
- Assigning the handler address to object properties.

Q.32 Define the term intrinsic events. AU : May-12

Ans. : Event is an activity that represents a change in the environment. For example mouse clicks, pressing a particular key of keyboard represents the events. Such events are called intrinsic events.

Q.33 List some HTML intrinsic attributes. AU : May-11, 12

Ans. : Some of the intrinsic attributes are listed in the following table

Intrinsic Attribute	Meaning
Onblur	This event is for losing the focus
onchange	On occurrence of some change this event occurs
onclick	When user clicks the mouse button this event occurs
ondblclick	When user double clicks the mouse button.

Q.34 Define event bubbling. **AU : May-10**

Ans. : Suppose, there is an element present inside another element. Then during the event handling, if the event which is present in the inner element is handled and then the event of the outer element is handled. This process of event handling is called event bubbling.

Q.35 List the types of event listeners in DOM2. **AU : Dec.-12**

Ans. : There are three types of event listeners in DOM2 -

1. **Capturing listeners :** The capturing listener is associated with the event that occurs at the root node in the document tree and propagates towards the target node. It is created with the call to addEventListener().
2. **Bubbling listeners :** The bubbling listener is associated with the event that starts at the target node and moves up the document tree to the root node. It is created with the call to addEventListener().
3. **Target listeners :** Target listener is the event listener which is added in the target node.

Q.36 What is meant by DHTML ? **AU : Dec.-13**

Ans. : The DHTML stands for Dynamic HTML. This is a markup language used to create interactive and animated web site.

Q.37 Define event programming. Name any two of its techniques. **AU : Dec.-15**

Ans. : • Event is an activity that represents a change in the environment. For example mouse clicks, pressing a particular key of keyboard represent the events. Event programming is technique in which such events are handled using the code.

- Event capturing and event bubbling are the two techniques of event propagation.

Q.38 Write appropriate JavaScript code to remove an element(current element) from a DOM. **AU : May-16**

Ans. :

```
<!DOCTYPE html>
<html>
<body>
 <div id="headers">
<h1 id="s1">Hello friends!!!</h1>
<h2 id="s2">How are you?</h2>
<h3 id="s3"> See you...</h3>
</div>
<script>
 var parent = document.getElementById("headers");
 var child = document.getElementById("s3");
 parent.removeChild(child);
</script>
</body>
</html>
```

Output

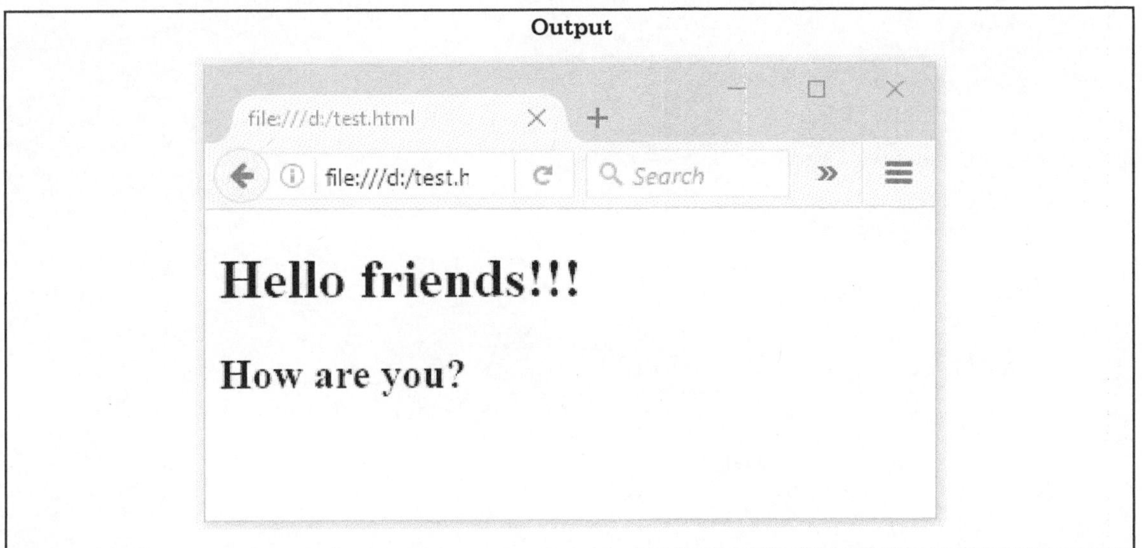
file:///d:/test.html
file:///d:/test.h
Search
Hello friends!!!
How are you?

❑❑❑

Notes

Unit III

5 Server Side Programming (Servlets)

Syllabus

Servlets : Java Servlet Architecture- Servlet Life Cycle - Form GET and POST actions- Session Handling - Understanding Cookies - Installing and Configuring Apache Tomcat Web Server - DATABASE CONNECTIVITY : JDBC perspectives, JDBC program example .

Contents

5.1 Introduction to Server Side Programming

- Server side technology deals with the data submitted by the client.
- Server side program basically **handles the request** made by the client. This program then **prepares the response** for the client.
- The server side programming also act as a link between backend database and front end client side programming.
- Various server side technologies include – servlet, JSP, ASP.NET, PHP and so on.

Difference between client side and server side scripting

Sr. No.	Server side scripting	Client side scripting
1.	The server side scripting is used to create the web pages that provide some services.	The client side scripting is used to create the web pages as a request or response to server. These pages are displayed to the user on web browser.
2.	These scripts generally run on web servers.	These scripts generally run on web browser.
3.	A user's request is fulfilled by running a script directly on the web server to generate dynamic HTML pages. This HTML is then sent to the client browser.	The processing of these scripts takes place on the end users computer. The source code is transferred from the web server to the users computer over the internet and run directly in the browser.
4.	Uses : Processing of user request, accessing to databases.	Uses : Making interactive web pages, for interacting with temporary storages such as cookies or local storage, sending request to server and getting the response and displaying that response in web browser.
5.	Example : PHP, ASP.NET, nearly all the programming languages including C++, Java and C#	Example : HTML, CSS, JavaScript(primarily)

5.2 Introduction to Servlets

AU : May-19, Marks 6

- Servlets are basically the Java programs that run on server. These are the programs that are requested by the XHTML documents and are displayed in the browser window as a response to the request.
- The servlet class is instantiated when web server begins the execution.
- The execution of servlet is managed by **servlet container,** such as Tomcat.

- The servlet container is used in java for dynamically generate the web pages on the server side. Therefore the servlet container is the part of a web server that interacts with the servlet for handling the dynamic web pages from the client.
- Servlets are most commonly used with HTTP (i.e. Hyper Text Transfer Protocol) hence sometimes servlets are also called as "HTTP Servlet".
- The main purpose of servlets is to add up the functionality to a web server.

Working of How Servlet Works ?

- Before learning the actual servlet programming it is very important to understand how servlet works.

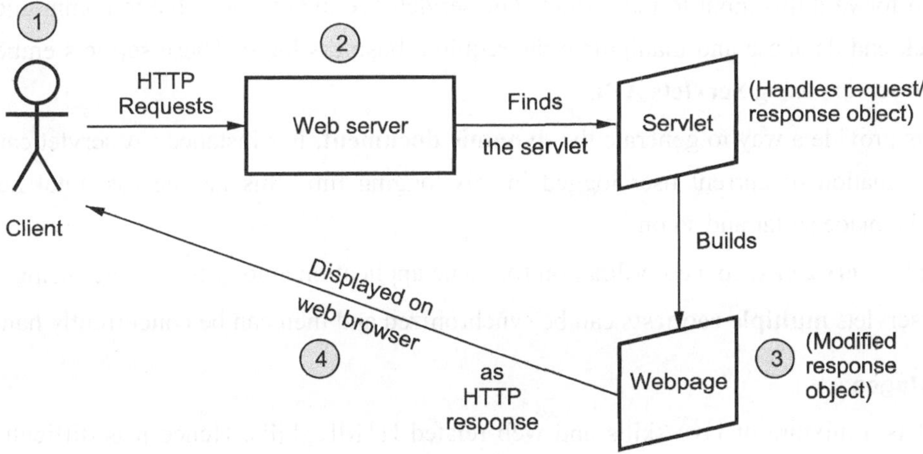

Fig. 5.2.1 How servlet works ?

1. When a client make a request for some servlet, he/she actually uses the **Web browser** in which request is written as a URL.
2. The web browser then sends this request to **Web server**. The web server first finds the requested servlet.
3. The obtained servlet gathers the relevant information in order to satisfy the client's request and builds a **web page** accordingly.
4. This web page is then **displayed** to the client. Thus the request made by the client gets satisfied by the servlets.

5.2.1 Need and Advantages

- Servlets can process and store the data submitted by an HTML form.
- Servlets are useful for providing the dynamic contents. For example retrieving and updating the databases.

- Servlets can be used in the cookies. Cookies are small programs which can make use of the information submitted on currently accessed web pages.
- Similarly servlets are used in session tracking. The session tracking are the useful programs that keeps track of all previously accessed the web pages.

Advantages

- The servlets are very **efficient** in their performance and get executed in the address space of the belonging web server.
- The servlets are **platform independent** and can be executed on different web servers.
- The servlets working is based on **Request-Response**. Any HTML form can take the user input and can forward this input to the servlet. The servlets are then responsible to communicate with the back-end database and manipulate the required business logic. These servlets embedded on the web servers using **Servlets API.**
- Servlets provide a way to generate the **dynamic document**. For instance : A servlet can display the information of current user logged in, his logging time, his last access, total number of access he made so far and so on.
- **Multiple users** can keep a co-ordination for some application among themselves using servlets.
- Using servlets **multiple requests** can be synchronized and then can be concurrently handled.

Disadvantages

- Servlet is a mixture of java skills and web related HTML skills. Hence it is difficult to write servlets.
- It slows down the application execution.
- The java runtime environment is required on the server, if you want to execute servlet application.

University Question

1. *Discuss the advantage and disadvantages of servlet.* **AU : May-19, Marks 6**

5.3 Java Servlet Architecture **AU : May-08,13,19, Marks 8**

- When we write a servlet program, it is necessary to - i) either implement **Servlet** interface or ii) extend a class that implements **Servlet** interface.
- While implementing **Servlet** interface we must include **javax.servlet** package. Hence the first line in out servlet program must be

```
import javax.servlet.*;
```

- **GenericServlet** class is a predefined implementation of **Servlet** interface. Hence we can extend GenericServlet class in our servlet program. Similarly, the **HttpServlet** class is a child class of **GenericServlet** class, hence we can extend this class as well while writing the servlet program.
- Hence following are the two ways by which we can write servlet program

```
import javax.servlet.*;
import javax.servlet.http.*;
import java.io.*;
public class Test extends
GenericServlet
{
  //body of servlet
}
```

```
import javax.servlet.*;
import javax.servlet.http.*;
import java.io.*;
public class Test extends HttpServlet
{
  //body of servlet
}
```

- The servlet gets the request from the client for some service. The servlet then processes the request and sends the response back to the client. In order to handle these issues **HttpServletRequest** and **HttpServletResponse** are used in servlet program.
- These requests are handled with the help of some methods that are popularly known as **methods of HttpServlet.** These methods are as follows

Method	Purpose
doGet	This method handles the HTTP GET request
doPost	This method handles the HTTP POST request
doPut	This method handles the HTTP Put request.
doDelete	This method handles the DELETE request.

The doGet and doPost methods

- The **doGet** method requests the data from the source.
- The **doPost** method submits the processed data to the source.
- The protocol of **doGet** method is as follows

```
protected void doGet(HttpServletRequest request, HttpServletResponse response)
    throws ServletException,IOException
```

- The **ServletException** and **IOException** are thrown to handle the Servlet problems gracefully.
- The **HttpServletRequest** request : contain the client request made by client.
- The **HttpServletResponse** response : contains the response made by servlet back to the client.
- The protocol of doPost method is same as doGet method. It is as follows -

```
protected void doPost(HttpServletRequest request, HttpServletResponse response) throws
ServletException,IOException
```

- The GET request is more efficient than the POST request.
- The GET request is less secure than the POST request.

How to Write Servlet Program ?

Open Notepad and write the first servlet code to display Greeting messages. It is as follows

FirstServlet.java

```
import java.io.*;
import javax.servlet.*;
import javax.servlet.http.*;

public class FirstServlet extends HttpServlet
{
 public void doGet(HttpServletRequest request,HttpServletResponse response)
 throws IOException,ServletException
 {
  response.setContentType("text/html");
  PrintWriter out=response.getWriter();
  out.println("<html>");
  out.println("<head>");
  out.println("<title>My First Servlet</title>");
  out.println("<body>");
  out.println("<h1>Hello How are U?</h1>");
  out.println("<h2>I am enjoying this Servlet Application</h2>");
  out.println("<h3>See You later!</h3>");
  out.println("</body>");
  out.println("</html>");
}
}
```

Program Explanation :

- In the above program, we have imported following files,

```
import java.io.*;
import javax.servlet.*;
import javax.servlet.http.*;
```

- Out of these files **java.io** package is useful for taking care of I/O operations.
- The **javax.servlet** and **javax.servlet.http** are important packages containing the **classes** and **interfaces** that are required for the operation of servlets. The most commonly used interface from **javax.servlet** package is **Servlet**. Similarly most commonly used class in this package is **GenericServlet.** The **ServletRequest** and **ServletResponse** are another two commonly used interfaces defined in **javax.servlet** package.

- In the **javax.servlet.http** package **HttpServletRequest** and **HttpServletResponse** are two commonly used interfaces. The **HttpServletRequest** enables the servlet to read data from the HTTP request and **HttpServletResponse** enables the servlet to write data to HTTP response. The **cookie** and **HttpServlet** are two commonly used classes that are defined in this package.
- We have given class name **FirstServlet** which should be derived from the class **HttpServlet.** (Sometimes we can derive our class from **GenericServlet**).
- Then we have defined **doGet method** to which the HTTP request and response are passed as parameters. The commonly used basic exceptions for the servlets are **IOException** and **ServletException.**
- The MIME type is specified as using the **setContentType()** method. This method sets the content type for the HTTP response to type. In this method "text/html" is specified as the MIME type. This means that the browser should interpret the contents as the HTML source code.
- Then an output stream is created using **PrintWriter().** The **getWriter()** method is used for obtaining the output stream. Anything written to this stream is sent to the client as a response. Hence using the object of output stream 'out', we can write the HTML source code in **println** method as HTTP response.

How to execute Servlet program ?

Step 1 : Compile the above program using the javac command at command prompt.

```
D:\test>javac FirstServlet.java
```

The class file for this program gets generated.

Step 2 : Before running any servlet program, it is necessary to have

1. JDK installed
2. Tomcat installed.
3. Class path for above two packages must be set.

For Tomcat installation, I prefer to install the package XAMPP. The XAMP contains a directory for tomcat. The XAMPP package contains Apache Web server, MySQL, PHP and Perl support. It can work on both Windows and Linux operating System.

Step 3 : Copy the class file generated in Step 1 to the path

C : \xampp\tomcat\webapps\examples\WEB-INF\classes

Step 4 : Go to the directory

C : \xampp\tomcat\webapps\examples\WEB-INF

Open **web.xml** file and edit it as follows

```
<servlet>
  <servlet-name>FirstServlet</servlet-name>
  <servlet-class> FirstServlet </servlet-class>
```

```
</servlet>
...
...
...
<servlet-mapping>
    <servlet-name> FirstServlet </servlet-name>
    <url-pattern>/servlet/ FirstServlet </url-pattern>
  </servlet-mapping>
```

The **web.xml** file is popularly known as **deployment descriptor**. This is basically the configuration file that describes how to map the URL of web application to servlet.

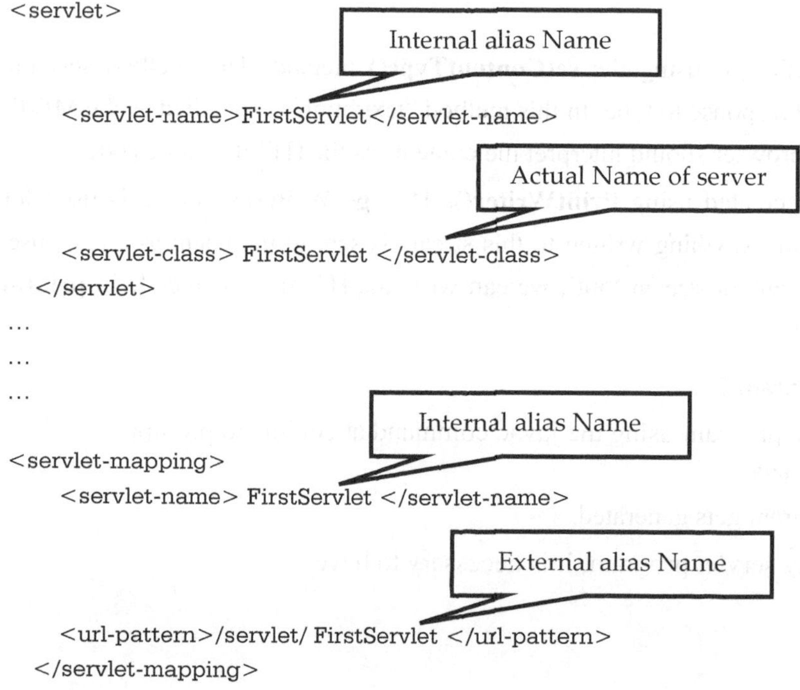


```
<servlet>
    <servlet-name>FirstServlet</servlet-name>
    <servlet-class> FirstServlet </servlet-class>
  </servlet>
...
...
...
<servlet-mapping>
    <servlet-name> FirstServlet </servlet-name>
    <url-pattern>/servlet/ FirstServlet </url-pattern>
  </servlet-mapping>
```

The Servlet comes with two alias names, internal and external. The internal name is used by the Tomcat and the external name is given (to be written in <FORM> tag of HTML file) to the client to invoke the Servlet on the server. That is, there exists alias to alias. All this is for security. Observe, the names are given in two different XML tags, in the web.xml file, to make it difficult for hacking.

To invoke the **FirstServlet** Servlet, the client calls the server with the name **servlet/FirstServlet**.

When **servlet/FirstServlet** call reaches the server, the Tomcat server opens the **web.xml** file to check the deployment particulars. Searches such a <servlet-mapping> tag that matches **servlet/FirstServlet**. **servlet/FirstServlet** is exchanged with **FirstServlet.**

Then, searches such a <servlet> tag that matches **FirstServlet** and exchanges with **FirstServlet class**. Now the server, loads **FirstServlet** Servlet, executes and sends the output of execution as response to client.

Step 5 : Start tomcat and xampp

Step 6 : Open web browser and type the command

http ://localhost/examples/servlet/FirstServlet

The output will be

Output

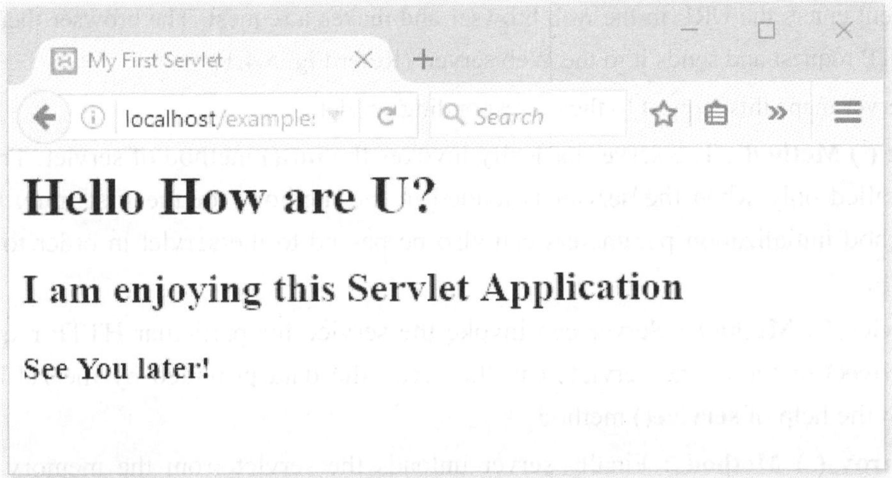

University Questions

1. *Explain about architecture of servlet.* **AU : May-13, Marks 6**
2. *Describe the servlet architecture and various information invoked by the servlet container.* **AU : May-08, Marks 8**
3. *Draw the servlet architecture and explain its working.* **AU : May-19, Marks 8**

5.4 Servlet Life Cycle

AU : May-18, Marks 13

In the life cycle of servlet there are three important methods. These methods are

1. Init

2. Service

3. Destroy

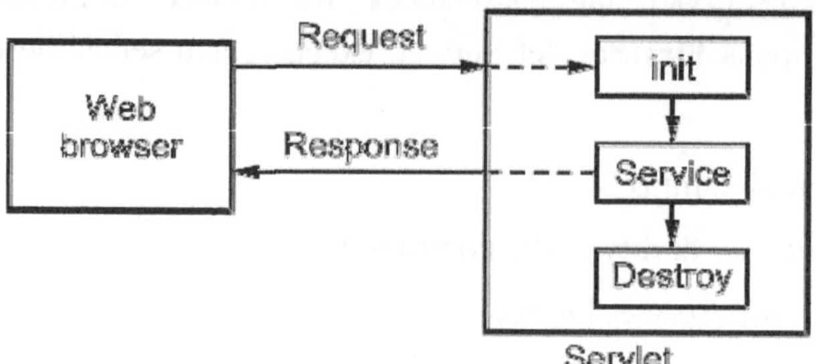

Fig. 5.4.1 Life cycle of servlet

- The client enters the URL in the web browser and makes a request. The browser then generates the HTTP request and sends it to the Web server. (Refer Fig. 5.4.1)
- Web server maps this request to the corresponding servlet.

1. **Init ( ) Method :** The server basically invokes the **init()** method of servlet. This method is called only when the servlet is loaded in the memory for the first time. Using this method initialization parameters can also be passed to the servlet in order to configure itself.
2. **service ( ) Method :** Server can invoke the service for particular HTTP request using **service()** method. The servlets can then read the data provided by the HTTP request with the help of **service()** method.
3. **destroy ( ) Method :** Finally server unloads the servlet from the memory using the **destroy()** method.

University Question

1. *Explain life cycle of servlets with suitable example.* **AU : May-18, Marks 13**

5.5 Servlet API

AU : Dec.-09, May-10, Marks 8

There are two packages used to implement the **Servlet**. These packages are

1) javax.servlet

2) javax.servlet.http

The classes and interfaces defined in these packages help in implementing the servlet.

Let us discuss them in detail -

5.5.1 The javax.servlet Package

This package is used to implement the servlet. Out of many other interfaces and classes defined in this package the most important interface is **Servlet** . All the servlet must implement this interface. The interfaces and classes that are defined in this package are enlisted below -

5.5.1.1 Interfaces

Interface	Description
Servlet	This interface defines all the life cycle methods.
ServletConfig	This interface obtains the initialization parameters.
ServletContext	Using this interface the events can be logged.
ServletRequest	This interface is useful in reading the data from the client request.
ServletResponse	This interface is useful in writing the data to the client response.

1. The Servlet Interface

This interface defines all the life cycle methods such as **init(),destroy()** and **service()**. All the servlets must implement this interface. Some of the methods provided by this interface are –

Method	Description
void init(ServletConfig s)	This method is called for initialising the servlet. The initialisation parameter is obtained from the ServletConfig interface.
void destroy()	This method is called when the servlet has to be unloaded.
ServletConfig getServletConfig()	This method is used to obtain the initialisation parameters.
void Service(ServletRequest req, ServletResponse res)	This method is used to implement the service that a servlet should provide. The clients request is processed and a response is given.
String getServletInfo()	This method is used to obtain description of the servlet.

2. The ServletConfig Interface

This interface is used to obtain the initialisation parameters. Various methods that are used by this interface are -

Method	Description
String getServletName()	This method is used to obtain the name of the servlet.
String getInitParameter(String *p*)	This method returns the value of the parameter *p*
Enumeration getinitParamernames()	This method returns the names of initialisation parameters.
ServletContext getServletContext()	This method returns the context for the servlet.

3. The ServletContext Interface

This is the interface that enables the servlet to log events and access information about their environment. Various methods of this interface are –

Method	Description
Object getAttribute(String *attribute_name*)	The value of the attribute *attribute_name* in the current session is returned.
void setAttribute(String *attribute_name*, object *value*)	The *attribute_name* is passed to the object *value.*
String getServerInfo()	This method returns the information about the server.
String log(String *str*)	Writes the *str* to the servlet log.
String getMimeType(String *file*)	It returns the MIME type of the file.

4. The ServletRequest Interface

The **ServletRequest** interface helps in gathering the information about the client. Various methods in ServletRequest are –

Method	Description
Object getAttribute(String *attribute_name*)	The value of the attribute *attribute_name* in the current session is returned.
int getContentlength()	It returns the content size of the request.
String getContentType()	It returns the type of the request.
getInputStream()	This method is used to read the binary data from

	the request.
getProtocol()	Returns the name of the protocol used.
getReader()	This method is useful for reading the text from the request.
getServerName()	It returns the name of the server on which the servlet is running.
int getServerPort()	It returns the port number of the server.

5. The ServletResponse Interface

This interface helps the servlet to formulate the response for the client's request. Various methods of this interface are -

Method	Description
String getCharacterEncoding()	This method returns the character encoding.
ServletOutputStream getOutputStream()	This method returns outputstream which is used to write the data for responding.
PrintWriter getWriter()	This method is used to write the character data to the response.
void setContentLength(int *size*)	This method sets the length of the content equal to the *size*.
void setContentType(String *Type*)	This methods sets the type of the content

5.5.1.2 Classes

The **javax.servlet** package contains following classes.

Class	Description
GenericServlet	This class implements the **Servlet** and **ServletConfig** interfaces.
ServletInputStream	This class provides the input stream for reading the client's request.
ServletOutputStream	This class provides the output stream for writing the client's response.
ServletException	This class is used to raise the exception when an error occurs.

1. The GenericServlet Class

This class is useful for implementing the life cycle methods. It implements the **servlet** and **ServletConfig** interfaces. It is called "Generic" because it does not assume that the protocol it will process will be HTTP. If we want to write our own protocol, then we must extend this class.

2. The ServletInputStream class

The **ServletInputStream** class extends the **InputStream**. This class provides an input stream which is used by a servlet for reading the data from a client request. For reading the bytes from a client the method used is **readLine**.

3. The ServletOutputStream class

The **ServletOutputStream** class extends the **OutputStream**. This class provides an output stream which is used by a servlet for writing the data for a client response. It also defines **print** and **println** method.

4. The ServletException class

The **javax.servlet** defines two **servlets ServletException** and **UnavailableException**

5.5.2 The javax.servlet.http Package

The javax.servlet.http package contains a number of interfaces and classes and their functionality makes it easy to build servlets. These servlets then work with HTTP requests and responses.

5.5.2.1 Interface

The following table describes the interfaces that are provided in this package

Interface	Description
HttpSession	The session data can be read or written using this interface.
HttpServletRequest	The servlet can read the information from the HTTP request using this interface.
HttpServletResponse	The servlet can write the data to HTTP response using this interface.
HttpSessionBindingListener	This interface tells the object about its binding with the particular session.

1. The HttpSession

At every HTTP session, the state information is gathered. The servlet can read or write this information using **HTTPSession** interface. This interface is implemented by the server.

Various methods used by this interface are as given below -

Method	Description
String getId()	This method returns the session ID.
Object getAttribute(String *attribute_name*)	The value of the attribute *attribute_name* in the current session is returned.
Enumeration getAttributeNames()	Returns the attribute names.

2. The HttpServletRequest

The **HTTPServletRequest** is used to obtain the information from client's HTTP request.

Method	Description
String getMethod()	It returns the HTTP method for the client request.
String getPathInfo()	Returns the path information about the servlet path.
HttpSession getSession()	Returns the current session.
String getHeader(String *fields*)	It returns the value of header fields.
Cookie [ ] getCookies()	It returns the information in the cookies in the request made.
String getAuth Type()	It returns the type of Authentication.

3. The HttpServletResponse

This **HtttpServletResponse** interface is used to formulate an HTTP response to the client. Various methods are -

Method	Description
void addCookie(Cookie *cookie)*	This method is used to add cookie in the response.
String encodeURL(String url)	This method is used to encode the specified URL.
Boolean containsHeader(String *f*)	This method returns **true** if the response header contains the field *f*.
void sendError(int *code*)	This method sends error code to the client.

4. The HttpSessionBindingListener

When particular listener gets bound or unbound from a value within **HttpSession** object then this class is required. It extends the **HttpSessionEvent**. Various methods that can be defined by this interface are –

Method	Description
Object getValue()	This function returns the value of bounded or unbounded attribute.
String getName()	This function returns the name being bound or unbound.
HttpSession getSession()	This function returns the session to which the listener can be bound or unbound.

5.5.2.2 Classes

The following table describes the classes that are provided in this package

Class	Description
Cookie	This class is used to write the cookies.
HttpServlet	It is used when developing servlets that receive and process HTTP requests.
HttpSessionEvent	This class is used to handle the session events.
HttpSessionBindingEvent	When a listener is bound to a value.

1) The Cookie class

A cookie is a small piece of information that is stored in the client's machine. Sometimes cookies are useful to keep track of the user using the client machine. Various methods used by this class are –

class	Description
String getValue()	This function returns a value of the cookie.
void setValue(String s)	This function sets the value to the cookie.
String getName()	This function returns the name.

2) The HttpServlet class

The **HttpServlet** class extends **GenericServlet**. It is used when developing servlets that receive and process HTTP requests. Various methods of this class are -

Class	Description
Void doGet(HttpServletRequest req, HttpServletResponse res)	This method performs HTTP get request.
Void doPost(HttpServletRequest req, HttpServletResponse res)	This method performs HTTP Post request.
Void doPut(HttpServletRequest req, HttpServletResponse res)	This method performs HTTP Put request.
Void service(HttpServletRequest req, HttpServletResponse res)	This method is invoked for processing HTTP request and response.

3) The HttpSessionEvent

This method encapsulates the session event.

4) HttpSessionBindingEvent

The **HttpSessionBindingEvent** class extends **HttpSessionEvent**. It is generated when a listener is bound to a value. The **getSession()** method obtains the session to which the listener is being bound or unbound.

University Questions

1. *List out the commonly used methods to HTTP servlet.* **AU : Dec.-09, Marks 6**
2. *Discuss four important methods of HTTP Servlet class.* **AU : May-10, Marks 8**

5.6 Form GET and POST Actions **AU : May-08,14, Dec.-09, Marks 8**

- Many times we need to pass some information from web browser to Web server. In such case, the HTML document containing the FORM is written which sends the data to the servlet present on the web server.
- To make the form works with Java servlet, we need to specify the following attributes for the <form> tag:

  (i) **method="method name":** to send the form data as an HTTP POST request to the server.

  (ii)**action="URL/address of the servlet":** specifies relative URL of the servlet which is responsible for handling data posted from this form.
- The browser uses two methods to pass this information to web server. These methods are GET Method and POST Method.

(i) **GET method :** The GET method sends user information along with ? symbol called query string. For instance

http://localhost/hello?user = aaaa&age = 20

In servlet, this information is processed using **doGet()** method.

(ii)**POST method :** This is the most reliable method of sending user information to the server from HTML form. Servlet handles this request using **doPost** method.

Difference between GET and POST

GET	POST
Using GET request limited amount of information can be sent.	Using POST large amount of information can be sent.
GET request is not secured as information is visible in URL	This is a secured request.
This request is can be bookmarked.	This request can not be bookmarked.
This request is more efficient.	This request is less efficient.

How does servlet read form data ?

Servlet makes use of following three methods to read the data entered by the user on the HTML form

1. **getParameter()** – You call request.getParameter() method to get the value of a form parameter.
2. **getParameterValues()** – Call this method if the parameter appears more than once and returns multiple values, for example checkbox.
3. **getParameterNames()** – Call this method if you want a complete list of all parameters in the current request.

Programming Examples

Ex. 5.6.1 : Write a HTML that shows the following list :

C,C++,JAVA,C#

Define a form that contains a select statement and submit button. If the user selects the java and press the submit the web page displays "The selected language is Java".

Write a servlet program using HttpServlet and doGet method.

Sol. : We will write two source files first one is the HTML file named **test.html** in which the list of all the desired languages is displayed along with the submit button. User has to select the language of his choice and then press the submit button.

This data made by this request will be received by the servlet named **my_choiceservlet.java** which reads the selected parameter and displays the message about the selection made. The source files are as follows -

test.html

```
<html>
    <body>
    <center>
    <form name="form1" method=GET
    action="http://localhost:4040/servlets-examples/servlet/my_choiceservlet">
     <b>Language:</b>
     <select name="Language" size="1">
        <option value="C">C</option>
        <option value="C++">C++</option>
        <option value="Java">Java</option>
        <option value="C#">C#</option>
     </select>
     <br><br>
     <input type="submit" value="Submit">
    </form>
    </body>
</html>
```

my_choiceservlet.java

```
import java.io.*;
importjavax.servlet.*;
importjavax.servlet.http.*;

public class my_choiceservlet extends HttpServlet
{
    public void doGet(HttpServletRequestreq,HttpServletResponse res)
    throwsServletException,IOException
    {
     String lang=req.getParameter("Language");
     res.setContentType("text/html");
     PrintWriter out=res.getWriter();
     out.println("The selected language is "+lang);
     out.close();
    }
}
```

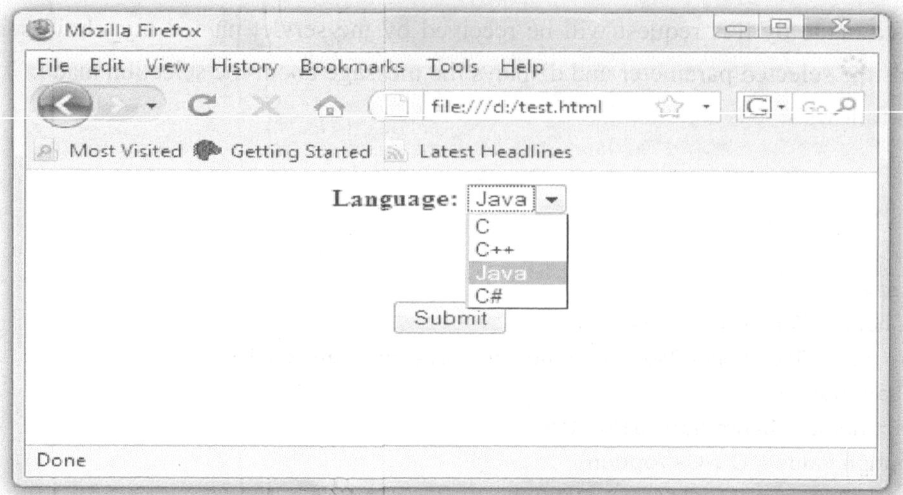

On clicking the submit button we will get following output.

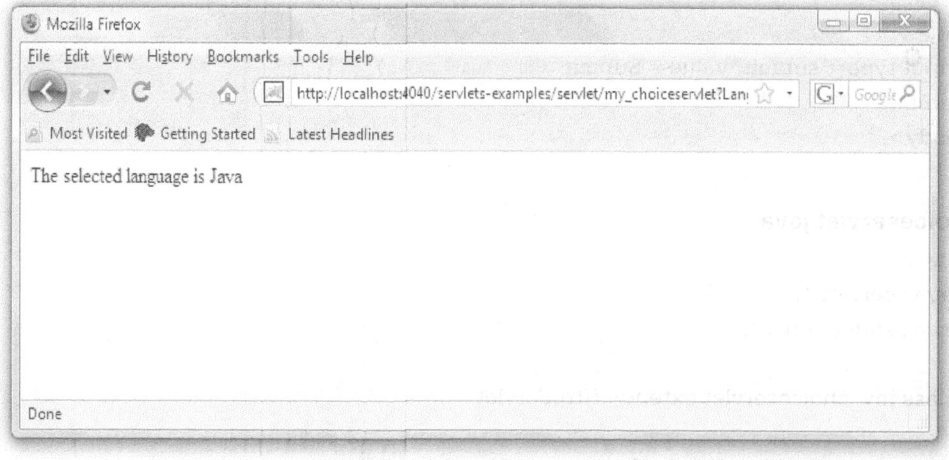

Ex. 5.6.2 : Write HTML form to read user name and password. This data is sent to the servlet. If the correct user name and password is given then welcome him/her by his/her name otherwise display the message for invalid user.

Sol. : Step 1 : Create HTML form for accepting user name and password

Input.html

```
<html>
<head>
</head>
<body>
<form action="http://localhost/examples/servlets/servlet/Welcome" method ="get">
User Name:<input type="text" name="uname"/>
```

```
<br/>
Password:<input type="password" name="pwd"/>
<input type="submit" value="Submit"/>
</form>
</body>
</html>
```

Step 2 : Create the servlet program to read user name and password and validate it.

Welcome.java

```
import java.io.*;
import javax.servlet.*;
import javax.servlet.http.*;

public class Welcome extends HttpServlet
{
    public void doGet(HttpServletRequest req,HttpServletResponse res)
    throws ServletException,IOException
    {
     PrintWriter out=res.getWriter();
     res.setContentType("text/html");

     String username=req.getParameter("uname");
     String password=req.getParameter("pwd");
     if ((username=="Ankita")&&(password=="1234"))
          out.print("Welcome "+username);
     else
        out.println("Invalid username");
    }
}
```

Ex. 5.6.3 : Write a servlet which accept two numbers using POST methods and display the maximum of them.

Sol. : Step 1 : The HTML document for inputting two numbers is as follows -

NumbersInput.html

```
<html>
<head>
<body>
<div align="center">
   <br> <br>
   <form action="http ://localhost/examples/servlets/servlet/MaxNumber" method="post">
    Enter First Number :
     <input type="text" value="" name="Number1" size='5'>
     <br/><br/> Enter Second Number :
```

```
      <input type="text" value="" name="Number2" size='5'>
      <br/> <br/> <br/>
      <input  type="submit" value="Submit">
    </form>
  </div>
  </body>
  </html>
```

Step 2 : The servlet code that handles the Post method and finds the maximum of the two input numbers is as follows -

MaxNumber.java

```
import java.io.*;
import javax.servlet.*;
import javax.servlet.http.*;

public class MaxNumber extends HttpServlet
  {
  protected void doPost(HttpServletRequest req, HttpServletResponse res) throws ServletException,
IOException
  {
      res.setContentType("text/html");
      PrintWriter out=res.getWriter();

      // get request parameters for userID and password
      int a = Integer.parseInt(req.getParameter("Number1"));
     int b = Integer.parseInt(req.getParameter("Number2"));

      if (a>b)
      out.println("<h4>The maximum number is:"+a+"</h4>");
     else
      out.println("<h4>The maximum number is :"+b+"</h4>");

  }
}
```

Step 3 : The output is as follows -

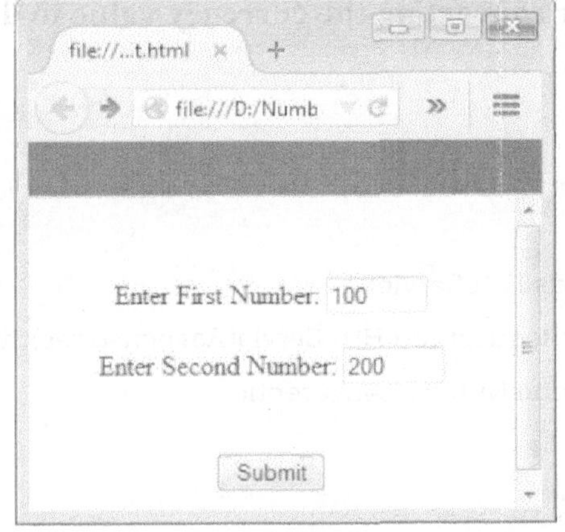

Ex. 5.6.4 Write the code for converting currencies to US Dollar. **AU : May-14, Marks 8**

Sol. :

Step 1 : We will write the simple HTML document, which will create the interface. **The user can** select **the type of currencies and will enter the value.**

```
<html>
 <body>
  <formname="form1"method="post"
action="http://localhost/examples/servlets/servlet/DollarDemo">
  Select the type of Currency:
   <Select name="currency">
    <option value="Euro">Euro</option>
    <option value="Pound">Pound</option>
    <option value="Rupees">Rupees</option>
   </select>
   <br/>  <br/>
   Enter the value:
   <input type="text" name="currencyVal" value=""/>
   <br/>  <br/>
   <input type="submit" value="Submit"/>
   </form>
 </body>
</html>
```

Step 2 : The java servlet for converting the currency value to dollar is as given below -

```
import java.io.*;
import java.net.*;
import javax.servlet.*;
import javax.servlet.http.*;
public class DollarDemo extends HttpServlet {
public void doPost(HttpServletRequest req,HttpServletResponse res)throws
    ServletException,IOException,NullPointerException
{
 res.setContentType("text/html");
 PrintWriter out=res.getWriter();
 String c=req.getParameter("currency");
 double RupeeValue,EuroValue,PoundValue;
 double DollarValue=0;
 String value=req.getParameter("currencyVal");

 if(c.equals("Rupees"))
 {
  RupeeValue=Double.parseDouble(value);
  DollarValue=RupeeValue/61;
 }
 if(c.equals("Euro"))
 {
  EuroValue=Double.parseDouble(value);
  DollarValue=EuroValue/0.77;
 }
 if(c.equals("Pound"))
 {
  PoundValue=Double.parseDouble(value);
  DollarValue=PoundValue*1.62;
 }
 out.println("<p> The dollar value= "+DollarValue+"</p>");
 out.close();
}
}
```

Output

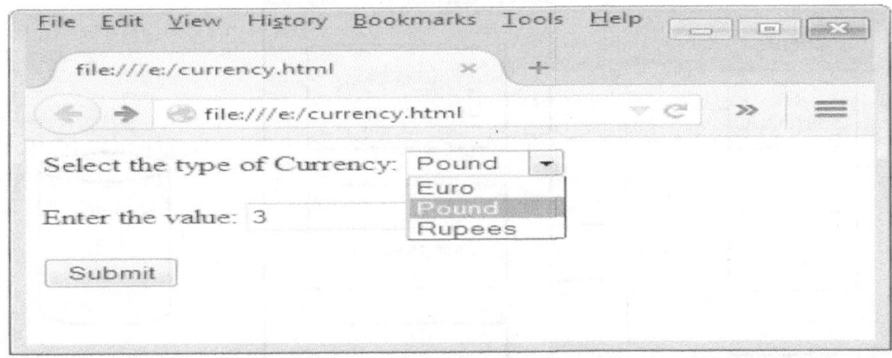

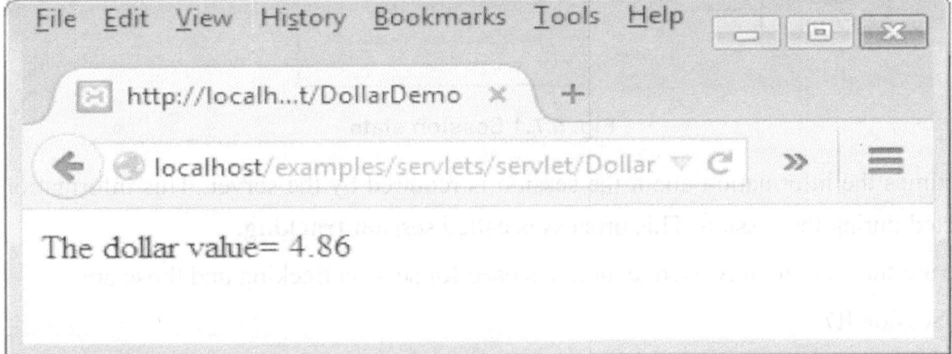

University Questions

1. *What is the difference between the HTTP-GET and HTTP-POST request ?* **AU : Dec.-09, Marks 2**
2. *Write the servlet program that handles the HTTP get request containing data that is supplied by the user as part of the request.* **AU : May-08, Marks 8**

5.7 Session Handling

AU : May-12,14, Marks 8

- When you open some application, use it for some time and then close it. This entire scenario is named as **session.**
- **Session state** is a server-based state mechanism that lets web applications store and retrieve objects of any type for each **unique user session.** That is, each browser session has its own session state stored as a serialized file on the server, which is deserialized and loaded into memory as needed for each request. Refer Fig. 5.7.1.
- Because server storage is a finite resource, objects loaded into memory are released when the request completes, making room for other requests and their session objects. This means there can be more active sessions on disk than in memory at any one time.

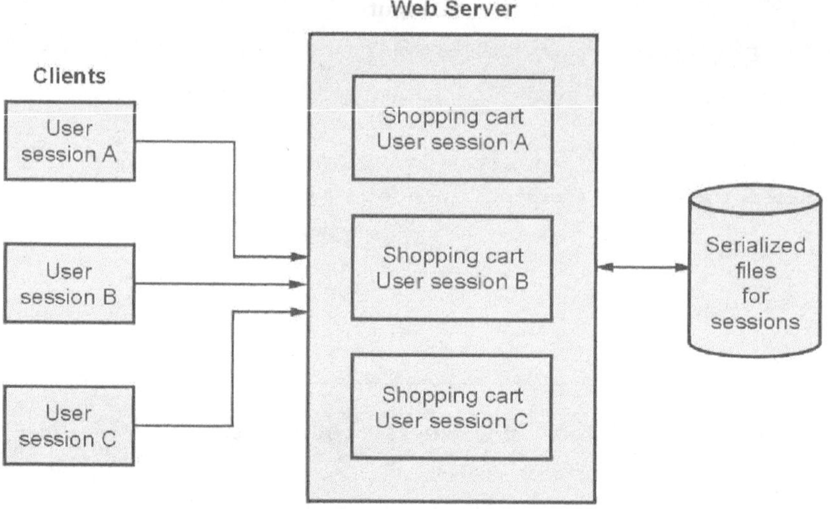

Fig. 5.7.1 Session state

- Sometimes the information about the session is required by the server. This information can be collected during the session. This process is called **session tracking.**
- There are three commonly used techniques used for session tracking and those are
  - Session ID
  - Cookies
  - URL Rewriting

5.7.1 Session Management using Session ID

AU : May-12,14, Marks 8

- **HTTP** is a **stateless protocol** in which each request is independent of the previous request. And HTTP is a protocol using which user can interact with the server via web browser and it cannot remember previously held communications but sometimes there is serious need to keep track of previous communication sessions. This can be achieved by **session tracking**.
- The **session tracking technique** is a mechanism by which we can keep track of previous sessions between server and the browser.
- For sending all state information to and fro between browser and server, usually an ID is used. This ID is basically a **session-ID.**
- Thus session-ID is passed between the browser and server while processing the information. This method of keeping track of all the information between server and browser using session-ID is called **session tracking.**
- In servlets, for creating the sessions **getSession()** method can be used. This method returns the object which stores the bindings with the names that use this object. And these bindings can be

managed using **getAttribute(), setAttribute(), removeAttribute()** methods. Actually in session tracking two things are playing an important role -

1) One is **HttpServletRequest** interface which supports **getSession()** method.
2) The another class is **HttpSession** class which supports the binding managing functions such as **getAttribute(), setAttribute(), removeAttribute()** and **getAttributeNames().**

Let us first discuss the servlet program which returns the number of previous sessions established between client and server. Note that any client can communicate with the server using some web browser only!

Ex. 5.7.1 : Write a servlet program to keep track of number of times user is visiting the page. Display the count appropriately.

Sol. : Servlet Program(SessionServletDemo)

```
import java.io.*;
import java.util.*;
import javax.servlet.*;
import javax.servlet.http.*;
public class SessionServletDemo extends HttpServlet
{
 public void doGet(HttpServletRequest req,HttpServletResponse res)
 throws ServletException,IOException
 {
  res.setContentType("text/html");
  HttpSession session=req.getSession();
  String heading;
  Integer cnt=(Integer)session.getAttribute("cnt");
  if(cnt==null)
  {
   cnt=new Integer(0);
    heading="Welcome You are accessing the page for the First Time";
  }
  else
  {
   heading="Welcome once again!";
   cnt=new Integer(cnt.intValue()+1);
  }

 session.setAttribute("cnt",cnt);
  PrintWriter out=res.getWriter();
  out.println("<html>");
  out.println("<head>");
  out.println("</head>");
  out.println("<body>");
```

```
out.println("<center>");
out.println("<h1>"+heading);
out.println("<h2> The number of previous access= "+cnt);
out.println("</center>");
out.println("</body>");
out.println("</html>");
}
}
```

Output

To get an output we will use following steps -

1. Compile the Servlet (i.e. a java program) using **javac.** This will generate a class file.
2. Copy this class file to C:*your tomcat directory\examples-folder\WEB-INF\classes*
3. Edit the **web.xml** file present at C:*your tomcat directory\examples-folder\WEB-INF* like this

```
...
<servlet>
    <servlet-name>SessionServletDemo</servlet-name>
    <servlet-class>SessionServletDemo</servlet-class>
  </servlet>
...
<servlet-mapping>
        <servlet-name>SessionServletDemo</servlet-name>
        <url-pattern>/servlet/SessionServletDemo</url-pattern>
</servlet-mapping>
```

4. Start tomcat server.
5. Open the web browser and give the URL for **SessionServletDemo.** Following output can be seen.

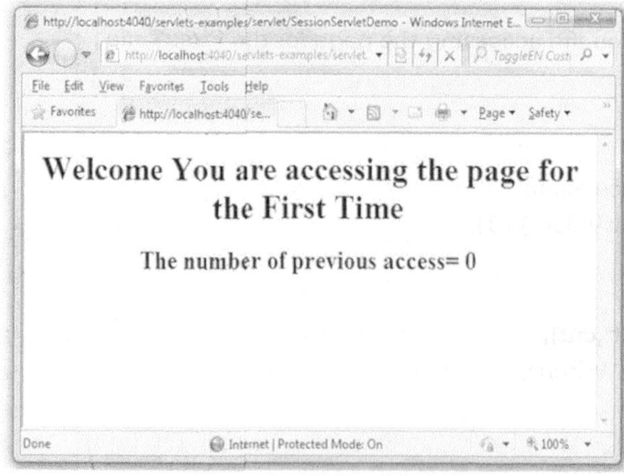

If you simply refresh your browser either by pressing F5 or clicking the refresh button then you will get following kind of output.

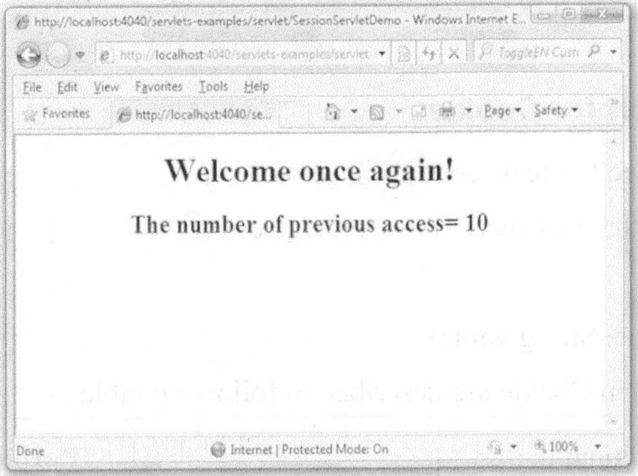

Program Explanation

1. Our class *SessionServletDemo* is inherited from **HttpServlet** class. And inside the **doGet()** method we can create an object *session* of **HttpSession** class. This method returns the current session for the corresponding request.
2. The **getAttribute(string** *attribute)* returns the value associated with the *attribute.* We can pass this *attribute* as a parameter to this method. If there is no attribute present then this method returns null. The data type of getAttribute() method is **void.**
3. The setAttribute(**string** *attribute,* **object** *value)* is a method which assigns the value passed as the object value to the attribute name. The data type of this method is **void.**

University Question

1. *What is session ? Explain the session tracking systems used.* **AU : May-12,14, Marks 8**

5.8 Understanding Cookie **AU : May-09,13,17,18,19, Dec.-16, Marks 16**

Definition : Cookies are some little information that can be left on your computer by the other computer when we access an internet.

- Generally this information is left on your computer by some advertising agencies on the internet. Using the information stored in the cookies these advertising agencies can keep track of your internet usage, liking of users.
- For the applications like on-line purchase systems once you enter your personal information such as your name or your e-mail ID then it can be remembered by these systems with the help of cookies.

- Sometimes cookies are very much dangerous because by using information from your local disk some malicious data may be passed to you. So it is upto you how to maintain your own privacy and security.

5.8.1 Servlet Support for Cookies

- The **cookie** class is used to create cookies in servlet.
- **Syntax :** The Syntax for constructor for cookies are
  - Cookie()
  - Cookie(String name, String value)
- Various methods used in Cookie are described in following table

S.N.	Method	Purpose
1.	public string getName()	It returns the name of the cookie.
2.	public String getValue()	It returns the value of the cookie.
3.	public string setName()	It sets or changes the name of the cookie.
4.	public String setValue()	It sets or changes the value of the cookie.
5.	public void addCookie(Cookie c)	The cookie is added in the response object of HttpServletResponse interface.
6.	public Cookie[] getCookies()	All the cookies can be returned using this method with the help of HttpServletRequest interface.

- In Servlet following steps are used to support for cookies

Step 1 : Creation of Cookies :

The cookie can be created in Servlet and added to response object using **addCookie** method

```
Cookie cookie=new Cookie("user","XYZ");//creating cookie object
response.addCookie(cookie);//adding cookie in the response
```

Step 2 : Reading Cookies :

The value from the cookie can be obtained using the **getName()** and **getValue()** methods.

```
    Cookie[ ] my_cookies=req.getCookies();
int n=my_cookies.length;
for(int i=0;i<n;i++)
{
String name=my_cookies[i].getName();
String value=my_cookies[i].getValue();
}
```

5.8.2 Examples

Below is simple HTML form in which a servlet is invoked. This servlet creates a cookie by the name **My_Cookie** and stores the value entered by you in the textbox of HTML form. You can further get the information stored in the cookie by another servlet program **getCookieServlet**. Hence we will write three programs -

1. Our normal HTML script in which some value is entered in the textbox.
2. The servlet program named mycookieservlet which will set a cookies and take the value entered by you in the HTML form.
3. The another servlet program named *getCookieServlet* which helps us to view the cookie.

HTML Program

```
<html>
<head>
<title>Demo of Cookie</title>
</head>
<body>
<form name="form1" method="post"
action="http ://localhost:8080/examples/servlet/mycookieservlet">
<h3> Enter the value for my Cookie: </h3>
<input type=text name="txt_data" size =30 value=" ">
<input type=submit  value="Submit">
</form>
</body>
</html>
```

Servlet Program [mycookieservlet.java]

```
import java.io.*;
import javax.servlet.*;
import javax.servlet.http.*;
public class mycookieservlet extends HttpServlet
{
public void doPost(HttpServletRequest req,HttpServletResponse res)
throws ServletException, IOException
{
String txt_data = req.getParameter("txt_data");
// Create cookie.
Cookie cookie = new Cookie("My_Cookie", txt_data);
// Adding cookie to HTTP response.
res.addCookie(cookie);
// Write friendly output to browser.
res.setContentType("text/html");
PrintWriter out = res.getWriter();
```

```
out.println("<h2>MyCookie has been set to : ");
out.println(txt_data);
out.println("<br><br><br>");
out.println("This page shows that the cookie has been added");
out.close();
}
}
```

We have first created an object of Cookie class using which the cookie can be added using **addCookie()** method.

Servlet Program[getcookieservlet.java]

```
import java.io.*;
import javax.servlet.*;
import javax.servlet.http.*;
public class getCookieServlet extends HttpServlet
{
 public void doGet(HttpServletRequest req,HttpServletResponse res)
 throws ServletException,IOException
{
Cookie[ ] my_cookies=req.getCookies();
res.setContentType("text/html");
PrintWriter out=res.getWriter();
out.println("<b>");
int n=my_cookies.length;
for(int i=0;i<n;i++)
{
String name=my_cookies[i].getName();
String value=my_cookies[i].getValue();
out.println("name= "+name);
out.println("and value= "+value);
}
out.close();
}
}
```

In the above program using **getName()** and **getValue()** functions we can get the name of the cookie as well as the value of the cookie respectively. The output of all the above given three programs is as given below -

Output

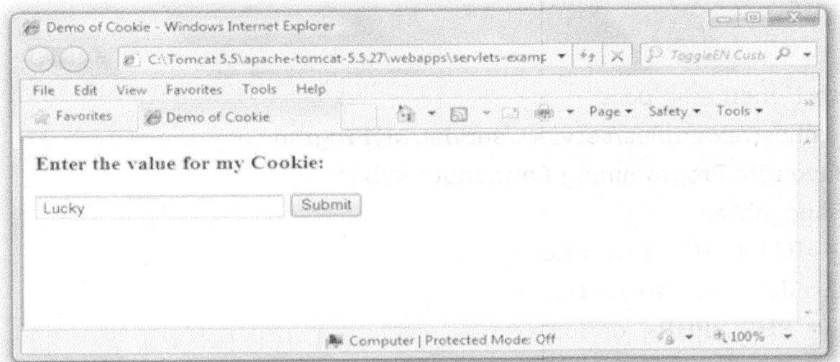

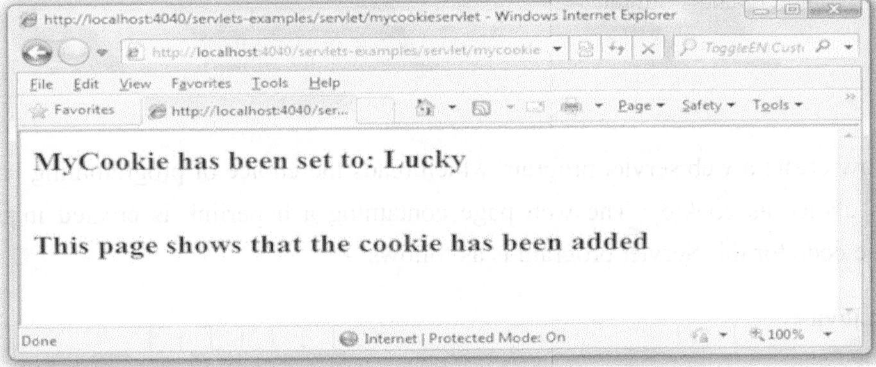

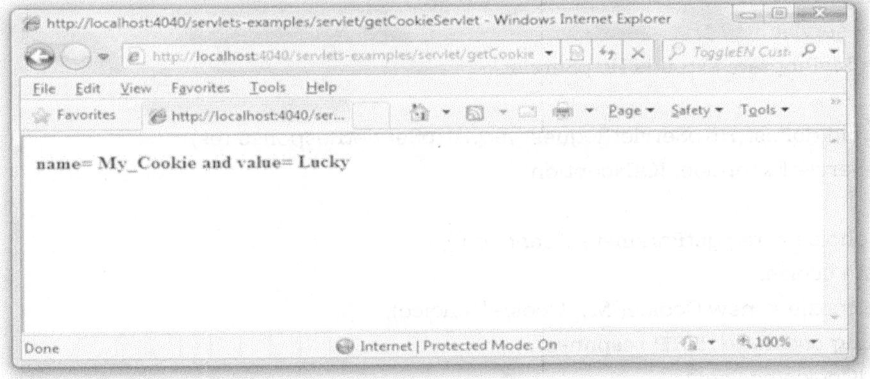

Ex. 5.8.1 Write a program that allows the user to select a favorite programming language and post the choice to the servlet. The response is a web page in which user can click a link to view list of book recommendations. The cookies previously stored on the client are read by the servlet and form a web page containing the book recommendation. Use servlet, cookies and HTML.

AU : May-17, Marks 16

Sol. :

Step 1 : Create an HTML page which allows the user to select the favourite programming language. The user can submit his choice by clicking the submit button.

InputForm.html

```
<html>
<body>
<form name="form1" method="post"
action="http://localhost/examples/servlets/servlet/MyProgram">
<h3> Enter the favourite Programming Language: </h3>
<select name="Lang_ch">
    <option value="C++">C++</option>
    <option value="Java">Java</option>
    <option value="PHP">PHP</option>
</select>
<input type=submit  value="Submit">
</form>
</body>
</html>
```

Step 2 : Now create a web servlet program which reads the choice of programming language and set this choice as cookie. The web page containing a hyperlink is created in this servlet program. The code for this Servlet program is as follows –

MyProgram.java

```
import java.io.*;
import javax.servlet.*;
import javax.servlet.http.*;
public class MyProgram extends HttpServlet
{
    public void doPost(HttpServletRequest req,HttpServletResponse res)
    throws ServletException, IOException
    {
     String choice = req.getParameter("Lang_ch");
     // Create cookie.
     Cookie cookie = new Cookie("My_Cookie", choice);
     // Adding cookie to HTTP response.
     res.addCookie(cookie);
     // Write friendly output to browser with web link
     res.setContentType("text/html");
     PrintWriter out = res.getWriter();
     out.println("<a href='ReadChoice'><p>Click Here to read about your
     favorite programming language </p></a>");
     out.println("<br><br><br>");
     out.println("This page shows that the cookie has been added");
     out.close();
    }
}
```

Step 3 : On clicking the hyperlink present in the above servlet, we can read the value of cookie(which is actually the name of the favorite programming language). The following program displays the recommended book for the programming language you have chosen. The code is as follows -

ReadChoice.java

```
import java.io.*;
import javax.servlet.*;
import javax.servlet.http.*;
public class ReadChoice extends HttpServlet
{
    public void doGet(HttpServletRequest req,HttpServletResponse res)
     throws ServletException,IOException
     {
      Cookie[] my_cookies=req.getCookies();
      res.setContentType("text/html");
      PrintWriter out=res.getWriter();
      out.println("<b>");
      int n=my_cookies.length;
      for(int i=0;i<n;i++)
      {
         String name=my_cookies[i].getName();
         String value=my_cookies[i].getValue();
         if(value.equals("PHP"))
         {
            out.println("<b>Programming Language: </b>"+value);
            out.println("<br/><b>Book Name: </b>"+"PHP and MySQL Web
            Development by Luke Welling and Laura Thompson");
         }
         else if(value.equals("Java"))
         {
            out.println("<b>Programming Language: </b>"+value);
            out.println("<br/><b>Book Name: </b>"+"The Complete
            Reference Java");
         }
         else
         {
            out.println("<b>Programming Language: </b>"+value);
            out.println("<br/><b>Book Name: </b>"+"C++
            Programming Language by Bjarne Stroustrup");
         }
      }
      out.close();
```

```
    }
}
```

Output

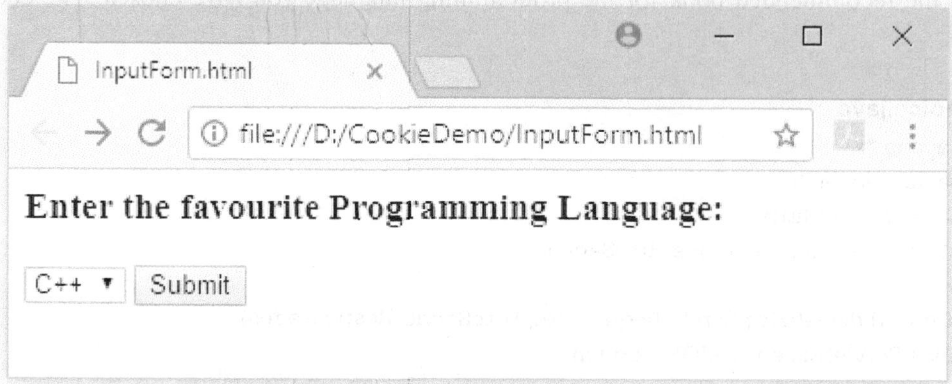
InputForm.html
file:///D:/CookieDemo/InputForm.html
Enter the favourite Programming Language:
C++
Submit

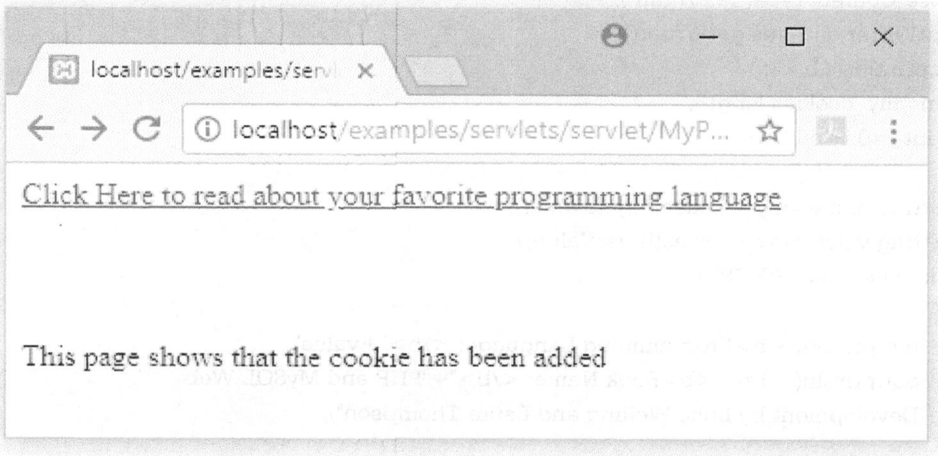
localhost/examples/serv
localhost/examples/servlets/servlet/MyP...
Click Here to read about your favorite programming language
This page shows that the cookie has been added

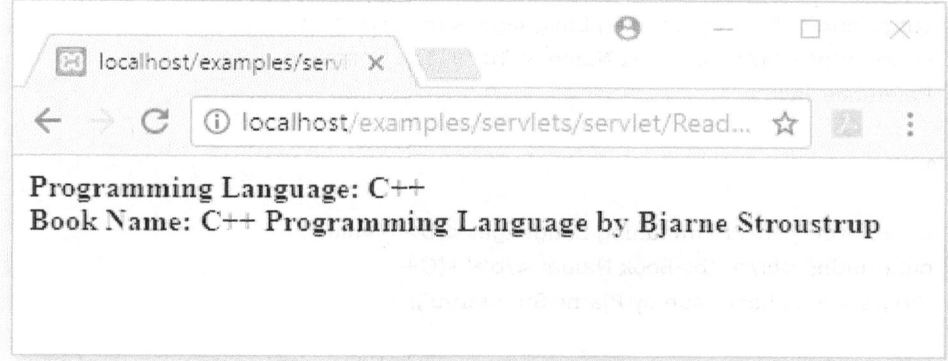
localhost/examples/serv
localhost/examples/servlets/servlet/Read...
Programming Language: C++
Book Name: C++ Programming Language by Bjarne Stroustrup

University Questions

1. *How to create cookies and retrieve its value ?* **AU : May-09, Marks 6**
2. *Write a servlet to illustrate the principles of cookies and explain ?* **AU : May-13, Marks 16**
3. *Explain the use of cookies for tracking requests with a program.* **AU : Dec.-16, Marks 8**
4. *What are cookies ? With examples differentiate session and persistent cookies and explain how to write and read cookies.* **AU : May-18, Marks 13**
5. *Explain cookies with suitable example.* **AU : May-19, Marks 5**

5.9 Installing and Configuring Apache Tomcat Web Server

- Tomcat is an open source web server and servlet contained developed by **Apache Software Foundation (ASF).**
- With the help of Tomcat we can execute Servlets, JSP Java EL and so on. Tomcat is developed and maintained by an open community of developers under **Apache License.** It is written in Java.
- Tomcat 4.X is released with following components -
  1. **Catalina :** The Catalina is Tomcat's servlet container. It helps to execute Servlets and Java Server Pages(JSP). This is the core component of Tomcat. When you start up Tomcat, you actually start up Catalina.
  2. **Coyote :** The Coyote is Tomcat's Web connector component. It listens for incoming connections to the server on specific TCP port and forwards the request to the Tomcat engine to process the request and sent back the response to the requesting client.
  3. **Jasper :** The Jasper is basically Tomcat's JSP engine. It parses the JSP files and compiles them to Java code as Servlets. At runtime, Jasper detects the changes to JSP files and recompiles them.

Features of Tomcat

Various features of Tomcat are -

1. It has reduced garbage collection.
2. It is useful for improving the performance and scalability.
3. The platform integration feature allows to work it on Windows and Unix.
4. It parses JSP efficiently.

Installation of Tomcat

Step 1 : Go to http://tomcat.apache.org/ then go to the Binary Distribution/Core/ and download the "zip" package (for example "apache-tomcat-7.0.40.zip", about 8MB).

Step 2 : Now unzip the downloaded file into a directory of our choice.

Step 3 : Check the installed directory to ensure it contains the following sub-directories :

- bin folder
- logs folder
- webapps folder
- work folder
- temp folder
- conf folder
- lib folder

Alternative

- We can install tomcat using XAMPP or LAMP package.
- XAMPP is a completely free, easy to install Apache distribution containing MariaDB, PHP, and Perl.
- This package has built in Tomcat web container, and MySQL database system.
- The XAMPP open source package has been set up to be incredibly easy to install and to use.

Configuring Tomcat

After downloading this software we need to **configure** it with the help of environment variables. The configuration of Tomcat can be done using following steps -

Step 1 : First of all set the environment variable JAVA_HOME. For that matter go to control panel–>System–>Advanced tab. You can click on Environment Variables and set the variable JAVA_HOME=C:\your_jdk_directory

For instance

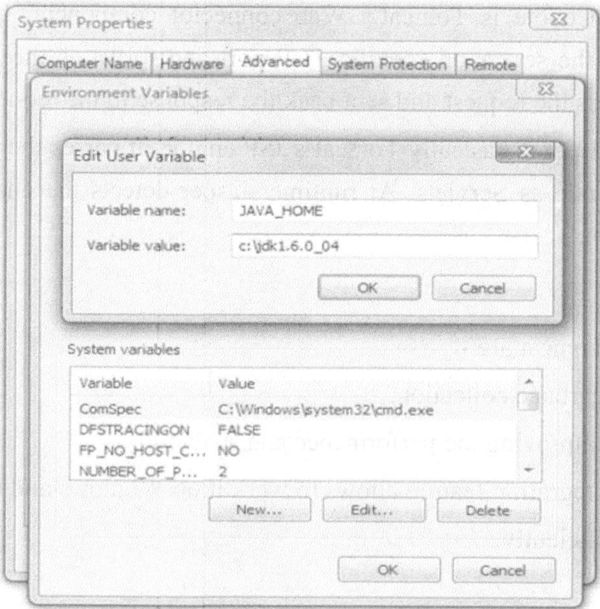

Step 2 : Then you can set the environment variable for CATALINA_HOME as the Tomcat's directory. This environment variable is needed to start the Tomcat server.

The configuration files of the Apache Tomcat Server are located in the "conf" sub-directory of our Tomcat installed directory.

There are four configuration XML files :

1. context.xml file
2. tomcat-users.xml file
3. server.xml file
4. web.xml file

Tomcat can be started by running the startup.bat file located in bin folder.

5.10 Database Connectivity

AU : Dec.- 9,10,12,18, May-13,16,17 Marks 16

JDBC is a Java API for database access. A servlet can connect to MYSQL and sends the SQL commands to the database and get the required data. Hence we will first get introduced with structured query language SQL.

5.10.1 Structured Query Language using MySQL

The MYSQL is a open source database product which can be downloaded from the web site.

After getting installed on the machine the command prompt window for MYSQL can appear. The screenshot is as follows –

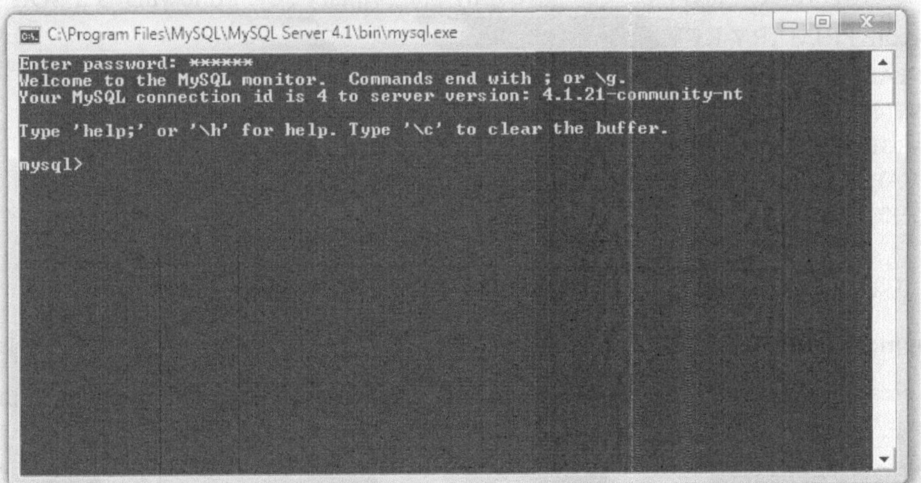

```
C:\Program Files\MySQL\MySQL Server 4.1\bin\mysql.exe
Enter password: ******
Welcome to the MySQL monitor.  Commands end with ; or \g.
Your MySQL connection id is 4 to server version: 4.1.21-community-nt

Type 'help;' or '\h' for help. Type '\c' to clear the buffer.

mysql>
```

Now let us go through some MYSQL query statements which are required while handling the database.

1. Creating database

```
mysql> CREATE DATABASE mydb;
Query OK, 1 row affected (0.15 sec)
```

2. Displaying all the databases

```
mysql> SHOW DATABASES;
+-------------+
| Database |
+-------------+
| mydb      |
| mysql      |
| students  |
| test        |
+--------------+
4 rows in set (0.06 sec)
```

3. Selecting particular database

```
mysql> USE MYDB;
Database changed
```

4. Creating table

We must create a table inside a database hence it is a common practice to use create table command after USE database command. While creating a table we must specify the table fields.

```
mysql> CREATE TABLE my_table(id INT(4),name VARCHAR(20));
Query OK, 0 rows affected (0.28 sec)
```

Use of Primary Key : The primary key contains the unique value. The primary key column can not contain NUL value. Each table can have only one primary key. Following is a SQL statement used to create PRIMARY KEY.

```
CREATE TABLE student_table(
roll_no INT(4) NOT NULL AUTO_INCREMENT,
name VARCHAR(50) NOT NULL,
address VARACHAR(50) NOT NULL,
PRIMARY KEY(roll_no)
);
```

In above example the roll_no acts as a primary key for the student_table.

5. Displaying a table

After creating the table using SHOW command we can see all the existing tables in the current database.

```
mysql> SHOW TABLES;
+----------------------+
| Tables_in_mydb |
+----------------------+
| my_table             |
+----------------------+
1 row in set (0.00 sec)
```

6. Displaying the table fields

For knowing the various fields of the table we may use following command

```
mysql> DESCRIBE my_table;
+---------+----------------+--------+------+---------- +---------+
| Field   | Type           | Null   | Key  | Default | Extra |
+---------+----------------+--------+------+----------+--------+
| id      | int(4)         | YES    |      | NULL     |        |
| name    | varchar(20)    | YES    |      | NULL     |        |
+---------+----------------+--------+------+---------- +-------- +
2 rows in set (0.07 sec)
```

7. Inserting values into the table

We can insert only one complete record at a time. It is as shown below -

```
mysql> INSERT INTO my_table
   -> VALUES(1,'SHILPA');
Query OK, 1 row affected (0.05 sec)
```

8. Displaying the contents of the table

```
mysql> SELECT * FROM my_table;
+------+------------+
|  id  | name       |
+------+------------+
|  1   | SHILPA     |
+-------+------------+
1 row in set (0.06 sec)
```

We can also write SELECT statement for selecting particular row by specifying some condition such as -

```
mysql> SELECT * FROM my_table where id=1;
or
mysql> SELECT * FROM my_table where name='SHILPA';
```

Thus we can insert the rows into the table by repeatedly giving the INSERT command.

If we want to get the records in sorted manner then we use ORDER BY clause

```
mysql> SELECT * FROM my_table;
+-------+---------------+
|  id   | name          |
+-------+---------------+
|  1    | SHILPA        |
|  2    | SUPRIYA       |
|  3    | YOGESH        |
|  4    | MONIKA        |
+-------+---------------+
4 rows in set (0.00 sec)
mysql> SELECT * FROM my_table ORDER BY name;
```

```
+------+-------------+
| id   | name        |
+------+-------------+
|    4 | MONIKA      |
|    1 | SHILPA      |
|    2 | SUPRIYA     |
|    3 | YOGESH      |
+------+-------------+
4 rows in set (0.00 sec)
```

9. Updating the record

For updating the record in the database following command can be used -

```
mysql> UPDATE my_table
    -> SET name='PRIYANKA'
    -> WHERE id=4;
Query OK, 1 row affected (0.05 sec)
Rows matched: 1  Changed: 1  Warnings: 0
mysql> SELECT * FROM my_table;
+------+--------------+
| id   | name         |
+-----+---------------+
|    1 | SHILPA       |
|    2 | SUPRIYA      |
|    3 | YOGESH       |
|    4 | PRIYANKA     |
+-----+---------------+
4 rows in set (0.00 sec)
```

10. Deleting record

For deleting particular record from a database

```
mysql> DELETE FROM my_table
    -> WHERE id=3;
Query OK, 1 row affected (0.04 sec)
```

Then use SELECT statement for displaying the contents of the table we use following command

```
mysql> SELECT * FROM my_table;
+------+---------------+
| id   |  name         |
+------+---------------+
|    1 | SHILPA        |
|    2 | SUPRIYA       |
|    4 | PRIYANKA      |
+------+---------------+
3 rows in set (0.00 sec)
```

11. For deleting the table

The table can be deleted using the command

mysql>drop table my_table;

12. Inner join

This query used to display the result from both the tables when at least one column from both the tables is matching-

For example

Consider table **Customer**

Cust_Id	Name	City
1	Rahul	Bombay
2	Priyanka	Pune
3	Supriya	Banglore

Consider table **Order**

Order_Id	Cust_Id	Order_Number
10	3	1234
20	1	5678
30	1	8900

Then we can make use of inner join query as follows -

```
SELECT Customer.Name, Customer.city, Order.Order_Number
FROM Customer
INNER JOIN Order
ON Customer.Cust_Id=Order.Order_Id
```

Name	City	Order_Number
Rahul	Bombay	5678
Rahul	Bombay	8900

13. Order By Clause

If we want to get the records in sorted manner then we use ORDER BY clause

mysql> SELECT * FROM my_table;

id	name
1	SHILPA
2	SUPRIYA

3	YOGESH
4	MONIKA

mysql> SELECT * FROM my_table ORDER BY name;

id	name
4	MONIKA
1	SHILPA
2	SUPRIYA
3	YOGESH

5.10.2 JDBC Perspectives

- JDBC stands for Java DataBase Connectivity.
- JDBC is nothing but an API (i.e. Application Programming Interface).
- It consists of various classes, interfaces, exceptions using which Java application can send SQL statements to a database. The SQL is a Structured Query Language used for accessing the database.
- JDBC is specially used for having connectivity with the RDBMS packages (such as Oracle or MYSQL) using corresponding JDBC driver.

The **JDBC API** is a set of classes, interfaces and exceptions used for establishing connection with data source. This JDBC API is defined in the **java.sql** and **javax.sql** packages. We use following core JDBC classes and interfaces that belong to **java.sql** package.

- **DriverManager** - When Java application needs connection to the database it invokes the **DriverManager** class. This class then loads JDBC **drivers** in the memory. The DriverManager also attempts to open a connection with the desired database. For JSP-MYSQL connectivity we can get DriverManager class as -

```
Class.forName("sun.jdbc.odbc.JdbcOdbcDriver");
```

1) **Connection** - This is an interface which represents connectivity with the data source. The **connection** is used for creating the **Statement** instance.

```
Connection conn=
DriverManager.getConnection("jdbc:mysql://localhost:3306/databaseName","userName","password");
```

2) **Statement** - This interface is used for representing the SQL statements. Some examples of SQL statements are
   - o SELECT * FROM students_table;
   - o UPDATE students_table set name='Neel' where roll_no='1';
   - o DELETE from students_table WHERE roll_no='10';

The code for statement is as follows -

```
Statement stmt=conn.createStatement();
stmt.executeQuery("select * from mytab");
```

There are two specialised Statement types: **PreparedStatement** and **CallableStatement.** The **PreparedStatement** represents the precompiled SQL statements.

For instance :

```
SELECT * from students_table WHERE name=?
```

The placeholder represented by ? is used in this type of statement. There are special type setter methods that assign the values to the placeholders before the SQL statement is executed.

CallableStatement is represents the stored procedures. These are similar to **PreparedStatement.** In this type of Statements we can assign the methods for the types of output arguments.

3) **ResultSet** - This interface is used to represent the database result set. After using SELECT SQL statement, the information obtained from the database can be displayed using **ResultSet.**

4) **SQLException** - For handling SQL exceptions this interface is used.

5.10.2.1 How JDBC Works ?

Following is a way by which JDBC works -

1) First of all Java application establishes connection with the data source.
2) Then Java application invokes classes and interfaces from JDBC driver for sending queries to the data source.
3) The JDBC driver connects to corresponding database and retrieves the result.
4) These results are based on SQL statements which are then returned to Java application.
5) Java application then uses the retrieved information for further processing.

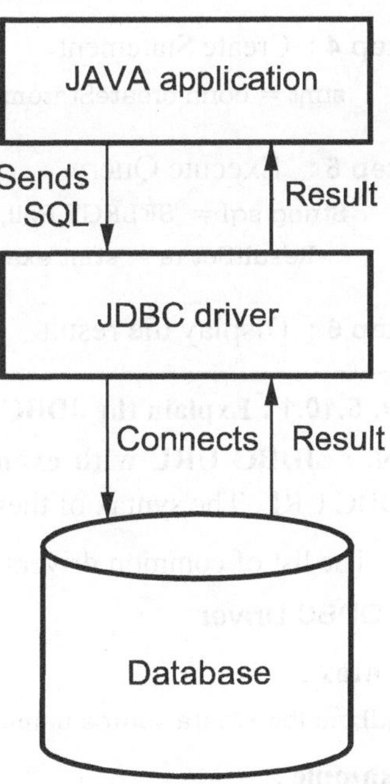

Fig. 5.10.1 Role of JDBC

5.10.2.2 Difference between JDBC and ODBC

The JDBC is similar to the ODBC i.e. Open Database Connectivity. But the ODBC is used for managing any kind of database and JDBC is specially created to support the Java programs.

5.10.2.3 Uses of JDBC

1. JDBC helps the client to store and retrieve the data to the databases.
2. JDBC allows the client to update the databases.

5.10.3 Connectivity between Database and Servlet

Following steps are used to connect JDBC to MYSQL

Step 1 : Import java.sql.* package in the JDBC program

Following line can be included in your JDBC program at the beginning.

```
import java.sql.*
```

Step 2 : Load JDBC Driver.

The JDBC driver for MYSQL can be loaded using following statement

```
Class.forName("com.mysql.jdbc.Driver");
```

Step 3 : Get connection using the Driver Manager

```
conn = riverManager.getConnection("jdbc:mysql://localhost:3306/my_database","root","password");
```

Step 4 : Create Statement

```
stmt = conn.createStatement();
```

Step 5 : Execute Query

```
String sql = "SELECT Roll,StudName FROM my_table";
    ResultSet rs = stmt.executeQuery(sql);
```

Step 6 : Display the result

Ex. 5.10.1 : Explain the JDBC URL with appropriate examples.

Sol. : JDBC URL with examples : The databases are referenced by Java runtime engine using JDBC URL. The syntax of these URLs depends on the database driver you are using.

The list of common drivers along with JDBC URL is

1. ODBC Driver

Syntax :

```
jdbc:odbc:<data source name>
```

Example :

```
jdbc:odbc:MyDataSource
```

2. MYSQL

Syntax :

```
jdbc:mysql://[host][:port]/[database]
```

Example :

jdbc:mysql://localhost:3306/Mydatabase

3. ORACLE

Syntax :

jdbc:oracle:<drivertype>:<user>/<password>@<database>

Example :

jdbc:oracle:thin:myuser/mypassword@localhost:mydatabse

5.10.4 JDBC Program Example

For executing following programs –

(1) JDK must be installed

(2) XAMPP must be installed

(3) Eclipse must be installed. Also add jar file **mysql-connector-java.** Get it downloaded from Internet and save it at suitable location. Then configure Eclipse to use MySQL, for that purpose :

  (i) Right click on your Project.

  (ii) Click on Properties->Java Build Path->Libraries.

  (iii) Click Add External JARs... button and select **mysql-connector-javaXXX.jar file.**

Ex. 5.10.2 Consider a database table with the following schema.(PNR No,status). Write a servlet program to display the status, given the PNR number. **AU : Dec.-09, Marks 10, Dec.-12, Marks 16**

Sol. : Java Program[PNRDemo.java]

```
import java.io.*;
import java.util.*;
import javax.sql.*;
import javax.servlet.*;
import javax.servlet.http.*;
import java.sql.Connection;
import java.sql.DriverManager;
import java.sql.ResultSet;
import java.sql.SQLException;
import java.sql.Statement;

public class PNRDemo extends HttpServlet
{
  public void service(HttpServletRequest request,HttpServletResponse response)
  throws IOException, ServletException
  {
   // connecting to database
   Connection con = null;
   Statement stmt = null;
   ResultSet rs = null;
```

```
 PrintWriter out = response.getWriter();
try
{
  Class.forName("sun.jdbc.odbc.JdbcOdbcDriver");
  con =DriverManager.getConnection ("jdbc:odbc:PNRDemo","","");
}catch(ClassNotFoundException e){e.printStackTrace();}
catch(SQLException e){e.printStackTrace();}
catch(Exception e){e.printStackTrace();}
try
{
    stmt = con.createStatement();
   rs = stmt.executeQuery("SELECT * FROM PNR_table");
  // displaying records
  response.setContentType("text/html");
   out.println("<html>");
   out.println("<head><title>PNR Status Display</title></head>");
   out.println("<body>");
  out.print("<center>");
  out.print("<h2>PNR Details </h2>");
  out.print("<table border=3>");
  out.print("<th>PNR No.</th>");
  out.print("<th>Status</th>");
  while(rs.next())
  {
   out.print("<tr>");
   out.print("<td>");
   out.print(rs.getObject(1).toString());
   out.print("</td>");
   out.print("<td>");
         out.print(rs.getObject(2).toString());
   out.print("</td>");
   out.print("</tr>");
  }
  out.print("</table>");
  out.print("</center>");
  out.println("</body></html>");
  }catch (SQLException e)  { }
finally {
  try {
   if(rs != null) {
    rs.close();
    rs = null;
   }
   if(stmt != null) {
    stmt.close();
    stmt = null;
   }
   if(con != null) {
    con.close();
```

```
            con = null;
          }
        } catch (SQLException e) {}
      }
      out.close();
    }//end of service function
  } //end of class
```

Output

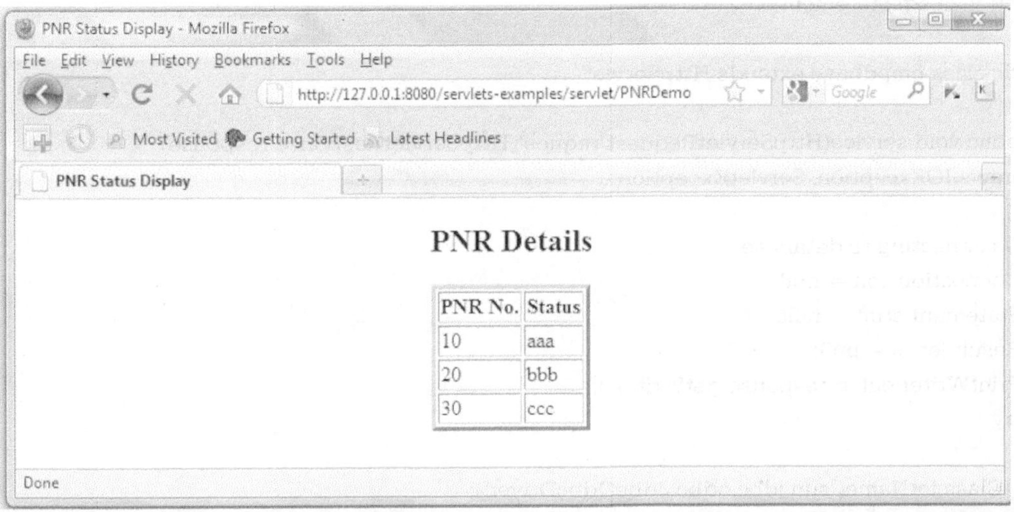

Ex. 5.10.3 Write a Java Servlet to display net salary of employee, Use JDBC connectivity to get employee details from database. **AU : May-13, Marks 16**

Sol. : Step 1 : Create a employees database as follows -

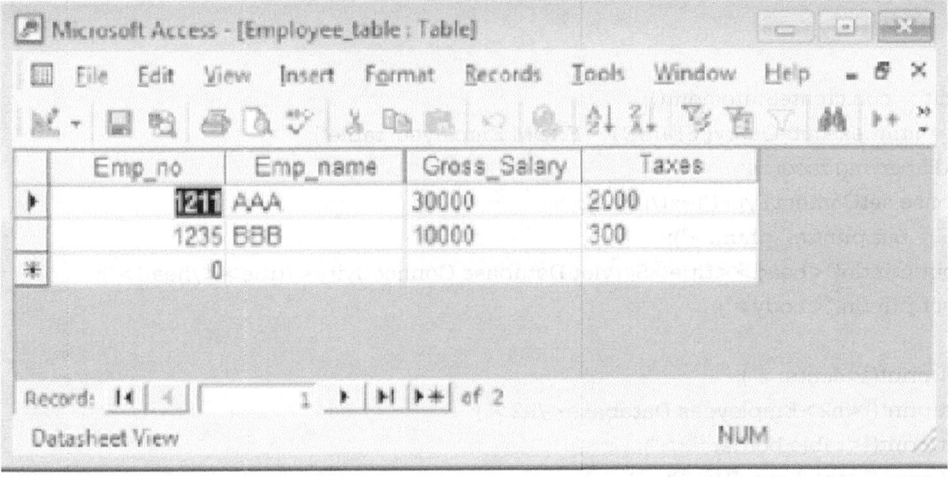

Emp_no	Emp_name	Gross_Salary	Taxes
1211	AAA	30000	2000
1235	BBB	10000	300
0			

Step 2 : The servlet for computing the net salary is as given below -

```
import java.io.*;
import java.util.*;
```

```
import javax.sql.*;
import javax.servlet.*;
import javax.servlet.http.*;
import java.sql.Connection;
import java.sql.DriverManager;
import java.sql.ResultSet;
import java.sql.SQLException;
import java.sql.Statement;

public class empdbase extends HttpServlet
{
   public void service(HttpServletRequest request,HttpServletResponse response)
   throws IOException, ServletException
   {
    // connecting to database
    Connection con = null;
    Statement stmt = null;
    ResultSet rs = null;
    PrintWriter out = response.getWriter();
    try
    {
      Class.forName("sun.jdbc.odbc.JdbcOdbcDriver");
      con =DriverManager.getConnection ("jdbc:odbc:Employees","","");
    }catch(ClassNotFoundException e){e.printStackTrace();}
    catch(SQLException e){e.printStackTrace();}
    catch(Exception e){e.printStackTrace();}
    try
    {

      stmt = con.createStatement();
      rs = stmt.executeQuery("SELECT * FROM Employee_table");
      // displaying records
   response.setContentType("text/html");
           out.println("<html>");
        out.println("<head><title>Servlet Database Connectivity</title></head>");
        out.println("<body>");

      out.print("<center>");
      out.print("<h2>Employees Database</h2>");
      out.print("<table border=3>");
      out.print("<th>Emp_ID</th>");
      out.print("<th>Name</th>");
      out.print("<th>Gross</th>");
      out.print("<th>Taxes</th>");
```

```
out.print("<th>Net Salary</th>");
while(rs.next())
{
  int tot=0;
    String gross=rs.getString(3);
     String deductions=rs.getString(4);

    int g=Integer.parseInt(gross);
    int d=Integer.parseInt(deductions);

tot=g-d;//net salary of employee
    out.print("<tr>");
    out.print("<td>");
    out.print(rs.getInt(1));
    out.print("</td>");
    out.print("<td>");
     out.print(rs.getString(2));
  out.print("</td>");
  out.print("<td>");
    out.print(g);
    out.print("</td>");
    out.print("<td>");
     out.print(d);
     out.print("</td>");
     out.print("<td>");
    out.print(tot);
    out.print("</td>");
     out.print("</tr>");
}
out.print("</table>");
out.print("</center>");
out.println("</body></html>");
}catch (SQLException e)  { }
finally {
try {
 if(rs != null) {
  rs.close();
  rs = null;
 }
 if(stmt != null) {
  stmt.close();
  stmt = null;
 }
 if(con != null) {
```

```
        con.close();
        con = null;
      }
    } catch (SQLException e) {}
  }
  out.close();
 }//end of service function
} //end of class
```

Ex. 5.10.3 Assume that a database has a table Employee with two columns EmployeeID and Name. Assume that the administrator user id and password to access the database table are, scott and tiger. Write a JDBC program that can query and print all the entries in the table Employee. Make the database connection using a type2 driver database.driver and connection string jdbc:db:oci

AU : May-16, Marks 16

Sol. : The JDBC code for displaying the employees in Employee table is as follows -

DisplayEmp.java

```
import java.io.*;
import java.util.*;
import javax.sql.*;
import javax.servlet.*;
import javax.servlet.http.*;
import java.sql.*;

public class DisplayEmp extends HttpServlet
{
  public void service(HttpServletRequest request,HttpServletResponse response)
      throws IOException, ServletException
  {
    response.setContentType("text/html");
    PrintWriter out = response.getWriter();
    out.println("<html>");
    out.println("<head><title>Servlet Database Connectivity</title></head>");
    out.println("<body>");
    // connecting to database
    Connection con = null;
    Statement stmt = null;
    ResultSet rs=null;
    try
    {

      Class.forName("oracle.jdbc.OracleDriver");
      String dbURL = "jdbc:oracle:oci:@my_database";
```

```
        Properties properties = new Properties();
        properties.put("user", "scott");
        properties.put("password", "tiger");
        properties.put("defaultRowPrefetch", "20");
        con =DriverManager.getConnection (dbURL,properties);
        stmt = con.createStatement();
        rs=stmt.executeQuery("select * from Employee");
        out.print("<table border=1>");
        out.print("<tr><td>EmployeeID</td><td>Name</td></tr>");
        while(rs.next())
        {
          //Retrieve by column name
          int id  = rs.getInt("ID");
          String name = rs.getString("Name");
          out.print("<tr><td>"+id+"</td><td>"+name);
          out.print("</td></tr>");
        }
        out.println("</table></body></html>");
      }catch (SQLException e)
      {
        throw new ServletException("Servlet Could not display records.", e);
      }
      catch (ClassNotFoundException e)
      {
        throw new ServletException("JDBC Driver not found.", e);
      }
      finally
      {
        try
        {
          if(rs != null)
          {
            rs.close();
            rs = null;
          }
          if(stmt != null)
          {
            stmt.close();
            stmt = null;
          }
          if(con != null)
          {
            con.close();
            con = null;
```

```
            }
         }
         catch (SQLException e) {}
      }//end of finally
      out.close();
   }//end of service function
} //end of class
```

Output

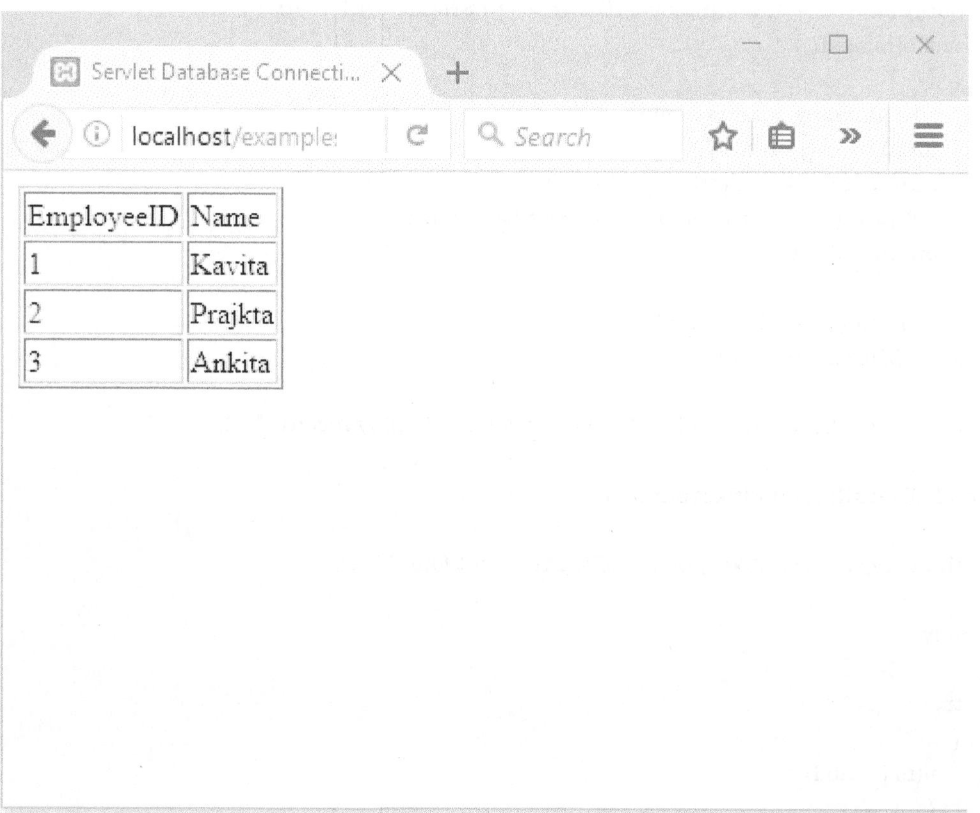

Ex. 5.10.4 Write complete query application for books database using JDBC. **AU : May-17, Marks 16**

Sol. :

```
import java.io.*;
import java.util.*;
import javax.sql.*;
import javax.servlet.*;
import javax.servlet.http.*;
import java.sql.*;
public class hms extends HttpServlet
{
public void service(HttpServletRequest request,HttpServletResponse response)
throws IOException, ServletException
```

```
{
// connecting to database
Connection con = null;
Statement stmt = null;
ResultSet rs = null;
PrintWriter out = response.getWriter();
try
{
Class.forName{"sun.jdbc.odbc.jdbcodbcDriver");
con =DriverManager.getConnection ("jdbc:odbc:books","","");
}catch(ClassNotFoundException e){e.printStackTrace();}
catch(SQLException e){e.printStackTrace();}
catch(Exception e){e.printStackTrace();}
try
{
stmt = con.createStatement();
rs = stmt.executeQuery("SELECT * FROM books_table");
// displaying records
response.setContentType("text/html");
out.println("<html>");
out.println("<head><title>Servlet Database Connectivity</title></head>");
out.println("<body>");
out.print("<center>");
out.print("<h2>Books Database</h2>");
out.print("<table border=3>");
out.print("<th>ISBN</th>");
out.print("<th>Name</th>");
out.print("<th>Author</th>");
out.print("<th>Publication</th>");
out.print("<th>Edition</th>");
while(rs.next())
{
 int tot=0;
 out.print("<tr><td>");
 out.print(rs.getString(1));
 out.print("</td><td>");
 out.print(rs.getString(2));
 out.print("</td><td>");
 out.print(rs.getString(3));
 out.print("</td><td>");
 out.print(rs.getString(4));
 out.print("</td><td>");
 out.print(rs.getString(5));
 out.print("</td></tr>");
```

```
  }
  out.print("</table>");
  out.print("</center>");
  out.println("</body></html>");
  }catch (SQLException e)  { }
  finally {
  try {
      if(rs != null) {
              rs.close();
              rs = null;
      }
      if(stmt != null) {
          stmt.close();
          stmt = null;
          }
        if(con != null) {
          con.close();
          con = null;
          }
      } catch (SQLException e) {}
  }
  out.close();
  }//end of service function
 } //end of class
```

University Question

1. *Explain in detail about Servlet Database Connectivity with an example of Student database.* **AU : Dec.-18, Marks 13**

Two Marks Questions with Answers

Q.1 What are servlets ? **AU : Dec.-17**

Ans. : Servlets are simple Java programs that run on the server. The servlets are used along with the http protocol. Hence sometimes they are also referred as http servlets. Servlets make use of standard packages such as javax.servlet and javax.servlet.http.

Q.2 What are the uses of servlets ?

Ans. : Following are the uses of servlets -

Servlets can process and store the data submitted by an HTML form.

Servlets are useful for providing the dynamic contents. For example retrieving and updating the databases.

Servlets can be used in the cookies and session tracking. Cookies are small programs which can make use of the information submitted on currently accessed web pages. Similarly session tracking are the useful programs that keeps track of all previously accessed the web pages.

Q.3 Explain the Servlet API life cycle methods in brief. AU : May-12, 13

Ans. : The **init** method is called when the servlet is loaded in the memory for the first time. Using this method the initialization parameters can also be passed to the servlet. Then using **service()** method the server can invoke the service for particular HTTP request.Finally the server unloads the servlet from the memory using **destroy()** method.

Q.4 Explain the difference between get request type and post request type. AU : May-12, 13

Ans. : In HTTP-GET request the **doGet** method is used. In HTTP-POST request the **doPost** request is used.

When user submits his request using doGet method then the URL string displays the request submitted by the user. But if the **doPost** method is used then URL string does not show the submitted contents.

Q.5 What is the use of web config file ?

Ans. : The web config file specifies the configuration for the web application. The URL for the servlets can be specified using the web config file. It is a XML file usually located in WEB-INF folder.

Q.6 Specify the need for client and server side scripting.

Ans. : The client side scripting is useful for presenting the data to the user or to submit the request to the server. Various scripting languages such as XHTML, JavaScript, DHTML are used as client side scripting languages. The applets can also be embedded in these scripts.

The server side scripting languages are used to process the request submitted by the client. The server side scripting can be done using servlets, JSP, ASP, PHP and so on.

Q.7 Explain cookies. AU : May-08, 10, 13, Dec.-12

Ans. : Cookies are some little information that can be left on your computer by the other computer when we access an internet. The information is stored in the cookies using the name value pair.

Q.8 What is JDBC ? AU : Dec.-17

Ans. : The JDBC stands for Java Database Connectivity. JDBC is nothing but an API(Application Programming Interface). It consists of various classes, interfaces, exceptions using which Java application can send SQL statements to a database. JDBC is specially used for the connectivity of Java with RDBMS packages.

Q.9 What is driver manager ?

Ans. : The driver manager is a class that connects the Java application or servlet to the JDBC driver. The driver manager also attempts to open a connection with the desired database using the method DriverManager.getConnection()

Q.10 What do you mean by result set ?

Ans. : The Result Set is a set of rows from a database, as well as meta-information about the query such as the column names, and the types and sizes of each column. The **ResultSet** interface is used to represent the database result set.

Q.11 What is the primary purpose of an HTTP get request ? **AU : May-10**

Ans. : The HTTP GET request makes use of doGet method. The user can submit his request using the doGet request. When user submits his request using doGet method the URL string is displayed along with the URL.

Q.12 How can you create JDBC statements ?

Ans. : The JDBC API classes are supported by the Java package Java.sql. Hence we must import java.sql.* using following statement -

```
import java.sql.*;
```

We have to use following statement for referring the JDBC-ODBC Bridge.

```
Class.forName("sun.jdbc.odbc.JdbcOdbcDriver") ;
```

There is a JDBC Driver Manager which connects your Java application or servlet to the JDBC driver. We can try to connect our Java program to our database with JDBC-ODBC Bridge using the **DriverManager.getConnection()** method, in which the first parameter is passed as ***jdbc:odbc:your_database_name.*** The JDBC-ODBC driver helps to translate the JDBC function calls into the ODBC function calls. The JDBC for any database can be implemented only when the ODBC driver is available. Note that JDBC-ODBC bridge is implemented in **sun.jdbc.odbc.**

The connection to this database can be done using the JDBC-ODBC driver with the help of following statement in our Java program.

```
DriverManager.getConnection("jdbc:odbc:My_database", "  ", "  ");
```

Where first parameter specifies the name of the database file, second parameter specifies the user name and the third parameter specifies the password.

Q.13 What are HTTP servlets ?

Ans. : The HTTP servlets are nothing but the servlets only. As servlets are commonly used with the HTTP(Hyper Text Transfer Protocol), they are also called as HTTP servlets.

Q.14 Name the two packages form which most of the servlet classes can be used.

Ans. : The javax.servlet and javax.servlet.http are the two packages from which the classes are used by the servlet.

Q.15 What are HttpServletRequest and HttpServletResponse ?

Ans. : The HttpServletRequest and HttpServletResponse are the two commonly used interfaces from the **javax.servlet.http** package. The HttpServletRequest enables the servlet to read data from the HTTP request and HttpServletResponse enables the servlet to write the data to the HTTP response.

Q.16 List the two commonly used exceptions used by the servlet.

Ans. : The two commonly used basic exceptions of servlet are **IOException and ServletException.**

Q.17 Write the code to return the full URL of a document. AU : Dec.-11

Ans. : The code will be

```
import java.io.*;
import javax.servlet.*;
import javax.servlet.http.*;
public class URLReturn extends HttpServlet
{
 public void doGet(HttpServletRequest req, HttpServletResponse res)
 throws ServletException, IOException
 {
  PrintWriter out= res.getWriter();
  String FullURL = req.getRequestURL().toString();
  String queryString = req.getQueryString();
  if (queryString != null)
  {
    FullURL += "?"+queryString;
  }
  out.println(FullURL);
 }
}
```

Q.18 How is session tracking is achieved by the URL rewriting ? AU : Dec.-11

Ans. : URL rewriting is a technique in which the information is embedded into the URL. When the user requests for some web page via the browser the Server responds to the browser by writing some session id. When the user requests for the another page using the same URL, then the server will come to know that the request is related to the previous page and the task will be considered to be in the same session. When browser gets closed then the session gets lost. In such a case URL will not be available. So when the user opens the browser again then server can not associate the current request with previous session and it will be treated as a new session. Thus using URL the session can be tracked.

Q.19 What is the difference between ServletContext and ServletConfig ? AU :May-11

Ans. : The **ServletContext** defines a set of methods that a servlet uses to communicate with its servlet container. The ServletContext object is contained within the **ServletConfig** object and during the initialization of servlet the web server provides it to servlet.

The ServletConfig object is created after a servlet is instantiated and its default constructor is read. It is created to pass initialization information to the servlet.

Q.20 State the use of ServletContext object. **AU : Dec.-13**

Ans. : The servletContext object can be used to communicate with the servlet container. When one ServletContext object is created then it can be accessed by all the servlets in the web container. For instance - if you want to share some data to all the servlets then you can share this data using the ServletContext object.

Q.21 What is a servlet container ? Specify its function. **AU : May-14**

Ans. : The servlet container is a part of web server. Its function is to generate the dynamic web pages on the server using the input provided by the user. Thus servlet container is an environment on the web server in which the servlets can be executed to provide information to its user dynamically.

Q.22 What are the two methods used to send a request to a server ? **AU : May-14**

Ans. : The HTTP GET and HTTP POST are the two methods used to send a request to a server.

Q.23 Write the code segment to store current server time in session using Java Servlet API **AU : May-16**

Ans. :

```
import java.io.*;
import java.util.*;
import javax.servlet.*;
import javax.servlet.http.*;
import java.util.*;
public class SessionServletDemo extends HttpServlet
{
 public void doGet(HttpServletRequest req,HttpServletResponse res)
 throws ServletException,IOException
 {
  res.setContentType("text/html");
  HttpSession session=req.getSession();
  String heading;
  Date now =new Date();
  Integer cnt=(Integer)session.getAttribute("cnt");
  if(cnt==null)
  {
   cnt=new Integer(0);
```

```
heading="Welcome You are accessing the page for the First Time.";
}
else
{
heading="Welcome once again!";
cnt=new Integer(cnt.intValue()+1);
}
session.setAttribute("cnt",cnt);
PrintWriter out=res.getWriter();
out.println("<html>");
out.println("<head>");
out.println("</head>");
out.println("<body>");
out.println("<center>");
out.println("<h1>"+heading+"</h1>");
String str=now.toString();
out.println("<br/>The current time is"+str);
out.println("<h2> The number of previous access= "+cnt+"</h2>");
out.println("</center>");
out.println("</body>");
out.println("</html>");
}
}
```

Output

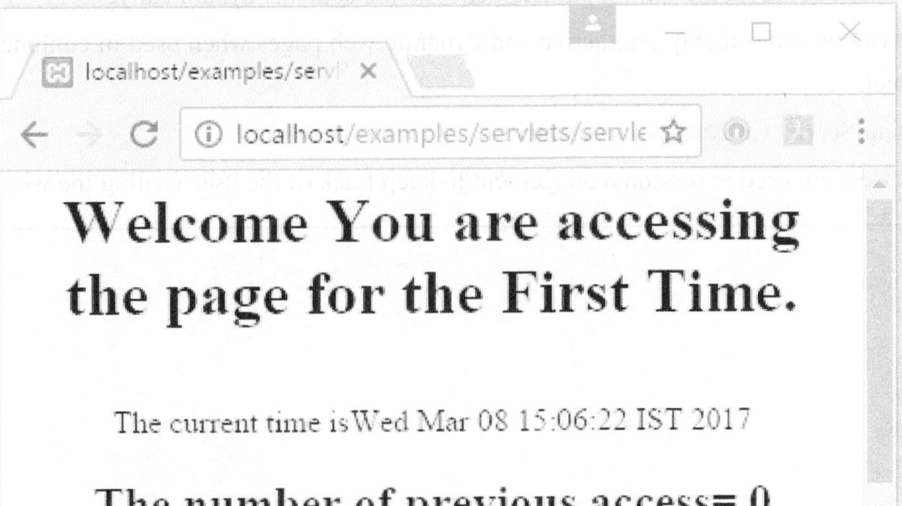

Q.24 Explain the servlet interface and its methods. **AU : Dec.-16**

Ans. : This interface defines all the life cycle methods such as **init(), destroy()** and **service().** All the servlets must implement this interface. Some of the methods provided by this interface are -

Method	Description
void init(ServletConfig s)	This method is called for initialising the servlet. The initialisation parameter is obtained from the **ServletConfig** interface.
void destroy()	This method is called when the servlet has to be unloaded.
ServletConfig getServletConfig()	This method is used to obtain the initialisation parameters.
void Service(ServletRequest req, ServletResponse res)	This method is used to implement the service that a servlet should provide. The clients request is processed and a response is given.

Q.25 Write the applications of servlets. **AU : May-19**

Ans. :

1. Servlet can accept the form input and generate the contents dynamically.
2. Servlet provides highly interactive and dynamic web pages when used in conjunction with applet.
3. Using Servlet Cookies can be created.
4. Servlets are used in session management to keep track of the user visiting the web page.

❑❑❑

Unit III

6 JSP

Syllabus

JSP : Understanding Java Server Pages-JSP Standard Tag Library (JSTL) - Creating HTML forms by embedding JSP code.

Contents

6.1 Understanding Java Server Pages

JSP stands for **Java Server Pages.**

It is an alternative way than the servlet to build the dynamic web pages. It is built on top of the Servlet.

Following are some advantages of Java Server pages -

1. JSP is useful for **server side programming.**
2. JSP can be used **along with servlets**. Hence **business logic** for any application can be developed using JSP.
3. **Dynamic contents** can be handled using JSP because JSP allows scripting and element based programming.
4. JSP allows creating and using our own **custom tag libraries**. Hence any application specific requirements can be satisfied using custom tag libraries. This helps the developer to develop any kind of application.
5. JSP is a **specification and not a product.** Hence developers can develop **variety of applications** and add up to performance and quality of software products. Due to this many companies are ready to invest in JSP technology.
6. JSP is an essential component of J2EE. Hence using JSP it is possible to develop simple as well as complex applications.

Difference between Servlet and JSP

Sr. No.	JSP	Servlet
1.	JSP is a scripting language that generates dynamic content.	Servlets are the Java programs that can be compiled to generate dynamic content.
2.	JSP runs slower than servlet.	Servlet runs faster than JSP.
3.	In Model View Controller JSP acts as view.	In Model View Controller servlet acts as controller.
4.	JSP can build custom tags.	There is no facility of creating custom tags.
5.	JSP can directly call Java beans.	Servlets have no facility of calling Java bean.
6.	It is easier to code in JSP.	The servlets are basically complex Java programs.

6.2 Document Structure of JSP

Every JSP document contains four elements -

1. **Template text :** The XML of HTML code can be directly used in JSP document. This is called the static or fixed part of the document. This markup is called template text. This part is not modified by JSP container.

2. **Action elements :** The action elements are used to create the documents dynamically. The action elements is written in the form i) Opening tag ii) Action body iii) Closing tag. For example.

<jsp:include>	This tag works as a subroutine. It includes the response from servlet or JSP when request is being processed.
<jsp:forward>	This tag helps in forwarding the current request to servlet or to JSP page.
<jsp:element>	This tag generated the XML elements dynamically.
<jsp:text>	This tag is used to handle template text. When JSP pages are written as XML documents then this tag is used.

3. **Directives :** JSP directives control the processing of entire JSP Page. It gives direction to the server regarding the processing of a page. The directive elements are enclosed within the <%@ .... %> delimiters. For example -

```
<%@page import="java.io.*" %>
<%@page language="java" %>
<%@page contentType="text/html" %>
```

4. **Scriptlets :** Scriptlets are nothing but java code enclosed within <% and %> tags. For example we can write following statement in JSP document

```
<p>
    <% out.print("JSP is eqaul to HTML and JAVA "); %> //Scriptlet
</p>
```

Example of JSP document

```
<%@ page language="java" contentType="text/html" %>
<html>
   <head>
      <title>Demo for Template Text</title>
   </head>
   <body bgcolor="gray">
      <h1>Twinkle Twinkle little stars</h1>
      <h2>How I wonder what you are!!!</h2>
      <li>like a diamond in the sky</li>
      <p>

<% out.print("JSP is eqaul to HTML and JAVA "); %>
      </p>
   </body>
</html>
```

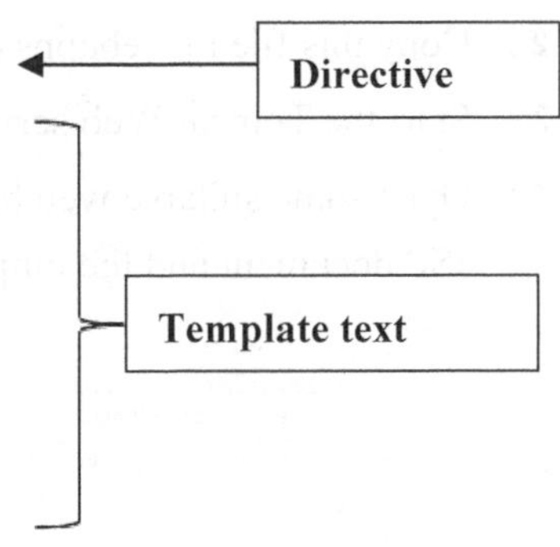

6.3 How to Write and Execute JSP Script ?

For execution of JSP pages following installations are needed.

1. **Java Development Kit :** Download and install the latest version of JDK.
2. **Tomcat WebServer :** The Tomcat is a web container provided by Apache Web server. Now a days XAMPP software package is installed for running JSP, Servlets and PHP programs.

Note that before running any JSP page it is essential to start the tomcat by double clicking the **startup.bat** file present in the tomcat directory.

Ex. 6.3.1 : Write a simple JSP page for displaying the message "This is my first JSP page!!!"

Sol. : We follow these steps to get the JSP page displayed -

Step 1 : First of all open some text editor like Notepad and type the following code.

hello.jsp

```
<%@ page language="java" contentType="text/html" %>
<%@ page import ="java.util.*" %>
<html>
<!-- This is basic JSP page -->
<title>JSP Demo </title>
<body>
<%-- Displaying the message on the browser --%>
    <% out.println("This my first JSP page!!!"); %>
   </body>
</html>
```

Step 2 : Copy this file to webapps directory of your tomcat folder.

Step 3 : Start the Tomcat Web server.

Step 4 : Open some suitable web browser like Firefox or Internet Explorer. Type the path for the JSP document and the output will be as follows -

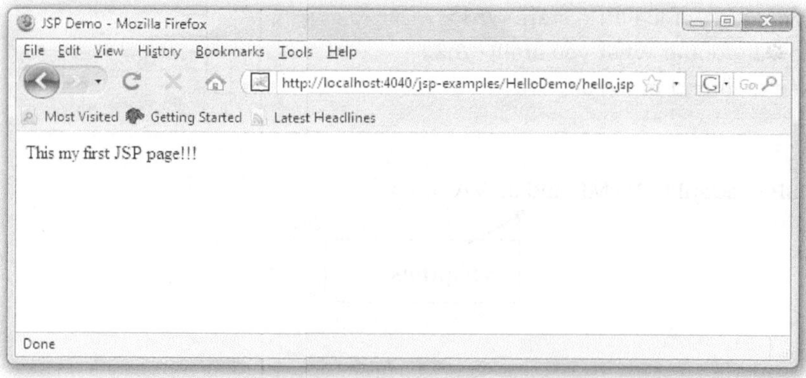

Script explanation

1. The first line is the **page directive** statement

```
<%@ page language="java" contentType="text/html" %>
```

using this line we are specifying that the language used in this script is Java and the contentType specifies the MIME type which is text/html.

2. Then on the next line we have imported the Java library package **java.util** using import statement -

```
<%@ page import ="java.util.*" %>
```

3. We can specify the JSP comments in two ways

```
<!—HTML style comment statement -->
<%-- JSP comment statement --%>
```

As JSP is commonly used along with HTML, it also supports the HTML comments.

4. For displaying the message on the web browser we have written the message using the Java statement

```
out.println("This my first JSP page!!!");
```

5. Normally any Java code must be written within <% and %>

6. Then all the corresponding tags are closed.

6.4 Declaration

- The JSP page that we write is turned into class definition. So when we declare a variable or method in JSP inside **Declaration Tag**.
- We can declare static member,instance variable and methods inside **Declaration Tag**.
- Syntax of Declaration Tag

```
<%! Declaration code %>
```

- For example -

```
<html>
    <head>
        <title>JSP Declaration Demo</title>
    </head>
    <%!
        String msg = "Hello";
    %>
    <body>
    Message is:
        <% out.println(msg); %>
    </body>
</html>
```

Output

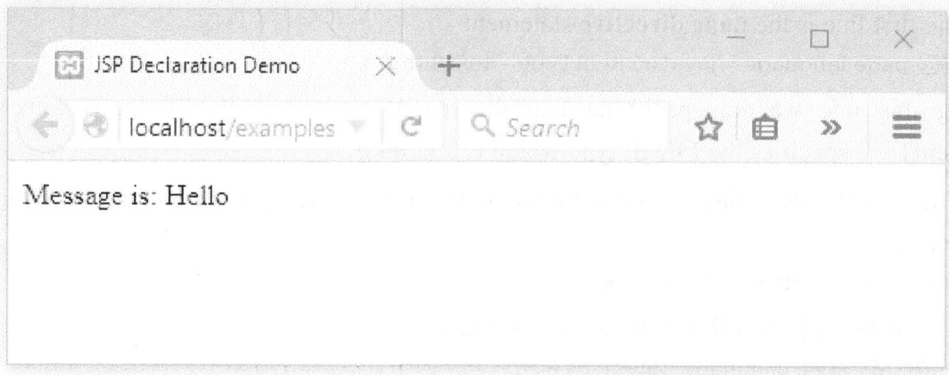

Explanation of Script :

(1) The above JSP code contains the declaration within <%!   %> tag.

(2) The variable **msg** of string type is declared and assigned with value as **"Hello"**

We can declare a function of a method in JSP just similar to variable. Following JSP example illustrates the use of function declaration and definition.

MethodDemo.jsp

```
<%@ page language="java" contentType="text/html" %>
<%!
    String msg="Hello";
%>
<%! public String MyFunction(String msg)
{
     return msg;
}
%>
<html>
<head>
    <title> Use of Method </title>
</head>
<body>
    <% out.print("Before function call: "+msg); %>
<br/>
    After function call: <%= MyFunction("Technical Publications") %>
</body>
</html>
```

Output

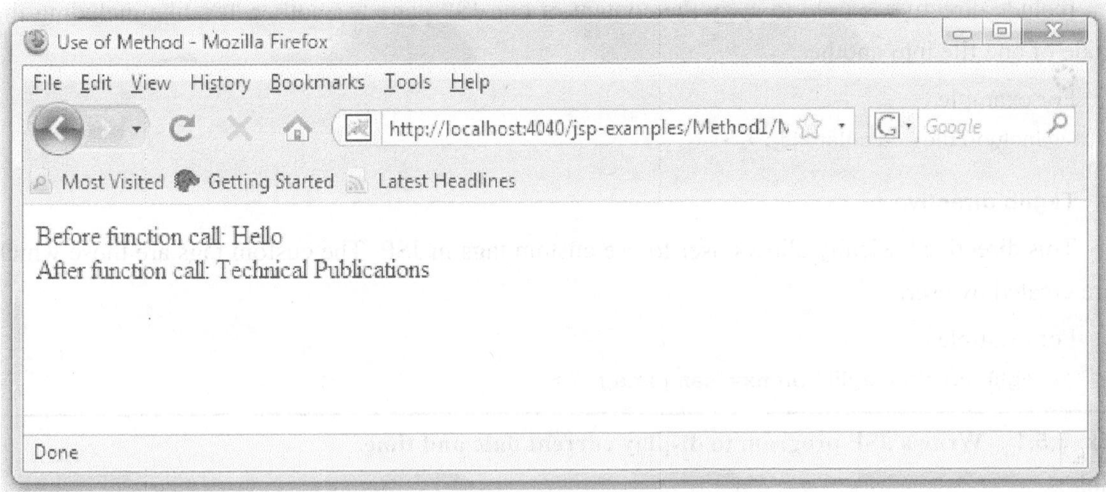

6.5 Directives

JSP directives control the processing of entire JSP Page. It gives direction to the server regarding the processing of a page.

Syntax

```
<%@ directive name [attribute name="value" attribute name="value" ........]%>
```

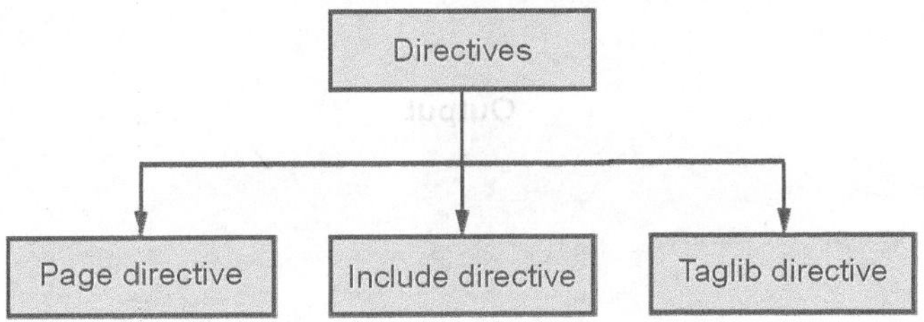

1. Page directive :

The page directive is used to provide the information about the page. Various attributes of page directive are -

i) import ii) language iii) contentType
iv) extends v) session vi) buffer
vii) autoFlush viii) isThreadSafe ix) info
x) errorPage xi) IsErrorPage

For example -

```
<%@page import="java.io.*" %>
<%@page language="java" %>
<%@page contentType="text/html" %>
```

2. Include directive :

Include directive is used to copy the content of one JSP page to another. It's like including the code of one file into another.

For example

```
<% @include file=calculate.jsp %>
```

3. Taglib directive :

This directive basically allows user to use custom tags in JSP. The custom tags are those which are created by user.

For example -

```
<%@ taglib uri="mytaglib" prefix="sampletag" %>
```

Ex. 6.5.1 : Write a JSP program to display current date and time.

Sol. :

DateDemo.jsp

```
<%@ page language="java" contentType="text/html" %>
<%@ page import ="java.util.*" %>
<html>
<body>Today's Date is:
            <%= new Date().toString() %>
</body>
</html>
```

Output

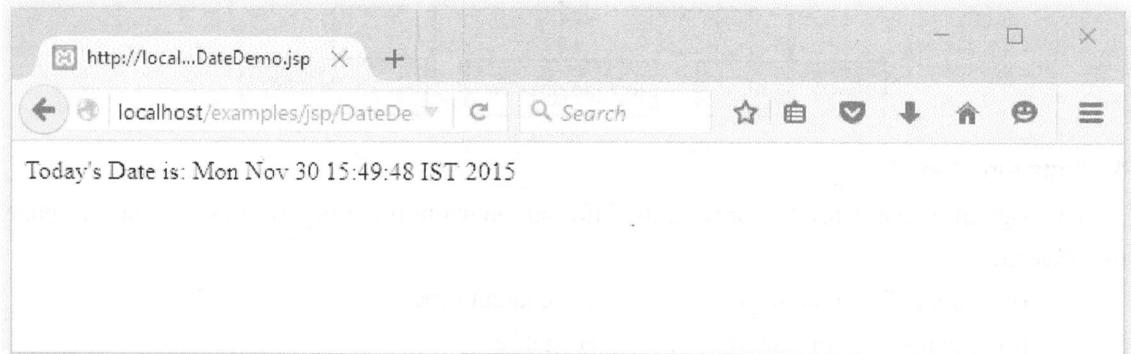

6.6 Comments in JSP

We can specify the JSP comments in two ways

```
<!—HTML style comment statement -->
<%-- JSP comment statement --%>
```

As JSP is commonly used along with HTML, it also supports the HTML comments.

6.7 Scripting Elements

There three types of scripting elements in JSP **1. Expression 2. Scriptlet 3.Declaration**

1. Expression

The expression tag is used to represent the expression in JSP page. The syntax of writing expression is -

```
<%= Java Expression %>
```

For example -

```
<html>
  <head>
    <title>JSP Expression Demo</title>
  </head>

 <body>
      Value of Expression is :
    <%= (10*20) %>
 </body>
</html>
```

Output

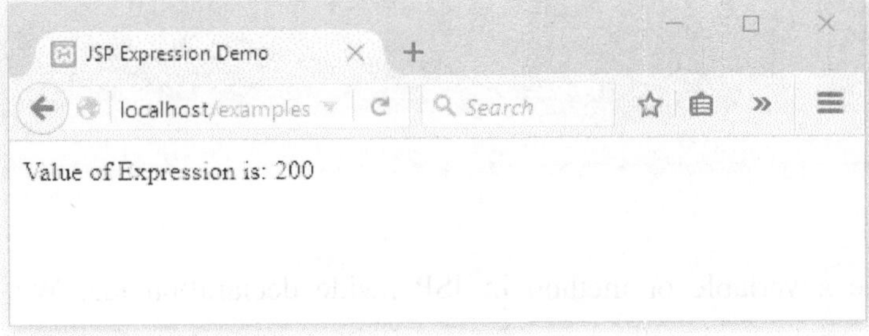

2. Scriptlet

The code that appears between the <% and %> delimiters is called *a scriptlet.* Scriptlets are nothing but java code **enclosed within** <% and %> tags.

The everything other than a JSP statement in the JSP is called template text. For example

Templatetext.jsp

```
<%@ page language="java" contentType="text/html" %>
<html>
        <head>
                <title>Demo for Tempplate Text</title>
        </head>
        <body bgcolor="gray">
                <h1>Twinkle Twinkle little stars</h1>
                <h2>How I wonder what you are!!!</h2>
```

```
                    <li>like a diamond in the sky</li>
                    <p>
                              <% out.print("JSP is eqaul to HTML and JAVA "); %>
                    </p>
          </body>
</html>
```

In the above code the boldfaced code is a template text. The output for the above code will be

Output

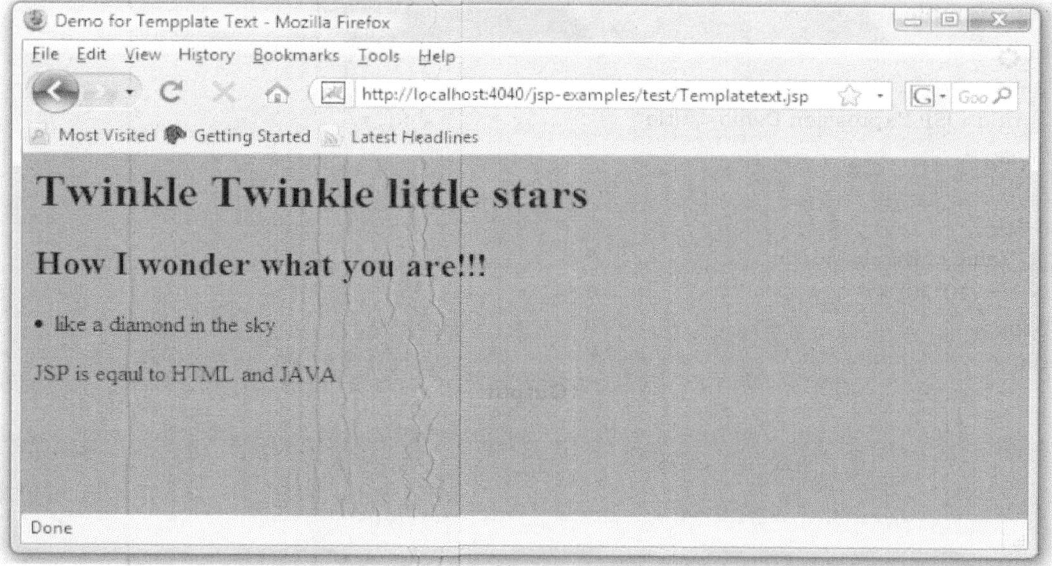

3. Declaration

We can declare a variable or method in JSP inside declaration tag. We can declare static member, instance variable and methods inside declaration tag. Syntax of declaration tag -

<%! Declaration code %>

For example -

```
<html>
   <head>
      <title>JSP Declaration Demo</title>
   </head>
   <%!
      String msg = "Hello";
   %>
   <body>
         Message is:
      <% out.println(msg); %>
   </body>
</html>
```

Output

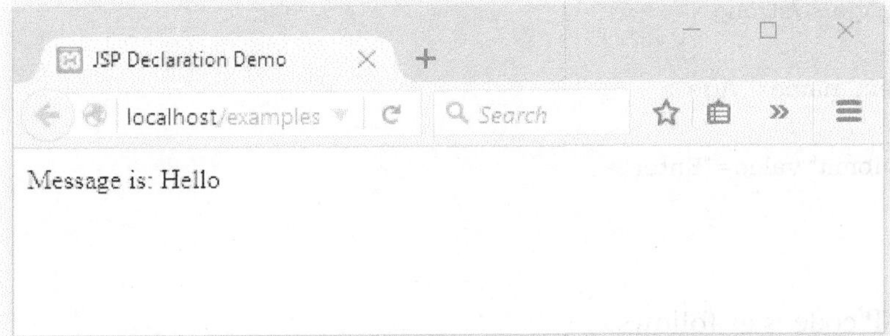

The above JSP code contains the declaration within <%! %> tag.

6.8 Creating HTML Forms by Embedding JSP Code AU : Dec.-15, May-19, Marks 19

- HTML form basically is a graphic user interface (GUI) which you present to get the input data from users. Once users submit the form from the client side, on the server side, you need to capture those data for further processing such as business logic validation, saving the data into the database and so on.
- Use of forms in JSP code enhances the interactivity of the web application. JSP code can handle the form data easily.
- The **request** object contains information about the request from the browser . It is actually used by JSP to obtain the information stored in the fields of the form.
- The **getParameter()** method of request object accepts the name of the form field and return field value. The returned value of the **getParameter()** method is always string type therefore if you have a form field that accepts the numerical value, you have to convert it.
- Following examples illustrate how to accept form data in JSP code.

Ex. 6.8.1 : Develop a simple JSP application that accepts user's age and displays a message according to the following rules :
i) Age<15 : Message : You are a kid!
ii) Age between 16 and 40 : You are young!
iii) Age above 40 : You are old!

Sol. : For developing this application we will create an HTML form for inputting the age value and then invoke the JSP page on which the appropriate messages are given based on the age.

Step 1 :

InputAge.html

```
<html>
<head>
</head>
<body>
```

```
<form method="get" action="AgeMessage.jsp">
<strong>Enter Age:</strong>
<br/>
<input type="text" name="Age">
<br/>
<input type="submit" value="Enter">
</form>
</body>
</html>
```

Step 2 : The JSP code is as follows -

AgeMessage.jsp

```
<html>
<body>
<%@ page language="java" contentType="text/html" %>
<%@page import="java.io.*" %>
<%
    String msg="";
    String age;
    int age_val;
    age=request.getParameter("Age");
    age_val=Integer.parseInt(age);
    if(age_val<15)
        msg+="You are a kid!";
    if((age_val>16)&&(age_val<40))
        msg+="You are young!";
    if(age_val>40)
        msg+="You are old!";
    out.println("<h3>"+msg+"</h3>");
%>
</body>
</html>
```

Step 3 : The output will be as follows -

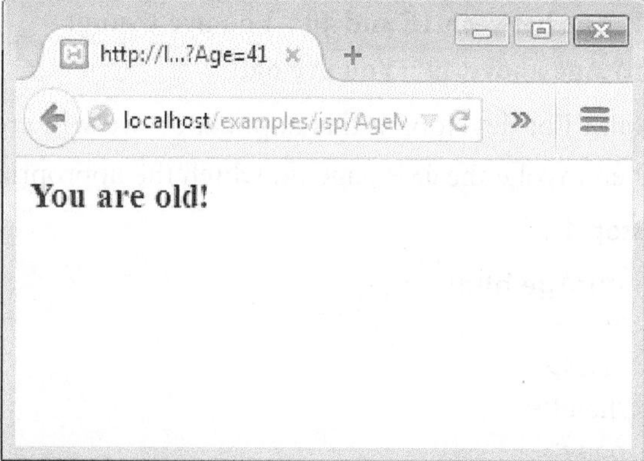

Ex.6.8.2 : Develop JSP program to display the grade of a student by accepting the marks of five subjects. **AU : May-19, Marks 19**

Sol. :

Step 1:

We will create an HTML form for inputting the marks of five subjects

```
<!DOCTYPE html>
<html>
<body>
<form action="http://localhost:8089/examples/jsp/Grade.jsp" method="post">
Rollno:<input type="text" name="RollNo"/>
<br/><br/>
First Name:<input type="text" name="FirstName"/>
<br/><br/>
Last Name:<input type="text" name="LastName"/>
<br/><br/>
Marks of Subject1:<input type="text" name="Marks1"/>
<br/><br/>
Marks of Subject2:<input type="text" name="Marks2"/>
<br/><br/>
Marks of Subject3:<input type="text" name="Marks3"/>
<br/><br/>
Marks of Subject4:<input type="text" name="Marks4"/>
<br/><br/>
Marks of Subject5:<input type="text" name="Marks5"/>
<br/><br/><br/><br/>
<input type="submit" value="Submit"/>
</form>
</body>
</html>
```

Step 2:

The JSP page will accept the marks and calculate the percentage. The code is as follows –

```
<%@ page language="java"%>
<%@ page import="java.io.*" %>
<%
    String Rollno=request.getParameter("RollNo");
    String Firstname=request.getParameter("FirstName");
    String Lastname=request.getParameter("LastName");
  String Marks1=request.getParameter("Marks1");
    int mk1=Integer.valueOf(Marks1);
  String Marks2=request.getParameter("Marks2");
    int mk2=Integer.valueOf(Marks2);
  String Marks3=request.getParameter("Marks3");
```

```
    int mk3=Integer.valueOf(Marks3);
  String Marks4=request.getParameter("Marks4");
    int mk4=Integer.valueOf(Marks4);
  String Marks5=request.getParameter("Marks5");
    int mk5=Integer.valueOf(Marks5);
    double total_marks=0,percentage;
    total_marks=mk1+mk2+mk3+mk4+mk5;
    percentage=total_marks/5;
    String grade=null;
    if(percentage>80)
    {
     grade="A";
    }
    else if(percentage>60 && percentage<=80)
    {
     grade="B";
}
    else if(percentage>40 && percentage<=60)
    {
     grade="C";
    }
    else
    {
     grade="D";
    }

%>
<html>
<head>
<title>
Display of Result
</title>
</head>
<body>
<h3>Total marks out of 500 =
<%
    out.print(total_marks);
%>
</h3>
<h3>Marks in Percentage =
<%
    out.print(percentage);
%>
</h3>
```

```
<h3>Grade =
<%
    out.print(grade);
%>
</h3>

</body>
</html>
```

Output

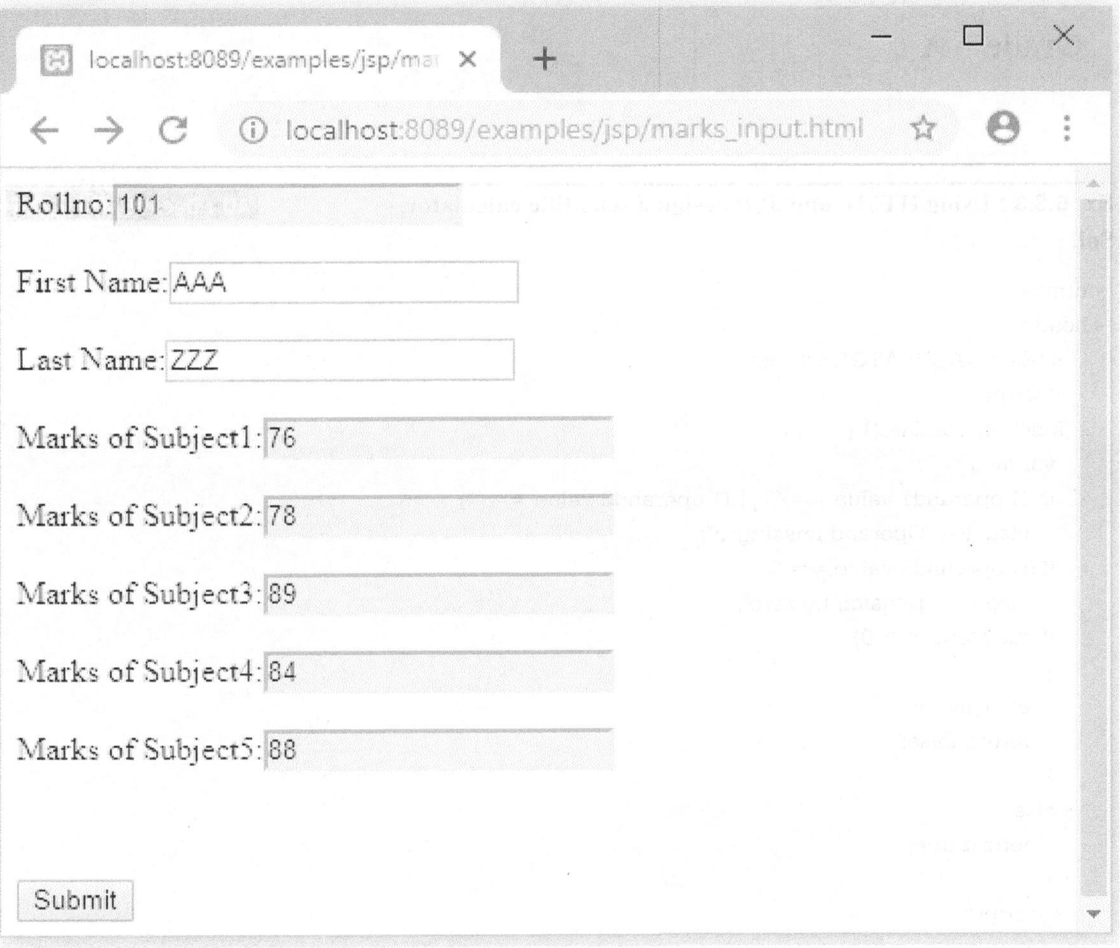

On clicking the Submit button we get,

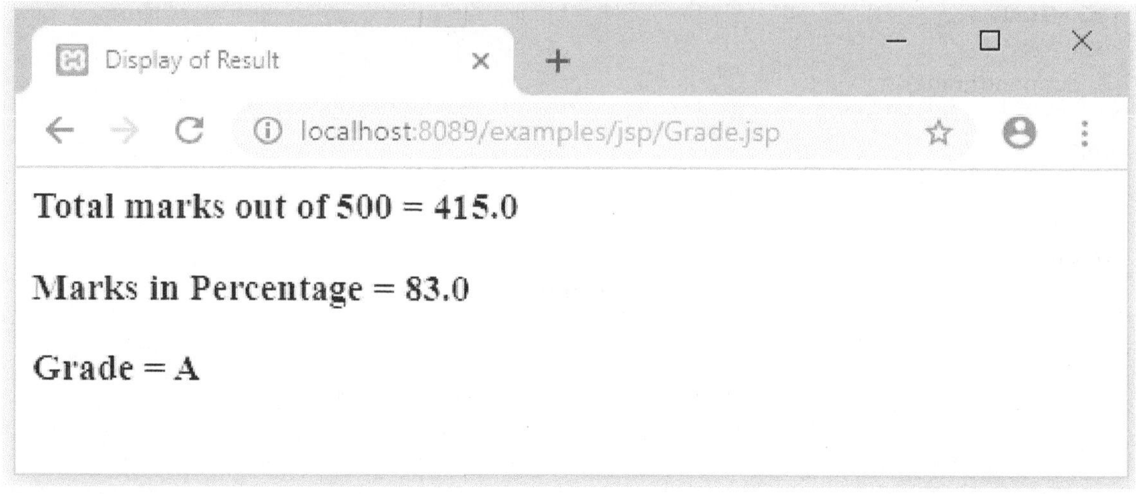

Ex. 6.8.3 : Using HTML and JSP design a scientific calculator. **AU : Dec.-15, Marks 16**

Sol. :

```
<html>
<head>
    <title>CACULATOR</title>
    <script>
    function Validate() {
     var msg = "";
     if (f1.operand1.value == "" || f1.operand2.value == "")
        msg += "Operand missing\n";
     if (f1.operand2.value == 0)
        msg += "Division by zero";
     if (msg.length > 0)
     {
        alert(msg);
        return false;
     }
     else
        return true;
    }
    </script>
</head>
<body>
    <%
    String op1 = "0",op2 = "0";
    int result = 0;
    String op = " ";
    char opchar = op.charAt(0);
    if (request.getParameter("op") != null)
```

```
{
 op = request.getParameter("op");
 opchar = op.charAt(0);
 op1 = request.getParameter("operand1");
 op2 = request.getParameter("operand2");
 switch(opchar)
 {
      case '+': result = Integer.parseInt(op1) + Integer.parseInt(op2);
            break;
      case '-': result = Integer.parseInt(op1) - Integer.parseInt(op2);
            break;
      case '*': result = Integer.parseInt(op1) * Integer.parseInt(op2);
            break;
      case '/': result = Integer.parseInt(op1) / Integer.parseInt(op2);
            break;
      case '%': result = Integer.parseInt(op1) % Integer.parseInt(op2);
            break;
 }
}
%>
<center>
<form method ="get" name ="f1" onsubmit = "return Validate()">
 <table border=7 bordercolor="black" bgcolor="gray">
   <p><br><br>
   <th> CALCULATOR </th>
   <tr align="center">
   <td>
     <input type ="text" size ="10" name ="operand1" value = <%= op1 %> />
     <input type ="text" size="10" name ="operand2" value = <%= op2 %> />
     <input type="text" name="Result" size="10" value="<%= result + "" %>">
   </td>
   </tr>
   <tr align="center">
   <td>
   <input type="hidden" name="op">
   <input type="button" value="+" onclick="ADD()">
   <input type="button" value="-" onclick="SUB()">
   <input type="button" value="*" onclick="MUL()">
   <input type="button" value="/" onclick="DIV()">
   <input type="button" value="mod" onclick="MOD()">
   <input type = submit value = "=" />
   </td></tr>
 </table>
</form>
```

```
<script language="JavaScript">
 function ADD() {
        document.f1.op.value = "+"
      }
      function SUB() {
        document.f1.op.value = "-"

      }
      function MUL() {
        document.f1.op.value = "*"
      }
 function DIV() {
        document.f1.op.value = "/"
      }
      function MOD() {
        document.f1.op.value = "%"
      }
 </script>
 </center>
</body>
</html>
```

Output

6.9 Actions and Templates

- The standard actions are those actions that can be defined by the JSP specification itself.
- Following is a list of standard actions

Action Element	Description
<jsp:useBean>	This tag is used to instantiate the object of java bean.
<jsp:setProperty>	This tag is used to set the property value for the java bean.
<jsp:getProperty>	This tag is used to get the property value from the java bean.
<jsp:include>	This tag works as a subroutine. It includes the response from servlet or JSP when request is being processed.
<jsp:param>	For adding the specific parameter to the request this tag is used. Normally this tag is used inside <jsp:include> or <jsp:forward>
<jsp:forward>	This tag helps in forwarding the current request to servlet or to JSP page.
<jsp:plugin>	This tag is used to generate HTML code and to embed the applet into it.
<jsp:attribute>	This tag sets the value of the action attribute
<jsp:element>	This tag generated the XML elements dynamically.

<jsp:text>	This tag is used to handle template text. When JSP pages are written as XML documents then this tag is used.
<jsp:body>	This tag is used to set the body element.

Let us now discuss the standard actions by creating appropriate JSP pages.

Include action

Using the **<jsp:include>** action we can include different files in current jsp pages.

For example -

Include_action.jsp

```
<html>
    <head>
        <title> Include action Demo </title>
    </head>
    <body>
        <h1>This page contains include action</h1>
        <jsp:include page="test_include.html" />
        <jsp:include page="test_jsp.jsp" />
    </body>
</html>
```

Now the static html page can be

test_include.html

```
<html>
<body>
    Hello How are you?
</body>
</html>
```

Now the JSP page for displaying dynamic content is

test_jsp.jsp

```
<html>
<body>
    <br>Time is <%= new java.util.Date().getHours()%>
    : <%= new java.util.Date().getMinutes()%>
    </body>
</html>
```

For getting the output, open the web browser and open our main JSP page **Include_action.jsp,** it is as follows -

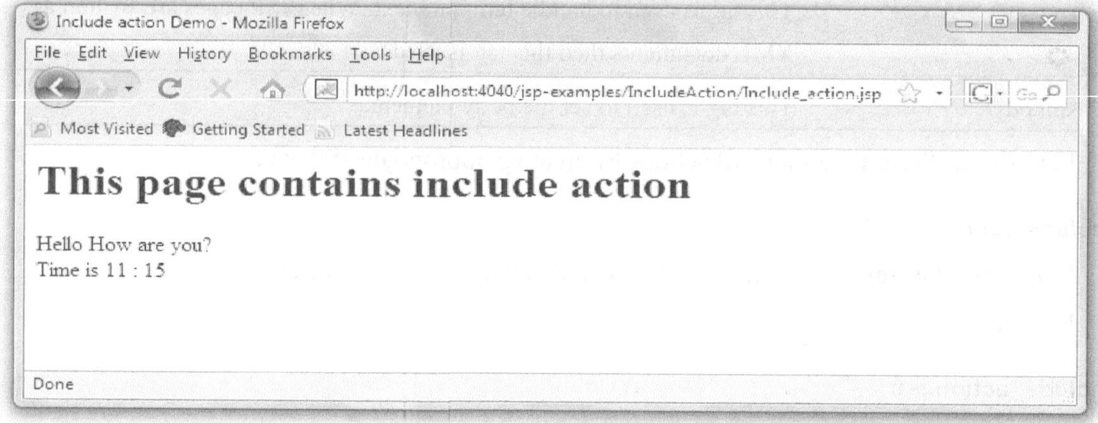

Forward action

- Using forward action we can forward the current request to corresponding JSP page or servlet.
- Here is a simple demonstration in which we have created two web pages the first one is a main JSP page named as first.jsp in which we are using JSP action forward. And forwarding the current request to an HTML page which is named as Second.html

first.jsp

```
<html>
    <head>
        <title> Forward action Demo </title>
    </head>
    <body>
        <h1>This page contains forward action</h1>
        <jsp:forward page="Second.html" />
    </body>
</html>
```

Second.html

```
<html>
<body>
    <strong>You are forwarded to Second page!!</strong>
</body>
</html>
```

For getting the output open the web page and open the main JSP page that is **first.jsp** and you will get the following output -

Output

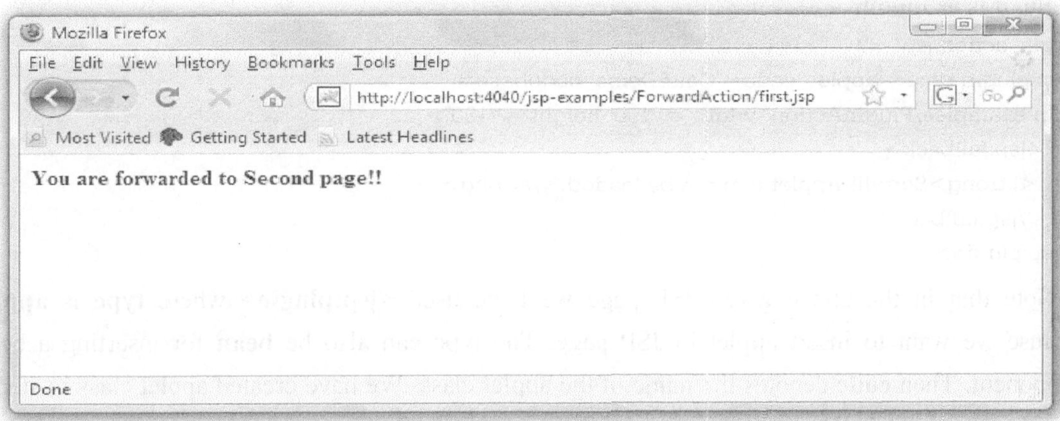

(3) Plugin Action

- The plugin action is used to embed an applet or a bean.
- In this section we will discuss how to embed an applet in the JSP page using **jsp:plugin**. We will follow these steps to use plugin action.

  Step 1: Let us write an applet program as follows -

  ColorDemo.java

```
import java.awt.*;
import java.applet.*;
public class ColorDemo extends Applet
{
 public void paint(Graphics g)
 {
  setBackground(Color.cyan);
  setForeground(Color.red);
  g.drawString("Its a colorful Applet",50,30);
  Color newColor=new Color(255,255,0);
   //creating red+green=yellow color
  g.setColor(newColor);
  g.drawString("Its a colorful Applet",50,70);
}
}
compile this code using the command
D:\> javac ColorDemo.java
```

Then corresponding class file i.e. ColorDemo.class gets generated. Now create a folder named **PluginAction** in your tomacat directory in the subfolder webapps/jsp-examples. Copy this class path in the **PluginAction** directory.

Step 2 : Now create a JSP page in **PluginAction** folder in which we are using the jsp action plugin. It is as follows -

```
Plugin_action.jsp
<jsp:plugin type="applet" code="ColorDemo" codebase=
"/jsp-examples/PluginAction" width = "190" height = "190">
    <jsp:fallback>
     <strong>Sorry!!! Applet can not be loaded.</strong>
    </jsp:fallback>
</jsp:plugin>
```

Note that in the above given JSP page we have used **<jsp:plugin>** where **type** is **applet** because we want to insert applet in JSP page. The type can also be **bean** for inserting a bean component. Then **code** denotes the name of the applet class. We have created applet class in step 1 and its name is **ColorDemo** hence we put the same name for the **code**. Then comes a **codebase** whose value is the directory name in which java class is located. Here the class file refers to the applet class file which we have created in Step 1.

Step 3 : For getting the output, open the web browser and open the jsp file Plugin_action.jsp and you can see that the desired applet is getting loaded -

Output

6.10 Use of Java Bean Classes

AU : May-13, Marks 10

- Java beans are reusable components. We can use simple Java bean in the JSP.
- Beans are used in the JSP pages as the instance of class. We must specify the scope of the bean in the JSP page. Here scope of the bean means the range time span of the bean for its existence in JSP.
- Bean is basically Java class with **getXX** and **setXX** methods.

Characteristics for JavaBean Class

(1) Java Bean class contains a default **no argument constructor**. This constructor must have the access specifier as **public.**

(2) It should be serializable and should **implement serializable interface.**

(3) It can have any number of properties which can be read or written. For these properties we write **getter and setter methods.**

JavaBean Properties

A JavaBean Property is a named attribute that can be accessed using the object.

The JavaBean properties can be accessed through two methods namely

(1) getPropertyName(): This method is called **accessor** method. It returns the property value. This method is written in some special way. For example – If the property is **rollNo** then the method name for **rollNo** is **getRollNo()**

(2) setPropertyName(): This is called **mutator** method. This method is generally used to assign the value to the properties. This method is written in some special way. For example – If the property is **rollNo** then method name will be **setRollNo()**

The read-only attribute is for **getPropertyName()** method and write-only attribute is for **setPropertyName()** method.

Example: Bean program using JSP for Employee Information.

Step 1: Create a Bean program in some package. I have created a folder(as a package) named **BeanProg**. The code for JavaBean class is written as follows –

Employee.java

```
package BeanProg;
public class Employee implements java.io.Serializable {
    private String empName=null;
    private int empNo=0;
    public Employee() { //no argument constructor
    }
    public String getEmpName() {
     return empName;
}
    public int getEmpNo() {
     return empNo;
    }
    public void setEmpName(String empName) {
     this.empName=empName;
    }
    public void setEmpNo(int empNo) {
```

```
        this.empNo=empNo;
    }
}
```

Step 2: The JSP code can be written as follows -

EmpBeanDemo.jsp

```
<html>
    <head>
     <title> JSP BEAN DEMO </title>
    </head>
    <body>
     <jsp:useBean id="empID" class="BeanProg.Employee">
        <jsp:setProperty name = "empID" property = "empName" value = "AAA"/>
           <jsp:setProperty name = "empID" property = "empNo" value = '10'/>
     </jsp:useBean>
     <p>Employee Name:
     <jsp:getProperty name = "empID" property = "empName"/>
     </p>
     <p>Employee Number:
     <jsp:getProperty name = "empID" property = "empNo"/>
     </p>
    </body>
</html>
```

Step 3: Start tomcat and open the JSP page in Web browser you will get the output as follows -

Output

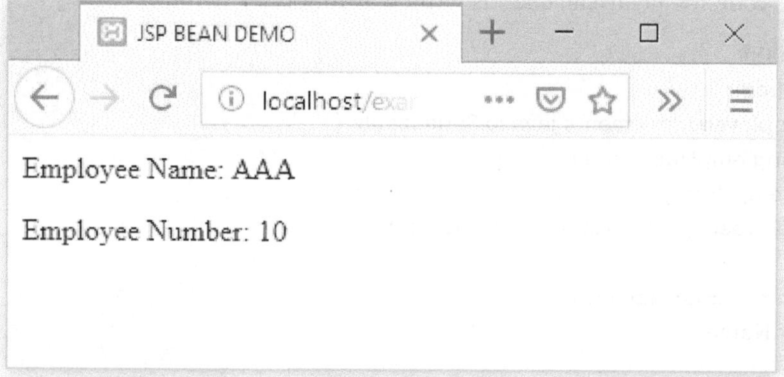

Ex. 6.10.1 Write a client server JSP program to find the simple interest and display the result in the client.

AU : May-13, Marks 10

Sol. : This program is created using following steps.

Step 1 : Create an simple HTML form for inputting the values of P, N and R. The HTML document for this is as given below

Input.html

```
<html>
<head><title>Input Form</title></head>
<body>
Enter following values:<br/>
<form method="post" action="interest.jsp">
Amount:<input type="text" name="amount" value="" size="10"/>
Period:<input type="text" name="period" value="" size="3"/>
Rate of Interest:<input type="text" name="rate" value="" size="3"/>
<input type="submit" value="Submit"/>
</form>
</body>
</html>
```

Step 2 : Create JSP page which acts as a client to receive the values for P,N and R. These values will be sent to the server Java program for calculating the simple interest. The calculated interest value is displayed by this same JSP page. The code for this is as follows -

Interest.jsp

```
<html>
<head>
    <title> Simple Interest Calculation Demo </title>
</head>
<body>
<jsp:useBean id="bean_id" class="interestcalcDemo.InterestDemo" scope="session" />
<% String s_p=request.getParameter("amount");
int p=Integer.parseInt(s_p);
    bean_id.setP(p);

String s_n=request.getParameter("period");
int n=Integer.parseInt(s_n);
bean_id.setN(n);

String s_r=request.getParameter("rate");
int r=Integer.parseInt(s_r);
    bean_id.setR(r);
%>
</form>
Amount =  <%= p%><br/>
Period =  <%= n%><br/>
Rate = <%= r%><br/>
<strong>Interest is now <%= bean_id.getI() %><br/></strong>
</body>
</html>
```

Calling server Java program for computing the simple interest.

Collecting values from **input.html** created in **Step 1** and sending them to sever program using method **set**

Obtaining interest value from server

Step 3 : Following is a Java bean program which acts as a Server. It calculated the simple interest using the formula (p*n*r)/100. This value is then returned to the client JSP program created in Step 2. The code for server java program is as follows -

InterestDemo.java

```
package interestcalcDemo;
public class InterestDemo
{
 public int p,n,r;
 public InterestDemo()
 {
     p=0;n=0;r=0;
 }
 public int getI()
 {
    int i=(p*n*r)/100;
    return i;
 }
public void setP(int p)
 {
    this.p=p;
 }
 public int getP()
 {
    return p;
 }
 public void setN(int n)
 {
   this.n=n;
 }
 public int getN()
 {
    return n;
 }
public void setR(int r)
 {
    this.r=r;
 }
 public int getR()
 {
    return r;
 }
}
```

Output

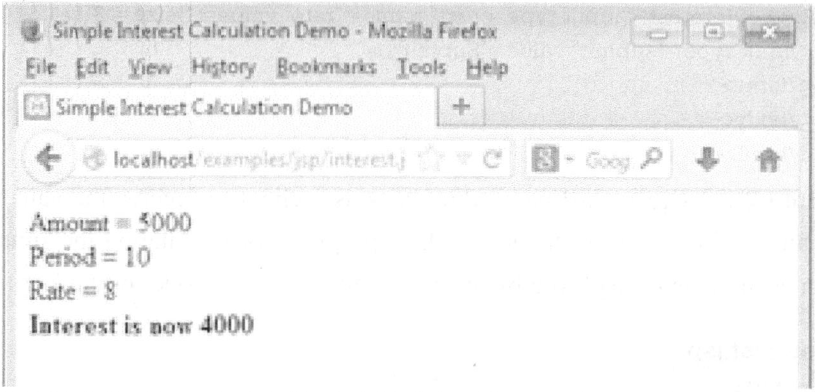

Simple Interest Calculation Demo - Mozilla Firefox
File Edit View History Bookmarks Tools Help
Simple Interest Calculation Demo
localhost/examples/jsp/interest.j

Amount = 5000
Period = 10
Rate = 8
Interest is now 4000

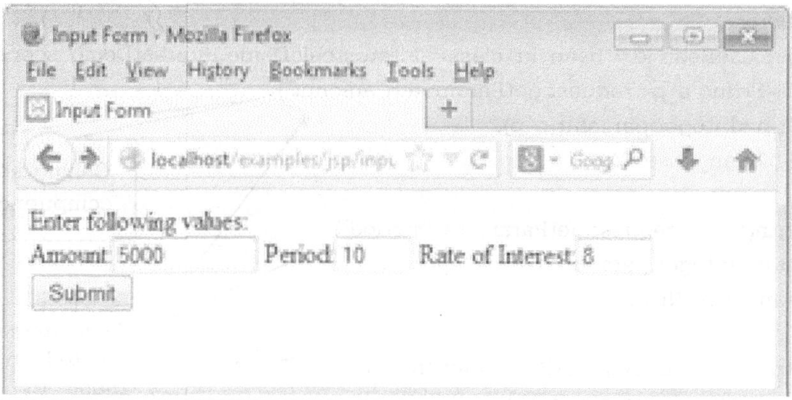

Input Form - Mozilla Firefox
File Edit View History Bookmarks Tools Help
Input Form
localhost/examples/jsp/inpu

Enter following values:
Amount: 5000 Period: 10 Rate of Interest: 8
Submit

6.11 JSP Standard Tag Libraries (JSTL)

- In JSP the tag library is specified by JSTL.
- JSTL stands for **JSP** **S**tandard **T**ag **L**ibrary.
- **J2EE** is typically used for server side programming using Java and JSTL is a component of J2EE web application development platform.
- The JSTL makes use of JSP along with a tag library.
- This tag library is useful for performing some common tasks such as condition execution, loop execution, data procession and so on.
- JSTL allows the programmer to embed the logic in JSP page without using JAVA code.
- The tag library makes use of some standard set of tags. We will discuss the use of core tag in JSP.

6.11.1 Types of Tags

- There are five types of tags used in JSTL. These are

Tag	Purpose	url, prefix and example
Core tag	It is used for performing basic input-output, looping operations, evaluating expressions and so on.	• The url for the core tag is http ://java.sun.com/jsp/jstl/core. • The prefix of core tag is c. **Example :** <%@ taglib prefix="c" uri="http //java.sun.com/jsp/jstl/core" %>
Function tag	This tag is used to support string manipulation and string length functions.	• The url for the functions tags is http ://java.sun.com/jsp/jstl/functions • The prefix is fn. **Example :** <%@ taglib prefix="fn" uri="http ://java.sun.com/jsp/jstl/functions" %>
XML tag	The xml tag is used for flow control and transformations.	• The url for the xml tags is http ://java.sun.com/jsp/jstl/xml • The prefix is x. **Example :** <%@ taglib prefix="x" uri="http ://java.sun.com/jsp/jstl/xml" %>
SQL tag	For supporting sql statements this tag is used.	• The url for the sql tags is http ://java.sun.com/jsp/jstl/sql • The prefix is sql. **Example :** <%@ taglib prefix="sql" uri="http ://java.sun.com/jsp/jstl/sql" %>

Formatting tag	For message formatting, date formatting this tag is useful	• The url for the xml tags is http ://java.sun.com/jsp/jstl/fmt • The prefix is fmt. **Example :** <%@ taglib prefix="fmt" uri="http ://java.sun.com/jsp/jstl/fmt" %>

6.11.2 Core Tags

- The core tag is used nearly in all the web applications.
- This tag is useful for performing basic input and output, for looping operation or for evaluating expressions. Various tags used in core library are -

  1. <c:out> 2. <c:set> 3. <c:if> 4.<c:choose> 5.<c:when>
  6. <c:otherwise> 7. <c:forEach> 8. <c:forTokens> 9. <c:url> 10.<c:redirect>
  11.<c:param> 12.<c:import>

  Let us understand the use of core tag with the help of programming examples.

Use of <c:out>

First.jsp

```
<%@ page contentType="text/html" %>
<%@ taglib prefix="c" uri="http://java.sun.com/jsp/jstl/core" %>
<html>
<body>
<form method=post action="first.jsp">
Name <input type=text name="text1" value=""><br><br>
<input type=submit value="Enter">
</form>
Name:<c:out value="${param.text1}" /><br>
</body>
</html>
```

Output

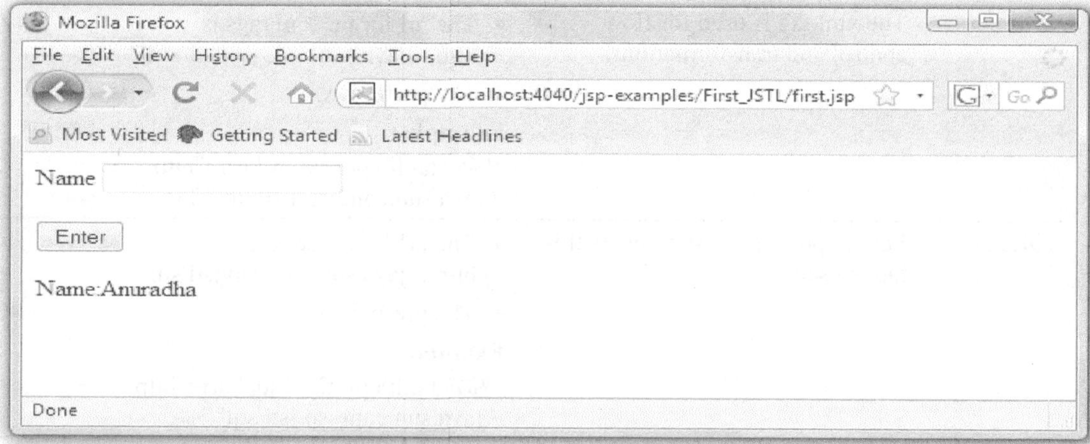

Script explanation

In above written JSP code

(1) we have used **taglib** directive with prefix **c**.

(2) Note that we must specify the **uri="http://java.sun.com/jsp/jstl/core"** for every core tag and prefix **"c"** .

(3) We have used **<c:out>** for outputting the value written in the text box of the form.

Use of <cset>

Second.jsp

```
<%@ page contentType="text/html" %>
<%@ taglib prefix="c" uri="http://java.sun.com/jsp/jstl/core" %>
<html>
<body bgcolor=pink>
<form   method=post   action=Second.jsp>
   <select name="combo1">
   <option value="">Select
    <option value="Apple">Apple
    <option value="Mango">Mango
    <option value="Banana">Banana
    <option value="Guava">Guava
</select>
<input type=submit value="Enter">
</form>
<c:set var="fruit"   value="${param.combo1}"   />
I like <strong> <c:out value="${fruit}" /> </strong> very much!!!
<br>
</body>
</html>
```

Output

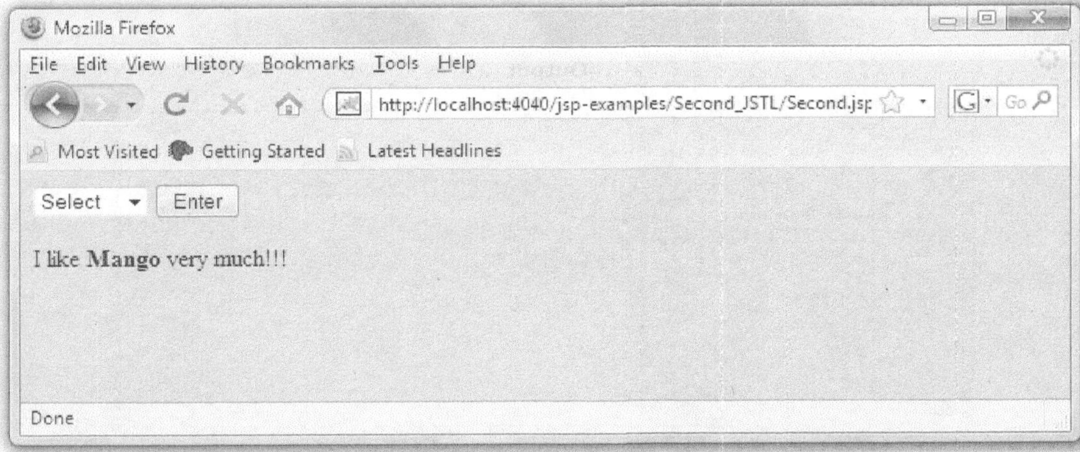

Use of <c:if>

Third.jsp

```
<%@ page contentType="text/html" %>
<%@ taglib prefix="c" uri="http://java.sun.com/jsp/jstl/core" %>
<html>
<body bgcolor=pink>
<form method=post action=Third.jsp>
   <select name="combo1">
   <option value="">Select
     <option value="Apple">Apple
     <option value="Mango">Mango
     <option value="Banana">Banana
     <option value="Guava">Guava
  </select>
<input   type=submit value="Enter">
</form>
<c:set var="fruit"   value="${param.combo1}"   />
<c:if test="${fruit == 'Apple'}" >
I like <strong><c:out value="${fruit}" /></strong> very much!!!
</c:if>
<c:if test="${fruit == 'Mango'}" >
I like <strong><c:out value="${fruit}" /></strong> very much!!!
</c:if>

<c:if test="${fruit == 'Banana'}" >
I like <strong><c:out value="${fruit}" /></strong> very much!!!
</c:if>

<c:if test="${fruit == 'Guava'}" >
I like <strong><c:out value="${fruit}" /></strong> very much!!!
</c:if>

<br>
</body>
</html>
```

Output

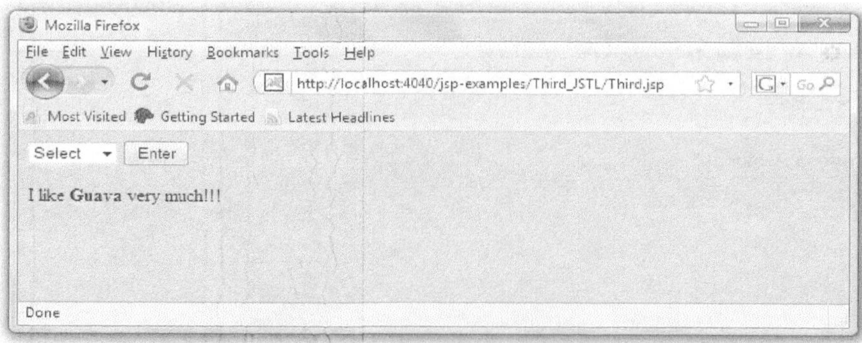

Use of <c:choose>,<c:when> <c:otherwise>

We can have select any item using **<c:choose>** tag. The <c:choose> contains the <c:when test> and <c:otherwise> tags for specifying the selection criteria. In the following example we will see how to make use of these tags. For a <c:when> tag the **test** is a standard variable being used.

Forth.jsp

```
<%@ page contentType="text/html" %>
<%@ taglib prefix="c" uri="http://java.sun.com/jsp/jstl/core" %>
<html>
<body bgcolor=pink>
<form method=post action=Forth.jsp>
   <select name="combo1">
   <option value="">Select
     <option value="Apple">Apple
     <option value="Mango">Mango
     <option value="Banana">Banana
     <option value="Guava">Guava
  </select>
<input  type=submit value="Enter">
</form>
<c:set var="fruit"  value="${param.combo1}"  />
<c:choose>
     <c:when test="${fruit == 'Apple'}" >
     I like <strong><c:out value="${fruit}" /></strong> very much!!!
     </c:when>

     <c:when test="${fruit == 'Mango'}" >
     I like <strong><c:out value="${fruit}" /></strong> very much!!!
     </c:when>
     <c:when test="${fruit == 'Banana'}" >
     I like <strong><c:out value="${fruit}" /></strong> very much!!!
     </c:when>

     <c:when test="${fruit == 'Guava'}" >
     I like <strong><c:out value="${fruit}" /></strong> very much!!!
     </c:when>
     <c:otherwise>
      Select any fruit of your choice
     </c:otherwise>
     </c:choose>
     <br>
     </body>
</html>
```

Output

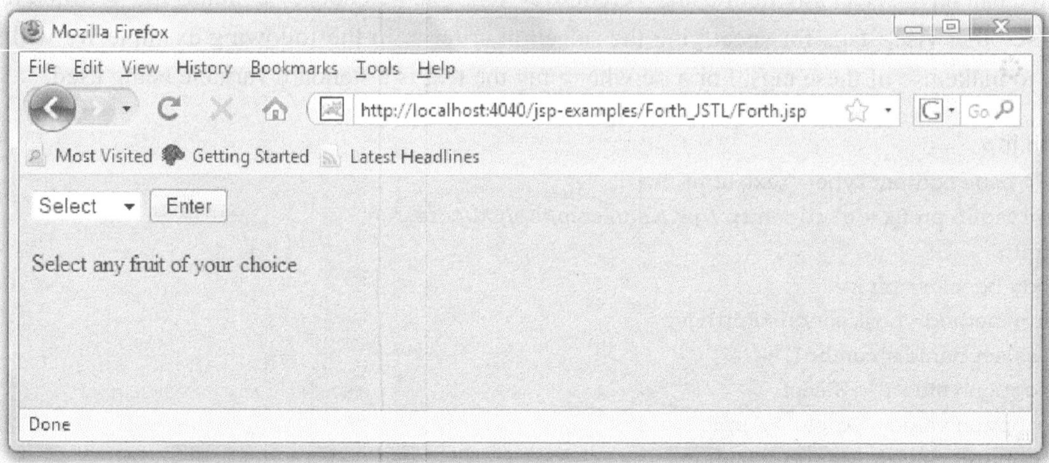

Use of <c:forEach>

This tag is specially used to denote the looping condition. Following code shows its demonstration.

Fifth.jsp

```
<%@ page contentType="text/html" %>
<%@ taglib prefix="c" uri="http://java.sun.com/jsp/jstl/core" %>
<html>
<body>
<% pageContext.setAttribute("Fruits",new String[] {"Apple","Mango","Banana","Guava"} );%>
<b>The various fruits are...</b>
<c:forEach   var="i" items="${Fruits}" varStatus="n">
<br/>
  <c:out value="${n.index}"  />
  <c:out value="${n.current}" />
</c:forEach>
</body>
</html>
```

In above code we have used <c:forEach> tag in which **items** denote the current String, var is a symbolic name for array varStatus is the symbolic name for current status. Using **index** we can display the index of each item in an array. By default array starts from index 0 and **current** is used to display the current element.

The output will be

Output

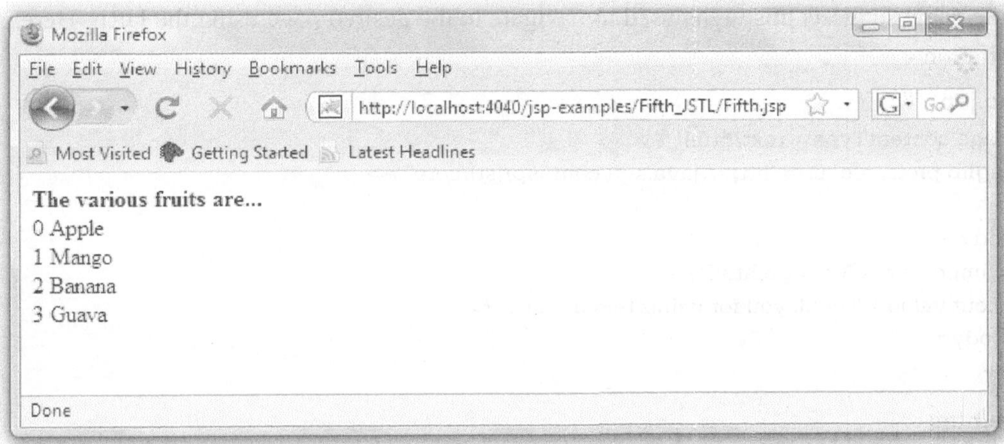

Let us see one more program which makes use of the tag **<c:forEach>**

for_loop.jsp

```
<%@ page contentType="text/html" %>
<%@ taglib prefix="c" uri="http://java.sun.com/jsp/jstl/core" %>
<html>
    <body>
     <b>The natural numbers are...</b>
     <c:forEach   var="i" begin="1" end="10">
       <br/>
       <c:out value="${i}" />
     </c:forEach>
    </body>
</html>
```

Output

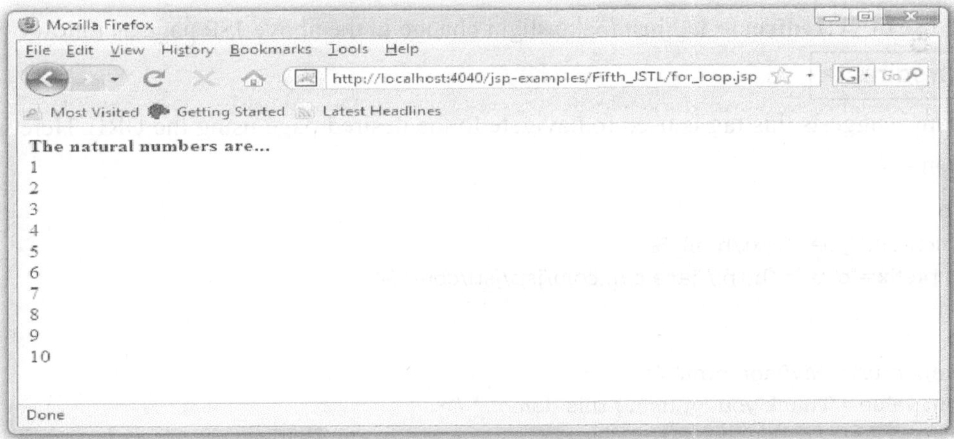

Use of <c:url>

As the name suggests this tag is used to navigate to the desired page using the URL. Here is its demonstration -

urldemo.jsp

```
<%@ page contentType="text/html" %>
<%@ taglib prefix="c" uri="http://java.sun.com/jsp/jstl/core" %>
<html>
    <body>
     <c:import url="MyPage.html" />
     <c:out value="Thank you for using this demo..." />
    </body>
</html>
```

MyPage.html

```
<html>
<body>
<h1>The visitors of this site are always wonderful persons!!</h1>
</body>
</html>
```

Output

To make use of **<c:redirect>** tag just make slight change in the above JSP page as follows -

Use of <c:redirect>

As the name suggests this tag is used to navigate to the desired page using the URL. Here is its demonstration -

urldemo.jsp

```
<%@ page contentType="text/html" %>
<%@ taglib prefix="c" uri="http://java.sun.com/jsp/jstl/core" %>
<html>
    <body>
        <c:import url="MyPage.html" />
        <c:out value="Thank you for using this demo..." />
    </body>
</html>
```

MyPage.html

```
<html>
<body>
<h1>The visitors of this site are always wonderful persons!!</h1>
</body>
</html>
```

Output

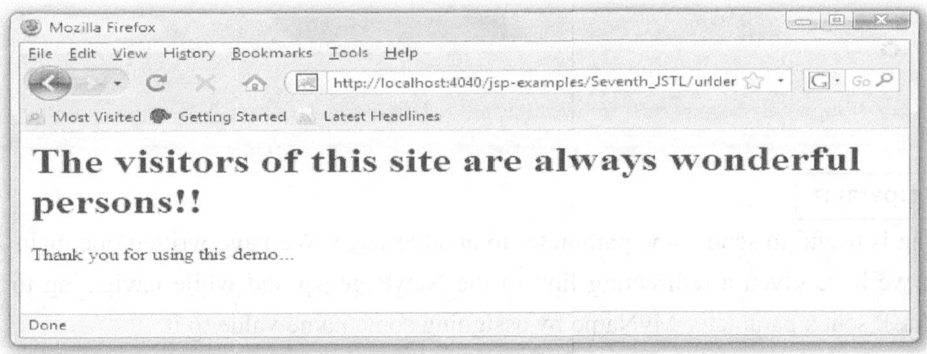

To make use of **<c:redirect>** tag just make slight change in the above JSP page as follows -

urldemo.jsp

```
<%@ page contentType="text/html" %>
<%@ taglib prefix="c" uri="http://java.sun.com/jsp/jstl/core" %>
<html>
    <body>
     <c:redirect url="http://localhost:4040/jsp-examples/Seventh_JSTL/MyPage.html" />
     <c:out value="Thank you for using this demo..." />
    </body>
</html>
```

MyPage.html

```
<html>
    <body>
        <h1>The visitors of this site are always wonderful persons!!</h1>
    </body>
</html>
```

The **Output** itself is self explanatory. Note that the string specified using **<c:out>** tag i.e. "Thank you for using this demo…" will not be displayed at all. That means using <c:redirect> we get navigated to designated page from the source web page and contents of source web page will not be displayed. Here is your output

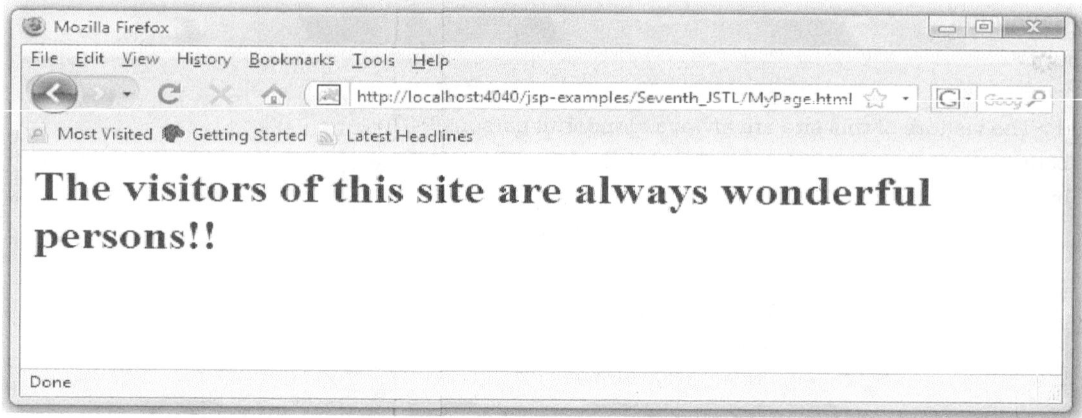

Use of <c:param>

This tag is useful to send some parameter to another page. We have written one main JSP page on which we have given a redirecting link to the NewPage.jsp and while navigating to this web page we have sent a parameter MyName by assigning some name value to it.

ParamDemo.jsp

```
<%@ page contentType="text/html" %>
<%@ taglib prefix="c" uri="http://java.sun.com/jsp/jstl/core" %>
<c:redirect url="http://localhost:4040/jsp-examples/Eighth_JSTL/NewPage.jsp" >
<c:param name="MyName" value="Parth" />
</c:redirect>
```

NewPage.jsp

```
<%@ taglib prefix="c" uri="http://java.sun.com/jsp/jstl/core" %>
<html>
    <body>
     <strong> Just look at the address bar of your Web browser </strong>
     <c:out value="${param.MyName}" />
    </body>
</html>
```

Output

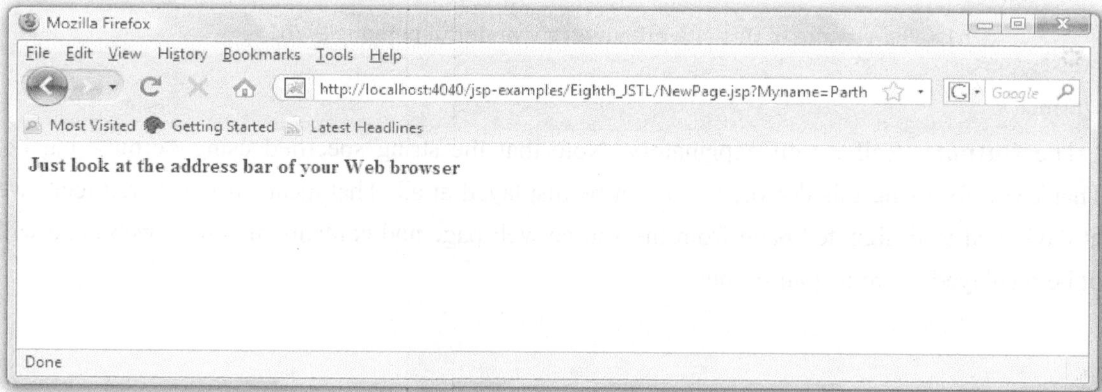

Use of <c:import>

This tag is very much similar to <c:url>

ImportDemo.jsp

```
<%@ page contentType="text/html" %>
<%@ taglib prefix="c" uri="http://java.sun.com/jsp/jstl/core" %>
<html>
<body>
    <c:import url="http://localhost:4040/jsp-examples/Nineth_JSTL/MyPage.html" />
    <c:out value="Thank you for using this demo..." />
</body>
</html>
```

MyPage.html

```
<html>
    <body>
     <h1>The visitors of this site are always wonderful persons!!</h1>
    </body>
</html>
```

Output

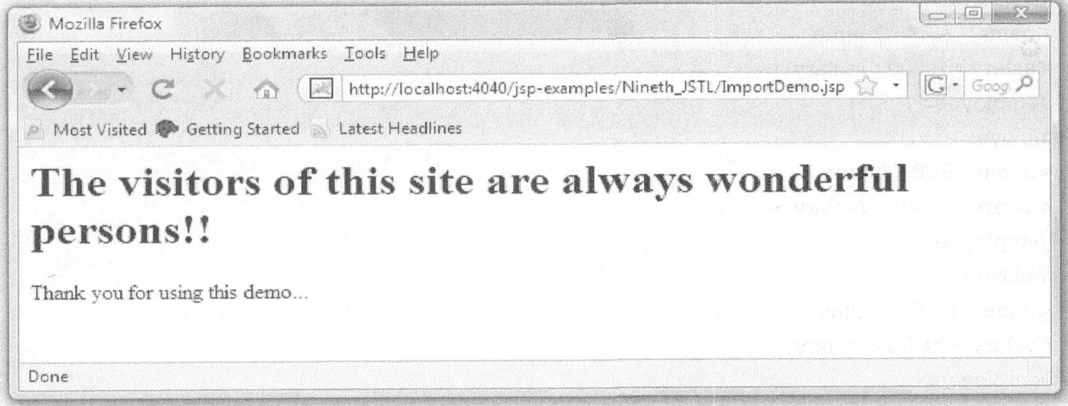

6.11.3 The XML tag

- The XML tag library is used to create and manipulate XML data in JSP page. It is also used to transform the xml data used in JSP page.
- **Syntax for JSTL XML tag is**
  <%@ taglib uri="http://java.sun.com/jsp/jstl/xml" prefix = "x" %>
- For execution of following code we need to copy following jar files in Tomcat's installation directory's lib folder -
  - XercesImpl.jar
  - Xalan.jar
  - xml-apis-1.4.01

(1) <x:out>:

The <x:out> tag is used for displaying the result of an xml Path expression and writes the result to JSP writer object. It is similar to the scriptlet tag <%= %> used in JSP.

Syntax :

```
<x:out attributes/>
```

Example

```
<%@ taglib prefix="c" uri="http://java.sun.com/jsp/jstl/core" %>
<%@ taglib prefix="x" uri="http://java.sun.com/jsp/jstl/xml" %>

<html>
<head>
 <title>XML Tags</title>
</head>
<body>
<h2>Employee Information:</h2>
<c:set var="employee">
<employees>
   <employee>
    <name>AAA</name>
    <salary>10000</salary>
   </employee>
 <employee>
    <name>BBB</name>
    <salary>20000</salary>
   </employee>
 <employee>
    <name>CCC</name>
    <salary>30000</salary>
   </employee>
</employees>
</c:set>
<x:parse xml="${employee}" var="output"/>
<b>Name of the Employee is</b>:
<x:out select="$output/employees/employee[1]/name" /><br>
<b>Salary is:</b>:
<x:out select="$output/employees/employee[2]/salary" />
</body>
</html>
```

(2) <x:parse>

It is used to parse the xml content and the result is been stored in specified variable.

Syntax :

```
<x:parse attributes> body content </x:parse>
```

Example

Step 1 : We will create an XML file for storing the employee information. It is as follows –

```
<employees>
<employee>
  <name>AAA</name>
  <salary>10000</salary>
</employee>
<employee>
  <name>BBB</name>
  <salary>20000</salary>
</employee>
<employee>
<name>CCC</name>
  <salary>30000</salary>
</employee>
</employees>
```

Step 2 : Now the JSP code to parse the above xml file is as given below –

```
<%@ taglib prefix="c" uri="http://java.sun.com/jsp/jstl/core" %>
<%@ taglib prefix="x" uri="http://java.sun.com/jsp/jstl/xml" %>

<html>
<head>
  <title>x:parse Tag</title>
</head>
<body>
<h2>Employees Detail</h2>
<c:import var="emp" url="employees.xml"/>

<x:parse xml="${emp}" var="output"/>
<p> Employee#1 </p>
<p>Name: <x:out select="$output/employees/employee[1]/name" /></p>
<p>Salary: <x:out select="$output/employees/employee[1]/salary" /></p>
<p> Employee#2 </p>
<p>Name: <x:out select="$output/employees/employee[2]/name" /></p>
<p>Salary: <x:out select="$output/employees/employee[2]/salary" /></p>
<p> Employee#3 </p>
<p>Name: <x:out select="$output/employees/employee[3]/name" /></p>
<p>Salary: <x:out select="$output/employees/employee[3]/salary" /></p>
</body>
</html>
```

Output

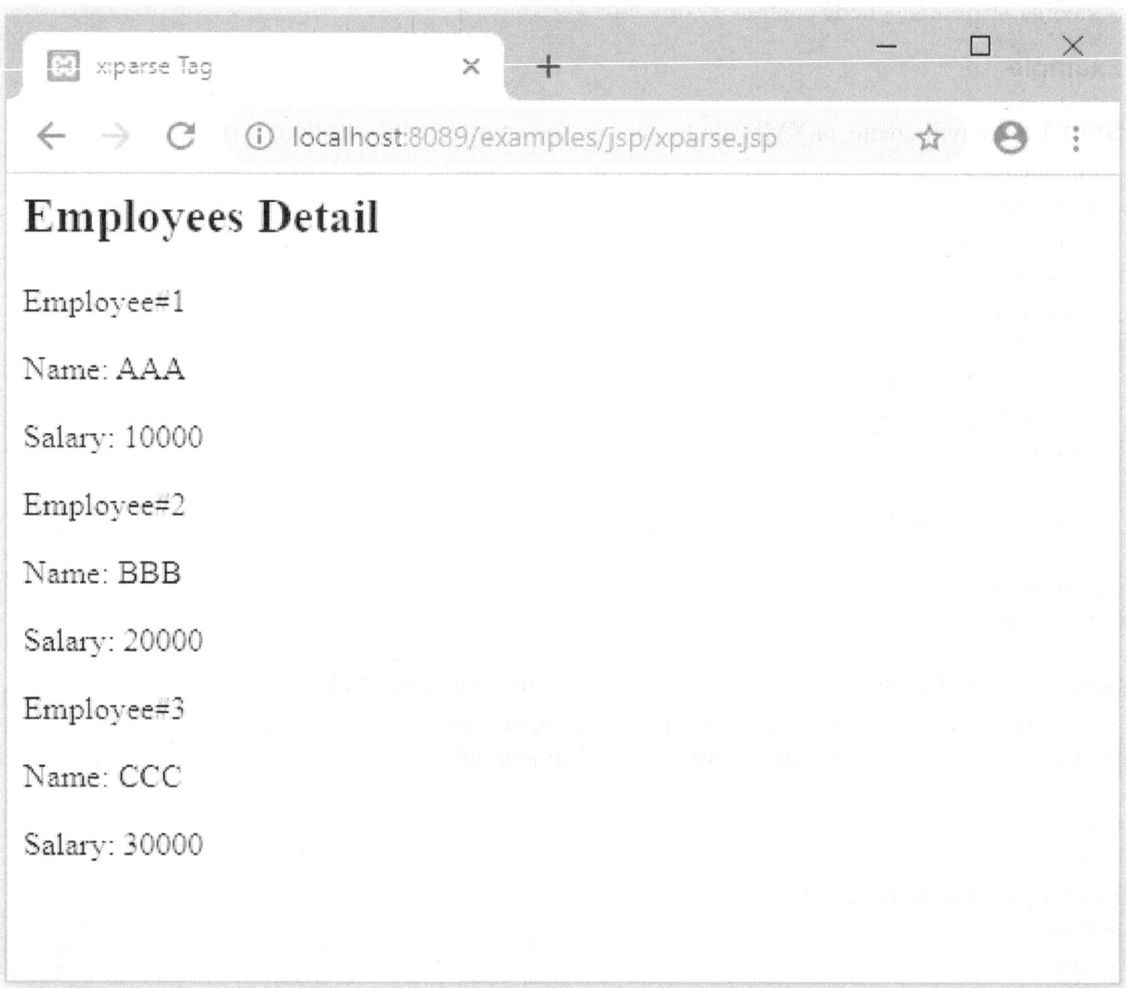

(3) <x:set>

The <x:set> tag is used to set a variable with the value of an XPath expression.

Syntax :

```
<x:set attributes/>
```

Example

```
<%@ taglib prefix="c" uri="http://java.sun.com/jsp/jstl/core" %>
<%@ taglib prefix="x" uri="http://java.sun.com/jsp/jstl/xml" %>

<html>
<head>
 <title>XML Tags</title>
</head>
```

```
<body>
<h2>Employee Information:</h2>
<c:set var="employee">
<employees>
   <employee>
     <name>AAA</name>
     <salary>10000</salary>
   </employee>
 <employee>
     <name>BBB</name>
     <salary>20000</salary>
   </employee>
 <employee>
     <name>CCC</name>
     <salary>30000</salary>
   </employee>
</employees>
</c:set>
<x:parse xml="${employee}" var="output"/>
<x:set var="e" select = "$output/employees/employee[2]/name"/><br>
<b>Name of the Second Employee is</b>:
<x:out select = "$e" />
</body>
</html>
```

Output

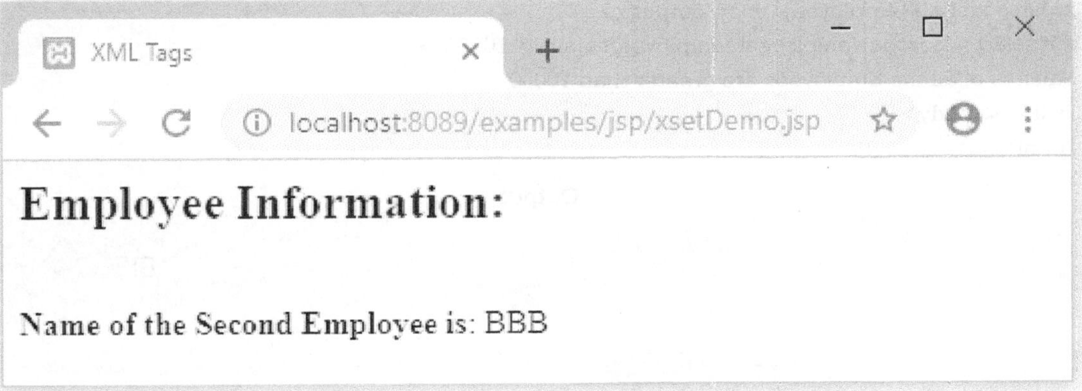

(4) <x:if>

The <x: if> tag evaluates an XPath expression and if the result is true then the body of the tag is evaluated.

Syntax :

```
<x:if attributes> body content </x:if>
```

Example

```
<%@ taglib prefix="c" uri="http://java.sun.com/jsp/jstl/core" %>
<%@ taglib prefix="x" uri="http://java.sun.com/jsp/jstl/xml" %>

<html>
<head>
 <title>XML Tags</title>
</head>
<body>
<h2>Employee Information:</h2>
<c:set var="employee">
<employees>
   <employee>
     <name>AAA</name>
     <salary>10000</salary>
   </employee>
 <employee>
     <name>BBB</name>
     <salary>20000</salary>
   </employee>
 <employee>
     <name>CCC</name>
     <salary>30000</salary>
   </employee>
</employees>
</c:set>
<x:parse xml="${employee}" var="output"/>
<x:if select="$output/employees/employee/salary > 10000">
  Salaries of all the Employees are greater than 10000
</x:if>  </body>
</html>
```

Output

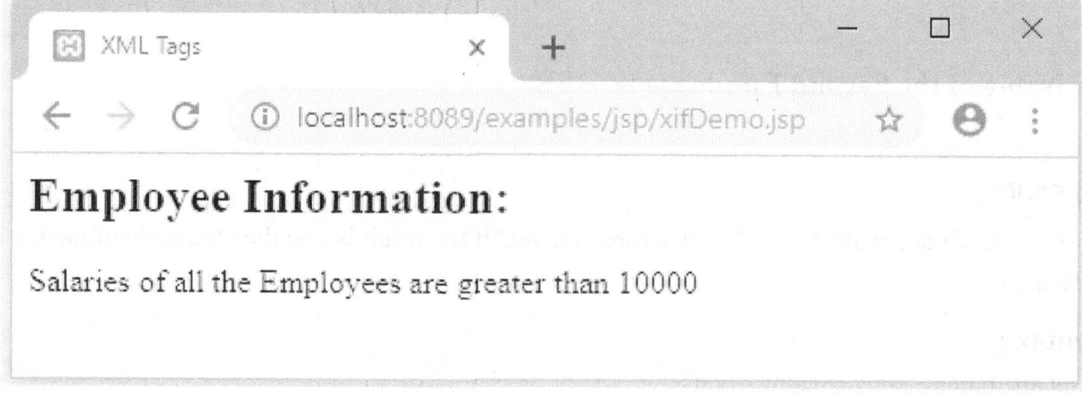

(5) <x:choose>, <x:when> and <x:otherwise>

The x:choose tag is XML tag used for checking conditional statements. The <x:when> tag is to check to see whether the expression evaluates to be true. This is the subtag of <x:choose> tag. This is the subtag of <x:choose> which is used with <x:when> tag. This tag includes its body when all of the conditions specified using <x:when> tags evaluated to false.

The <x:when> and <x:otherwise> works like if-else statement. But it must be placed inside <x:choose> tag.

Syntax :

```
<x:choose> body content </x:choose>
<x:when attribute> body content </x:when>
<x:otherwise> body content </x:otherwise>
```

Example

```
<%@ taglib prefix="c" uri="http://java.sun.com/jsp/jstl/core" %>
<%@ taglib prefix="x" uri="http://java.sun.com/jsp/jstl/xml" %>

<html>
<head>
 <title>XML Tags</title>
</head>
<body>
<h2>Employee Information:</h2>
<c:set var="employee">
<employees>
   <employee>
     <name>AAA</name>
     <salary>10000</salary>
   </employee>
 <employee>
     <name>BBB</name>
     <salary>20000</salary>
   </employee>
 <employee>
     <name>CCC</name>
     <salary>30000</salary>
   </employee>
</employees>
</c:set>
<x:parse xml="${employee}" var="output"/>

<x:choose>
  <x:when select="$output//employee/name = 'XXX'">
```

```
    The Name of the Employee is XXX
  </x:when>
  <x:when select="$output//employee/name = 'BBB'">
    The Name of the Employee is BBB
  </x:when>
  <x:otherwise>
    There is no such employee in the department!!!!
  </x:otherwise>
</x:choose>

</body>
</html>
```

Output

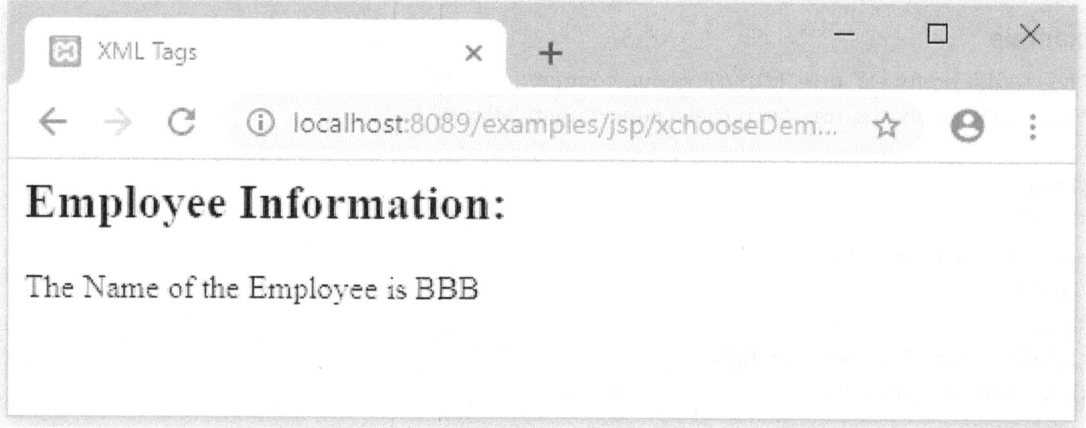

(6) <x:transform>: This tag is used to transform XML data based on XSLT script.

Example

Step 1 : Create an XSLT file as follows

```
<?xml version="1.0"?>
<xsl:stylesheet xmlns:xsl="http://www.w3.org/1999/XSL/Transform" version="1.0">
<xsl:output method="html" indent="yes"/>
<xsl:param name="bgColor"/>

<xsl:template match="/">
 <html>
 <body>
  <xsl:apply-templates/>
 </body>
 </html>
</xsl:template>
```

```
<xsl:template match="employees">
 <table border="1" width="30%" bgColor="{$bgColor}">
  <xsl:for-each select="employee">
   <tr>
    <td>
     <b><xsl:value-of select="name"/></b>
    </td>
    <td>
     <xsl:value-of select="salary"/>
    </td>
   </tr>
  </xsl:for-each>
 </table>
</xsl:template>
</xsl:stylesheet>
```

Step 2 : Create a JSP page containing the XML transform tag is as follows –

```
<%@ taglib prefix="c" uri="http://java.sun.com/jsp/jstl/core" %>
<%@ taglib prefix="x" uri="http://java.sun.com/jsp/jstl/xml" %>

<html>
<head>
 <title>XML Tags</title>
</head>
<body>
<h2>Employee Information:</h2>
<c:set var="employee">
<employees>
  <employee>
   <name>AAA</name>
   <salary>10000</salary>
  </employee>
 <employee>
   <name>BBB</name>
   <salary>20000</salary>
  </employee>
 <employee>
   <name>CCC</name>
   <salary>30000</salary>
  </employee>
</employees>
</c:set>
```

```
<c:import url="employees_info.xsl" var="i" />
<x:transform xml="${employee}" xslt="${i}"/>
</body>
</html>
```

(7) <x:param>:

This tag is subtag of <x:transform> tag which is used with transform tag to set a parameter in the XSLT stylesheet.

Syntax :

```
<x:param name="name" value="value"></x:param>
```

Example

Step 1 : Create an XSLT file as follows

```
<?xml version="1.0"?>
<xsl:stylesheet xmlns:xsl="http://www.w3.org/1999/XSL/Transform" version="1.0">
<xsl:output method="html" indent="yes"/>
<xsl:param name="bgColor"/>

<xsl:template match="/">
  <html>
  <body>
   <xsl:apply-templates/>
  </body>
  </html>
</xsl:template>

<xsl:template match="employees">
<table border="1" width="30%" bgColor="{$bgColor}">
    <xsl:for-each select="employee">
      <tr>
        <td>
          <b><xsl:value-of select="name"/></b>
        </td>
        <td>
          <xsl:value-of select="salary"/>
        </td>
      </tr>
    </xsl:for-each>
  </table>
</xsl:template>
</xsl:stylesheet>
```

Step 2 : Create a JSP page containing the XML param tag is as follows -

```
<%@ taglib prefix="c" uri="http://java.sun.com/jsp/jstl/core" %>
<%@ taglib prefix="x" uri="http://java.sun.com/jsp/jstl/xml" %>

<html>
<head>
 <title>XML Tags</title>
</head>
<body>
<h2>Employee Information:</h2>
<c:set var="employee">
<employees>
   <employee>
     <name>AAA</name>
     <salary>10000</salary>
   </employee>
 <employee>
     <name>BBB</name>
     <salary>20000</salary>
   </employee>
 <employee>
     <name>CCC</name>
     <salary>30000</salary>
   </employee>
</employees>
</c:set>

<c:import url="employees_info.xsl" var="i" />
<x:transform xml="${employee}" xslt="${i}">
     <x:param name="bgColor" value="pink"/>
</x:transform>
</body>
</html>
```

6.11.4 The SQL tag

- The JSTL sql tags provide SQL support.
- The prefix sql is used for using this tag.
- Syntax
- <%@ taglib uri="http://java.sun.com/jsp/jstl/sql" prefix="sql" %>
- Various tag attributes used are -

SQL Tags	Description
sql:setDataSource	It is used for creating a simple data source suitable only for prototyping.
sql:query	It is used for executing the SQL query defined in its SQL attribute or the body.
sql:update	It is used for executing the SQL update defined in its SQL attribute or in the tag body.
sql:param	It is used for sets the parameter in an SQL statement to the specified value.
sql:dateParam	It is used for sets the parameter in an SQL statement to a specified java.util.Date value.
sql:transaction	It is used to provide the nested database action with a common connection.

6.12 JSP and Database Connectivity

AU : Dec.-18, Marks 15

While accessing JSP database from JSP page we should have some database package installed. In this section we will consider the connectivity of JSP with the MYSQL database. We will follow following steps to get access the database using JSP page with some assumptions -

Assumptions

- TOMCAT web server is installed.
- MYSQL server is installed.
- JDK is installed.

Step 1 : Create a database named students in MYSQL using following command.

```
mysql>CREATE DATABASE students;
```

Then create a table named students_table in the students database as follows -

```
C:\Program Files\MySQL\MySQL Server 4.1\bin\mysql.exe

mysql> use students;
Database changed
mysql> CREATE TABLE students_table(roll_no INT(4) NOT NULL AUTO_INCREMENT,
    -> name VARCHAR(50) NOT NULL,
    -> address VARCHAR(50) NOT NULL,
    -> phone VARCHAR(15) NOT NULL,
    -> PRIMARY KEY(roll_no)
    -> );
Query OK, 0 rows affected (0.08 sec)

mysql> _
```

If you would like to see the structure of created table then give following command -

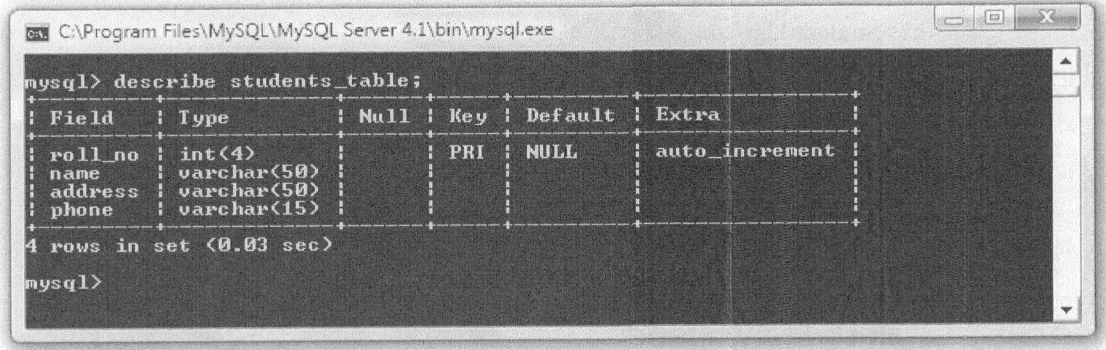

```
C:\Program Files\MySQL\MySQL Server 4.1\bin\mysql.exe

mysql> describe students_table;
+----------+-------------+------+-----+---------+----------------+
| Field    | Type        | Null | Key | Default | Extra          |
+----------+-------------+------+-----+---------+----------------+
| roll_no  | int(4)      |      | PRI | NULL    | auto_increment |
| name     | varchar(50) |      |     |         |                |
| address  | varchar(50) |      |     |         |                |
| phone    | varchar(15) |      |     |         |                |
+----------+-------------+------+-----+---------+----------------+
4 rows in set (0.03 sec)

mysql>
```

Step 2 :For establishing the connectivity between JSP and MYSQL using JDBC driver what we need is to download the MYSQL JDBC connector. Download this connector from https://dev.mysql.com/downloads/connector/j/3.1.html

Copy the jar file named **mysql-connector-java-3.1.14-bin.jar** to the C:/your_tomcat_directoy/common/lib.

Step 3 : Start tomcat server.

Step 4 : The code for JSP is as follows -

StudentForm.jsp

```
<%@ page language="java" import="java.sql.*" %>
<%@ page import="java.io.*" %>
   <%
   Connection conn=null;
   ResultSet rs=null;
   Statement stmt=null;
   Class.forName("com.mysql.jdbc.Driver").newInstance();
   conn=
   DriverManager.getConnection("jdbc:mysql://localhost:3306/students","root","system");
   out.write("Connected to mysql!!!");
   stmt=conn.createStatement();
   if(request.getParameter("action") != null)
   {
      String Studname=request.getParameter("Studname");
      String Studaddress=request.getParameter("Studaddress");
      String Studphone=request.getParameter("Studphone");
      stmt.executeUpdate("insert into students_table(name,address,phone) values('
      "+Studname+"','"+Studaddress+"','"+Studphone+"')" );
      rs=stmt.executeQuery("select * from students_table");
   %>
      <html>
      <body>
```

```
<center>
        <h2>Student List</h2>
        <table border="1" cellspacing="0" cellpadding="0">
        <tr>
            <td><b>Roll No</b></td>
            <td><b>Student Name</b></td>
            <td><b>Address</./b></td>
            <td><b>Phone</./b></td>
        </tr>
            <%
             int num=1;
             while(rs.next()){
            %>
          <tr>
            <td><%=num%></td>
            <td><%=rs.getString("name")%></td>
            <td> <%=rs.getString("address")%></td>
            <td> <%=rs.getString("phone")%></td>
          </tr>
          <%
           num++;
           }
           rs.close();
          stmt.close();
          conn.close();
         %>
    </table>
</center>
</body>
</html>
<%}else{%>
<html>
<head>
<title>Student Registartion Demo</title>
<script language="javascript">
  function validation(Form_obj)
     {
      if(Form_obj.Studname.value.length==0){
      alert("Please,fill up the remaining information!!");
      Form_obj.Studname.focus();
      return false;
     }
     if(Form_obj.Studaddress.value.length==0){
     alert("Please,fill up the remaining information!!");
     Form_obj.Studaddress.focus();
     return false;
```

```
        }
        if(Form_obj.Studphone.value.length==0){
        alert("Please,fill up the remaining information!!");
        Form_obj.Studphone.focus();
        return false;
        }
        return true;
        }
        </script>
</head>
<body>
        <center>
        <form action="StudentForm.jsp" method="post"
        name="entry" onSubmit="return validation(this)">
                <input type="hidden" value="list" name="action">
                <table border="3" cellpadding="0" cellspacing="0">
                        <tr>
                        <td>
                        <table>
                            <tr>
                               <td colspan="2" align="center">
                               <h2>Student Entry Form</h2></td>
                               </tr>
                               <tr>
                               <td colspan="2"> </td>
                               </tr>
                               <tr>
                               <td>Student Name:</td>
                               <td><input name="Studname"
                               type= "text" size="50"></td>
                               </tr>
                               <tr>
                               <td>Address:</td>
                               <td><input name="Studaddress" type="text"
                                                 size="50"></td>
                               </tr>

                               <td>Phone:</td>
                               <td><input name="Studphone"
                               type="text" size="15"></td>
                               </tr>

                               <tr>
                               <td colspan="2" align="center">
                               <input type="submit" value="Submit"></td>
                               </tr>
```

6

```
                    </table>
                            </td>
                            </tr>
                    </table>
                </form>
            </center>
        </body>
    </html>
<%}%>
```

Output

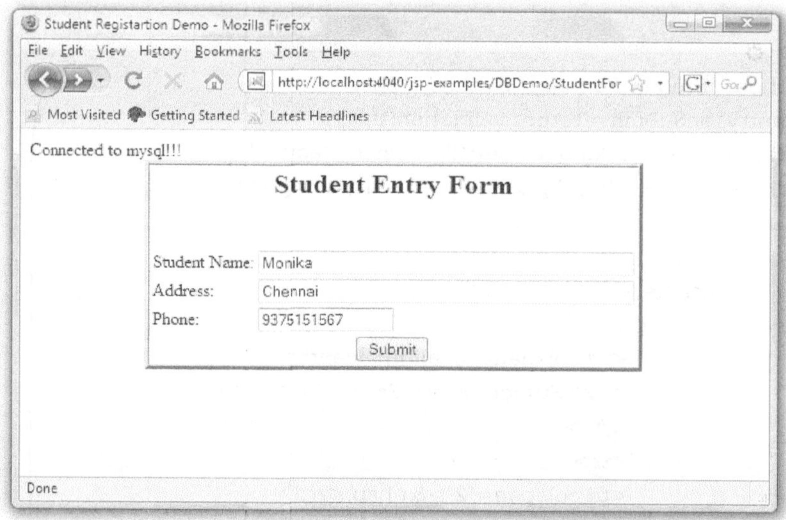

Just click the Submit button and you will get the display of all the records from the students_table.

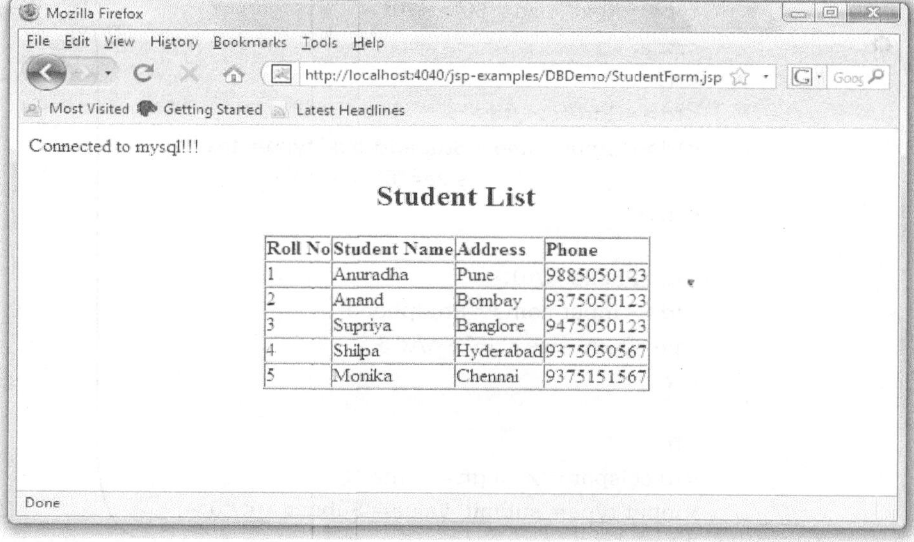

We can verify this table using backend database MYSQL as follows -

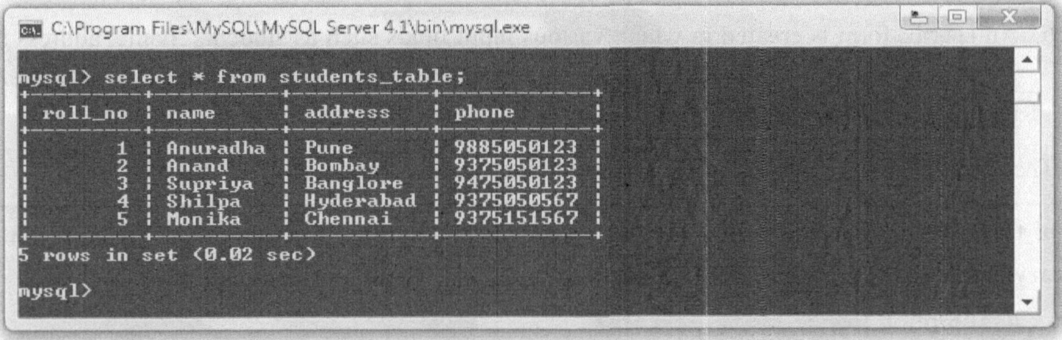

```
C:\Program Files\MySQL\MySQL Server 4.1\bin\mysql.exe

mysql> select * from students_table;
+---------+----------+-----------+------------+
| roll_no | name     | address   | phone      |
+---------+----------+-----------+------------+
|       1 | Anuradha | Pune      | 9885050123 |
|       2 | Anand    | Bombay    | 9375050123 |
|       3 | Supriya  | Banglore  | 9475050123 |
|       4 | Shilpa   | Hyderabad | 9375050567 |
|       5 | Monika   | Chennai   | 9375151567 |
+---------+----------+-----------+------------+
5 rows in set (0.02 sec)

mysql>
```

Script explanation

In above code, I have marked some steps by numbering them out. Let us understand these steps -

1. In this step required JDBC classes and interfaces such as **Connection, ResultSet, Statement** are initialised. These classes and interfaces are defined in the package **java.sql.*.** That is why we must import them hence at the beginning of the program we did this job!
2. Here the object of the JDBC driver is instantiated. We have already downloaded the MYSQL JDBC connector (*as described in Step 2*). Hence the we specify it as

```
Class.forName("com.mysql.jdbc.Driver").newInstance();
```

3. Then using **DriverManager** class we are getting connected to the MYSQL database. Note that this **DriverManager** class is defined in **java.sql.*** package. Using getConnection method we are actually getting connected to the MYSQL database.

```
DriverManager.getConnection("jdbc:mysql://localhost:3306/students","root","system");
```

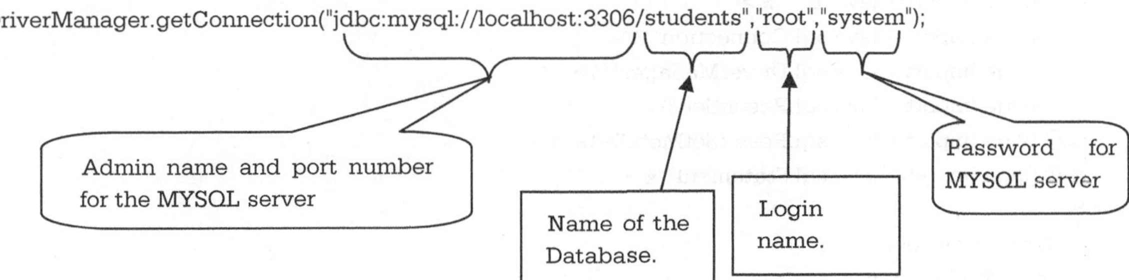

Note that the above given parameters in **getConnection** method may vary as per your database name, login name for your SQL server and the password. Then, a **createStatement** is used. It creates on object using which SQL statements can be sent to database.

4. Now we are retrieving the fields from the **form** (*this form is created on the same JSP page*) using **request.getParameter** method.
5. We then insert the values in the table using Insert query using **executeUpdate** method.

After inserting the values the table in the database can be displayed using the **Select** * query. For this purpose we have used **executeQuery** method.

6. An HTML form is created in which various input fields such as students' name, address and phone number are given. User can enter the required values in these fields. These values can be further used by **Insert** query.

The above code also has a provision of validating the user input.

Ex. 6.12.1 : Write a program that lists all books and the authors for those books from technical library database [Assume database schema].

Sol. : Assumption :

1. The database named **books** is created.
2. The table in the books database is **books_info** which is as given below -

ISBN	name	author
1	DSF	Tannebaum
11	DC	Kelvin
22	OS	Peterson
42	Unix Programming	Bach
55	Java Server Pages	Hans Bergsten
57	DAA	Coreman

input.jsp

```
<%@ page language="java" import="java.sql.*" %>
<%@ page import="java.io.*" %>
<%@ page import="java.sql.Connection" %>
<%@ page import="java.sql.DriverManager" %>
<%@ page import="java.sql.ResultSet"%>
<%@ page import="java.sql.ResultSetMetaData" %>
<%@ page import="java.sql.Statement" %>
<%
    Connection conn=null;
    ResultSet rs=null;
    Statement stmt=null;
    Class.forName("com.mysql.jdbc.Driver").newInstance();
    conn=DriverManager.getConnection("jdbc:mysql://localhost:3306/books","root","system");
    out.write("Connected to mysql!!!");
    stmt=conn.createStatement();
    rs=stmt.executeQuery("select * from books_info");
%>
```

```
<html>
<body>
<center>
<h2>Books List</h2>
<table border="1" cellspacing="0" cellpadding="0">
<tr>
 <td><b>ISBN</b></td>
 <td><b>Book Name</b></td>
 <td><b>Author</./b></td>
</tr>
<%
   while(rs.next())
   {
%>
<tr>
  <td><%=rs.getString("ISBN")%></td>
  <td><%=rs.getString("name")%></td>
  <td> <%=rs.getString("author")%></td>
</tr>
<%
}
rs.close();
stmt.close();
conn.close();
%>
</table>
</center>
</body>
</html>
```

Output

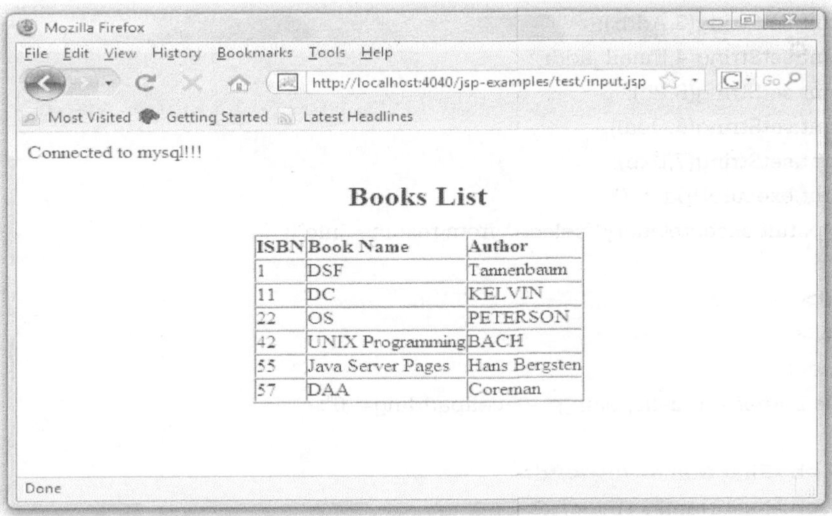

ISBN	Book Name	Author
1	DSF	Tannenbaum
11	DC	KELVIN
22	OS	PETERSON
42	UNIX Programming	BACH
55	Java Server Pages	Hans Bergsten
57	DAA	Coreman

Ex. 6.12.2 : Design HTML forms by embedding JSP code for submission of a resume to a job portal website with appropriate database connectivity.

AU : Dec.-2018, Marks 15

Sol. :

```
<%@ page language="java" import="java.sql.*" %>
<%@ page import="java.io.*" %>
<%@ page import="java.sql.*"%>
<%
    Connection conn=null;
    ResultSet rs=null;
    PreparedStatement pstmt=null;
    Class.forName("com.mysql.jdbc.Driver").newInstance();
    conn=DriverManager.getConnection("jdbc:mysql://localhost:3306/resume","root","");
    if(request.getParameter("action")!=null)
    {
        String Firstname=request.getParameter("FirstName");
        String Lastname=request.getParameter("LastName");
        String Addr=request.getParameter("Address");
        String Email_addr=request.getParameter("Email");
        String Ph=request.getParameter("Phone");
        String Qual=request.getParameter("Qual");
        String Exp=request.getParameter("Exp");
          Exp=Exp+" years";
          String myquery="insert into resume_info
          (First_Name,Last_Name,Address,
          Email,Phone,Qualification,Experience) values (?,?,?,?,?,?,?)";
          pstmt= conn.prepareStatement(myquery);
          pstmt.setString(1,Firstname);
          pstmt.setString(2,Lastname);
          pstmt.setString(3,Addr);
          pstmt.setString(4,Email_addr);
          pstmt.setString(5,Ph);
          pstmt.setString(6,Qual);
          pstmt.setString(7,Exp);
          pstmt.executeUpdate();
          rs=pstmt.executeQuery("select * from resume_info");
%>
        <html>
        <body>
        <center>
        <table border="1" cellspacing="0" cellpadding="0">
        <tr>
        <td><b>First Name</b></td>
        <td><b>Last Name</b></td>
```

```
<td><b>Address</.b></td>
<td><b>Email</.b></td>
<td><b>Phone</.b></td>
<td><b>Qualification</.b></td>
<td><b>Experience</.b></td>
</tr>
<%
while(rs.next())
{
  %>
<tr>
  <td><%=rs.getString("First_Name")%></td>
  <td><%=rs.getString("Last_Name")%></td>
  <td> <%=rs.getString("Address")%></td>
  <td> <%=rs.getString("Email")%></td>
  <td> <%=rs.getString("Phone")%></td>
  <td> <%=rs.getString("Qualification")%></td>
  <td> <%=rs.getString("Experience")%></td>
</tr>
<%
}
rs.close();
pstmt.close();
conn.close();
%>
</table>
</center>
</body>
</html>
<%}else{%>
<html>
     <head>
     <title>Resume Details</title>
     <script language="javascript">
          function validation(Form_obj)
               {
               if(Form_obj.FirstName.value.length==0){
               alert("Please,fill up the remaining information!!");
               Form_obj.FirstName.focus();
               return false;
               }
               if(Form_obj.LastName.value.length==0){
               alert("Please,fill up the remaining information!!");
               Form_obj.LastName.focus();
```

```
        return false;
        }
        if(Form_obj.Address.value.length==0){
        alert("Please,fill up the remaining information!!");
        Form_obj.Address.focus();
        return false;
        }
        if(Form_obj.Email.value.length==0){
        alert("Please,fill up the remaining information!!");
        Form_obj.Email.focus();
        return false;
        }
        if(Form_obj.Phone.value.length==0){
        alert("Please,fill up the remaining information!!");
        Form_obj.Phone.focus();
        return false;
        }
        if(Form_obj.Qual.value.length==0){
        alert("Please,fill up the remaining information!!");
        Form_obj.Qual.focus();
        return false;
        }
        if(Form_obj.Exp.value.length==0){
        alert("Please,fill up the remaining information!!");
        Form_obj.Exp.focus();
        return false;
        }

        return true;
        }
        </script>
    </head>
    <body>
        <center>
        <form action="http://localhost:8089/examples/jsp/Resume.jsp" method="post"
        name="entry" onSubmit="return validation(this)">
        <input type="hidden" value="list" name="action">
            <table border="3" cellpadding="0" cellspacing="0">
                <tr>
                <td>
                <table>
                  <tr>
                  <td colspan="2" align="center">
                  <h2>Resume Details</h2></td>
```

```
                    </tr>
                    <tr>
                    <td colspan="2"> </td>
                    </tr>
                    <tr>
                    <td>First Name:</td>
size="50"></td>
                    </tr>
                    <tr>
                    <td>Last Name:</td>
                    <td><input name="LastName" type= "text"
size="50"></td>
                    </tr>

                    <tr>
                    <td>Address:</td>
                    <td><input name="Address" type="text"
size="50"></td>
                    </tr>

                    <tr>
                    <td>Email:</td>
                    <td><input name="Email" type="text" size="20"></td>
                    </tr>

<tr>
                    <td>Phone:</td>
                    <td><input name="Phone" type="text" size="15"></td>
                    </tr>

                    <tr>
                    <td>Qualification:</td>
                    <td><input name="Qual" type="text" size="30"></td>
                    </tr>

                    <tr>
                    <td>Experience(in Years):</td>
                    <td><input name="Exp" type="text" size="15"></td>
                    </tr>
                    <tr>
                    <td colspan="2" align="center">
                    <input type="submit" value="Submit"></td>
                    </tr>
               </table>
```

```
                        </td>
                        </tr>
                    </table>
            </form>
            </center>
        </body>
    </html>
<%}%>
```

Output

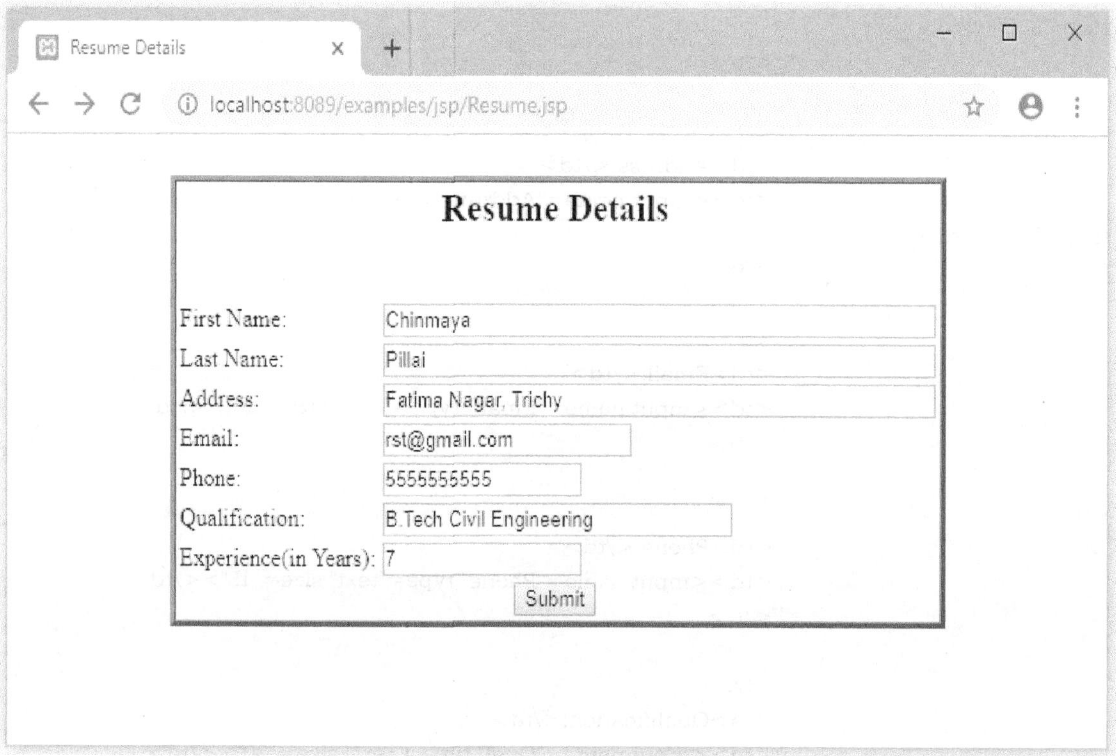

Click Submit button, and you will get the following output

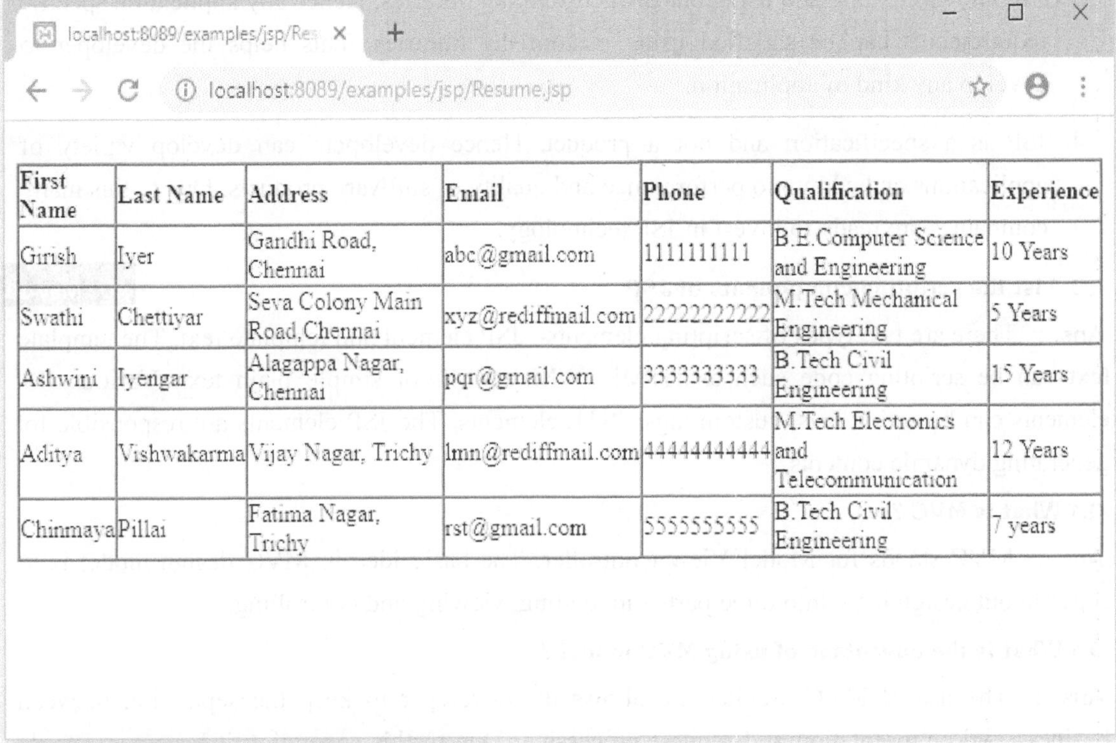

First Name	Last Name	Address	Email	Phone	Qualification	Experience
Girish	Iyer	Gandhi Road, Chennai	abc@gmail.com	1111111111	B.E.Computer Science and Engineering	10 Years
Swathi	Chettiyar	Seva Colony Main Road,Chennai	xyz@rediffmail.com	2222222222	M.Tech Mechanical Engineering	5 Years
Ashwini	Iyengar	Alagappa Nagar, Chennai	pqr@gmail.com	3333333333	B.Tech Civil Engineering	15 Years
Aditya	Vishwakarma	Vijay Nagar, Trichy	lmn@rediffmail.com	4444444444	M.Tech Electronics and Telecommunication	12 Years
Chinmaya	Pillai	Fatima Nagar, Trichy	rst@gmail.com	5555555555	B.Tech Civil Engineering	7 years

Two Marks Questions with Answers

Q.1 List any three advantages of Java Servlet over JSP. **AU : Dec.-08**

Ans. : Following are the three advantages of Java Servlet -

1. Java servlets contain pure Java code and there is no mixing of HTML tags.
2. Java servlets execute faster than JSP.
3. Servlet can act as a model-view and controller all at the same time. It can handle different dynamic pages.

Q.2 What are the advantages of JSP ?

OR Give the advantage of using JSP for server side programming . **AU : May-12**

Ans. : Following are some advantages of JSP –

1. JSP can be used along with servlets. Hence business logic for any application can be developed using JSP.
2. Dynamic contents can be handled using JSP because JSP allows scripting and element based programming.

3. JSP allows creating and using our own custom tag libraries. Hence any application specific requirements can be satisfied using custom tag libraries. This helps the developer to develop any kind of application.

4. JSP is a specification and not a product. Hence developers can develop variety of applications and add up to performance and quality of software products. Due to this many companies are ready to invest in JSP technology.

Q.3 List the scripting components of JSP. **AU : May-10**

Ans. : There are two types of scripting elements- JSP element and template text. The template text can be scripting code such as HTML, WML, XML or simple plain text. Various JSP elements can be action tags, custom tags, JSTL elements. The JSP elements are responsible for generating dynamic contents.

Q.4 What is MVC ?

Ans. : MVC stands for Model View Controller. The basic idea in MVC design model is to separate out design logic into three parts - modelling, viewing and controlling.

Q.5 What is the advantage of using MVC model ?

Ans. : The use of MVC architecture allows the developer to keep the separation between business logic, presentation and request processing. Due to this separation it becomes easy to make changes in presentation without disturbing the business logic. The changes in presentation are often required for accommodating the new presentation interfaces.

Q.6 What are the types of directive in JSP ? **AU : May-08**

Ans. : There are three types of directives in JSP.

1. page directive : Using page directive we can specify the language used by the JSP. For example : <%@page language="java"%>
2. include directive : This directive is used to include a file in the JSP page. For example : <%@include file="/dingdong.jsp"%>
3. taglib directive : The taglib is used to use the custom tags in the JSP pages. For example : <%@taglib uri="/WEB-INF/Mytag.tld" prefix="my" %>

Q.7 What are the standard action elements in JSP ?

Ans. : The standard actions are those actions that can be defined by the JSP specification itself. For example –

Action Element	Description
<jsp:useBean>	This tag is used to instantiate the object of java bean.

<jsp:setProperty>	This tag is used to set the property value for the java bean.
<jsp:getProperty>	This tag is used to get the property value from the java bean.
<jsp:include>	This tag works as a subroutine. It includes the response from servlet or JSP when request is being processed.

Q.8 What is the use of 'param' variable in JSP ? **AU : Dec.-09**

Ans. : For adding the specific parameter to the request the param tag is used. Normally this tag is used inside <jsp:include> or <jsp:forward>

Q.9 Explain in brief about Java scriplet. **AU: May-11**

Ans. : Java scriplets allow the developer to embed the Java code in JSP page. The syntax of scriplet can be -

```
<% any Java code %>
```

The tags <% and %> are used for embedding thes Java code.

Q.10 Write about javax.servlet.jsp.tagext package.

Ans. : It supports the classes and interfaces that are required for Java Server Pages tags libraries. Various classes and interfaces from the tag library are

Classes	Description
TagSupport	When a tag has to be implemented then we can extend the new tag handler class using this base class.
TagInfo	It provide the tag information for the tag in a tag library.
BodyTagSupport	When we want to create tag handlers for defining the body tag then this base class is used.

Interface	Description
Tag	This is the simple interface for defining the tag handler which does not want to manipulate its body.

The JSP tag library contains -

1. Various tag handler classes handling the request.
2. Tag library descriptors in .tld files.
3. Additional classes and interfaces.

Q.11 List methods in Request object.

Ans. : Various methods that are defined by the Request object are enlisted below -

Methods	Meaning
getAttribute(String *att*)	It returns the value of the attribute.
getAttributeNames()	For retrieving the names of the all attributes that are associated with the current session, this method is used.
getCookies()	It returns all the cookies sent by the client during the request.
getHeader(String *header*)	It returns the value of the requested header.
getHeaderNames()	It returns the header named of the requested header.
getMethod()	It returns the HTTP methods mentioned during the request. The HTTP methods are GET and POST.
getParameter(String *param*)	It returns the value of requested parameter.
getParameterNames()	It returns the names of all the parameters that are associated with the current session.
getQueryString	For returning the query string used during the request, this method is invoked.
setAttribute	For setting the object to the named attribute this method is used.

Q.12 Write two differences between JSP and servlet. **AU: May-13**

Ans. :

Sr. No.	JSP	Servlet
1.	JSP is an HTML in which the Java code is embedded.	Servlets are basically Java programs in which the HTML is embedded.
2.	JSP is a scripting language which generates the dynamic contents.	Servlets are Java programs that are compiled to generate dynamic web contents.
3.	In Model View Controller architecture(MVC) the JSP acts as a View.	In Model View Controller architecture(MVC) the servlet acts as a controller.
4.	JSP makes use of custom tags that can call the Java beans directly.	Servlet does not support for the custom tags.

Q.13 What are the advantages of JSP over Servlets ? **AU : Dec.-18**

Ans. : i) JSP can build custom tags. ii) JSP can call Java bean.

Unit IV

7 PHP

Syllabus

An introduction to PHP : PHP - Using PHP- Variables - Program control- Built-in functions - Form Validation - Regular Expressions - File handling – Cookies - Connecting to Database

Contents

7.1 Introduction to PHP

7.1.1 Origins and Uses of PHP

- PHP was developed in 1994 by Apache group.
- PHP stands for PHP : **H**ypertext **P**reprocessor.
- PHP is a server-side scripting language. It is mainly used for form handling and database access.
- It is free to download and use.

7.1.2 Overview

- PHP is a server side scripting language embedded in XHTML. It is an alternative to CGI, ASP, ASP.NET and JSP.
- The extension to the PHP files are .php, .php3 or .phtml.
- The php processor works in **two modes**. If the PHP processor finds XHTML tags in the PHP script then the code is simply copied to the output file. But when the PHP processor finds the PHP code in the script then that code is simply interpreted and the output is copied to the output file.
- If you click for view source on the web browser you can never see the PHP script because the output of PHP script is send directly to the browser but you can see the XHTML tags.
- PHP makes use of dynamic typing that means there is no need to declare variables in PHP. The type of variable gets set only when it is assigned with some value.
- PHP has large number of library functions which makes it flexible to develop the code in PHP.

7.1.3 Installation of PHP

- There are various methods of getting PHP installed on your machine.
- The PHP requires the Apache Web server to execute its code. The Apache web server is an open source software and can be easily downloaded from the Internet. The site for getting the Apache web server is **http://httpd.apache.org/download.cgi**.
- Then PHP can be installed on you machine from the web site **http://www.php.net**.
- Another approach which is the most efficient way to install Apache, PHP, MYSQL on you machine is to use the packages like XAMPP(The X stands for any OS) or WAMPP(the W stands for Windows OS). These packages support the Apache, PHP, MYSQL, PERL.
- I have installed the XAMPP package. The root directory can be accessed using the **http://localhost/**

7.2 General Syntactic Characteristics

- PHP code can be embedded in the XHTML document. The code must be enclosed within **<?php** and >
- If the PHP script is stored in some another file and if it needs to be referred then **include** construct is used. For instance :

```
Include("myfile.inc")
```

- The variable names in PHP begin with the $ sign.
- Following are some reserved keywords that are used in PHP.

and	default	false	if	or	this
break	do	For	include	require	true
case	else	foreach	list	return	var
class	elseif	function	new	static	virtual
continue	extends	gloabal	not	switch	while
					xor

- The **comments** in PHP can be #,//, /* …*/
- The PHP statements are terminated by semicolon.

Open some suitable text editor like Notepad and type the following code. Save your code by the extension .php.

It is expected that the PHP code must be stored in **htdocs** folder of Apache.

As I have installed **xampp**, I have got the directory c:\xampp\htdocs. I have created a folder named php-examples inside the htdocs and stored all my PHP documents in that folder.

Hence when I want to get the output of the PHP code I always give the URL

http://localhost/php-examples/programmName.php

The http://localhost refers to the path **c:\xampp\htdocs**

Following is the first example of PHP script

PHP Document[FirstCode.php]

```
<html>
 <head>
  <title> PHP Demo </title>
 </head>
 <body>
  <?php
  $i=10;
```

```
    echo "<h3>Welcome to first PHP Document</h3>";
    echo "The value of variable is = $i";
  ?>
 </body>
</html>
```

Output

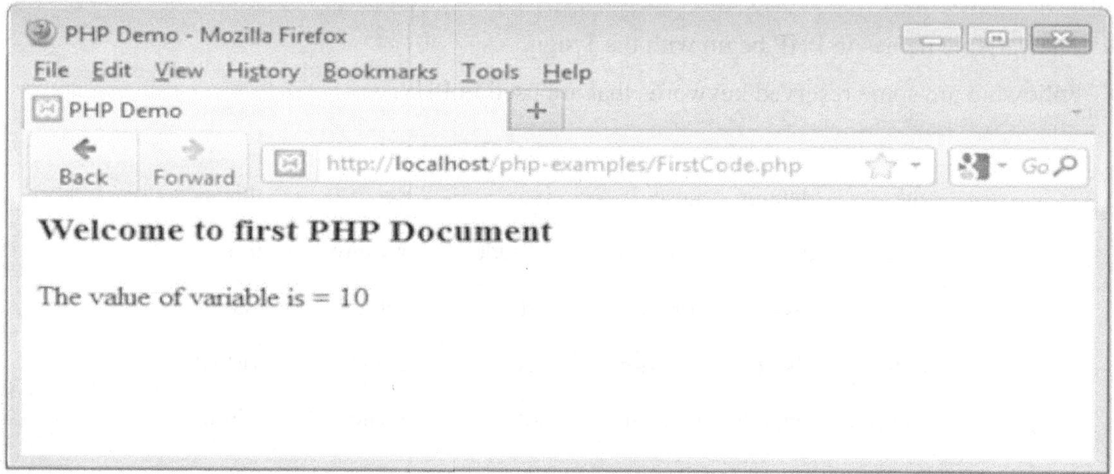

7.2.1 Variables

- Variables are the entities that are used for storing the values.
- PHP is a dynamically typed language. That is PHP has no type declaration.
- The value can be assigned to the variable in following manner -

```
$variable_name=value
```

- If the value is not assigned to the variable then by default the value is NULL. The unsigned variables are called **unbound variable.**
- If the unbound variable is used in the expression then its NULL value is converted to the value 0.
- Following are some rules that must be followed while using the variables -
    1. The variable must start with letter or underscore _, but it should not begin with a number.
    2. It consists of alphanumeric characters or underscore.
    3. There should not be space in the name of the variable.
    4. While assigning the values to the variable the variable must start with the $. For example

    ```
    $marks=100;
    ```

- Using the function **IsSet** the value of the variable can be tested. That means if IsSet($marks) function returns **TRUE** then that means some value is assigned to the variable **marks.**

- If the unbound variable gets referenced then the error reporting can be done with the help of a function **error_reporting(7)**. The default error reporting level is 7.

7.3 Data Type

7.3.1 Integer Type

- For displaying the integer value the Integer type is used.
- It is similar to the **long** data type in C.
- The size is 32 bit.

7.3.2 Double Type

- For displaying the real values the double data type is used.
- It includes the numbers with decimal point, exponentiation or both. The exponent can be represented by E or e followed by integer literal.
- It is not compulsory to have digits before and after the decimal point. For instance .123 or 123. is allowed in PHP.

7.3.3 String Type

- There is no character data type in PHP. If the character has to be represented then it is represented using the string type itself; but in this case the string is considered to be of length 1.
- The string literals can be defined using either single or double quotes.
- In single quotes the escape sequence or the values of the literals can not be recognized by PHP but in double quotes the escape sequences can be recognized. For example

  ```
  'The total marks are= $marks'
  ```

  will be typed as it is but

  ```
  "The total marks are= $marks"
  ```

  will display the value of $marks variable.

7.3.4 Boolean Type

- There are only two types of values that can be defined by the Boolean type and those are TRUE and FALSE.
- If Boolean values are used in context of integer type variable then TRUE will be interpreted as 1 and FALSE will be interpreted as 0.
- If Boolean values are used in context of double type then the FALSE will be interpreted as 0.0.

7.4 Type Conversion

- PHP supports for both implicit and explicit type conversion.
- The implicit type conversion is called **coercion**. In implicit type conversion the context of expression determines the data type that is expected or required.

Implicit conversion

- The coercion takes place between integer and double types and between Boolean and other scalar type.
- The coercion is also between the numeric and string types. That means whenever a numeric value appears in string context then it is converted to string type, similarly when the string value appears in numeric context it is automatically converted to numeric type.
- When the double value is converted to integer the fractional part is eliminated and the value is not rounded.

Explicit conversion

- There are three ways by which the explicit conversion takes place.

1. The syntax is

```
(datatype)$variable_name
```

For example -

```
(int)$marks
```

2. The syntax is -

```
Conversion_function($variable_name)
```

For example -

```
Intval($marks)
```

3. The syntax is -

```
settype($variable_name,"datatype")
```

For example -

```
settype($marks,"integer");
```

- The **gettype** function is useful to obtain the data type of the variable.

7.5 Displaying Output

- The PHP is a server side scripting language and is used to submit the web page to the client browser. Hence it is a standard method of embedding the PHP code within the XHTML document. That means we can use the XHTML tags in PHP while displaying the output.
- The **print** function is used to create simple unformatted output. For example: The string can be displayed as follows

```
print "I am proud of my <b>country</b>"
```

The numeric value can also be displayed using the **print**. For example -

```
print(100);
```

It will display the output as 100.

- PHP also makes use of the **printf** function used in C. For example

```
printf("The student %d has %f marks",$roll_no,$marks);
```

- Following is a simple PHP document which makes use of the statements for displaying the output.

PHP Document[OutputDemo.php]

```
<html>
<head>
    <title> Output Demo</title>
</head>
<body>
 <?php
    print "<h2>Welcome to my Website </h2>";
    print "<hr/>";
    $roll_no=1;
    $name="AAA";
    printf("<b>The roll number: %d</b>",$roll_no);
  print "<br/><b>";
    printf("The name: %s",$name);
    print "</b>";
?>
</body>
</html>
```

Output

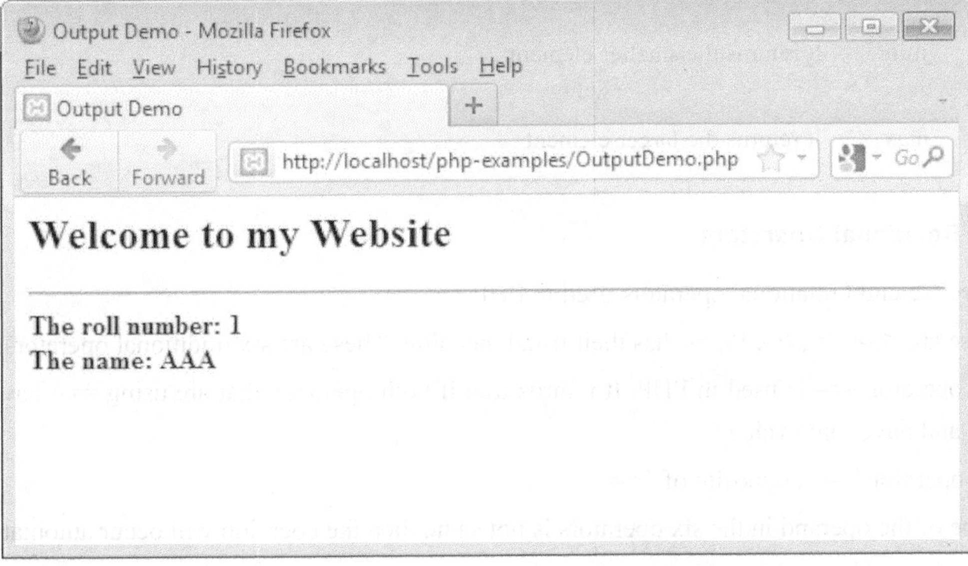

7.6 Operators

7.6.1 Arithmetic Operators

- PHP supports the collection of arithmetic operators such as +,-,/,*,%,++ and – with their usual meaning.
- While using the arithmetic operators if both the operands are integer then the result will be integer itself.
- If either of the two operands is double then the result will be double.
- PHP has large number of predefined functions. Some of these functions are enlisted in the following table -

Function	Purpose
floor	The largest integer less than or equal to the parameter is returned For example floor(4.9) will return 4,
ceil	The smallest integer greater than or equal to the parameter is returned For example ceil(4.9) will return 5,
round	Nearest integer is returned.
abs	Returns the absolute value of the parameter.
min	It returns the smaller element .
max	It returns the larger element .

7.6.2 Relational Operators

- There are eight relational operators used in PHP.
- These are <, >, <=, >=, !=, == has their usual meaning. These are six traditional operators.
- The operator === is used in PHP. It returns true if both operands that are using === have same type and have same value.
- The operator !== is opposite of ===.
- If one of the operand in the six operators is not same then the coercion will occur automatically.

7.6.3 Boolean Operators

- The Boolean operators are

Operator	Meaning
and &&	The binary AND operation is performed.
or ||	The binary OR operation is performed.
xor	The XOR operation will be performed.

7.6.4 String Operators

- Concatenation is the only one **operator** used in string. It is denoted by dot.
- Strings are treated as the array of characters. The first position of the character is indexed as 0.
- The sample PHP script that stores the string in a variable is as given below -

PHPScript[stringDemo1.php]

```
<?php
$s="I like PHP";
echo $s;
?>
```

Output

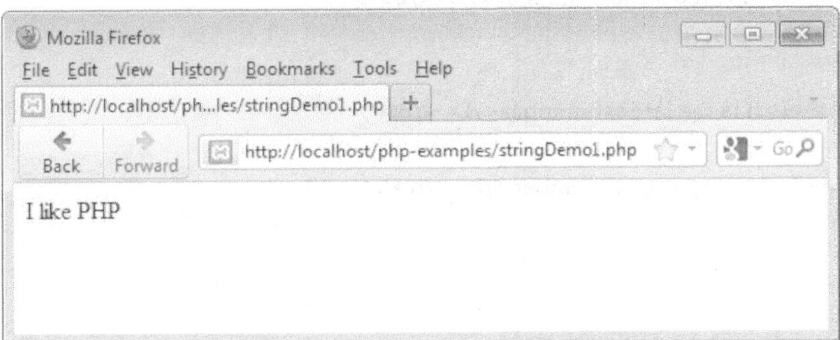

Note that the variable **s** is assigned with the string. The string is given in a double quotes. Then using the **echo** whatever string is stored in the variable **s** is displayed on the console.

Review Question

1. *Explain various operators used in PHP.*

7.7 Program Control

- The control statements in PHP are similar to the control statements that are used in C.
- The control statements include if statements, while, do while and for loops.

7.7.1 The Selection Statement

- The **if** statement, the **if ... else** statement or **if...elseif** statements are used in selection statements. Following is an example of it.

PHPDocument[selection.php]

```
<html>
<head>
    <title>Selection Demo</title>
</head>
<body>
<?php
    print "<h2>Selection Statement </h2>";
    $a=10;
    $b=20;
    $c=30;
    if($a>$b)
    if($a>$c)
    print "<b><I>a is the largest number </I></b>";
else
     print "<b><I> c is the largest number</I></b>";
    else
    if($b>$c)
     print "<b><I>b is the largest number</I></b>";
else
    print "<b><I>c is the largest number</I></b>";
?>
</body>
</html>
```

Output

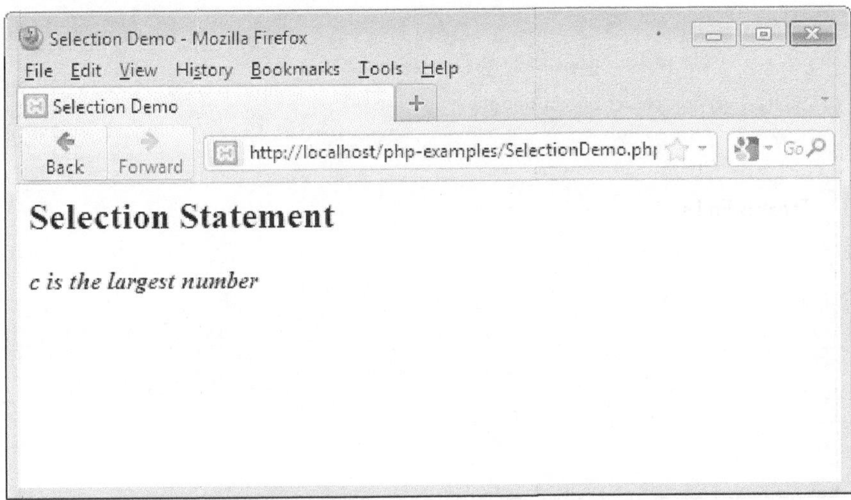

- Similar to **if** statement the **switch** statement can also be used for selection. Following is a simple PHP script for demonstrating switch statement -

PHPDocument[SwitchDemo.php]

```
<?php
$today = getdate();
switch($today['weekday'])
{
    case "Monday":print "Today is Monday";
     break;
    case "Tuesday":print "Today is Tuesday ";
     break;
    case "Wednesday":print "Today is Wednesday ";
     break;
    case "Thursday":print "Today is Thursday";
     break;
    case "Friday":print "Today is Friday";
     break;
    case "Saturday":print "Today is Saturday";
     break;
    case "Sunday":print "Today is Sunday ";
     break;
default: print "Invalid input";
}
?>
```

Output

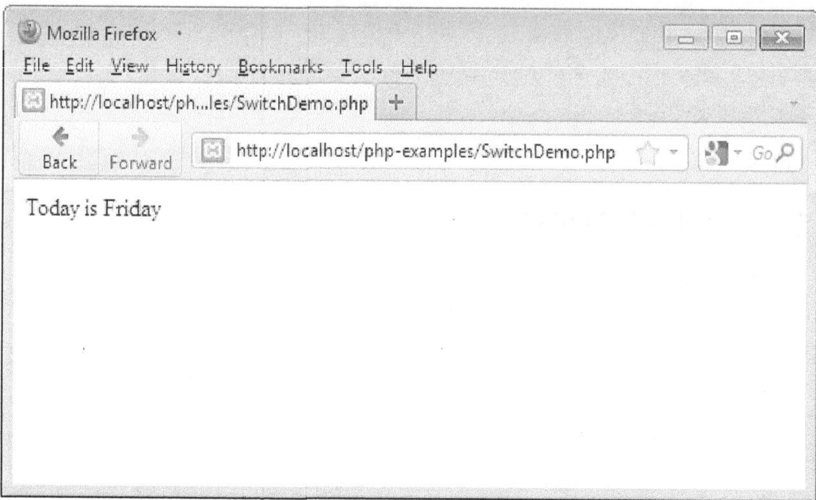

7.7.2 Looping Structure

- The **while**, for and **do-while** statements of PHP are similar to JavaScript.
- Following is a simple PHP script which displays the first 10 number.

PHPDocument[LoopDemo1.php]

```
<?php
$i=1;
print "The numbers are ...";
print "<br/>";
while($i<=10)
{
    print $i;
    print "<br/>";
    $i++;
}
?>
```

Output

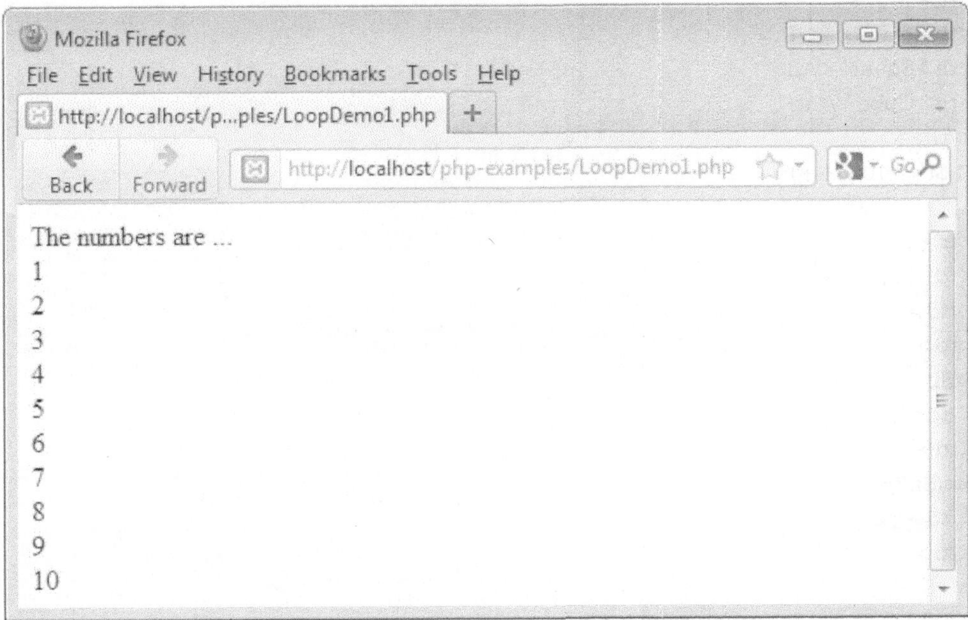

Similarly we can modify the above script by using do-while and for loop as follows –

do ...while

```
<?php
$i=1;
print "The numbers are ...";
print "<br/>";
do
{
    print $i;
    print "<br/>";
    $i++;
}while($i<=10);
?>
```

for

```
<?php
print "The numbers are ...";
print "<br/>";
for($i=1;$i<n)
{
    print $i;
    print "<br/>";
    $i++;
}
?>
```

Ex.7.7.1 Write a PHP script to display the squares and cubes of 1 to 10 numbers.

Sol. :

```
<html>
<head>
<title>Square and Cube Table </title>
</head>
<body>
<center>
<?php
```

```
print "<table border =1>";
print "<tr>";
print "<th>Number</th>";
print "<th>Square</th>";
print "<th>Cube</th>";
print "</tr>";
for($i=1;$i<=10;$i++)
{
print "<tr>";
print "<td>$i";
print "</td>";
print "<td>";
print $i*$i;
print "</td>";
print "<td>";
printpow($i,3);
print "</td>";
print "</tr>";
}
print "</table>";
?>
</center>
</body>
</html>
```

Output

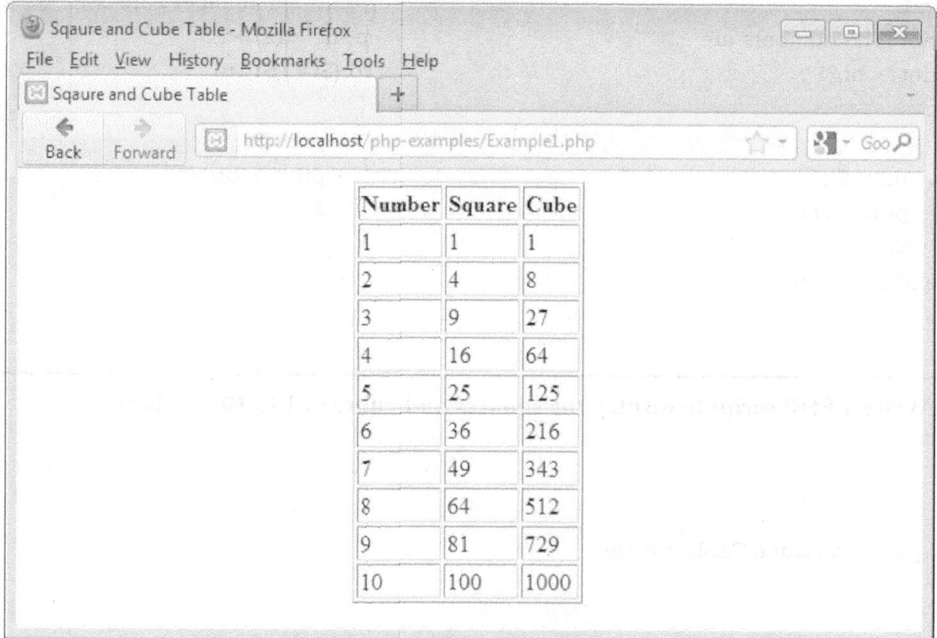

Number	Square	Cube
1	1	1
2	4	8
3	9	27
4	16	64
5	25	125
6	36	216
7	49	343
8	64	512
9	81	729
10	100	1000

Ex.7.7.2 Write a PHP script to compute the sum and average of N numbers.

Sol. :

```
<html>
<head>
<title> Sum and Average </title>
</head>
<body>
<center>
<?php
$sum=0;
for($i=1;$i<=10;$i++)
{
        $sum+=$i;
}
$avg=$sum/10;
print "The Sum is:  $sum";
print "<br/>";
print "the Average is: $avg";
?>
</center>
</body>
 </html>
```

Output

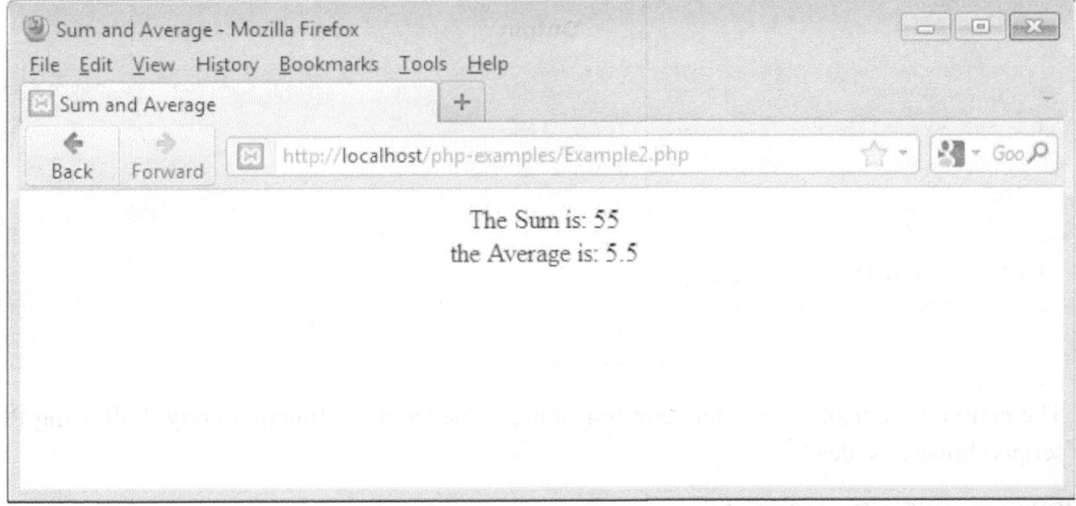

7.8 Functions

The functions in PHP are very much similar to the functions in C. Let us discuss it in detail.

7.8.1 General Characteristics of Functions

- The syntax of the function definition is as follows -

```
functionname_of_function(parameter list)
{
statements to be executed in function
 ...
 ...
 ...}
```

- The function gets executed only after the call to that function. The call to the function can be from anywhere in the PHP code. For example -

PHPDocument[FunDemo1.php]

```
<?php
functionmyfun()
{
    print "<i>This statement is in myfun()</i>";
}
print "<b>The Function Demo Program</b>";
print "<br/>";
myfun();
?>
```

Output

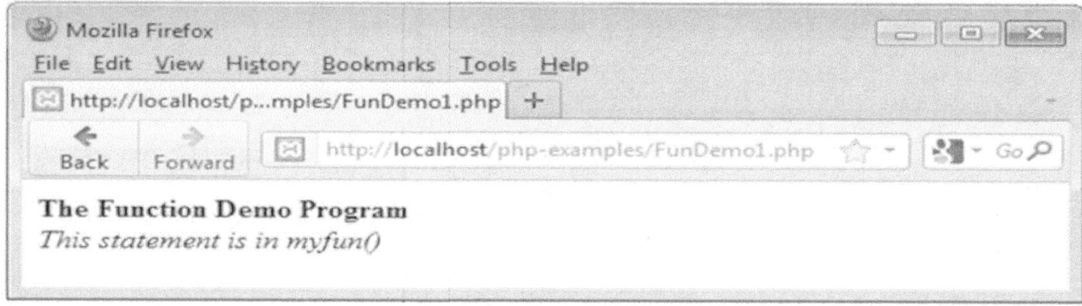

- The **return** statement is used for returning some value from the function body. Following PHP scripts shows this idea.

PHPDocument[FunDemo2.php]

```
<?php
function Addition()
{
    $a=10;
```

```
    $b=20;
    $c=$a+$b;
   return $c;
}
print "<b>The Function Demo Program with return statement</b>";
print "<br/>";
print "10+20= ".Addition();
?>
```

Output

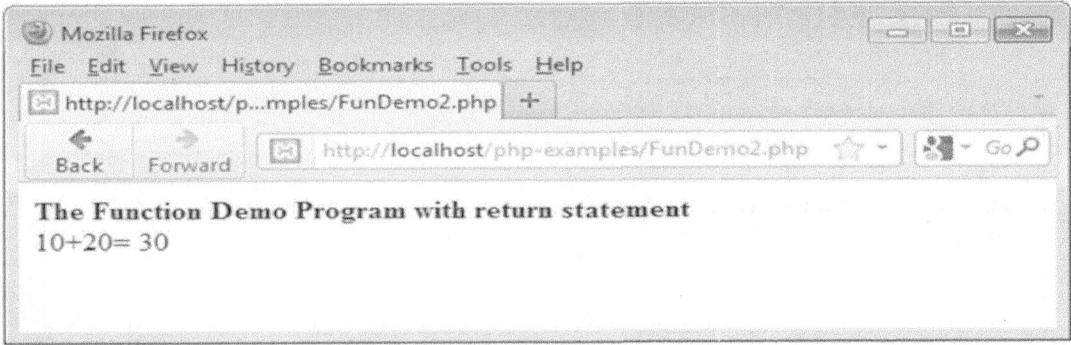

7.8.2 Parameters

- The parameters that we pass to the function during the call is called the **actual parameter.** These parameters are generally the expressions.
- The parameters that we pass to the function while defining it is called the **formal parameters.** These are generally the variables. It is not necessary that the number of actual parameters should match with the number of formal parameters.
- If there are few actual parameter and more formal parameters then the value of formal parameter will be some unbounded one.
- If there are many actual parameters and few formal parameters then the excess of actual parameters will be ignored.
- The default parameter passing technique in PHP is pass by value. The parameter passing by value means the values of actual parameters will be copied in the formal parameters. But the values of formal parameters will not be copied to the actual parameters.
- Following PHP script illustrates the functions with parameters.

PHP Document[FunDemo3.php]

```
<?php
function Addition($a,$b)
{
    $c=$a+$b;
```

```
        return $c;
}
print "<b>The Function Demo Program with parameter passing and return
statement</b>";
print "<br/>";
$x=10;
$y=20;
print "10+20= ".Addition($x,$y);
?>
```

Output

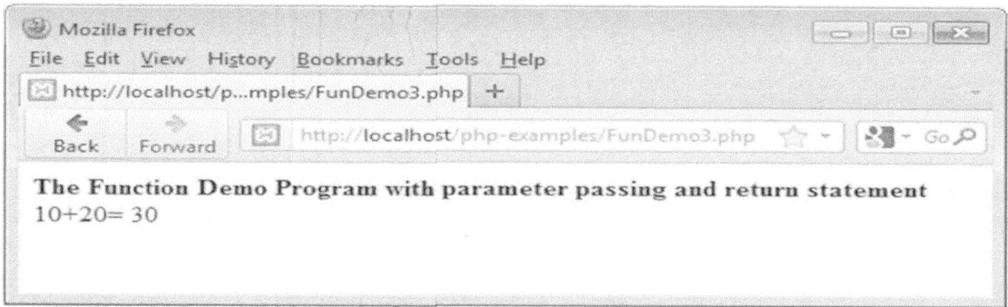

Review Question

1. *Write a short note on life time of variable in PHP.*

7.9 Arrays

- Array is a collection of similar type of elements, but in PHP you can have the elements of mixed type together in single array.
- In each PHP, each element has two parts **key** and **value.**
- The key represents the index at which the value of the element can be stored.
- The **keys** are positive integers that are in ascending order.

7.9.1 Array Creation

- There are two ways to create an array in PHP.
- The first way is to use the construct **array.** For example -

```
$mylist=array(10,20,30,40,50);
```

- The second way is to assign the value directly to the array. For example -

```
$mylist[0]=10;
```

- An empty array can also be created using the **array** construct. For example -

```
$mylist=array();
```

- We can have mixed type of elements in the array. It is as follows -

$mylist=array("Archana" => "Pune", "Shilpa =>89.33);

7.9.2 Accessing Array Elements

- Using an array subscript we can access the array element. The value of subscript is enclosed within the square brackets. For example -

```
$Citycode['Pune']=005;
$Name[0]="Chitra";
```

- Multiple values can be set to a single scalar variable using array. For example -

```
$people=array("Meena","Teena","Heena");
list($operator,$accountant,$manager)=$people;
```

- By this assignment Meena becomes operator, Teena becomes accountant and Heena becomes the manager.

7.9.3 Functions for Dealing with Arrays

- The **unset** function is used to remove particular element from the array. For example consider following PHP document.

PHP Document[ArrayFunDemo1.php]

```
<?php
$mylist=array(10,20,30,40,50);
unset($mylist[1]);
for($i=0;$i<=4;$i++)
{
    print $mylist[$i];
    print " ";
}
?>
```

Output

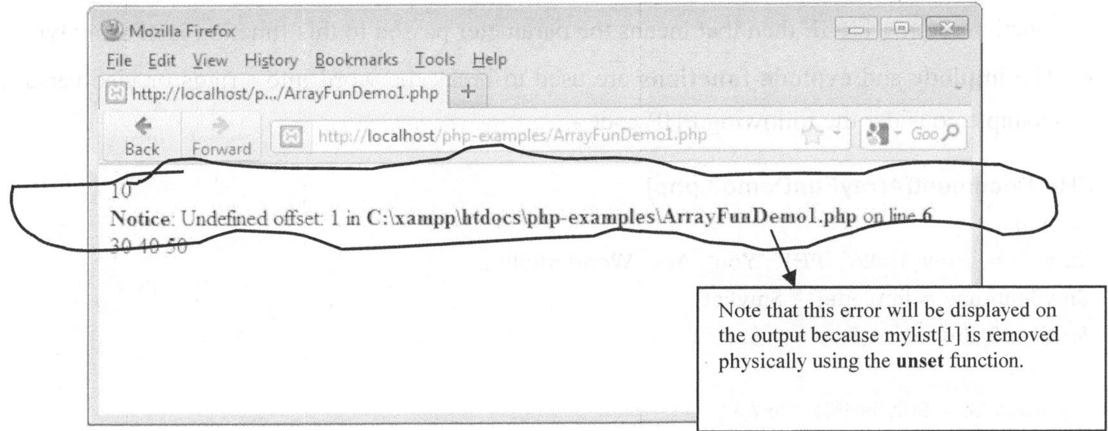

- The functions **array_keys** and **array_values** are used to return the array keys and the values at corresponding key. For example consider the following PHP document -

PHPDocument[ArrayFunDemo2.php]

```
<?php
$mylist=array(10=>"AAA",20=>"BBB",30=>"CCC",40=>"DDD",50=>"EEE");
$Roll=array_keys($mylist);
$Name=array_values($mylist);
print_r($Roll);
print "<br/>";
print_r($Name);
?>
```

Output

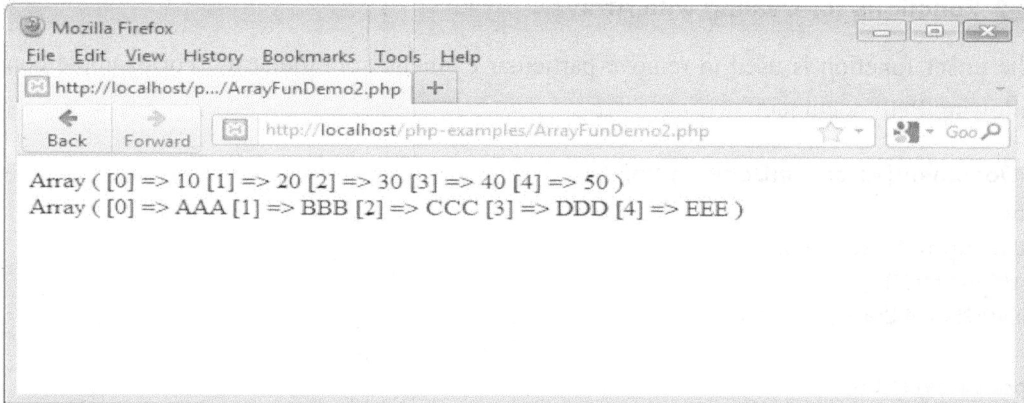

- The existence of particular key can be checked by using the **array_key_exists** function. This function returns the Boolean value.
- The **is_array** returns the Boolean value. This function takes a variable as a parameter. If the function returns TRUE then that means the parameter passed to this function is of array type.
- The **implode** and **explode functions** are used to break the word into strings or vice versa. For example consider the following PHP code -

PHP Document[ArrayFunDemo3.php]

```
<?php
$mylist = array("Hello", "PHP","You","Are","Wonderful!!!");
$mySentence = implode(" ", $mylist);
for($i = 0; $i< count($mylist); $i++)
{
    echo "$i = $mylist[$i] <br />";
}
echo "The sentence is  = $mySentence<br />";
```

```
print "<hr/>";
$newSentence="I Like Programming In It";
$chunks=explode(" ",$newSentence);
echo "The new sentence = $newSentence";
print "<br/>";
echo "The first chunk=$chunks[0]";
print "<br/>";
echo "The second chunk=$chunks[1]";
print "<br/>";
echo "The third chunk=$chunks[2]";
print "<br/>";
?>
```

Output

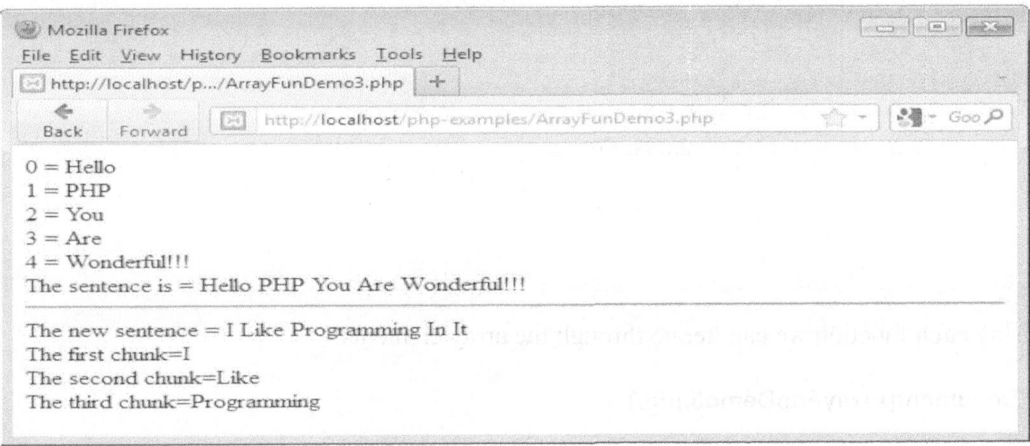

7.9.4 Sequential Access to Array Elements

- The array element reference start at the first element and every array maintains an internal pointer using which the next element can be easily accessible.
- This helps to access the array elements in sequential manner.
- The pointer **current** is used to point to the current element in the array. Using the next function the **next** subsequent element can be accessed. Following PHP code illustrates this idea -

PHP Document[ArrayFunDemo4.php]

```
<?php
$mylist = array("Hello", "PHP","You","Are","Wonderful!!!");
$myval=current($mylist);
print("The current value of the array is <b>$myval</b>");
print "<br/>";
$myval=next($mylist);
```

```
print("The next value of the array is <b>$myval</b>");
print "<br/>";
$myval=next($mylist);
print("The next value of the array is <b>$myval</b>");
print "<br/>";
$myval=next($mylist);
print("The next value of the array is <b>$myval</b>");
print "<br/>";
$myval=next($mylist);
print("The next value of the array is <b>$myval</b>");
?>
```

Output

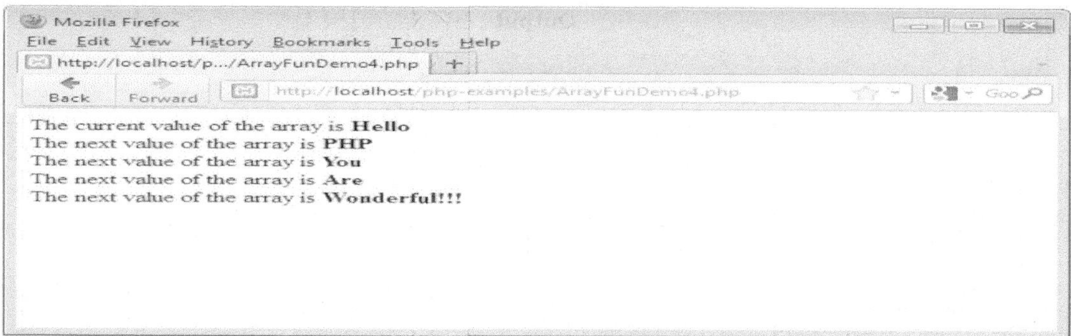

- Using **each** function we can iterate through the array elements.

PHP Document[ArrayFunDemo5.php]

```
<?php
$mylist = array("Hello", "PHP","You","Are","Wonderful!!!");

while($myval=each($mylist))
{
    $val=$myval["value"];
    print("The current value of the array is <b>$val</b>");
    print "<br/>";
}
?>
```

Output

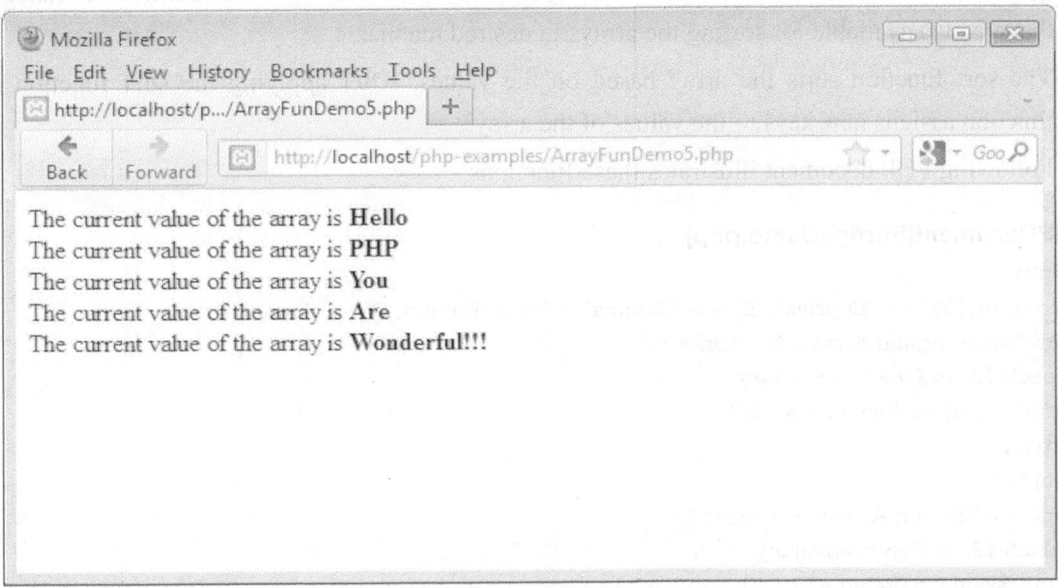

- The **foreach** function is used to iterate through all the elements of the loop. The syntax of foreach statement is as follows -

```
foreach($array as $value)
{
statements to be executed
}
```

- The above code can be modified and written as follows -

PHP Document[ArrayFunDemo6.php]

```
<?php
$mylist = array("Hello", "PHP","You","Are","Wonderful!!!");

foreach($mylist as $value)
{
    print("The current value of the array is <b>$value</b>");
    print "<br/>";
}
?>
```

The output will be the same as above.

7.9.5 Sorting Arrays

- Sorting is a process in which the elements of arrays in some specific order. There are two types ordering which are followed in sorting - ascending order and descending order.

- Basically PHP uses **sort** function for sorting the array elements. There are some other functions that are also available for sorting the arrays in desired manner.
- The sort function sorts the array based on the values. After applying the **sort** function this function assigns new keys to the values of the array.
- Following PHP document illustrates these functions -

PHPDocument[SortingDemo.php]

```
<?php
$A = array("A" => "Supriya", "B" => "Monika", "C" => "Kumar","D"=>"Archana");
print "<b>Original Array:<b><br/>";
foreach($A as $key => $value )
print(" [$key] =>$value <br />");
sort($A);
print "<br/>";
print "<b>Sorted Array:<b><br/>";
foreach($A as $key=>$value)
print("[$key]=>$value <br />");
?>
```

Output

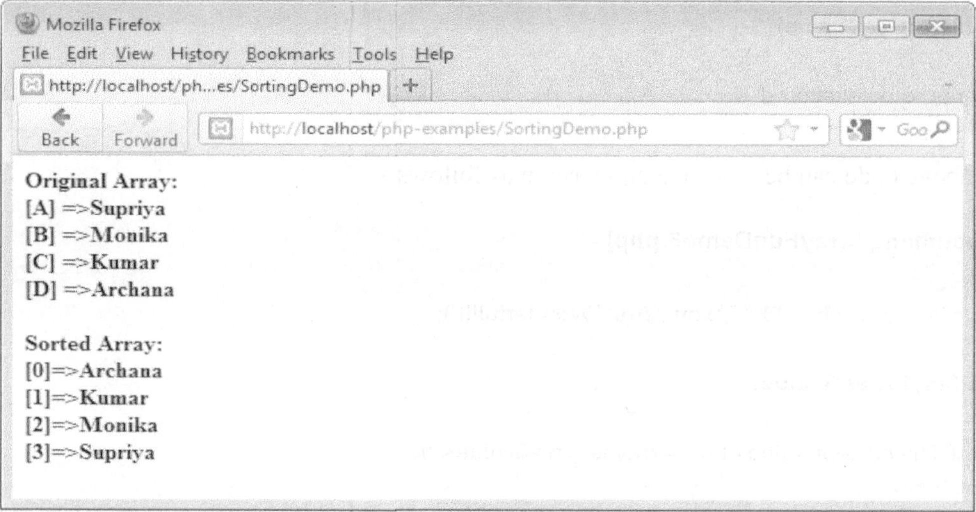

- The **asort()** function sorts an array by the values. But the original keys are kept.
- The **ksort** function sorts the array by keys but each value's original key is retained.
- Following PHP illustrates both of these functions -

PHP Document[SortingDemo1.php]

```
<?php
$A = array("A" => "Supriya", "B" => "Monika", "C" => "Kumar","D"=>"Archana");
```

```
print "<b>Original Array:<b><br/>";
foreach($A as $key => $value )
    print(" [$key] =>$value <br />");
asort($A);
print "<br/>";
print "<b>Sorted Array by asort function:<b><br/>";
foreach($A as $key=>$value)
    print("[$key]=>$value <br />");
print "<hr/>";
$B = array(30 => "CCC", 20 => "BBB", 40 => "DDD",10=>"AAA");
print "<b>Original Array:<b><br/>";
foreach($A as $key => $value )
    print(" [$key] =>$value <br />");
ksort($A);
print "<br/>";
print "<b>Sorted Array by ksort function:<b><br/>";
foreach($A as $key=>$value)
    print("[$key]=>$value <br />");
?>
```

Output

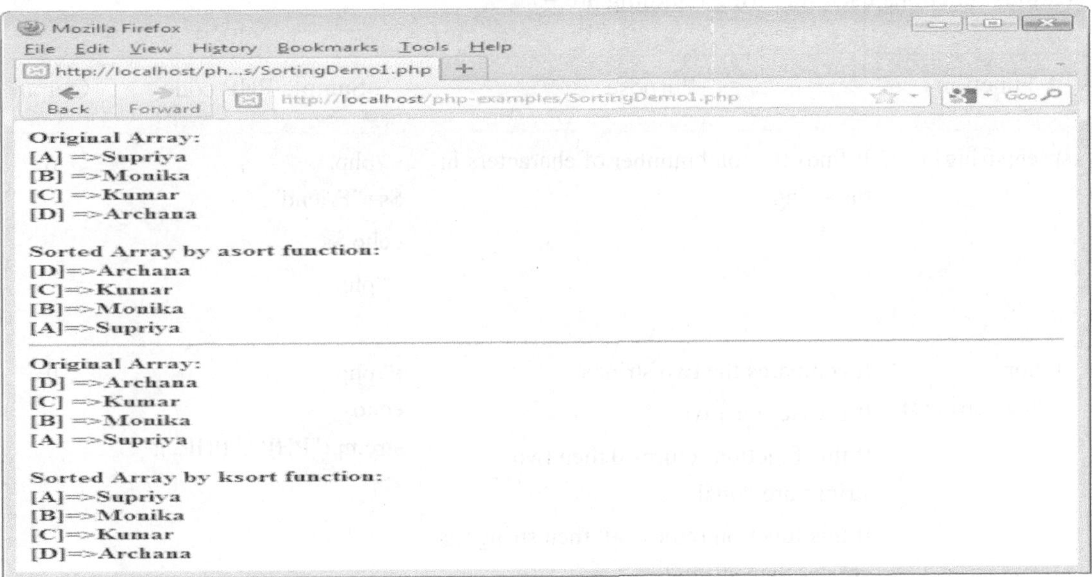

7.10 Built in Functions

AU : Dec.-15, Marks 16

PHP has number of predefined functions.

7.10.1 Functions based on Basic Operations

These function help in performing basic operations such floor, ceil, round and so on.

Function	Purpose
floor	The largest integer less than or equal to the parameter is returned. For example floor(4.9) will return 4,
ceil	The smallest integer greater than or equal to the parameter is returned. For example ceil(4.9) will return 5,
round	Nearest integer is returned.
abs	Returns the absolute value of the parameter.
min	It returns the smaller element .
max	It returns the larger element .

7.10.2 String Handling Functions

Various functions used for string handling are –

Function	Purpose	Sample PHP code	Output
strlen(string1)	It finds the total number of characters in the string	<?php $s=”Friend”; echo $s <?php	6
strcmp (string1,string2)	It compares the two strings. It is case sensitive. If this function returns 0 then two strings are equal. If this function returns >0 then string1 is greater than string2. If this function returns <0 then string1 is less than string2.	<?php echo strcmp("PHP”,”PHP”); ?>	0
strtolower (string1)	This function converts the characters in string1 to lower case.	<?php echo strtolower("PHP."); ?>	php

strtoupper (string1)	This function converts the characters in string1 to upper case.	<?php echo strtolower("php"); ?>	PHP
trim(string1)	This function eliminates the white space from both the ends of the string.	<?php $str = " PHP "; echo "<h3>: $str</h3>"; echo "<h3>:".trim($str); echo "</h3>"; ?>	: PHP : PHP

Ex.7.10.1 Write a PHP program to do string manipulations.

AU :Dec.-15, Marks 16

Sol. : For this program we will apply various built in string manipulating functions to the string. The PHP code is as follows –

```
<?php
    $Str1="PHP is Fun";
    $length = strlen($Str1);
    echo "<b> Length:</b>The length of string: $Str1 is = $length";
    echo "<br/><b>Position: </b>The position of word Fun in the $Str1 is ".strpos($Str1,'Fun');
    $Str1="Hello";
    $Str2="hello";
    if(strcmp($Str1,$Str2))
     echo "<br/><b>Comparison: </b> The two strings $Str1 and $Str2 are not equal";
    else
     echo "<br/><b>Comparision: </b> The two strings $Str1 and $Str2 are equal";
    $Str1="HELLO";
    echo "<br/><b>Changing Case: </b> The string $Str1 becomes ".strtolower($Str1);
    echo "<br/><b>Reversing String: </b> The string $Str1 is reversed as ".strrev($Str1);
    $Str1="Hello";
    $Str2="Friend";
    echo "<br/><b>Concatenating strings: </b> The string $Str1 and $Str2 are concatenated ".$Str1.$Str2;
    echo "<br/><b>Replacing all instances of string: </b> The string tictactoe is now ";
    echo str_replace("t","p","tictactoe");
    $Str1="PHP is fun";
    $newstring=substr_replace($Str1,"FUN",7,9);
    echo "<br><b>Replacing substring: </b> $Str1 becomes $newstring";
?>
```

Output

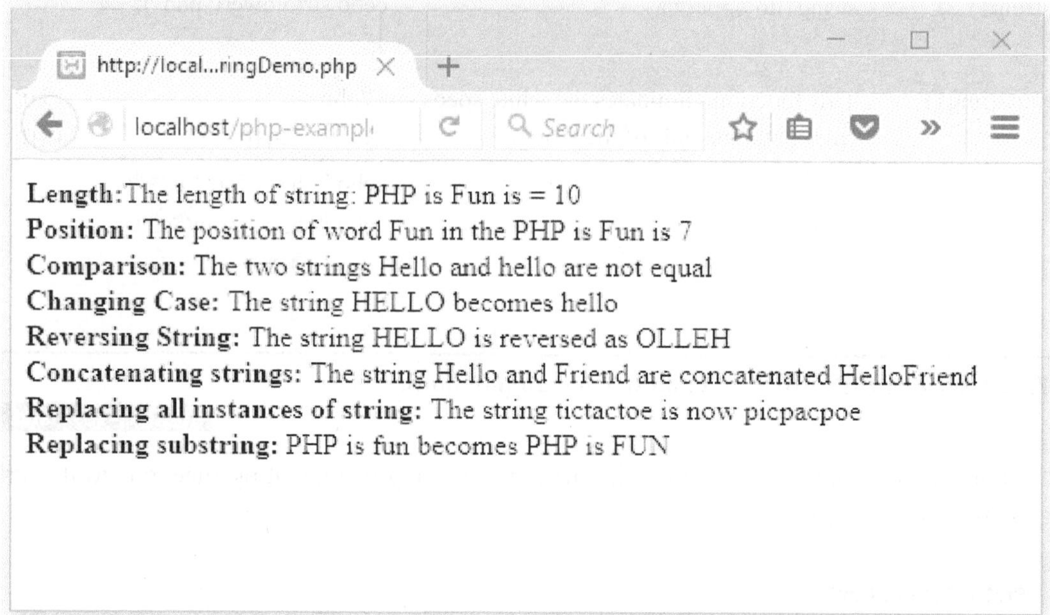

7.10.3 Data Type Conversion Functions

Syntax :

```
Conversion_function($variable_name)
```

Example :

```
Intval($marks)
```

Syntax :

```
settype($variable_name,"datatype")
```

Example :

```
settype($marks,"integer");
```

- The **gettype** function is useful to obtain the data type of the variable.

7.10.4 Array Handling Functions

Function	Purpose
array()	Creates an array.
array_change_key_case(array,nameof case)	Changes the elements of array from lower to upper or from upper to lower case.

array_fill()	Fills the array with values.
array_keys()	Returns all the keys of the array.
array_merge()	Merges one or more arrays into one array.
array_search()	Searches array for given value and returns the keys.
array_value()	Returns the values of array.
count()	Returns the elements in array.
current()	Returns current element in an array.
each()	Returns current key and value pair from array.
end()	Returns last element value form array.
next()	Advances the internal pointer of the array to point to the next element.
sizeof()	Returns the total number of elements.
sort()	This function is for sorting the array.

7.11 Form Validation

- PHP is used for form handling. For that purpose the simple form can be designed in HTML and the values of the fields defined on the form can be transmitted to the PHP script using GET and POST methods.
- For forms that are submitted via "GET" method, we can obtain the form via the **$_GET** array variable.
- For forms that are submitted via "POST" method, we can obtain the form via the **$_POST** array variable.

Ex. 7.11.1 Create HTML form with one textbox to get user's name. Also write PHP code to show length of entered name when, the HTML form is submitted.

Sol. :

Step 1 : The HTML form can be created as follows.

```
<!DOCTYPE html>
<html>
<head><title> HTML-PHP DEMO</title>
</head>
<body>
  <form method="post"
   action="http://localhost/getdata.php">
```

```
    Name: <input type="text" name="myname" size="20"/>
    <br/>
    <input type="submit" name="submit"
    value="submit"/>
  </form>
</body>
</html>
```

Step 2 : The PHP script to display the length of submitted name is as written below.

```
<?php
print "The name is: ";
print $_POST["myname"];
$len= strlen($_POST["myname"]);
print "<br/> The length of name is: ";
print $len;
?>
```

Output

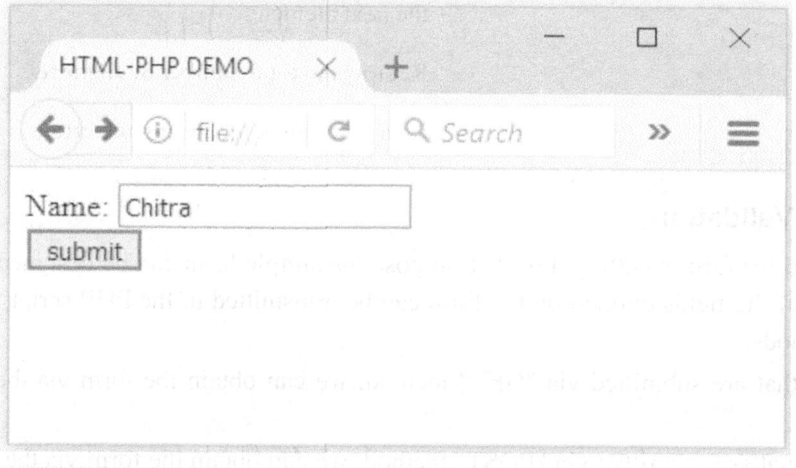

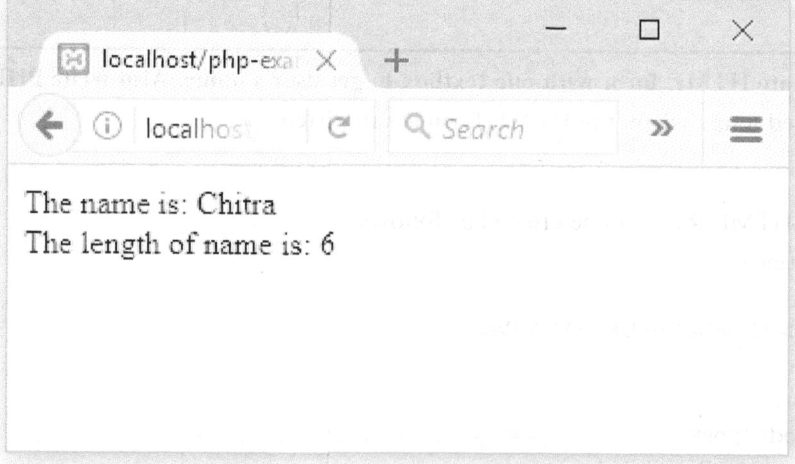

Ex. 7.11.2 Create HTML form to enter one number. Write PHP code to display the message about number is odd or even.

Sol. :

Step 1 : The HTML form for accepting number is created as below -

```
<!DOCTYPE html>
<html >
 <head><title> HTML-PHP DEMO</title>
</head>
<body>
   <form method="post" action="http://localhost/getdata.php">
     Enter Number: <input type="text" name="mynum"  size="5"/>
      <br/>
   <input type="submit" name="submit" value="submit"/>
   </form>

</body>
</html>
```

Step 2 : The PHP script deciding whether the number is even or odd is as given below -

```
<?php
print "The number is: ";
print $_POST["mynum"];
$a= $_POST["mynum"];
if($a%2==1)
 print "<br/> The number is odd ";
else
 print "<br/> The number is even ";
?>
```

Output

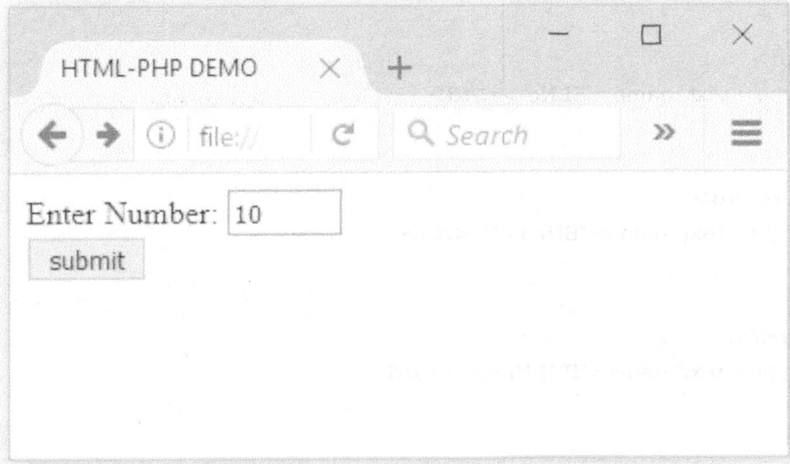

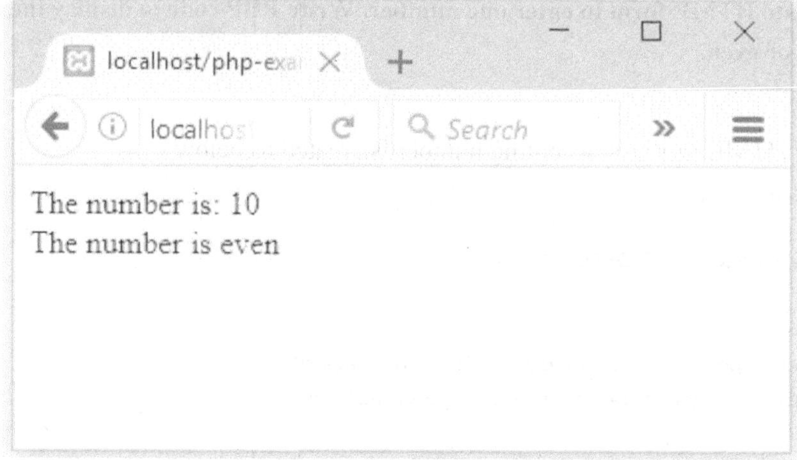

Ex. 7.11.3 Create a form containing information sl.no, title of the book, publishers, quantity, price read the data from the form and display it using PHP script.

Sol. :

Step 1 : Create an HTML page for inputting the data. Following is the code for HTML script .

HTML Document[input.html]

```
<!doctype html>
<html>
<head>
<title> Book Order Form </title>
</head>
<body>
<h3> Enter the Book Data </h3>
<form method="post" action="http://localhost/php-examples/formdemo.php">
<table>
<tr>
<td>Sr.No.</td>
<td><input type="text" name="SLNo"></td>
</tr>
<tr>
 <td>Book name</td>
 <td><input type="text" name="BName"></td>
</tr>
<tr>
 <td>Publisher</td>
 <td><input type="text" name="PUBName"></td>
</tr>
<tr>
 <td>Price</td>
```

```
<td><input type="text" name="Price"></td>
</tr>
<td>Quantity</td>
<td><input type="text" name="Qty"></td>
</tr>
<tr>
<td><input type="submit" value="Submit"></td>
<td><input type="submit" value="Clear"></td>
</tr>
</table>
</form>
</body>
</html>
```

Step 2 : Create a PHP script which will read out the data entered by the user using HTML form. The code is as follows -

PHP Document[formdemo.php]

```
<html>
<head>
<title>Book Information</title>
</head>
<body>
<?php
$BName=$_POST["BName"];
$PUBName=$_POST["PUBName"];
$Price=$_POST["Price"];
$Qty=$_POST["Qty"];
?>
<center>
<h3> Book Data </h3>
<table border=1>
<tr>
<th>Book name</th>
<th>Publisher</th>
<th>Price</th>
<th>Quantity</th>
</tr>
<tr>
<td><?php print ("$BName"); ?></td>
<td><?php print ("$PUBName"); ?></td>
<td><?php printf("%3.2f",$Price); ?></td>
<td><?php printf("%d",$Qty); ?></td>
</tr>
```

```
</table>
</center>
</body>
</html>
```

Step 3 : Open some suitable web browser and enter the address for the HTML file which you have created in step 1.

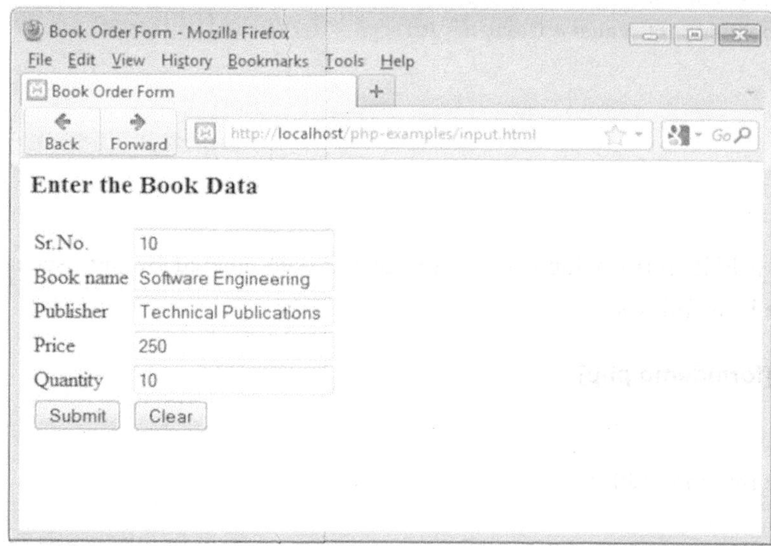

Now click on the Submit button and the PHP file will be invoked. The output will then be as follows -

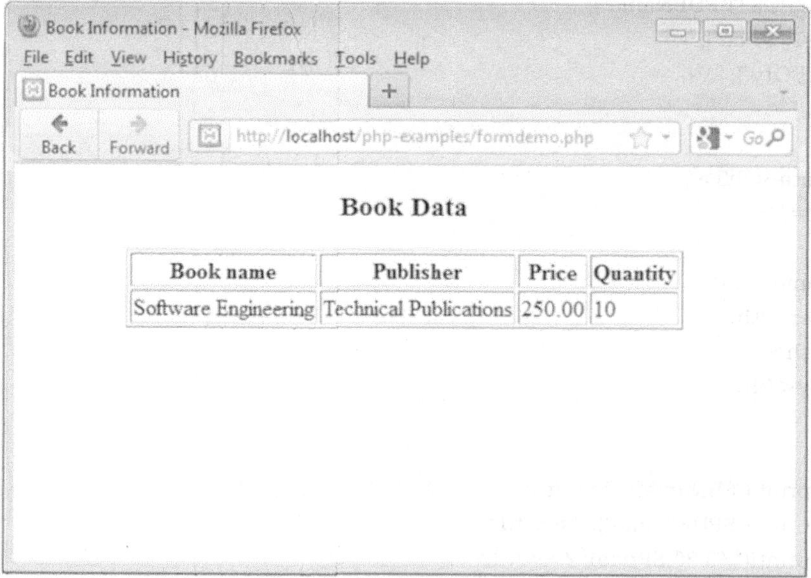

Ex. 7.11.4 Write a PHP program to accept a positive integer 'N' through a HTML form and to display the sum of all the numbers from 1 to N **AU : April-14, Marks 8**

Sol. :

```
<html>
    <head>
     <title> PHP Demo </title>
    </head>
    <body>
     <form method="post">
        <input type="text" name="num"/>
        <input type="submit" value="Submit"/>
     </form>
    </body>
</html>
<?php
    //getting values from HTML form
    $n = intval($_POST['num']);
    $sum=0;
    for($i=1;$i<=$n;$i++)
     $sum=$sum+$i;
    echo "The sum of all numbers from 1 to ".$n." is ".$sum;
?>
```

Output

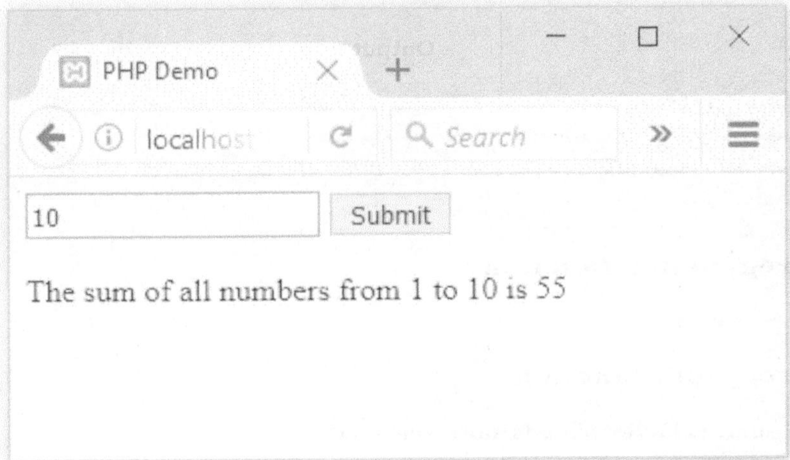

7.12 Regular Expressions

AU : Dec.-16, 17, May-17, Marks 10

- The pattern matching technique which is used in PHP is of two types -The first one is based on **POSIX regular expression** and the another is based on **Perl regular expression.**
- There is a **preg_match** function which is used to check the matching of the pattern from the text. It takes two parameters the first parameter is the pattern to be matched and the second parameter is the text against which the pattern is to be matched.

- The **preg_split** is the function that splits the string into the chunks.
- Following is a PHP script in which both of these functions are discussed.

PHP Document[PatternMatchDemo.php]

```
<?php
print "<h3>Use of preg_match function</h3>";
if (preg_match("/gram/", "I like Programming in PHP!"))
      print "The pattern is matching <br />";
else
      print "The pattern does not match <br />";
print "<h3>Use of preg_split function</h3>";
$text ="Hello:friends:how:are:you?";
print "The original string is<b> $text</b>";
print "<br/>";
print "The split is as follows ...<br/>";
$chunks=preg_split("/:/",$text);
while($myval=each($chunks))
{
    $val=$myval["value"];
    print("<b>$val</b>");
    print "<br/>";
}
?>
```

Output

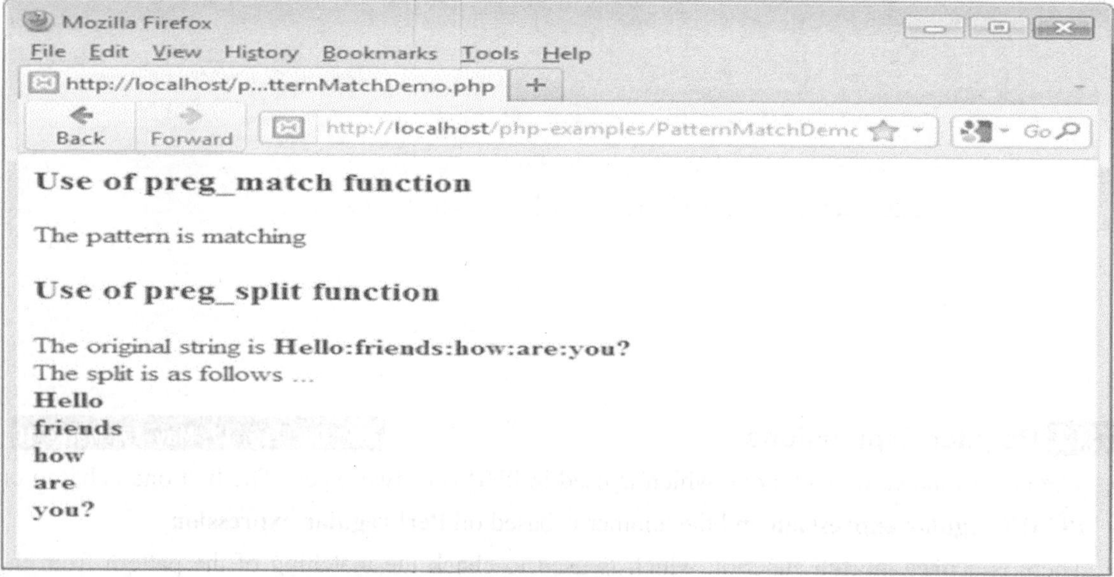

Ex. 7.12.1 Explain the string comparison capability of PHP using regular expression with an example. **AU : Dec.-16, Marks 10**

Sol. : The preg_match function is used to compare two strings using regular expression. The first parameter to this function is a regular expression and second parameter is the string which is used for matching with the regular expression.

Following PHP program illustrates, the matching of date pattern using regular expression.

Example program in PHP

```
<?php
$regex = "/[a-zA-Z]+ \d+/";
if (preg_match($regex, "May 16"))
{
   // The expression "[a-zA-Z]+ \d+" matches the date string
   echo "The date is matching with given regular expression!";
}
else
 {
   // If preg_match() returns false, then the regex does not
   // match the string
   echo "The regex pattern does not match.";
}
?>
```

Output

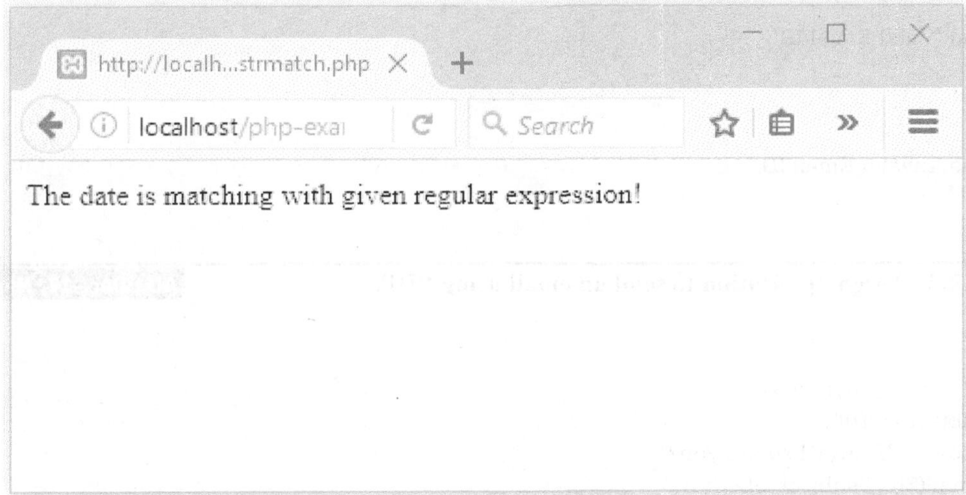

Ex. 7.12.2 Write a PHP program that tests whether an email address is input correctly. Verify that the input begins with a series of characters followed by the @ character, another series of characters, a period '.' And a final series of characters. Test your program with both valid and invalid email address. **AU : May-17, Marks 8**

Sol. : Step 1 : The HTML form containing the text box for inputting the email address is created as follows –

```
<html>
<head>
    <title> Inserting Data into Database Table</title>
</head>
<body>
    <form method = "post" action = "http://localhost/php-examples/ValidateEmail.php ">
    <label>Email</label>
    <input type="text" name="email" />
    <br />
    <input type="submit" value="Submit">
    </form>
</body>
</html>
```

Step 2 : The PHP script that validates the given email address using regular expression is as follows –

ValidateEmail.php

```
<?php
$reg = '/^[_a-z0-9-]+(\.[_a-z0-9-]+)*@[a-z0-9-]+(\.[a-z0-9-]+)*(\.[a-z]{2,3})$/';
$email=$_POST["email"];
if (preg_match($reg, $email))
{
    echo "Valid Email ID";
}
else
{
    echo "Invalid Email ID.";
}
?>
```

Ex. 7.12.3 Design application to send an email using PHP. **AU : Dec.-17, Marks 15**

Sol. :

```
<?php
    $to = "xyz@mysite.com";
    $subject = "Hi!";
    $body = "Hi,\n\nHow are you?";
    if (mail($to, $subject, $body))
    {
     echo("<p>Email successfully sent!</p>");
    }
    else
    {
     echo("<p>Failure in Email delivery!!!</p>");
    }
?>
```

7.13 File Handling

PHP is known as a server-side scripting language. Hence file handling functions such as create, read, write, append are some file related operations that are supported by PHP.

7.13.1 Opening and Closing Files

- The first step in file handling is opening of the file.
- It takes two parameters - The first parameter of this function contains the name of the file to be opened and the second parameter specifies in which mode the file should be opened.

Modes	Description
r	Read only. Starts reading from the beginning of the file.
r+	Read/Write. Starts reading from the beginning of the file.
w	Write only. Opens and clears the contents of file; or creates a new file if it is not created
w+	Read/Write. Opens and clears the contents of file; or creates a new file if it is not created.
a	Append. Opens and writes to the end of the file or creates a new file if it is not created.
a+	Read/Append. Preserves file content by writing to the end of the file.

For example :

```
$my_file = 'file.txt';
$file_handle = fopen($my_file, 'a') or die('Cannot open file:  '.$my_file);
```

The **fopen** function returns TRUE if the required file is opened.

7.13.2 Reading from File

- The **fread** is the function which is used to read the file.
- It takes two parameters. The first parameter is the handle to the file and the second parameter is the number of bytes to be read. The **filesize** is the function which takes the filename as the parameter. For example -

```
$mystring = fread($file_handle, filesize("file.txt"));
```

- There is another function named **file_get_contents** using which the contents of the file can be obtained.

- The **fgets()** function is used to read a single line from the file. For example, following code displays the contents of the file line by line.

```
while(!feof($file_handle))
{
    echo fgets($file_handle). "<br />";
}
```

7.13.3 Writing to a File

- The **fwrite** is the function which is used to write the contents to the file.
- It takes two parameters - the first parameter is the handle to the file and the second parameter is the number of bytes to be written. For example -

```
$Written_string = fread($file_handle, $my_data);
```

Ex. 7.13.1 Create a form containing information sl.no, title of the book, publishers, quantity, price read the data from the form and write onto the file using PHP script.

Sol. : Step 1 : We will create a input form for the user to enter the data. The HTML code is as follows. (It is the same HTML form which we have discussed in the last section)

HTML Document[input.html]

```
<!doctype html public "-//w3c//dtd html 4.0 transitional//en">
<html>
<head>
<title> Book Order Form </title>
</head>
<body>
<h3> Enter the Book Data </h3>
<form method="post" action="http://localhost/php-examples/formdemo.php">
<table>
<tr>
<td>Sr.No.</td>
<td><input type="text" name="SLNo"></td>
</tr>
<tr>
 <td>Book name</td>
 <td><input type="text" name="BName"></td>
</tr>
<tr>
 <td>Publisher</td>
 <td><input type="text" name="PUBName"></td>
</tr>
<tr>
 <td>Price</td>
```

```
<td><input type="text" name="Price"></td>
</tr>
<td>Quantity</td>
<td><input type="text" name="Qty"></td>
</tr>
<tr>
<td><input type="submit" value="Submit"></td>
<td><input type="submit" value="Clear"></td>
</tr>
</table>
</form>
</body>
</html>
```

Step 2 : Following is a simple PHP script which displays the data and then writes it to the file.

PHP Document

```
<html>
<head>
<title>Book Information</title>
</head>
<body>
<?php
$BName=$_POST["BName"];
$PUBName=$_POST["PUBName"];
$Price=$_POST["Price"];
$Qty=$_POST["Qty"];
?>
<center>
<h3> Book Data </h3>
<table border=1>
<tr>
<th>Book name</th>
<th>Publisher</th>
<th>Price</th>
<th>Quantity</th>
</tr>
<tr>
<td><?php print ("$BName"); ?></td>
<td><?php print ("$PUBName"); ?></td>
<td><?php printf("%3.2f",$Price); ?></td>
<td><?php printf("%d",$Qty); ?></td>
</tr>
</table>
</center>
```

```
<?php
$my_file = 'file.txt';
$file_handle = fopen($my_file, 'a') or die('Cannot open file:  '.$my_file);
fwrite($file_handle, $BName);
fwrite($file_handle, "\r\n");
fwrite($file_handle, $PUBName);
fwrite($file_handle, "\r\n");
fwrite($file_handle, $Price);
fwrite($file_handle, "\r\n");
fwrite($file_handle, $Qty);
fclose($file_handle);
?>
<p>The contents are written to the file <u>file.txt<u></p>
</body>
</html>
```

Step 3 : Now open the web browser and type the address of the html file which you have created in step 1. On clicking the submit button on the this input form the data will be displayed as follows -

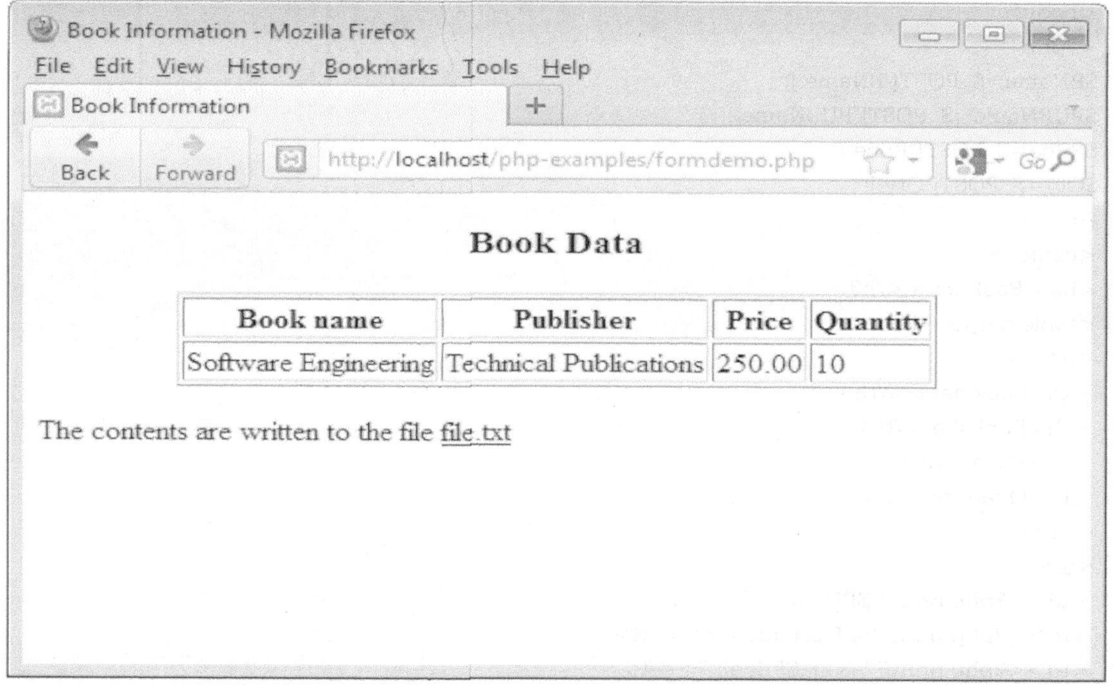

Step 4 : Open the current directory folder(The folder in which your html and PHP scripts are present) . You will obtain a text file file.txt. Just Open the file and see the contents. I have got the following contents -

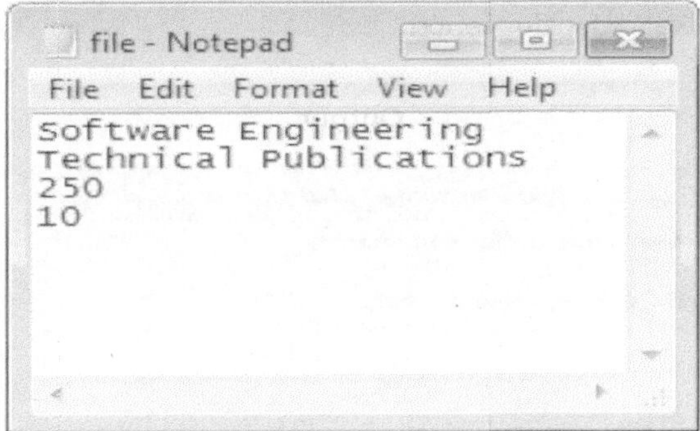

Review Questions

1. *Explain different file modes in PHP.*
2. *Explain how to perform read and write operations in PHP ?*

7.14 Cookies

AU : May-18

In this section we will discuss how to create and read cookies.

7.14.1 Introduction to Cookies

- Cookie is a small file that server embeds in the user's machine.
- Cookies are used to identify the users.
- A cookie consists of **a name** and **a textual value**. A cookie is created by some software system on the server.
- In every HTTP communication between browser and server a header is included. The header stores the information about the message.
- The header part of http contains the cookies.
- There can be one or more cookies in browser and server communication.

7.14.2 PHP Support for Cookies

- PHP can be used to create and retrieve the cookies.
- The cookie can be set in PHP using the function called setcookie()
- The syntax for the cookie is -

```
setcookie(name,value,expire_period,path,domain)
```

- Following is a simple PHP document which illustrates how to set the cookies -

PHP Document[CookieSetDemo.php]

```
<?php
$Cookie_period=time()+60*60*24*30;
```

```
setcookie("Myname", "Monika", $Cookie_period);
?>
```

Output

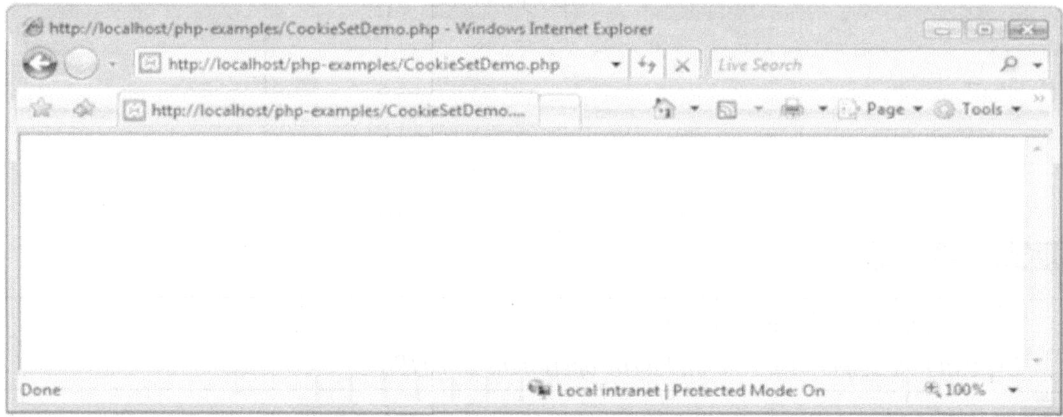

Note that you have got the blank screen it indicates that the cookie is set. In above PHP document we have set the PHP script for one month. Just observer the third parameter of the setcookie function.

Now you can retrieve the cookie and read the value to ensure whether or the cookie is set.

PHP Document[CookieReadDemo.php]

```
<html>
 <head><title>Reading Cookies</title>
<body>
 <?php
if (isset($_COOKIE["Myname"]))
  echo "<h3>Welcome " . $_COOKIE["Myname"]."!!!</h3>";
else
  echo "<h3>Welcome guest!</h3>";
?>
</body>
</html>
```

Output

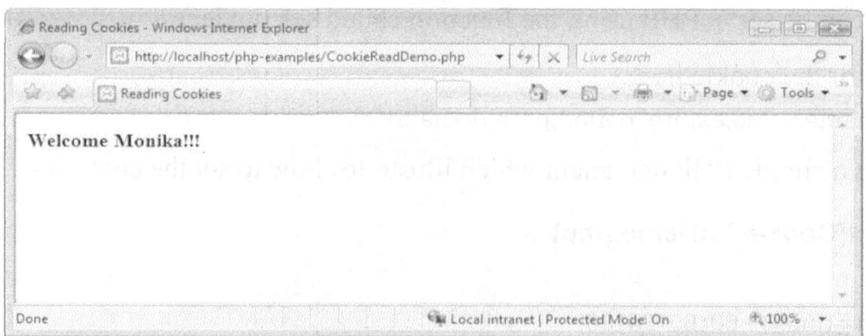

Program Explanation

The isset function is used for checking whether or not the cookie is set. Then using the $_COOKIE the value of the cookie can be retrieved.

Review Questions

1. *What are cookies and how are they used ?* **AU : May 18, Marks 3**

7.15 Connecting to Database

7.15.1 Connecting to Database

The PHP function **mysql_connect** connects to the MySQL server. There are three parameters that can be passed to this function. For example –

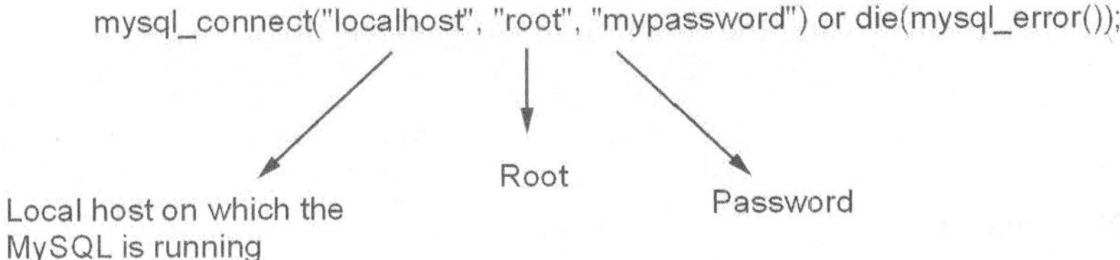

For example

```
<?php
// Make a MySQL Connection
$conn=mysql_connect("localhost:3306/mydb","root","mypassword");
if(!$conn)
{
die('error in connection'.mysql_error());
}
else
{
print"connected";
}
mysql_close($conn); //closing the database
?>
```

The database can be closed using the function **mysql_close**

7.15.2 Creating Database

We can create a database using the function **mysql_query**. The **mysql_error()** function is used to obtain the error messages if any command gets failed.

For example -

```
<?php
// Make a MySQL Connection
$conn=mysql_connect("localhost ","root","mypassword");
if(!$conn)
```

```
{
die('error in connection'.mysql_error());
}
//Create a database
if(mysql_query("CREATE DATABASE mydb",$conn))
    {
    print "Database created";
    }
    else
    {
     print "Error creating database: " . mysql_error();
    }
mysql_close($conn); //closing the database
?>
```

7.15.3 Selecting Database

The database can be selected using the function **mysql_select_db().**

For example -

```
<?php
// Make a MySQL Connection
$conn=mysql_connect("localhost:3306/mydb ","root","mypassword");
if(!$conn)
{
die('error in connection'.mysql_error());
}
//Select a database
mysql_select_db("mydb", $conn);
mysql_close($conn); //closing the database
?>
```

7.15.4 Listing Database

There are various databases present in the MySQL which can be displayed using the function **mysql_list_db().**

For example -

```
<?php
// Make a MySQL Connection
$conn=mysql_connect("localhost:3306/mydb ","root","mypassword");
if(!$conn)
{
die('error in connection'.mysql_error());
}
```

```
//Show databases
$db_lists=mysql_list_db($conn)
while($i=$mysql_fetch_object($db_list))
{
echo $i->Database. "\n"; //Present Databases will be displayed
}
mysql_close($conn); //closing the database
?>
```

7.15.5 Listing Table Names

The tables are present inside the databases. The function **mysql_list_tables** function is used to display the tables present in the database or we can use **mysql_query**

For example -

```
<?php
// Make a MySQL Connection
$conn=mysql_connect("localhost ","root","mypassword");
if(!$conn)
{
die('error in connection'.mysql_error());
}
$table_list=mysql_query("SHOW TABLES FROM mydb",$con)
if(!$table_list)
{
 print "Error!!! " . mysql_error();
}
while($i=$mysql_fetch_row($table_list))
{
echo $i[0]. "\n"; //Listing the tables
}
mysql_close($conn); //closing the database
?>
```

7.15.6 Creating a Table

Before creating the table a database must be created and within which the table can be created. Note that before creating a table the desired database must be selected.

```
<?php
// Make a MySQL Connection
$conn=mysql_connect("localhost ","root","mypassword");
if(!$conn)
{
die('error in connection'.mysql_error());
}
```

```
//Create a database
if(mysql_query("CREATE DATABASE mydb",$con))
    {
    print "Database created";
    }
    else
    {
    print "Error creating database: " . mysql_error();
    }
mysql_select_db("mydb",$conn); //before creating table select the database
$query="CREATE TABLE my_table
       (
        id INT(4),
        name VARCHAR(20)
        )";
mysql_query($query,$conn);//Execution of Query

mysql_close($conn); //closing the database
?>
```

7.15.7 Inserting Data

Using PHP we can insert the data in the database created in the MySQL.

For example -

```
<?php
// Make a MySQL Connection
$conn=mysql_connect("localhost","root","mypassword");
if(!$conn)
{
die('error in connection'.mysql_error());
}
mysql_select_db("mydb",$conn); //select the database
$query=" INSERT INTO my_table (id,name)  VALUES(1,'SHILPA')";
mysql_query($query,$conn);//Execution of Query
$query=" INSERT INTO my_table (id,name)  VALUES(2,'MONIKA')";
mysql_query($query,$conn);//Execution of Query

mysql_close($conn); //closing the database
?>
```

Sometimes values that can be inserted in the table can be obtained from some another script and these values might be present in the variables. Insertion of such data can be done using $_POST variables. It is as shown below -

```
<?php
// Make a MySQL Connection
```

```
$conn=mysql_connect("localhost","root","mypassword");
if(!$conn)
{
die('error in connection'.mysql_error());
}
mysql_select_db("mydb",$conn); //select the database
$query=" INSERT INTO my_table (id,name)
   VALUES('$_POST[MyID]','$_POST[MyName]')";
mysql_query($query,$conn);//Execution of Query

mysql_close($conn); //closing the database
?>
```

We can display these records using the SELECT query. For example-

```
<?php
// Make a MySQL Connection
$conn=mysql_connect("localhost ","root","mypassword");
if(!$conn)
{
die('error in connection'.mysql_error());
}
mysql_select_db("mydb",$conn); //select the database
//Execution of Query for displaying the data
$result=mysql_query("SELECT * FROM my_table");
while($row = mysql_fetch_array($result))
      {
        echo $row['id'] . " " . $row['name'];         //Each record will be displayed line by line

        echo "<br />";
      }
mysql_close($conn); //closing the database
?>
```

7.15.8 Altering Table

The ALTER table command is useful for various reasons such as to add some columns in the existing table, to delete some column from the table, for changing the size of some field or to change the name of some column. In the following example we are adding one column named **addr** to the existing table **my_table**

```
<?php
// Make a MySQL Connection
$conn=mysql_connect("localhost","root","mypassword");
if(!$conn)
{
die('error in connection'.mysql_error());
}
```

```
mysql_select_db("mydb",$conn); //select the database
$query=" ALTER TABLE my_table ADD COLUMN addrVARCHAR(30)";
mysql_query($query,$conn);//Execution of Query
mysql_close($conn); //closing the database
?>
```

7.15.9 Deleting Database

We can delete the values from the database using the DELETE query.

For example -

```
<?php
// Make a MySQL Connection
$conn=mysql_connect("localhost","root","mypassword");
if(!$conn)
{
die('error in connection'.mysql_error());
}
mysql_select_db("mydb",$conn); //select the database
$query=" DELETE FROM my_table WHERE id=1";
mysql_query($query,$conn);//Execution of Query
mysql_close($conn); //closing the database
?>
```

Similarly we can delete a database using the query DROP.

For example -

```
<?php
// Make a MySQL Connection
$conn=mysql_connect("localhost","root","mypassword");
if(!$conn)
{
die('error in connection'.mysql_error());
}
mysql_select_db("mydb",$conn); //select the database
$query=" DROP DATABASE mydb";
mysql_query($query,$conn);//Execution of Query
mysql_close($conn); //closing the database
?>
```

Examples

Ex. 7.15.1 Write a PHP script to create a new database table with 4 fields of your choice and perform following database operations

1. Insert 2. Delete 3. Update 4. Display

Sol. : We will create a table in the database test. The name of the table ismytable. Then we will insert the record into the table using the INSERT command, update particular field of the record using the command UPDATE and delete the record using the command DELETE.

The PHP script is as follows -

PHPDocument[DBDemo.php]

```
<?php
// Make a MySQL Connection
mysql_connect("localhost", "root", "mypassword") or die(mysql_error());
mysql_select_db("test") or die(mysql_error());
echo "Connected to database!";
mysql_query("CREATE TABLE mytable(id INT NOT NULL AUTO_INCREMENT, PRIMARY KEY(id),
name VARCHAR(30),
phoneINT,emailIdVARCHAR(30))")
or die(mysql_error());
print "<br/>";
echo "Table Created!";

// Insert a row of information into the table
mysql_query("INSERT INTO mytable
(name, phone,emailId) VALUES('Priyanka', '11111','abc123@gmail.com' ) ")
or die(mysql_error());

mysql_query("INSERT INTO mytable
(name, phone,emailId) VALUES('Kumar', '22222','pqr11@yahoo.com' ) ")
or die(mysql_error());

mysql_query("INSERT INTO mytable
(name, phone,emailId) VALUES('Archana', '33333','xyz@rediffmail.com' ) ")
or die(mysql_error());
print "<br/>";
echo "Data Inserted!";
$result =mysql_query("SELECT * FROM mytable")
or die(mysql_error());
print "<br/>";
print "<b>User Database</b>";
echo "<table border='1'>";
echo "<tr><th>ID</th><th>Name</th><th>Phone</th><th>Email-ID</th>
</tr>";
while($row = mysql_fetch_array( $result ))
    {
    // Print out the contents of each row into a table
    echo "<tr><td>";
```

```
    echo $row['id'];
    echo "</td><td>";
    echo $row['name'];
    echo "</td><td>";
    echo $row['phone'];
    echo "</td><td>";
    echo $row['emailId'];
    echo "</td></tr>";
}
echo "</table>";
$result = mysql_query("UPDATE mytable SET phone='55555' WHERE phone='22222'")
or die(mysql_error());

print "<br/>";
echo "Data Updated!";
$result =mysql_query("SELECT * FROM mytable")
or die(mysql_error());
print "<br/>";
print "<b>User Database</b>";
echo "<table border='1'>";
echo "<tr><th>ID</th><th>Name</th><th>Phone</th><th>Email-ID</th>
</tr>";
while($row = mysql_fetch_array( $result ))
{
// Print out the contents of each row into a table
echo "<tr><td>";
echo $row['id'];
echo "</td><td>";
echo $row['name'];
echo "</td><td>";
echo $row['phone'];
echo "</td><td>";
echo $row['emailId'];
echo "</td></tr>";
}
echo "</table>";
$result = mysql_query("DELETE FROM mytable WHERE phone='33333'")
or die(mysql_error());
print "<br/>";
echo "Data Deleted!";
$result =mysql_query("SELECT * FROM mytable")
or die(mysql_error());
print "<br/>";
print "<b>User Database</b>";
```

```
echo "<table border='1'>";
echo "<tr><th>ID</th><th>Name</th><th>Phone</th><th>Email-ID</th>
</tr>";
while($row = mysql_fetch_array( $result ))
    {
    // Print out the contents of each row into a table
    echo "<tr><td>";
    echo $row['id'];
    echo "</td><td>";
    echo $row['name'];
    echo "</td><td>";
    echo $row['phone'];
    echo "</td><td>";
    echo $row['emailId'];
    echo "</td></tr>";
}
echo "</table>";
?>
```

Output

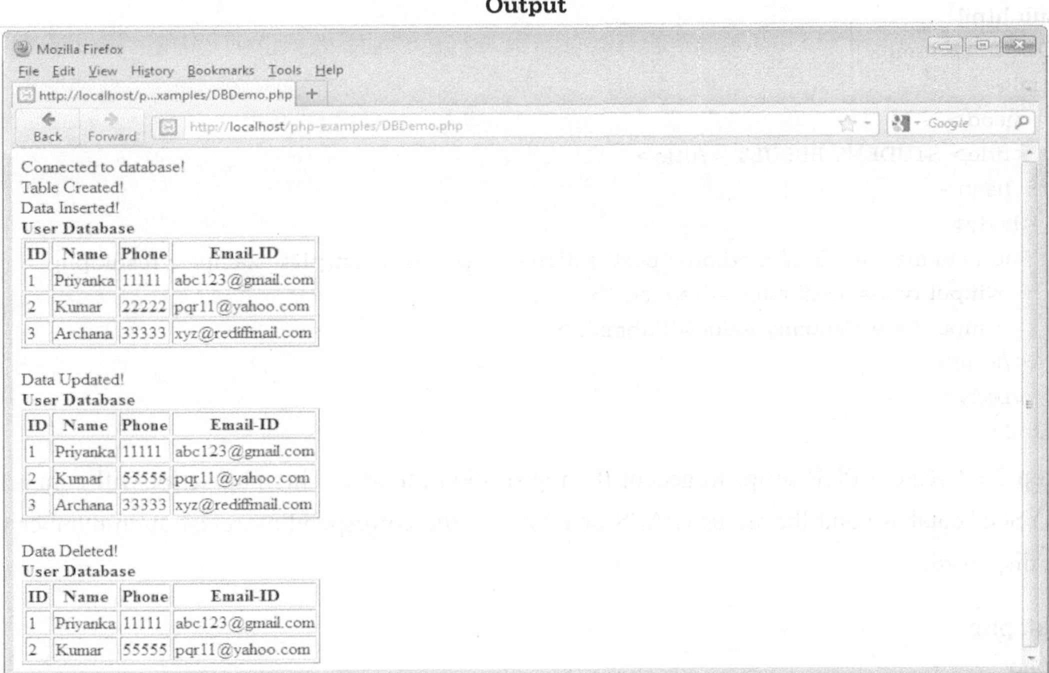

Ex. 7.15.2 Create a HTML form "result.html" with a text box and a submit button to accept registration number of the student. Write a "result.php" code to check the status of the result from the table to display whether the student has "PASS" or "FAIL" status. Assume that the MYSQL database "my_db" has the table "result_table" with two columns REG NO and STATUS **AU : May-13, Marks 8**

Sol. :

Step 1 : Create a database named my_db. Create a table result_table for this database and insert the values in this table. The table is created as follows –

Sr. No.	REG_NO	STATUS
1	101	PASS
2	102	FAIL
3	103	PASS
4	104	FAIL
5	105	PASS

Table 7.15.1

Step 2 : Create an HTML form to accept the registration number, the HTML document is as follows -

result.html

```
<!DOCTYPE html>
<html>
    <head>
     <title> STUDENT RESULT </title>
    </head>
    <body>
     <form name="myform" method="post" action="http://localhost/php-examples/result.php">
        <input type="text" name="reg_no"/>
        <input type="submit" value="Submit"/>
     </form>
    </body>
</html>
```

Step 3 : Create a PHP script to accept the registration number. This php script will connect to MYSQL database and the status (PASS or FAIL) of the corresponding registration number will be displayed.

result.php

```
<?php
// Make a MySQL Connection
$conn=mysql_connect("localhost","root","");
if(!$conn)
{
die('error in connection'.mysql_error());
}
```

```
mysql_select_db("my_db",$conn); //select the database
//Execution of Query for displaying the data
$reg_no = intval($_POST['reg_no']);

$result=mysql_query("SELECT REG_NO,STATUS FROM result_table where REG_NO=$reg_no ");
 while($row = mysql_fetch_array($result))
  {
   echo $row['REG_NO'] . " is " . $row['STATUS'];
   echo "<br />";
  }
mysql_close($conn); //closing the database
?>
```

Step 4 : Load the HTML form created in Step 2 and click the submit button by entering some registration number.

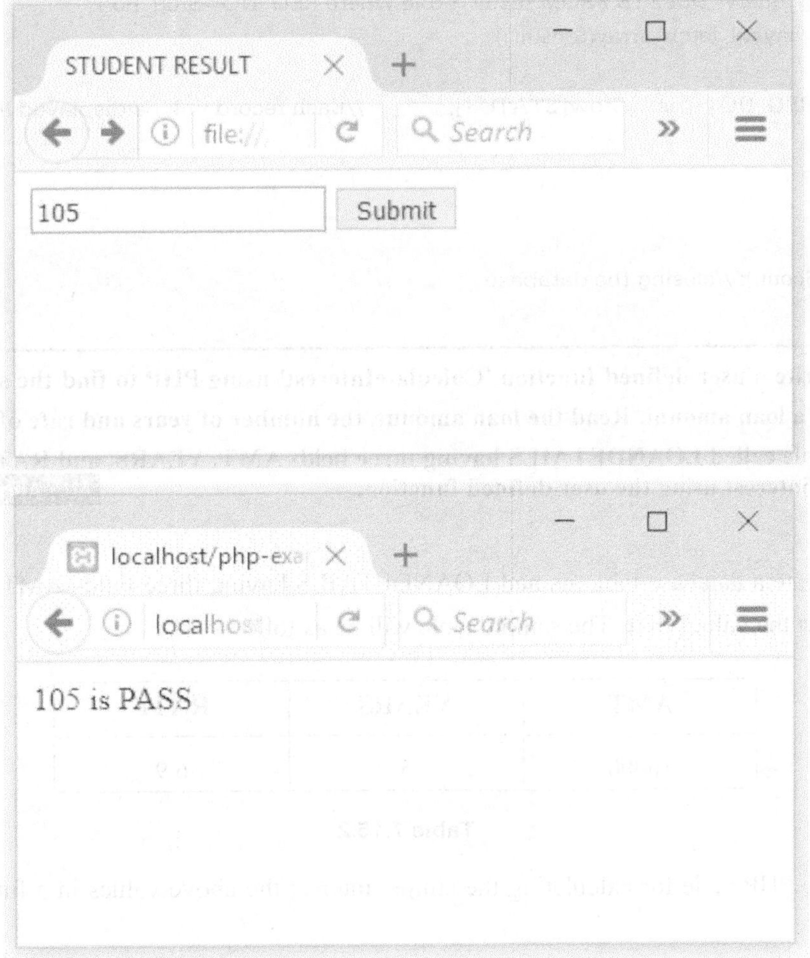

Ex. 7.15.3 Write a PHP program to delete a record from result_table(Refer example 7.15.2)

AU : May-13, Marks 8

Sol. :

```
<?php
// Make a MySQL Connection
$conn=mysql_connect("localhost","root","");
if(!$conn)
{
die('error in connection'.mysql_error());
}
mysql_select_db("my_db",$conn); //select the database
//Execution of Query for displaying the data
$reg_no = intval($_POST['reg_no']);

$result=mysql_query("DELETE FROM result_table where REG_NO=$reg_no");
 while($row = mysql_fetch_array($result))
  {
   echo $row['REG_NO'] . " is " . $row['STATUS'];          //Each record will be displayed line by line

   echo "<br />";
  }

mysql_close($conn); //closing the database
?>
```

Ex. 7.15.4 Write a user defined function 'CalculateInterest' using PHP to find the simple interest to be paid for a loan amount. Read the loan amount, the number of years and rate of interest from a database table called LOANDETAILS having three fields AMT, YEARS, and RATE, and Calculate the interest using the user defined function.

AU : April-14, Marks 8

Sol. :

Step 1 : Create a database table named LOANDETAILS having three fields AMT, YEARS and RATE. Insert the values in it. The sample table will be as follows –

AMT	YEARS	RATE
10000	5	6.9

Table 7.15.2

Step 2 : The PHP code for calculating the simple interest the above values in a function will be as follows -

Interest.php

```
<?php
function CalculateInterest()
{
    // Make a MySQL Connection
    $conn=mysql_connect("localhost","root","");
    if(!$conn)
    {
     die('error in connection'.mysql_error());
    }
    mysql_select_db("my_db",$conn); //select the database
    //Execution of Query for displaying the data
    $result=mysql_query("SELECT * FROM LOANDETAILS");
    $row = mysql_fetch_array($result);
    $amount= $row['AMT'];
    $rate= $row['RATE'];
    $years= $row['YEARS'];
     $interest=($amount * $rate *$years)/100;
    mysql_close($conn); //closing the database
    return $interest;
}
print "Simple Interest =".CalculateInterest();
?>
```

Output

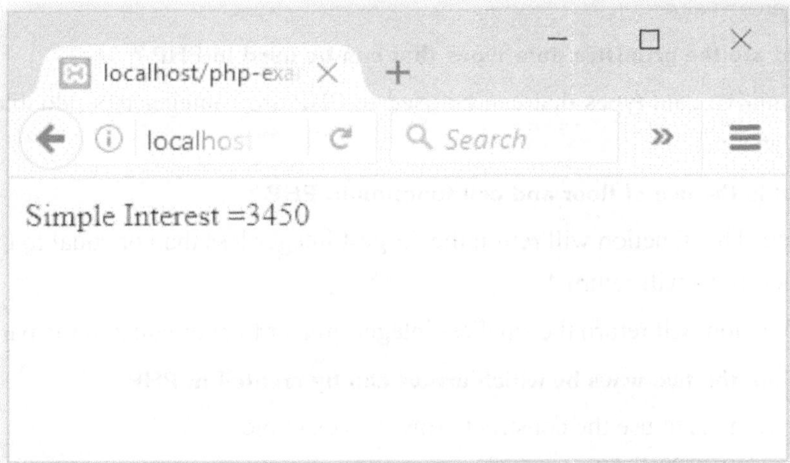

Review Question

1. *Write and explain various PHP modules to insert, delete and update the records in MySQL database.*

Two Marks Questions with Answers

Q.1 What is PHP stands for ?

Ans. : The PHP stands for PHP:Hypertext Preprocessor

Q.2 Explain the working of PHP processor.

Ans. : The PHP processor works in two modes. If the PHP processor finds XHTML tags in the PHP script then the code is simply copied to the output file. But when the PHP processor finds the PHP code in the script then that code is simply interpreted and the output is copied to the output file

Q.3 How will you embed the PHP code in the HTML?

Ans. : The PHP code can be embedded in the HTML by using <? and >. The code must be enclosed within <? >

Q.4 How do you write the comment statements in PHP ?

Ans. : The comments in PHP can be #, // or /* .... */

Q.5 What do you understand by variable in PHP. Explain how a value can be assigned to the variable ?

Ans. : The variables are the entities that are used to assign the values to the variables. The value can be assigned to the variable in the following manner -

```
$variable_name=value
```

Q.6 What are the primitive data types that can be used in PHP ?

Ans. : The primitive data types that can be used in PHP are - integer type, double type, string type and boolean type.

Q.7 What is the use of floor and ceil function in PHP ?

Ans. : **1. floor :** This function will return the largest integer less than or equal to the parameter. For example floor(4.9) will return 4

2. ceil : This function will return the smallest integer greater than or equal to the parameter.

Q.8 Explain the two ways by which arrays can be created in PHP.

Ans. : The first way is to use the construct array. For example -

```
$mylist=array(10,20,30,40,50);
```

The second way is to assign the value directly to the array. For example -

```
$mylist[0]=10;
```

Q.9 How will you construct the empty array ?

Ans. : The empty array can be created using the array construct. For example -

```
$mylist=array();
```

Q.10 What is the use of foreach function in PHP ?

Ans. : The foreach function is used to iterate through all the elements of the loop. The syntax of foreach statement is as follows -

```
foreach($array as $value)
{
statements to be executed
}
```

Q.11 What is the use of asort() and ksort() function ?

Ans. : The asort() function sorts an array by the values. But the original keys are kept. The ksort function sorts the array by keys but each value's original key is retained.

Q.12 Explain the concept of regular expressions in PHP.

Ans. : The pattern matching technique which is used in PHP is of two types - The first one is based on POSIX regular expression and the another is based on Perl regular expression.

Q.13 Explain the use of prg_match in PHP.

Ans. : There is a preg_match function which is used to check the matching of the pattern from the text. It takes two parameters the first parameter is the pattern to be matched and the second parameter is the text against which the pattern is to be matched.

Q.14 What are Cookies ? Give its uses. **AU : Dec.-15**

Ans. : • Cookie is a small file that server embeds in the user's machine.

- A cookie consists of **a name** and **a textual value.** A cookie is created by some software system on the server.

Uses

- Cookies are used to identify the users.
- In every HTTP communication between browser and server a header is included. The header stores the information about the message. Thus the header part of http contains the cookies.

Q.15 Name any four built in functions in PHP. **AU : Dec.-15**

Ans. :

Function	Purpose
Floor	The largest integer less than or equal to the parameter is returned. For example floor(4.9) will return 4,
Ceil	The smallest integer greater than or equal to the parameter is returned. For example ceil(4.9) will return 5,
strlen(string1)	It finds the total number of characters in the string
array()	Creates an array.

Q.16 When should the super global arrays in PHP be used ? Which super global array in PHP would contain a HTML Form's POST data ? AU : May-16

Ans. : • When we need to create an array which is accessible by all the elements regardless of its scope, then, PHP stores all global variables in an array called $GLOBALS[*index*]. The ***index*** holds the name of the variable.

- PHP $_POST is widely used to collect form data after submitting an HTML form with method="post".

Q.17 What is PHP ? AU : Dec.-16

Ans. : Refer Q.1 and Q.2.

Q.18 Differentiate echo() and print() function.

Ans. : Both the echo and print are used to display output in PHP. The difference between the two is

print()	echo()
Print doesn't pass multiple argument	echo can pass multiple string separated as (,)
print always returns 1	echo does not return any value.
It is slower than echo.	It is faster than print

Q.19 What do you mean by QueryString in PhP ?

Ans. : QueryString is a string obtained when we pass data from one page to another. The query string is visible to the user if GET method is used.

Q.20 How can a PHP program determine the type of browser that a web client is using ? AU : May -17

Ans. :

```
<html>
<body>
<?php
echo $_SERVER['HTTP_USER_AGENT'];
$browser = get_browser();
print($browser);
?>
</body>
</html>
```

Q.21 List out the advantages of PHP. AU : Dec -17

Ans. : i) It is widely used as a server side web development language.

ii) It is an open source technology and help the web developers by support community and abundant extension library.

iii) It is easy to use due to C like syntax.

iv) It is relatively fast.

v) It has built in database connection modules.

vi) It can be run on many platforms including Windows, Linux and Mac.

❑❑❑

Notes

Unit IV

8 XML

Syllabus

XML : Basic XML - Document Type Definition - XML Schema DOM and Presenting XML, XML Parsers and Validation, XSL and XSLT Transformation, News Feed (RSS and ATOM)

Contents

8.1 Introduction to XML

- XML stands for e**X**tensible **M**arkup **L**anguage.
- This scripting language is similar to HTML. That means, this scripting language contains various tags. But these tags are not predefined tags, in-fact user can define his own tags.
- Thus HTML is designed for **representation of data** on the web page whereas the XML is designed for **transport or to store data.**

Uses of XML

1. XML is used to display the meta contents i.e. XML describes the content of the document.
2. XML is useful in exchanging data between the applications.
3. The data can be extracted from database and can be used in more than one application. Different applications can perform different tasks on this data.

Advantages of XML

1. XML document is human readable and we can edit any XML document in simple text editors.
2. The XML document is language neutral. That means a Java program can generate an XML document and this document can be parsed by Perl.
3. Every XML document has a tree structure. Hence complex data can be arranged systematically and can be understood in simple manner.
4. XML files are independent of an operating system.

Goals of XML

Following are the goals of XML -

1. User must be able to define and use his own tag. This allows us to restrict the use of the set of tags defined by proprietary vendors.
2. Allow user to build his own tag library based on his web requirement.
3. Allow user to define the formatting rules for the user defined tags.
4. XML must support for storage or transport of data.

Features of XML

Following are some features which are most suitable for creating web related applications.

- XML is EXtesible Markup Language intended for **transport** or storage of the data.
- The most important feature of XML is that user is able to **define and use his own tag.**
- XML contains only data and does not contain any formatting information. Hence document developers **can decide how to display the data.**

- XML permits the document writer to create the tags for any type of information. Due to this virtually any kind of information can be such as mathematical formulae, chemical structures, or some other kind of data can be described using XML.
- Searching sorting, rendering or manipulating the XML document is possible using Extended Stylesheet Language (XSL).
- The XML document can be validated using some external tools.
- Some commonly used web browsers like Internet Explorer and Firefox Mozilla provide support to the tags in XML. Hence XML is not at all vendor specific or browser specific.

Difference between XML and HTML

Sr. No.	HTML	XML
1.	HTML stands for Hypertext Markup Language.	XML stands for eXtensible Markup Language.
2.	HTML is designed to display data with the focus on look and feel of data.	XML is used to transport and store data, with focus on what data is.
3.	HTML is case insensitive.	XML is case sensitive.
4.	HTML has predefined tags.	XML has custom tags can be defined and the tags are invented by the author of the XML document.
5.	As HTML is for displaying the data it is static.	As XML is for carrying the data it is dynamic.
6.	It can not preserve white space.	It can preserve the white space.

8.2 Building Block of XML Document

Elements and Attributes

- Various building blocks of XML are -

1. Elements

The basic entity is **element.** The elements are used for defining the tags. The elements typically consist of opening and closing tag. Mostly only one element is used to define a single tag.

2. Attribute

The attributes are generally used to specify the values of the element. These are specified within the double quotes.

For example -

```
<flag type="True">
```

The type attribute of the element flag is having the value True.

3. CDATA

CDATA stands for Character Data. This character data will be parsed by the parser.

4. PCDATA

It stands for Parsed Character Data (i.e. text).

8.2.1 Declaring Elements

- The element type data can be declared using the **ELEMENT**.
- The syntax for defining the ELEMENT is,

```
<!ELEMENTelt_name (elt1,elt2,..)>
```

XML Document [Internal_Elt.xml]

```
<?xml version="1.0" encoding="UTF-8"?>
<!DOCTYPE student [
<!ELEMENT student (name,address,std,br,marks)>
<!ELEMENT name (#PCDATA)>
<!ELEMENT address (#PCDATA)>
<!ELEMENTstd (#PCDATA)>
<!ELEMENTbr EMPTY>
<!ELEMENT marks (#PCDATA)>
]>
<student>
        <name>Anand</name>
        <address>Pune</address>
        <std>Second</std>
        <br />
        <marks>70 percent</marks>
</student>
```

Here we are defining the DTD internally

Output

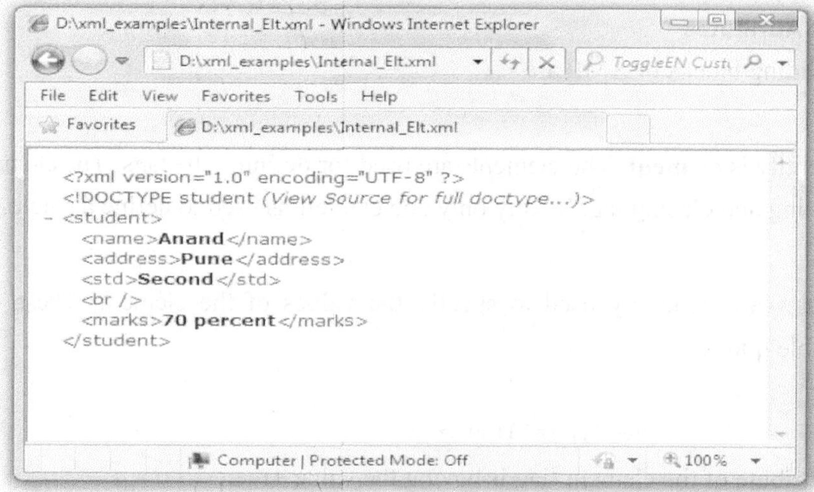

- The ELEMENT must be defined in the beginning of the XML file. It must be enclosed within ***<!DOCTYPEroot_element ....>***
- There are various ways by which the actual element can be **defined**. It is enlisted in the following table -

Category	Syntax	Description
Empty	<!ELEMENT elt_nameEMPTY>	Empty elements can be declared.
Character data	<!ELEMENT elt_name (#PCDATA)>	Character data can be declared.
Any content	<!ELEMENT elt_nameANY>	Any combination of data can be declared.
Sequence	<!ELEMENTelt_name(elt1,elt2,...)>	Sequence of elements that must appear in specific order.

- Sometimes we can define the ELEMENT along with the iterator characters. The iterator characters are the special character which are associated with some meaning.
- Some commonly used iterator characters are as given below -

Iterator character	Meaning	Example
?	The preceding choice appears zero or once.	<!ELEMENT(marks?)> The child element marks can appear for zero or one time.
*	The preceding choice appears for any number of time(zero or more times).	<!ELEMENT (person*)> The person can appear for any number of times.
+	The preceding choice appears for at least once (one or more times).	<!ELEMENT (person+)> The person can appear for at least once.

8.2.2 Declaring Attributes

- The attribute type declaration is done using the string ATTLIST.
- The attribute type specifies the type of data which can be used for specifying the attribute. The syntax for specifying the attribute declaration is as follows -

```
<!ATTLISTelement_nameattribute_nameattribute_typedefault_value>
```

- **For example**

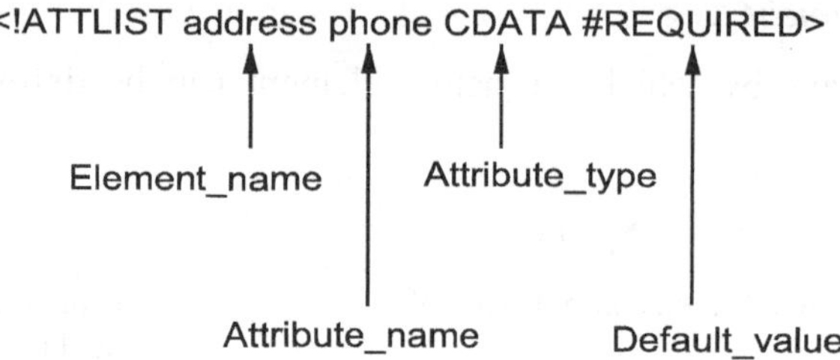

- The XML document containing attributes is as given below -

XML Document [Internal_Attr.xml]

```
<?xml version="1.0" encoding="UTF-8"?>
<!DOCTYPE student [
<!ELEMENT student (name,address,std,marks)>
<!ELEMENT name (#PCDATA)>
<!ELEMENT address (#PCDATA)>
<!ELEMENTstd (#PCDATA)>
<!ELEMENT marks (#PCDATA)>

<!ATTLIST address phone CDATA #REQUIRED>

]>
<student>
	<name>Anand</name>
	<address phone="9898123123">Pune</address>
	<std>Tenth</std>
	<br />
	<marks>70 percent</marks>
</student>
```

Using **ATTLIST** the attribute can be defined.

Output

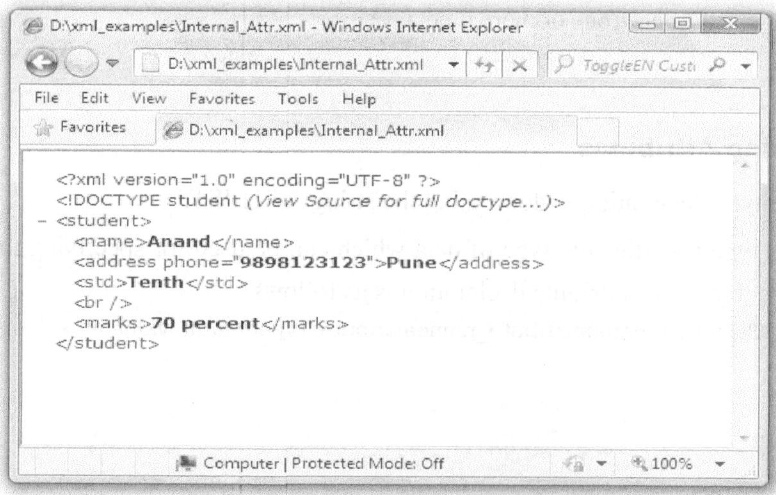

- Following are some **attribute type** –

Attribute_Type	Syntax	Description
Character data	CDATA	Attribute value is character data.
Enumerated	(str1|str2|...)	Attribute value must be one from an enumerated list.
Identifier	ID	Attribute value is a unique id.
Identifier reference	IDREF	Attribute value is the id of another element.
Identifier reference list	IDREFS	Attribute value is a list of other ids.
Name token	NMTOKEN	Attribute value is a valid XML name.
Name token list	NMTOKENS	Attribute value is a list of valid XML names.

The default_values are -

Default_Value	Meaning
Value	Default value can be defined. For example - <!ATTLIST Index flag="0"> In XML document <Index flag="1" /> If the **flag** is not assigned with any value then by default it will be 0.
#REQUIRED	Required attribute forces the attribute to be present even if there is no default value.
#IMPLIED	The default value is not provided and attribute can be optionally used.
#FIXED value	The attribute value is fixed and cannot be changed.

8.2.3 Declaring Entities

- The attribute type declaration is done using the string **ENTITY**.
- Inside the XML file at the beginning the entity can be defined using the <!DOCTYPE ...> and with the help of string ENTITY. Following XML document demonstrates it -

XML Document [EntityDemo.xml]

```
<?xml version="1.0" encoding="UTF-8"?>
<!DOCTYPE Book[
<!ENTITY writer "Puntambekar">
<!ENTITYnbsp " ">
<!ENTITY title "Web Technologies">
```

```
]>
<Book>&writer; &title;</Book>
```

Output

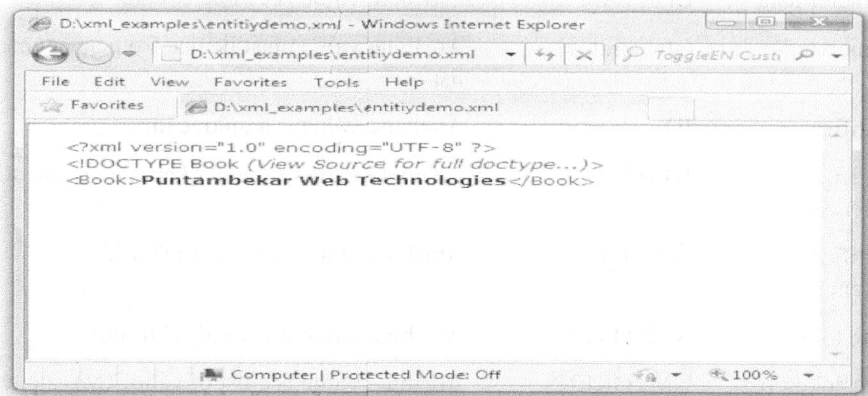

Note that we can define the predefined entities ** ** along with the other entity declaration.

The entity can be used using following syntax.

```
&name_of_entity;
```

In above script we have used two entities namely **writer** and **title**. For displaying the space within these two entities we have used an entity **nbsp** and for defining it we have used **#160.**

University Question

1. *What are the features of elements and attributes in XML ?*

8.3 Rules

- **Rules that must be followed while writing XML -**

  Here are some rules that must be followed while writing the XML programs -

1. XML is a **case sensitive**. For example -

   ```
   <hobby>I like drawing</Hobby>or
   <Hobby>I like drawing</hobby>
   ```

   is not allowed because the words **hobby** and **Hobby** are treated differently.

2. In XML each **start tag** must have **matching end tag**. For example-

   ```
   <staring> XML is funny to write
   <simple> It is simple to implement </simple>
   ```

   That means a closing tag is a must.

3. The elements in XML must be **properly nested**. For example-

   ```
   <one><two>Hello how are you?</one></two>   is wrong but
   <one><two>Hello how are you?</two></one>   is correct
   ```

8.4 Namespace

AU : May-10,12, Marks 8

- Sometimes we need to create two different elements by the same name. The xml document allows us to create **different elements** which are having the **common name**. This technique is known as **namespace**.
- In some web documents it becomes necessary to have the same name for two different elements. Here different elements mean the elements which are intended for different purposes. In such a case support for namespace technique is very much helpful.
- **For example :** Consider the following xml document -

namespacedemo.xml

```
<File-Description>
    <text fname="input.txt">
        <describe>It is a text file</describe>
    </text>
    <text fname="flower.jpg">
        <describe>It is an image file</describe>
    </text>
</File-Description>
```

The above document does not produce any error although the element **text** is used for two different attribute values. The output will be,

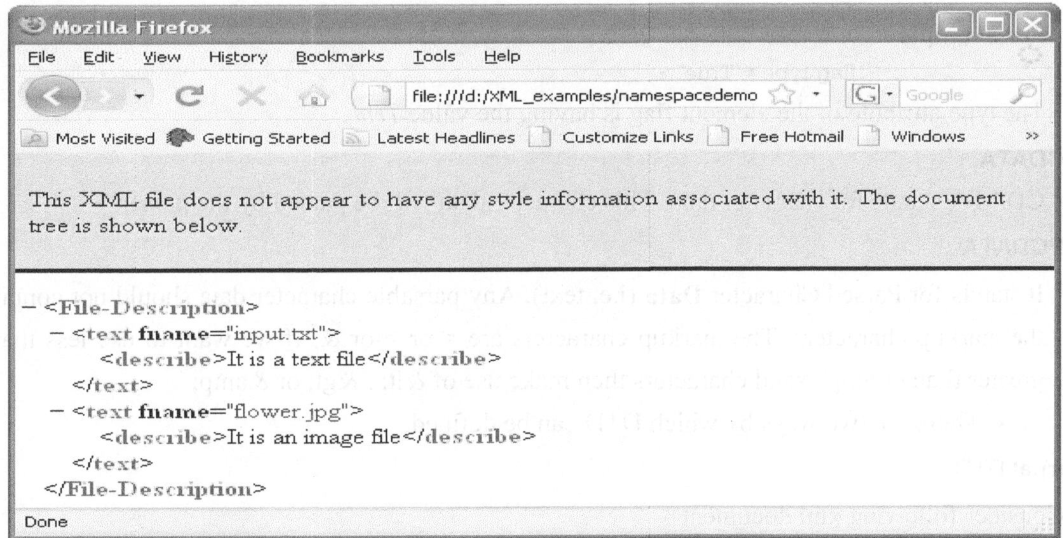

University Questions

1. *Why should namespaces be used in XML ? Explain with an example.* AU : May-10, Marks 8
2. *Explain the role of XML name space with examples.* AU : May-12, Marks 8

8.5 Document Type Definition

AU : May-11,19 Marks 13

- The document type definition is used to define the basic building block of any xml document.
- Using DTD we can specify the various elements types, attributes and their relationship with one another.
- Basically DTD is used to specify the set of rules for structuring data in any XML file.
- **For example :** If we want to put some information about some students in XML file then, generally we use tag **student** followed by his/her **name, address, standard and marks.** That means we are actually specifying the manner by which the information should be arranged in the XML file. And for this purpose the Document Type Definition is used.
- Various building blocks of XML are –

1. Elements

The basic entity is **element.** The elements are used for defining the tags. The elements typically consist of opening and closing tag. Mostly only one element is used to define a single tag.

2. Attribute

The attributes are generally used to specify the values of the element. These are specified within the double quotes.

For example -

```
<flag type="True">
```

The type attribute of the element flag is having the value *True*.

3. CDATA

CDATA stands for character data. This character data will be parsed by the parser.

4. PCDATA

It stands for Parsed Character **Data** (i.e. text). Any parsable character data should not contain the markup characters. The markup characters are < or > or &. If we want to use less than, greater than or ampersand characters then make use of < , > or &

- There are two ways by which DTD can be defined.

Internal DTD

Consider following xml document –

XML Document [DTDDemo1.xml]

```
<?xml version="1.0" encoding="UTF-8"?>
<!DOCTYPE student [
<!ELEMENT student (name,address,std,marks)>
<!ELEMENT name (#PCDATA)>
<!ELEMENT address (#PCDATA)>
<!ELEMENT std (#PCDATA)>
<!ELEMENT marks (#PCDATA)>
```

Here we are defining the DTD internally

```
]>
<student>
<name>Anand</name>
        <address>Pune</address>
        <std>Second</std>
        <marks>70 percent</marks>
</student>
```

Output

This XML file does not appear to have any style information associated with it. The document tree is shown below.

```
– <student>
     <name>Anand</name>
     <address>Pune</address>
     <std>Second</std>
     <marks>70 percent</marks>
  </student>
```

External DTD

In this type, an external DTD file is created and its name must be specified in the corresponding XML file. Following XML document illustrates the use of external DTD.

Step 1 : Creation of **DTD file [*student.dtd*]**

Open some suitable text editor or a notepad. Type following code into it -

```
<!ELEMENT student (name,address,std,marks)>
<!ELEMENT name (#PCDATA)>
<!ELEMENT address (#PCDATA)>
<!ELEMENT std (#PCDATA)>
<!ELEMENT marks (#PCDATA)>
```

Now save this file as ***student.dtd***

Step 2 : Creation of XML document -

XML Document [*DTDDemo.xml*]

Now create a XML document as follows -

```
<?xml version="1.0"?>
<!DOCTYPE student SYSTEM "student.dtd">
<student>
        <name>Anand</name>
```

The external DTD file is created

```
        <address>Pune</address>
        <std>Second</std>
        <marks>70 percent</marks>
</student>
```

Step 3 : Using some web browser open the XML document.

Output

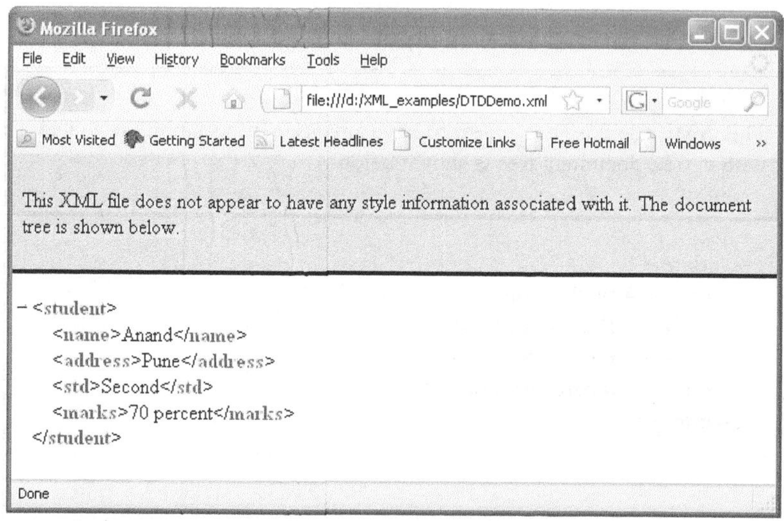

Ex. 8.5.1 : Create a DTD for a catalog of four stroke motorbikes, where each motor bike has the following child elements -make, model, year, colo, engine, chasis number and accessories. The engine element has the child elements engine number, number of cylinders, type of fuel. The accessories element has the attributes like disc brake,auto-start and radio, each of which is required and has the possible values yes and no.

Sol. :

automobile.dtd

```
<!ELEMENT Catalog (MotorBike)*>
<!ELEMENT MotorBike (make, model, year,color, engine,chasis-num,accessories ) >
<!ELEMENT make (#PCDATA)>
<!ELEMENT model (#PCDATA)>
<!ELEMENT year (#PCDATA)>
<!ELEMENT color (#PCDATA)>
<!ELEMENT engine (engin-num,cylinders-num,fuel-type)>
<!ELEMENT chasis-num (#PCDATA)>
<!ELEMENT accessories (#PCDATA)>
<!ATTLIST accessories disc-brake (yes|no) #REQUIRED
                auto-start (yes|no) #REQUIRED
                radio (yes|no) #REQUIRED>
```

Ex. 8.5.2 : Consider a hospital management system. Write a DTD program to consolidate and show the bill to be paid by the inpatients (Assume your own data).

AU : May-11, Marks 10

Sol. : Patients.xml

```
<?xml version="1.0" encoding="UTF-8"?>
<!DOCTYPE Patients [
<!ELEMENT Patients (Patient)*>
<!ELEMENT Patient (Name, Address,Test,Date,Doctor,Bill)>
<!ELEMENT Name (#PCDATA)>
<!ELEMENT Address (#PCDATA)>
<!ELEMENT Test (#PCDATA)>
<!ELEMENT Date (#PCDATA)>
<!ELEMENT Doctor (#PCDATA)>
<!ELEMENT Bill (#PCDATA)>
]>
<Patients>
        <Patient>
                <Name>Anuradha</Name>
                <Address>Pune</Address>
                <Test>ECG</Test>
                <Date>1-1-2010</Date>
                <Doctor>Mr.XYZ</Doctor>
                <Bill>Rs.500</Bill>
        </Patient>
        <Patient>
                <Name>Archana</Name>
                <Address>Mumbai</Address>
                <Test>Blood Test</Test>
                <Date>10-3-2010</Date>
                <Doctor>Mr.PQR</Doctor>
                <Bill>Rs.100</Bill>
        </Patient>
</Patients>
```

Merits of DTD

1. DTDs are used to define the structural components of XML document
2. These are relatively simple and compact.
3. DTDs can be defined inline and hence can be embedded directly in the XML document.

Demerits of DTD

1. The DTDs are very basic and hence cannot be much specific for complex documents.
2. The language that DTD uses is not an XML document. Hence various frameworks used by XML cannot be supported by the DTDs.

3. The DTD cannot define the type of data contained within the XML document. Hence using DTD we cannot specify whether the element is numeric, or string or of date type.
4. There are some XML processor which do not understand DTDs.
5. The DTDs are not aware of namespace concept.

University Question

1. *Explain the types of DTD in XML with an example.*

AU : May-19, Marks 13

8.6 XML Schema

AU : May-16, 17, Marks 8

- The XML schemas are used to represent the **structure of XML document.**
- The goal or purpose of XML schema is to define the building blocks of an XML document. These can be used as an alternative to XML DTD.
- The XML schema language is called as **XML Schema Definition (XSD) language**.
- XML schema defines elements, attributes, elements having child elements, order of child elements. It also defines fixed and default values of elements and attributes.
- XML schema also allows the developer to use **data types.**

How to write a simple schema ?

Step 1 : We will first write a simple xsd file in which the desired structure of the XML document is defined. I have named it as ***StudentSchema.xsd***

This file contains the complex type with four child simple type elements.

XML Schema [StudentSchema.xsd]

```
<?xml version="1.0"?>
<xs:schema xmlns:xs="http://www.w3.org/2001/XMLSchema">
              <xs:element name="Student">
  <xs:complexType>
   <xs:sequence>
   <xs:element name="name" type="xs:string"/>
   <xs:element name="address" type="xs:string"/>
   <xs:element name="std" type="xs:string"/>
   <xs:element name="marks" type="xs:string"/>
   </xs:sequence>
  </xs:complexType>
 </xs:element>
</xs:schema>
```

Script Explanation :

1) The **xs** is qualifier used to identify the schema elements and types.
2) The document element of schema is **xs:schema.** The **xs:schema** is the root element. It takes the attribute **xmlns:xs** which has the value **http://www.w3.org/2001/XMLSchema.** This declaration indicates that document should follow the rules of XML schema. The XML schema rules are defined by the W3 recommendation in year 2001.
3) Then comes **xs:element** which is used to define the xml element. In above case the element **Student** is of complex type who have four child elements : *name, address, std* and *marks*. All these elements are of simple type **string.**

Step 2 : Now develop XML document in which the desired values to the XML elements can be given. I have named this file as **MySchema.xml**

XML Document [MySchema.*xml]*

```
<?xml version="1.0" encoding="UTF-8"?>
<Student xmlns:xsi="http://www.w3.org/2001/XMLSchema-instance"
xsi:noNamespaceSchemaLocation="StudentSchema.xsd">
<name>Anand</name>
<address>Pune</address>
<std>Second</std>
<marks>70 percent</marks>
</Student>
```

Program Explanation :

1) In above XML document, the first line is typical in which the version and encoding is specified.
2) There is **xmlns:xsi** attribute of document which indicates that XML document is an instance of XML schema. And it has come from the namespace "http://www.w3.org/2001/XMLSchema-instance."
3) To tie this XML document with the some Schema definition we use the attribute **xsi:noNamespace SchemaLocation.** The value that can be passed to this attribute is the name of xsd file "StudentSchema.xsd".
4) After this we can define the child elements.

Step 3 : See the output in the browser window as follows -

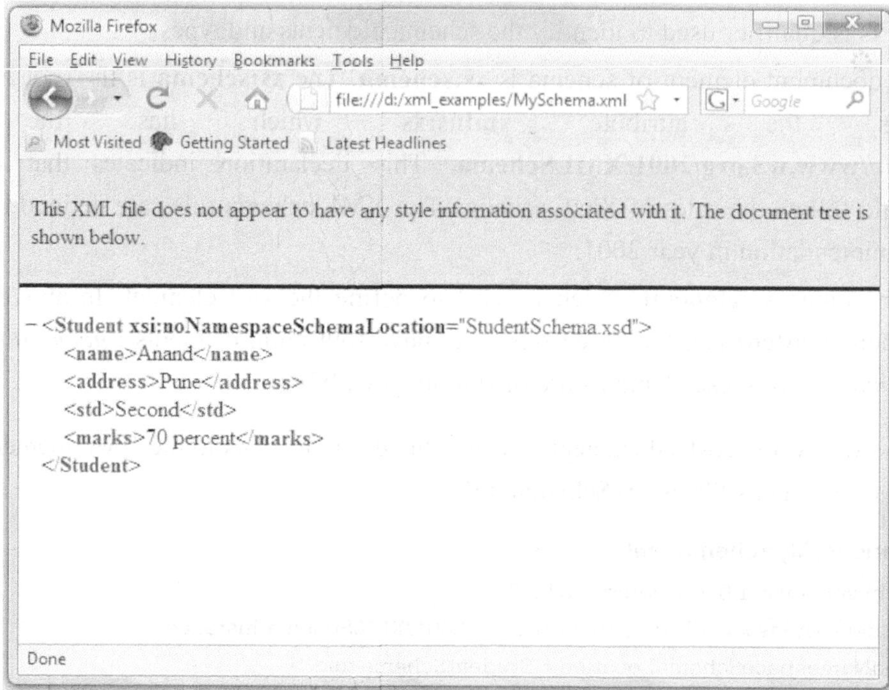

8.6.1 Data Types

Various data types that can be used to specify the data types of an element are :

- String
- Date
- Numeric
- Boolean

Let us discuss each of these data types with the help of examples -

1. String data type

The string data type is used to define the **element** containing characters, lines, tabs or white spaces. Following schema definition illustrates this data type.

We can write a schema definition in which the data type of element **Student_Name** is declared as of string type.

XML Schema [stringType.xsd]

```
<?xml version="1.0" encoding="UTF-8"?>
<xs:schema xmlns:xs="http://www.w3.org/2001/XMLSchema" >
    <xs:element name="Student_Name" type="xs:string" />
</xs:schema>
```

2. Date data type

For specifying the date we use date data type. The format of this date is yyyy-mm-dd where yyyy denotes the year, mm denotes the month and dd specifies the day. While specifying the date if any entry is single digit then it must be with leading zero. All the entries (i.e. yyyy,mm and dd) must be present.

Here is an illustration.

XML Schema [dateType.dtd]

```
<?xml version="1.0" encoding="UTF-8"?>
<xs:schema xmlns:xs="http://www.w3.org/2001/XMLSchema">
    <xs:element name="Date_of_Birth" type="xs:date"/>
</xs:schema>
```

XML Document [dateTypeDemo.xml]

```
<?xml version="1.0" encoding="UTF-8"?>
<Date_of_Birth xmlns:xsi="http://www.w3.org/2001/XMLSchema-instance"
xsi:noNamespaceSchemaLocation="dateType.xsd">
2009-09-01
</Date_of_Birth>
```

We can also specify the time by specifying the time as follows -

XML Document

```
<?xml version="1.0" encoding="UTF-8"?>
<Date_of_Birth xmlns:xsi="http://www.w3.org/2001/XMLSchema-instance"
xsi:noNamespaceSchemaLocation="dateType.xsd">
2009-09-01-01:57
</Date_of_Birth>
```

3. Numeric

If we want to use numeric value for some element then we can use the data types as either **decimal** or **integer.**

XML Schema [decimal Type.xsd]

```
<?xml version="1.0" encoding="UTF-8"?>
<xs:schema xmlns:xs="http://www.w3.org/2001/XMLSchema">
    <xs:element name="My_Marks" type="xs:decimal"/>
</xs:schema>
```

XML Document [decimal Type Demo.xml]

```
<?xml version="1.0" encoding="UTF-8"?>
<My_Marks xmlns:xsi="http://www.w3.org/2001/XMLSchema-instance"
xsi:noNamespaceSchemaLocation="decimalDemo.xsd">
```

```
99.99
</My_Marks>
```

Using decimal data type we can specify the value that may contain some decimal point. We can have another data type called integer which is used to specify the numeric values that are without any decimal point.

XML Schema [integer Type.xsd]

```
<?xml version="1.0" encoding="UTF-8"?>
<xs:schema xmlns:xs="http://www.w3.org/2001/XMLSchema">
    <xs:element name="My_Number" type="xs:integer"/>
</xs:schema>
```

4. Boolean

For specifying the true or false values we must use the boolean data type.

XML Schema [booleantype.xsd]

```
<?xml version="1.0" encoding="UTF-8"?>
<xs:schema xmlns:xs="http://www.w3.org/2001/XMLSchema">
        <xs:element name="Flag" type="xs:boolean"/>
</xs:schema>
```

8.6.2 Advantages and Disadvantages of Schema

Advantages of schema

1. The schemas are more specific.
2. The schema provide the support for data types.
3. The schema is aware of namespaces.
4. The XML schema is written in XML itself and has a large number of built in and derived types.
5. The XML schema is the W3C recommendation. Hence it is supported by various XML validator and XML processors.

Disadvantages of schema

1. The XML schema is complex to design and hard to learn.
2. The XML document cannot be if the corresponding schema file is absent.
3. Maintaining the schema for large and complex operations sometimes slows down the processing of XML document.

Advantages of schema over DTD

1. Both the schemas and DTDs are useful for defining structural components of XML. But the DTDs are basic and cannot be much specific for complex operations. On the other hand schemas are more specific.
2. The schemas provide support for defining the type of data. The DTDs do not have this ability. Hence content definition is possible using schema.
3. The schemas are namespace aware and DTDs are not.
4. The XML schema is written in XML itself and has a large number of built in and derived types.
5. The schema is the W3C recommendation. Hence it is supported by various XML validator and XML processors but there are some XML processors which do not support DTD.
6. Large number of web applications can be built using XML schema. On the other hand relatively simple and compact operations can be built using DTD.

University Questions

1. *Explain the role of XML schema in building web services in detail.* **AU : May-12, Marks 8**
2. *Briefly discuss how data types are represented in XML schema.* **AU : Dec.-12, Marks 8**

8.7 DOM and Presenting XML

AU : May-10, Marks 8, Dec.-18, Marks 13

What is DOM ?

Document Object Model (DOM) is a set of platform independent and language neutral Application Programming Interface (API) which describes how to access and manipulate the information stored in XML or in HTML documents.

Thus XML DOM is for

- **Loading** the XML document.
- **Accessing** the elements of XML document.
- **Deleting** the elements of XML document.
- **Changing** the elements of XML document.

1. Loading an XML file

We will write a simple script by which any desired XML file can be loaded. Note that these scripts are dependant upon the browser in which these are getting opened. We will write the following script which can be opened in any browser like internet explorer or Mozilla Firefox.

Step 1 : Open some simple text editor like Notepad and type the following script. I have named it as first.html

```
<html>
<!--Simple DOM example for loading some xml file -->
<body>
<script type="text/javascript">
try
 {
 xmlDocument=new ActiveXObject("Microsoft.XMLDOM");
 }
catch(e)
 {
 try
  {
  xmlDocument=document.implementation.createDocument("","",null);
  }
 catch(e) {alert(e.message)}
 }
try
 {
 xmlDocument.async=false;
 xmlDocument.load("student.xml");
 document.write("XML Document student.xml is loaded");
 }
catch(e) {alert(e.message)}
</script>
</body>
</html>
```

The **load** function is used to load the desired XML file. Note that when we specify some xml file for loading then it must be present at the current path. As an illustration the **student.xml** file is given as below -

XML Document [student.xml]

```
<?xml version="1.0" ?>
<student>
        <Roll_No>10</Roll_No>
```

```
        <Personal_Info>
                <Name>Parth</Name>
                <Address>Pune</Address>
                <Phone>1234567890</Phone>
        </Personal_Info>
        <class>Second</class>
        <Subject>Mathematics</Subject>
        <Marks>100</Marks>
</student>
```

Step 2 : Then open some web browser like Firefox or Internet explorer and the output for the above script can be seen as follows -

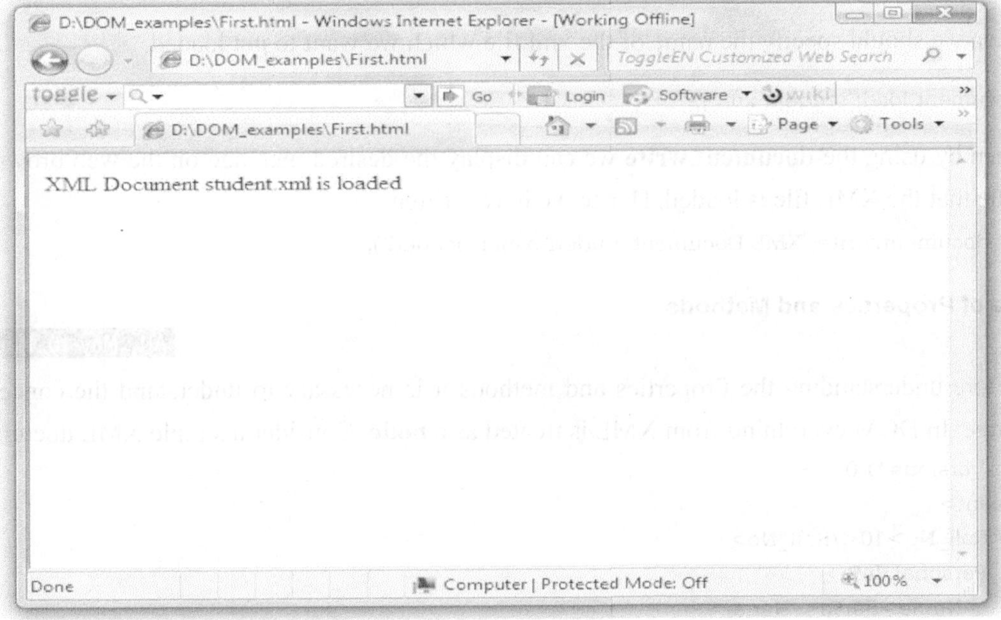

Script Explanation

There is an XML parser which reads any XML file. All the modern web browsers like Internet explorer have built in XML parser. The parser converts the XML into javascript accessible object. Hence we have mentioned the script type as -

```
<script type="text/javascript">
```

The parser reads the XML file, stores it into a memory and converts it into the XML DOM object. These objects can be accessible by the **JavaScript**.

Internet Explorer 5 and above have the built in XML parser. Hence in above given script we have written -

```
xmlDocument=new ActiveXObject("Microsoft.XMLDOM");
```

This statement means create an empty XML document object. We have taken this object in the variable **xmlDocument**.

After getting the document loaded fully in the memory the parser will continue for execution of the script, hence we must set -

```
xmlDocument.async=false;
```

Then we should specify the name of the xml file which we want to get loaded.

```
xmlDocument.load("student.xml");
```

Then by using the **document.write** we can display the desired message on the web browser to indicate that the XML file is loaded. Hence we have written

```
document.write("XML Document student.xml is loaded");
```

2. Use of Properties and Methods

AU : May-10, Marks 8

Before understanding the Properties and methods it is necessary to understand the concept of node tree. In DOM everything from XML is treated as a **node**. Consider a simple XML document,

```
<?xml version="1.0" ?>
<student>
    <Roll_No>10</Roll_No>
    <Personal_Info>
       <Name>Parth</Name>
       <Address>Pune</Address>
       <Phone>1234567890</Phone>
    </Personal_Info>
    <class>Second</class>
    <Subject>Mathematics</Subject>
    <Marks>100</Marks>
</student>
```

We can draw a node tree for this document as follows -

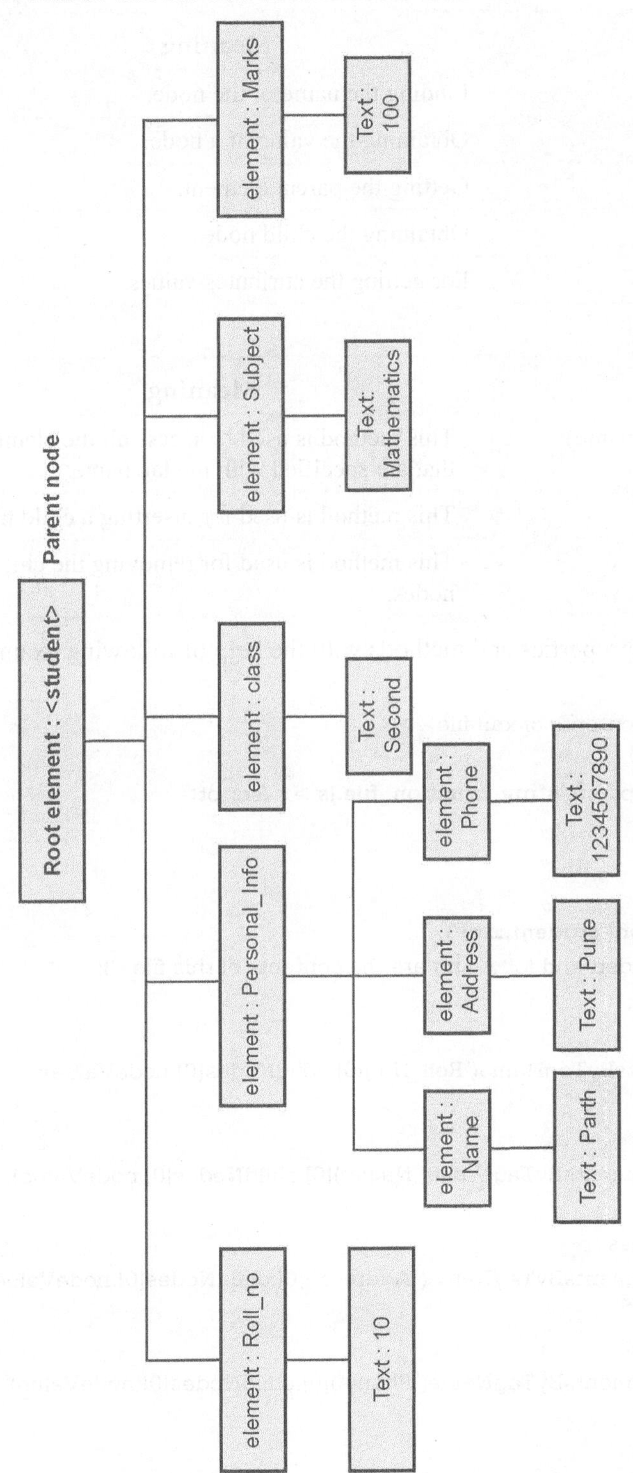

Fig. 8.7.1 Node-tree for student.XML

Various properties are

Property	Meaning
nodeName	Finding the name of the node.
nodeValue	Obtaining the value of a node.
parentNode	Getting the parent element.
childNodes	Obtaining the child nodes.
attributes	For getting the attributes values.

Various methods are

Method	Meaning
getElementsByTagName(name)	This method is used to access all the elements that are specified with the tag name.
appendChild(node)	This method is used for inserting a child node.
removeChild(node)	This method is used for removing the child nodes.

Let us understand the use of properties and methods with the help of following example -

```
<html>
<!-- loading and accessing the contents of xml file -->
<head>
    <script type="text/javascript" src="my_function_file.js"></script>
</head>
<body>
<script type="text/javascript">
  xmlDocument=My_Function("student.xml");
  document.write("xml File loaded and following are the contents of this file -");
    document.write("</br>");
   document.write("Roll_No :
   "+xmlDocument.getElementsByTagName("Roll_No")[0].childNodes[0].nodeValue);
   document.write("</br>");
   document.write("Name :
      "+xmlDocument.getElementsByTagName("Name")[0].childNodes[0].nodeValue);
   document.write("</br>");
      document.write("Address :
      "+xmlDocument.getElementsByTagName("Address")[0].childNodes[0].nodeValue);
   document.write("</br>");
      document.write("Phone :
      "+xmlDocument.getElementsByTagName("Phone")[0].childNodes[0].nodeValue);
   document.write("</br>");
      document.write("class :
      "+xmlDocument.getElementsByTagName("class")[0].childNodes[0].nodeValue);
```

```
document.write("</br>");
    document.write("Subject :
    "+xmlDocument.getElementsByTagName("Subject")[0].childNodes[0].nodeValue);
document.write("</br>");
    document.write("Marks :
    "+xmlDocument.getElementsByTagName("Marks")[0].childNodes[0].nodeValue);
document.write("</br>");
    </script>
    </body>
    </html>
```

Output

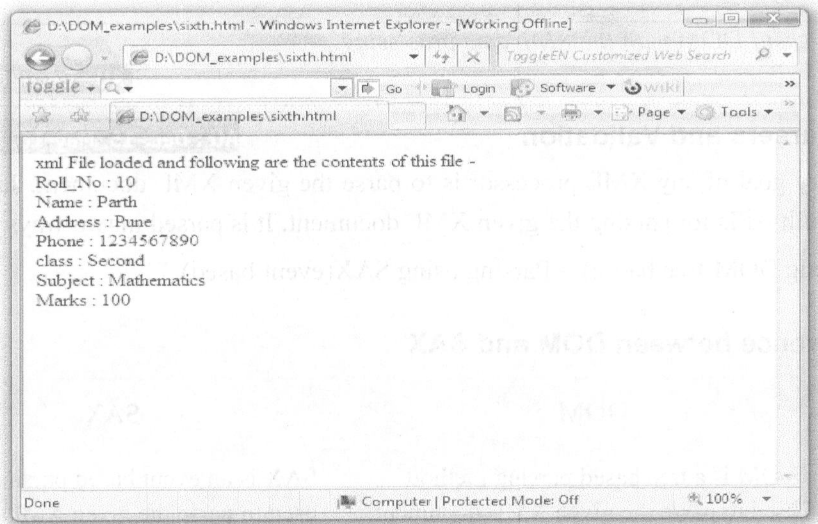

Script Explanation

In above given script, we have specified an external file **my_function_file.js** in the head section. This is a file in which the function My_Function is defined. This function performs the task of loading an XML document **student.xml**

We will first obtain a document object using the statement,

```
xmlDocument=My_Function("student.xml");
```

Note that **xmlDocument** is a document object referring the document **student.xml**. Using this object we can use the properties and methods. The method **getElementsByTagName** is used and to this method the parameter will be a tag names such as “Roll_No”, “Name” “class” and so on.

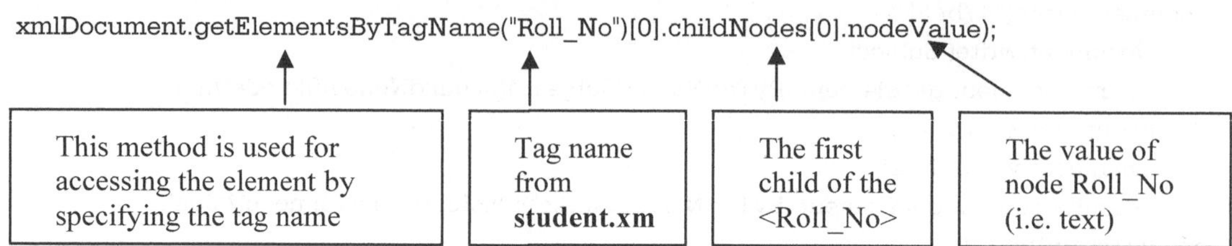

Hence as an output we can see the value of every element. That means the contents of **student.xml** file will be displayed.

University Question

1. *Explain about DOM with the XML data processing.*

AU : Dec.-2018, Marks 13

8.8 XML Parsers and Validation

AU : Dec.-15, May-16, 17, Marks 8

The primary goal of any XML processor is to parse the given XML document. Java has a rich source of in-built APIs for parsing the given XML document. It is parsed in two ways -

- Parsing using DOM(tree based)
- Parsing using SAX(event based)

8.8.1 Difference between DOM and SAX

Sr. No.	DOM	SAX
1.	DOM is a tree based parsing method used to parse the given XML document.	SAX is an event based parsing method used to parse the given XML document.
2.	In this method, the entire XML document is stored in the memory before actual processing. Hence it requires more memory.	In this method, the parsing is done by generating the sequence of events or it calls handler functions.
3.	The DOM approach is useful for smaller applications because it is simpler to use but it is certainly not used for larger XML documents because it will then require larger amount of memory.	Although SAX development is much more challenging, it is useful for parsing the large XML document because the approach is event based, xml gets parsed node by node and does not require large amount of memory.
4.	We can insert or delete a node.	We can insert or delete a node.
5.	Traversing is done in any direction in DOM approach.	Top to bottom traversing is done in this approach.

Features of XML Parsers

1. XML parser is a library that provides methods (or interfaces) for client applications to work with XML documents.
2. It validates the document.
3. It checks for well formedness.
4. DOM is a tree based parsing method.
5. SAX is event based parsing method.
6. In DOM approach the entire XML document is stored in the memory before actual processing.
7. In SAX the sequence of events or handler functions are called for parsing the XML document.
8. In DOM , the XML document is traversed in any direction and in SAX the XML document is traversed from top to down.

8.8.2 DOM based XML Processing

Using DOM API the XML document can be processed. The DOM API is defined in the **package or.w3c=.dom.*.** Using this API a DOM object tree is created from the input XML document and this tree helps in parsing the XML document.

Ex. 8.8.1 : Write XML document for checking Well Formedness of XML document using DOM API.

Sol. :

Java Program [parsing_DOMDemo.java]

```
import java.io.*;
import javax.xml.parsers.*;        } (1)
import org.w3c.dom.*;
import org.xml.sax.*;

public class Parsing_DOMDemo
{
    static public void main(String[] arg)
    {
        try
        {

            System.out.print("Enter the name of XML document ");
        BufferedReader input = new BufferedReader(new          } (2)
        InputStreamReader(System.in));
            String file_name = input.readLine();
            File fp = new File(file_name);
```

```
        if(fp.exists())
            {
            try
             {
              DocumentBuilderFactory Factory_obj =
               DocumentBuilderFactory.newInstance();
                DocumentBuilder builder = Factory_obj.newDocumentBuilder();     3
                InputSource ip_src = new InputSource(file_name);
                Document doc = builder.parse(ip_src);
                System.out.println(file_name + " is well-formed!");
             }
             catch (Exception e)
             {
             System.out.println(file_name + " isn't well-formed!");            4
             System.exit(1);
             }
            }
            else
           {
            System.out.print("File not found!");
           }
     }
     catch(IOException ex)
     {
     ex.printStackTrace();
     }
  }
}
```

Program Explanation

1. In above Java program we have to import some useful packages initially. Those are described as follows -

- The **java.io** package provides the interface for performing simple input and output operations.
- The **javax.xml.parsers.*** package provides the classes allowing the processing of XML documents. It supports various classes such as **DocumentBuilder** and **DocumentBuilderFactory**.
- The pacakge **org.w3c.dom.*** provides the interfaces for Document Object Model which is a component API of JAVA API for XML processing.
- The package **org.xml.sax.*** provides the classes and interfaces for the Simple API for XML (SAX) which is a component API of JAVA API.

2. Reading the name of XML document using the command prompt. Using the input stream for the **BufferReader** class we can read the contents from the command prompt.

3. **DocumentBuilderFactory** is a factory API an application can obtain parser. This parser basically produces DOM object tree from given XML document. Using the object of DocumentBuilderFactory an instance for **DocumentBuilder** is created. The object of **DocumentBuilder** is used to invoke a method **parse**. This method takes as XML document as an input, parses it. If the XML document is well formed then appropriate message will be displayed. In an XML document if every starting tag has an ending tag then that document is said to be well formed otherwise it is not.
4. In the **try** block we are calling the method **parse** for parsing the XML document. If the XML document is not well formed then the control of the program will go to **catch** block.

We will consider following XML document for executing above program -

student1.xml

```
<?xml version="1.0" ?>
<student>
    <Roll_No>10</Roll_No>
    <Personal_Info>
     <Name>Parth</Name>
     <Address>Pune</Address>
     <Phone>1234567890</Phone>
    </Personal_Info>
    <class>Second</class>
    <Subject>Mathematics</Subject>
    <Marks>100

    <Roll_No>20</Roll_No>
    <Personal_Info>
     <Name>Anuradha</Name>
     <Address>Banglore</Address>
     <Phone>90901233</Phone>
    </Personal_Info>
    <class>Fifth</class>
    <Subject>English</Subject>
    <Marks>90</Marks>

    <Roll_No>30</Roll_No>
    <Personal_Info>
     <Name>Anand</Name>
     <Address>Mumbai</Address>
     <Phone>90901256</Phone>
    </Personal_Info>
    <class>Fifth</class>
    <Subject>English</Subject>
    <Marks>90</Marks>
</student>
```

Purposely made this statement like this! (It is not well formed)

For getting the output go to the command prompt and give the commands as shown in the following screenshot.

Output

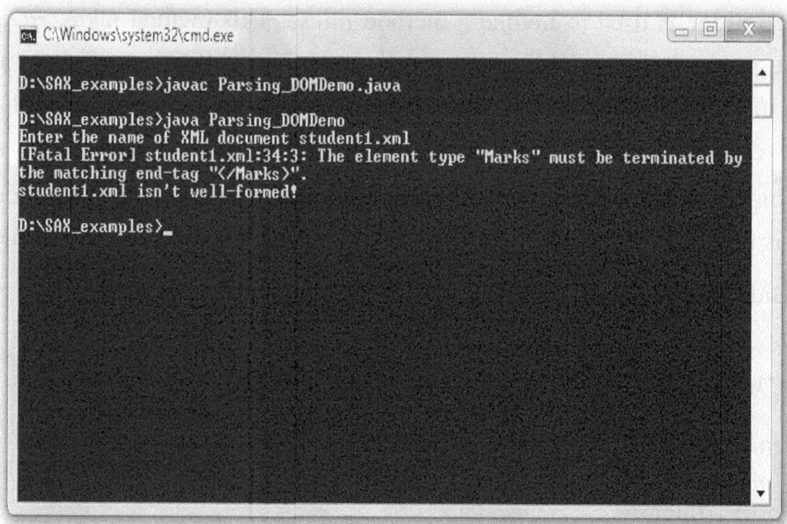

Naturally if we correct the statement like this,

```
<Marks>100</Marks>
```

Then we will get the **output** as follows -

```
D:\SAX_examples>javac Parsing_DOMDemo.java

D:\SAX_examples>java Parsing_DOMDemo
Enter the name of XML document student1.xml
student1.xml is well-formed!
D:\SAX_examples>
```

8.8.3 Event-Oriented Parsing : SAX

AU : Dec.-15, May-16,17, Marks 8

Now we will discuss simple Java programs that can be built to parse the given XML document using the event based API i.e. SAX

Ex. 8.8.2 : Write XML document for checking Well Formedness of XML document using SAX API.

Sol. :

Java Program [Parsing_SAXDemo.java]

```
import java.io.*;
import org.xml.sax.*;
import org.xml.sax.helpers.*;          (1)

public class Parsing_SAXDemo
```

```
{
    public static void main(String[] args) throws IOException
    {
    try
    {
          System.out.print("Enter the name of XML document ");
      BufferedReader input = new BufferedReader(new
      InputStreamReader(System.in));                                  } (2)
          String file_name = input.readLine();
          File fp = new File(file_name);
          if (fp.exists())
    {
       try
    {
       XMLReader reader = XMLReaderFactory.createXMLReader();
       reader.parse(file_name);                                       } (3)
       System.out.println(file_name + " is well-formed.");
    }
       catch (Exception e)
    {
       System.out.println(file_name + " is not well-formed.");        } (4)
       System.exit(1);
    }

       }
       else
       {
           System.out.println("File is not present: " + file_name);
       }
    }
    catch (IOException ex){ex.printStackTrace();}
    }
}
```

Program Explanation (The numbered steps are explained as follows)

1. In above Java program we have to import some useful packages initially. Those are described as follows -

- The **java.io** package provides the interface for performing simple input and output operations.
- The package **org.xml.sax.*** provides the classes and interfaces for the Simple API for XML (SAX) which is a component API of JAVA API.
- The package **org.xml.sax.helpers.*** provides the helper classes for Simple API for XML(i.e. SAX) which is a component of JAVA API for processing XML.

2. Reading the name of XML document using the command prompt. Using the input stream for the **BufferReader** class we can read the contents from the command prompt.
3. The **XMLReaderFactory** helps in creating an XML reader. This reader then parses xml document using the appropriate callbacks. Using **createXMLReader** an object **reader** is created using which we can call the method **parse** for parsing the XML document.

4. In the **try** block we are calling the method **parser** for parsing the XML document. If the XML document is not well formed then the control of the program will go to **catch** block.

A sample XML document that can be parsed using above program is as given below -

student.xml

```
<?xml version="1.0" ?>
<student>
    <Roll_No>10</Roll_No>
    <Personal_Info>
        <Name>Parth</Name>
        <Address>Pune</Address>
        <Phone>1234567890</Phone>
    </Personal_Info>
    <class>Second</class>
    <Subject>Mathematics</Subject>
    <Marks>100</Marks>
</student>
```

Output

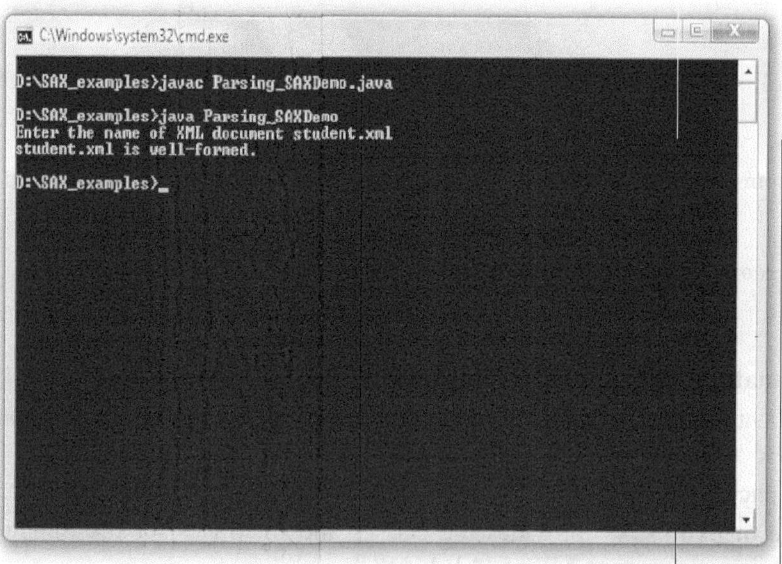

University Questions

1. *Explain XML parsers and validation.* **AU : Dec.-15, Marks 8**
2. *List the essential features of XML parsers.* **AU : May-16, Marks 8**
3. *Discuss the merits and demerits of DOM and SAX parsers with neat examples.* **AU : May-17, Marks 8**

8.9 XSL and XSLT Transformation

- The XSLT stands for **XSL** Transformations and XSL stands for eXtensible Stylesheet Language.
- An XSLT is a W3C recommendation.
- The XSLT is used for defining the XML document transformations and presentations. Hence XSL decides how an XML document should look on the web browser.
- XSL consists of three parts :
  1. XSLT is a language for **transforming XML documents.**
  2. XPath is a language for **navigating in XML documents.** In other words we can reach to any node of XML document using XPath.
  3. XSL-FO is a language for formatting XML documents for **displaying it in desired manner.**

8.9.1 Transforming XML into XSLT

- Using XSLT we can decide the way by which we want the element to get displayed.
- XSLT uses **XPath** to find information in an XML document. XPath is used to navigate through elements and attributes in XML documents. We can sort these elements, hide or display particular element and can apply some decision making logic on these elements.
- XSLT processors **take two input documents** one is **XML document** and another is **XSLT document.** The XSLT document is nothing but a program and XML document is nothing but the input data, thus this program works on the XML input data. Then some or whole part of the XML document is selected, modified and merged with XSLT program document in order to produce another document.
- This newly produced document is provided as input to the XSLT processor which in turn produce another document called the **XSL document.**
- The XSL document is used along with the application so that particular application can be displayed on the web browser in some desired manner.

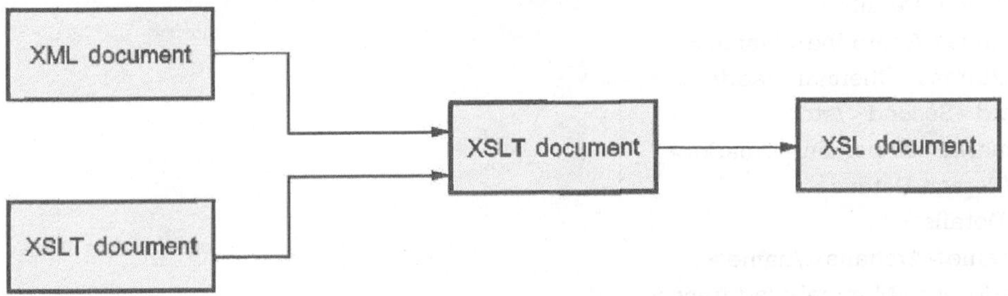

Fig. 8.9.1 Processing of XSLT document

- The XSLT document makes use of **templates** using which particular code can be described in XML document.
- XML document and then particular code in XSLT is executed when the match is found.
- XSLT processor processes the XML document sequentially by reading each line one by one.
- The XSLT model can be described as **template driven** or **data driven** model.

8.9.2 XSL Elements

1. The <xsl:template>

- The <xsl:template> is for building the templates.
- The **match** attribute is associated with the template element. The match attribute can also be used to define a template for the entire XML document. The **match="/"** defines the whole document.
- In the following example we store the XML elements in the tabular form using the <xsl:template> and <match>

Step 1 : Write a simple XML document. One sample example is as below -

Open Notepad and write the following code. Save it by the name SimpleXml.xml

XML Document[SimpleXml.xml]

```
<?xml version="1.0" encoding="UTF-8"?>
<?xml-stylesheet type="text/xsl" href="SimpleXml.xsl"?>
<Student>
<Person-Details>
      <name>Anand</name>
      <address>Pune</address>
      <std>Second</std>
      <marks>70 percent</marks>
</Person-Details>
      <Person-Details>
      <name>Anuradha</name>
      <address>Chennai</address>
      <std>Second</std>
      <marks>90 percent</marks>
      </Person-Details>
<Person-Details>
      <name>Archana</name>
      <address>Mumbai</address>
      <std>Forth</std>
      <marks>80 percent</marks>
</Person-Details>
<Person-Details>
```

We have defined this file in step 2

```
        <name>Monika</name>
        <address>Delhi</address>
        <std>Tenth</std>
        <marks>77 percent</marks>
</Person-Details>
        </Student>
```

Step 2 : Now create a XSL stylesheet. Note that this document must have file name extension as **.xsl.** Open notepad and save following code in it.

XSLT Document [SimpleXml.xsl]

```
<?xml version="1.0" encoding="ISO-8859-1"?>
<xsl:stylesheet version="1.0"
xmlns:xsl="http://www.w3.org/1999/XSL/Transform">
<xsl:template match="/">
<html>
<body>
<h2>Students Database</h2>
<table border="1">
<trbgcolor="gray">
<th>Name</th>
<th>Address</th>
<th>Standard</th>
<th>Marks</th>
</tr>
<trbgcolor="pink">
<td>**</td>
<td>**</td>
<td>**</td>
<td>**</td>
</tr>
</table>
</body>
</html>
</xsl:template>
</xsl:stylesheet>
```

Step 3 : Open the web browser and the output will be as follows -

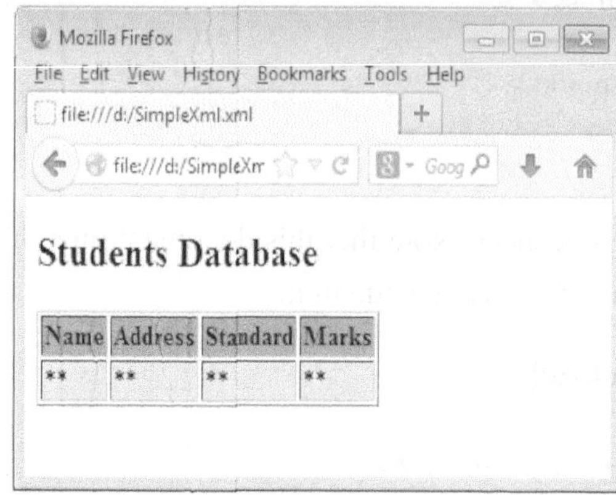

2. The <xsl:value-of>

The **value-of** is used to extract the value of xml element and add it to output stream of the XSL transformation. Following example illustrates this

Step 1 : Keep the same xml[**SimpleXml.xml**] file which you have created in section 8.9.2 (1) Step 1.

Step 2 : Create the xsl file as follows -

```
<?xml version="1.0" encoding="ISO-8859-1"?>
<xsl:stylesheet version="1.0"
xmlns:xsl="http://www.w3.org/1999/XSL/Transform">
<xsl:template match="/">
<html>
<body>
<h2>Students Database</h2>
<table border="1">
<trbgcolor="gray">
<th>Name</th>
<th>Address</th>
<th>Standard</th>
<th>Marks</th>
</tr>
<trbgcolor="pink">
<td><xsl:value-of select="Student/Person-Details/name"/></td>
<td><xsl:value-of select="Student/Person-Details/address"/></td>
<td><xsl:value-of select="Student/Person-Details/std"/></td>
<td><xsl:value-of select="Student/Person-Details/marks"/></td>
</tr>
</table>
</body>
</html>
```

```
</xsl:template>
</xsl:stylesheet>
```

Step 3 : Open the web browser and the output will be as follows -

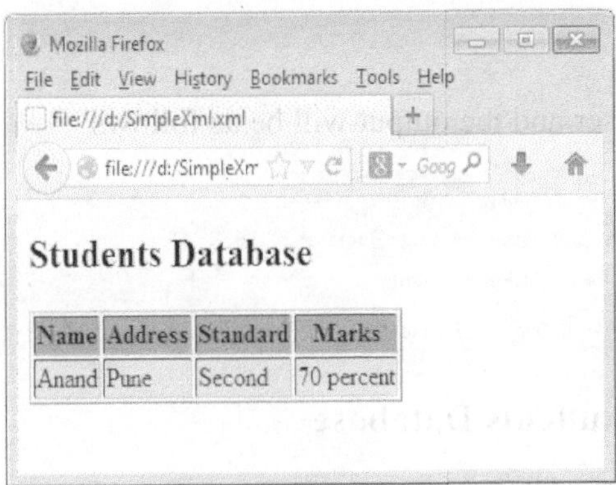

3. The <xsl:for-each>

The **for-each** element allows to traverse through each element of the node

Step 1 : Keep the same xml[**SimpleXml.xml**] file which you have created in section 8.9.2(1) Step 1.

Step 2 : Now create .xsl document illustrating <xsl:for-each>. It is as follows -

```
<?xml version="1.0" encoding="ISO-8859-1"?>
<xsl:stylesheet version="1.0"
xmlns:xsl="http://www.w3.org/1999/XSL/Transform">
<xsl:template match="/">
<html>
<body>
<h2>Students Database</h2>
<table border="1">
<trbgcolor="gray">
<th>Name</th>
<th>Address</th>
<th>Standard</th>
<th>Marks</th>
</tr>
<xsl:for-each select="Student/Person-Details" >
<trbgcolor="pink">
<td><xsl:value-of select="name"/></td>
<td><xsl:value-of select="address"/></td>
<td><xsl:value-of select="std"/></td>
<td><xsl:value-of select="marks"/></td>
</tr>
</xsl:for-each>
```

```
</table>
</body>
</html>
</xsl:template>
</xsl:stylesheet>
```

Step 3 : Open the web browser and the output will be as follows -

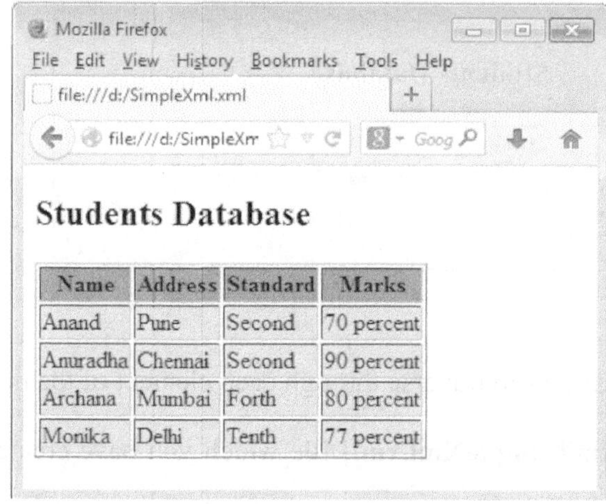

4. The <xsl:sort>

We can also display the sorted data using **<xsl:sort>.**

Step 1 : Keep the same xml[**SimpleXml.xml**] file which you have created in section 8.9.2 (1) Step 1.

Step 2 : Create the .xsl file as follows –

SimpleXml.xsl

```
<?xml version="1.0" encoding="ISO-8859-1"?>
<xsl:stylesheet version="1.0"
xmlns:xsl="http://www.w3.org/1999/XSL/Transform">
<xsl:template match="/">
<html>
<body>
<h2>Students Database</h2>
<table border="1">
<trbgcolor="gray">
<th>Name</th>
<th>Address</th>
<th>Standard</th>
<th>Marks</th>
</tr>
```

```
<xsl:for-each select="Student/Person-Details">
<xsl:sort select="marks"/>
<trbgcolor="pink">
<td><xsl:value-of select="name"/></td>
<td><xsl:value-of select="address"/></td>
<td><xsl:value-of select="std"/></td>
<td><xsl:value-of select="marks"/></td>
</tr>
</xsl:for-each>
</table>
</body>
</html>
</xsl:template>
</xsl:stylesheet>
```

Output

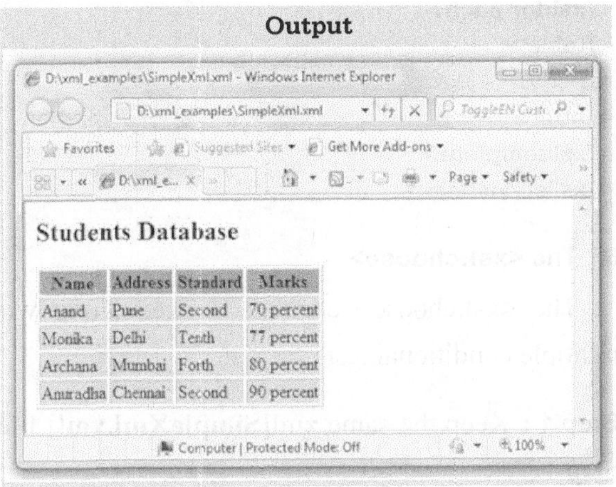

5. The <xsl:if>

For selection specific record based on some condition the <xsl:if> is used.

Step 1 : Keep the same xml[**SimpleXml.xml**] file which you have created in section 8.9.2(1) Step 1.

Step 2 : Create the .xsl file as follows –

```
<?xml version="1.0" encoding="ISO-8859-1"?>
<xsl:stylesheet version="1.0"
xmlns:xsl="http://www.w3.org/1999/XSL/Transform">
<xsl:template match="/">
<html>
<body>
<h2>Students Database</h2>
<table border="1">
<trbgcolor="gray">
<th>Name</th>
<th>Address</th>
<th>Standard</th>
<th>Marks</th>
</tr>
<xsl:for-each select="Student/Person-Details" >
<xsl:if test="marks>77">
<trbgcolor="pink">
<td><xsl:value-of select="name"/></td>
<td><xsl:value-of select="address"/></td>
<td><xsl:value-of select="std"/></td>
<td><xsl:value-of select="marks"/></td>
</tr>
</xsl:if>
```

```
</xsl:for-each>
</table>
</body>
</html>
</xsl:template>
</xsl:stylesheet>
```

6. The <xsl:choose>

The <xsl:choose> element is used along with <xsl:when> and <xsl:otherwise> to express multiple conditional tests.

Step 1 : Keep the same xml**[SimpleXml.xml]** file which you have created in section 8.9.2 (1) Step 1.

Step 2 : Create the .xsl file as follows –

```
<?xml version="1.0" encoding="ISO-8859-1"?>
<xsl:stylesheet version="1.0"
xmlns:xsl="http://www.w3.org/1999/XSL/Transform">
<xsl:template match="/">
<html>
<body>
<h2>Students Database</h2>
<table border="1">
<trbgcolor="gray">
<th>Name</th>
<th>Marks</th>
</tr>
<xsl:for-each select="Student/Person-Details">
<tr>
<td><xsl:value-of select="name"/></td>
<xsl:choose>
<xsl:when test="marks &lt; 77">
<td bgcolor="pink">
<xsl:value-of select="marks"/></td>
</xsl:when>
<xsl:otherwise>
<td><xsl:value-of select="marks"/></td>
</xsl:otherwise>
</xsl:choose>
</tr>
</xsl:for-each>
</table>
</body>
</html>
</xsl:template>
</xsl:stylesheet>
```

8.10 Displaying XML Document using CSS

- Cascading Style Sheet(CSS) is used to apply the style to HTML elements. Similarly we can apply the style to XML elements using CSS style
- The document structure can be specified in DTD file.
- The style sheet can be specified in a separate CSS file.
- **For example :** Following is a web application that represent the book database displaying Book Title, Author Name, publication, Edition, ISBN, Price in different fonts and color

Step 1 : Create a DTD file name *Catalog.dtd*

```
<?xml version="1.0" encoding="UTF-8"?>
<!ELEMENT Catalog (Book)*>
<!ELEMENT Book ( Title, Author, Publication, Edition, ISBN, Price ) >
<!ELEMENT Title (#PCDATA)>
<!ELEMENT Author (#PCDATA)>
<!ELEMENT Publication (#PCDATA)>
<!ELEMENT Edition (#PCDATA)>
<!ELEMENT ISBN (#PCDATA)>
<!ELEMENT Price (#PCDATA)>
```

Step 2 : Create a CSS file and name it as library.css

```
Catalog
{
font-family:arial;
color:red;
font-size:16pt
}
Book
{
display:block;
font-family:times new roman;
color:blue;
font-size:14pt
}
Title
{
font-family:arial;
color:maroon;
font-size:12pt
}
Author
{
font-family:arial;
color:magenta;
```

```
}
Publication,Edition,ISBN,Price
{
display:block;
font-family:arial;
color:black;
font-size:10pt;
margin-left: 20pt
}
```

Step 3 : Finally create a XML document and name it as CSSDemo.css as follows -

XML Document

```
<?xml version="1.0" encoding="UTF-8"?>
<?xml-stylesheet type="text/css" href="library.css"?>
<!DOCTYPE Catalog SYSTEM "Catalog.dtd">
<Catalog>
        <Book>
                <Title>XML Bible</Title>
                <Author>Winston</Author>
                <Publication>Wiely</Publication>
                <Edition>Fifth Edition</Edition>
                <ISBN>0-7645-4760-7</ISBN>
                <Price>$40.5</Price>
        </Book>
        <Book>
                <Title>Artificial Intelligence</Title>
                <Author>S.Russel</Author>
                <Publication>Princeton hall</Publication>
                <Edition>Sixth Edition</Edition>
                <ISBN>0-13-1038-5-2</ISBN>
                <Price>$63</Price>
        </Book>
        <Book>
                <Title>Java 2</Title>
                <Author>Watson</Author>
                <Publication>BPB Publications</Publication>
                <Edition>Third Edition</Edition>
                <ISBN>0-41-1058-7-2</ISBN>
                <Price>$63</Price>
        </Book>

        <Book>
                <Title>HTML in 24 hours</Title>
                <Author>Sam Peter</Author>
                <Publication>SAM Publications</Publication>
                <Edition>Fifth Edition</Edition>
                <ISBN>0-672-32841-0</ISBN>
```

Here both **CSS** and **DTD** files are used externally

```
        <Price>$50</Price>
    </Book>
</Catalog>
```

Step 4 : Finally execute the XML document on the web browser and you can see following sort of output -

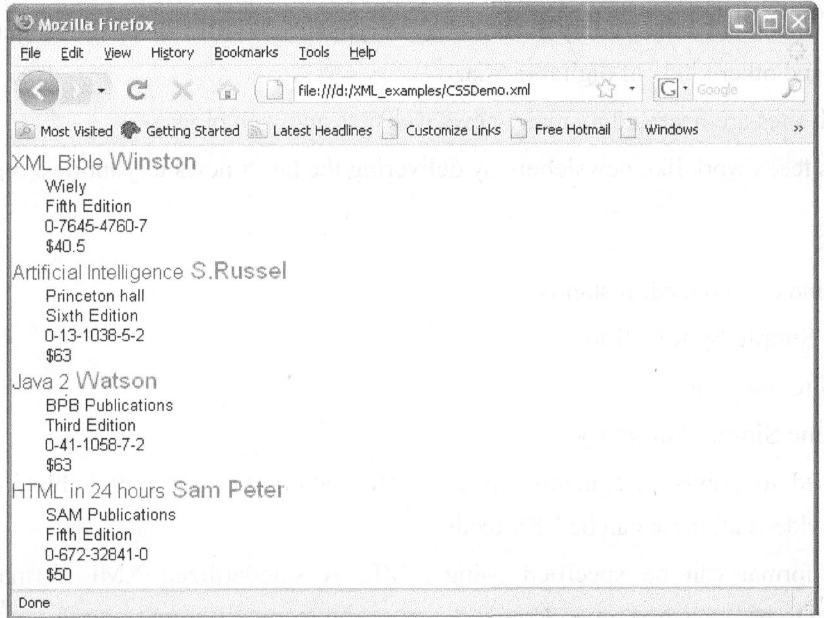

8.11 News Feed (RSS and ATOM)

AU : May-19, Marks 13

News feed or Web feed is a kind of document(or some data format) which is providing updated contents to its users. The news feed lets web sites continuously **feed** you the updated news.

Suppose you are interested in Cricket. You could visit the websites that show information on Cricket, Cricket match schedule, Score, information about the players and so on. Depending on your interests you may have to visit several websites to get the information you want. By subscribing to a News feed or web feed, you can conveniently get a feed on the topic *"cricket"* without having to go to particular website as well as catch up on all the history sites you are interested in without visiting each site.

How it works ?

- There are **content providers or distributors.** They publish feed links on their sites.
- Several web feeds are collected together at one spot. This spot is called **aggregator.**
- The **end users** can register with an **aggregator program** running on their own machines. This is just similar to the task as dragging the link from the web browser to the aggregator.

- When instructed, the **aggregator** asks all the servers in its feed list if they have new content; if so, the aggregator either makes a note of the new content or downloads it.
- Aggregators can be scheduled to check for new content periodically.
- Web feeds are an example of pull technology although they may appear to push content to the user.
- The kinds of content delivered by a web feed are typically HTML (webpage content) or links to webpages and other kinds of digital media.
- These Web sites are operated by many news websites and web blogs.
- Thus news feeds work like newsletters by delivering the latest news to your desktop.

8.11.1 RSS

- RSS is a kind of web feed. It stands for
    - Really Simple Syndication
    - Rich Site Summary
    - Real time Simple Summary
- RSS is used to publish frequently updated information. For instance - blog entires, news headlines, videos all these can be RSS feeds.
- The RSS format can be specified using XML. A standardized XML format allows the information to be published once. Then it is viewed by many different programs.

How it works ?

- RSS headlines are simple text files.
- The web master submits these files to a special feed server.
- This RSS feed server, in turn, pushes the text file to the screens of its subscribers.
- Time span is usually 30 seconds to 30 minutes before the subscribers see the updates. In most cases, the lag is not even noticeable.
- Most RSS readers are free to use and easy to learn. User can setup the screen using the reader tool. The users subscribe to a feed by using the feed's URL or by clicking the RSS icon. Thus the subscription process is initiated.
- Various examples of RSS reader are - Newsgator.com, Google Reader, My Yahoo Reader.

Example of RSS <item> element

- The most commonly used elements in RSS are <channel>,<item>,<link> and <description>.
- The <channel> element describes the RSS feed. This element has three child elements.
- <title> : This element is for defining the title of channel element.

- <link> : This element defines the hyperlink to channel.
- <description> : This element describes the channel.
- Each <channel> element has one or more <item> elements. The item element defines the article or story in RSS field.
- Following is a simple XML document which makes used of RSS<item> to describe the book store collection.

```
<?xml version="1.0" encoding="ISO-8859-1" ?>
<rss version="2.0">
<channel>
<title>Books Store</title>
<link>http://www.myreadings.com</link>
<description>This book store has a huge collection of books</description>
<item>
<title>Engineering Books</title>
<link>http://www.myreadings.com/engineering</link>
<description>Collection of books on Engineering Subjects</description>
</item>
</channel>
</rss>
```

Advantages of using web feeds

1. User need not have to specify their email addresses while subscribing the web feed. Hence there are no unlike email threats such as spam or phishing.
2. User need not have to send the unsubscribe information. He simply removes the feed from aggregator in order to stop getting news from the feed.
3. The feeds are obtained in sorted manner.

8.11.2 ATOM

- Atom is an XML - based file format used to **syndicate** content.
- Atom was originally developed as an alternative to RSS 2.0, and is designed for improving the shortcomings of the RSS format.
- Atom is much more robust and feature rich than RSS.
- Web feeds are used by the blogging community to share recent entries' headlines, full text, and even attached multimedia files.
- Users visiting a web site with an atom feed can discover a file described as "atom.xml" in the URL that can be copied and pasted into an aggregator to subscribe to the feed.
- In particular, many **blog** and **wiki** sites offer their web feeds in the atom format.

8.11.3 Difference between RSS and ATOM

Sr. No.	RSS	Atom
1.	RSS contain either a plain text or escaped HTML as a payload.	Atom contains variety of payloads such as escaped HTML, XML, DHTML, references to external contents such as documents, audio or video streams, and so on.
2.	RSS shows the date timestamp of data when the feed was created and last updated.	Atom shows the date timestamp when website was last updated.
3.	RSS vocabulary elements are unusual in other XML vocabularies.	Atom allows the reuse of elements outside the atom feed document.
4.	RSS makes use of two publishing protocols - Blogger protocol and MetaWeblog.	Atom has only one standardized protocol.
5.	RSS adopts loose approach about data.	Atom uses restrictive approach about data.
6.	RSS has more complicated aggregating and extracting process.	Atom has easier aggregating and extracting process.
7.	RSS is not a standardized feature.	Atom is a standardized feature.
8.	The browser is left to figure out whether the RSS feed contains plain text or escaped HTML.	Atom feeds explicitly indicates the content

University Question

1. *Discuss the following in detail.*

i) RSS, ii) ATOM

AU : May-19, 7+6 Marks

Two Marks Questions with Answers

Q.1 What is XML ?

Ans. : The XML stands for eXtensible Markup Language. The XML is designed to transport or to store the data.

Q.2 What is the difference between XML and HTML ?

Ans. : The difference between HTML and XML is that HTML is designed for representation of data on the web page whereas XML is designed transport or to store the data. The HTML has its predefined tags whereas the XML does not have predefined tags.

Q.3 What are goals of XML?

Ans. : Following are the goals of XML -

1. User must be able to define and use his own tag. This allows us to restrict the use of the set of tags defined by proprietary vendors.
2. Allow user to build his own tag library based on his web requirement.
3. Allow user to define the formatting rules for the user defined tags.
4. XML must support for storage or transport of data.

Q.4 Explain the following terms related to XML :
i) XML parsing ii) XML browsers iii) XML editors iv) XML validators

AU : May-17

Ans. :

i) **XML parsing :** This is a technique in which the XML parser reads the XML file into the memory and converts into XML DOM object.

ii) **XML browser :** The XML browser visualizes the elements in XML document. The user can browse through or can associate external interfaces with the XML elements. For examples the XML file can be viewed using Internet Explorer or Firefox browser.

iii) **XML editors :** XML editors allow the developer to write error free XML document by editing it. The plain text editor like notepad can also be used for editing the XML document. But there are some graphical XML editors like XML Spy or oXygen that present the content to the user in a more user-friendly format.

iv) **XML validators :** The validation of XML document is done by XML parser. It can be done using two approaches.

i) Checking the well formedness of XML document - That means if any bracket is missing or additional is tested by checking the well formedness of the XML document.

ii) Checking the validity of XML elements.

Q.5 Discuss the important features of XML which makes it more suitable for creating web related services.

Ans. : Following are some features which are most suitable for creating web related applications.

1. XML is EXtesible Markup Language intended for transport or storage of the data.

2. The most important feature of XML is that user is able to define and use his own tag. This allows us to restrict the use of the set of tags defined by proprietary vendors. On the other hand other markup languages like HTML or SGML requires a predefined set of tags.
3. XML contains only data and does not contain any formatting information. Hence document developers can decide how to display the data.
4. XML permits the document writer to create the tags for any type of information. Due to this virtually any kind of information can be such as mathematical formulae, chemical structures, or some other kind of data can be described using XML.
5. Searching sorting, rendering or manipulating the XML document is possible using eXtended Stylesheet Language (XSL).
6. The XML document can be validated using some external tools.
7. Some commonly used web browsers like Internet Explorer and Firefox Mozilla provide support to the tags in XML. Hence XML is not at all vendor specific or browser specific.

Q.6 What are the advantages of XML ?

AU : May-17

Ans. :

1. XML document is human readable and we can edit any XML document in simple text editors.
2. The XML document is language neutral. That means a Java program can generate an XML document and this document can be parsed by Perl.
3. Every XML document has a tree structure. Hence complex data can be arranged systematically and can be understood in simple manner.
4. XML files are independent of an operating system.

Q.7 What is XML element ?

Ans. : The basic entity in XML is element. The elements are used to define tags.

The elements typically consist of opening and closing tag. Mostly only one element is used to define a single tag.

The syntax of writing any element for opening tag is

<element name>

The syntax of writing any closing element for closing tag is

< /element name >

Every XML must have a single root element.

Q.8 Why DTD's ?

AU : May-09

Ans. : The document type definition is used to define the basic building block of any xml document. Using DTD we can specify the various elements types, attributes and their relationship with one another. Basically DTD is used to specify the set of rules for structuring data in any XML file.

For example : If we want to put some information about some students in XML file then, generally we use tag student followed by his/her name, address, standard and marks. That means we are actually specifying the manner by which the information should be arranged in the XML file. And for this purpose the Document Type Definition is used.

Q.9 What is meant by namespace ?

AU : Dec.-09, 12, May-11

Ans. : The xml document allows us to create different elements which are having the common name. This technique is known as namespace.

For example : Consider the following XML document

XML Document

```
<File-Description>
<text fname="input.txt">
   <describe>It is a text file</describe>
</text>
<text fname="flower.jpg">
   <describe>It is an image file</describe>
   </text>
</File-Description>
```

The above document does not produce any error although the element text is used for two different attribute values.

Q.10 What is CDATA ?

Ans. : The CDATA stands for Character Data. The character data will be parsed by the parser.

Q.11 What is PCDATA ?

Ans. : It stands for Parsed Character Data (i.e. text). Any Parsable character data should not contain the markup characters. The markup characters are < or > or &. If we want to use less than, greater than or ampersand characters then make use of < , > or &

Q.12 What are the merits of DTD ?

Ans. :

1. DTDs are used to define the structural components of XML document
2. These are relatively simple and compact.
3. DTDs can be defined inline and hence can be embedded directly in the XML document.

Q.13 What are the demerits of DTD ?

Ans. :

1. The DTDs are very basic and hence cannot be much specific for complex documents.
2. The language that DTD uses is not an XML document. Hence various frameworks used by XML cannot be supported by the DTDs.
3. The DTD cannot define the type of data contained within the XML document. Hence using DTD we cannot specify whether the element is numeric, or string or of date type.
4. There are some XML processor which do not understand DTDs.
5. The DTDs are not aware of namespace concept.

Q.14 What is XSL and why it is used ?

AU : May-08

Ans. : XSL stands for eXtensible Stylesheet Language. The XSL decided how an XML document should look on web browser.

Q.15 What is the difference between DOM and SAX ? [Refer section 8.8.1]

AU : May-13

Q.16 What are the two methods of parsing the XML document ?

Ans. : The XML document is parsed using two approaches -

1) Tree based 2) Event based.

The tree based parsing is done using DOM and th Event based parsing is done using SAX.

Q.17 What is the importance of SAX ?

Ans. : The SAX stands for Simple API for XML. It allows to access the information of XML document using sequence of events. This API is basically used for parsing the XML document.

Q.18 How is XML parsing done with SAX ?

AU : Dec.-11

Ans. : The XML parsing can be done with SAX using following steps -

A Java program can make use of following steps.

1) Using the **BufferedReader** class the contents of XML document are read.
2) Then using **XMLReadFactory** XML reader is created. This reader parses the XML document using appropriate callbacks.
3) Using **createXMLReader** an object **reader** is created.
4) With the help of this object the method parse is invoked for parsing the XML document.

Q.19 What does XSLT mean ?

AU : May-12

Ans. : The XSLT stands for eXtensible Stylesheet Language Transformation. It is a W3C recommendation.

Q.20 What is the purpose of XSLT ?

AU : Dec.-11

Ans. : The purpose of XSLT is to define the XML document transformations and presentations. Thus using XSLT the XML document can be transformed into XHTML documents or some other XML document.

Q.21 What is Xpath ?

AU : Dec.-12

Ans. : The XSLT uses the Xpath to navigate in XML document. In other words we can reach to any node of XML document using XPath.

Q.22 What is XSL-FO ?

Ans. : The XSL-FO is a language for formatting XML document for displaying it in desired manner.

Q.23 What is the use of CSS for XML document ?

Ans. : In XML user defined tags are used. The cascading style sheet can be embedded within the XML document using which the desired style can be applied to the user defined tags. Thus the XML document can be presented in the desired style using the CSS.

Q.24 What is XML Parse Tree ?

AU : Dec.-15

Ans. : The XML document form a tree structure that starts from root node to branches.

The XML parse tree is a DOM model in which everything from XML is treated as node.

This tree is created for parsing the XML document.

Various properties such as nodeName, nodeValue, parentNode, childNodes and so on are used while parsing the XML document.

Q.25 Why is XSLT an important tool in development of web applications ?

AU : May-16

Ans. : The XSLT stands for XSL Transformations. It is used for defining the XSL document transformations and presentations. Thus XSLT decides how an XML document should look on web browser.

Q.26 What is XML parser ?

AU : Dec 17

Ans. : XML parser is a parser that is designed to read XML and check the well formedness of the document. The XML parser also validates the document.

Q.27 What is Well formed XML document ? **AU : May-18**

Ans. : Refer section 8.3.

Q.28 What are the different data types used in XML Schema ?

Ans. :

Data Types	Description
String	The string is a collection of characters. This data type is used to define the elements containing characters, lines, tabs or white spaces. It is denoted by **type=xs:string**
Date	For specifying the date we use this data type. The format is yyyy-mm-dd where y denotes year, m denotes month and d denotes the day. It is specified using **type=xs:date**
Numeric	For specifying the numeric values this data type is used. This can be denoted as either **type=xs:decimal** or **type=xs:integer**
Boolean	For specifying the true or false values the Boolean data type is used. It is denoted as **type=xs:boolean**

Q.29 Compare DTD and Schema. **AU : May-10**

Ans. :

1. Both the schemas and DTDs are useful for defining structural components of XML. But the DTDs are basic and cannot be much specific for complex operations. On the other hand schemas are more specific.
2. The schemas provide support for defining the type of data. The DTDs do not have this ability. Hence content definition is possible using schema.
3. The schemas are namespace aware and DTDs are not.
4. The XML schema is written in XML itself and has a large number of built in and derived types.
5. The schema is the W3C recommendation. Hence it is supported by various XML validator and XML processors but there are some XML processors which do not support DTD.
6. Large number of web applications can be built using XML schema. On the other hand relatively simple and compact operations can be built using DTD.

Q.30 What is the purpose of XML schema ? **AU : May-13**

Ans. : The XML schemas are used to represent the structure of XML document. The purpose of XML schema is to define the building blocks of an XML document.

Q.31 Explain the term XML schema. **AU : Dec.-13**

Ans. : The XML schema are used to represent the structure of XML document. The goal of XML schema is to define building blocks of an XML document.

Q.32 What is RSS ?

Ans. : RSS stands for Really Simple Syndication. It is used to publish frequently updated information. For instance - blog entires, news headlines, videos all these can be RSS feeds.

Q.33 How RSS is more important than email ? Comment.

Ans. : By offering an RSS feed user can have an ability to embed his/her contents on other sites. An email subscription is when people subscribe to your new posts via email. RSS is more important than email because - 1. RSS feeds won't get trapped in your email spam filter, and 2. They have no file size limits. They are 100 % deliverable.

Q.34 List the steps to get your RSS file up on the web.

Ans. : To get the RSS file up on the web following steps are used -

1. Name the RSS file with an extension .xml.
2. Validate the RSS file.
3. Upload the RSS file to a web directory on your web server.
4. Copy the RSS or XML buttons to your web directory.

Q.35 What are the advantages of web feeds ?

Ans. : Following are the advantages of web feeds -

1. User need not have to specify their email addresses while subscribing the web feed. Hence there are no unlike email threats such as spam or phishing.
2. User need not have to send the unsubscribe information. He simply removes the feed from aggregator in order to stop getting news from the feed.
3. The feeds are obtained in sorted manner.

Q.36 What is atom ?

Ans. : Atom is an XML based file format used to syndicate content. It is developed as an alternative to RSS but it is more robust and is feature rich than RSS.

Q.37 What is news feed ?

Ans. : News feed is a kind of document(or some data format) which is providing updated contents to its users.

Q.38 What is the use of web feed ? **AU : May-18**

Ans. : The web feed provides very efficiently the updated information on the topic of user's interest.

For instance - By subscribing to a News feed or web feed, you can conveniently get a feed on the topic *"cricket"* without having to go to particular website as well as catch up on all the history sites you are interested in without visiting each site.

Q.39 What is the advantage of RSS document ? **May 2018**

Ans. : Following are the advantages of RSS feed.

1. The main benefit of RSS is that instead of having to go out to each individual website and see if there is any new content, content comes to you in one centralized location.
2. It gives you the latest updates. This saves surfing time.
3. It is spam free.
4. It can be used as an advertising or marketing tool.

❑❑❑

Unit V

9 AJAX

Syllabus

AJAX : Ajax Client Server Architecture - XML Http Request Object - Call Back Methods.

Contents

9.1 AJAX Client Server Architecture

AU : Dec.-15, 16, May-16, 19 Marks 16

9.1.1 Introduction to AJAX

- AJAX is a **A**synchronous **Ja**va **Script** and XML
- Here
  - o **Asynchronous** means, the execution of script does not disturb the user's work.
  - o **JavaScript** because, it makes use of Javascripting to do the actual work.
  - o **XML** because along with JavaScript the XML is also supported to perform the given task in AJAX.
- It is not a new programming language but it is a kind of web document which adopts certain standards.
- AJAX allows the developer to exchange the data with the server and updates the part of web document without reloading the web page.

9.1.2 Architecture

- When user makes a request, the browser creates a object for the **HttpRequest** and a request is made to the server over an internet.
- The Server processes this request and sends the required data to the browser.
- At the browser side the returned data is processed using JavaScript and the web document gets updated accordingly by sending the appropriate response.

Following Fig. 9.1.1 illustrates this working.

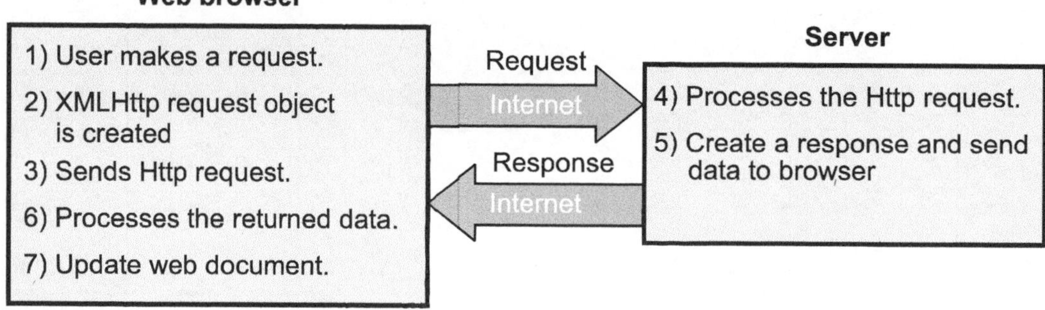

Fig. 9.1.1 Working of AJAX

Similarities and Differences

Sr.No.	Traditional Web Application Architecture	Ajax Based Web Application Architecture
1.	The web applications architectures are based on HTTP request response protocol.	

2.	At the client side the browser client has only one component and that is – user interface.	At the client side the browser client has user interface and AJAX Engine due to which the client gets quick response from the server.
3.	The architecture is based on client server communication.	
4.	It makes use of synchronous communication. The client has to wait to get the response from the server then only client can make the request to the server. It is start-stop-start-stop kind of communication.	By adding a new layer of AJAX Engine at the client side, it eliminates the start-stop-start-stop nature of communication and makes the communication asynchronous.
5.	With traditional web application architecture user cannot get rich user interface experience.	With AJAX architecture user gets rich user interface experience.
6.	It is less responsive.	It is more responsive.
7.	Building web application is simple.	The development time is more while designing the Ajax based web application.
8.	Limited use of JavaScript, CSS and XML technologies. In fact - Most user actions in the interface trigger an HTTP request back to a web server.	Extensive use of JavaScript, CSS and XML - i) standards-based presentation using XHTML and CSS; ii) Dynamic display and interaction using the Document Object Model(DOM); iii) Data interchange and manipulation using XML and XSLT; iv) Asynchronous data retrieval using XMLHttpRequest; v) JavaScript binding everything together

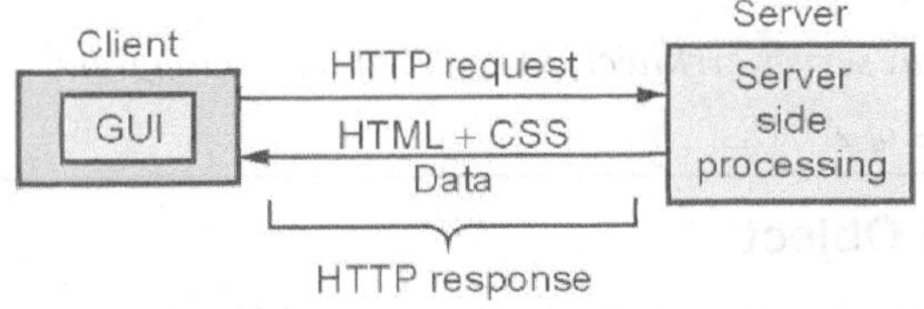

Fig. 9.1.2 Traditional web application architecture

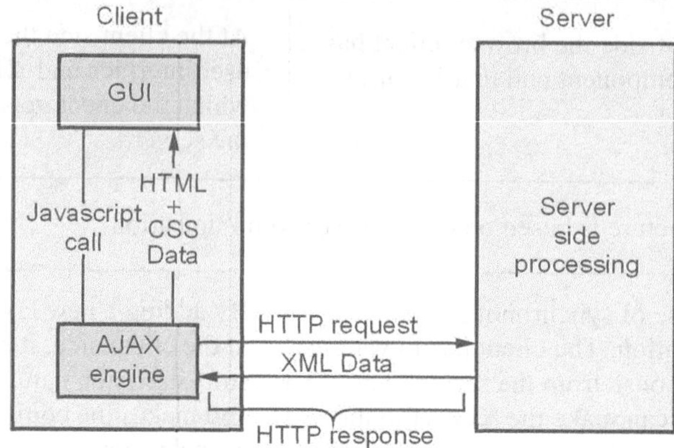

Fig. 9.1.3 AJAX web application architecture

Merits of AJAX

1. Response time is faster, hence increases performance and speed.
2. XMLHttpRequest object call as a asynchronous HTTP request to the Server for transferring data both side. It's used for making requests to the non-Ajax pages.
3. It is used in form validation.
4. It performs fetching of data from database and storing of data into database without reloading page.

Demerits of AJAX

1. It has browsing compatibility issues.
2. It is impossible to bookmark AJAX updated page contents.
3. Search engine would not crawl AJAX generated content. Hence, Search Engines like Google cannot index AJAX pages.

University Questions

1. *Discuss Ajax client server architecture in detail.* **AU : Dec.-15, Marks 16**
2. *Compare and contrast the traditional web application architecture and AJAX based web application architecture.* **AU : May-16, Marks 16**
3. *Explain the Ajax client server architecture in detail with a diagram.* **AU : Dec.-16, Marks 8**
4. *List the pros and cons of AJAX.* **AU : May-19, Marks 5**

9.2 XMLHttpRequest Object

AU : May-17, 19 Marks 10

- XMLHttpRequest object is an important element in AJAX.
- XMLHttpRequest is an API which is used by JavaScript, VBScript and some other scripting languages.

- The methods of XMLHttpRequest are used in transferring data between a Web browser and a web server.
- It is because of XMLHttpRequest object, to update parts of web page without reloading the whole page.

Syntax

```
Variable = new XMLHttpRequest();
```

Various Methods of XMLHttpRequest object

Method	Purpose
new XMLHttpRequest()	Creates new XMLHttpRequest object.
Open(method, URL, async,user,pwd)	To make request this method is used. method: The request can be GET or POST URL: The location of file async: true(for asynchronous) and false(synchronous) user: user name(optional) pwd:password(optional)
send()	sends the request to the server.
send(string)	sends the request to the server.
setRequestHeader()	Adds the label- value pair to the header.

Various Properties of XMLHttpRequest object

Property	Description
readyState	Specifies the ready state of XMLHttpRequest 0: request not initialized 1: server connection established 2: request received 3: processing request 4: request finished and response is ready
onreadystatechange	When readystate property changes the onreadystatechange event listener will be automatically invoked
responseText	Returns the response data as a string
status	Returns the status number. Following is the meaning of various numbers returned by the status property

	200: "OK" 403: "Forbidden" 404: "Not Found"
statusText	Returns the status text as "OK", or "Forbidden"

Ex. 9.2.1 Create an XMLHttpRequest to retrieve data from an XML file and display the data in an HTML table. The data to be retrieved is a collection of stationary items stored in an XML file.

AU : May -17, Marks 10

Sol. : Step 1 : Create an xml file storing the stationary items. The code is as follows -

```
/ELEMENTS>
<STATIONARY>
<ITEM>Notebook</ITEM>
<PRICE>40</PRICE>
</STATIONARY>
<STATIONARY>
<ITEM>Punching Machine</ITEM>
<PRICE>60</PRICE>
</STATIONARY>
<STATIONARY>
<ITEM>Pencil Box</ITEM>
<PRICE>40</PRICE>
</STATIONARY>
<STATIONARY>
<ITEM>Eraser</ITEM>
<PRICE>5</PRICE>
</STATIONARY>
</ELEMENTS>
```

Step 2 : The XML file displaying the stationary items in a tabular form is as given below –

```
test.html
<!DOCTYPE html>
<html>
<body>
<button type="button" onclick="loadXMLDoc()">Display Stationary Items</button>
<br><br>
<table id="demo" border="1"></table>
<script>
function loadXMLDoc()
{
 if(window.XMLHttpRequest)
 {
     xmlhttp = new XMLHttpRequest();
 }
       else
```

```
{
    xmlhttp = new ActiveXObject("Microsoft.req");//to execute on Inter. Explorer
 }
 xmlhttp.onreadystatechange = function()
 {
     if (this.readyState == 4 && this.status == 200) {
     myFunction(this);
}
};
     xmlhttp.open("GET","stationary.xml",true);
   xmlhttp.send();
}
function myFunction(xml)
{
 var i;
     var xmlDoc = xml.responseXML;
      var table="<tr><th>Item</th><th>Price(Rs.)</th></tr>";
     var x = xmlDoc.getElementsByTagName("STATIONARY");
     for (i = 0; i <x.length; i++)
      {
    table += "<tr><td>" +
    x[i].getElementsByTagName("ITEM")[0].childNodes[0].nodeValue +
    "</td><td>" +
    x[i].getElementsByTagName("PRICE")[0].childNodes[0].nodeValue +
    "</td></tr>";
 }
 document.getElementById("demo").innerHTML = table;
}
</script>
</body>
</html>
```

Output

/d:/test.ht

file:///

Display Stationary Items

Item	Price(Rs.)
Notebook	40
Punching Machine	60
Pencil Box	40
Eraser	5

University Question

1. *Explain the XMLHttpRequest object methods.* **AU : May-19, Marks 8**

9.3 Call Back Methods

- Callback functions are used to handle responses from the server in Ajax. A callback function can be either a named function or an anonymous function.
- We can set the value of event handler onreadystatechange equal to anonymous function as follows –

```
req.onreadystatechange=function()
{
    if (req.readyState==4 && req.status==200)
    {
      document.getElementById("myID").innerHTML=req.responseText;
    }
}
```

- We can write the call back function as named function using following steps –

Step 1 : Create XMLHttpRequest obect in global space

```
var req = new XMLHttpRequest();
```

Step 2 : Write a function which acts as a callback function

```
function myCallBkFun()
{
    if (req.readyState==4 && req.status==200)
     {
     Cosole.log(req.responseText);
     }
}
```

Step 3 : Now we can set the value of onreadystatechange property to the name of the call back function.

```
//assigning call back function to onreadystatechange property
req. onreadystatechange=myCallBkFun;
```

9.4 Coding AJAX Script **AU : Dec.-18, Marks 13**

Let understand how AJAX works with the help of programming example

```
<html>
 <head>
  <script type="text/javascript">
   function MyFun()
```

```
{
    if (window.XMLHttpRequest)
  {
    req=new XMLHttpRequest();
  }
  else
   {
     req=new ActiveXObject("Microsoft.req");
   }
  req.onreadystatechange=function()
   {
     if (req.readyState==4 && req.status==200)
      {
           document.getElementById("myID").innerHTML=req.responseText;
      }
   }
   req.open("GET","newdata.txt",true);
   req.send();
}
</script>
</head>
<body>
<div id="myID">This text can be changed</div>

<button type="button" onclick="MyFun()">Change</button>
</body>
</html>
```

(Callouts in the listing: 2 – the XMLHttpRequest/ActiveXObject block; 3 – the readyState check; 4 – req.open; 5 – req.send; 1 – the button.)

Script Explanation (Above numbered steps are explained here)

In above script, we have written some text which can be replaced by some another text on button click.

1. On button click a function **MyFun** is invoked. Thus client triggers the event.
2. **XMLHttpRequest** object is used to exchange data with a server. This object allows the user to change/update the parts of the web page without reloading it fully. The modern web browsers such as IE7+, FireFox,Chrome have built in **XMLHttpRequest** but old web browsers make use of **ActiveXObject**.
3. When a request to a server is sent, then **onreadystatechange** event is triggered.

The **readyState** property holds the status of the XMLHttpRequest. The **readystate=4** means request is finished and response is ready. The **status = 200** means "OK"

The DOM is modified and response is modified using the statement

```
document.getElementById("myID").innerHTML=req.responseText;
```

4. The request can be sent to the server by using two functions **open()** and **send()**.

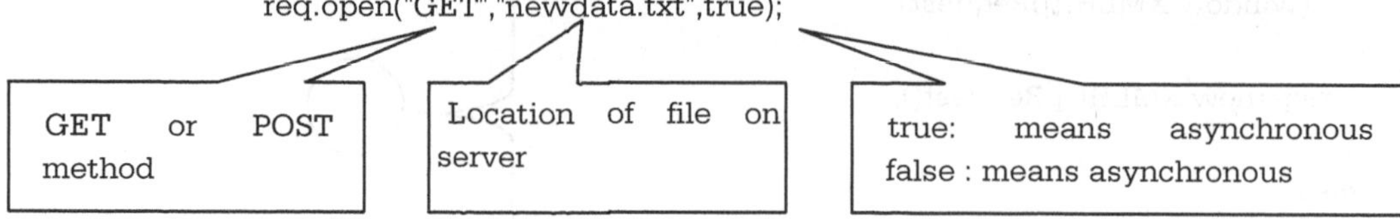

Asynchronous communication allows fast processing of the data.

The **newdata.txt** file contains some updating text using which our web page can be updated.

newdata.txt

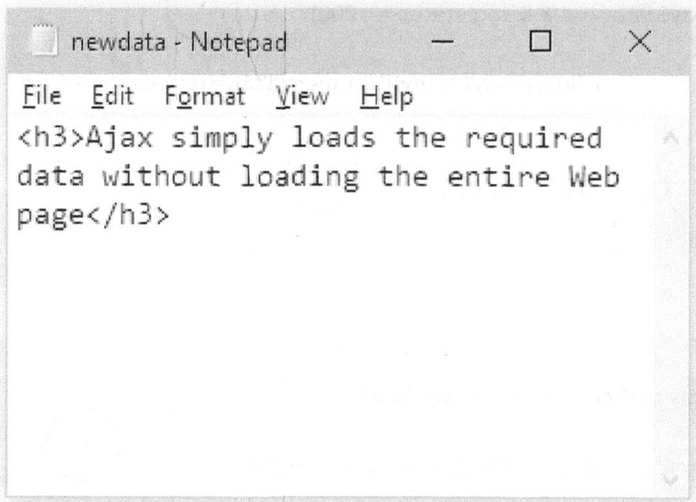

5. The **send()** method sends the request to the server.

Output

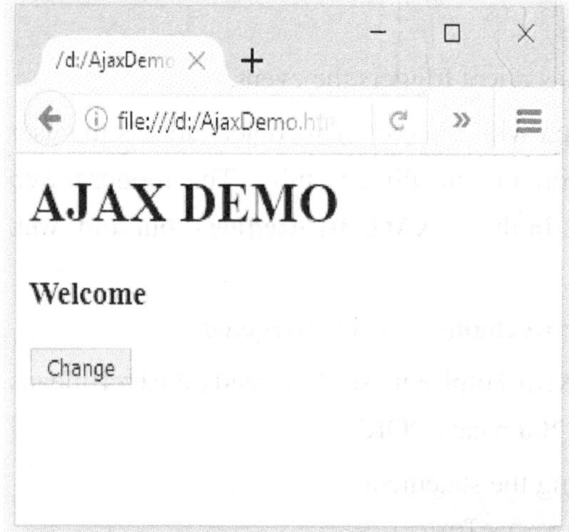

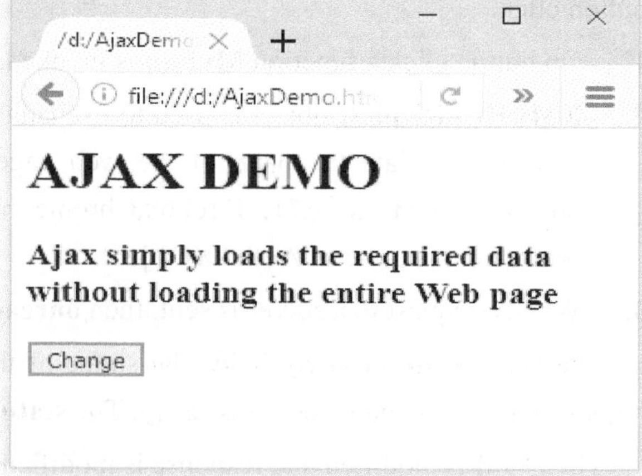

Ex. 9.4.1 : Write AJAX script to obtain the student information stored in XML document. The information should be displayed on clicking the button. It should be displayed in tabular form.

Sol. :

Step 1 : Create an XML file for storing the student information. The XML file is as follows

Student.xml

```
<Student>
    <student_data>
     <Name>AAA</Name>
     <Marks>45</Marks>
    </student_data>
    <student_data>
     <Name>BBB</Name>
     <Marks>55</Marks>
    </student_data>
    <student_data>
     <Name>CCC</Name>
     <Marks>67</Marks>
    </student_data>
    <student_data>
     <Name>DDD</Name>
     <Marks>84</Marks>
    </student_data>
</Student>
```

Step 2 : Create a AJAX script as follows –

AjaxXMLDemo.html

```
<!DOCTYPE html>
<html>
<body>
<h1>STUDENT INFORMATION</h1>
<button type="button" onclick="MyFun()">Click</button>
<br><br>
<table border="1" id="demo"></table>
<script>
function MyFun()
{
    var xhttp = new XMLHttpRequest();
    xhttp.onreadystatechange = function()
    {
     if (this.readyState == 4 && this.status == 200)
     {
```

```
            Load_XML_File(this);
        }
    };
    xhttp.open("GET", "Student.xml", true);
    xhttp.send();
}
function Load_XML_File(xml)
{
    var i;
    var xmlDoc = xml.responseXML;
    var table="<tr><th>Name</th><th>Marks</th></tr>";
    var x = xmlDoc.getElementsByTagName("student_data");
    for (i = 0; i <x.length; i++)
    {
     table += "<tr><td>" +
     x[i].getElementsByTagName("Name")[0].childNodes[0].nodeValue +
     "</td><td>" +
     x[i].getElementsByTagName("Marks")[0].childNodes[0].nodeValue +
     "</td></tr>";
    }
    document.getElementById("demo").innerHTML = table;
}
</script>
</body>
</html>
```

Step 3 : Open the web browser and the output will be as follows –

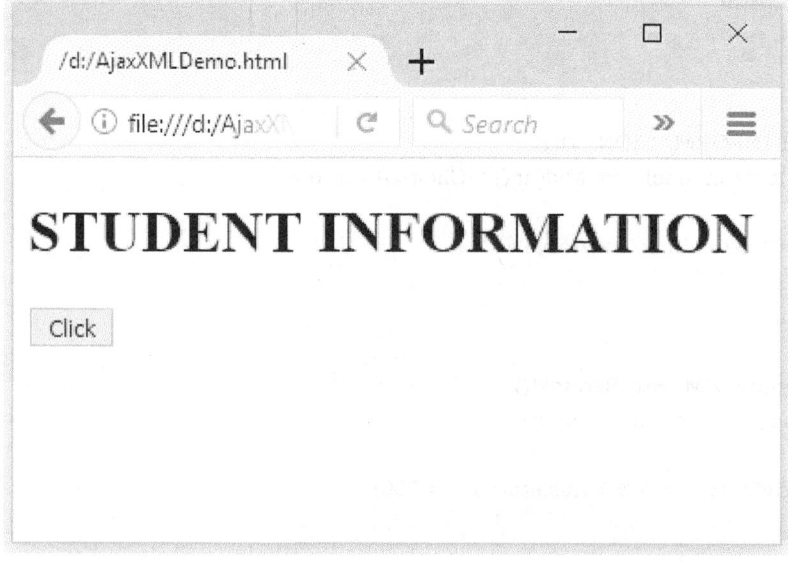

On clicking the button we will get

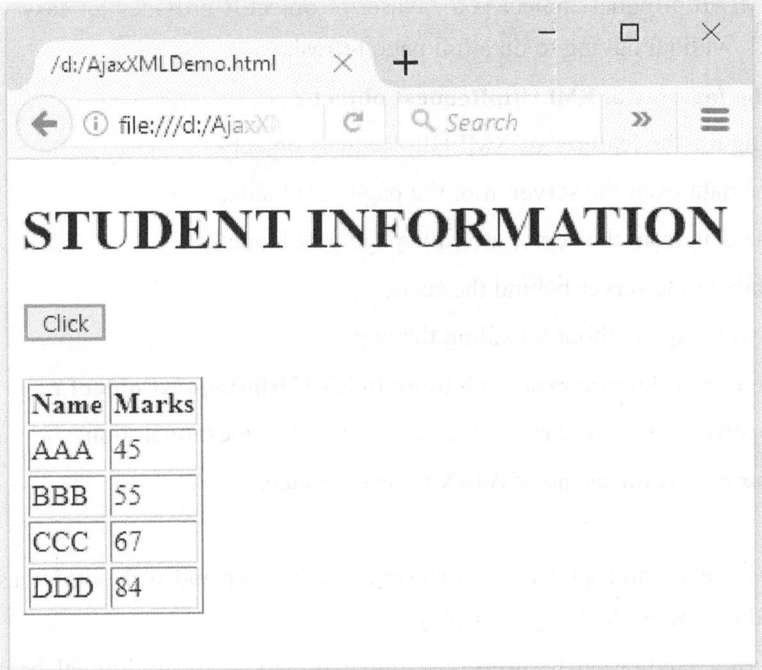

University Question

1. *Explain about the object that helps AJAX reload parts of a web page without reloading the whole page.* **AU : Dec.-18, Marks 13**

Two Marks Questions with Answers

Q.1 What is AJAX ?

Ans. : AJAX is a Asynchronous Java Script. It is not a new programming language but it is a kind of web document which adopts certain standards. AJAX allows the developer to exchange the data with the server and updates the part of web document without reloading the web page.

Q.2 What is Http Request Object ?

Ans. : XMLHttpRequest is an API which is used by JavaScript, VBScript and some other scripting languages.

The methods of XMLHttpRequest are used in transferring data between a Web browser and a web server.

Q.3 What is call back method in AJAX ? **AU : May - 19**

Ans. : Callback functions are used to handle responses from the server in Ajax. A callback function can be either a named function or an anonymous function.

Q.4 What is the use of XMLHttp Request object ? **AU : Dec.-17**

Ans. : The XMLHttpRequest object is a Javascript object.It provides an easy way to retrieve data from a URL without having to do a full page refresh.

Q.5 What are the features of XMLHttpRequest object ?

Ans. : Following are the features of XMLHttpRequest object -

1. Requests the data from the server after the page gets loaded.
2. Receives the data from the server after the page gets loaded.
3. Sends the data to the server behind the scene.
4. Update the web page without reloading the page.

Q.6 What is the use of the property readyState in XMLHttpRequest object ?

Ans. : This property is used to retrive the current state of request operation.

Q.7 List any four merits for usage of AJAX in web service. **AU : Dec.-15**

Ans. :

1) AJAX allows easier and quicker interaction between user and web service as the pages are not reloaded for the contents to be displayed.
2) It allows easier navigation to users in comparison to using traditional back and forward button on a browser.
3) Traffic to and from the server is reduced a considerable amount.
4) The web service becomes more responsive and interactive as the user gets the response without clicking any buttons.
5) If one section of a page encounters any error, other sections do not get affected and the data entered by the user is also not lost.

Q.8 What is the role of a callback function in performing a partial page update in an AJAX application ? **AU : May-16**

Ans. : Partial page update are a part of callback functions which process returned data from a server and only update the parts of the page the callback says to update.

Unit V

10 Introduction to Web Services

Syllabus

Introduction- Java web services Basics – Creating, Publishing, Testing and Describing a Web services (WSDL)-Consuming a web service, Database Driven web service from an application –SOAP.

Contents

10.1 Introduction to Web Services

> **Definition :** The Web Services are the software systems that are displayed by the web browser using the web protocol. These software systems are used by the some software applications rather than by end-users directly.

- Web service is a software system designed which is **independent** of specific hardware or software on which it is running.
- **Examples** of a web service are -
  1. **Credit card validation system -** For using this service the client simply enters the ID and password for the credit card and web service reports the validity of it.
  2. **Whether forecast system -** The clients submits the location and the web service returns the information about current whether as well as it may report some predictions.
  3. **Currency converter -** The client enter the source and destination currency along with the amount and appropriate converted information will be displyed.

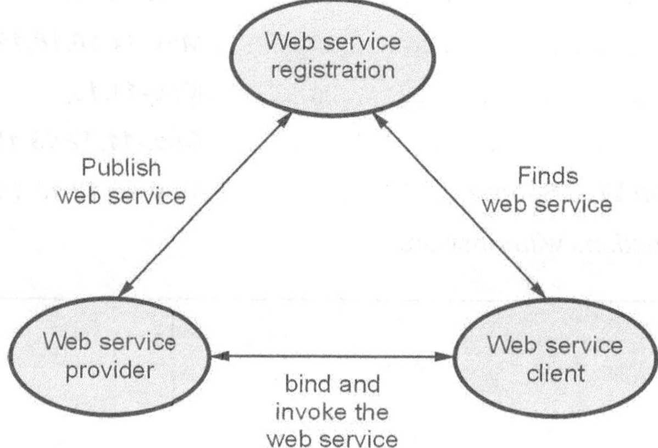

Fig. 10.1.1 Basic web service model

Following are the steps that a web service model follows -

Step 1 : In the first step, a service provider **publishes** a web service in the **web service registry**.

Step 2 : A web client who demands for some web service **searches** in the registry. After finding a match for the desired web service in the registry. After finding a match for the desired web service in the registry, the client chooses it.

Step 3 : The client **binds** to the corresponding web service provider and **invokes** for the service.

10.2 Java Web Service Basics

AU : Dec.-12, Marks 8

10.2.1 Concept of RPC

- RPC stands for **Remote Procedure Call**. This technique is basically used in distributed client-server applications.
- By using RPC one can call the any procedure situated in some remote machine. Thus, this technique facilitates that the procedure need not exist in the same address space as the calling procedure.
- Following scenario illustrates the working of RPC.

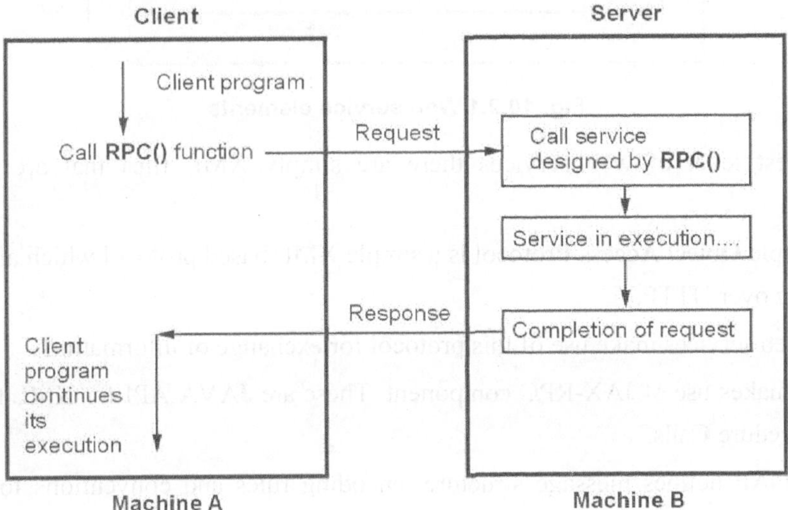

- RPC is similar to the procedure call.
- When a RPC is called the calling arguments are passed to the remote procedure and the caller waits for the response.
- The client makes a remote procedure call by sending a request to the server.
- At the server end, when the request arrives, server calls dispatch routine and process for the requested service. Finally it sends the replay to the client and then client program continues its execution.

10.2.2 JAX-RPC

The role of various components such as XML, SOAP, WSDL, UDDI in web service building is as shown below -

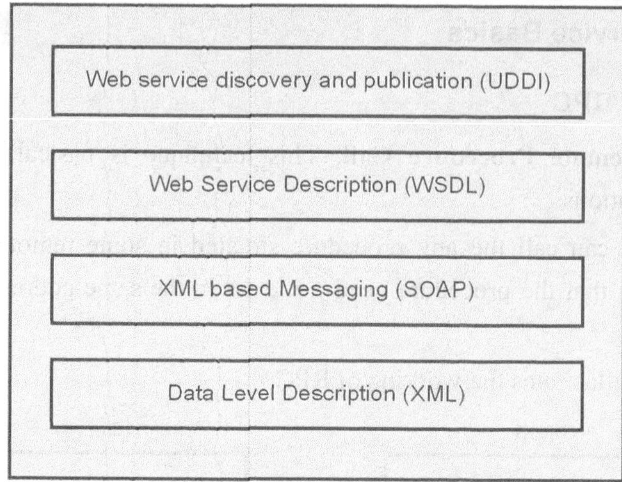

Fig. 10.2.1 Web service elements

- At the lowest level of web services there are simply XML files that are for data level description.
- SOAP - **S**imple **O**bject **A**ccess **P**rotocol is a simple XML based protocol which allows exchange of messaging over HTTP.

  Typically web services make use of this protocol for exchange of information .

The SOAP makes use of JAX-RPC component. These are **JA**VA **A**PI for **X**ML that makes use of **R**emote **P**rocedure **C**alls.

Basically SOAP defines message structure, encoding rules and conventions for exchange of information in RPC programming model.

The following table describes core JAX-RPC interfaces and classes.

Interface / Class	Description
Service	Main client interface. Used for both static and dynamic invocations.
Service Factory	This is a factory class which is used to create services
Stub	It is used by client for invoking the web services.
Call	For invoking the web services the call is used.
JAXRPCException	This exception is thrown when an error occurs while invoking web service.

- At the higher level very important element of web service lies i.e. WSDL. The **W**eb **S**ervice **D**escription **L**anguage is used for abstract description of web services. This description is provided in XML document. When the client wants to make use of web service, the users of the client make read this description file and understand what input data is needed to perform the web service. Such a special file is called WSDL i.e. seb services Description Language.

- UDDI i.e. **U**niversal **D**escription and **D**iscovery **I**ntegration, provides a directory of web services, so that client can easily discover the services of their choices. The UDDI maintains a registry in which the web services are registered.

In this chapter we will learn how to develop a simple web service using JAX-RPC. Further we will learn how to build a **web client** for using this service.

University Question

1. *Explain the basic concept of RPC.* **AU : Dec.-12, Marks 8**

10.3 Creating, Publishing, Testing Web Service **AU : May-12,14, Dec.-13, 16, Marks 16**

In this section We will Create two Web Projects – one for Server and other for Client.

The Server defines the web service and client invokes this web service

We can develop a web service using Apache Axis2 and Eclipse.

Prerequisite :

(1) JDK must be installed.

(2) Eclipse must be installed

(3) Apache Server, Tomcat must be installed. Install the software package XAMPP for this purpose.

Configuring Tomcat to Eclipse

Step A : To integrate Tomcat Server with your Eclipse, Select **File->New->Other...** from Eclipse main menu.

Step B: Select Server->Server and click Next

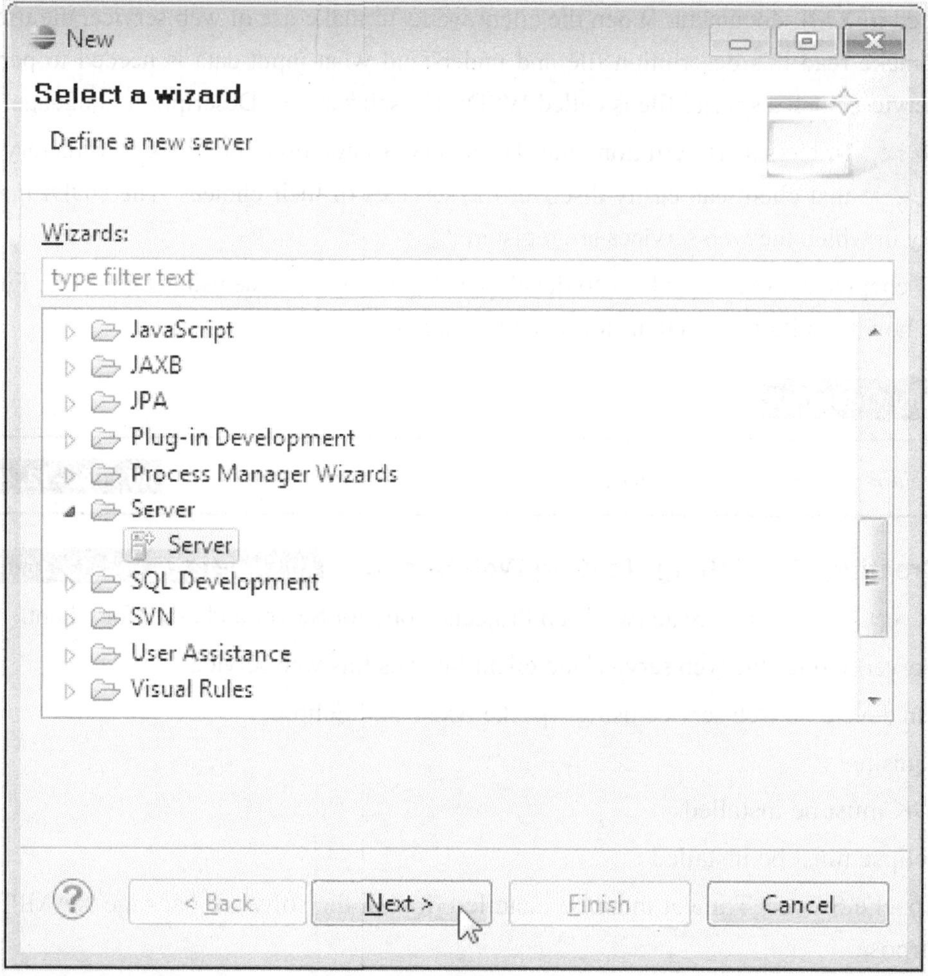

Step (3) Select Tomcat Version XX and click **Next**

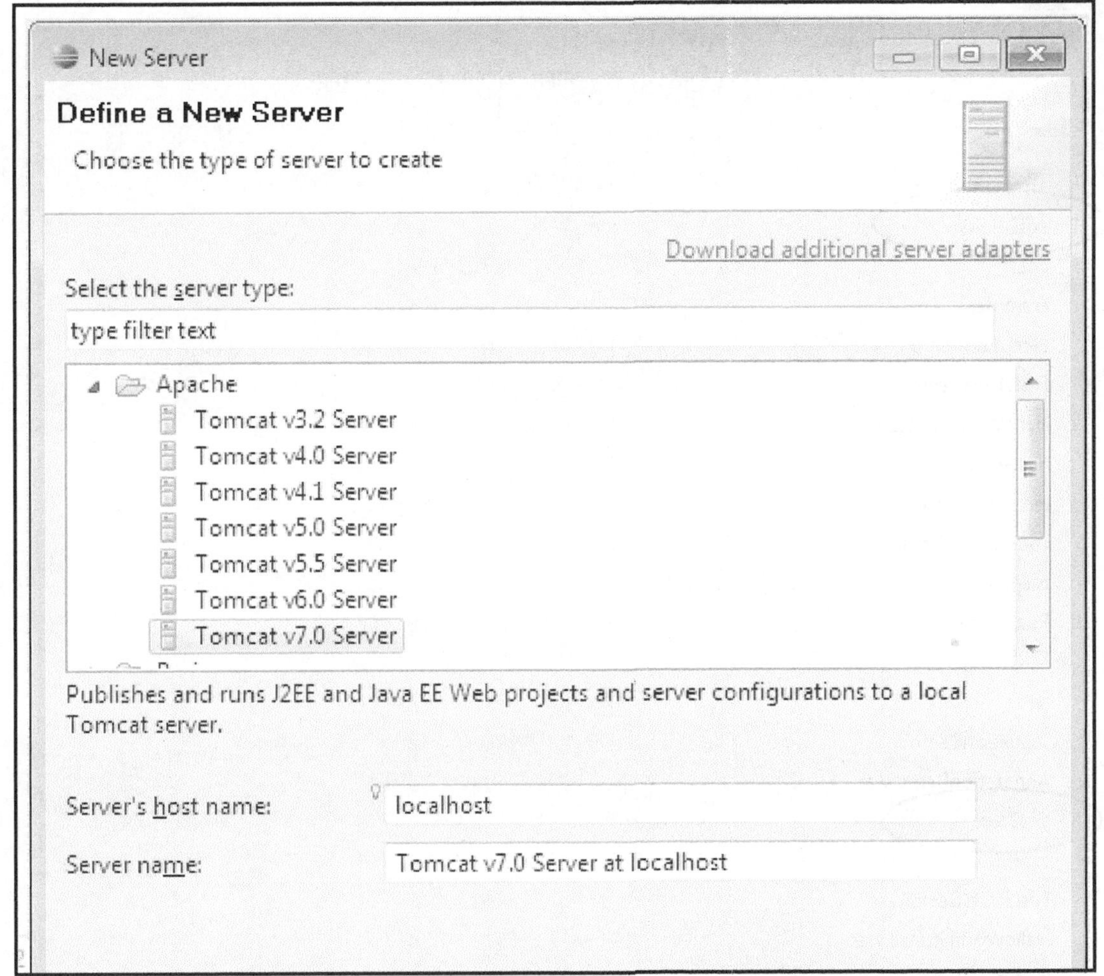

Step C: Browse to the folder of Tomcat. If XAMP is installed then it is c:\XAMPP\tomcat

Step D: Click **Finish**

(4) Install Axis2.

Installation of Axis 2 :

Step 1: Open the web browser and get the axis2 package using following URL

http://axis.apache.org/axis2/java/core/download.html

Step 2 : Click on Binary Distribution Link and download axis2-1.7.9-bin.zip. Also download axis2-1.7.9-war.zip

Step 3 : Unzip both the folders and copy these folders at your c:\tompcat-directory\webapps folder. Following screenshot helps in understanding the location

File Home Share View

This PC > Local Disk (C:) > xampp > tomcat > webapps >

Name	Date modified	Type	Size
AnnotationDemo	10-Feb-18 1:07 PM	File folder	
axis2-1.7.9	07-Apr-19 4:55 PM	File folder	
docs	27-Nov-15 11:45 A...	File folder	
examples	22-Apr-17 10:51 AM	File folder	
ExceptionDemo	10-Feb-18 1:08 PM	File folder	
FirstStrutsDemo	10-Feb-18 1:08 PM	File folder	
HelloWorldStruts2	10-Feb-18 1:08 PM	File folder	
host-manager	27-Nov-15 11:45 A...	File folder	
InceptorDemo	10-Feb-18 1:08 PM	File folder	
LocalizationDemo	10-Feb-18 1:08 PM	File folder	
manager	27-Nov-15 11:45 A...	File folder	
ResultTypeDemo	10-Feb-18 1:08 PM	File folder	
ROOT	22-Apr-17 10:54 AM	File folder	
temp	08-Apr-19 2:15 PM	File folder	
ValidationDemo	10-Feb-18 1:08 PM	File folder	
AnnotationDemo.war	12-Nov-17 1:04 PM	WAR File	4,584 KB
axis2.war	07-Apr-19 4:56 PM	WAR File	19,515 KB
ExceptionDemo.war	12-Nov-17 6:06 AM	WAR File	4,153 KB
FirstStrutsDemo.war	11-Nov-17 2:26 PM	WAR File	4,153 KB
HelloWorldStruts2.war	11-Nov-17 1:50 PM	WAR File	4,153 KB
InceptorDemo.war	11-Nov-17 4:28 PM	WAR File	4,154 KB
LocalizationDemo.war	12-Nov-17 4:31 AM	WAR File	4,154 KB
ResultTypeDemo.war	11-Nov-17 5:15 PM	WAR File	4,153 KB
ValidationDemo.war	11-Nov-17 9:12 PM	WAR File	4,154 KB

Configuring Axis2 in Eclipse

Step 1 : Open the Eclipse.

Step 2 : Click on **Window -> Preferences.**

Step 3 : Locate **Web Services.** Click **Axis2 Preferences.**

Step 4 : Set the location of Axis2 folder with the help of **Browse..** button. It is your Webapps folder in Tomcat directory. On successful deploying of Axis2, we get "Axis2 runtime loaded successfully" message. Click **Apply** and then **Ok** button.

Following screenshot illustrates it.

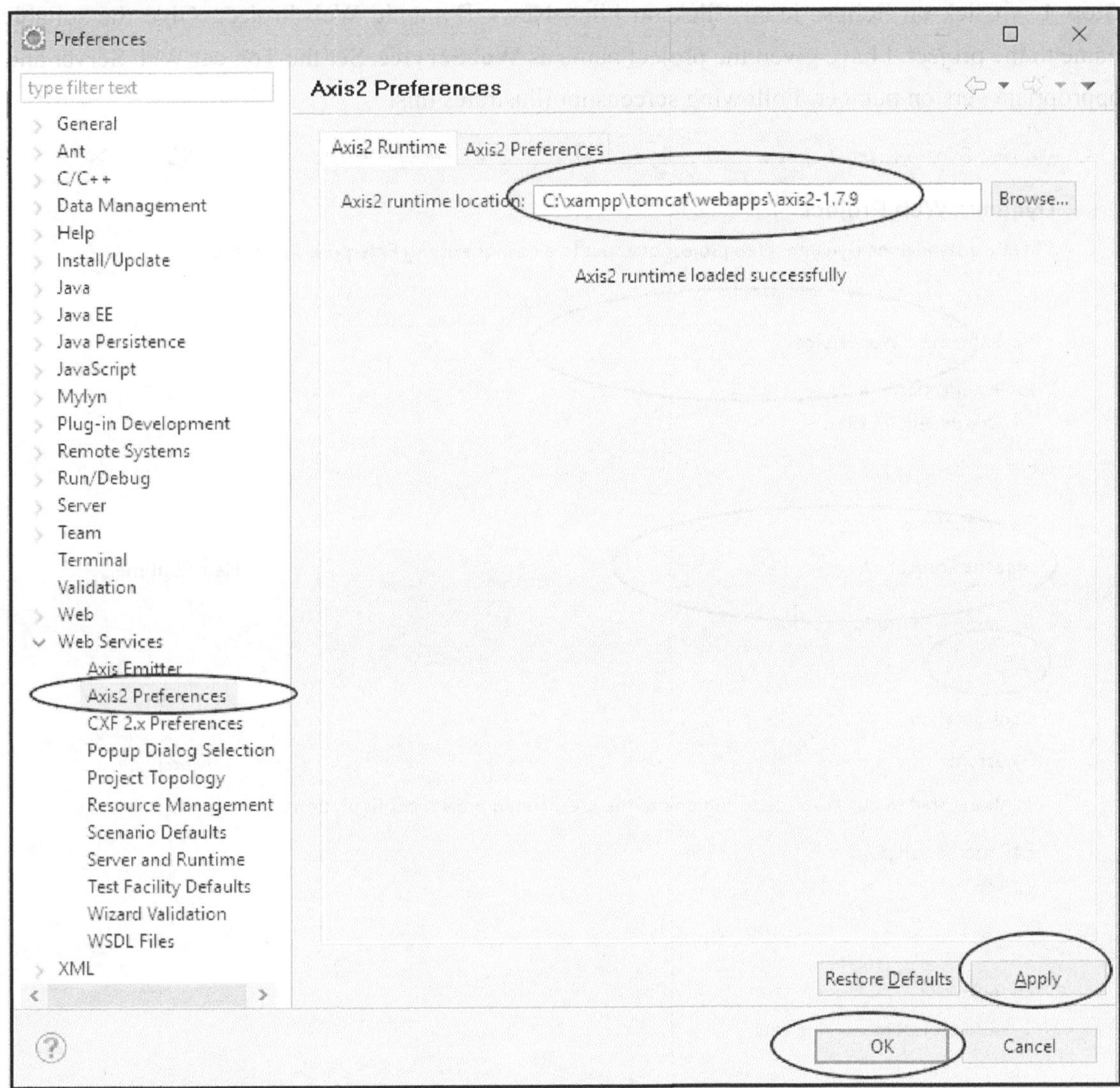

Let us now discuss step by step - how to create a simple Web Service.

Ex. 10.3.1 Create a web service in java environment to return the sum of two integers with necessary deployment procedures.

AU : May-14, Marks 16

Sol. :

Stage I : Creating Server

Step 1 : Click on Eclipse icon. Click on File->New->Dynamic Web Project. Give the suitable name to the project. I have given the project name as **WebService**. Set the Tomcat Web Server and appropriate version number. Following screenshot illustrates this.

Click **Finish** button.

Step 2 : Locate **src** folder under the project in WebService project. The snapshot of Project Explorer is as shown below

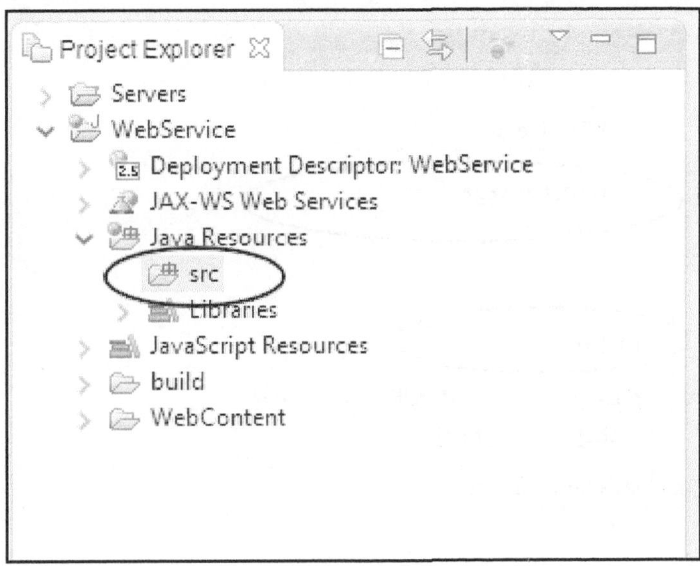

Right click on **src** folder Select **New-> Class**

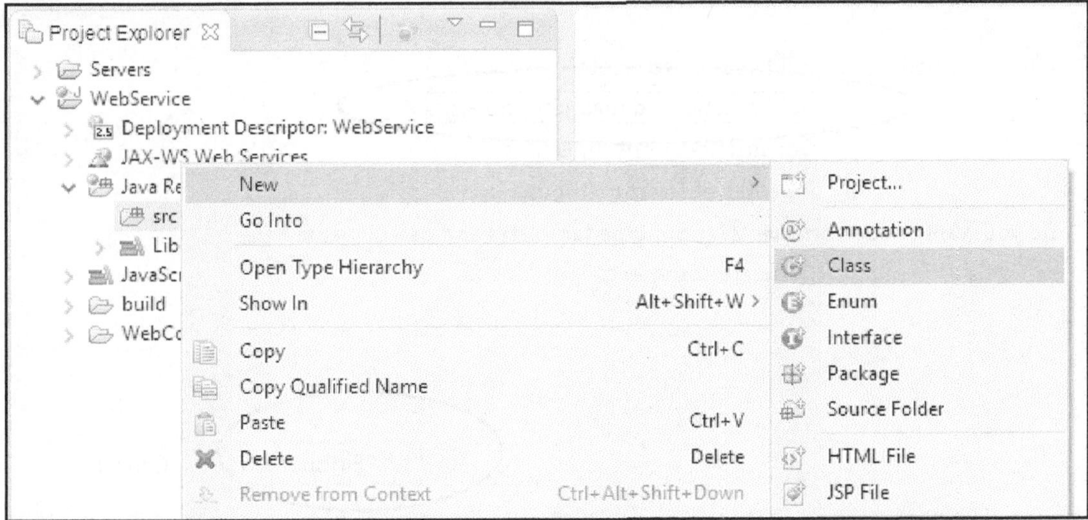

A New Class Window opens up. Give suitable Package name, Class name and uncheck the check box for void main function. Then click **Finish** button. It is illustrated by following screenshot.

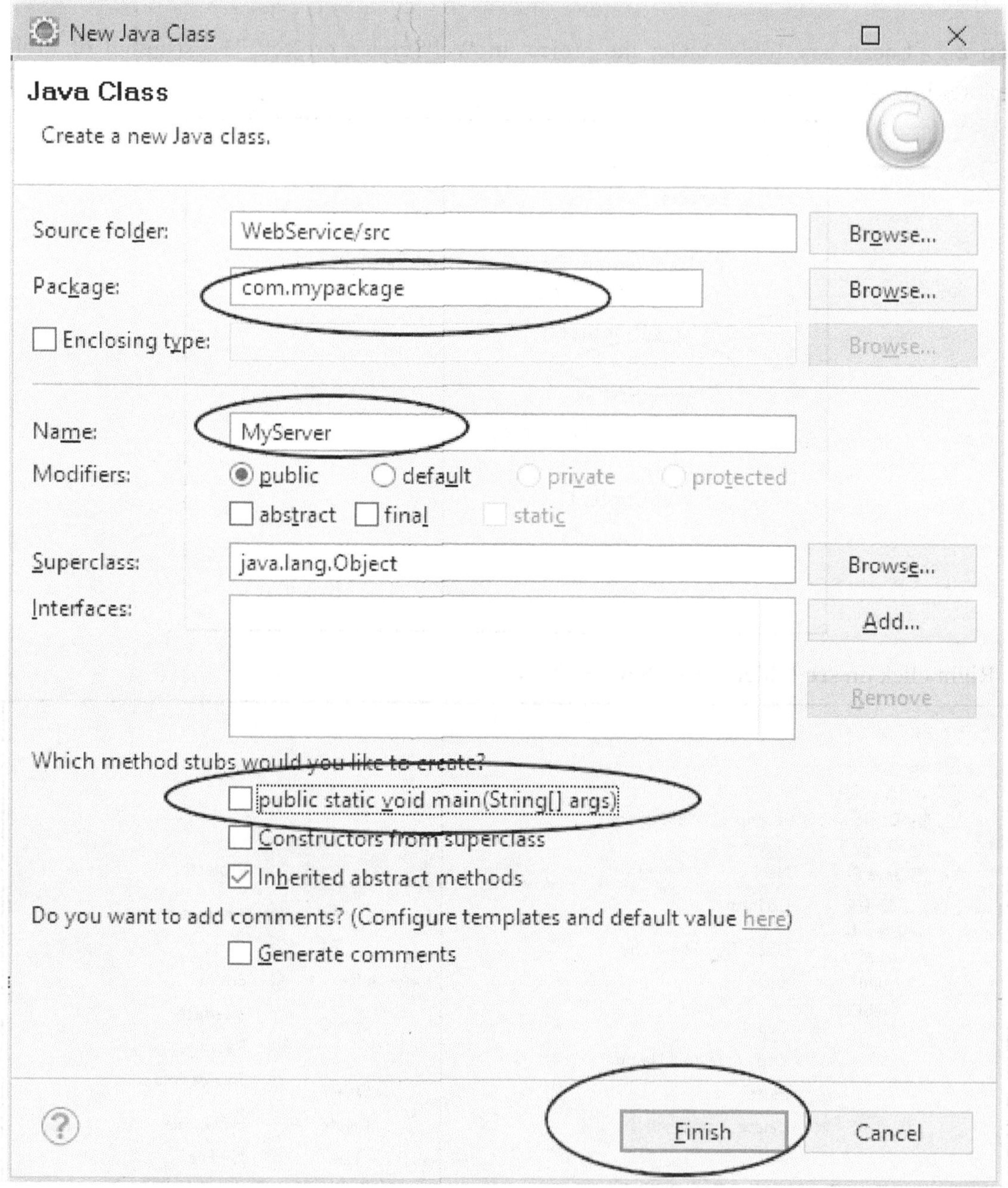

New Java Class

Java Class

Create a new Java class.

Source folder: WebService/src Browse...

Package: com.mypackage Browse...

Enclosing type: Browse...

Name: MyServer

Modifiers: public default private protected

abstract final static

Superclass: java.lang.Object Browse...

Interfaces: Add...

Remove

Which method stubs would you like to create?

public static void main(String[] args)

Constructors from superclass

Inherited abstract methods

Do you want to add comments? (Configure templates and default value here)

Generate comments

Finish Cancel

Step 3 : Now write the following code for **MyServer.java**

```
package com.mypackage;

public class MyServer {
    public int add(int a,int b){
```

```
      return a+b;
    }
}
```

Save the above code.

Step 4 : Now right click on **src** folder. Click **New->other->Web Services->Web Service.** Then click **Next** button

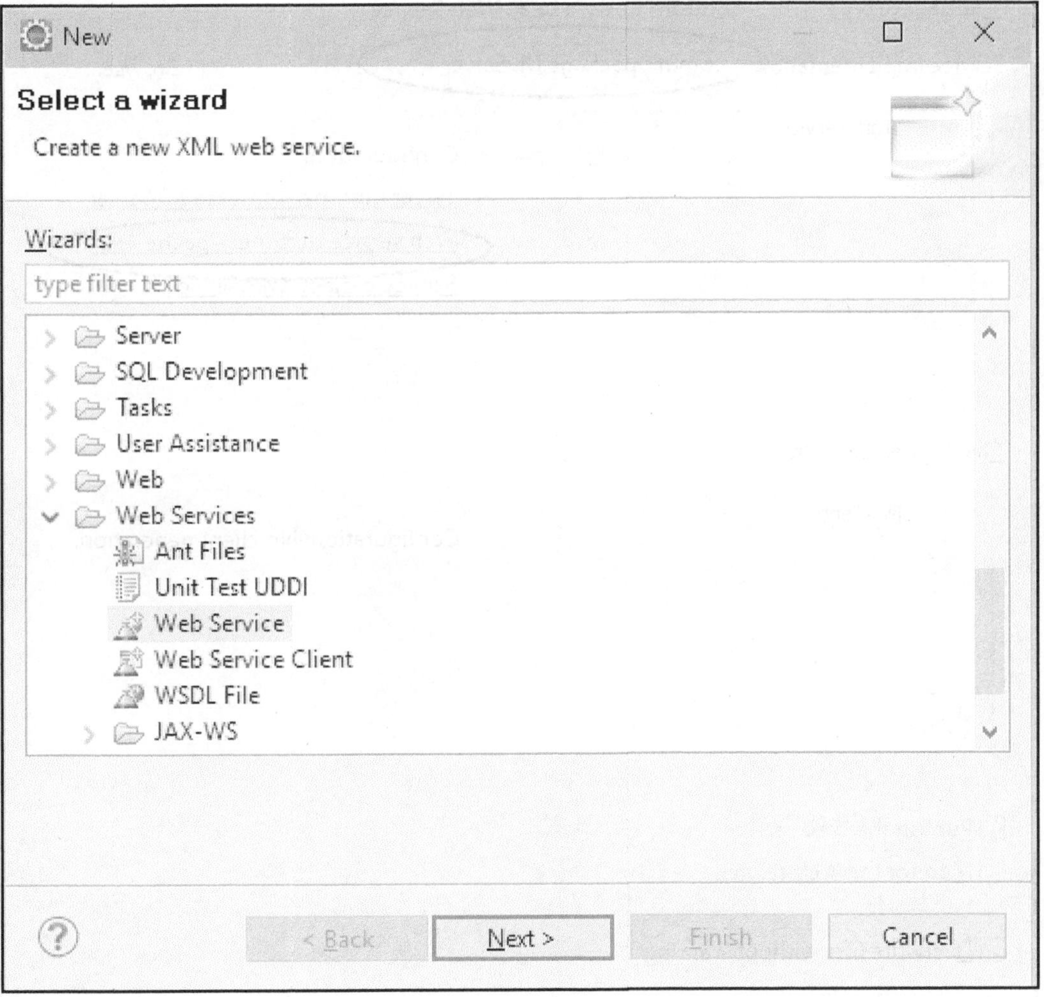

The **Web Services** window will appear. Write the name of service implementation and click on **Web service runtime:Apache Axis.** Following screenshot shows this -

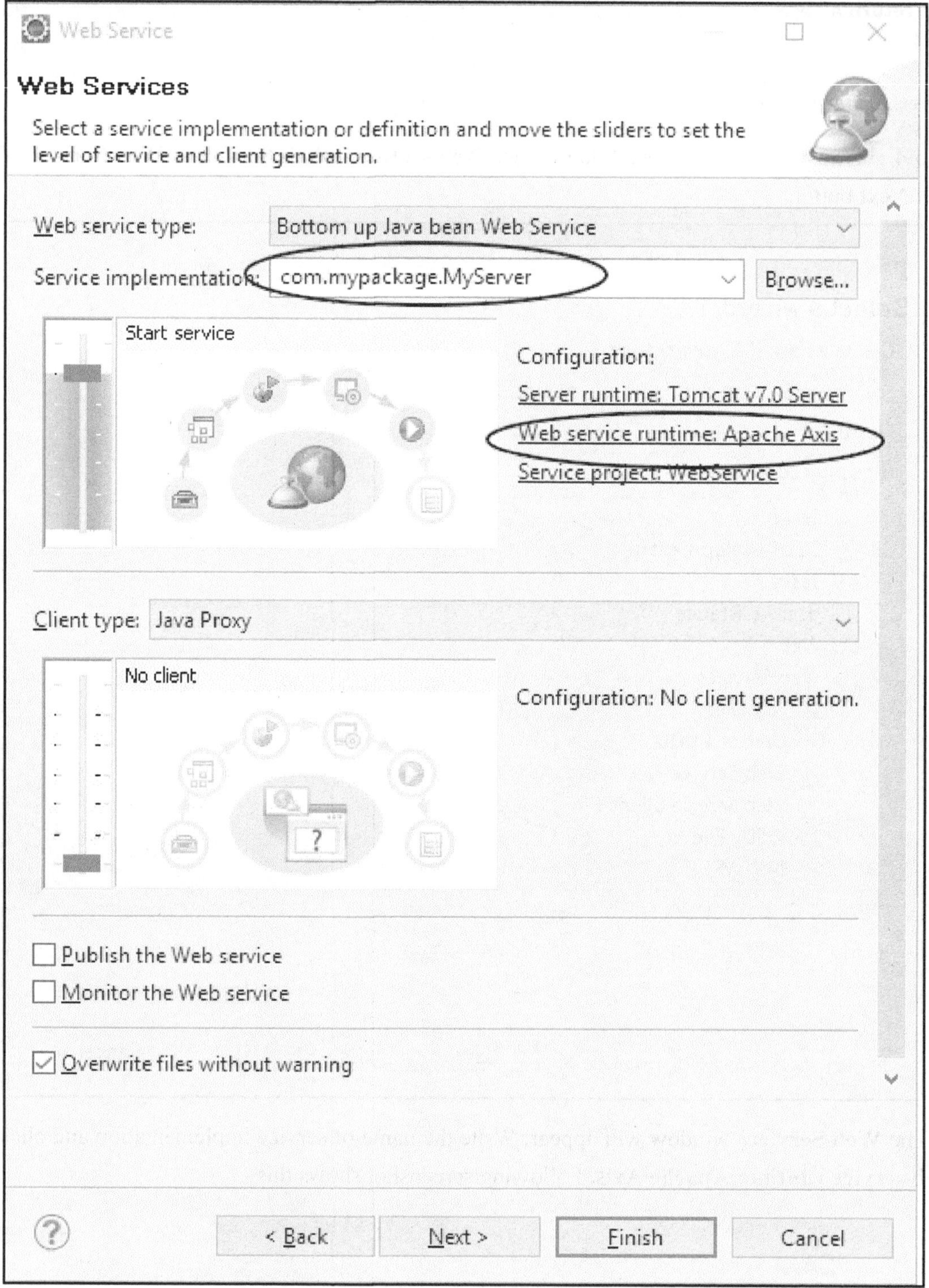

Click on **Apache Axis2** and then click **Ok** button. Refer following screenshot.

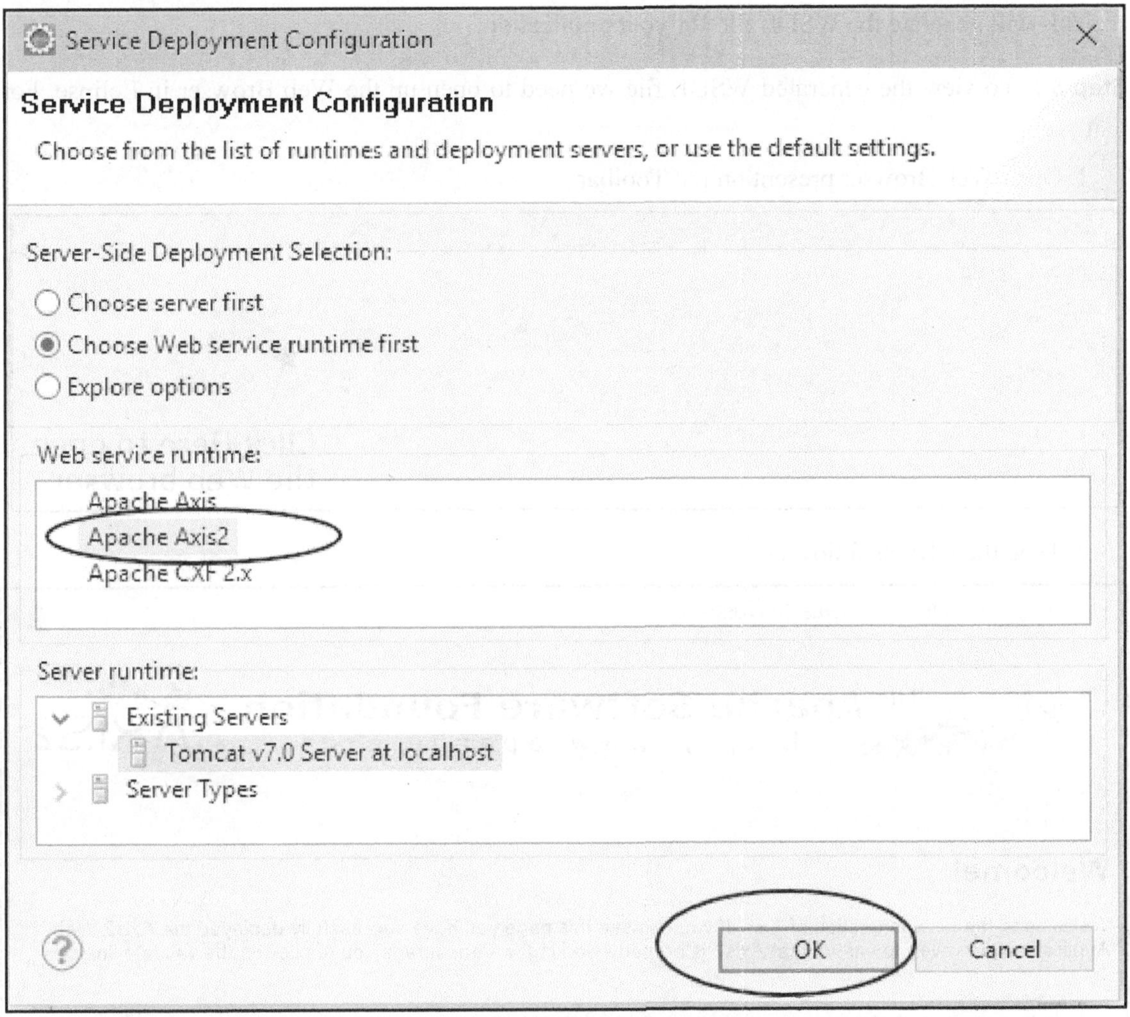

Service Deployment Configuration
Service Deployment Configuration
Choose from the list of runtimes and deployment servers, or use the default settings.
Server-Side Deployment Selection:
Choose server first
Choose Web service runtime first
Explore options
Web service runtime:
Apache Axis
Apache Axis2
Apache CXF 2.x
Server runtime:
Existing Servers
Tomcat v7.0 Server at localhost
Server Types
OK
Cancel

Then click on Finish button. You will get the progress window as,

Progress Information
Operation in progress...
Installing Axis2 Web Services Core facet...
Cancel
Details >>

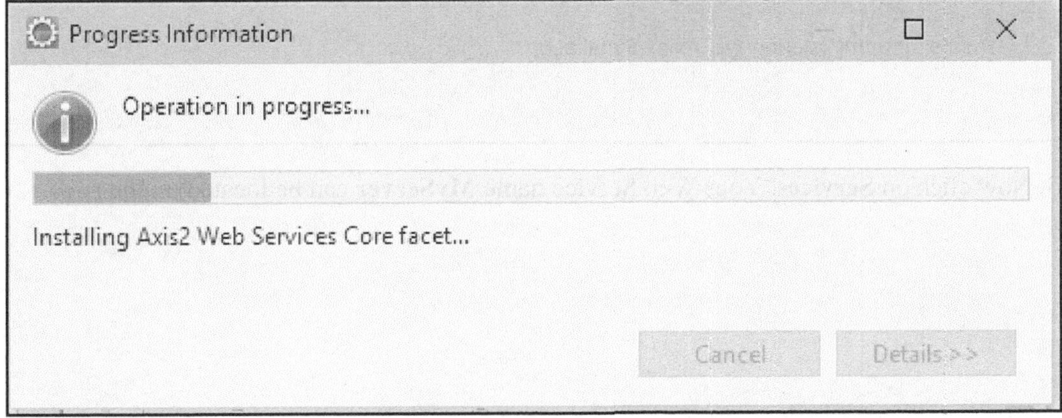

This will generate the WSDL file for your application.

Step 5 : To view the generated WSDL file we need to open up the Web Browser in Eclipse. For that

1. Open Web Browser present on the Toolbar

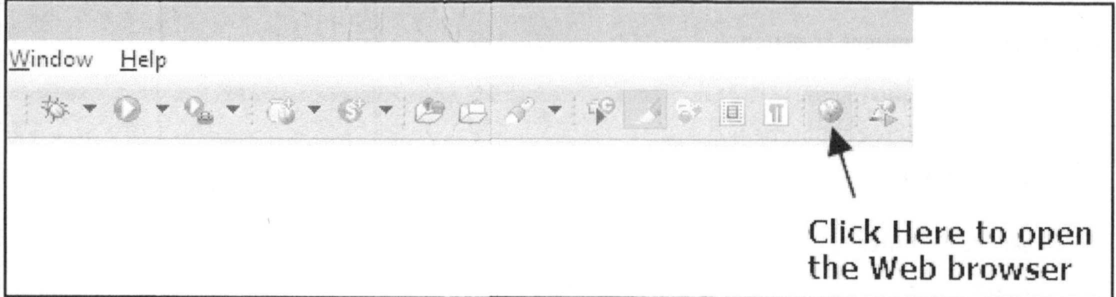

2. Type the URL as follows -

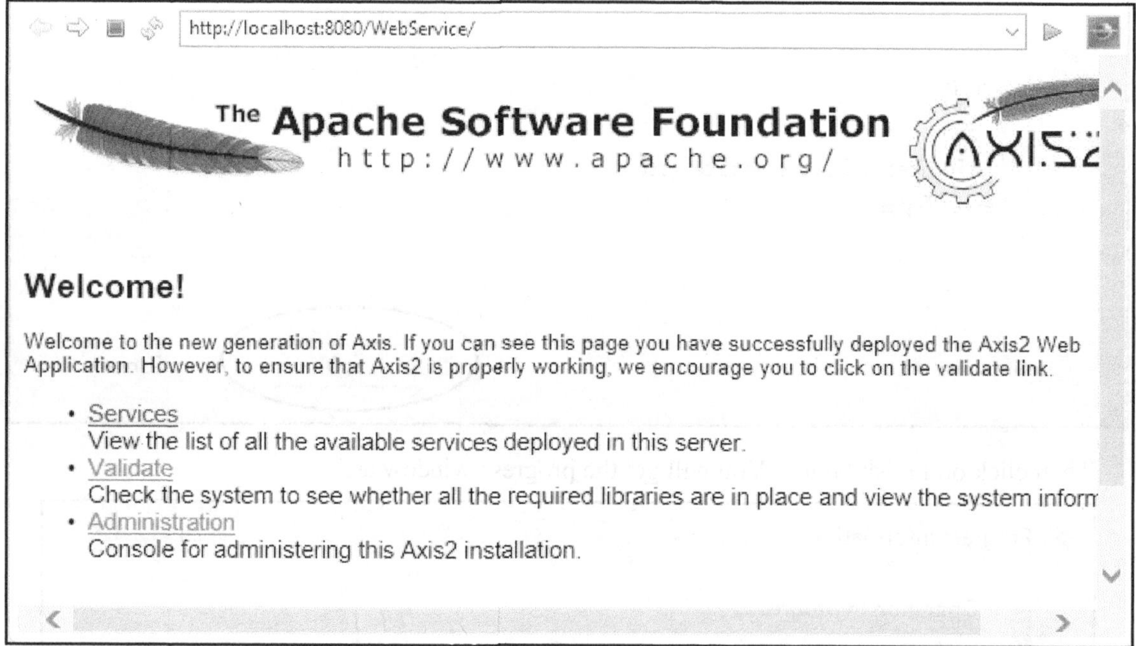

3. Now click on **Services**. Your Web Service name **MyServer** can be located on the page.

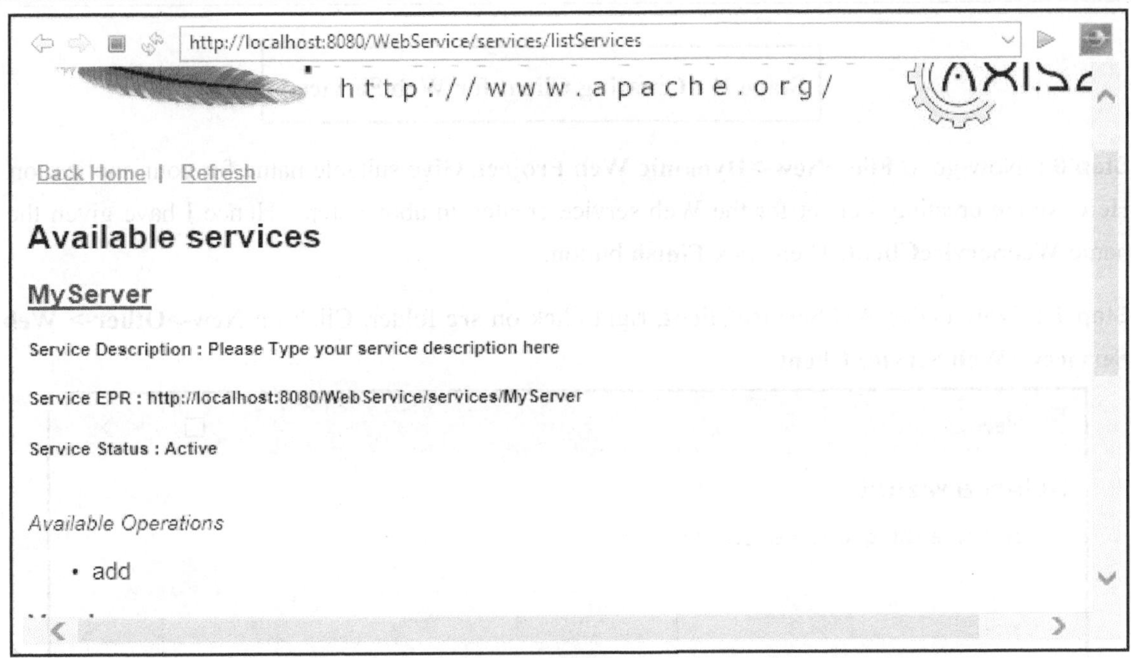

4. Just click on **MyServer** link another web page will be opened up in the browser. This is actually your WSDL file. Copy the full URL for WSDL file marked in screenshot given below. Save this URL in some Notepad file. Note that: We need this URL during the creation of Client.

http://localhost:8080/WebService/services/MyServer?wsdl

```
<?xml version="1.0" encoding="UTF-8"?>
- <wsdl:definitions targetNamespace="http://mypackage.com"
  xmlns:wsaw="http://www.w3.org/2006/05/addressing/wsdl"
  xmlns:mime="http://schemas.xmlsoap.org/wsdl/mime/"
  xmlns:http="http://schemas.xmlsoap.org/wsdl/http/"
  xmlns:soap12="http://schemas.xmlsoap.org/wsdl/soap12/"
  xmlns:soap="http://schemas.xmlsoap.org/wsdl/soap/"
  xmlns:ns1="http://org.apache.axis2/xsd"
  xmlns:xs="http://www.w3.org/2001/XMLSchema"
  xmlns:ns="http://mypackage.com"
  xmlns:wsdl="http://schemas.xmlsoap.org/wsdl/">
      <wsdl:documentation> Please Type your service description here
          </wsdl:documentation>
    - <wsdl:types>
      - <xs:schema targetNamespace="http://mypackage.com"
        elementFormDefault="qualified" attributeFormDefault="qualified">
        - <xs:element name="add">
          - <xs:complexType>
            - <xs:sequence>
                  <xs:element name="a" type="xs:int"/>
```

Stage II : Creating Client for Web Service

Step 6 : Now go to **File->New->Dynamic Web Project**. Give suitable name for your application. Here we are creating a client for the Web service created in above steps. Hence I have given the name **WebServiceClient**. Then click **Finish** button.

Step 7 : Now under **WebServiceClient**, right click on **src** folder. Click on **New->Other-> Web Services->Web Service Client**

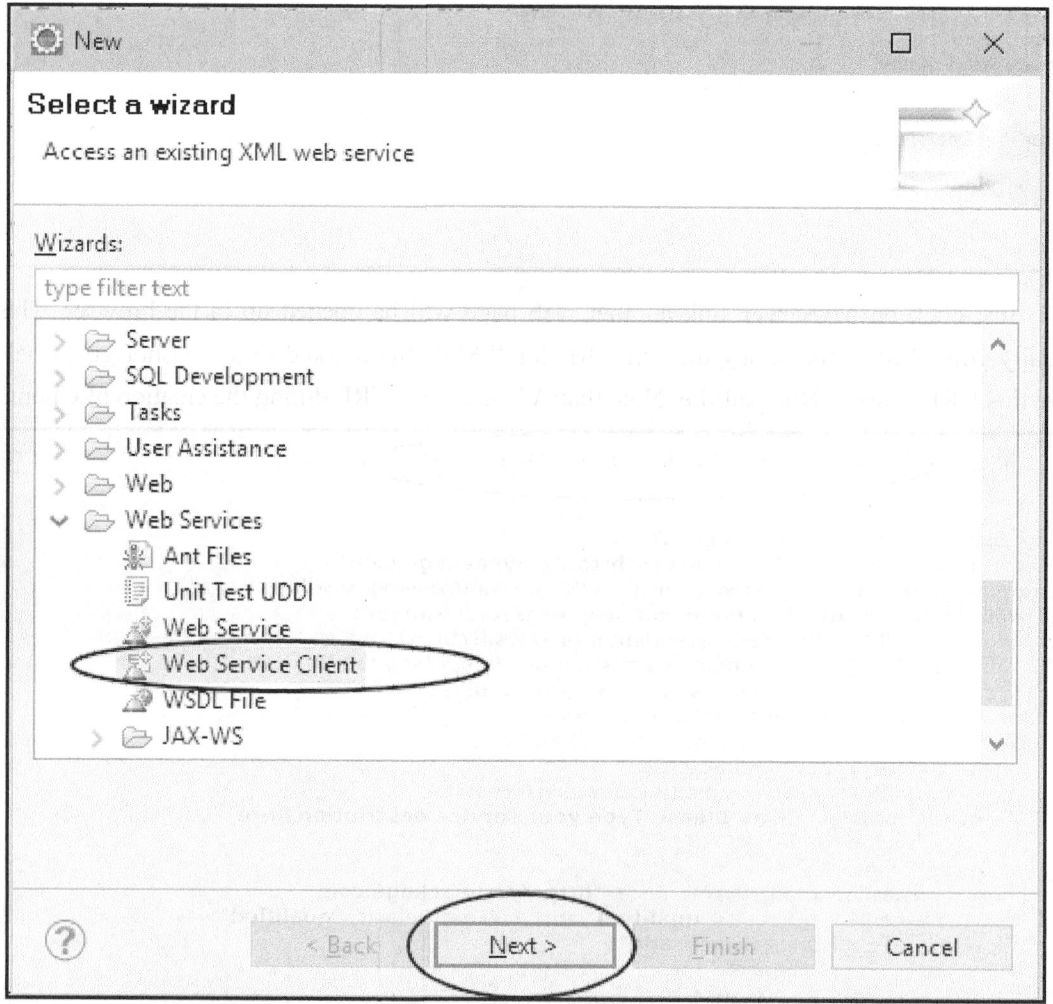

Click the **Next** button. Now on **Web Services** window. Copy the URL of WSDL which you have copied in Step 5(4).

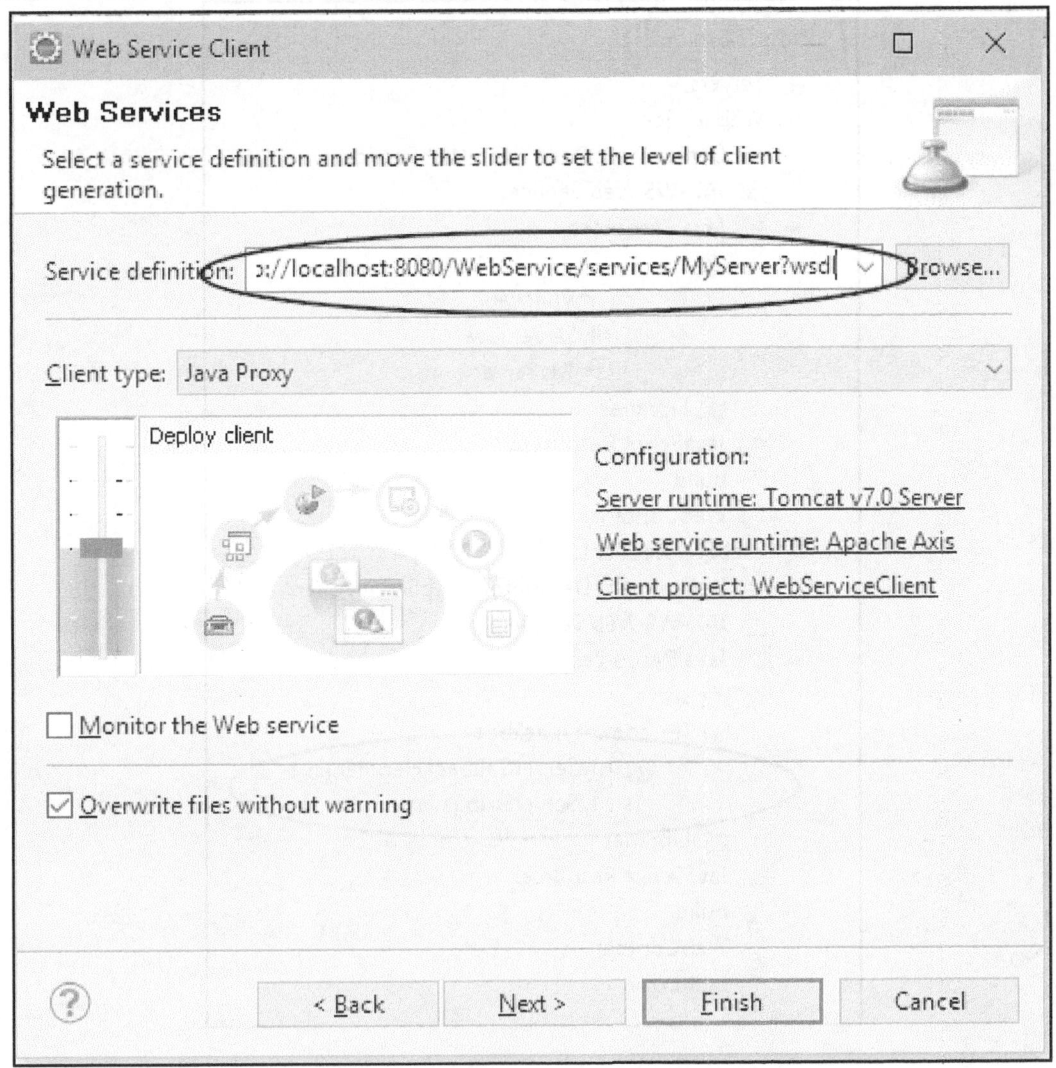

Then Select **Web Service runtime:Apache Axis**. Set it to **Apache Axis2** click **OK** button. Then Click on **Finish** button. You will get Progress Information and then two files will get generated. These are as shown in following screenshot.

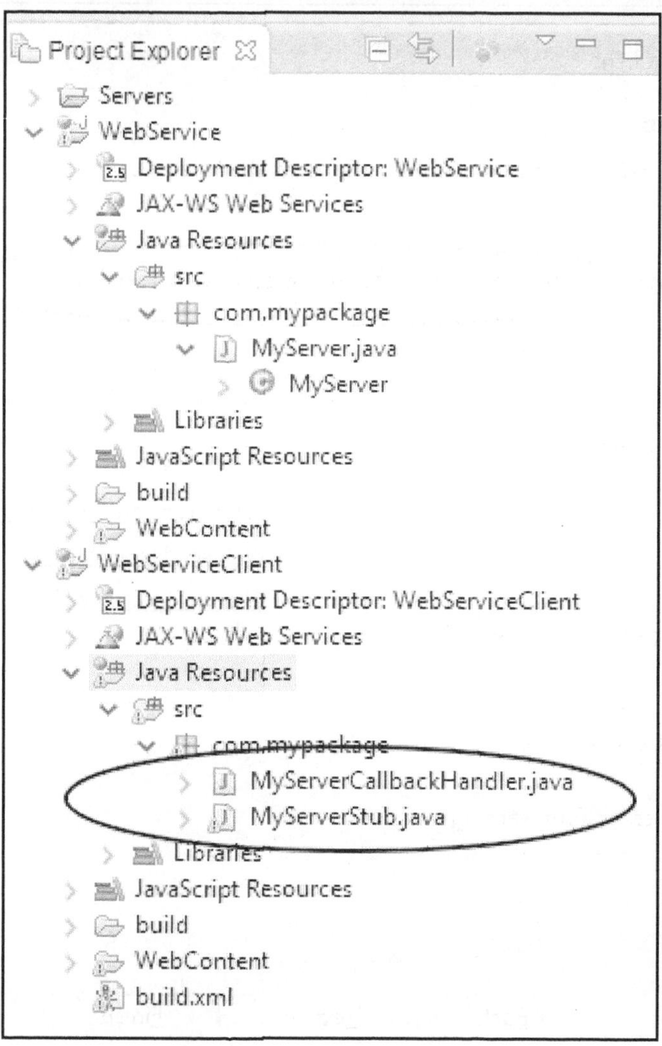

Step 8 : Now right click on **src** folder of **WebServiceClient**. Click on **New->Class**. The **New Java Class** window will appear. Set appropriate package name, class name and Check for void main method. Here is the screenshot.

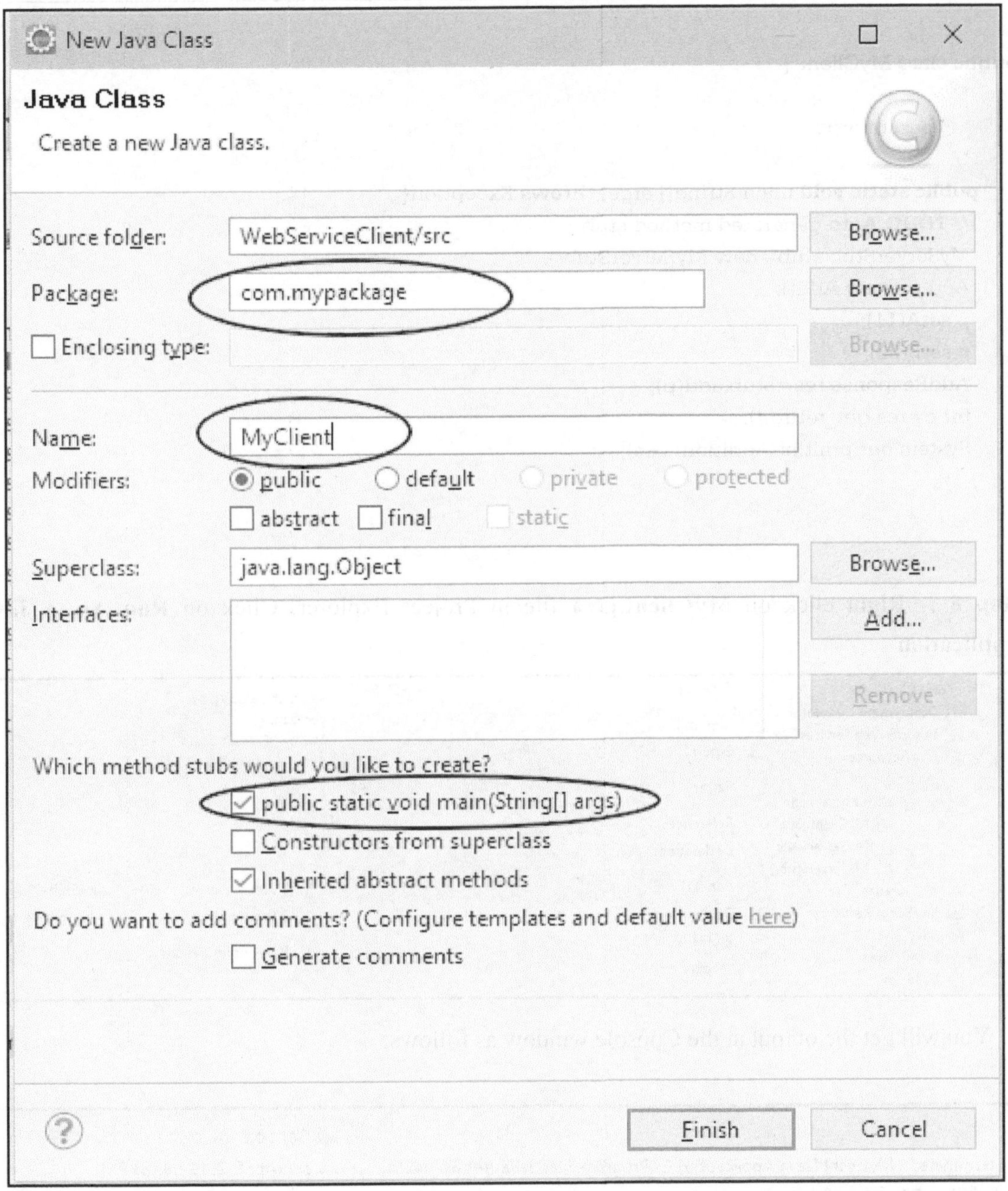

New Java Class

Java Class

Create a new Java class.

Source folder: WebServiceClient/src Browse...

Package: com.mypackage Browse...

Enclosing type: Browse...

Name: MyClient

Modifiers: public default private protected

abstract final static

Superclass: java.lang.Object Browse...

Interfaces: Add...

Remove

Which method stubs would you like to create?

public static void main(String[] args)

Constructors from superclass

Inherited abstract methods

Do you want to add comments? (Configure templates and default value here)

Generate comments

Finish Cancel

Click on **Finish** button. You can now write the Java Client code for web service. The code is as follows,

MyClient.java

```
package com.mypackage;
import com.mypackage.MyServerStub.Add;
import com.mypackage.MyServerStub.AddResponse;
```

```
public class MyClient {
    /**
     * @param args
     */
    public static void main(String[] args) throws Exception{
     // TODO Auto-generated method stub
     MyServerStub stub=new MyServerStub();
     Add p=new Add();
     p.setA(11);
     p.setB(22);
     AddResponse res=stub.add(p);
     int c=res.get_return();
     System.out.println("Addition: "+c);
    }
}
```

Step 8 : Right click on **MyClient.java** file in Project Explorer. Click on **Run As -> Java Application**

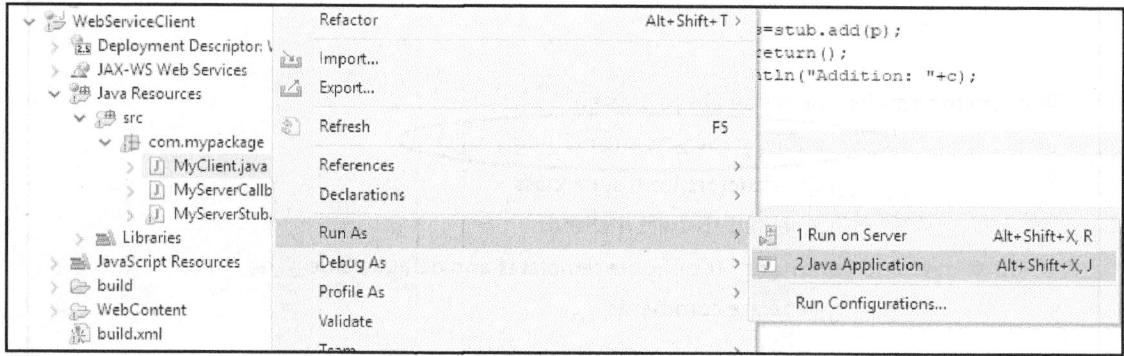

You will get the output at the Console window as follows,

```
Markers  Properties  Servers  Data Source Explorer  Snippets  Console
<terminated> MyClient [Java Application] C:\Program Files\Java\jre1.8.0_141\bin\javaw.exe (Apr 8, 2019 1:38:35 PM)
Addition: 33
```

Troubleshooting :

We may get following error on running the above client

```
Exception in thread "main" org.apache.axis2.AxisFault:...
...
...
```

To overcome through this Exception, we need to make some changes in **services.xml** file. It can be located in the Web Services folder. To locate this **xml** file, follow the path as

Web Content-> WEB-INF-> Services->MyServer->META-INF. Locate services.xml

Change following lines

```
<messageReceivermep="http://www.w3.org/2004/08/wsdl/in-only"
class="org.apache.axis2.rpc.receivers.RPCInOnlyMessageReceiver" />
<messageReceivermep="http://www.w3.org/2004/08/wsdl/in-out"
class="org.apache.axis2.rpc.receivers.RPCMessageReceiver"/>
```

To

```
<messageReceivermep="http://www.w3.org/ns/wsdl/in-only"
class="org.apache.axis2.rpc.receivers.RPCInOnlyMessageReceiver" />
<messageReceivermep="http://www.w3.org/ns/wsdl/in-out"
class="org.apache.axis2.rpc.receivers.RPCMessageReceiver"/>
```

Stop the Apache Tomcat Server and start it again. Now Run your **MyClient.java** file as Java Application and you will get the required output.

University Questions

1. *Explain the creation of Java web service in detail with examples.* **AU : May-12, Marks 16**
2. *Explain in detail the steps in the creation, publishing and testing of a web services in detail.* **AU : Dec.-13, Marks 16**

10.4 Describing Web Services : WSDL

AU : Dec.-11,15, May-14,16,18,19, Marks 16

- The WSDL is a Web Service Descriptor Language which is based on XML.
- The purpose of this file is to describe the web service and the method of accessing it.
- WSDL is a W3C recommendation.
- It contain various definitions. Following elements are described in WSDL file.

Elements	Description
types	It specifies the data types of the symbols used by the web service.
messages	It specifies the messages used by the web service.
portType	It specifies the name of the operation(function) defined by the web service
binding	It specifies the name of the protocol of the web service, typically it is SOAP.

1) Types

If we declare and use some variable in the web service then their data types can be specified.

For example -

```
<?xml version="1.0" encoding="UTF-8"?>
<definitions name="SimpleCalculator" targetNamespace="http://tempuri.org/wsdl" >
 <types>
  <schema targetNamespace="http://tempuri.org/types">
   <import namespace="http://schemas.xmlsoap.org/soap/encoding/"/>
    <complexType name="CalciClass">
     <sequence>
      <element name="operator1" type="double"/>
      <element name="operator2" type="double"/>
      <element name="operation" type="String"/>
     </sequence>
   </complexType>
  </schema>
 </types>
```

2) Messages

The messages define the **part** of the element along with the data types. The message name specified the name of the function.

In following example the **HelloFun** is a name of the function which is declared in the interface named **MyInterface**. The return parameter is specified by **name="MyInterface_HelloFunResponse".**

For example -

```
<?xml version="1.0" encoding="UTF-8"?>
<definitions name="SimpleHelloMessage" targetNamespace="http://tempuri.org/wsdl" > <types/>
 <message name="MyInterface_HelloFun">
   <part name="String_1" type="xsd:string"/>
  </message>
 <message name="MyInterface_HelloFunResponse">
   <part name="result" type="xsd:string"/>
 </message>
```

3) PortTypes

This is an important element of the WSDL file. It defined various **operations** that can be performed by the web service.

Various operation types are -

Elements	Description
one-way	This operation will send the message but it will not get any response.
request-response	This operation will send a message and will receive a response.
Solicit-response	This operation will send a message and will wait for a response.
Notification	This operation will send a message and will not wait for a response.

The messages in portTypes define the name of the operation along with the prefix **tns** where tns stands for TypeNamespace.

4) Binding

The binding defines the message format and details of the protocol.

```
<?xml version="1.0" encoding="UTF-8"?>
<definitions name="SimpleHelloMessage" targetNamespace="http://tempuri.org/wsdl" >  <types/>
...
...
 <binding name="MyInterfaceBinding" type="tns:MyInterface">
   <soap:binding transport="http://schemas.xmlsoap.org/soap/http" style="rpc"/>
    <operation name="HelloFun">
...
...
...
```

There are three main elements -

binding

The binding defines **name** which defines the name of the binding and **type** attributes specifies the port which is typically the name of the interface file.

soap:binding

The soap:binding defines **transport** and **style** attributes. The style is remote procedure call which allows the distributed clients to access the web service.

operation

The operations defines the port operations. Each operation contains the **soap:operation, input** and **output** elements. The **soap:body** element provides the communication details such as whether or not the associated message is encoded and if it is encoded then the **encodingStyle** is specified.

5) Service

The service element specifies the name for overall web service.

```
<?xml version="1.0" encoding="UTF-8"?>
<definitions name="SimpleHelloMessage" targetNamespace="http://tempuri.org/wsdl" >
 <types/>
...
...
....
  <service name="SimpleHelloMessage">
    <port name="MyInterfacePort" binding="tns:MyInterfaceBinding">
      <soap:address location="REPLACE_WITH_ACTUAL_URL"/>
    </port>
  </service>
</definitions>
```

University Questions

1. *Describe the significance and working of WSDL with an example.* **AU : Dec.-11, Marks 16**
2. *Explain WSDL structure and its elements.* **AU : May-14, Marks 8**
3. *Write short note on WSDL .* **AU : Dec.-15, Marks 8**
4. *Describe the structure of a WSDL document, its elements and their purposes with appropriate examples.* **AU : May-16, Marks 16**
5. *Give the basic structure of WSDL and show how they are used to create, publish, test and describe web services.* **AU : May 18, Marks 13**
6. *Describe the major elements of a WSDL document.* **AU : May 19, Marks 7**

10.5 SOAP

AU : May-11,19, Dec.-11,12, 13,15,16,18, Marks 16

Simple Object Access Protocol (SOAP) is a protocol based on XML. It is used by the web services for exchange of information. It is a W3C recommendation.

This exchange of information is done over HTTP. This is a platform and language independent protocol.

The client-server communication is based on RPC. The HTTP does not designed to handle the distributed objects that are required by the RPC. Hence another application protocol is build over HTTP which popularly known as SOAP. SOAP allows to talk different applications that are running in two different operating systems.

10.5.1 Structure of SOAP

The structure of the SOAP is defined by four building blocks.

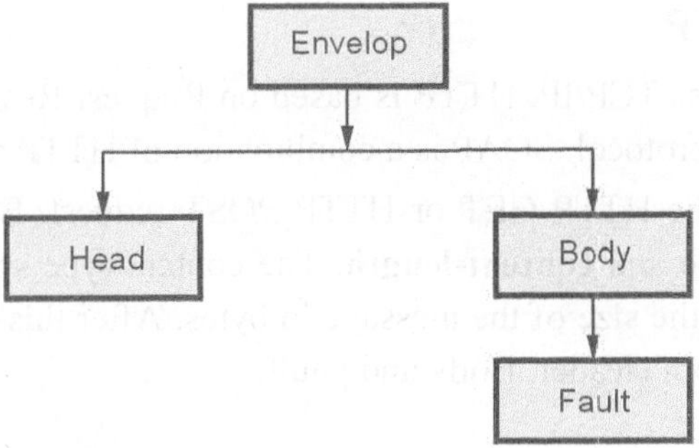

Fig. 10.5.1 SOAP building blocks

1) Envelop

The Envelop is the root of any SOAP document. It identifies that the XML document as a SOAP message. It defines two things - **Namespace** and **encodingStyle**. The Namespace value can be given as -

xmlns:soap="http://www.w3.org/2001/12/soap-envelope".

The encoding style is useful to define the data types used in the document. For example the value of encoding can be given as -

soap:encodingStyle="http://www.w3.org/2001/12/soap-encoding"

2) Header

The SOAP header field is optional. It contains the header information. The header contains three attributes such as **mustUnderstand, actor** and **encodingStyle**

The **mustUnderstand** attribute specifies 0 or 1. If the value is 1 then it means that the receiver should process the header.

Normally the SOAP message travels over a message path having the endpoints at the two ends. The SOAP **actor** is used to specify the URI for this endpoint.

The **encodingStyle** is useful to define the data types used in the document

The SOAP header defines how the recipient should process the SOAP message.

3) Body

The required SOAP Body element contains the actual SOAP message intended for the ultimate endpoint of the message.

4) Fault

This is optional element of the SOAP message. It is used to represent the error code. It consists of elements such as **faultcode** which is a code for fault. The **faultstring** message gives the details about the fault.

10.5.2 SOAP and HTTP

HTTP communicates over TCP/IP. HTTP is based on Request-Response mechanism. SOAP is a HTTP Request-Response protocol. SOAP is a combination of HTTP and XML.

The SOAP request can be HTTP GET or HTTP POST request. Each request consists of two HTTP headers :**content-type** and **content-length**. The content-type specifies the MIME type and the content-length specifies the size of the message in bytes. After this header the body part begins which defines SOAP Envelop, Header, Body and Fault.

Example

The SOAP request can be

```
POST /mycreation HTTP/1.0
Host: www.mywebsite.com
Content-Type: text/xml; charset=utf-8
Content-Length: 500
<?xml version="1.0"?>
<SOAP-ENV:Envelope
xmlns:SOAP-ENV="http://www.w3.org/2001/12/soap-envelope"
SOAP-ENV:encodingStyle="http://www.w3.org/2001/12/soap-encoding">
  <SOAP-ENV:Body xmlns:m="http://www.mywebsite.com/mycreation">
   <m:GetDetails>
     <m:Name>ABCD</m:Name>
   </m:GetDetails>
  </SOAP-ENV:Body>
</SOAP-ENV:Envelope>
```

The SOAP response can be

```
HTTP/1.0 200 OK
Content-Type: text/xml; charset=utf-8
Content-Length: 500
<?xml version="1.0"?>
 <SOAP-ENV:Envelope
 xmlns:SOAP-ENV="http://www.w3.org/2001/12/soap-envelope"
 SOAP-ENV:encodingStyle="http://www.w3.org/2001/12/soap-encoding">
   <SOAP-ENV:Body xmlns:m="http://www.mywebsite.com/mycreation">
     <m:GetDetailsResponse>
        <m:ItemDetails>This is a my new creation</m:ItemDetails>
     </m:GetDetailResponse>
   </SOAP-ENV:Body>
  </SOAP-ENV:Envelope>
```

10.5.3 SOAP Encoding

SOAP makes use of XML Schema to encode the programming constructs. Following are examples of SOAP encoding.

1. Encoding of Struct Data

Following is a code fragment which can be encoded as follows -

```
<xs:element name="Student">
<xs:complexType>
  <xs:sequence>
  <xs:element name="Name" type="xs:string"/>
  <xs:element name="RollNo" type="xs:integer"/>
   <xs:element name="address" type="tns:Address"/>
  </xs:sequence>
  <xs:element name="Address">
 <xs:complexType>
   < xs:sequence>
    < xs:element name="street" type="xsd:string"/>
   < xs:element name="city" type="xsd:string"/>
   < xs:element name="country" type="xsd:string"/>
  </ xs:sequence>
</xs:complexType>
</e:element>
```

The following is an example of how the preceding schema definition could be subsequently used in a SOAP encoding.

```
        <e:Student>
  <Name>AAA</Name>
  <RollNo>11</RollNo>
 <address>
               <street>XYZ Road</street>
               <city>PQR City</city>
               <country>India</country>
 </address>
</e:Student>
```

2. Encoding of Arrays

An array in SOAP is of type **SOAP-ENC:Array**

```
  <element name="myArray"
  type="SOAP-ENC:Array"/>
```

The preceding schema can be represented in SOAP encoding as follows -

```
<myArray SOAP-ENC:arrayType="xsd:int[3]">
  <number>1</number>
  <number>2</number>
  <number>3</number>
</myArray>
```

The above encoding shows that there is an array of three integers. All these members of array are called **number**.

10.5.4 RPC Representation

- The RPC (Remote Procedure Call) is a mechanism used when the client makes a call to a method that resides on another machine. The SOAP has a support for RPC representation.
- The **style** attribute of **soap:binding** element in the WSDL document makes use of string "rpc" to denote that the communication with the client is in RPC style.

```
<soap:binding transport="http://schemas.xmlsoap.org/soap/http"
 style="rpc"/>
```

- The **soap:body** element indicated using an encoding specified by SOAP 1.1 to represent RPC.
- In SOAP specified representation of RPC calls, the call is modeled as **struct.**
- The specified structure used in SOAP representation of RPC call has a name for the remote procedure call and has one accessor for each parameter that is to be passed to the procedure. This struct us then encoded as XML markup. This markup is then made a child of SOAP body element.

For example – Following is a soap document sent by the client to display message web service.

```
<?xml version="1.0" encoding ="UTF-8"?>
<env:Envelop
 xmlns:env="http://schemas.xmlsoap.org/soap/envelop/"
 xmlns:xsd="http://www.w3.org/2001/XMLSchema"
 xmlns:xsi="http://www.w3.org/2001/XMLSchema-instance"
 xmlns:enc="http:// schemas.xmlsoap.org/soap/encoding/"
 xmlns:ns0="http://tempuri.org/wsdl"
 xmlns:ns1="http://tempuri.org/types"
 env:encodingStyle="http:// schemas.xmlsoap.org/soap/encoding/">
 <env:Body>
   <ns0:HelloMsg>          ← Call to procedure which is RPC
    <msg_1 xsi: type=:xsd:string">Welcome</msg_1>
   </ns0:HelloMsg>
</env:Body>
</env:Envelop>
```

University Questions

1. *Describe major elements of SOAP.* **AU : May-11, Marks 8, Dec.-11, 13, Marks 16**
2. *Briefly discuss how SOAP encodes struct data and arrays.* **AU : Dec.-12, Marks 8**
3. *Explain the SOAP elements and their RPC representation in detail.* **AU : Dec.-13, Marks 16**
4. *Write short notes on SOAP.* **AU : Dec.-15, Marks 8**
5. *Define SOAP and explain the building blocks of a SOAP message in detail.* **AU : Dec.-16, Marks 8**
6. *Describe SOAP, UDDI, and WSDL in detail.* **AU : Dec.-18, Marks 7**
7. *Write in brief about the SOAP.* **AU : May-19, Marks 6**

10.6 Database Driven Web service

- The database driven web service technology is a database approach to web services.
- It works in the following two directions :
  - o Accessing database resources as a Web service
  - o Consuming external Web services from the database.
- Database mechanism provides easy access to remote content and applications regardless of the platform and location of web service provider.
- The client application can query and retrieve data from database through a web service.
- It is possible to access and manipulate database tables from a web service client.
- Following Fig. 10.6.1 illustrates the web service call-in to the database.

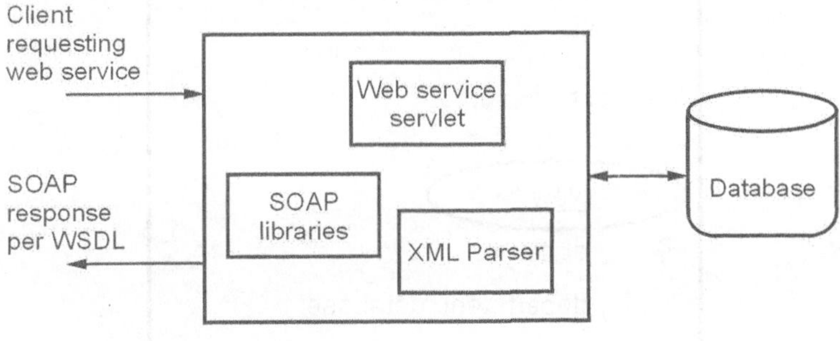

Fig. 10.6.1 Database driven Web service application

Let us understand working of a web service through a database with the help of following example –

Ex. 10.6.1 : Consider a case where we have two web services - an airline service and a travel agent and the travel agent is searching for an airline. Implement this scenario using web services and database.

Sol. : This application is created in three stages -

- First stage is creation of database in MySQL,
- Second stage is creation of Web service
- Third stage is creation of client for the created web service.

Stage I : Creating a Database

The database in MySQL can be created as follows – Note that the database name is **Reservation_database** and the table name is **Airways_table**.

- It is very simple to create a database in MySQL, if you have installed XAMPP. For creating database you simply need to start XAMP.
- Open the web browser and type the URL http://localhost/phpmyadmin/
- At the left hand Pane Click On **New** and create a database named **reservation_database**

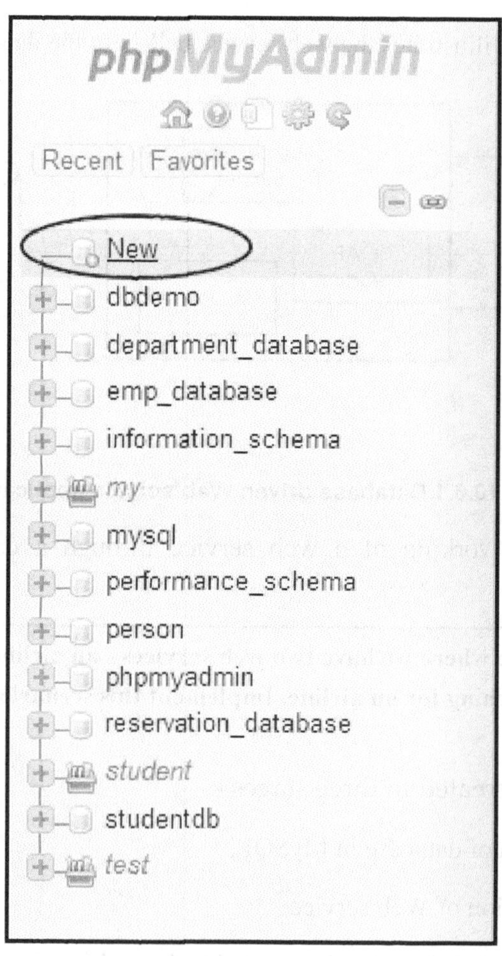

Under this database the table named **Airways_table** can be created by using **Insert** Operation The table is as follows -

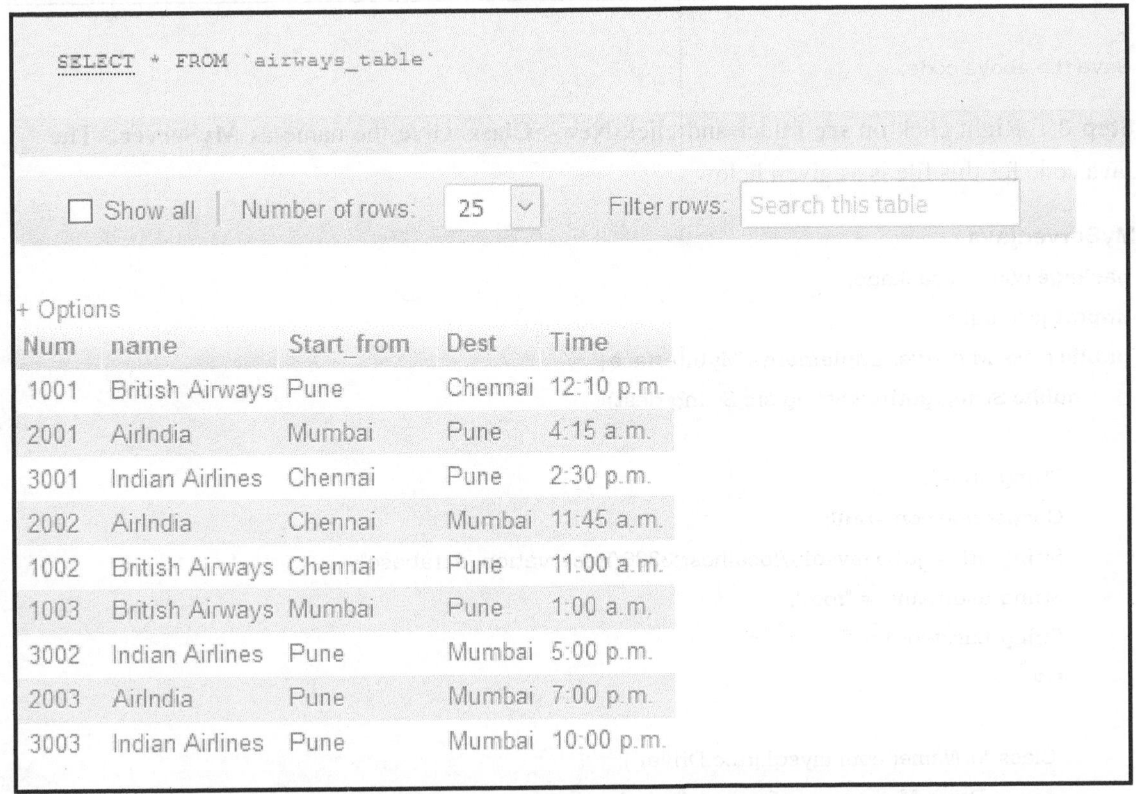

SELECT * FROM `airways_table`

Show all | Number of rows: 25 Filter rows: Search this table

+ Options

Num	name	Start_from	Dest	Time
1001	British Airways	Pune	Chennai	12:10 p.m.
2001	AirIndia	Mumbai	Pune	4:15 a.m.
3001	Indian Airlines	Chennai	Pune	2:30 p.m.
2002	AirIndia	Chennai	Mumbai	11:45 a.m.
1002	British Airways	Chennai	Pune	11:00 a.m.
1003	British Airways	Mumbai	Pune	1:00 a.m.
3002	Indian Airlines	Pune	Mumbai	5:00 p.m.
2003	AirIndia	Pune	Mumbai	7:00 p.m.
3003	Indian Airlines	Pune	Mumbai	10:00 p.m.

Stage II : Creating Web Service

Step 1 : Start Eclipse. Click on **File->New->Dynamic Web Project**. Give the suitable name to the project.

Set the Tomcat Web Server and appropriate version number. By clicking

Window → Preferences → Server → Runtime Environment.

Step 2 : Locate **src** folder under the project in **WebService** project. Right click on **src** folder and click **New->Interface**. Give the name as **MyInterface.** The code for this interface is as given below –

MyInterface.java

```
package com.mypackage;
import java.rmi.RemoteException;
public interface MyInterface extends java.rmi.Remote
{
   public String getInfo(String src,String dest)throws java.rmi.RemoteException;
```

```
}
```

Save the above code.

Step 3 : Right click on **src** folder and click **New->Class**. Give the name as **MyServer.** The Java code for this file is as given below -

MyServer.java

```
package com.mypackage;
import java.sql.*;
public class MyServer implements MyInterface{
      public String getInfo(String src,String dest)
      {
        String str="";
        Connection con=null;
        String url = "jdbc:mysql://localhost:3306/Reservation_database";
        String username = "root";
        String password = "";
        try
        {
         Class.forName("com.mysql.jdbc.Driver");
         con = DriverManager.getConnection(url, username, password);
         Statement s=con.createStatement();

        if(src.equals("Mumbai"))
        {
         if(dest.equals("Pune"))
           s.executeQuery("SELECT * FROM Airways_table WHERE Start_from='Mumbai' AND
Dest='Pune'");
         else if(dest.equals("Chennai"))
           s.executeQuery("SELECT * FROM Airways_table WHERE Start_from='Mumbai' AND
Dest='Chennai'");
        }
        else if(src.equals("Pune"))
        {
         if(dest.equals("Mumbai"))
           s.executeQuery("SELECT * FROM Airways_table WHERE Start_from='Pune' AND
Dest='Mumbai'");
         else if(dest.equals("Chennai"))
           s.executeQuery("SELECT * FROM Airways_table WHERE Start_from='Pune' AND
Dest='Chennai'");
```

```
        }
        else if(src.equals("Chennai"))
        {
         if(dest.equals("Pune"))
          s.executeQuery("SELECT * FROM Airways_table WHERE Start_from='Chennai' AND Dest='Pune'");
         else if(dest.equals("Mumbai"))
          s.executeQuery("SELECT * FROM Airways_table WHERE Start_from='Chennai' AND Dest='Mumbai'");
        }
        ResultSet rs=s.getResultSet();
        str+="<table border=1>";
        while(rs.next())
        {
         str+="<tr><b>";
         str+="<td>";
         str+=rs.getString("name");
         str+="</td>";
         str+="<td>";
         str+=rs.getString("Time");
         str+="</td>";
         str+="</tr></b>";
        }
        str+="</table>";

       }catch(ClassNotFoundException ex)
       {
        System.out.println(ex);
       }
       catch(SQLException ex)
       {
        System.out.println(ex);
       }
       return str;
      }
     }
```

Save the above code.

The snapshot of Project Explorer is as shown as follows :

Project Explorer

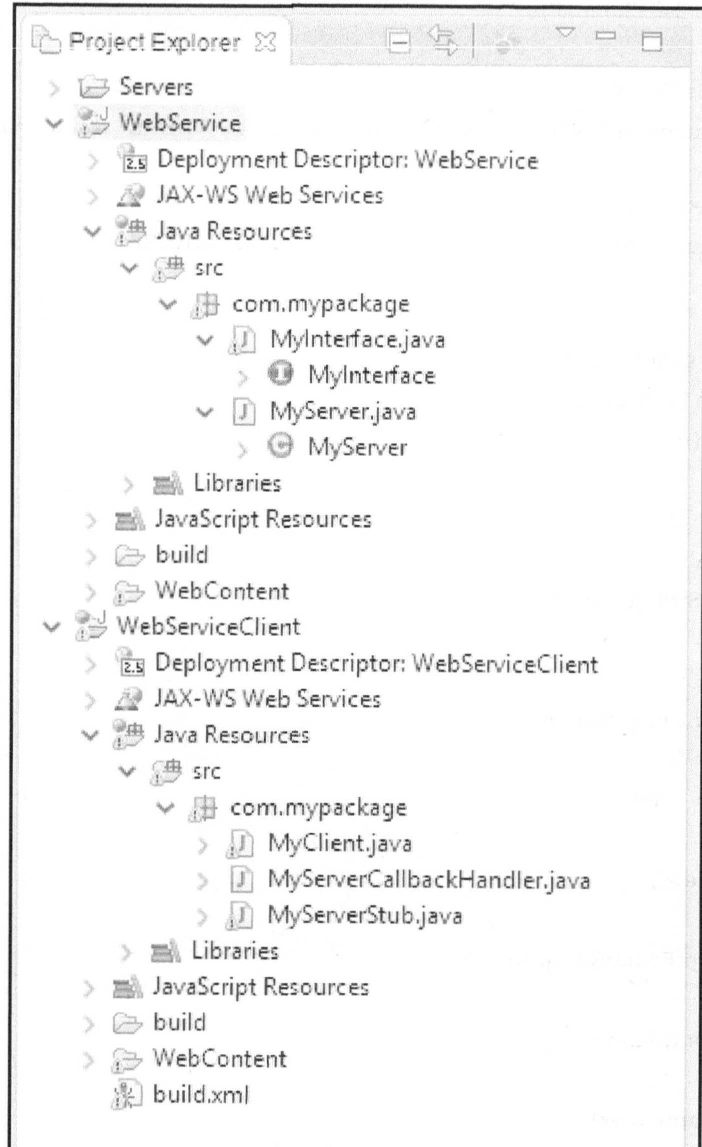

To establish connectivity between Database(Created in Stage I) and above Servlet created in Eclipse, we need some configuration. This can be done in following steps -

- Download **mysql-connector-jaxaXXX.jar** file from internet at suitable location.
- Right click on your Project.
- Click on **Properties->Java Build Path->Libraries.**
- Click Add External JARs… button and select **mysql-connector-javaXXX.jar** file.

- Following screenshot illustrates these steps.

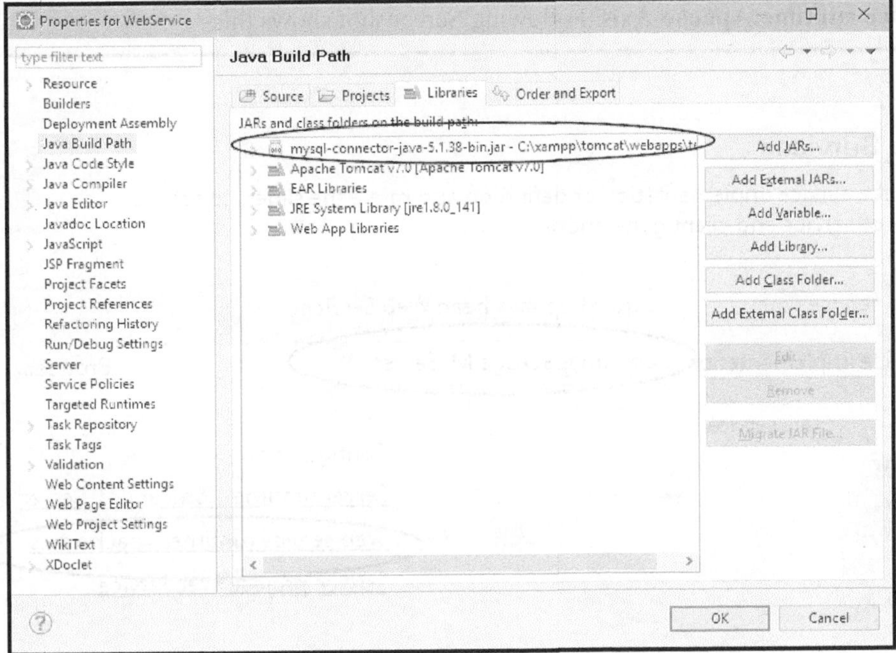

Step 4 : Now right click on **src** folder in Project Explorer under your **WebService.** Click **New->other->Web Services->Web Service.** Then click **Next** button

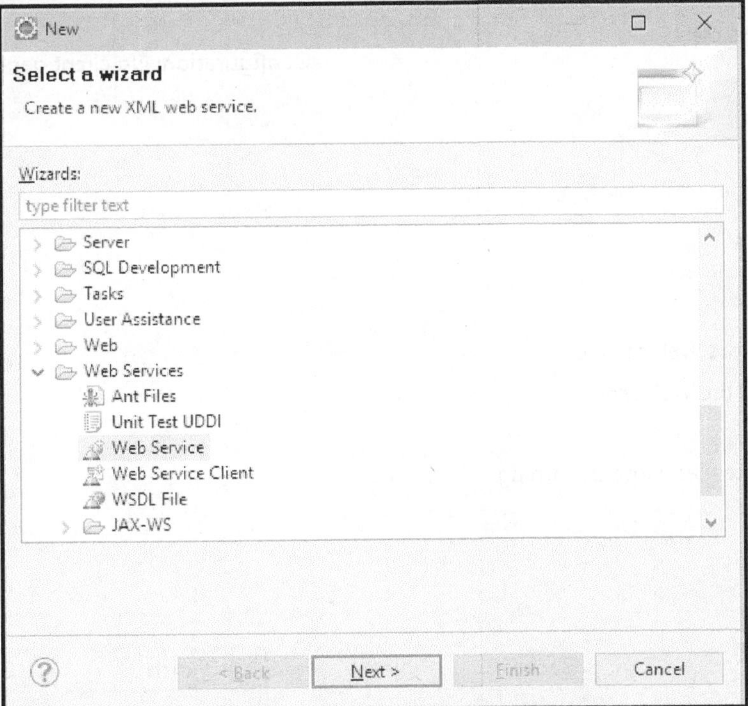

The **Web Services** window will appear. Write the name of service implementation and click on **Web service runtime:Apache Axis.** Following Screenshot shows this-

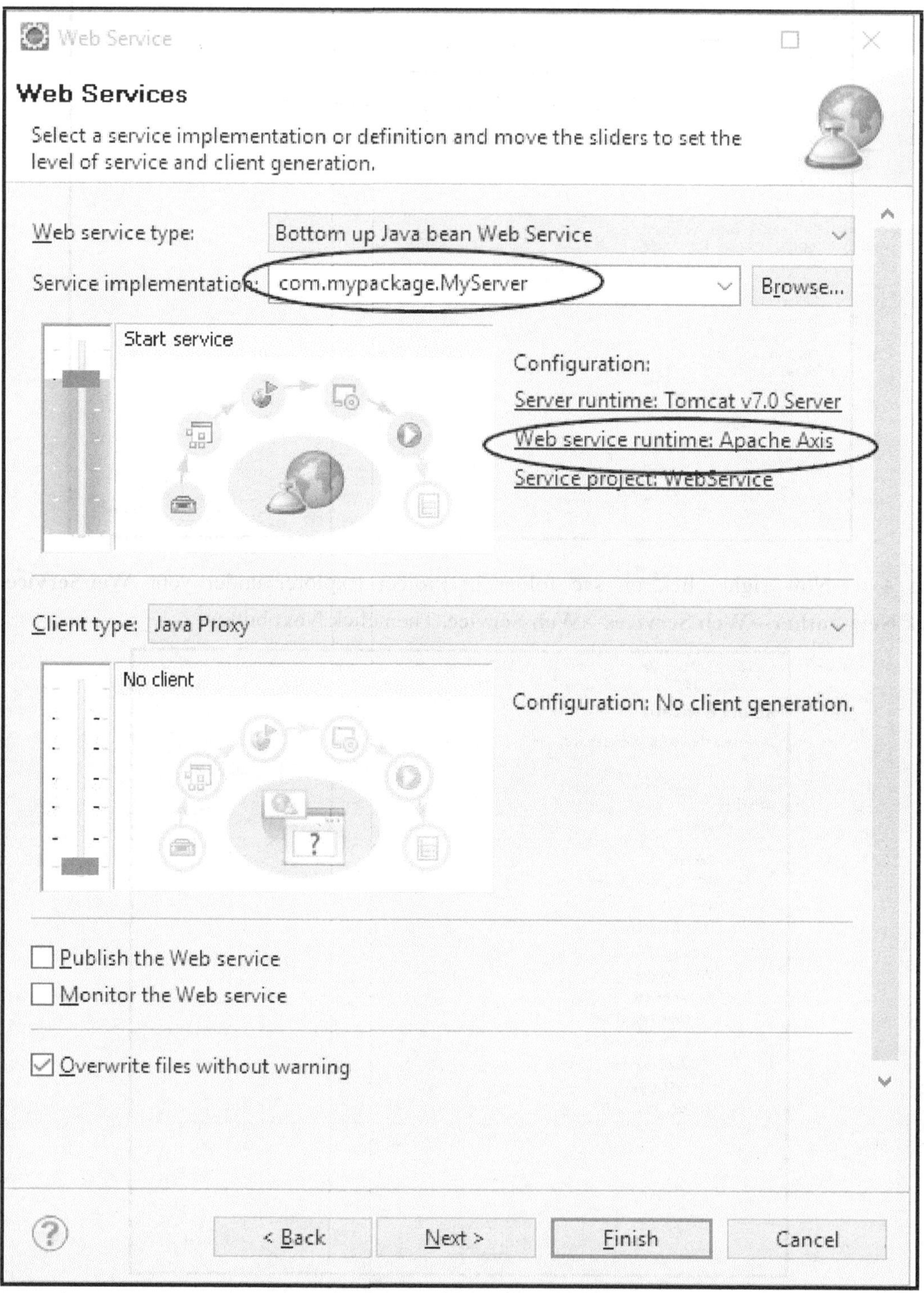

Click on **Apache Axis2** and then click **Ok** button. Refer following screenshot

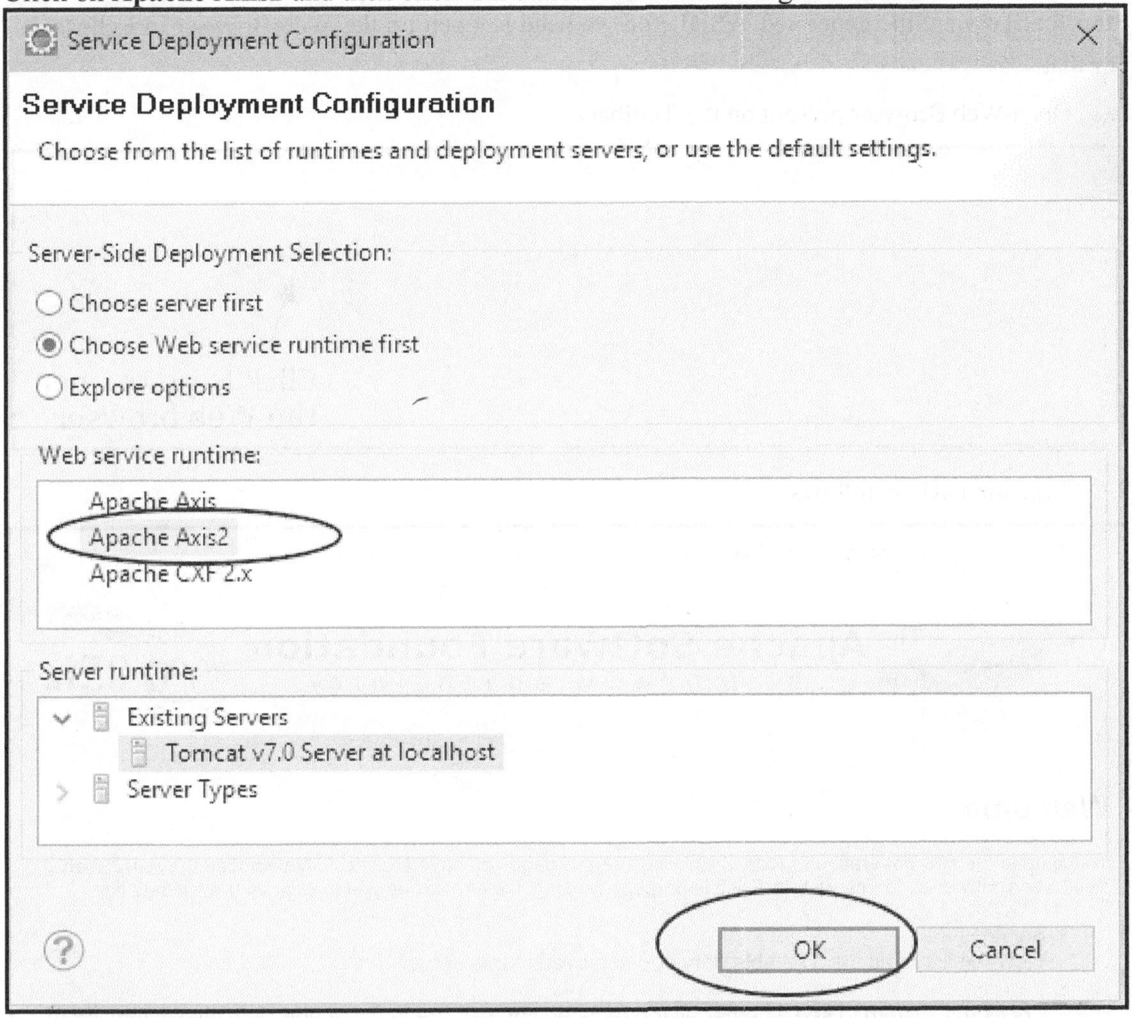

Service Deployment Configuration
Service Deployment Configuration
Choose from the list of runtimes and deployment servers, or use the default settings.
Server-Side Deployment Selection:
Choose server first
Choose Web service runtime first
Explore options
Web service runtime:
Apache Axis
Apache Axis2
Apache CXF 2.x
Server runtime:
Existing Servers
Tomcat v7.0 Server at localhost
Server Types
OK
Cancel

Then click on Finish button. You will get the progress window as

Progress Information
Operation in progress...
Installing Axis2 Web Services Core facet...
Cancel
Details >>

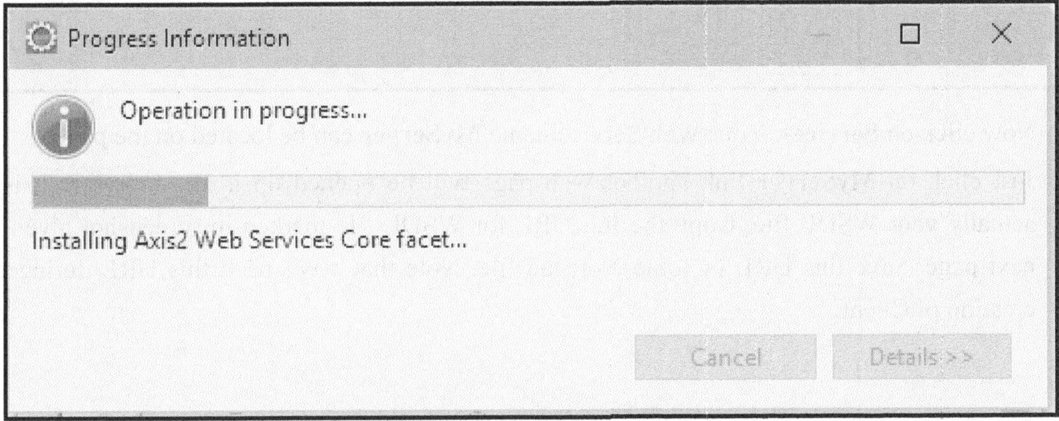

This will generate the WSDL file for your application.

Step 5 : To view the generated WSDL file we need to open up the Web Browser in Eclipse. For that

1. Open Web Browser present on the Toolbar

2. Type the URL as follows -

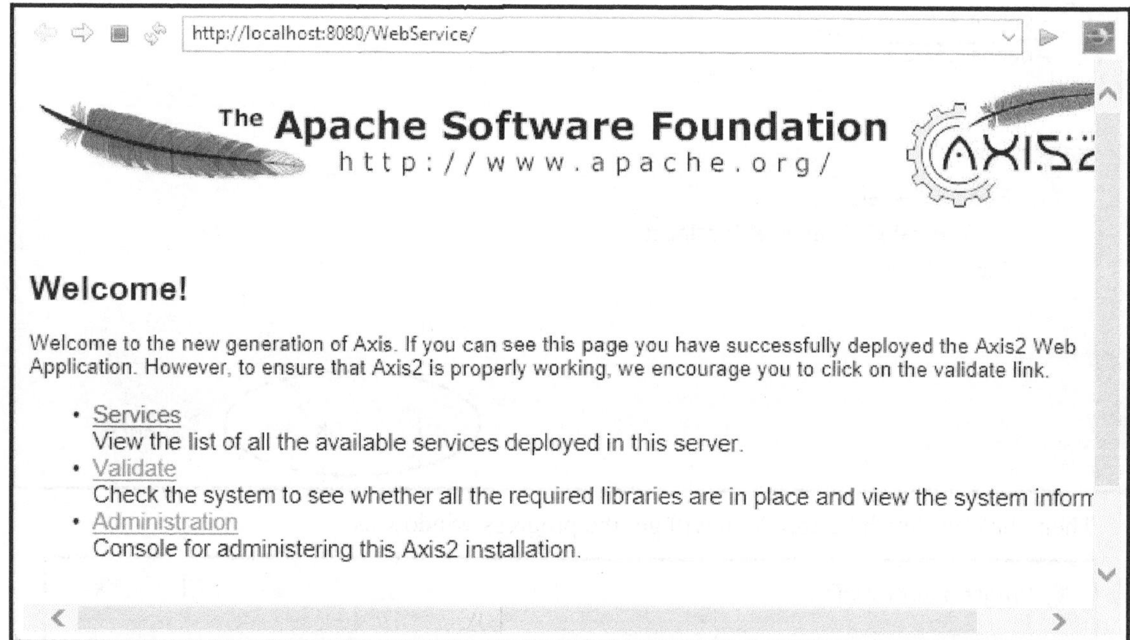

3. Now click on **Services**. Your Web Service name **MyServer** can be located on the page.
4. Just click on **MyServer** link another web page will be opened up in the browser. This is actually your WSDL file. Copy the full URL for WSDL file marked in screenshot given on next page. Save this URL in some Notepad file. Note that : We need this URL during the creation of Client.

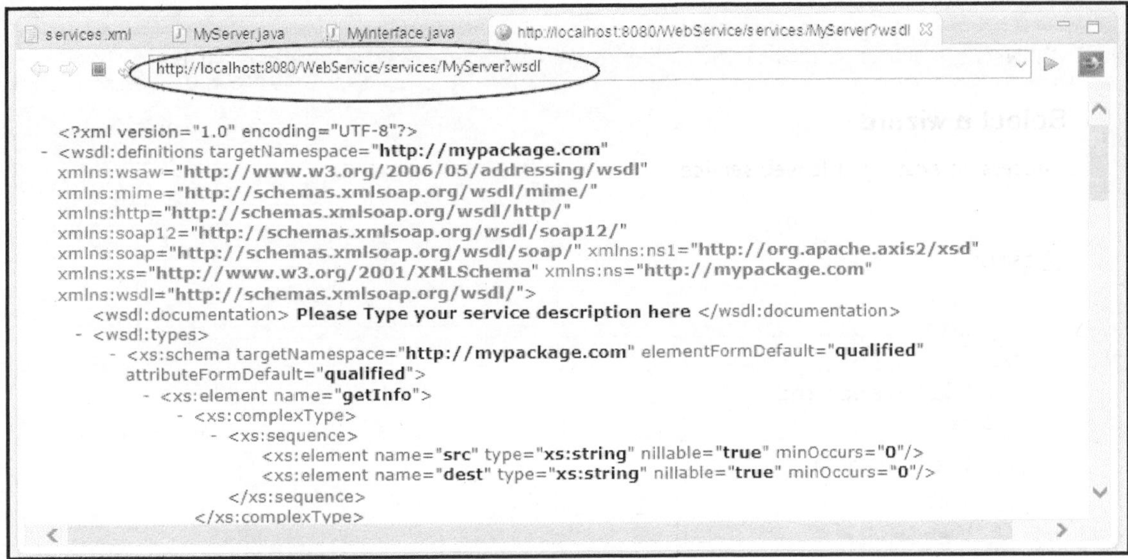

Thus we have created the Web Service.

Stage III : Creating Client for Web Service

Step 6 : Create a simple Java servlet for which invokes the web service. For that purpose go to **File->New->Dynamic Web Project**. Give suitable name for your application. Here we are creating a client for the Web service created in above steps. Hence I have given the name **WebServiceClient**. Then click **Finish** button

Step 7 : Now under **WebServiceClient**, right click on **src** folder. Click on **New->Other-> Web Services->Web Service Client**

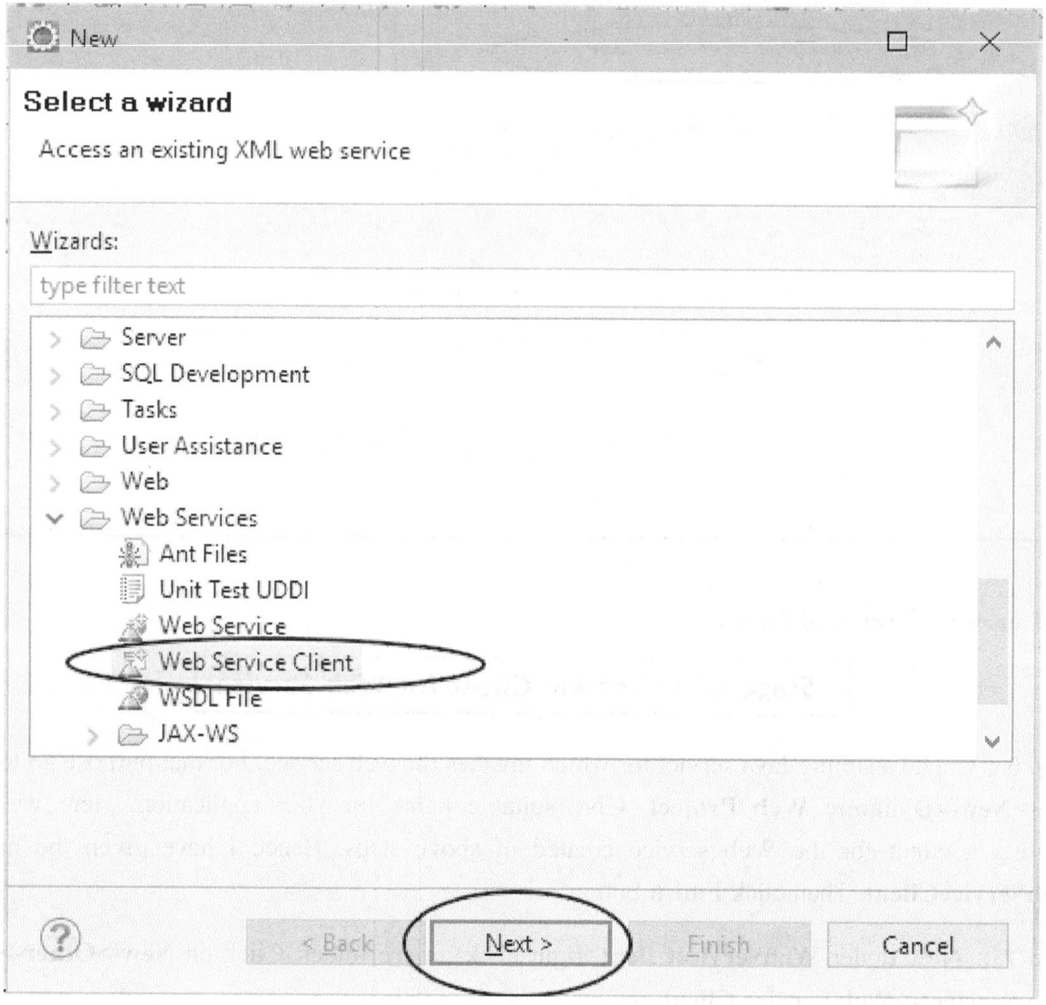

Click the **Next** button. Now on **Web Services** window. Copy the URL of WSDL which you have copied in Step 5(4).

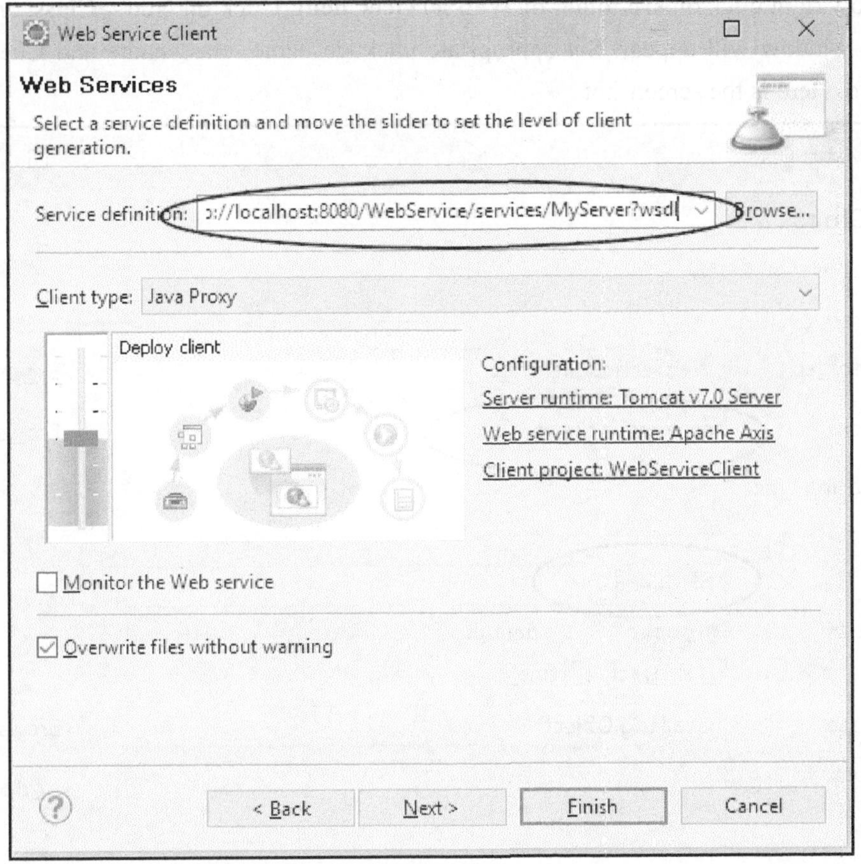

Then Select **Web Service runtime:Apache Axis**. Set it to **Apache Axis2** click **OK** button. Then Click on **Finish** button. You will get Progress Information and then two files will get generated namely **MyServerCallBackHandler.java** and another **MyServerStub.java**. Following is a snapshot of **Project Explorer** Window -

Step 8 : Now right click on **src** folder of **WebServiceClient**. Click on **New->Class**. The **New Java Class** window will appear. Set appropriate package name, class name and Check for void main method. Here is the screenshot

Click on **Finish** button. You can now write the Java Client code for web service. The code in as follows

MyClient.java

```
package com.mypackage;
import java.io.*;
import javax.servlet.*;
import javax.servlet.http.*;
import com.mypackage.MyServerStub.GetInfo;
import com.mypackage.MyServerStub.GetInfoResponse;

public class MyClient extends HttpServlet
{
      public void doGet(HttpServletRequest req,HttpServletResponse res)
        throws IOException,ServletException
      {
        res.setContentType("text/html");
        PrintWriter out=res.getWriter();
        String s=req.getParameter("Src_name");
        String d=req.getParameter("Dest_name");

        MyServerStub stub=new MyServerStub();
        GetInfo p=new GetInfo();
        p.setSrc(s);
        p.setDest(d);
        GetInfoResponse response = stub.getInfo(p);
        String result=response.get_return();
        out.println("<html>");
        out.println("<body bgcolor='khaki' >");
        out.println ( result );
        out.println("</body>");
        out.println("</html>");

      }
  }
```

Save the above code.

Step 9 : Update the web.xml file. Here is it -

web.xml

(Location: WebServiceClient->Web Content->WEB-INF->web.xml]

```
<?xml version="1.0" encoding="UTF-8"?>
<web-appxmlns:xsi="http://www.w3.org/2001/XMLSchema-instance"
xmlns="http://java.sun.com/xml/ns/javaee"
xmlns:web="http://java.sun.com/xml/ns/javaee/web-app_2_5.xsd"
xsi:schemaLocation="http://java.sun.com/xml/ns/javaee     http://java.sun.com/xml/ns/javaee/web-
app_2_5.xsd" id="WebApp_ID" version="2.5">
```

```
<display-name>WebServiceClient</display-name>
<welcome-file-list>
   ...
   ...
   ...

<servlet>
  <servlet-name>MyClient</servlet-name>
  <servlet-class>com.mypackage.MyClient</servlet-class>
</servlet>
<servlet-mapping>
  <servlet-name>MyClient</servlet-name>
  <url-pattern>/servlet/com.mypackage.MyClient</url-pattern>
</servlet-mapping>

   ...
   ...
   ...
<servlet-name>AxisAdminServlet</servlet-name>
  <servlet-class>org.apache.axis2.transport.http.AxisAdminServlet</servlet-class>
  <load-on-startup>100</load-on-startup>
</servlet>
  <servlet-mapping>
  <servlet-name>AxisAdminServlet</servlet-name>
  <url-pattern>/axis2-admin/*</url-pattern>
</servlet-mapping>
</web-app>
```

Step 10 : Now create a simple HTML file which will invoke the client servlet program(Created in step 8) . This file can be at any desired location. For instance I have stored this file in my D:\ drive.

Input.html

```
<!DOCTYPE html>
<html>
<head>
<title>AIRLINE RESERVATION SERVICE</title>
</head>
<body bgcolor ="khaki">
<h4>Travel Agent should fill up following information to get information about the Airline</h4>
  <form name="form1" method="GET" action
"http://localhost:8080/WebServiceClient/servlet/com.mypackage.MyClient">
  <table>
  <tr>
```

```
    <td><b>Source city: </b></td>
    <td><input type="text" name="Src_name" size="20" value=""/></td>
   </tr>
   <tr>
    <td><b>Destination city: </b></td>
    <td><input type="text" name="Dest_name" size="20" value=""/></td>
   </tr>
   <tr>
    <td><input type="submit" value="Submit"/></td>
   </tr>
   </table>
   </form>
  </body>
</html>
```

Save the above code.

Step 11 : Open the web browser and invoke the above created HTML file This HTML file is for Travel agent. He/she will use it for searching the desired airline. In this application our criteria for searching the airline is – **Source city** and **destination city**. This criterion may change from developers point of view.

Output

file:///D:/input.html

Travel Agent should fill up following information to get information about the Airline

Source city: Pune

Destination city: Mumbai

Submit

Indian Airlines	5:00 p.m.
AirIndia	7:00 p.m.
Indian Airlines	10:00 p.m.

Two Marks Questions with Answers

Q.1 What do you means by the term web service ? **AU : May-17, Dec.-17**

Ans. : The web services are the software systems that are displayed on the web browser using the web protocol. These software systems are used by some software applications rather than by end-users directly. For example: Weather forecast system, currency converters.

Q.2 What is SOAP ?

OR What is the need of SOAP ? **AU : May-17**

Ans. : The SOAP stands for Simple Object Access Protocol. It is simple XML based protocol which allows applications to exchange information over HTTP. Typically web services make use of this protocol for exchange of information.

Q.3 What is meant by WSDL ? **AU : May-11, Dec.-12**

OR State the use of WSDL **AU : May-12, Dec.-13, 16**

Ans. : Web services provide a special file to its client in which the interface is described. This description is provided in XML document. When a client wants to make use of this web service, the users of this client read this description file and understand what input data is needed to perform the web service. Such a special file is called **WSDL** i.e Web Services Description Languages.

Q.4 List some examples of web services. **AU : May-12**

Ans. : Following are some examples of web services -

1. Whether forecast system.
2. Currency converter.

3. Electronic payment processing system.

4. Credit card validation system

5. Resource management system.

Q.5 List some web service technologies.

Ans. : Following are some web service technologies -

1. Apache Axis 2. SOAP 3. JAX-RPC 4. .Net Framework.

Q.6 List the basic concepts behind JAX-RPC technology. AU : Dec.-11

Ans. : The JAX-RPC are the higher level technologies of web services. These are JAVA API for XML (JAX) based on Remote Procedure Call (RPC).

Q.7 What is PortType in WSDL ?

Ans. : This is an important element of WSDL file. It defines various operations that can be performed by web service.

Q.8 What is the purpose of element 'binding' in WSDL ?

Ans. : The binding in WSDL specifies the name of the protocol of the web service. Typically it is SOAP.

Q.9 What is UDDI ? AU : Dec.-11

Ans. : The UDDI stands for Universal Description, Discovery and Integration. It is XML based specification for registry of web services. It is platform independent framework.

Q.10 What are the elements of SOAP building block ?

Ans. : The following are the elements of SOAP architecture -

1. Envelop 2. Header 3. Body 4. Fault

Q.11 Explain how SOAP is related to HTTP ?

Ans. : The HTTP is a protocol which communicates over TCP/IP. It is based on request-response mechanism. SOAP is protocol which is a combination of both HTTP and XML. The SOAP request can be HTTP GET or HTTP POST. The SOAP request consists of two HTTP headers content-type and content-length the body of this request consists of SOAP Envelop, Header, Body and Fault.

Q.12 Give an example of a web service registry and its function. AU : Dec.-12

Ans. : The Universal Description and Discovery Integration (UDDI) provides a directory of web services so that client can easily discover the services of their choices. The UDDI maintains a registry in which the web services are registered.

Q.13 What is service endpoint interface in RPC ? AU : May-14

Ans. : A Service Endpoint Interface (SEI) is a Java interface that declares the methods that a client can invoke while using the service. The method parameters and return type specified by the SEI must be supported by the Remote Procedure Call (RPC).

Q.14 Specify how UDDI is utilized in Web Service ? **AU : May-14**

Ans. : The UDDI provides a directory of web services so that client can easily discover the services of their choices. The UDDI maintains a registry in which the web services are registered.

Q.15 What is a web service ? Give any four examples. **AU : Dec.-15**

Ans. : The Web Services are the software systems that are displayed by the web browser using the web protocol. These software systems are used by the some software applications rather than by end-users directly.

Examples are

1. Credit Card Validation System
2. Whether Forecast System
3. Currency Converter
4. Rate of Interest Calculator
5. Income Tax Calculator

Q.16 Draw the structure of SOAP messages. **AU : May-16**

Ans. : Refer Fig. 10.5.1.

Q.17 List out data types that are available in Web-Service.

Ans : Various data types that are available in web service are - boolean, byte, short, int, long, float, double, decimal, string.

Q.18 Define complex types.

Ans. : Complex types are objects created by the developer. For example, an object called Customer with the properties CustID and name is a complex type.

Q.19 Differentiate between SOAP and HTTP.

Ans. :

SOAP	HTTP
Simple Object Access protocol, is a protocol specification for exchanging structured information in the implementation of web services in computer networks.	The Hypertext Transfer Protocol (HTTP) is an application protocol used for communication for the World Wide Web.
It is used to build simple and useful APIs called web services.	It is used to transfer data using internet.
It uses XML information.	It relies on structured text.

Q.20 Why do web services need enhanced security ?

Ans. : Web services are widely used in diverse applications to fulfill the user requirements. Hence reliability of data, confidentiality and data nonrepudiation, user authentication are the most required features. Hence web services need enhanced security.

❑❑❑

Notes

Internet Programming Lab

Contents

Experiment 1 : Create a web page with the following using HTML

1) To embed a map in a web page.

2) To fix the hot spots in that map.

3) Show all the related information when the hot spots are clicked.

Sol. :

```
<html>
<body>
<p>
<b>Some Popular Planets from Solar system</b>
</p>
<img src="C:\Documents and Settings\User\My Documents\My Pictures\solar system.jpg"
width="145" height="126"
usemap="#solarmap">
<map id="solarmap" name="solarmap">
<area shape="rect"
coords="10,10,40,25"
alt="Mercury"
href="D:\\HTML_Examples\Mercury.html">
<area shape="rect"
coords="35,20,75,55"
alt="venus"
href="D:\\HTML_Examples\venus.htm">
<area shape="rect"
coords="65,55,115,85"
alt="Earth"
href="D:\\HTML_Examples\earth.htm">
<area shape="rect"
coords="90,85,135,120"
alt="Saturn"
href="D:\\HTML_Examples\saturn.htm">
</map>
<p><b>Note:</b> Some Planets from our solar system are displayed here click on any planet
and you will get some useful information about them</p>
</body>
</html>
```

This sets the image width and height.

Hot spot for each planet is set.

Output

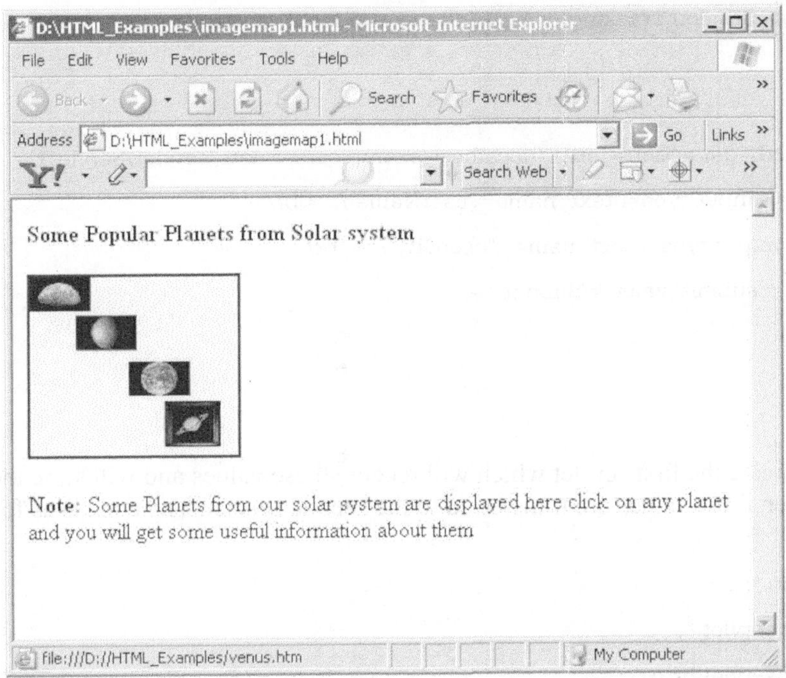

Experiment 2 : Create a web page with the following.

1. Cascading style sheets. 2. Embedded style sheets.

3. Inline style sheets. Use our college information for the web page.

Sol. : Refer section 3.4.

Experiment 3 : Validate the registration, user login, user profile, and payment by credit card pages using JavaScript.

Sol. : Refer section 4.17.

Experiment 4 : Write programs in Java using Servlet :

(i) To invoke servlets from HTML forms

(ii) Session tracking using hidden form fields and session tracking for hit count.

Sol. : (i) Refer section examples in section 5.6.

(ii) (a) **Session tracking using hidden form fields**

The hidden form fields are created to store the data entered by the user. The session is created in which the values entered by the user using the interface can be passed over the servlets and the last servlet will display the values entered by the user.

Step 1 : Create a graphical user interface for allowing the user to enter the data. Here is the code **GUI.html.**

```
<html>
```

```
<head>
    <title> Session Tracking using Hidden Form Field</title>
</head>
<body>
<form method=get action="http://localhost/examples/servlets/servlet/Servlet1">
Enter Name: <input type="text" name="userName"/><br/>
Enter City: <input type="text" name="userCity"/><br/>
<input type="submit" value="Submit"/>
</form>
</body>
</html>
```

Step 2 : Now create the first servlet which will receive these values and will store them in hidden form fields. Then these values are transferred to the second servlet. The code is as follows

Servlet1.java

```
import java.io.*;
import javax.servlet.*;
import javax.servlet.http.*;
public class Servlet1 extends HttpServlet
{
  public void doGet(HttpServletRequest request, HttpServletResponse response)
  {
    try
    {
      response.setContentType("text/html");
      PrintWriter out = response.getWriter();

      String n=request.getParameter("userName");
      String c=request.getParameter("userCity");

      //creating form that have invisible textfield
      out.print(" <form action=http://localhost/examples/servlets/servlet/Servlet2> ");
      out.print(" <input type='hidden' name='uname' value='"+n+"'>" );
      out.print("<input type='hidden' name='ucity' value='"+c+"'>");
      out.print("<input type='submit' value='Just Click Here'>");
```

```
        out.print("</form>");
        out.close();
      }
      catch(Exception e)
      {
        System.out.println(e);
      }
    }
  }
```

Step 3 : The second Servlet will display these values with greeting message. The code for Second servlet is as follows -

Servlet2.java

```
import java.io.*;
import javax.servlet.*;
import javax.servlet.http.*;
public class Servlet2 extends HttpServlet
{
  public void doGet(HttpServletRequest request, HttpServletResponse response)
  {
    try
    {
      response.setContentType("text/html");
      PrintWriter out = response.getWriter();

      //Getting the value from the hidden field
      String n=request.getParameter("uname");
      out.println("Hello "+n);
      String c=request.getParameter("ucity");
      out.println("You are from "+c);
      out.close();
    }
    catch(Exception e){System.out.println(e);}
  }
}
```

Step 4 : Now compile both the java servlets by using following command

```
D:\>javac Servlet1.java

D:\> javac Servlet2.java
```

The class files will get generated. Copy these class files to Tomcat's classes folder in the WEB-INF directory.

Step 5 : Then edit **web.xml** file as follows -

```
...
<servlet>
   <servlet-name>Servlet1</servlet-name>
   <servlet-class>Servlet1</servlet-class>
</servlet>

<servlet>
   <servlet-name>Servlet2</servlet-name>
   <servlet-class>Servlet2</servlet-class>
</servlet>
...
<servlet-mapping>
   <servlet-name>Servlet1</servlet-name>
   <url-pattern>/servlets/servlet/Servlet1</url-pattern>
</servlet-mapping>
<servlet-mapping>
   <servlet-name>Servlet2</servlet-name>
   <url-pattern>/servlets/servlet/Servlet2</url-pattern>
</servlet-mapping>
```

Step 6 : Open the web browser and invoke the HTML document created in Step 1.

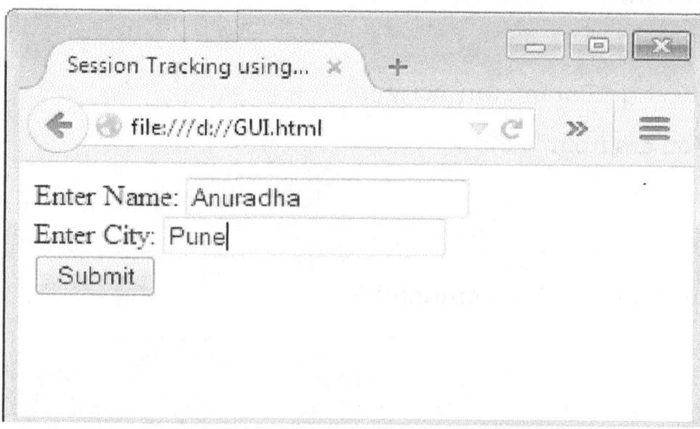

Click Submit button.

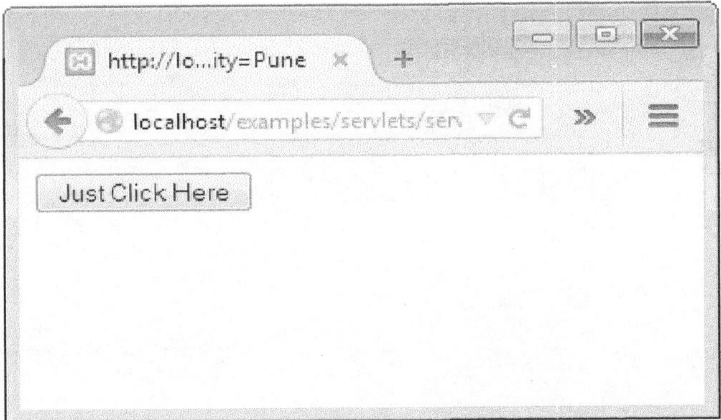

Click the button.

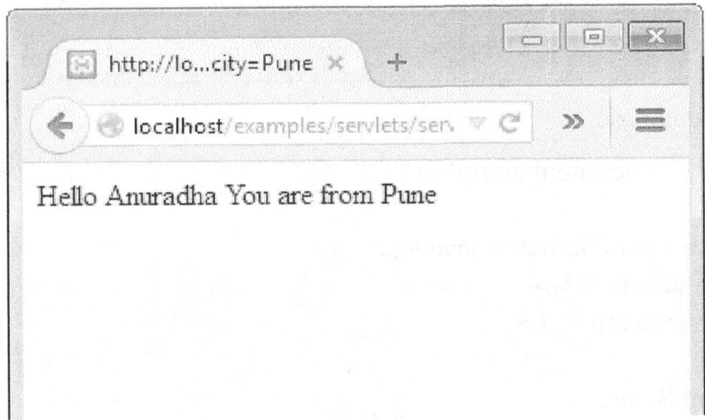

Thus session is maintained by keeping track of user name and city.

(b) Session tracking for a hit count.

Sol. : Refer example 5.7.1.

Experiment 5 : Write programs in Java to create three-tier applications using servlets for conducting on-line examination for displaying student mark list. Assume that student information is available in a database which has been stored in a database server.

Sol. :

Step 1 : Create a database in MS-Access. For instance, I have created a student database in MS-Access. Inside this database create a table. This table is as follows.

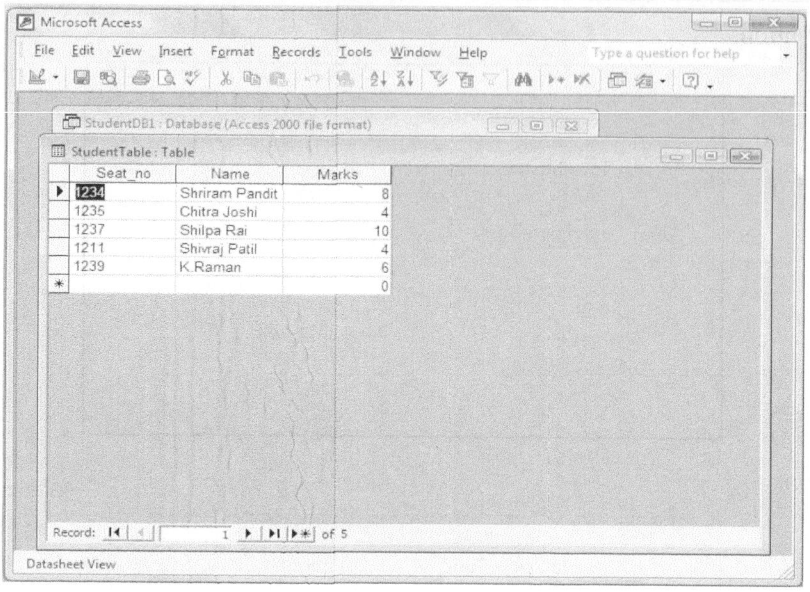

Create a DSN for this database.

Step 2 : Now write a JSP document as follows -
Exam.jsp

```
<%@ page language="java" import="java.sql.*" %>
<%@ page import="java.io.*" %>
<%@ page import="java.util.*" %>
    <%
    String SeatNum,Name;
    String ans1,ans2,ans3,ans4,ans5;
    int a1,a2,a3,a4,a5;
    a1=a2=a3=a4=a5=0;
    Connection connect=null;
    Statement stmt=null;
    ResultSet rs=null;
    Class.forName("sun.jdbc.odbc.JdbcOdbcDriver");
    String url = "jdbc:odbc:StudentDB1";
    connect = DriverManager.getConnection(url, " ", " ");
        if(request.getParameter("action")!=null)
        {
            SeatNum = request.getParameter("Seat_no");
            Name = request.getParameter("Name");
            ans1 =request.getParameter("group1");
            if(ans1.equals("True"))
            a1=2;
            else
            a1=0;
            ans2 = request.getParameter("group2");
```

```
if(ans2.equals("True"))
  a2=0;
else
  a2=2;
ans3 = request.getParameter("group3");
if(ans3.equals("True"))
  a3=0;
else
  a3=2;
ans4 = request.getParameter("group4");
if(ans4.equals("True"))
  a4=2;
else
  a4=0;
ans5 = request.getParameter("group5");
if(ans5.equals("True"))
  a5=0;
else
  a5=2;
int Total=a1+a2+a3+a4+a5;

   stmt = connect.createStatement();
String query = "INSERT INTO StudentTable (" + "Seat_no,Name,Marks" +  ") VALUES ('"
+SeatNum + "', '" + Name + "', '"+Total+ "')";
int result = stmt.executeUpdate(query);
stmt.close();
stmt = connect.createStatement();
query = "SELECT * FROM StudentTable WHERE Name="+"'"+Name+"'";
rs = stmt.executeQuery(query);
%>
<html><head><title>Student Mark List</title></head>
 <body bgcolor=khaki>
  <center>
        <h2>Students Marksheet</h2>
        <h3>Name of the College:ABC College of Engineering</h3>
        <table border="1" cellspacing="0" cellpadding="0">
        <tr>
         <td><b>Seat_No</b></td>
         <td><b>Name</b></td>
         <td><b>Marks</b></td>
        </tr>
        <%
         while(rs.next())
         {
        %>
```

```
            <tr>
             <td><%=rs.getInt(1)%></td>
             <td> <%=rs.getString(2)%></td>
             <td> <%=rs.getString(3)%></td>
            </tr>
           <%
          }
         rs.close();
           stmt.close();
           connect.close();
         %>
           </table>
   </center>
   <br/> <br/><br/>
         <table>
              <tr><td><b>Date:<%=new java.util.Date().toString() %></td></tr>
               <tr><td><b>Signature: X.Y.Z. <b></td></tr>
          </table>
         <div>
<a href="http://127.0.0.1:8080/jsp-examples/StudExam/Exam.jsp">Click here to go back</a>
      </body>
       </html>
      <%}else{%>
       <html>
         <head><title>Online Examination</title>
              <script language="javascript">
              function validation(Form_obj)
              {
               if(Form_obj.Seat_no.value.length==0)
               {
                 alert("Please,fill up the Seat Number");
                 Form_obj.Seat_no.focus();
                 return false;
               }
                          if(Form_obj.Name.value.length==0)
               {
                 alert("Please,fill up the Name");
                 Form_obj.Name.focus();
                 return false;
               }
                          return true;
             }
         </script>
        </head>
```

```
<body bgcolor=lightgreen>
<center>
  <h1>OnLine Examination</h1>
</center>
    <form action="Exam.jsp" method="post"
    name="entry" onSubmit="return validation(this)">
    <input type="hidden" value="list" name="action">
     <table>
      <tr>
        <td><h3>Seat Number:</h3></td>
        <td><input type="text" name="Seat_no"></td>
      </tr>
      <tr>
       <td><h3>Name:</h3></td>
       <td><input type="text" name="Name" size="50"></td>
      </tr>
      <hr/>
      <tr>
       <td><b>Total Marks:10(Each question carries equal marks) </b></td>
           <td></td><td></td><td></td><td><b>Time: 15 Min.</b></td>
      </tr>
      </table>
      <hr/>
       <b>1. Apache is an open source web server</b><br/>
       <input type="radio" name="group1" value="True">True
       <input type="radio" name="group1" value="False">False<br>
       <br/>

       <b>2. In Modern PC there is no cache memory.</b><br/>
       <input type="radio" name="group2" value="True">True
       <input type="radio" name="group2" value="False">False<br>
       <br/>

       <b>3. Tim-Berner Lee is the originator of Java.</b><br/>
       <input type="radio" name="group3" value="True">True
       <input type="radio" name="group3" value="False">False<br>
       <br/>

       <b>4.JPG is not a video file extension.</b><br/>
       <input type="radio" name="group4" value="True">True
       <input type="radio" name="group4" value="False">False<br>
       <br/>

       <b>5. HTTP is a statefull protocol</b><br/>
```

```
        <input type="radio" name="group5" value="True">True
        <input type="radio" name="group5" value="False">False<br>
        <hr/>

        <center>
         <input type = "submit" value="Submit">
         <input type = "reset" value="Clear"><br><br>
        </center>
      </form>
    <%}%>
```

Step 3 : This file must be saved at C:*your_tomcat_directory*\webapps\jsp-examples. Create a folder at this location and in that folder store the above written JSP file. For example I have created a folder named **StudExam** at the location **C:\Tomcat \jsp-examples.** Create a folder at this location and saved my JSP file as **Exam.jsp.**

Then start running your tomcat.

Now open a suitable web browser and executed the JSP program by typing the URL

http://127.0.0.1:8080/jsp-examples/StudExam/Exam.jsp

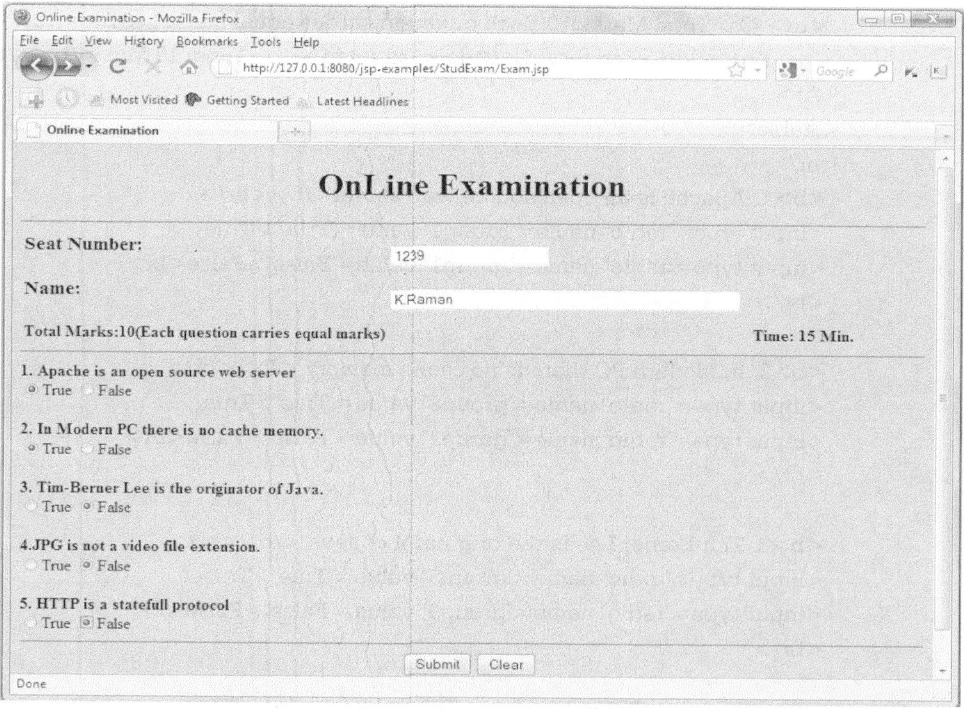

After inputting the data appropriately, Click the **Submit** button. And a Mark sheet will be displayed as follows –

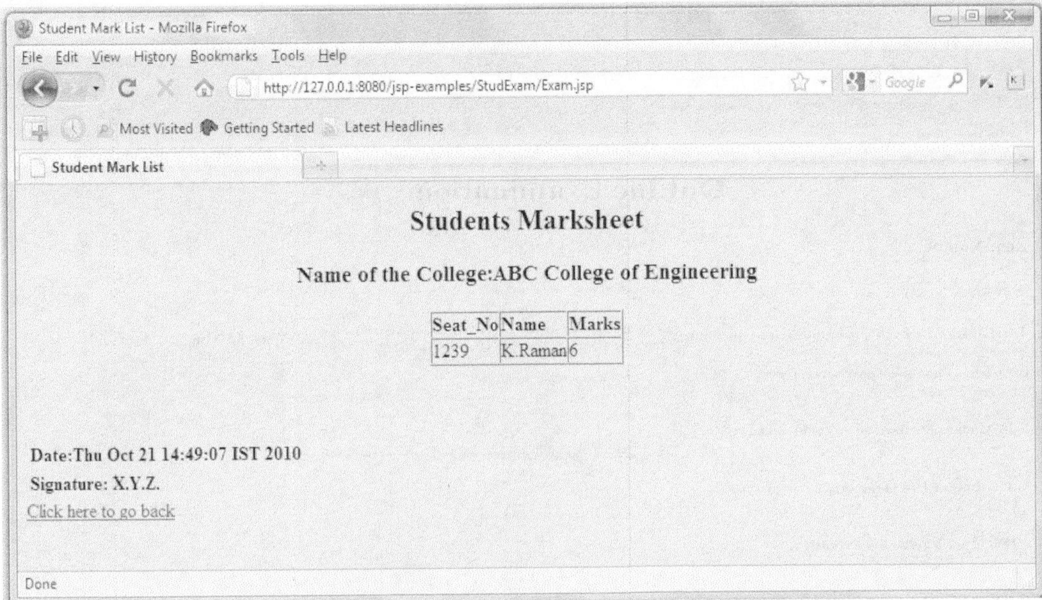

Validation

The form validation is also done in above JSP script. Following Output illustrate such validations.

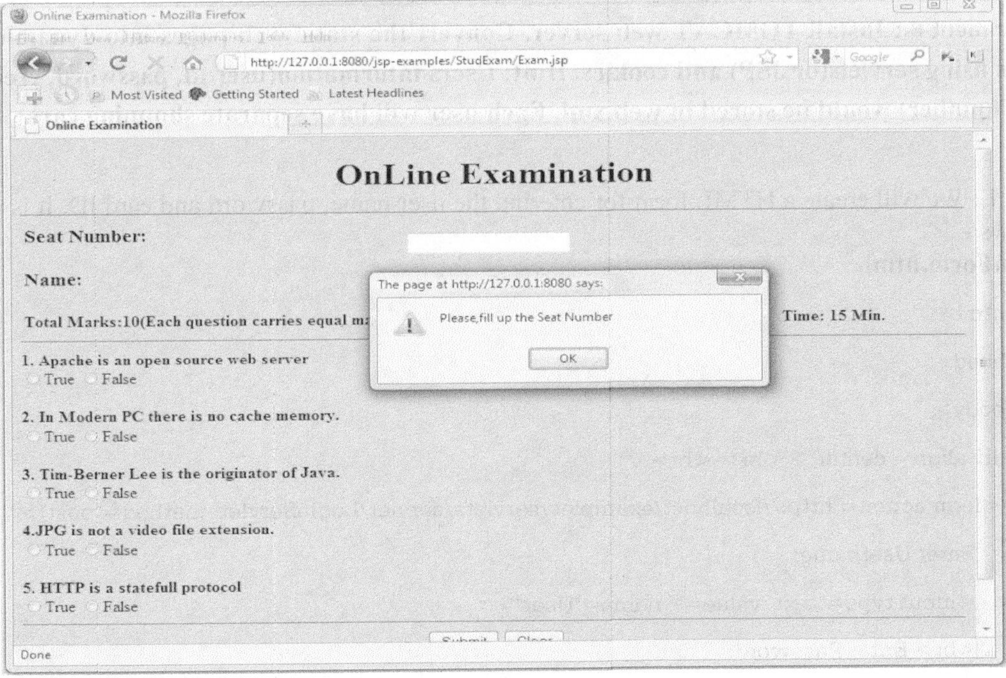

Similarly if you do not enter the name then,

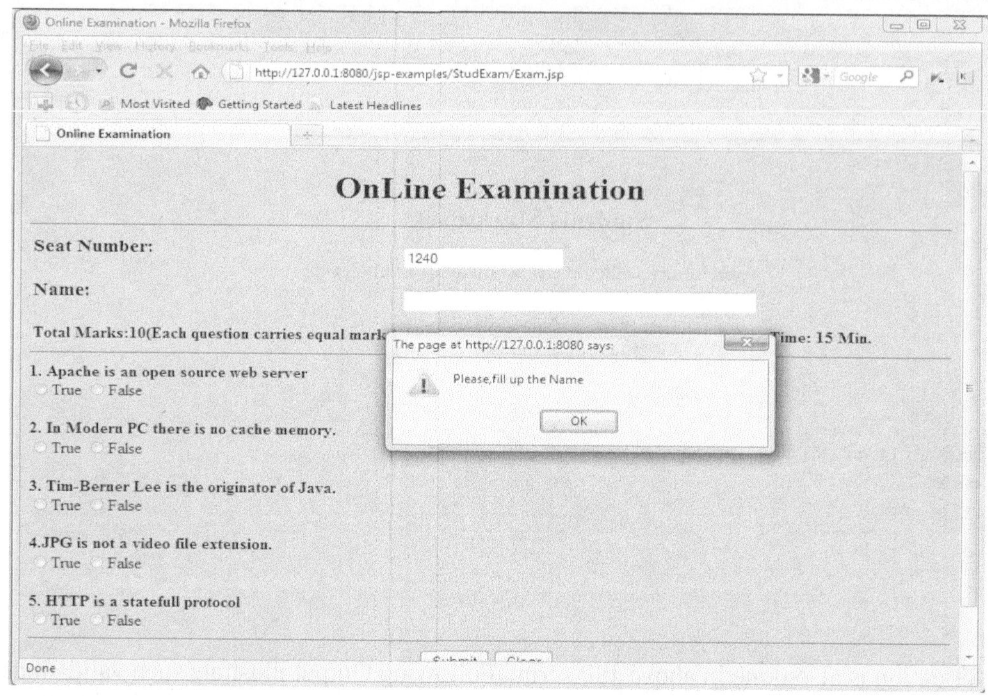

Experiment 6 : Install TOMCAT web server. Convert the static web pages into dynamic web pages using servlets(or JSP) and cookies. Hint: Users information(user id, password, credit card number) would be stored in web.xml. Each user will have separate shopping cart.

Sol. :

Step 1 : We will create a HTML form for entering the user name, password and card ID. It is as follows -

LoginForm.html

```
<html>
<head>
<body>
<div align="center"> <br> <br>
  <form action="http://localhost/examples/servlets/servlet/LoginServlet" method="post">
    Enter Username:
    <input type="text" value="" name="User">
    <br> Enter Password:
    <input type="password" value="" name="Password">
     <br> Enter Card ID:
    <input type="text" value="" name="CardID">
```

```
<br> <br> <br>
    <input type="submit" value="Login">
  </form>
</div>
</body>
</html>
```

Step 2 : From the above HTML form, the servlet program is invoked in which the validity of the user name, password and card id is checked. If it is a valid user then the welcome message will be displayed otherwise the "invalid user" message will be displayed. In this servlet we set the cookies in which the current user name is stored. The code for this servlet is as follows -

LoginServlet.java

```
import java.io.*;
import javax.servlet.*;
import javax.servlet.http.*;

public class LoginServlet extends HttpServlet
{
  protected void doPost(HttpServletRequest req, HttpServletResponse res) throws ServletException, IOException
  {
     res.setContentType("text/html");
     PrintWriter out=res.getWriter();

     // get request parameters for userID and password
     String usr = req.getParameter("User");
     String pwd = req.getParameter("Password");
     String card = req.getParameter("CardID");

     boolean flag=true;//flag is maintained to track of invalid user/password

   //get user names, passwords and cardIDs from web.xml
 String[] userID = getInitParameter("usernames").split(",");
 String[] password = getInitParameter("passwords").split(",");
```

In **web.xml** file we have stored
<init-param>
<param-name>usernames</param-name>
<param-value>user1,user2,user3</param-value>
</init-param>

Similarly passwords and CardIDs are stored.
Refer next step i.e. **step 3**

```
String[] cardids = getInitParameter("cardIDs").split(",");
int i;
  for(i=0;i<userID.length;i++)
  {
    if (userID[i].equals(usr) && password[i].equals(pwd) && cardids[i].equals(card))
    {
    flag=false;
      Cookie MyCookie = new Cookie("CurrentUser",usr);
      // setting cookie to expiry in 60 mins
      MyCookie.setMaxAge(60 * 60);
    res.addCookie(MyCookie);
      res.sendRedirect("http://localhost/examples/servlets/servlet/LoginSuccess");
    }
  }
  if(flag==true)//invalid user name or password
  {
        out.println("<h4>Invalid user,Please try again by clicking following link</h4>");

        out.println("<ahref='http://localhost/examples/LoginForm.html'>"+"LoginForm.html")
;
  }
 }
}
```

Step 3 : Compile the above servlet **LoginServlet.java** and copy its class file in tomcats folder at C:\tomcatdirectory\webapps\examples\WEB-INF\classes.

Then edit the **web.xml** in WEB-INF folder. We must store the user information such as user name, password and Card ID in the **web.xml** using **init-param**. Following is a snapshot of the **web.xml** file -

```
...
<servlet>
  <init-param>
    <param-name>usernames</param-name>
    <param-value>user1,user2,user3</param-value>
  </init-param>
```

```
<init-param>
   <param-name>passwords</param-name>
   <param-value>pwd1,pwd2,pwd3</param-value>
</init-param>
<init-param>
   <param-name>cardIDs</param-name>
   <param-value>111,222,333</param-value>
</init-param>

<servlet-name>LoginServlet</servlet-name>
<servlet-class>LoginServlet</servlet-class>
</servlet>
...
<servlet-mapping>
   <servlet-name>LoginServlet</servlet-name>
   <url-pattern>/servlets/servlet/LoginServlet</url-pattern>
</servlet-mapping>
```

Step 4 : On successful login, the information from the cookie is checked and shopping cart page for corresponding user can be displayed.

LoginSuccess.java

```
import java.io.*;
import javax.servlet.*;
import javax.servlet.http.*;
public class LoginSuccess extends HttpServlet
{
   protected void doGet(HttpServletRequest req,HttpServletResponse res)
         throws ServletException,IOException
   {
     Cookie[] my_cookies=req.getCookies();
     res.setContentType("text/html");
     PrintWriter out=res.getWriter();
```

```
        out.println("<b>");
        String userName = null;

        if (my_cookies != null)
        {
          for (Cookie cookie : my_cookies)
          {
            if (cookie.getName().equals("CurrentUser"))
              userName = cookie.getValue();

          }
        }
        out.print("<h3>Login Success!!!Welcome </h3>");
        out.print("<h2>This is a Shopping cart for "+userName+"</h2>");
        out.close();
    }
}
```

Step 5 : Compile the above servlet **LoginSuccess.java** and copy its class file in tomcat's folder at C:\tomcatdirectory\webapps\examples\WEB-INF\classes.
Then edit the **web.xml** in WEB-INF folder as follows -

```
...
<servlet>
   <servlet-name>LoginSuccess</servlet-name>
   <servlet-class>LoginSuccess</servlet-class>
</servlet>
...

<servlet-mapping>
   <servlet-name>LoginSuccess</servlet-name>
   <url-pattern>/servlets/servlet/LoginSuccess</url-pattern>
</servlet-mapping>
```

Step 6 : Start tomcat web server. Open the web browser and display the login form created in step 1.

Click the Login button.

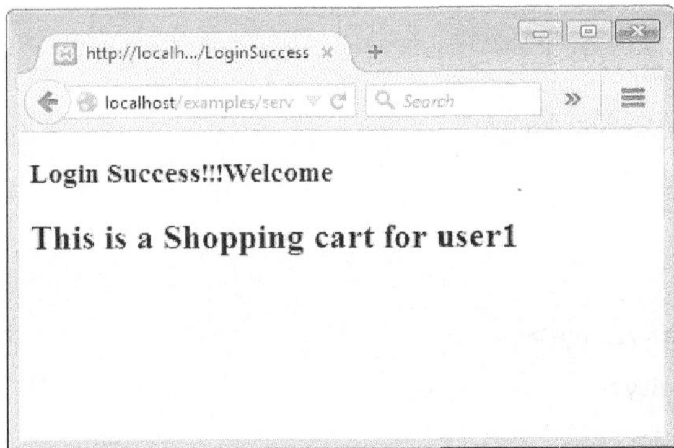

If we enter some wrong user name/password or Card ID then we will get following output.

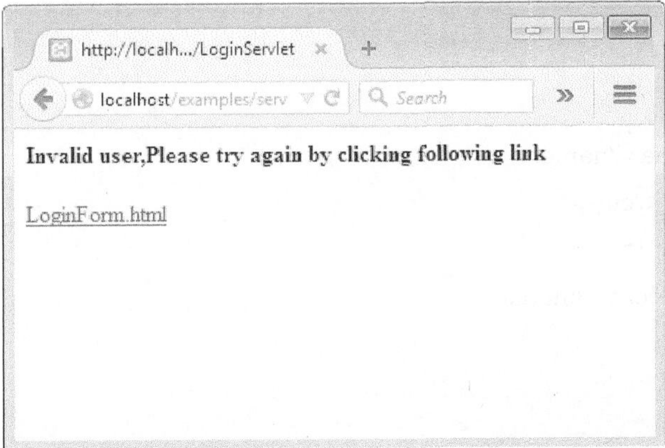

Experiment 7 : Redo previous task using JSP by converting static web page into dynamic web pages. Create database with user information and book information. The book catalogue must be dynamically loaded from the database.

Sol. : Refer section 6.12 and example 6.12.1.

Experiment 8 : Create and save an XML document at the server, which contains 10 users information. Write a program which takes user Id as an input and returns the User details by taking the user information from the XML document.

Sol. :

Step 1 : Create an xml file containing the user information. It is as follows -
(Note that for the sake of simplification, the information of four users is taken in following xml file, you can extend it to 10 users.)

UserInfo.xml

```
<?xml version="1.0" encoding="UTF-8"?>
<Student>
 <Person-Details>
      <id>101</id>
      <name>Anand</name>
      <city>Pune</city>
      <std>Second</std>
      <marks>70 percent</marks>
 </Person-Details>
 <Person-Details>
      <id>102</id>
      <name>Anuradha</name>
      <city>Chennai</city>
      <std>Second</std>
      <marks>90 percent</marks>
 </Person-Details>
 <Person-Details>
      <id>103</id>
      <name>Archana</name>
      <city>Mumbai</city>
      <std>Forth</std>
      <marks>80 percent</marks>
 </Person-Details>
 <Person-Details>
      <id>104</id>
      <name>Monika</name>
      <city>Delhi</city>
      <std>Tenth</std>
      <marks>77 percent</marks>
```

```
</Person-Details>
</Student>
```

Step 2 : Now we will write an HTML file in which the user ID is taken as an input. This HTML document will then load the xml file created in Step 1 and will retrieve the information of the user whose ID provided.

InputFrom.html

```
<!DOCTYPE html>
<html>
<head>
</head>
<body>
<script type="text/javascript">
function Display()
{

  if (window.XMLHttpRequest)
  {
  // code for IE7+, Firefox, Chrome, Opera, Safari
    xmlhttp=new XMLHttpRequest();
  }
  xmlhttp.open("GET","UserInfo.xml",false);
  xmlhttp.send();
  xmlDoc=xmlhttp.responseXML;
  var x=xmlDoc.getElementsByTagName("Person-Details");
  var key_id=document.getElementById('key').value;
  for(i=0;i<x.length;i++)
  {
   if(key_id.match(x[i].getElementsByTagName("id")[0].childNodes[0].nodeValue))
    j=i;
  }
  document.write("<h3> User Details are...</h3>");
  document.write
 ("<table border='3'><tr><th>ID</th><th>Name</th><th>City</th><th>Standard
  </th><th>Marks</th></tr>");
  document.write("<tr><td>");
  document.write(x[j].getElementsByTagName("id")[0].childNodes[0].nodeValue);
  document.write("</td><td>");
  document.write(x[j].getElementsByTagName("name")[0].childNodes[0].nodeValue);
```

```
        document.write("</td><td>");
        document.write(x[j].getElementsByTagName("city")[0].childNodes[0].nodeValue);
        document.write("</td><td>");
        document.write(x[j].getElementsByTagName("std")[0].childNodes[0].nodeValue);
        document.write("</td><td>");
        document.write(x[j].getElementsByTagName("marks")[0].childNodes[0].nodeValue);
        document.write("</td></tr>");
        document.write("</table>");
    }
    </script>
    <form name='myform'>
    Enter ID :<input type='text' id='key' /><br/>
    <input type='button' value='submit' onclick='Display()' />
    </form>
    </body>
    </html>
```

Output

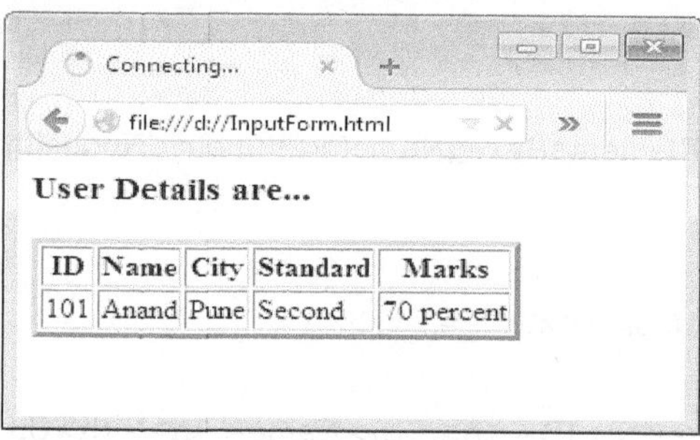

ID	Name	City	Standard	Marks
101	Anand	Pune	Second	70 percent

Experiment 9 : (i) Validate the form using PHP regular expression

(ii) PHP stores the form data into database.

Solution:

(i) Refer example 7.12.2

(ii) Refer example 7.15.1

SOLVED MODEL QUESTION PAPER

[As per New Syllabus]

Internet Programming

Semester - VI (CSE)

Time : Three Hours] [Maximum Marks : 100

Answer ALL Questions

PART A - (10 × 2 = 20 Marks)

Q.1 *List some basic internet protocols.* **[Refer Two Marks Q.6 of Chapter 1]**

Q.2 *Enlist any four features of HTML 5.* **[Refer section 2.2.1]**

Q.3 *Mention the need for cascading style sheet.* **[Refer Two Marks Q.6 of Chapter 3]**

Q.4 *List any four methods of date object.* **[Refer Two Marks Q.21 of Chapter 4]**

Q.5 *What are servlets ?* **[Refer Two Marks Q.1 of Chapter 5]**

Q.6 *Write two differences between JSP and servlet.*
[Refer Two Marks Q.12 of Chapter 6]

Q.7 *Name any four built in functions in PHP.* **[Refer Two Marks Q.15 of Chapter 7]**

Q.8 *What are the merits of DTD ?* **[Refer Two Marks Q.12 of Chapter 8]**

Q.9 *What is HTTP request object ?* **[Refer Two Marks Q.2 of Chapter 9]**

Q.10 *List some examples of web services.* **[Refer Two Marks Q.4 of Chapter 10]**

PART B - (5 × 13 = 65 Marks)

Q.11 a) *i) Explain the various internet protocols used for client server communication.* **[Refer section 1.2]**

ii) Enlist different functions of web server. **[Refer section 1.6]**

OR

b) *i) Explain the client server communication mechanism in detail.* **[Refer section 1.7]**

ii) Differentiate between HTML and HTML 5. **[Refer section 2.2.2]**

Q.12 a) *i) State and explain any four HTML elements in detail.* **[Refer section 2.3]**

ii) Write HTML code which includes table, hyperlink, character formatting ordered and unordered list to display your resume. **[Refer example 2.5.7]**

OR

b) *Create a HTML document for a company home page and explain.*
[Refer example 2.6.2]

Q.13 a) *i) Explain date and time control in HTML5.* **[Refer section 2.9.9]**

ii) Explain how to use audio and video controls in HTML5 with illustrative example. **[Refer section 2.12]**

OR

b) *Explain positioning of elements in CSS.* **[Refer section 3.5]**

Q.14 a) *i) Write a JavaScript to find and print the largest and smallest values among 10 elements of an array.* **[Refer example 4.8.6]**

ii) Write a JavaScript to check input string is palindrome or not. **[Refer example 4.9.4]**

OR

b) *i) Use a one-dimensional array and write a script to solve following problem. Read in 20 numbers, each of which is between 1 and 100. As each number is read, print it only if it is not a duplicate of a number that has already been read.* **[Refer example 4.10.2]**

ii) Explain life cycle of servlets with suitable example. **[Refer sections 5.4]**

Q.15 a) *i) Write HTML form to read user name and password. This data is sent to the servlet. If the correct user name and password is given then welcome him/her by his/her name otherwise display the message for invalid user.* **[Refer example 5.6.2]**

ii) Explain JSP directives. **[Refer section 6.5]**

OR

b) *i) Briefly discuss how data types are represented in XML schema.* **[Refer section 8.6]**

ii) Write short note on SOAP. **[Refer section 10.5]**

PART - C (1 × 15 = 15 Marks)

Q.16 a) *Write AJAX script to obtain the student information stored in XML document. The information should be displayed on clicking the button. It should be displayed in tabular form.* **[Refer example 9.4.1]**

OR

b) *Write a PHP script to create a new database table with 4 fields of your choice and perform following database operations -*

1. *Insert*
2. *Delete*
3. *Update*
4. *Display* **[Refer example 7.15.1]**

□□□